Adobe

Adobe Illustrator CC

2018 release

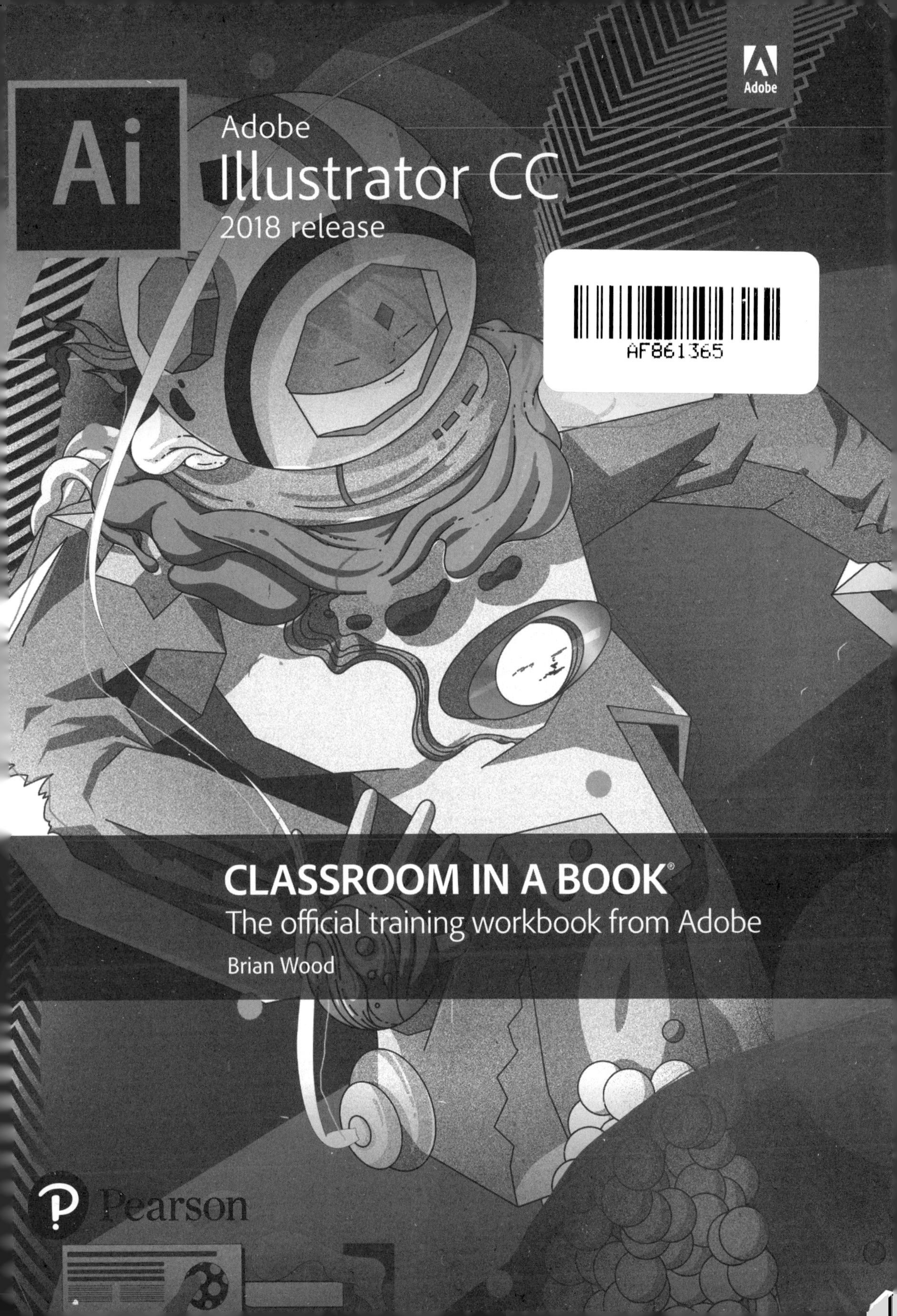

CLASSROOM IN A BOOK®

The official training workbook from Adobe

Brian Wood

Pearson

Original edition, entitled *Adobe Illustrator CC Classroom in A Book (2018 Release),* 1st Edition, by Wood, Brian, published by Pearson Education, Inc, publishing as Adobe Press,

ISBN 978-93-528-6900-8

First Impression

Published by Pearson India Education Services Pvt. Ltd, CIN: U72200TN2005PTC057128.

Head Office: 15th Floor, Tower-B, World Trade Tower, Plot No. 1, Block-C, Sector 16, Noida 201 301, Uttar Pradesh, India.
Registered Office: 4th Floor, Software Block, Elnet Software City, TS 140, Block 2 & 9, Rajiv Gandhi Salai, Taramani, Chennai 600 113, Tamil Nadu, India.
Fax: 080-30461003, Phone: 080-30461060
Website: in.pearson.com; Email: companysecretary.india@pearson.com

Printed in India at Shree Maitrey Printech Pvt. Ltd., Noida

WHERE ARE THE LESSON FILES?

Purchase of this Classroom in a Book in any format gives you access to the lesson files you'll need to complete the exercises in the book.

You'll find the files you need on your **Account** page at peachpit.com on the **Registered Products** tab.

1 Go to www.peachpit.com/register.

2 Sign in or create a new account.

3 Enter the ISBN: 9780134852492.

4 Answer the questions as proof of purchase.

5 The lesson files can be accessed through the Registered Products tab on your Account page.

6 Click the Access Bonus Content link below the title of your product to proceed to the download page. Click the lesson file links to download them to your computer.

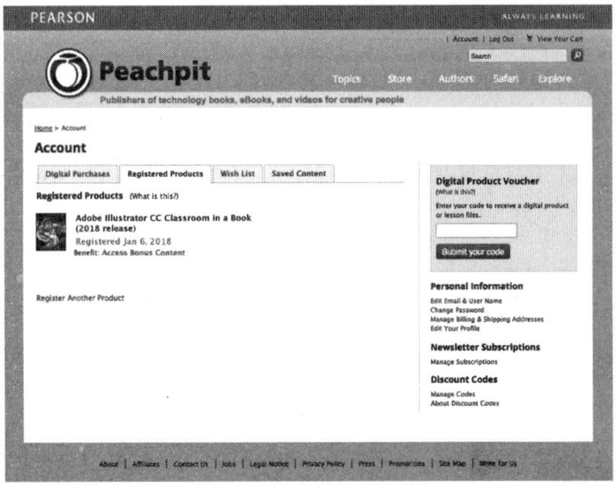

CONTENTS

2 TECHNIQUES FOR SELECTING ARTWORK 62

3 USING SHAPES TO CREATE ARTWORK FOR A POSTCARD 84

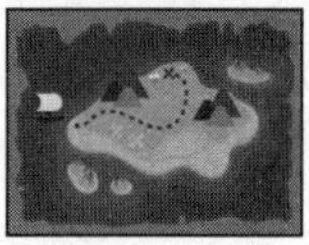

BULLSEYE
COFFEE

7 USING COLOR TO ENHANCE SIGNAGE 204

8 ADDING TYPE TO A POSTER 238

FOR SALE
$450,000

MTN RIDGE
BIKE TOURS

GETTING STARTED

Adobe® Illustrator® CC is the industry-standard illustration application for print, multimedia, and online graphics. Whether you are a designer or a technical illustrator producing artwork for print publishing, an artist producing multimedia graphics, or a creator of web pages or online content, Adobe Illustrator offers you the tools you need to get professional-quality results.

About Classroom in a Book®

Adobe Illustrator CC Classroom in a Book® (2018 release) is part of the official training series for Adobe graphics and publishing software developed with the support of Adobe product experts. The features and exercises in this book are based on Illustrator CC (2018 release).

The lessons are designed so that you can learn at your own pace. If you're new to Adobe Illustrator, you'll learn the fundamentals you need to master to put the application to work. If you are an experienced user, you'll find that Classroom in a Book® teaches many advanced features, including tips and techniques for using the latest version of Adobe Illustrator.

Although each lesson provides step-by-step instructions for creating a specific project, there's room for exploration and experimentation. You can follow the book from start to finish or do only the lessons that correspond to your interests and needs. Each lesson concludes with a review section to quiz you on what was covered.

Prerequisites

Before beginning to use *Adobe Illustrator CC Classroom in a Book® (2018 release)*, you should have working knowledge of your computer and its operating system. Make sure that you know how to use the mouse and standard menus and commands and also how to open, save, and close files. If you need to review these techniques, see the printed or online documentation for macOS or Windows.

Installing the program

● **Note:** When instructions differ by platform, macOS commands appear first and then the Windows commands, with the platform noted in parentheses. For example, "press Option (macOS) or Alt (Windows) and click away from the artwork."

Before you begin using *Adobe Illustrator CC Classroom in a Book® (2018 release),* make sure that your system is set up correctly and that you've installed the required software and hardware.

You must purchase the Adobe Illustrator CC software separately. For complete instructions on installing the software, visit http://helpx.adobe.com/illustrator.html. You must install Illustrator from Adobe Creative Cloud onto your hard disk. Follow the onscreen instructions.

Fonts used in this book

The Classroom in a Book® lesson files use fonts that are part of the Typekit Portfolio plan included with your Creative Cloud subscription, and trial Creative Cloud members have access to a selection of fonts from Typekit for web and desktop use.

For more information about fonts and installation, see the Adobe Illustrator CC Read Me file on the Web at http://helpx.adobe.com/illustrator.html.

Online content

Your purchase of this Classroom in a Book® includes online materials provided by way of your Account page on peachpit.com.

Lesson files

To work through the projects in this book, you will need to download the lesson files from peachpit.com. You can download the files for individual lessons, or it may be possible to download them all in a single file.

Web Edition

The Web Edition is an online interactive version of the book providing an enhanced learning experience. Your Web Edition can be accessed from any device with a connection to the Internet, and it contains the following:

- The complete text of the book
- Hours of instructional video keyed to the text
- Interactive quizzes

In addition, the Web Edition may be updated when Adobe adds significant feature updates between major Creative Cloud releases. To accommodate the changes, sections of the online book may be updated, or new sections may be added.

Accessing the lesson files and Web Edition

If you purchased an eBook from peachpit.com or adobepress.com, your Web Edition will automatically appear on the Digital Purchases tab on your Account page. Click the Launch link to access the product. Continue reading to learn how to register your product to get access to the lesson files.

If you purchased an eBook from a different vendor or you bought a print book, you must register your purchase on peachpit.com in order to access the online content:

1. Go to www.peachpit.com/register.
2. Sign in or create a new account.
3. Enter the ISBN: **9780134852492**.
4. Answer the questions as proof of purchase.
5. The Web Edition will appear on the Digital Purchases tab on your Account page. Click the Launch link to access the product.

The Lesson Files can be accessed through the Registered Products tab on your Account page. Click the Access Bonus Content link below the title of your product to proceed to the download page. Click the lesson file links to download them to your computer.

Restoring default preferences

● **Note:** If finding the preferences file proves difficult, please contact me at brian@brianwoodtraining.com for assistance.

The preferences file controls how command settings appear on your screen when you open the Adobe Illustrator program. Each time you quit Adobe Illustrator, the position of the panels and certain command settings are recorded in different preference files. If you want to restore the tools and settings to their original default settings, you can delete the current Adobe Illustrator Prefs file. Adobe Illustrator creates a new preferences file, if one doesn't already exist, the next time you start the program and save a file.

You must restore the default preferences for Illustrator before you begin each lesson. This ensures that the tools function and the defaults are set exactly as described in this book. When you have finished the book, you can restore your saved settings, if you like.

To delete or save the current Illustrator preferences file

● **Note:** In Windows, the AppData folder is hidden by default. You will most likely need to enable Windows to show hidden files and folders. For instructions, refer to your Windows documentation.

The preferences file is created after you quit the program the first time and is updated thereafter. *After launching Illustrator*, you can follow these steps:

1 Exit Adobe Illustrator CC.

2 Locate the file named Adobe Illustrator Prefs for macOS as follows:

- [startup drive]/Users/[username]/Library/Preferences/Adobe Illustrator 22 Settings/en_US**.

3 Locate the file named Adobe Illustrator Prefs for Windows as follows:

- [startup drive]\Users\[username]\AppData\Roaming\Adobe\Adobe Illustrator 22 Settings\en_US**\x86 or x64.

*On macOS, the Library folder is hidden by default. To access this folder, in the Finder hold down the Option key, and choose Library from the Go menu in the Finder.

**The folder name may be different depending on the language version you have installed.

▶ **Tip:** To quickly locate and delete the Adobe Illustrator preferences file each time you begin a new lesson, create a shortcut (Windows) or an alias (macOS) to the Adobe Illustrator 22 Settings folder.

For more information, refer to Illustrator help: https://helpx.adobe.com/illustrator/kb/preference-file-location-illustrator.html

If you can't find the file, that's because either you haven't started Adobe Illustrator CC yet or you have moved the preferences file. The preferences file is created after you quit the program the first time and is updated thereafter.

4 Copy the file and save it to another folder on your hard disk (if you want to restore those preferences) or delete it.

5 Start Adobe Illustrator CC.

To restore saved preferences after completing the lessons

1 Exit Adobe Illustrator CC.

2 Delete the current preferences file. Find the original preferences file that you saved and move it to the Adobe Illustrator 22 Settings folder.

Note: You can move the original preferences file rather than renaming it.

Additional resources

Adobe Illustrator CC Classroom in a Book® (2018 release) is not meant to replace documentation that comes with the program or to be a comprehensive reference for every feature. Only the commands and options used in the lessons are explained in this book. For comprehensive information about program features and tutorials, please refer to these resources:

Adobe Illustrator Learn & Support: helpx.adobe.com/illustrator.html (accessible in Illustrator by choosing Help > Illustrator Support Center) is where you can find and browse tutorials, help, and support on Adobe.com.

Adobe Forums: forums.adobe.com lets you tap into peer-to-peer discussions, questions, and answers on Adobe products.

Adobe Create Magazine: create.adobe.com offers thoughtful articles on design and design issues, a gallery showcasing the work of top-notch designers, tutorials, and more.

Resources for educators: www.adobe.com/education and edex.adobe.com offer valuable information for instructors who teach classes on Adobe software. Find solutions for education at all levels, including free curricula that can be used to prepare for the Adobe Certified Associate exams.

Also check out these useful links:

Adobe Illustrator CC product home page: See www.adobe.com/products/illustrator.

Adobe Add-ons: creative.adobe.com/addons is a central resource for finding tools, services, extensions, code samples, and more to supplement and extend your Adobe products.

Adobe Authorized Training Centers

Adobe Authorized Training Centers offer instructor-led courses and training on Adobe products. A directory of AATCs is available at training.adobe.com/trainingpartners.

WHAT'S NEW IN ADOBE ILLUSTRATOR CC (2018 RELEASE)

Adobe Illustrator CC (2018 release) is packed with new and innovative features to help you produce artwork more efficiently for print, web, and digital video publication. The features and exercises in this book are based on Illustrator CC (2018 release). In this section, you'll learn about many of these new features—how they function and how you can use them in your work.

New Properties panel

The new Properties panel in Illustrator lets you view settings and controls in the context of your current task or workflow. This new panel has been designed with ease of use in mind, ensuring that you have access to the right controls right when you need them.

The Properties panel is available by default in the Essentials workspace. You can also choose Window > Properties to view it.

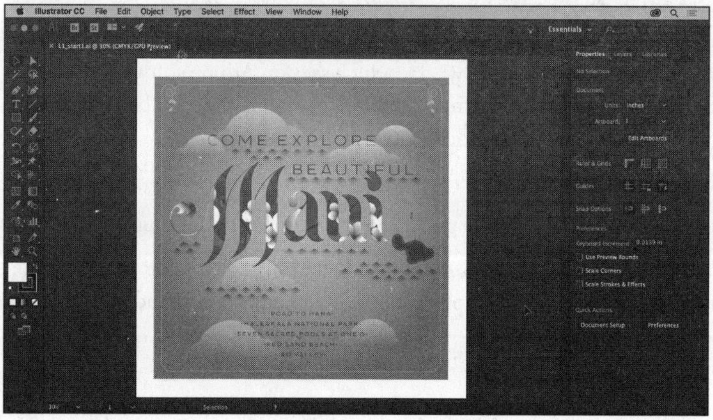

Puppet Warp tool

Puppet Warp lets you twist and distort parts of your artwork, to make transformations that appear natural. You can add, move, and rotate pins to seamlessly transform your artwork into different positions and stances using the new Puppet Warp tool in Illustrator.

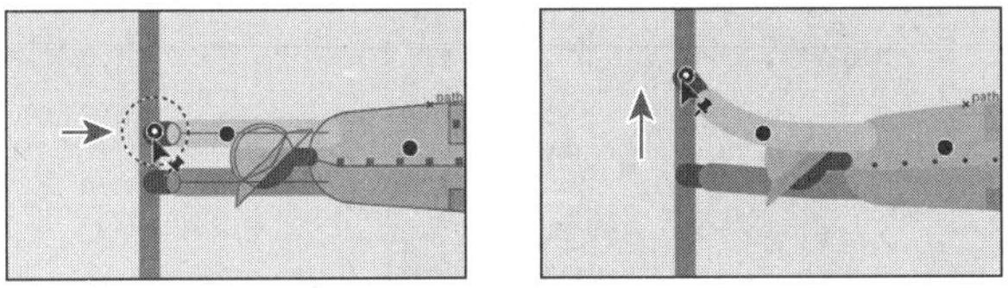

Artboard Improvements

There are a lot of artboard improvements in Illustrator CC (2018 release). The following is a list of those improvements and new features:

- Artboards are much easier to work with in this release of Illustrator CC.
- You can now create 1 to 1,000 artboards per document depending on the size of your artboards.
- You can also now select multiple artboards.
- Artboards can now be aligned and distributed.

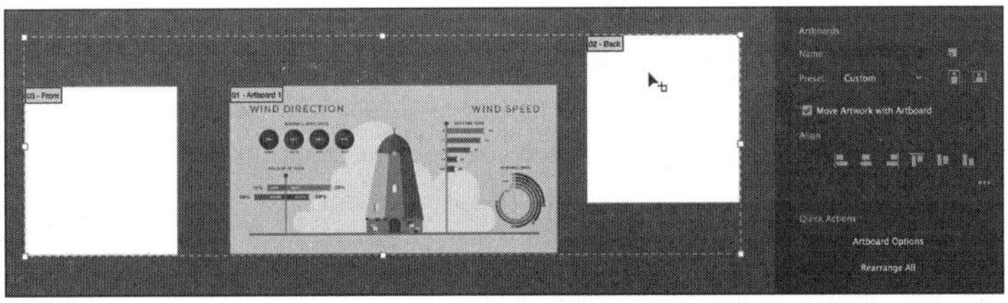

Variable fonts

Illustrator now supports Variable Fonts, a new OpenType font format supporting custom attributes like weight, width, slant, optical size, etc. This release of Illustrator ships with several variable fonts for which you can adjust weight, width, and slant using convenient slider controls available when you click in the Character panel, Character Styles panel, and Paragraph Styles panel.

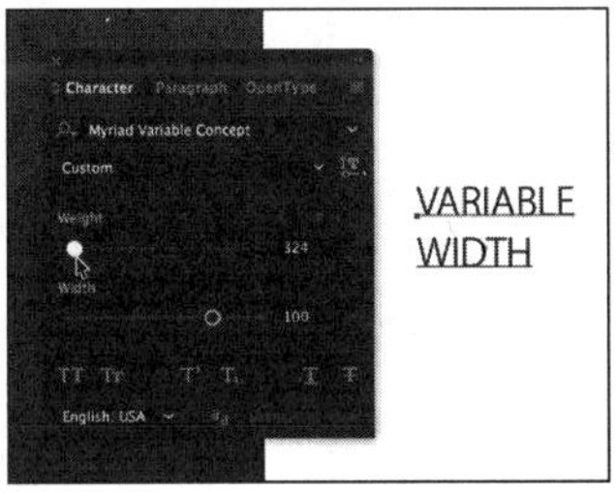

Note: To learn more about the Variable Fonts, visit helpx.adobe.com/illustrator/using/fonts.html.

Enhanced export experience

You can now collect objects in the Asset Export panel for export as a single asset or multiple assets. Simply drag your artwork to the Asset Export panel. Alternatively, right-click a piece of artwork and then choose Collect for Export > As Multiple Assets from the context menu.

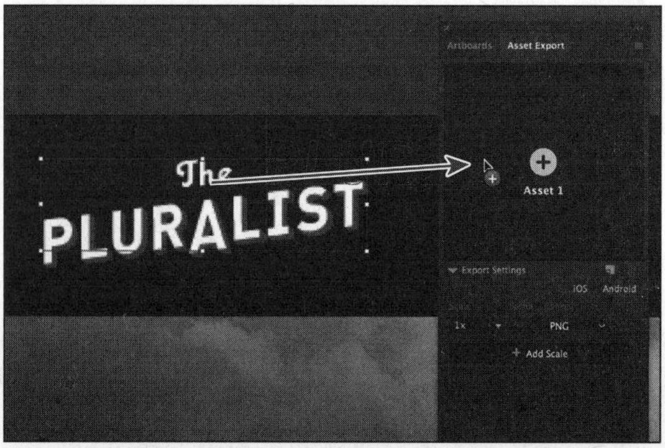

Add and share text assets using Creative Cloud libraries

Now, you can add text objects from your Illustrator documents to Creative Cloud libraries and then share them with other users and across applications. Text assets in a library retain the character/paragraph styles and other attributes originally applied to them. You can reuse text assets in libraries across Illustrator or InDesign documents. However, if a text object has effects and appearances applied to it, you must add it to the library as a graphics asset to preserve them.

Other enhancements

- You can now disable zoom to selection. Choose Illustrator CC > Preferences > Selection & Anchor Display (macOS) or Edit > Preferences > Selection & Anchor Display (Windows) and then deselect the Zoom To Selection option.
- You can now preview font characteristics, such as size, style, leading, and tracking in real time by simply hovering over the font characteristics in the Properties panel, Control panel, and Character panel.
- A new swatch is now a Global swatch by default.
- The New Document dialog box displays the units of measurement in the text boxes, such as Width and Height. You can use the formulas to add, subtract, multiply, and divide for quick computations of the preset dimensions in the New Document dialog box. You can also specify the Color Mode, Raster Effects, and Preview Mode settings of your document.
- You can now use the Path > Join command (Command+J [macOS] or Ctrl+J [Windows]) in Illustrator to join the end points of compound paths and artwork in different groups.

This list touches on just a few of the new and enhanced features of Illustrator CC (2018 release), yet still exemplifies Adobe's commitment to providing the best tools possible for your publishing needs. We hope you enjoy working with Illustrator CC (2018 release) as much as we do.

—The *Adobe Illustrator CC Classroom in a Book® (2018 release)* team

A QUICK TOUR OF ADOBE ILLUSTRATOR CC (2018 RELEASE)

Lesson overview

In this interactive demonstration of Adobe Illustrator CC (2018 release), you'll get an overview of the main features of the application.

This lesson takes approximately 45 minutes to complete. Please log in to your account on peachpit.com to download the lesson files for this chapter, or go to the "Getting Started" section at the beginning of this book and follow the instructions under "Accessing the lesson files and Web Edition."

Your Account page is also where you'll find any updates to the chapters or to the lesson files. Look on the Lesson & Update Files tab to access the most current content.

In this demonstration of Adobe Illustrator CC, you'll be introduced to some key fundamentals for working in the application.

Getting started

For the first lesson of this book, you'll get a quick tour of the most widely used tools and features in Adobe Illustrator CC, offering a sense of the many possibilities. Along the way, you'll create artwork for a condominium flyer. First, you'll open the final artwork to see what you will create in this lesson.

● **Note:** If you have not already downloaded the project files for this lesson to your computer from your Account page, make sure to do so now. See "Getting Started" at the beginning of the book.

● **Note:** If a Tour window appears after opening the document, you can simply close it.

1 To ensure that the tools and panels function exactly as described in this lesson, delete or deactivate (by renaming) the Adobe Illustrator CC preferences file. See "Restoring default preferences" in the "Getting Started" section at the beginning of the book.

2 Start Adobe Illustrator CC.

3 Choose File > Open, or click Open in the Start workspace that is showing. Open the L00_end.ai file in the Lessons > Lesson00 folder.

4 Choose View > Fit Artboard In Window to see an example of the artwork you'll create in this lesson. Leave the file open for reference, if you'd like.

Creating a new document

● **Note:** Learn more about creating and editing artboards in Lesson 5, "Transforming Artwork."

In Illustrator, you can start a new document using a series of preset options, depending on your needs. In this case, you will print the artwork you create as a postcard, so you will choose the Print preset to start.

1 Choose File > New.

2 In the New Document dialog box, select the Print category along the top of the dialog box.

Click the Letter document preset.

In the Preset Details area on the right, change the following:

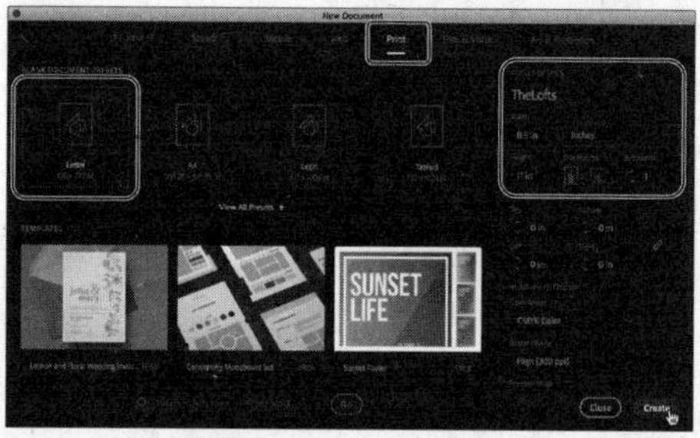

- Name: **TheLofts**
- Units (to the right of Width): **Inches**
- Width: **8.5 in** (the default setting)
- Height: **11 in** (the default setting)

3 Click Create, and a new, blank document opens.

4 Choose File > Save As. In the Save As dialog box, leave the name as TheLofts.ai, and navigate to the Lessons > Lesson00 folder. Leave the Format option set to Adobe Illustrator (ai) (macOS) or the Save As Type option set to Adobe Illustrator (*.AI) (Windows), and click Save.

5 In the Illustrator Options dialog box that appears, leave the Illustrator options at their default settings and then click OK.

6 Choose Window > Workspace > Reset Essentials.

Note: If you don't see Reset Essentials in the Workspace menu, choose Window > Workspace > Essentials before choosing Window > Workspace > Reset Essentials.

Drawing a shape

Drawing shapes is the cornerstone of Illustrator, and you'll create many of them in the coming lessons. To start your project, you'll create a rectangle.

Note: Learn more about creating and editing shapes in Lesson 3, "Using Shapes to Create Artwork for a Postcard."

1 Choose View > Fit Artboard In Window.

The white area you see is called the *artboard*, and it's where your printable artwork will go. Artboards are like pages in Adobe InDesign®.

2 Select the Rectangle tool (▭) in the Tools panel on the left. Move the pointer into the upper-left part of the artboard (see the red X in the figure). Click and drag down and to the right. When the gray measurement label next to the pointer shows a width of *approximately* 6.5 inches and a height of 7 inches, release the mouse button. The shape will be selected.

Note: You can also create shapes by clicking the artboard with a shape tool and modifying shape properties before they are created.

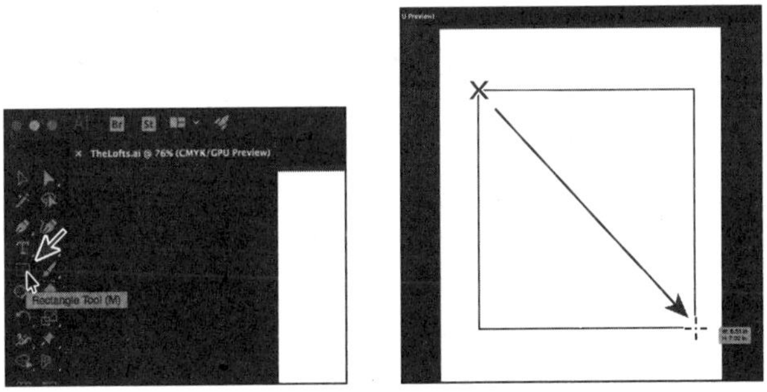

Editing shapes

Most shapes are *live*, which means you can edit them without switching away from the drawing tool, like the Rectangle tool. Next, you'll round the corners of the rectangle you just drew.

1 With the rectangle still selected, drag the bottom, middle point on the rectangle down until you see a height of about 7.6 inches.

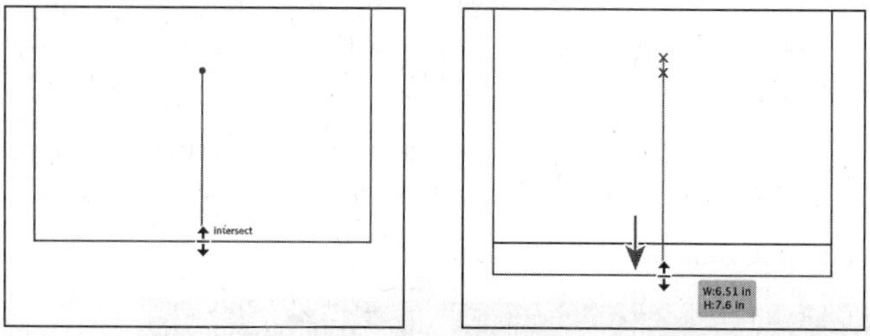

2 Move the pointer over the center of the shape (the blue circle). When the pointer changes (), drag the rectangle into the approximate center of the artboard.

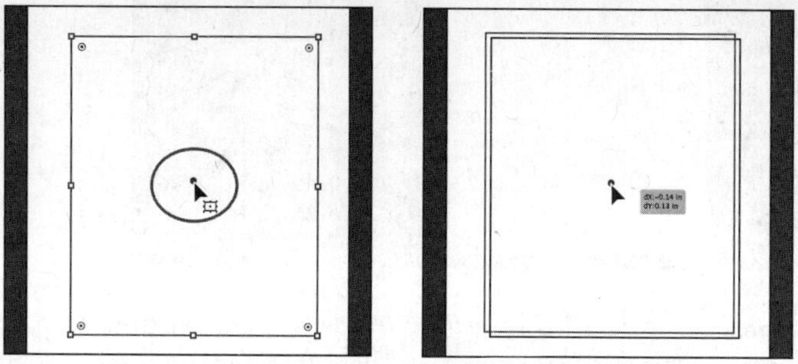

▶ **Tip:** You can also round all of the corners independently. You'll learn more about creating and editing Live Shapes in Lesson 3, "Using Shapes to Create Artwork for a Postcard."

3 With the rectangle still selected, click and drag the upper-right corner widget (⦿) toward the center of the rectangle. When the gray measurement label shows a value of approximately 0.4 in, release the mouse button.

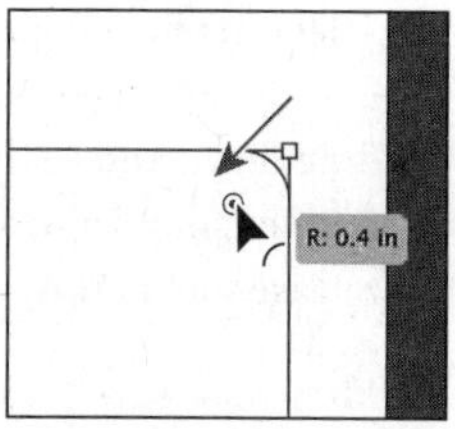

A lot of the different types of shapes you can create have widgets, like the corner widgets, for editing properties such as the number of sides on a polygon, adding pie angles to ellipses, and more.

4 Choose File > Save to save the document.

Applying and editing color

Applying color to artwork is a common Illustrator task. Shapes you create can have a stroke (border) and a fill. There are many ways in Illustrator to create your own colors and edit colors that come with each document by default, called *swatches*. In this section, you'll change the fill of the selected shape and edit the color you apply.

Note: Learn more about fill and stroke in Lesson 7, "Using Color to Enhance Signage."

1 With the rectangle still selected, click the Fill color box to the left of the word "Fill" in the Properties panel to the right of the Document window. In the panel that opens, make sure that the Swatches option (▦) is selected at the top of the panel to show the default swatches. Move the pointer over an orange swatch, and when a tooltip appears ("C=0, M=50, Y=100, K=0"), click to apply the orange color to the *fill* of the shape.

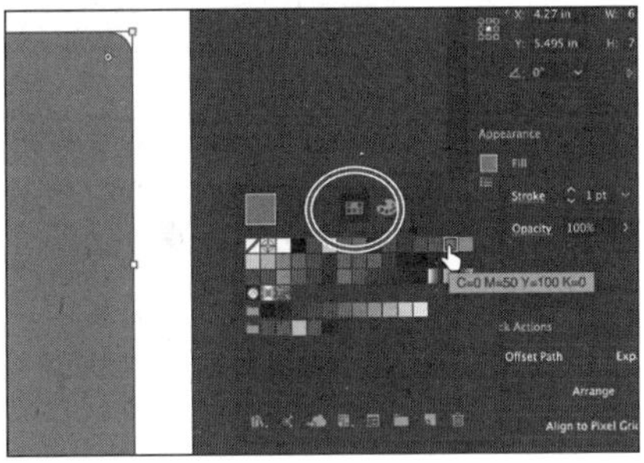

While you can use the predefined swatches, you can also create your own colors and save them as swatches to reuse them later.

2 With the swatches still showing for the fill, double-click the orange swatch you just applied to the shape to edit the color.

3 In the Swatch Options dialog box, change the values to C=**0**, M=**0**, Y=**0**, K=**8** and select Preview to see the change to the shape. Click OK to edit the swatch color for the rectangle. Press Escape to hide the Swatches panel.

Note: Going forward, you'll find you need to hide panels such as the Fill color panel before you continue. You can press Escape to do this.

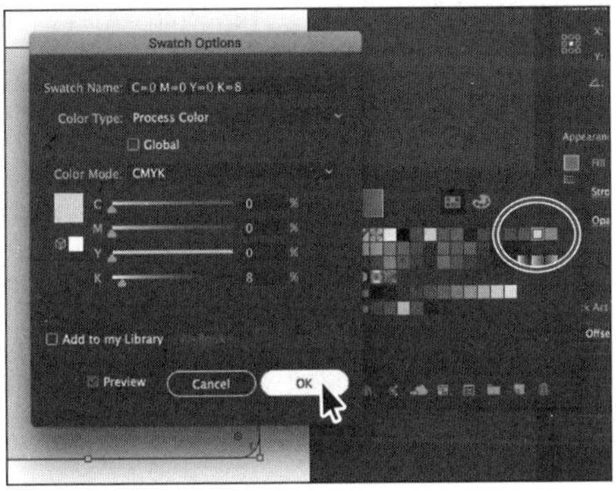

Editing strokes

● **Note:** Learn more about working with strokes in Lesson 3, "Using Shapes to Create Artwork for a Postcard."

A stroke can be the visible outline (border) of artwork like shapes and paths. There are a lot of appearance properties you can change for a stroke, including width, color, dashes, and more. In this section, you'll adjust the stroke of the rectangle.

1 With the rectangle still selected, click the color box ( ) to the left of the word "Stroke" in the Properties panel. In the panel that appears, make sure the Swatches option ( ) is selected to show the default colors that come with the document. Click to apply a medium gray color.

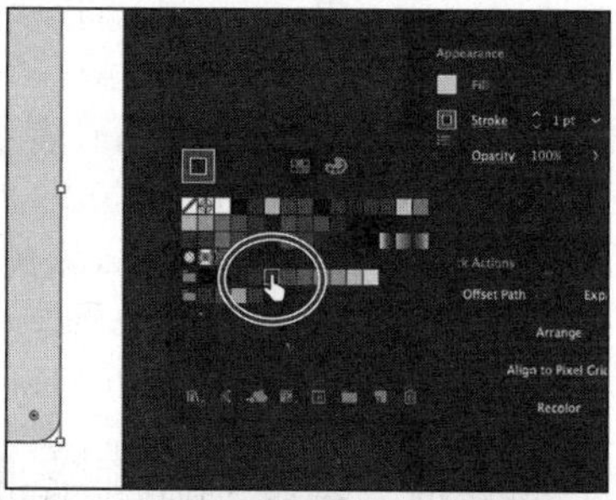

2 Click the word "Stroke" in the Properties panel to open the Stroke panel. Change the following options:

- Stroke Weight: **3 pt**
- Align Stroke: **Align Stroke to Outside** ( )
- Dashed Line: **Selected**
- Dash: **50 pt**, Gap: **3 pt**. After typing the Gap value, press Enter or Return.

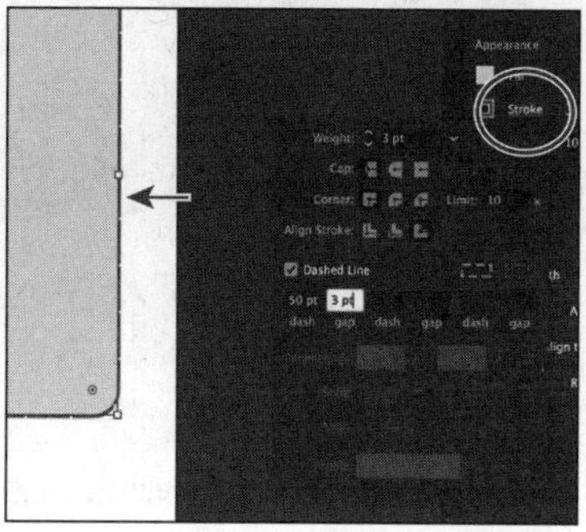

3 Choose Object > Lock > Selection to temporarily lock the rectangle so that it can't be selected.

Working with layers

● **Note:** Learn more about working with layers and the Layers panel in Lesson 9, "Organizing Your Artwork with Layers."

Layers allow you to organize and more easily select artwork. Next, using the Layers panel, you'll start to organize your artwork.

1 Choose Window > Layers to show the Layers panel to the right of the document.

2 Double-click the text "Layer 1" (the layer name) in the Layers panel. Type **Background**, and press Return or Enter to change the layer name.

Naming layers can be helpful when organizing content. Currently, the rectangle you created is on this layer.

3 Click the Create New Layer button (■) at the bottom of the Layers panel to create a new, blank layer.

4 Double-click the new layer name, Layer 2, and type **Content**. Press Return or Enter to change the layer name.

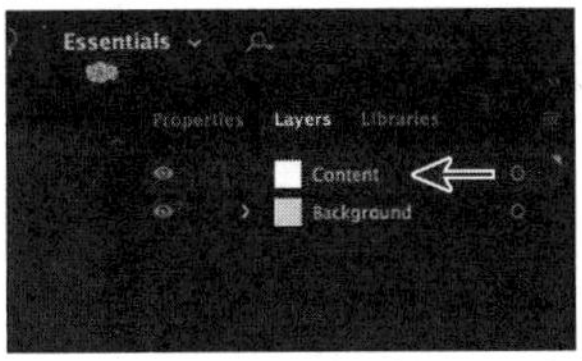

5 Click the Content layer to make sure it's selected in the Layers panel. Any new artwork will be put on the selected layer.

Transforming artwork

In Illustrator, there are a number of ways to move, rotate, skew, scale, distort, and shear (and more) artwork so you can get it just the way you want. This is called *transforming* artwork and is something you'll do next to a building icon you create.

● **Note:** Learn more about transforming artwork in Lesson 5, "Transforming Artwork."

1 Select the Line Segment tool (/) in the Tools panel on the left. In the middle of the artboard, to create a line, drag from left to right. As you drag, press and hold the Shift key to make the line straight. When you see a D (Distance) of 1.5 inches in the gray label next to the pointer, release the mouse button *and then* the key.

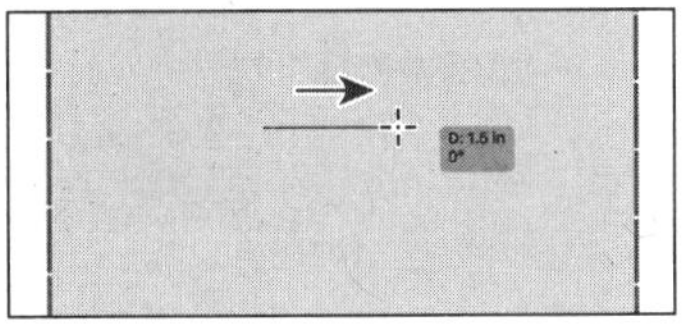

2 Press the letter D to set the default fill color (white), stroke color (black), and stroke weight (1 pt) for the line.

3 Choose View > Zoom In twice to zoom in to the selected line.

4 Click the Properties panel tab on the right side of the workspace to see the Properties panel. Change the stroke weight of the selected line by choosing 14 pt from the stroke weight menu.

▶ **Tip:** You can also choose Window > Properties to open the Properties panel.

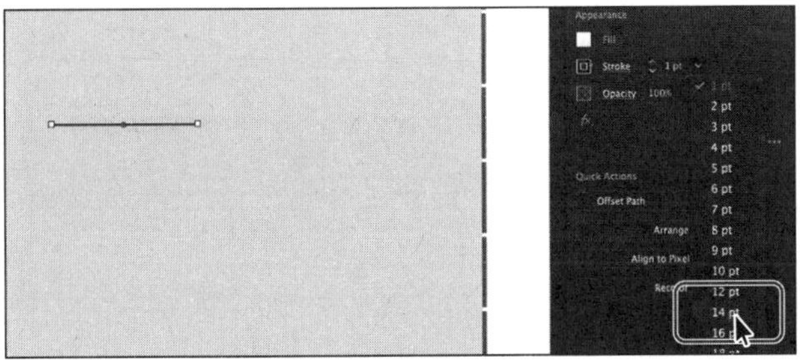

5 Move the pointer just above the line and drag from the left edge of the line to the right, while pressing the Shift key, to create a straight line. Release the mouse button *and then* the key.

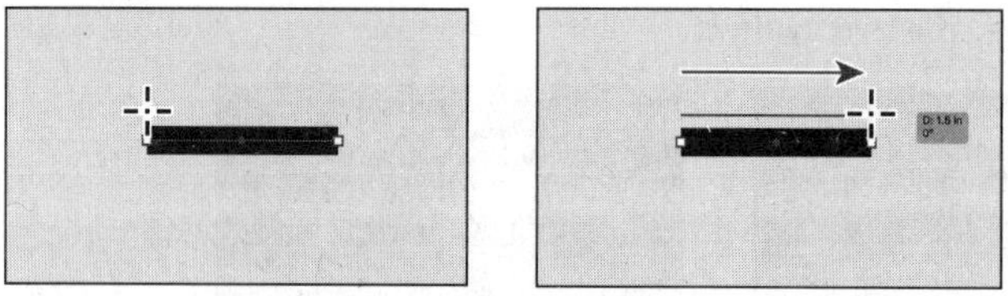

6 Change the stroke weight of the new line to 3 pt in the Properties panel by choosing it from the stroke weight menu. Now you'll make copies of the line.

7 With the line selected, choose Object > Transform > Move. In the Move dialog box, change the Vertical value to **–0.3**. Select Preview and then click Copy.

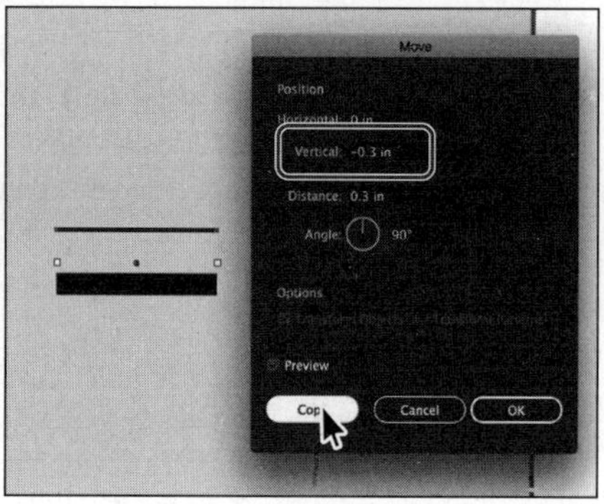

8 Choose Object > Transform > Transform Again to repeat the last Move transformation on the selected line, and make another copy of the line.

9 With the last line copy selected, select the Rotate tool ( ) in the Tools panel on the left. Click the left end of the line to set a point to rotate around there (see the first part of the following figure). Move the pointer to the right of the line and drag counterclockwise to rotate the line a little. When you see an angle of around 10 degrees in the gray label next to the pointer, stop dragging.

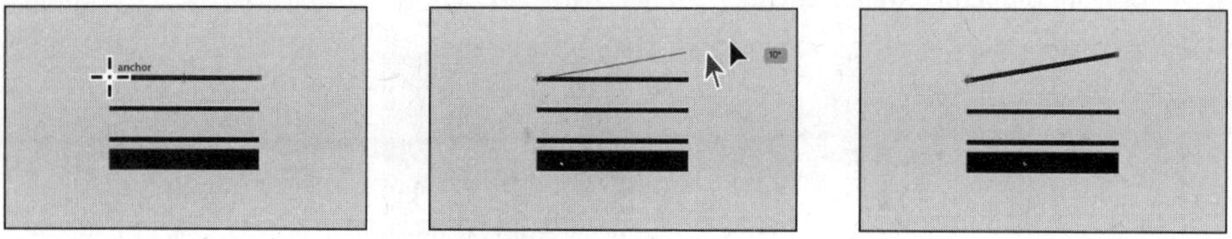

10 Choose Select > Deselect.

Creating a blend

You can blend two distinct objects to create and distribute shapes evenly between two objects. For instance, to create a fence, you could blend two rectangles together, and Illustrator will create all the copies between the two original rectangles. Next, you'll create the rest of the building icon using a blend.

Note: Learn more about working with blends in Lesson 10, "Gradients, Blends, and Patterns."

1 Select the Line Segment tool (/) in the Tools panel again. Move the pointer over the top line you rotated (see the first part of the following figure). Drag straight down to create a new line. As you drag, press and hold the Shift key to make it straight. When the pointer reaches the bottom thinner line, release the mouse button *and then* the key.

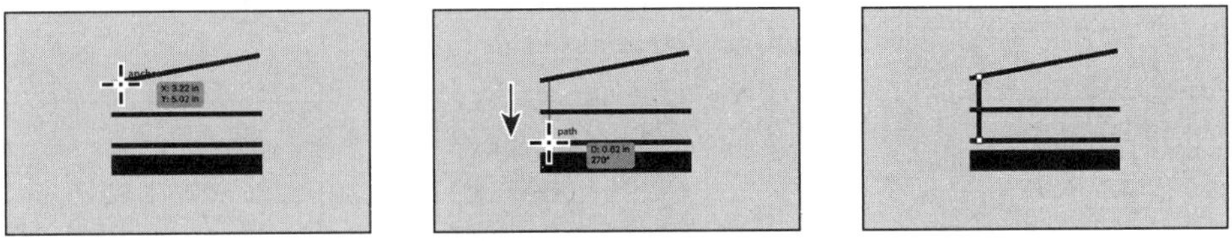

2 Change the stroke weight to **1** in the Properties panel to the right.

3 Position the pointer over the center widget (the center circle) of the selected line. When the pointer changes (), press and hold Option+Shift (macOS) or Alt+Shift (Windows), and drag to the right. Drag until you almost reach the right end of the lines. Release the mouse button and then release the keys.

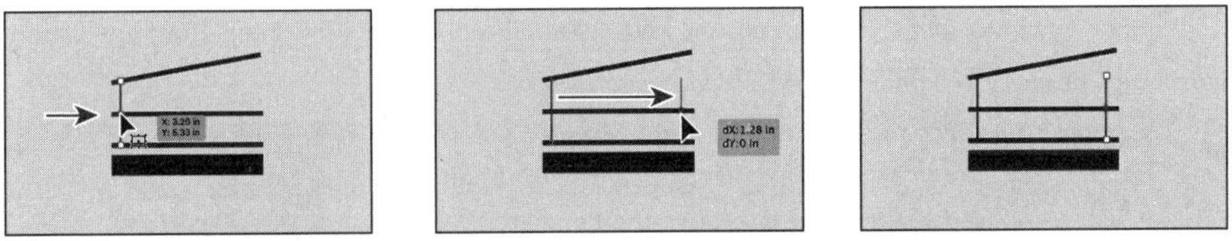

4 Move the pointer over the top of the new line and drag straight up to extend the line to the top line. When the line you are extending touches the top line, the word "intersect" may appear.

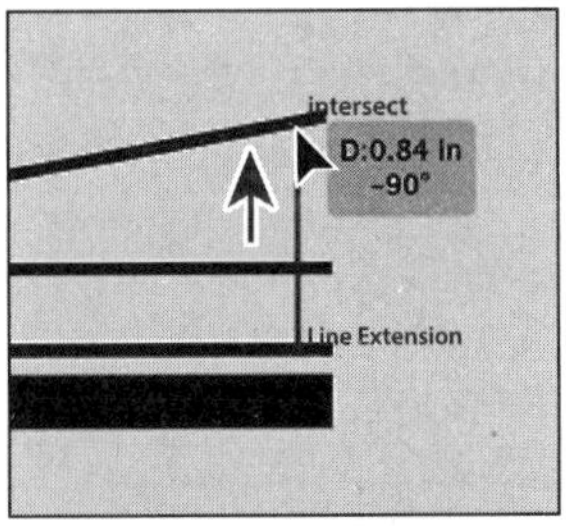

Tip: There are lots of keyboard commands that can help you work more efficiently in Illustrator. The Option (Alt) key copies a shape, and the Shift key constrains the movement to 0, 45, or 90 degrees.

5 Double-click the Blend tool () in the Tools panel to set a few settings for the tool. In the Blend Options dialog box, choose Specified Steps from the Spacing menu, and change the value to the right to **5**. Click OK.

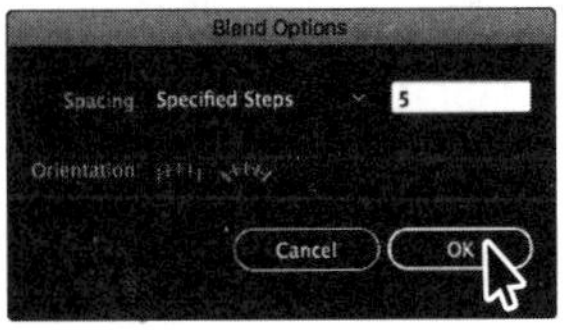

6 Click the vertical line on the left when you see the cursor look like this: . Then click the vertical line to the right when the cursor looks like this: . This creates a blend of the two lines, with five copies between them.

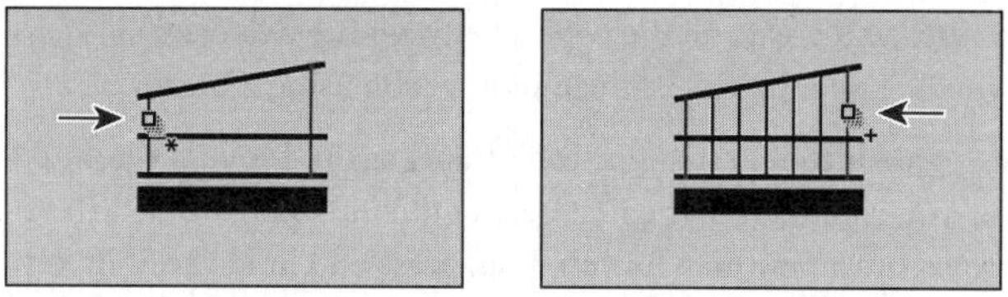

7 Select the Selection tool () in the Tools panel, and drag across all of the artwork for the building icon. Click the Group button in the Properties panel to keep it all together and treat it as a single object.

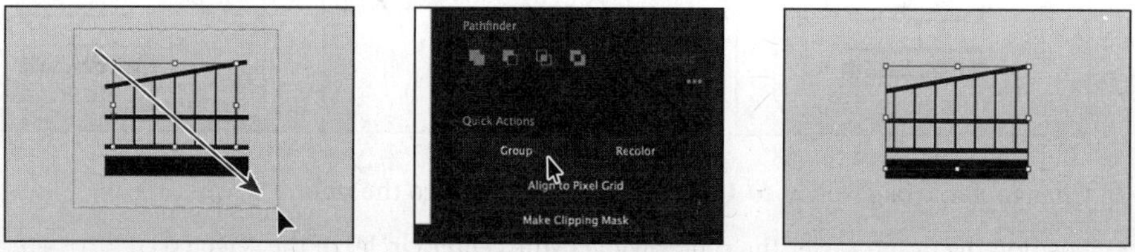

Drawing with the Pencil tool

Note: Learn more about working with the Pencil tool and other drawing tools in Lesson 6, "Creating an Illustration with the Drawing Tools."

The Pencil tool () lets you draw freeform paths that contain curves and straight lines. The paths you draw with the Pencil tool are editable later. Now you'll draw a bush with the Pencil tool.

1 Click and hold down on the Shaper tool () in the Tools panel on the left, and in the tools menu that appears, select the Pencil tool ().

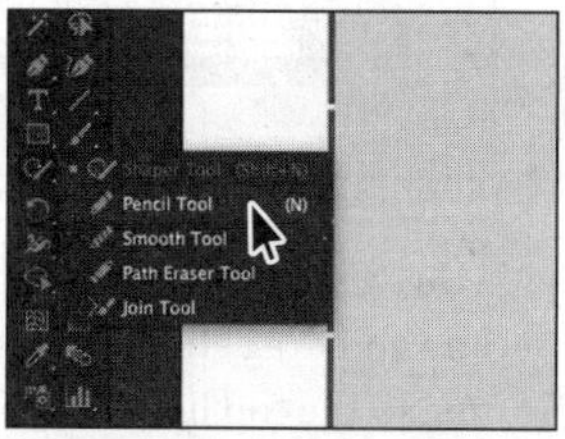

For the next step, don't worry about matching what you see in the figures. Just have some fun.

2 To the left of the building icon, click and drag to create a bush. When the pointer approaches where you started drawing, a circle will appear next to the Pencil tool (), indicating that the path will be closed. Release the mouse button to close the path. Leave the path selected.

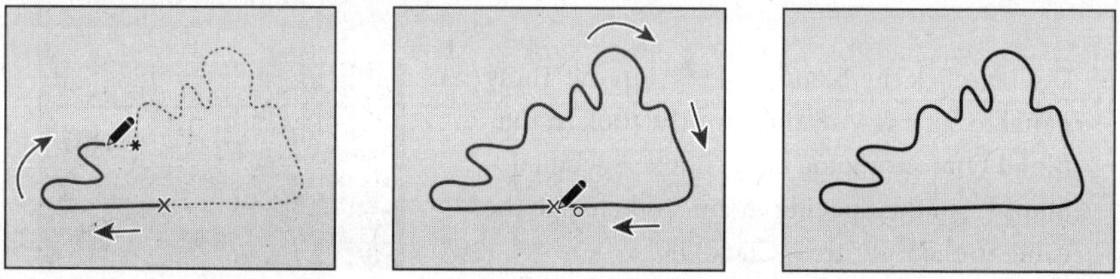

3 Click the Fill color box in the Properties panel to the right to reveal a panel. Make sure that the Swatches option (▦) is selected, and click to apply a blue/green color to the *fill* of the shape.

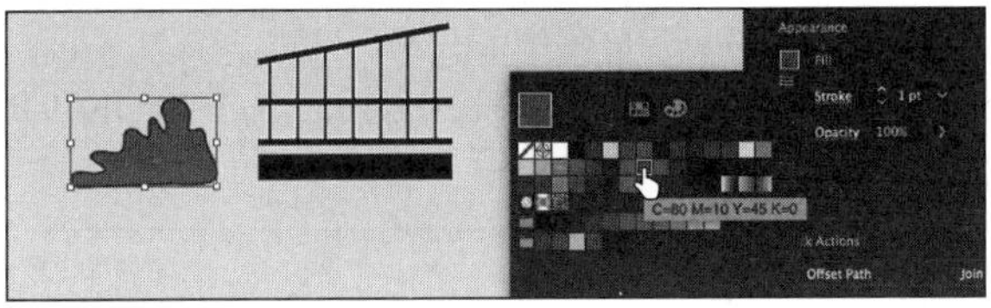

4 Change the stroke weight to **0** below the fill color in the Properties panel.

5 Select the Selection tool in the Tools panel, and drag the bush shape to the left of the building icon. Press the Shift key and drag a corner of the box around the bush, called a *bounding box*, to scale it in proportion to the building icon (see the figure for sizing). When finished resizing, release the mouse button and then the key.

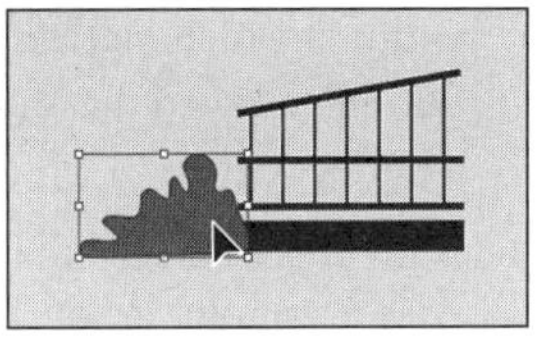

● **Note:** The Shift key maintains the proportions of the artwork as you scale it.

6 With the bush selected, choose Edit > Copy and then Edit > Paste. Drag the bush copy to the right of the building icon.

7 Click the Flip Along Horizontal Axis option (▶◀) in the Properties panel.

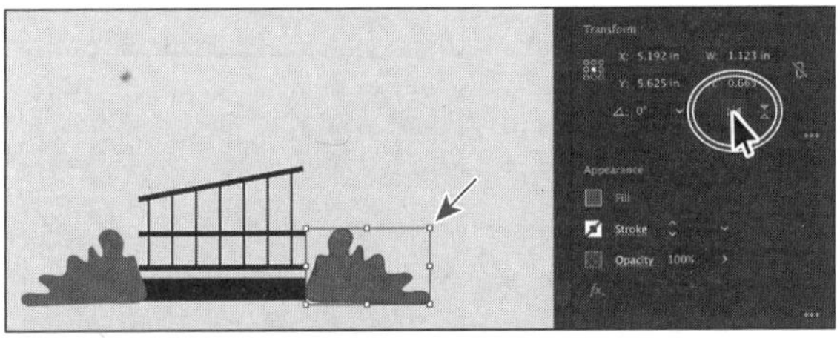

8 Drag across the building icon and the two bush shapes to select them. Choose Object > Group to keep them together.

▶ **Tip:** You could have also clicked the Group button in the Properties panel like you did earlier in the lesson.

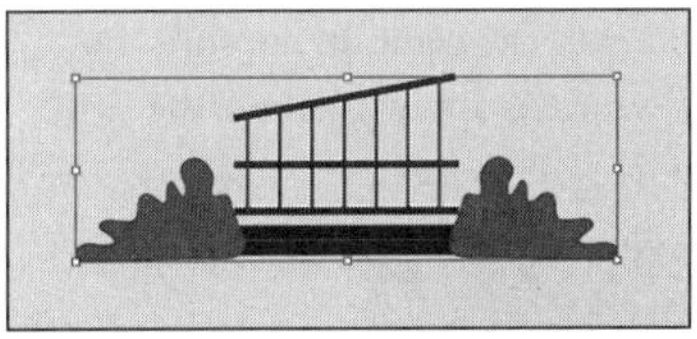

Creating shapes using the Shape Builder tool

● **Note:** Learn more about working with the Shape Builder tool in Lesson 4, "Editing and Combining Shapes and Paths."

The Shape Builder tool (◐) is an interactive tool for creating complex shapes by merging and erasing simpler shapes. Next, you'll make a cloud by creating a few circles and using the Shape Builder tool to combine them.

1 Click and hold down on the Rectangle tool (■) in the Tools panel on the left. Select the Ellipse tool (●) in the menu that appears.

2 Press and hold the Shift key, and drag above the building icon and bushes. When the gray measurement label next to the pointer shows a height and width of 1 inch, release the mouse button and then the Shift key to create a perfect circle.

3 With the circle selected, choose Edit > Copy and then Edit > Paste to paste a copy. Choose Edit > Paste two more times to create a few more copies.

4 Select the Selection tool (▶), and drag each of the circles on top of one another into a cloud shape.

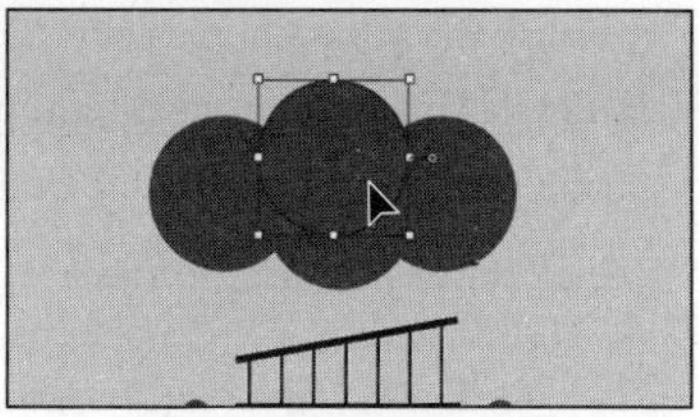

5 With a circle selected, drag a corner of the bounding box around the circle to make it smaller. Do the same for a few of the other circles, making them all different sizes. Drag to arrange them into a cloud shape.

6 Move the pointer above and to the left of the circles. Drag across all of the circles to select them.

7 Click the Fill color box in the Properties panel to the right, make sure the Swatches option (■) is selected, and click white to apply it. Leave the circles selected.

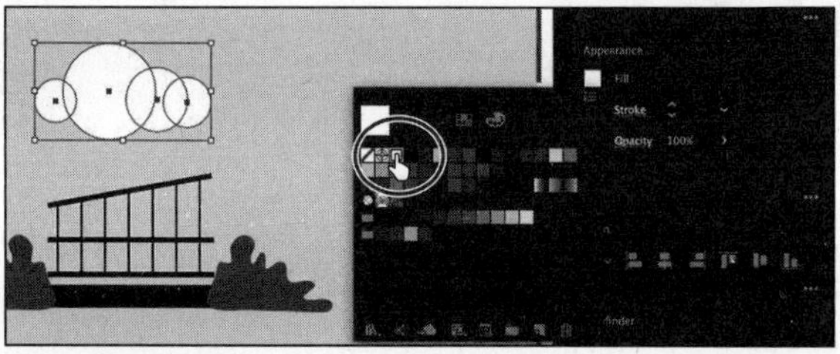

8 Select the Shape Builder tool ( ) in the Tools panel on the left. Position the pointer to the left and above all of the selected circles (see the red X in the figure). Press the Shift key and drag to the right and down across all the selected circles. Release the mouse button and then the Shift key to combine the shapes.

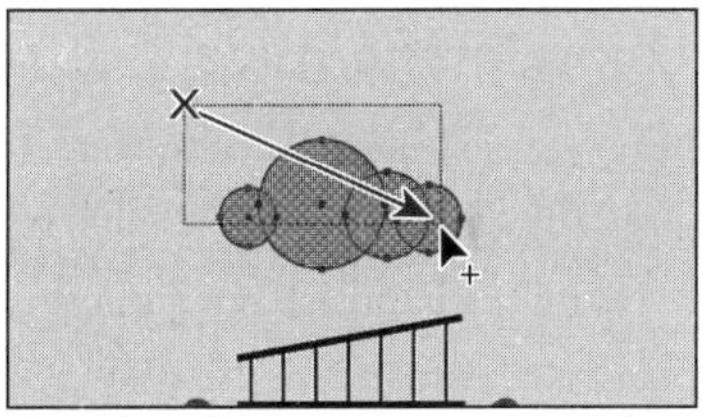

9 Choose Object > Hide > Selection to temporarily hide the cloud.

10 Choose File > Save.

Placing an image in Illustrator

In Illustrator, you can place raster images, like JPEG and Adobe Photoshop® files, and either link to them or embed them. Next, you'll place an image of hand-drawn text.

1 Choose View > Fit Artboard In Window.

2 Choose File > Place. In the Place dialog box, navigate to the Lessons > Lesson00 folder, and select the HandLettering.psd file. Make sure that the Link option in the dialog box is selected, and click Place.

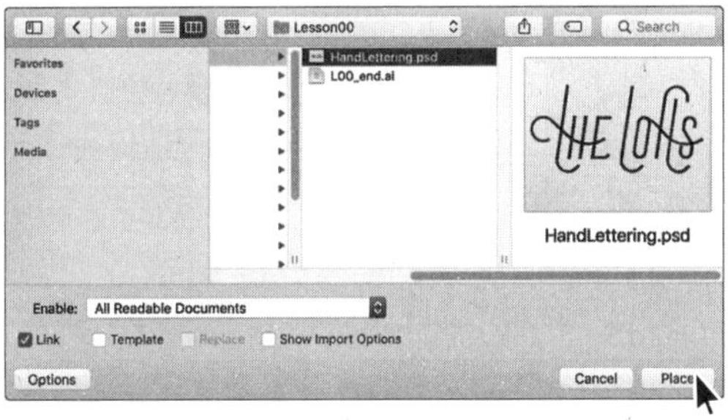

3 With the loaded graphics cursor, click in the upper-left corner of the rectangle to place the image. Leave it selected.

● **Note:** Learn more about placing images in Lesson 14, "Using Illustrator CC with Other Adobe Applications."

● **Note:** On macOS, if you don't see the Link option in the dialog box, click the Options button.

Using Image Trace

● **Note:** Learn more about Image Trace in Lesson 3, "Using Shapes to Create Artwork for a Postcard."

You can use Image Trace to convert raster images into vector artwork. Next, you'll trace the Photoshop file you just placed.

1 With the hand-lettering image still selected, click the Image Trace button in the Properties panel to the right and choose Black and White Logo from the menu.

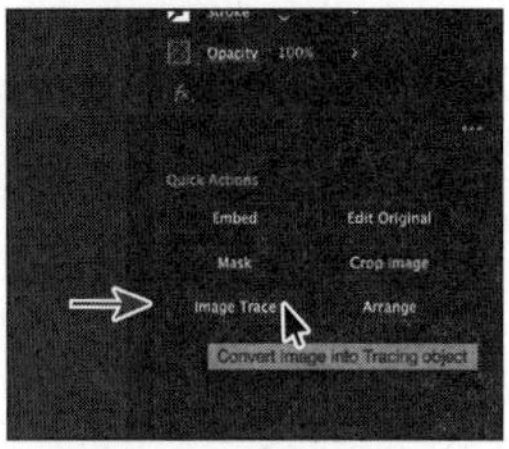

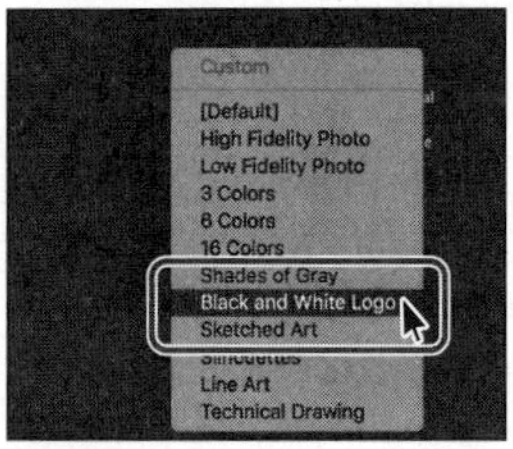

▶ **Tip:** Another method for converting the hand-drawn lettering is by using the Adobe Capture® CC app. To learn more about Adobe Capture, visit http://www.adobe.com/products/capture.html.

2 Click the Image Trace panel button (▤) in the Properties panel. In the Image Trace panel that opens, click the toggle arrow to the left of Advanced (circled in the following figure). Select Ignore White near the bottom of the panel to remove the white. Close the Image Trace panel by clicking the small X at the top.

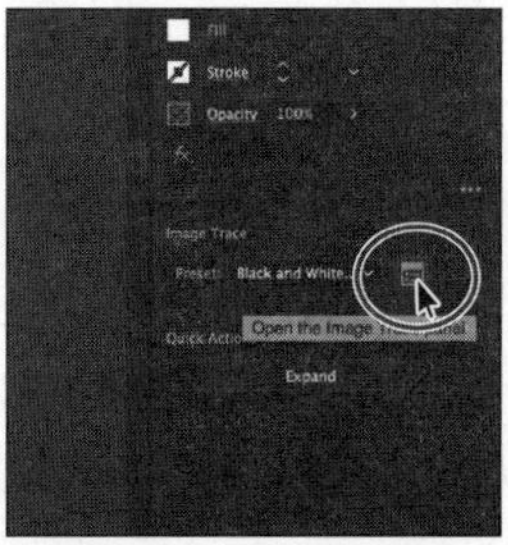

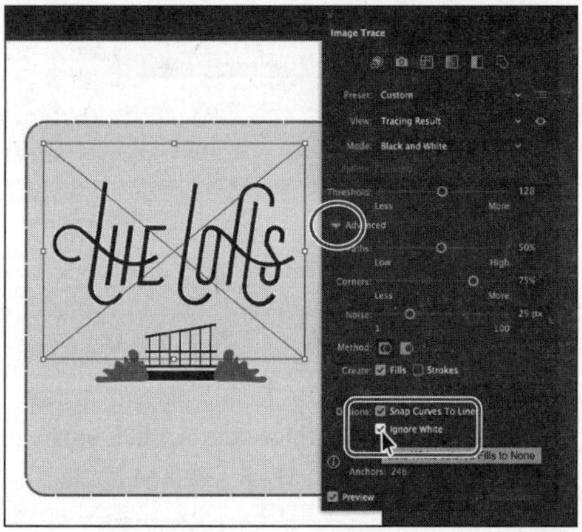

● **Note:** The hand lettering for this project was created by Danielle Fritz (www.behance.net/danielle_fritz).

3 With the lettering still selected, click the Expand button in the Quick Actions section of the Properties panel to make the object a series of editable vector shapes that are grouped together.

4 Select the Selection tool (▶). Move the pointer onto the lettering and drag it so that it's above the building icon and bushes, if it isn't already. Leave the hand-lettering shapes selected.

Creating and editing gradients

Gradients are color blends of two or more colors that you can apply to the fill or stroke of artwork. Next, you will apply a gradient to the lettering.

● **Note:** Learn more about working with gradients in Lesson 10, "Gradients, Blends, and Patterns."

1 With the lettering still selected, click the Fill color box in the Properties panel to the right, make sure the Swatches option (▦) is selected, and select the white-to-black swatch with the tooltip "White, Black." Leave the panel with the swatches showing.

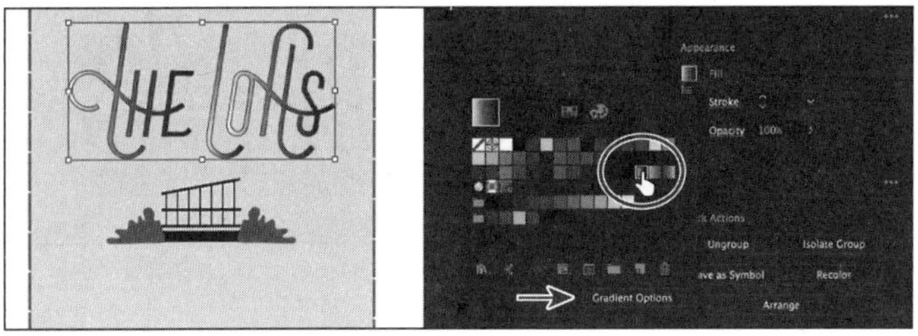

2 At the bottom of the panel with the swatches, click the Gradient Options button to open the Gradient panel. An arrow is pointing to the button in the previous figure.

You may need to drag the Gradient panel by the title bar at the top to see the whole thing.

3 In the Gradient panel, click the Fill box to make sure you are editing the fill (circled in the following figure). Double-click the little white color stop (▯) on the left side of the gradient slider in the Gradient panel (an arrow is pointing to it in the figure). In the panel that appears, click the Swatches button (▦) (if it's not already selected), and select the dark gray swatch with the tooltip "C=0, M=0, Y=0, K=70."

4 Press the Escape key to hide the color swatches.

5 Select the Gradient tool (■) in the Tools panel on the left. While pressing the Shift key, starting at the red X in the figure, click and drag down across the lettering to reposition and resize the gradient. Release the mouse button and then the key.

6 Choose Select > Deselect, and click the X at the top of the Gradient panel to close it.

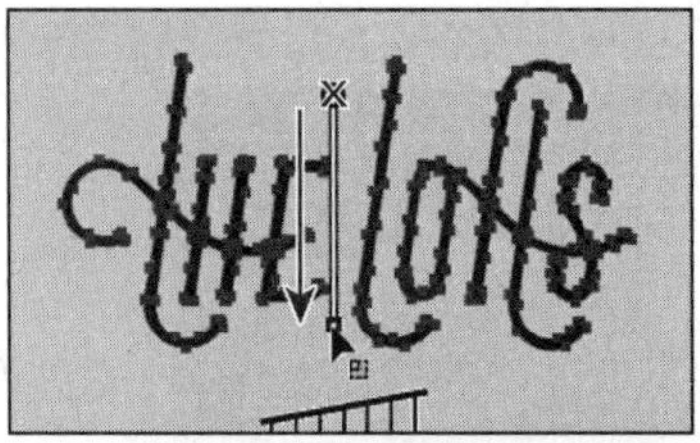

Working with type

● **Note:** Learn more about working with type in Lesson 8, "Adding Type to a Poster."

Next, you'll add some text to the project and change the formatting. You'll choose a Typekit font that requires an Internet connection. If you don't have an Internet connection, you can simply choose another font you have.

1 Select the Type tool (T) in the Tools panel on the left, and click in a blank area at the top of the artboard, above the "THE LOFTS" lettering. A text area will appear with the selected placeholder text, "Lorem ipsum." Type **on59th** (with no space between "on" and "59th").

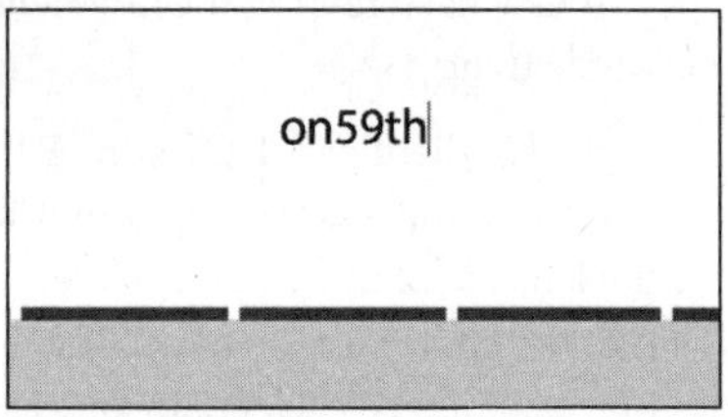

2 With the cursor still in the text, choose Select > All to select all of the text.

3 In the Properties panel to the right, click the Fill color box. In the panel that appears, make sure the Swatches option is selected, and click to select the darker gray swatch with the tooltip "C=0 M=0 Y=0 K=70."

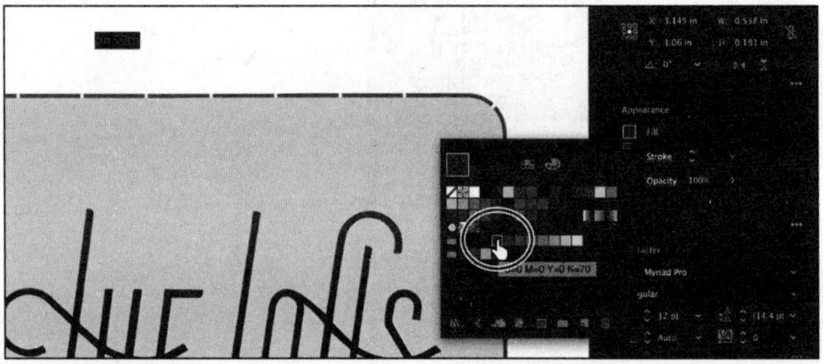

4 In the Character section of the Properties panel, select the font size, and type **20**. Press Return or Enter to accept the size change.

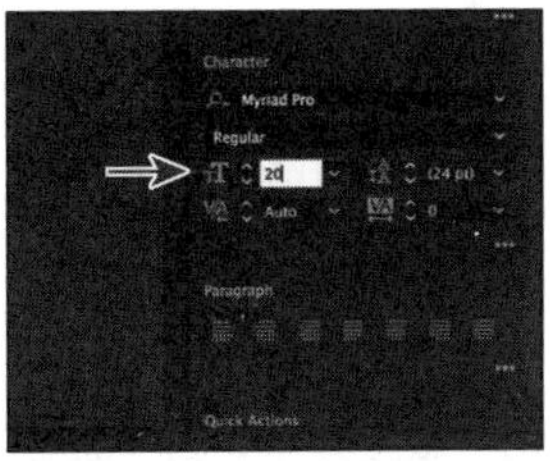

Next, you'll apply a Typekit font. You'll need an Internet connection. If you don't have an Internet connection or access to the Typekit fonts, you can choose any other font from the Font Family menu.

5 Click the arrow to the right of the Font Family field in the Properties panel. Click the Add Fonts From Typekit button to sync a font from Typekit.

The Typekit.com website should open in your default web browser, and you should be signed in to the site with your Creative Cloud ID.

6 Type **Raleway** in the Search Typekit field (or another font, if you can't find that one). Click Raleway in the search results menu that appears.

● **Note:** If you are taken to the Typekit.com home page, you can simply click Browse. It may also ask you to log in with your Creative Cloud (Adobe) ID.

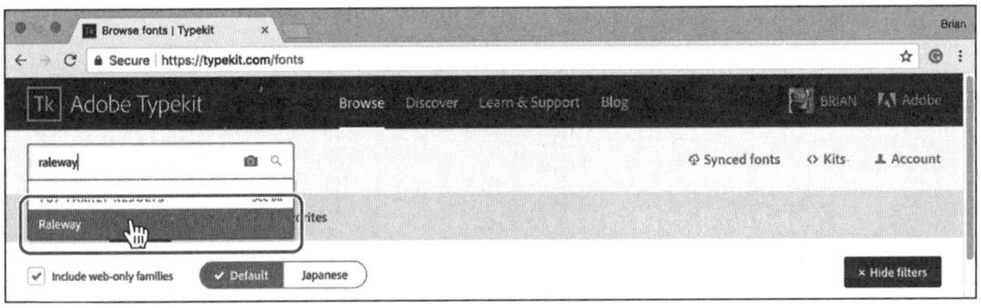

7 Scroll down on the next page that appears, if necessary, to find the Raleway Light font. Click the Sync button to the right of the font name to sync it to your machine.

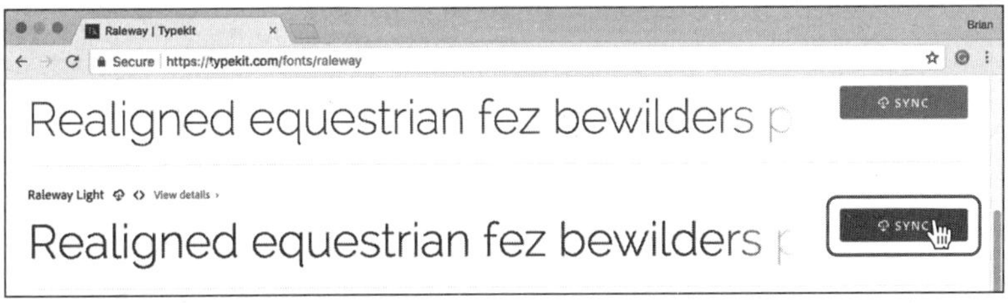

If you run into syncing issues, in the Creative Cloud desktop application, you will be able to see any messages indicating that font syncing is turned off (turn it on in that case) or any other issues.

● **Note:** It may take a few minutes for the font to sync with your computer.

8 Close the browser window, and return to Illustrator. With the text still selected, click to insert the cursor in the Font Family field in the Properties panel on the right (circled in the following figure). Begin typing **raleway**.

9 Position the pointer over the words "Raleway Light" in the menu that appears to show a live preview on the selected text. Click Raleway Light to apply it.

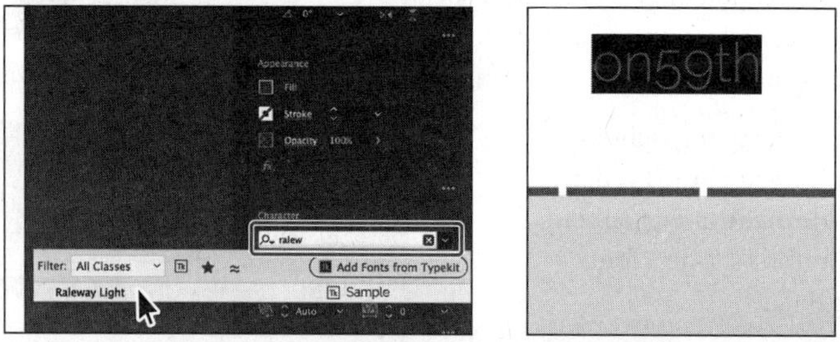

10 With the Type tool selected, click in the text; then drag across the "59" text and change the font size to **50** in the Properties panel on the right.

● **Note:** When selecting text this way, you may accidentally add new text. If that happens, choose Edit > Undo Type, move the pointer between the "n" and "5," and drag to the left to select the text.

11 Drag across the text "on," to select it. In the Properties panel on the right, click More Options (■) in the Character section to show more options. Change Baseline Shift to **18**.

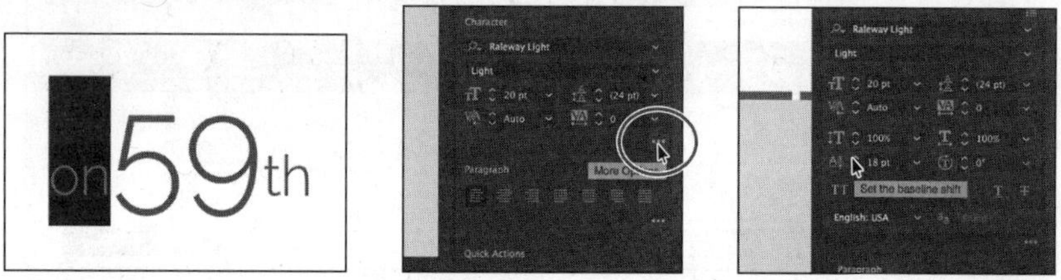

12 Drag across the "th" text to select it. In the Properties panel on the right, click More Options (■) in the Character section to show more options. Change Baseline Shift to **18**.

13 Select the Selection tool (▶) in the Tools panel, and drag the text below the hand lettering text but above the building icon and bushes. If you need to, you can drag all of the content so it looks like the figure.

14 Choose File > Save.

Aligning artwork

Illustrator makes it easy to align or distribute multiple objects relative to each other, the artboard, or a key object. In this section, you'll align several objects to the center of the artboard.

● **Note:** Learn more about aligning artwork in Lesson 2, "Techniques for Selecting Artwork."

1 Choose Object > Unlock All to unlock the rectangle in the background.

2 Select the Selection tool (▶) in the Tools panel, and choose Select > All.

3 Click the Align To Selection option ( ) in the Properties panel to the right of the document, and choose Align To Artboard.

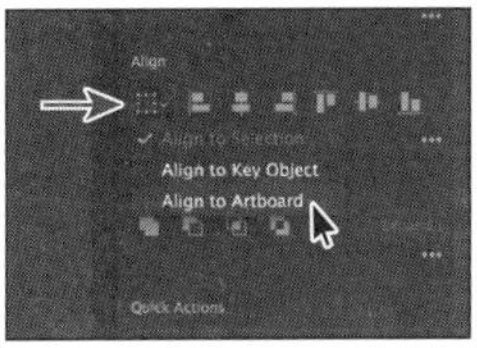

The selected content will now align to the artboard.

4 Click the Horizontal Align Center button ( ) to align the selected artwork to the horizontal center of the artboard.

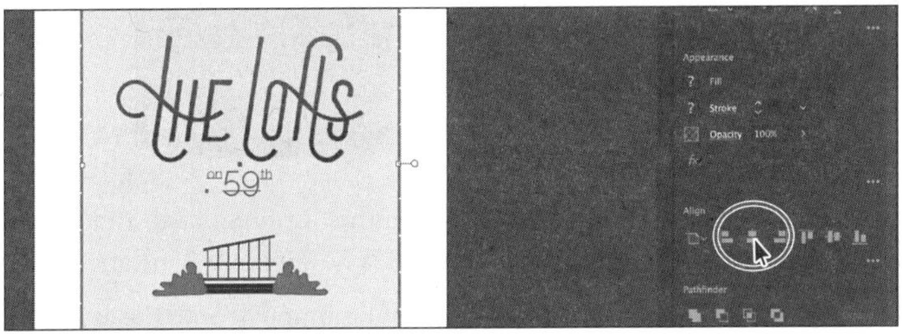

5 Choose Select > Deselect.

Working with brushes

Brushes let you stylize the appearance of paths. You can apply brush strokes to existing paths, or you can use the Paintbrush tool ( ) to draw a path and apply a brush stroke simultaneously.

● **Note:** Learn more about working with brushes in Lesson 11, "Using Brushes to Create a Poster."

1 With the Selection tool (▶) selected, click in the gray rectangle in the background to select it.

2 Choose Window > Brush Libraries > Borders > Borders_Lines to open the Borders_Lines collection of brushes in a panel.

3 Click the brush named "Multilines 1.4" in the panel to apply it to the stroke of the shape.

4 Click the X in the corner of the Borders_Lines panel to close it.

5 Choose Select > Deselect.

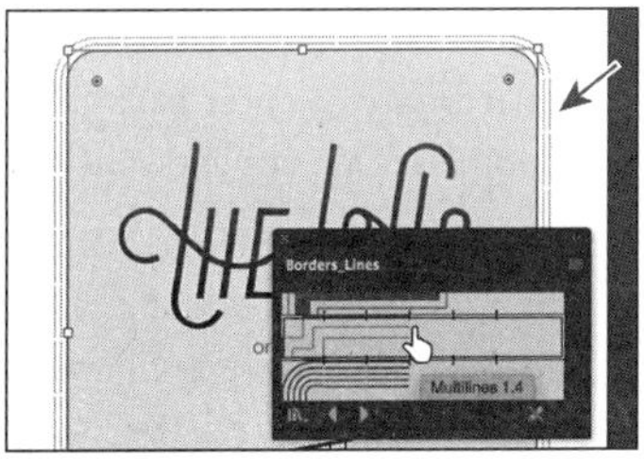

● **Note:** The brush you apply is a pattern brush, which means that it repeats artwork (in this case) along the path. The brush artwork is scaled on the path based on the stroke weight.

Working with symbols

● **Note:** Learn more about working with symbols in Lesson 13, "Creating Artwork for a T-Shirt."

A *symbol* is reusable art stored in the Symbols panel. Symbols are useful because they can help you save time and can save on file size as well. You will now create a symbol from the cloud artwork.

1 With the Selection tool (▶) selected, choose Object > Show All to see the cloud. The cloud shape should be selected.

2 Choose Window > Symbols to open the Symbols panel. Click the New Symbol button (◼) at the bottom of the panel to save the selected cloud as a symbol.

3 In the Symbol Options dialog box that appears, name the symbol **Cloud**, and click OK. If a warning dialog box appears, click OK as well.

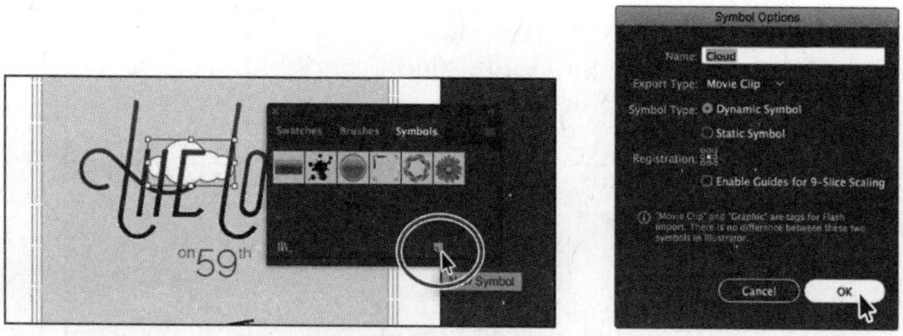

The artwork now appears as a saved symbol in the Symbols panel, and the cloud on the artboard you used to create the symbol is now a symbol instance.

● **Note:** Your cloud symbol instances may be in different locations than those in the figure. That's okay.

4 From the Symbols panel, drag the cloud symbol thumbnail onto the artboard *three times* and arrange them however you like in the background. Click the X at the top of the Symbols panel group to close it.

5 Resize a few of clouds, making them different sizes, by dragging a corner of the symbol instance with the Shift key held down. Release the mouse button and then the key.

▶ **Tip:** You could have also clicked the Edit Symbol button in the Properties panel to the right of the document.

6 Double-click one of the cloud instances on the artboard to enter Isolation mode. In the dialog box that appears, click OK.

7 Click to select the cloud shape. Click the Fill color box in the Properties panel to the right of the document with the Color Mixer option (◼) selected so you can see the CMYK sliders. Change the values to C=**20**, M=**0**, Y=**0**, K=**0** to create a light blue color. Press the Escape key to hide the panel.

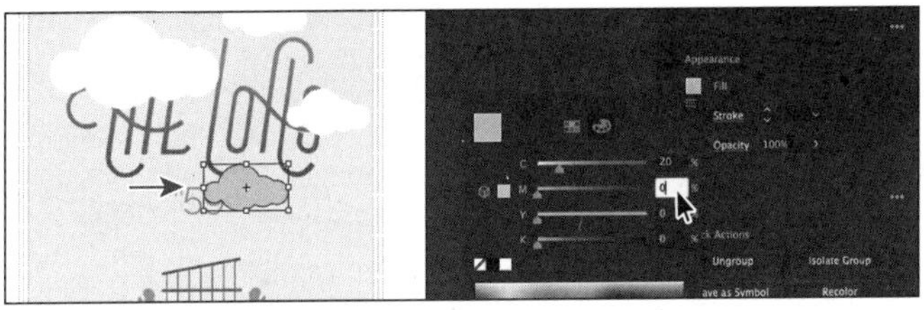

8 Double-click in a blank area of the document window to exit the editing (Isolation) mode, and notice that the other clouds have changed as well.

9 Click one of the cloud instances on the artboard, and choose Select > Same > Symbol Instance to select all of them. Choose Object > Group.

10 Click the Arrange button in the Properties panel, and choose Send To Back.

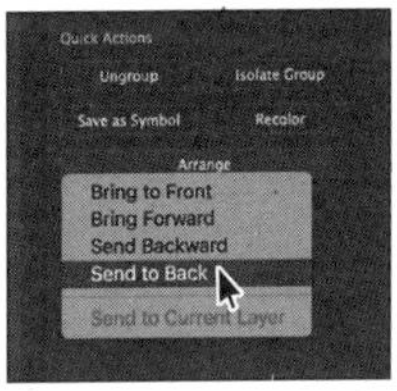

Working with effects

Effects alter the appearance of an object without changing the base object. Next, you'll apply a subtle Drop Shadow effect to the lettering you traced earlier.

● **Note:** Learn more about effects in Lesson 12, "Exploring Creative Uses of Effects and Graphic Styles."

1 With the Selection tool (▶), click the "THE LOFTS" lettering.

2 Click the Effect option (fx) in the Properties panel on the right, and choose Stylize > Drop Shadow. In the Drop Shadow dialog box, set the following options (if necessary):

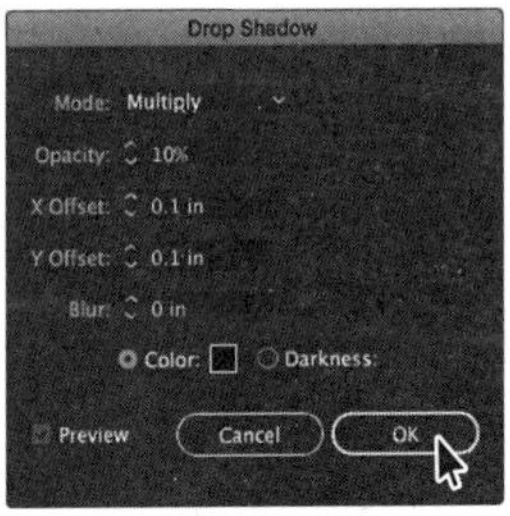

● **Note:** Choose the Stylize option in the Illustrator Effects section of the Effect menu.

- Mode: **Multiply** (the default setting)
- Opacity: **10%**
- X Offset and Y Offset: **0.1 in**
- Blur: **0**

3 Select Preview to see it applied to the artwork and then click OK.

4 Choose Select > Deselect.

5 Choose File > Save and then choose File > Close.

1 GETTING TO KNOW THE WORK AREA

Lesson overview

In this lesson, you'll explore the workspace and learn how to do the following:

- Open an Adobe Illustrator CC file.
- Work with the Tools panel.
- Work with panels.
- Reset and save your workspace.
- Use viewing options to change the display magnification.
- Navigate multiple artboards and documents.
- Explore document groups.
- Find resources for using Illustrator.

This lesson takes approximately 45 minutes to complete. Please log in to your account on peachpit.com to download the lesson files for this chapter, or go to the "Getting Started" section at the beginning of this book and follow the instructions under "Accessing the lesson files and Web Edition."

Your Account page is also where you'll find any updates to the chapters or to the lesson files. Look on the Lesson & Update Files tab to access the most current content.

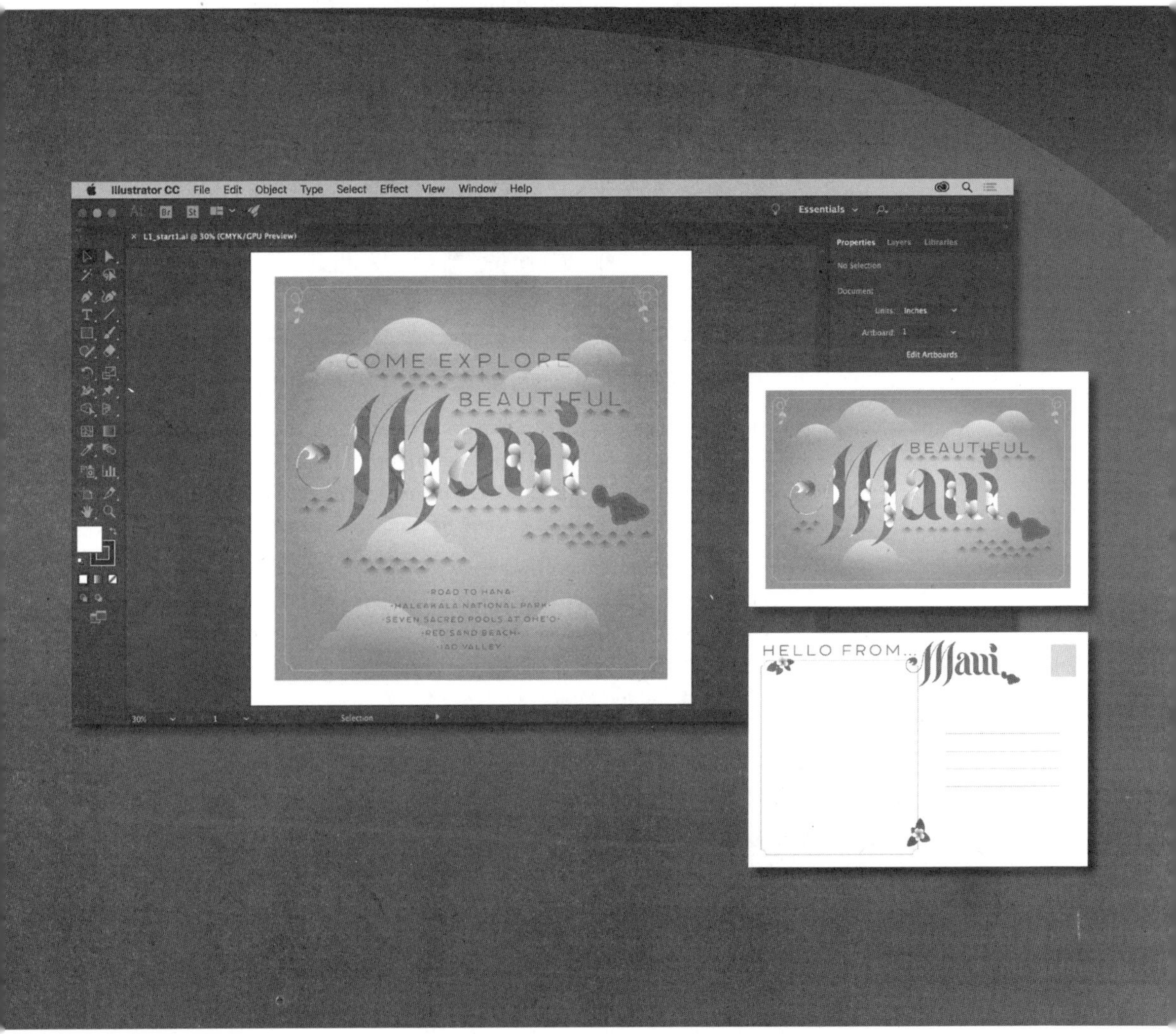

To make the most of the extensive drawing, painting, and editing capabilities of Adobe Illustrator CC, it's important to learn how to navigate the workspace. The workspace consists of the Application bar, menus, Tools panel, Properties panel, Document window, and other default panels.

Introducing Adobe Illustrator

In Illustrator, you primarily create and work with vector graphics (sometimes called vector shapes or vector objects). *Vector graphics* are made up of lines and curves defined by mathematical objects called *vectors*. You can freely move or modify vector graphics without losing detail or clarity because they are resolution-independent.

An example of vector artwork.

Editing vector artwork.

In other words, vector graphics maintain crisp edges when they are resized, printed to a PostScript printer, saved in a PDF file, or imported into a vector-based graphics application. As a result, vector graphics are the best choice for artwork, such as logos, that will be used at various sizes and in various output media.

▶ **Tip:** To learn more about bitmap graphics, search for "Importing bitmap images" in Illustrator Help (Help > Illustrator Help).

Illustrator also allows you to incorporate *bitmap images*—technically called *raster images*—that use a rectangular grid of picture elements (pixels) to represent the visual. Each pixel is assigned a specific location and color value. Pictures you take on your phone camera are considered raster images. Raster images can be created and edited in a program like Adobe Photoshop.

Example of a raster image and a zoomed-in portion to show the pixels.

Starting Illustrator and opening a file

In this first lesson, you'll begin by exploring Illustrator. You'll open a few art files during this lesson, but before you begin, you'll restore the default preferences for Adobe Illustrator CC. This is something you will do at the start of each lesson in this book to ensure that the tools function and the defaults are set exactly as described in this lesson.

1 To delete or deactivate (by renaming) the Adobe Illustrator CC preferences file, see "Restoring default preferences" in the "Getting Started" section at the beginning of the book.

Note: If finding the preferences file proves difficult, please contact me at brian@brianwoodtraining.com for assistance.

2 Double-click the Adobe Illustrator CC icon to launch Adobe Illustrator.

With Illustrator open, you will see a start screen showing resources for Illustrator, and more.

3 Choose File > Open or click the Open button in the Start screen. In the Lessons > Lesson01 folder on your hard disk, select the L1_start1.ai file, and click Open. You will use the L1_start1.ai file to practice navigating, zooming, and investigating an Illustrator document and the workspace.

Note: If you have not already downloaded the project files for this lesson to your computer from your Account page, make sure to do so now. See the "Getting Started" section at the beginning of the book.

4 Choose Window > Workspace > Essentials, make sure it's selected, and then choose Window > Workspace > Reset Essentials to reset the workspace.

The Reset Essentials command ensures that the workspace, which includes all of the tools and panels, is set to the default settings.

Note: If a Tour window appears after opening the document, you can simply close it. Do the same thing going forward for each lesson.

5 Choose View > Fit Artboard In Window.

An artboard is the area that contains your printable artwork and is similar to a page in Adobe InDesign®. This command fits the whole artboard into the Document window so that you can see the entire artboard.

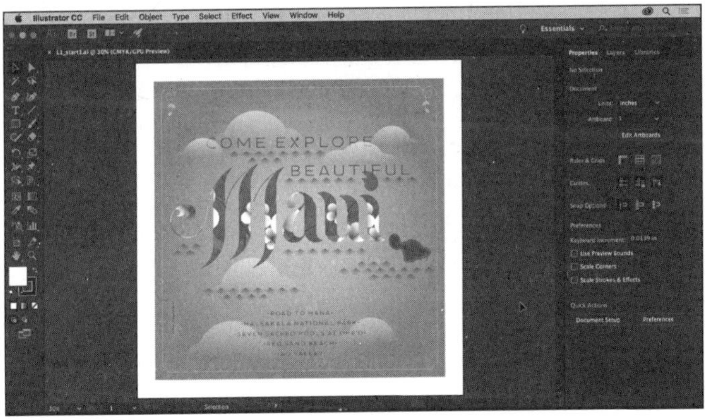

When the file is open and Illustrator is fully launched, the menus, Application bar, Tools panel, and panels appear on the screen.

Exploring the workspace

● **Note:** The figures in this lesson are taken using the macOS operating system and may look slightly different from what you see, especially if you are using Windows.

You create and manipulate your documents and files using various elements, such as panels, bars, and windows. Any arrangement of these elements is called a *workspace*. When you first start Illustrator, you see the default workspace, which you can customize for the tasks you perform. You can create and save multiple workspaces—one for editing and another for viewing, for example—and switch among them as you work.

Below, the areas of the default workspace are described:

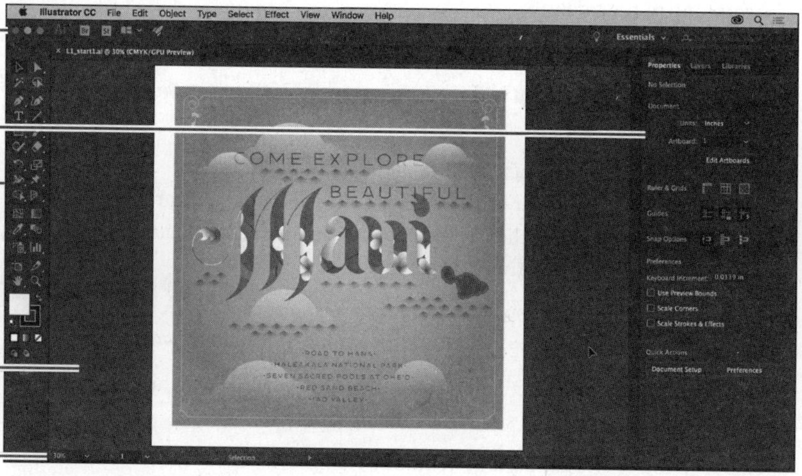

A. The **Application bar** across the top by default contains application controls, the Workspace Switcher, and Search. On Windows, the menu items appear *inline* with the Application bar—see the following figure.

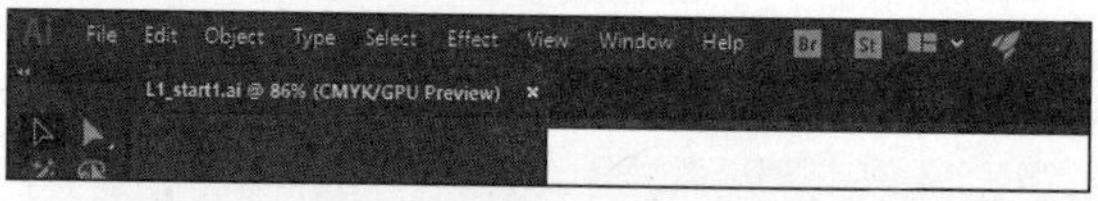

B. **Panels** help you monitor and modify your work. Certain panels are displayed by default, and you can display any panel by choosing it from the Window menu.

C. The **Tools panel** contains tools for creating and editing images, artwork, page elements, and more. Related tools are grouped together.

D. The **Document window** displays the file(s) you're working on.

E. The **Status bar** appears at the lower-left edge of the Document window. It displays information, zooming, and navigation controls.

Getting to know the Tools panel

The Tools panel on the left side of the workspace contains tools for selecting, drawing and painting, editing, and viewing, as well as the Fill and Stroke boxes, drawing modes, and screen modes. As you work through the lessons, you'll learn about the specific function of many of these tools.

Note: The Tools panel shown here and throughout this lesson has two columns. You may see a one-column Tools panel, depending on your screen resolution and workspace.

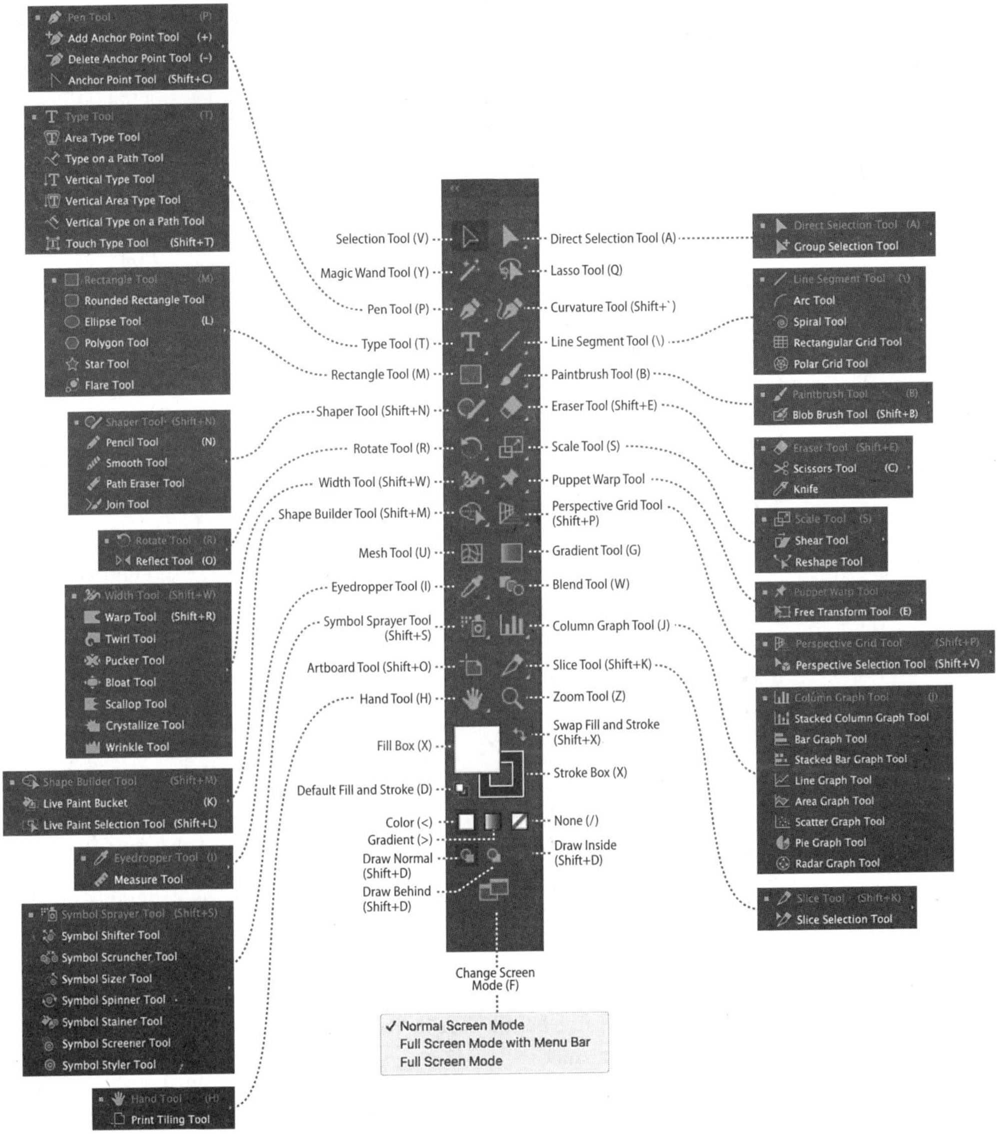

▶ **Tip:** You can modify the default keyboard shortcuts that Illustrator comes with. To do this, choose Edit > Keyboard Shortcuts. For more information, see "Keyboard Shortcuts" in Illustrator Help (Help > Illustrator Help).

▶ **Tip:** You can turn the tooltips on or off by choosing Illustrator CC > Preferences > General (macOS) or Edit > Preferences > General (Windows) and deselecting Show Tool Tips.

1 Position the pointer over the Selection tool ( ) in the Tools panel. Notice that the name (Selection Tool) and keyboard shortcut (V) are displayed in a tooltip.

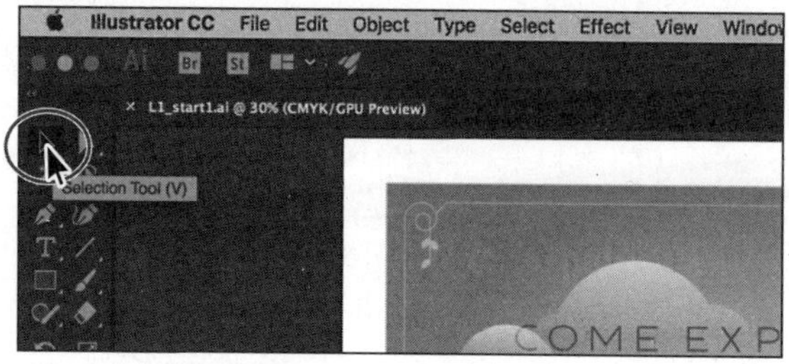

2 Move the pointer over the Direct Selection tool ( ), and click and hold down the mouse button until a tools menu appears. Release the mouse button and then click the Group Selection tool to select it.

Any tool in the Tools panel that displays a small triangle contains additional tools that can be selected in this way.

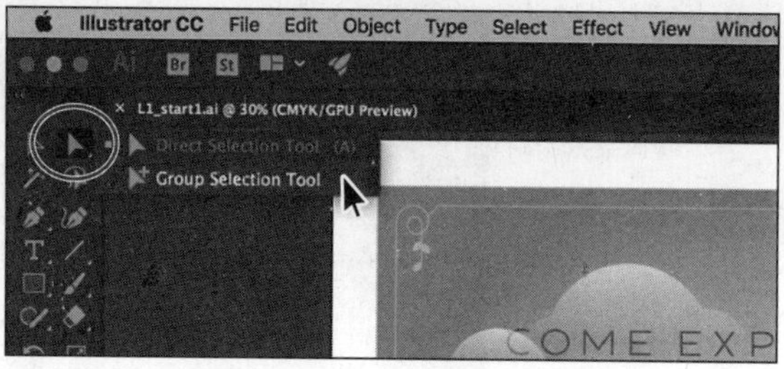

▶ **Tip:** You can also select hidden tools by pressing the Option key (macOS) or the Alt key (Windows) and clicking the tool in the Tools panel. Each click selects the next hidden tool in the tool sequence.

3 Click and hold down the mouse button on the Rectangle tool ( ) to reveal more tools. Click the arrow at the right edge of the hidden tools panel to separate the tools from the Tools panel so that you can access them at all times.

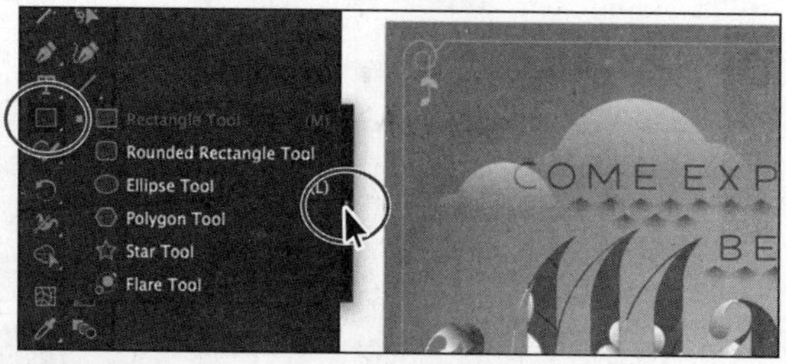

4 Click the Close button (X) in the upper-left corner (macOS) or upper-right corner (Windows) on the floating tool panel's title bar to close it. The tools return to the Tools panel.

▶ **Tip:** You can also collapse the floating tool panels or dock them to the workspace or each other.

Next, you'll learn how to resize and float the Tools panel. In the figures in this lesson, the Tools panel is a double column by default. As I said before, you may see a single-column Tools panel to start with, depending on your screen resolution and workspace, and that's okay.

5 Click the double arrow in the upper-left corner of the Tools panel to either expand the one column into two columns or collapse the two columns into one (depending on your screen resolution).

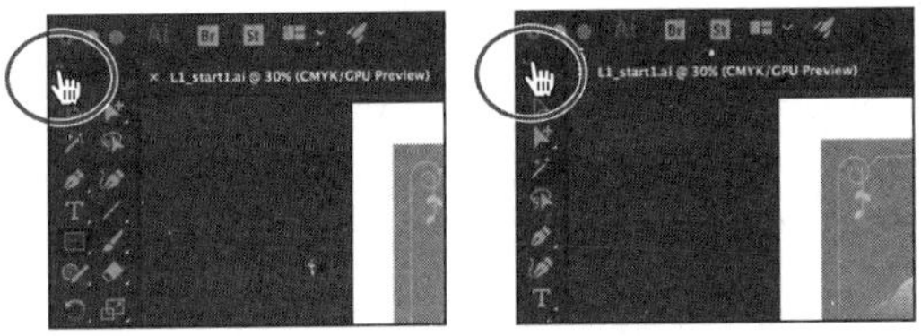

6 Click the same double arrow again to expand (or collapse) the Tools panel.

7 Click the dark gray title bar at the top of the Tools panel or the dashed line beneath the title bar, and drag the Tools panel into the workspace. The Tools panel is now floating in the workspace.

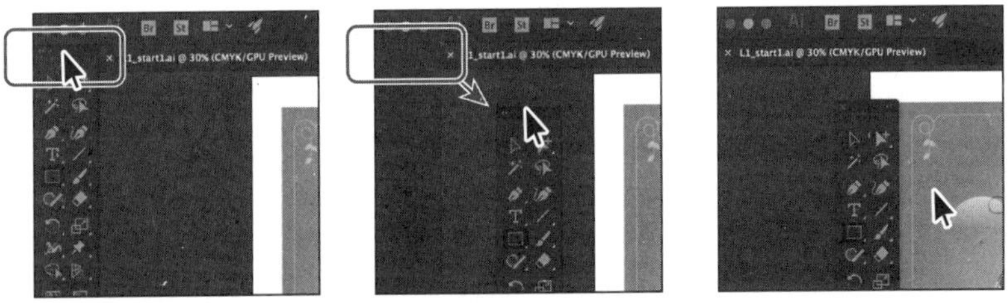

▶ **Tip:** You can click the double arrow at the top of the Tools panel or double-click the title bar at the top of the Tools panel to switch between two columns and one column. Just be careful not to click the X or it will close! If you close it, choose Window > Tools > Default to open it again.

8 To dock the Tools panel again, drag its title bar or the dashed line below it to the left side of the Application window. When the pointer reaches the left edge, a translucent blue border, called the *drop zone*, appears. Release the mouse button to dock the Tools panel neatly into the side of the workspace.

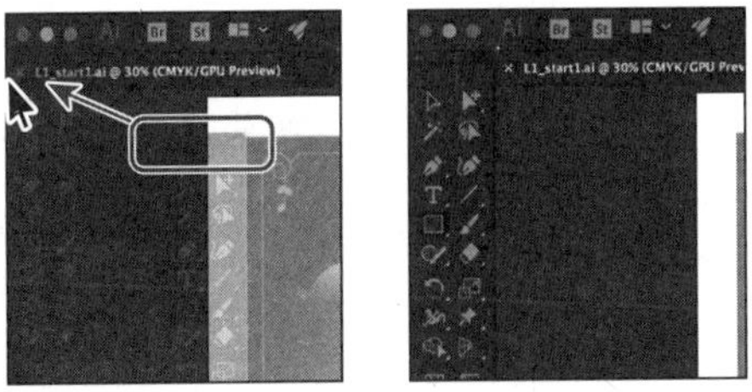

Custom tools panels

You may find yourself using a specific set of tools most of the time. In Illustrator, you can create custom tools panels that contain the tools you use most often.

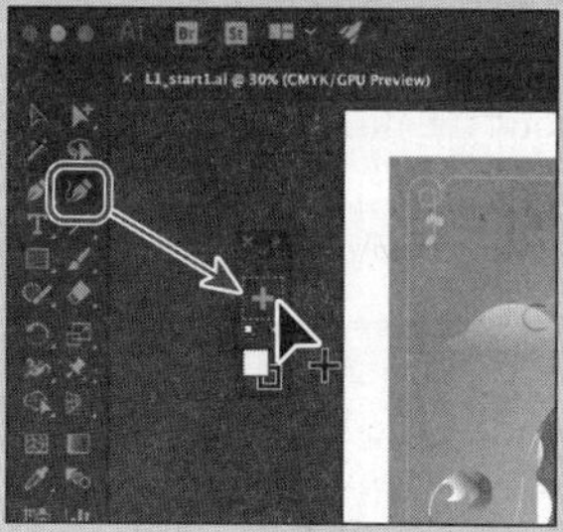

By choosing Window > Tools > New Tools Panel, you can create a custom tools panel. They are saved with Illustrator and can be closed and opened, regardless of which document is open. They are free-floating and can also be docked and saved in a custom workspace you create.

Each new custom tools panel has stroke and fill controls at the bottom and a plus sign (+) where you can drag copies of tools from the main Tools panel onto the custom panel you are creating and drag them off to remove it.

Working with the Properties panel

When starting Illustrator for the first time and opening a document, you'll see the Properties panel on the right side of the workspace. The Properties panel displays properties for the active document when nothing is selected, and appearance properties for content you select. It puts all of the most commonly used options in one place, and it's a panel you will be using quite a bit.

1 Select the Selection tool ( ) in the Tools panel, and look in the Properties panel on the right.

At the top of the Properties panel, you will see "No Selection." This is called the Selection Indicator and is a great place to look and see what type of content is selected (if any). The properties in the Properties panel are currently for the current document properties and program preferences.

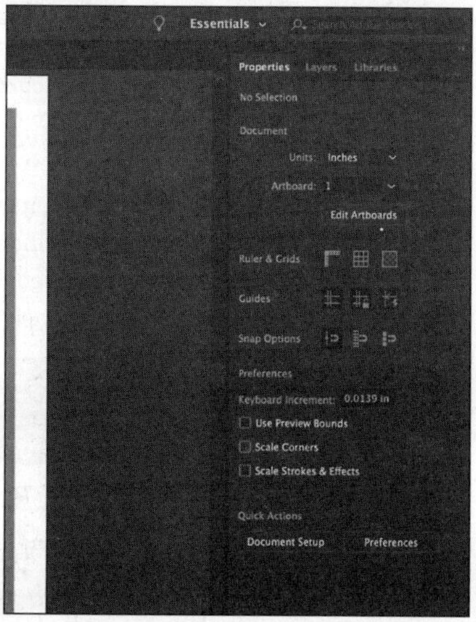

2 Move the pointer into the blue background in the artwork, and click to select it.

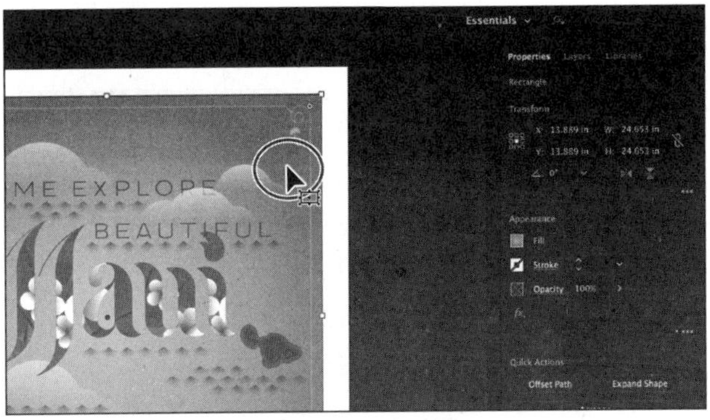

In the Properties panel, you should now see appearance options for the selected artwork. You can change the size, position, color, and much more for the artwork you selected. The artwork selected is a rectangle, as indicated by "Rectangle" at the top of the panel.

3 Click the underlined word "Opacity" in the Properties panel to open the Transparency panel options. Words that are underlined in the Properties panel will show more options when you click them.

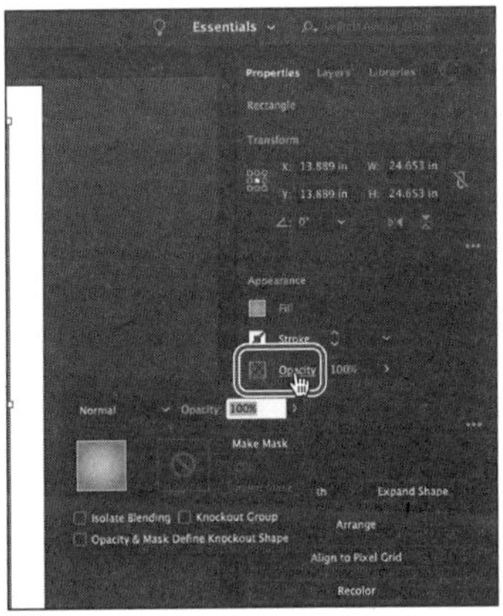

4 Press Escape to hide the Transparency panel, if necessary.

5 Choose Select > Deselect to deselect the rectangle.

The Properties panel once again shows the default properties when nothing is selected.

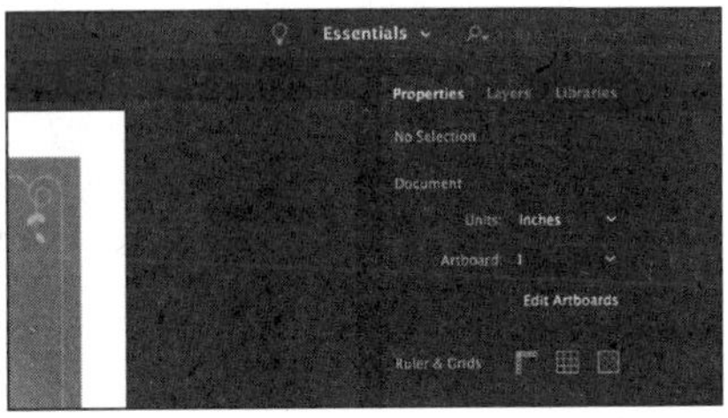

Working with panels

Panels in Illustrator, like the Properties panel, give you quick access to many of the tools and options that make modifying artwork easier. All of the panels available in Illustrator are listed alphabetically in the Window menu. Next, you'll experiment with hiding, closing, and opening panels.

1 Click the Layers panel tab to the right of the Properties panel tab.

The Layers panel appears with two other panels—the Properties panel and the Libraries panel. They are all part of the same panel group.

▶ **Tip:** To find a hidden panel, choose the panel name from the Window menu. A checkmark to the left of the panel name indicates that the panel is already open and in front of other panels in its panel group. If you choose a panel name that is already selected in the Window menu, the panel and its group either close or collapse.

▶ **Tip:** To expand or collapse the panel dock, you can also double-click the panel dock title bar at the top.

2 Click the double arrow at the top of the dock to collapse the panels.

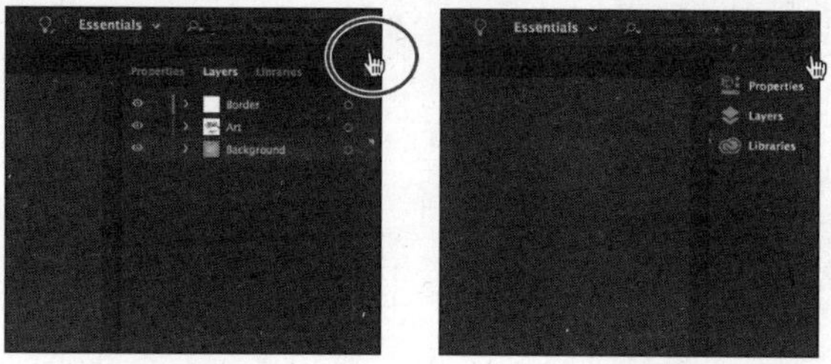

You can use this method of collapsing the panels so you have more area to work on your document.

3 Drag the left edge of the docked panels to the right until the panel text disappears.

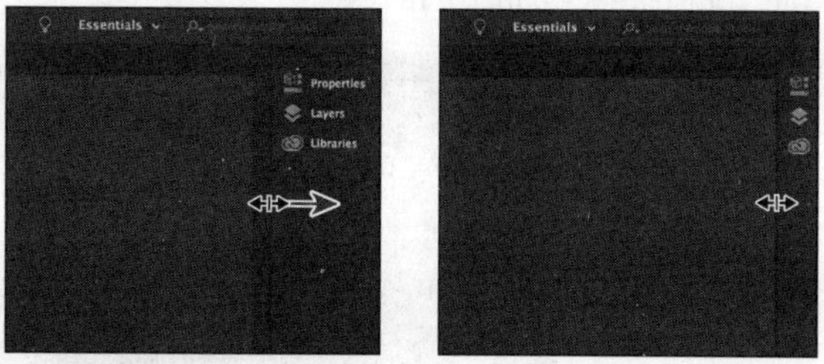

This hides the panel names and collapses the panel dock to icons only. In order to open a panel when collapsed as an icon, you can click a panel icon.

4 Click the double arrow again to expand the panels.

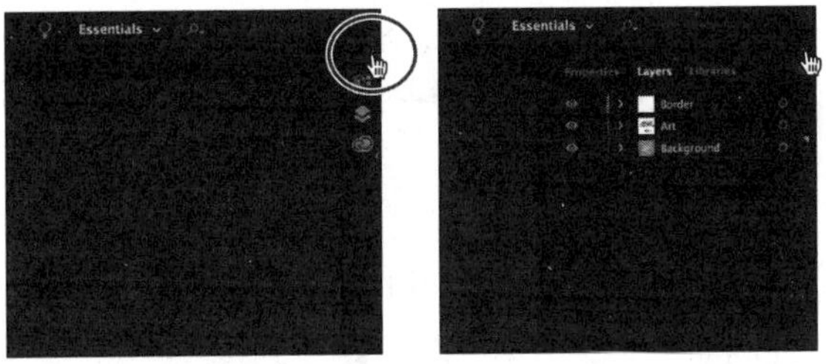

5 Choose Window > Workspace > Reset Essentials to reset the workspace.

Docking panels

Panels in Illustrator can be moved around in the workspace and organized to match your working needs. Next, you'll open a new panel and dock it with the default panels on the right side of the workspace.

1 Click the Window menu at the top of the screen to see all of the panels available in Illustrator. Choose Align in the Window menu to open the Align panel and the other panels grouped with it by default.

   Panels you open that do not appear in the default workspace are free-floating. That means they are not docked and can be moved around. You can dock free-floating panels on the right or left side of the workspace.

2 Drag the Align panel group by the title bar above the panel names to position the group closer to the docked panels on the right.

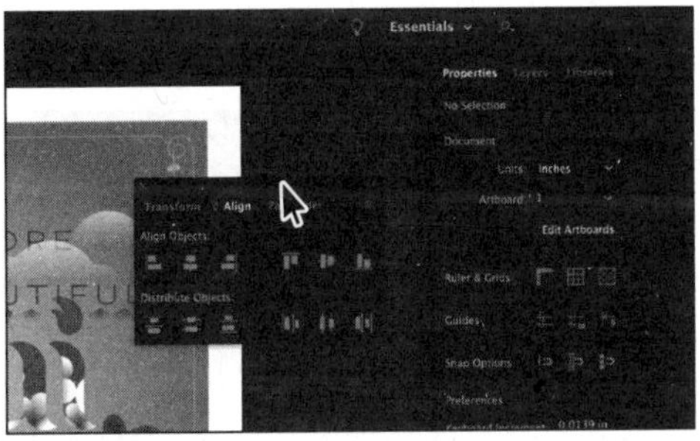

   Next, you'll dock the Align panel with the Properties panel.

3 Drag the Align panel tab away from the panel group and onto the panel tabs (Properties, Layers, and Libraries) at the top of the docked panels. When a blue highlight appears around the entire panel dock, release the mouse button to dock the panel.

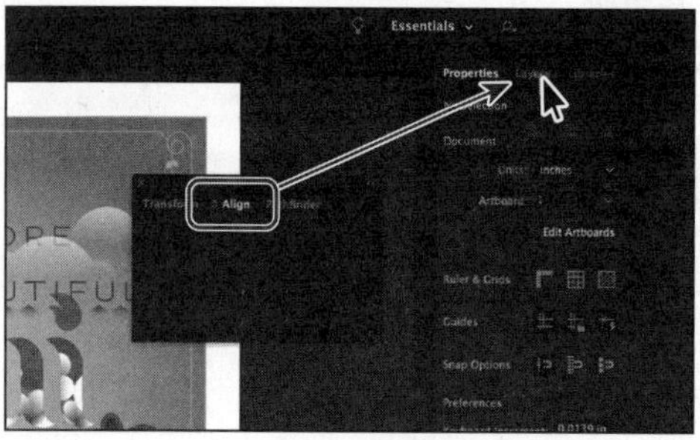

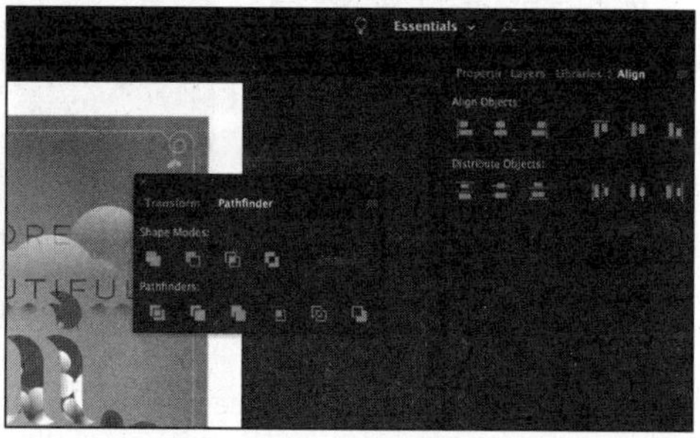

▶ **Tip:** You can also dock panels next to each other on the right or left side of the workspace. This is a great way to conserve space.

4 Click the X at the top of the Transform and Pathfinder panel group, which is free-floating, to close it.

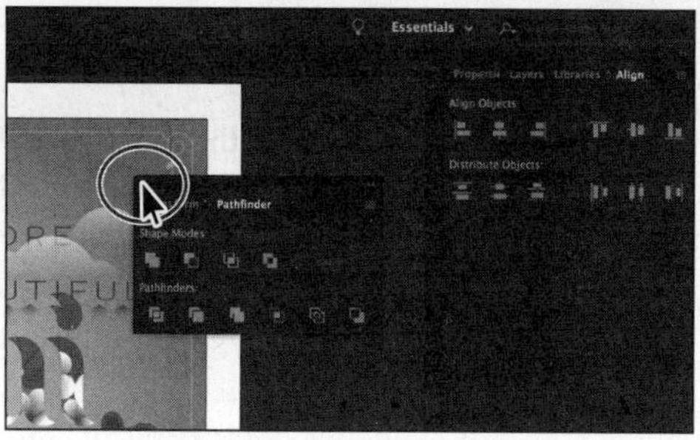

Aside from adding panels to the dock on the right, you can also remove them.

5 Drag the Align panel by the panel tab, to the left, away from the dock of panels, and release the mouse button.

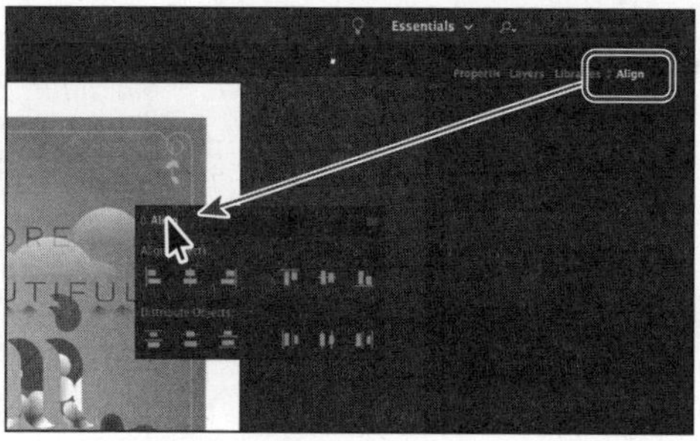

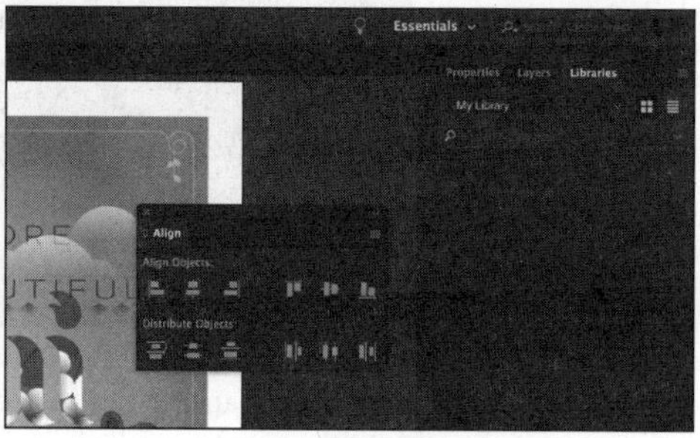

6 Click the X at the top of the Align panel to close it.

7 Click the Libraries panel tab on the right to show that panel, if it isn't already.

Switching workspaces

When you first launch Illustrator, the Essentials workspace is showing. Illustrator comes with a host of other default workspaces that can be used to set the workspace for a variety of tasks. Next, you'll switch workspaces to another default workspace to learn about some new panels.

1 Click the workspace switcher in the Application bar above the docked panels to change the workspace.

 You'll see a number of workspaces listed, each with a specific purpose, that will open panels and arrange the workspace to make it most conducive to that type of work.

▶ **Tip:** Press Tab to toggle between hiding and showing all panels. You can hide or show all panels at once, except for the Tools panel, by pressing Shift+Tab to toggle between hide and show.

2 Choose Layout from the workspace switcher menu to switch workspaces.

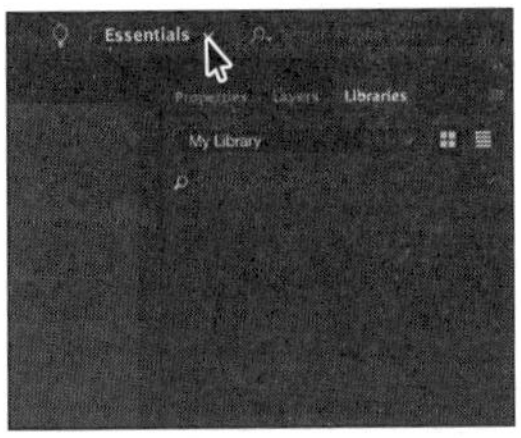

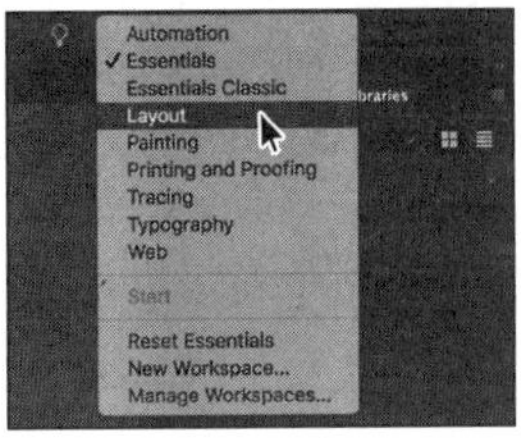

 You'll notice a few major changes in the workspace. One of the biggest is the Control panel that's now docked at the top of the workspace, just above the Document window (an arrow is pointing to it in the following figure). Similar to the Properties panel, it offers quick access to options, commands, and other panels relevant to the currently selected content.

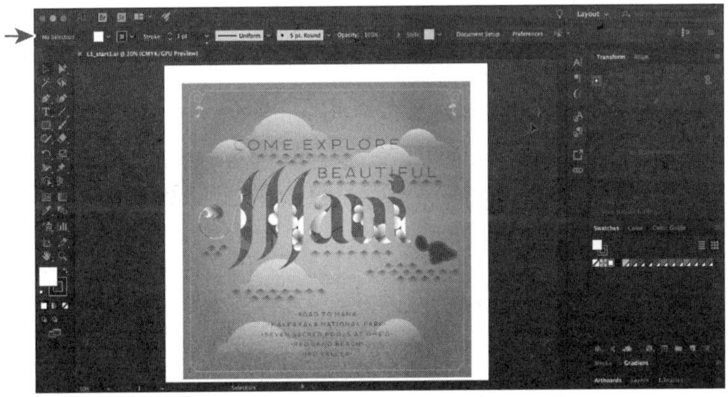

 Also, notice all of the collapsed panel icons on the right side of the workspace. In workspaces like Essential, you can create groups of panels that are stacked one on another. This way, you can have a lot more panels showing.

3 Choose Essentials from the workspace switcher above the docked panels to switch back to the Essentials workspace.

4 Choose Reset Essentials from the workspace switcher in the Application bar.

When you choose a previous workspace to switch to, it remembers any changes you made, like selecting the Libraries panel. To completely reset a workspace, Essentials in this case, to the default settings, you can choose to reset it.

Saving a workspace

So far, in this lesson, you've reset the workspace and chosen a different workspace. You can also set up the panels the way you like and save your own custom workspace. Next, you'll dock a new panel and create your own workspace.

1 Choose Window > Artboards to open the Artboards panel group.

2 Drag the Artboards panel by the panel tab onto the Properties panel tab at the top of the dock on the right. When a blue highlight appears around the entire panel dock, release the mouse button to dock the Artboards panel.

3 Click the X at the top of the free-floating Asset Export panel to close it.

4 Choose Window > Workspace > New Workspace. Change Name to **My Workspace** in the New Workspace dialog box, and click OK.

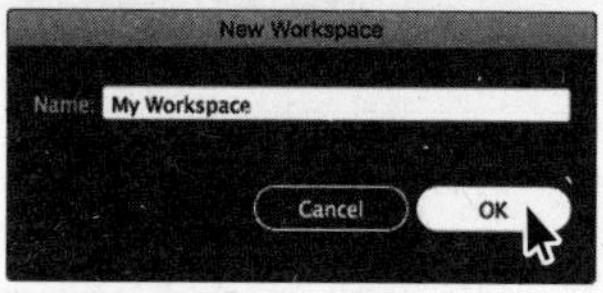

The name of the workspace could be anything, as long as it makes sense to you. The workspace named "My Workspace" is now saved with Illustrator until you remove it.

5 Choose Window > Workspace > Essentials.

6 Choose Window > Workspace > Reset Essentials.

Notice that the panels return to their default positions.

7 Choose Window > Workspace > My Workspace. Toggle between the two workspaces using the Window > Workspace command, and return to the Essentials workspace before starting the next exercise.

● **Note:** To delete saved workspaces, choose Window > Workspace > Manage Workspaces. Select the workspace name, and click the Delete Workspace button.

▶ **Tip:** To change a saved workspace, reset the panels as you'd like them to appear and then choose Window > Workspace > New Workspace. In the New Workspace dialog box, name the workspace with the original name. A message appears in the dialog box warning that you will overwrite an existing workspace with the same name if you click OK.

Using panel and context menus

Most panels in Illustrator have more options available in a panel menu, found by clicking the panel menu icon (▤ or ▤) in the upper-right corner of a panel. These additional options can be used to change the panel display, add or change panel content, and more. Next, you'll change the display of the Swatches panel using its panel menu.

1 With the Selection tool (▶) selected in the Tools panel on the left, click the blue shape in the background of the artwork again.

2 Click the Fill color box, to the left of the word "Fill," in the Properties panel.

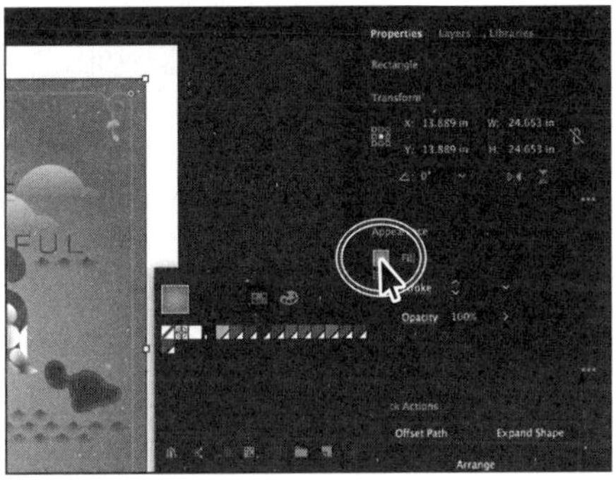

3 In the panel that appears, make sure that the Swatches option (▦) is selected. Click the panel menu icon (▤) in the upper-right corner, and choose Small List View from the panel menu.

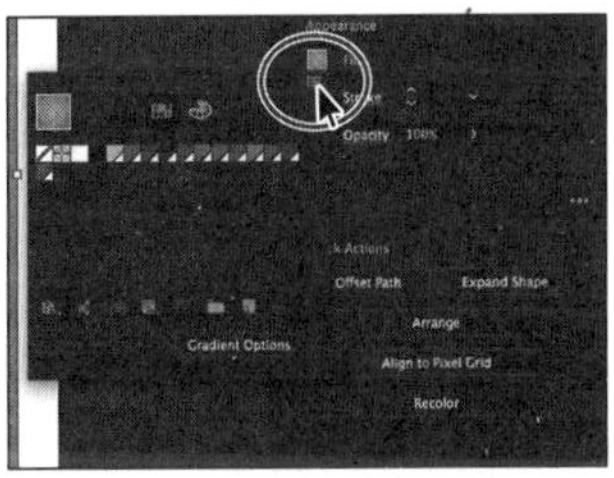

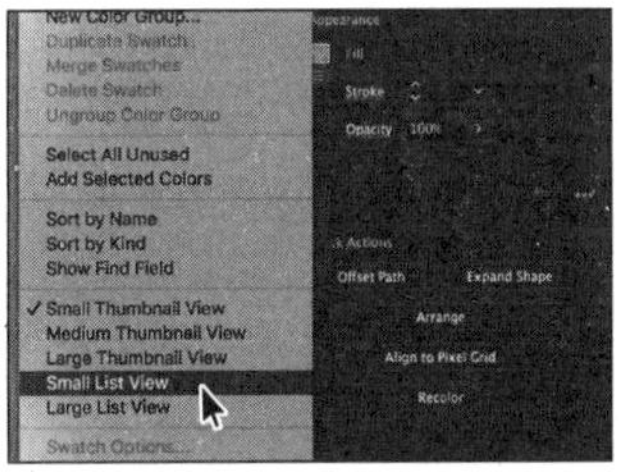

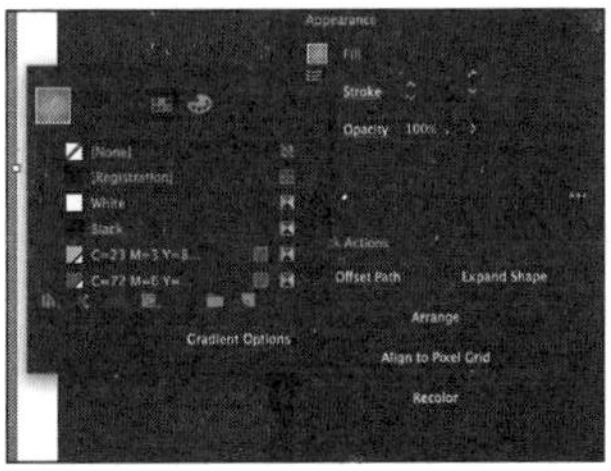

This displays the swatch names, together with thumbnails. Because the options in the panel menu apply only to the active panel, only the Swatches panel view is affected.

4 Click the same panel menu icon (▤) in the panel showing, and choose Small Thumbnail View to return the swatches to their original view.

In addition to the panel menus, context-sensitive menus display commands relevant to the active tool, selection, or panel. Usually the commands in a context menu are available in another part of the workspace, but using a context menu can save you time.

5 Choose Select > Deselect.

● **Note:** If you position the pointer over the tab or title bar for a panel and right-click, you can close a panel or a panel group in the context menu that appears.

6 Position the pointer over the dark gray area surrounding the white area of the artboard. Then, right-click to show a context menu with specific options.

The context-sensitive menu you see may contain different commands, depending on what the pointer is positioned over.

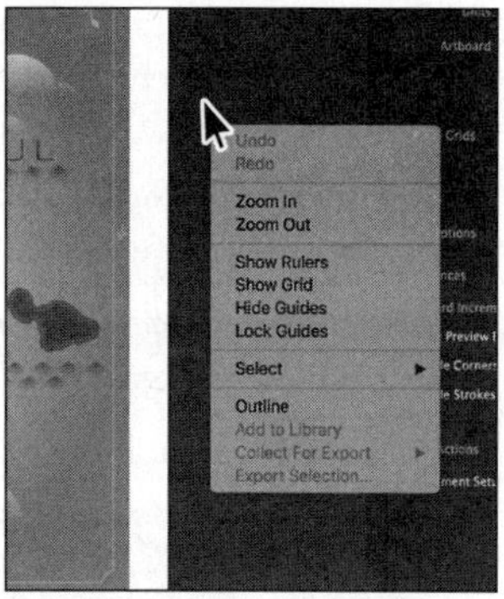

Adjusting the user-interface brightness

Similar to Adobe InDesign or Adobe Photoshop, Illustrator supports a brightness adjustment for the application user interface. This is a program preference setting that allows you to choose a brightness setting from four preset levels.

To edit the user-interface brightness, you can choose Illustrator CC > Preferences > User Interface (macOS) or Edit > Preferences > User Interface (Windows).

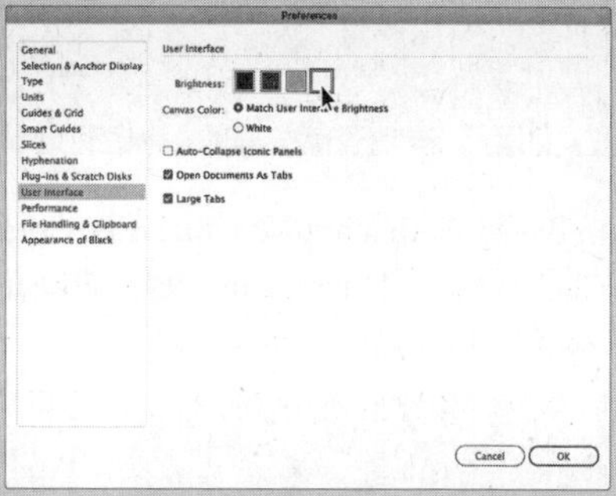

Changing the view of artwork

When working in files, it's likely that you'll need to change the magnification level and navigate among artboards. The magnification level, which can range from 3.13% to 64000%, is displayed in the title bar (or document tab) next to the filename and in the lower-left corner of the Document window.

There are a lot of ways to change the zoom level in Illustrator, and in this section you'll explore several of the most widely used methods.

Using view commands

To enlarge or reduce the view of artwork using the View menu, do one of the following:

- Choose View > Zoom In to enlarge the display of the artwork.
- Choose View > Zoom Out to reduce the view of the artwork.

Tip: You can also zoom in using the keyboard shortcut Command++ (macOS) or Ctrl++ (Windows). That's Command *and* + (macOS) or Ctrl *and* + (Windows). You can also zoom out using the keyboard shortcut Command+– (macOS) or Ctrl+– (Windows). That's Command *and* – (macOS) or Ctrl *and* – (Windows).

Each time you choose a Zoom option, the view of the artwork is resized to the closest preset zoom level. Using any of the viewing tools and commands affects only the display of the artwork, not the actual size of the artwork. The preset zoom levels appear in a menu in the lower-left corner of the Document window, identified by a down arrow next to a percentage. If you have artwork selected, using the View > Zoom In view command will zoom into what is selected.

You can also use the View menu to fit the *active* artboard to your screen, to fit all artboards into the view area, or to view artwork at actual size. The active artboard is the selected artboard. Artboards represent the regions that can contain printable artwork (similar to pages in a program like Adobe InDesign). The artboard is indicated by a red line I added to the following figure.

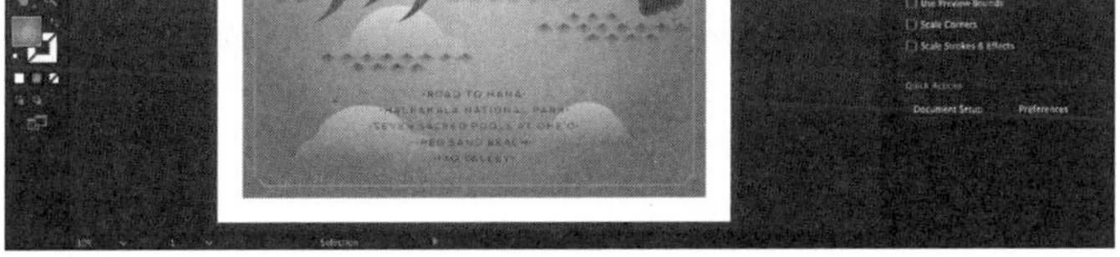

▶ **Tip:** You can also double-click the Hand tool (✋) in the Tools panel to fit the active artboard in the Document window.

▶ **Tip:** You can also double-click the Zoom tool (🔍) in the Tools panel to display artwork at 100%.

1 Choose View > Fit Artboard In Window.

By choosing View > Fit Artboard In Window or by using the keyboard shortcut Command+0 (macOS) or Ctrl+0 (Windows), the artboard is centered in the Document window.

2 Choose View > Actual Size to display the artwork at actual size.

The artwork is displayed at 100%. The actual size of your artwork determines how much of it can be viewed onscreen at 100%.

3 Choose View > Fit Artboard In Window before continuing to the next section.

Using the Zoom tool

In addition to the View menu options, you can use the Zoom tool (🔍) to magnify and reduce the view of artwork to predefined magnification levels.

1 Select the Zoom tool (🔍) in the Tools panel and then move the pointer into the Document window.

Notice that a plus sign (+) appears at the center of the Zoom tool pointer.

2 Position the Zoom tool over the text "Maui" in the center of the artboard and click once.

The artwork is displayed at a higher magnification. Notice that where you clicked is now in the center of the Document window.

3 Click two more times on the Maui text. The view is increased again, and you'll notice that the area you clicked is magnified.

4 With the Zoom tool still selected, hold down the Option (macOS) or Alt (Windows) key. A minus sign (–) appears at the center of the Zoom tool pointer. With the Option or Alt key pressed, click the artwork twice to reduce the view of the artwork.

Using the Zoom tool, you can also drag in the document to zoom in and out. By default, if your computer meets the system requirements for GPU Performance and it's enabled, zooming is animated. To find out if your computer meets the system requirements, see the sidebar titled "GPU Performance" following this section.

5 Choose View > Fit Artboard In Window.

6 With the Zoom tool still selected, click and drag from the left side of the document to the right to zoom in. The zooming is animated. Drag from right to left to zoom out.

7 Double-click the Hand tool (✋) in the Tools panel to fit the artboard in the Document window.

The Zoom tool is used frequently during the editing process to enlarge and reduce the view of artwork. Because of this, Illustrator allows you to select it using the keyboard at any time without first deselecting any other tool you may be using.

- To access the Zoom tool using your keyboard, press Command+spacebar (macOS) or Ctrl+spacebar (Windows).
- To access the Zoom Out tool using your keyboard, press Command+Option+spacebar (macOS) or Ctrl+Alt+spacebar (Windows).

GPU Performance

The graphics processing unit (GPU), found on video cards and part of display systems, is a specialized processor that can rapidly execute commands for manipulating and displaying images. GPU-accelerated computing offers faster performance across a broad range of design, animation, and video applications.

The GPU Performance in Illustrator feature has a preview mode called GPU Preview, which enables rendering of Illustrator artwork on the graphics processor.

This feature is available on compatible Mac and Windows computers. This feature is turned on by default for documents, and options can be accessed in Preferences by clicking the GPU Performance icon in the Application bar.

To learn more about GPU performance, visit https://helpx.adobe.com/illustrator/kb/gpu-performance-preview-improvements.html.

● **Note:** If your computer does *not* meet the system requirements for GPU Performance, you will instead draw a dotted rectangle, called a *marquee*, when dragging with the Zoom tool.

▶ **Tip:** With the Zoom tool selected, if you move the pointer into the Document window and press the mouse button for a few seconds, you can zoom in using the animated zoom. Once again, this will work if your computer meets the system requirements for GPU Performance and it's enabled.

● **Note:** In certain versions of macOS, the keyboard shortcuts for the Zoom tool (🔍) open Spotlight or the Finder. If you decide to use these shortcuts in Illustrator, you may want to turn off or change those keyboard shortcuts in the macOS System Preferences.

Scrolling through a document

In Illustrator, you can use the Hand tool (✋) to pan to different areas of a document. Using the Hand tool allows you to push the document around much like you would a piece of paper on your desk. This can be a very useful way to move around in a document with a lot of artboards or when you are zoomed in. In this section, you'll access the Hand tool using a few methods.

1 With the Hand tool (✋) selected in the Tools panel, drag down in the Document window. As you drag, the artwork moves with the hand.

   As with the Zoom tool (🔍), you can select the Hand tool with a keyboard shortcut without first deselecting the active tool.

2 Click any other tool except the Type tool (T) in the Tools panel, and move the pointer into the Document window. Hold down the spacebar on the keyboard to temporarily select the Hand tool and then drag to bring the artwork back into the center of your view.

● **Note:** The spacebar shortcut for the Hand tool (✋) does not work when the Type tool (T) is active *and* the cursor is in text. To access the Hand tool when the cursor is in text, press the Option (macOS) or Alt (Windows) key.

Touch workspace

In Adobe Illustrator CC, the Touch workspace is designed for touch-enabled devices on Windows 8 or newer. The touch layout has a cleaner interface that allows you to comfortably use a stylus or your fingertip to access the tools and controls of the Touch workspace.

You can create logos, create icons, explore custom lettering and typography, create UI wireframes, and more. The Touch workspace brings traditional drawing templates and French curves to the Illustrator workspace. These shapes project a scalable, movable outline that can be traced against to quickly create refined curves.

At any time (on a supported device), you can immediately switch between the Touch and traditional workspaces to access the full range of Illustrator tools and controls. For more information on working with touch devices and Illustrator, visit Help (Help > Illustrator Help).

On a touch device such as a Direct touch device (a touchscreen device), Indirect touch device (the trackpad on a Mac), a touchpad, or a Wacom Intuos5 (and later) device, you can also use standard touch gestures (pinch and swipe) to do the following:

- Pinch in or out, using two fingers (like the thumb and forefinger) to zoom
- Place two fingers on the document, and move the fingers together to pan within the document
- Swipe or flick to navigate artboards
- In Artboard Editing mode, use two fingers to rotate the artboard by 90°

Viewing artwork

When you open a file, it is automatically displayed in Preview mode, which shows how the artwork will print. Illustrator offers other ways of viewing your artwork, such as outlines and rasterized. Next, you'll take a look at the different methods for viewing artwork and understand why you might view artwork that way.

1 Choose View > Fit Artboard In Window.

When you're working with large or complex illustrations, you may want to view only the outlines, or *paths*, of objects in your artwork so that the screen doesn't have to redraw the artwork each time you make a change. This is called Outline mode. Outline mode can also be helpful when selecting objects, as you will see in Lesson 2, "Techniques for Selecting Artwork."

2 Choose View > Outline.

Only the outlines of objects are displayed. You can use this view to find and select objects that might not be visible in Preview mode.

▶ **Tip:** You can press Command+Y (macOS) or Ctrl+Y (Windows) to toggle between Preview and Outline modes.

3 With Outline mode still showing, choose View > GPU Preview (or View > Preview On CPU if GPU Preview is not supported) to see all the attributes of the artwork.

4 Choose View > Overprint Preview to view any lines or shapes that are set to overprint.

This view is helpful for those in the print industry who need to see how inks interact when set to overprint.

● **Note:** When switching between viewing modes, visual changes may not be readily apparent. Zooming in and out (View > Zoom In and View > Zoom Out) may help you see the differences more easily.

5 Choose View > Fit Artboard In Window.

6 Choose 400% from the zoom level menu in the lower-left corner of the application window.

7 Choose View > Pixel Preview.

When you turn on Pixel preview, Overprint preview is turned off. Pixel preview can be used to see how the artwork will look when it is rasterized and viewed onscreen in a web browser. Note the "jagged" edge on some of the artwork. An arrow is pointing to it in the figure.

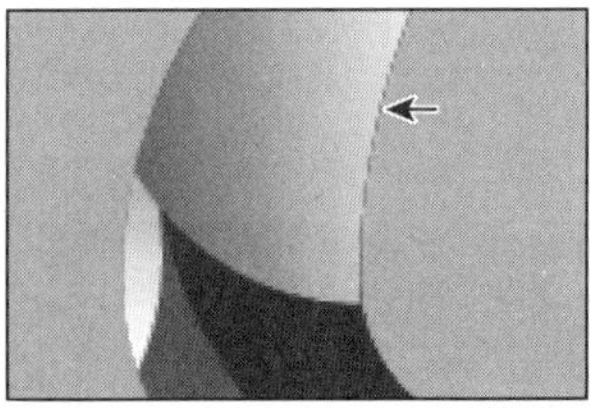

8 Choose View > Pixel Preview to turn off Pixel preview.

9 Choose View > Fit Artboard In Window to make sure that the entire active artboard is fit in the Document window, and leave the document open.

Zooming and panning with the Navigator panel

The Navigator panel is another way to navigate a document with a single artboard or multiple artboards. This is useful when you need to see all artboards in the document in one window and to edit content in any of those artboards in a zoomed-in view. You can open the Navigator panel by choosing Window > Navigator. It is in a free-floating group in the workspace.

The Navigator panel can be used in several ways, including the following:

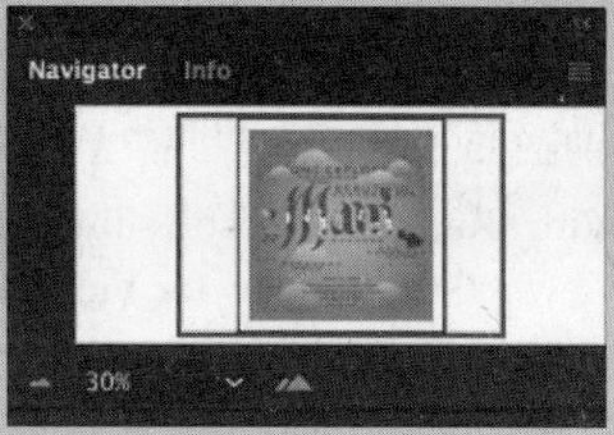

- The red box in the Navigator panel, called the *proxy view area*, indicates the area of the document that is being shown.
- Type in a zoom value or click the mountain icons to change the magnification of your artwork.
- Position the pointer inside the proxy view area of the Navigator panel. When the pointer becomes a hand (✋), drag to pan to different parts of the artwork.

Navigating artboards

Artboards represent the regions that can contain printable artwork (similar to pages in a program like Adobe InDesign). You can use artboards to crop areas for printing or placement purposes. Multiple artboards are useful for creating a variety of things, such as multipage PDFs, printed pages with different sizes or different elements, independent elements for websites, video storyboards, or individual items for animation in Adobe® Animate CC or Adobe After Effects® CC. You can easily share content among designs, create multipage PDFs, and print multiple pages by creating more than one artboard.

Note: Learn how to work more with artboards in Lesson 5, "Transforming Artwork."

Illustrator allows for up to 1,000 artboards within a single file (depending on their size). Multiple artboards can be added when you initially create an Illustrator document, or you can add, remove, and edit artboards after the document is created. Next, you will learn how to efficiently navigate a document that contains multiple artboards.

1 Choose File > Open. In the Open dialog box, navigate to the Lessons > Lesson01 folder, and select the L1_start2.ai file on your hard disk. Click Open to open the file.

2 Choose View > Fit All In Window to fit all artboards in the Document window. Notice that there are two artboards in the document that contain the designs for the front and back of a postcard.

The artboards in a document can be arranged in any order, orientation, or artboard size—they can even overlap. Suppose that you want to create a four-page brochure. You can create different artboards for every page of the brochure, all with the same size and orientation. They can be arranged horizontally or vertically or in whatever way you like.

3 Select the Selection tool (▶) in the Tools panel, and click to select the "HELLO FROM" text objects on the artboard on the right.

4 Choose View > Fit Artboard In Window.

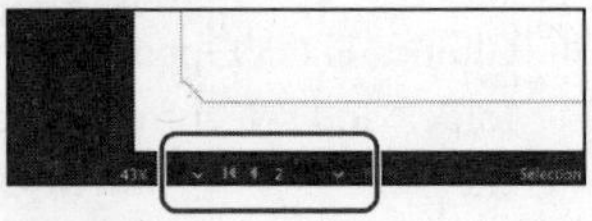

When you select artwork, it makes the artboard that the artwork is on the *active*, or selected, artboard. By choosing the Fit Artboard In Window command, the currently active artboard is fit in the Document window. The active artboard is identified in the Artboard Navigation menu in the lower-left corner of the Document window. Currently it is artboard 2.

5 Choose Select > Deselect to deselect the text.

6 Choose 1 from the Artboard Navigation menu in the Properties panel.

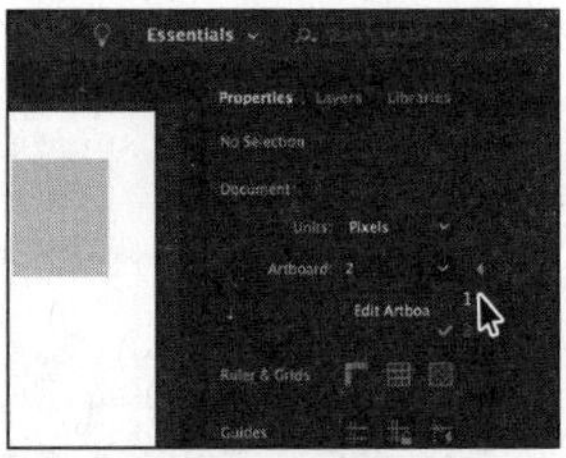

Notice the arrows to the right of the Artboard Navigation menu in the Properties panel. You can use these to navigate to the previous (◀) and next (▶) artboards. Those arrows plus a few others also appear in the Status bar below the document.

7 Click the Next navigation button (▶) in the Status bar below the document to view the next artboard (artboard 2) in the Document window.

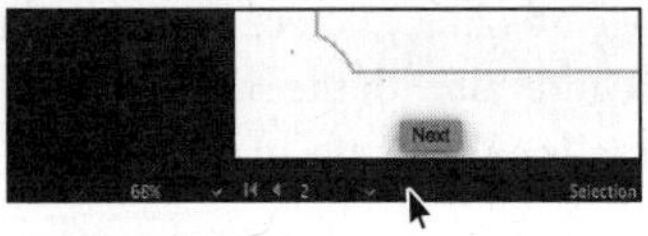

● **Note:** You'll learn all about Artboard Editing mode in Lesson 5, "Transforming Artwork."

The Artboard Navigation menu and navigation arrows always appear in the Status bar below the document, but only appear in the Properties panel when not in Artboard Editing mode, the Selection tool is selected, and nothing is selected.

Using the Artboards panel

Another method for navigating multiple artboards is to use the Artboards panel. The Artboards panel lists all artboards currently in the document and allows you to navigate between artboards, rename artboards, add or delete artboards, edit artboard settings, and more. Next, you'll open the Artboards panel and navigate the document.

1 Choose Window > Artboards to open the Artboards panel.

2 Double-click the number 1 that appears to the left of the name "Front" in the Artboards panel. The artboard named Front is now fit in the Document window.

● **Note:** Double-clicking the artboard name in the Artboards panel allows you to change the name of the artboard. Clicking the artboard icon (or) to the right of the artboard name in the panel allows you to edit artboard options.

3 Double-click the number 2 to the left of the name "Back" in the Artboards panel to show the second artboard in the Document window.

Notice that when you double-click to navigate to an artboard, that artboard is also fit in the Document window.

4 Click the X at the top of the Artboards panel group to close it.

Arranging multiple documents

There will be times when you open more than one Illustrator document at a time. When you open more than one document, the Document windows are tabbed. You can arrange the open documents in other ways, such as side by side, so that you can easily compare or drag items from one document to another. You can also use the Arrange Documents menu to quickly display your open documents in a variety of configurations.

You should currently have two Illustrator files open: L1_start1.ai and L1_start2.ai. Each file has its own tab at the top of the Document window. These documents are considered a group of Document windows. You can create document groups to loosely associate files while they are open.

1 Click the L1_start1.ai document tab to show L1_start1.ai in the Document window.

● **Note:** Be careful to drag directly to the right. Otherwise, you could undock the Document window and create a new group. If that happens, choose Window > Arrange > Consolidate All Windows.

2 Drag the L1_start1.ai document tab to the right of the L1_start2.ai document tab. Release the mouse button to see the new tab order.

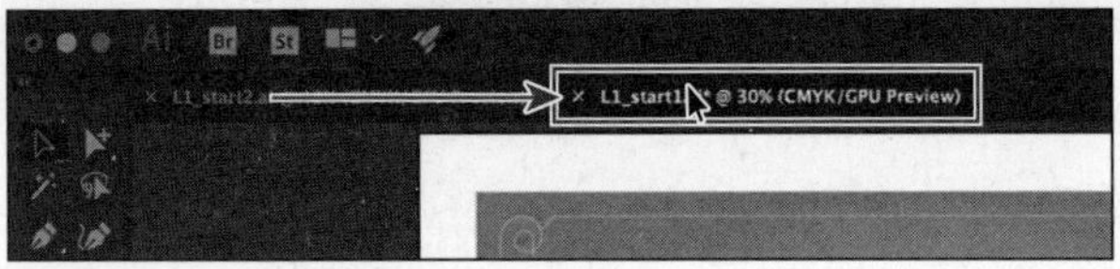

Dragging the document tabs allows you to change the order of the documents. This can be very useful if you use the document shortcuts to navigate to the next or previous document.

▶ **Tip:** You can cycle between open documents by pressing Command+~ (next document) and Command+Shift+~ (previous document) (macOS) or by pressing Ctrl+F6 (next document) and Ctrl+Shift+F6 (previous document) (Windows).

To see both of the documents at the same time, maybe to drag artwork from one to the other, you can arrange the Document windows by cascading or tiling them. *Cascading* allows you to cascade (stack) different document groups. *Tiling* shows multiple Document windows at one time, in various arrangements. Next, you'll tile the open documents so that you can see both documents at one time.

● **Note:** On macOS, the Application Frame needs to be turned on (Window > Application Frame) for tiling to work in this step.

3 Choose Window > Arrange > Tile.

This shows both Document windows arranged in a pattern.

● **Note:** Your documents may be tiled in a different order. That's okay.

4 Click in the Document window on the left to activate the document, and choose View > Fit Artboard In Window. Do the same for the Document window on the right.

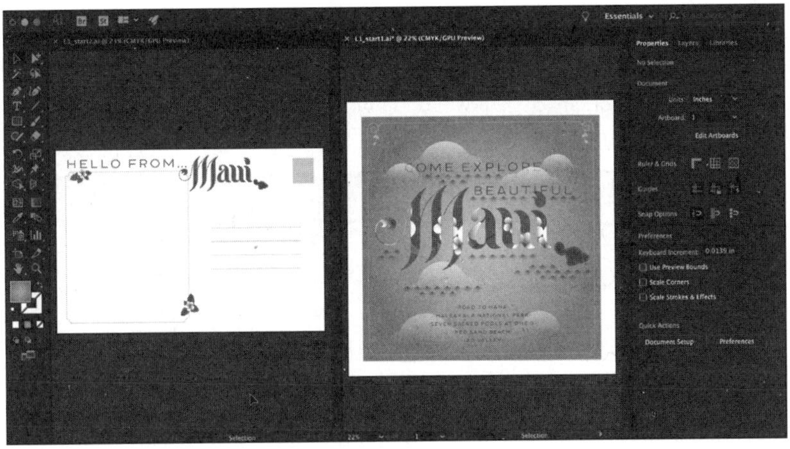

With documents tiled, you can drag the dividing line between each of the Document windows to reveal more or less of a particular document. You can also drag artwork between documents, which copies them from one document to another.

To change the arrangement of the tiled windows, it's possible to drag document tabs to new positions. However, it's easier to use the Arrange Documents menu to quickly arrange open documents in a variety of configurations.

5 Click the Arrange Documents button ( ) in the Application bar to display the Arrange Documents menu. Click the Consolidate All button ( ) to bring the documents back together.

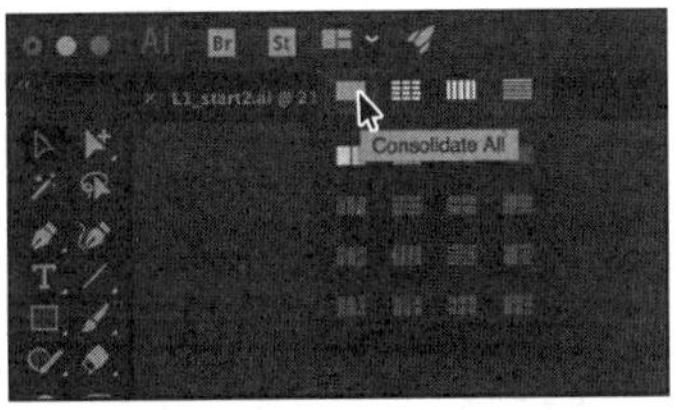

6 Click the Arrange Documents button ( ) in the Application bar to display the Arrange Documents menu again. Click the 2-Up vertical button ( ) in the Arrange Documents menu.

7 Click to select the L1_start1.ai tab, if it is not already selected. Then, click the Close button (X) on the L1_start1.ai document tab to close the document. If a dialog box appears asking you to save the document, click Don't Save (macOS) or No (Windows).

8 Choose File > Close to close the L1_start2.ai document without saving.

● **Note:** In Illustrator, all the workspace elements are grouped in a single, integrated window that lets you treat the application as a single unit. When you move or resize the Application frame or any of its elements, all the elements within it respond to each other so none overlaps another. If you are using a Mac and prefer the traditional, free-form user interface, you can turn off the Application frame by choosing Window > Application Frame to toggle it on or off.

● **Note:** On Windows, menus appear in the Application bar.

▶ **Tip:** You can also choose Window > Arrange > Consolidate All Windows to return the two documents to tabs in the same group.

Finding resources for using Illustrator

▶ **Tip:** The Learn panel, which contains instructional content, was added just prior to release. To access it, open a file and either choose Window > Learn or click the Learn icon (■) in the Application bar.

To access Illustrator tutorials, close all open files and click the Learn tab at the top of the Start workspace. You will find links to video and written tutorials on a variety of Illustrator-related topics.

For complete and up-to-date information about using Illustrator panels, tools, and other application features, visit the Adobe website. By choosing Help > Illustrator Help, you'll be connected to the Illustrator Help website, where you can search Illustrator Help and support documents, as well as other websites relevant to Illustrator users. Community Help brings together active Adobe product users, Adobe product team members, authors, and experts to give you the most useful, relevant, and up-to-date information about Adobe products.

Data recovery

When you restart Illustrator after a program crash, you have the option of recovering work-in-progress files so that your hours of work are not wasted. The recovered files are opened with the "[Recovered]" in the filename.

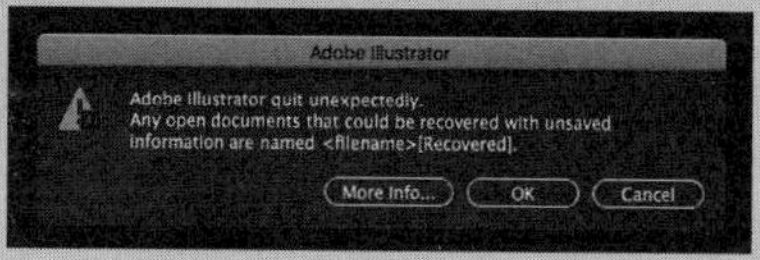

You can turn data recovery on and off as well as set options such as how often to save recovery data in the program preferences (Illustrator CC > Preferences > File Handling & Clipboard [macOS] or Edit > Preferences > File Handling & Clipboard [Windows]).

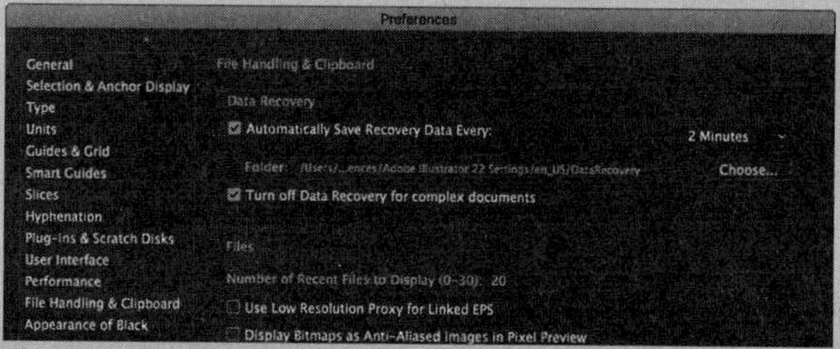

Review questions

1 Describe two ways to change the view of a document.

2 How do you select a tool in Illustrator?

3 How do you save panel locations and visibility preferences?

4 Describe a few ways to navigate among artboards in Illustrator.

5 Describe how arranging Document windows can be helpful.

Review answers

1 You can choose commands from the View menu to zoom in or out of a document or to fit it to your screen; you can also use the Zoom tool (🔍) in the Tools panel and click or drag over a document to enlarge or reduce the view. In addition, you can use keyboard shortcuts to magnify or reduce the display of artwork. You can also use the Navigator panel to scroll artwork or to change its magnification without using the Document window.

2 To select a tool, you can either click the tool in the Tools panel or press the keyboard shortcut for that tool. For example, you can press V to select the Selection tool (▶) from the keyboard. Selected tools remain active until you click a different tool.

3 You can save panel locations and visibility preferences by choosing Window > Workspace > New Workspace to create custom work areas and to make it easier to find the controls that you need.

4 To navigate among artboards in Illustrator, you can choose the artboard number from the Artboard Navigation menu at the lower-left of the Document window; with nothing selected, the Selection tool selected, and while not in Artboard Editing mode, you can choose the artboard number from the Artboard Navigation menu or use the Artboard Navigation arrows in the Properties panel; you can use the Artboard Navigation arrows in the lower-left of the Document window to go to the first, previous, next, and last artboards; you can use the Artboards panel to navigate to artboards; or you can use the Navigator panel to drag the proxy view area to navigate between artboards.

5 Arranging Document windows allows you to tile windows or to cascade document groups (cascading wasn't discussed in the lesson). This can be useful if you are working on multiple Illustrator files and you need to compare or share content among them.

2 TECHNIQUES FOR SELECTING ARTWORK

Lesson overview

In this lesson, you'll learn how to do the following:

- Differentiate between the various selection tools and use different selection techniques.
- Recognize Smart Guides.
- Save selections for future use.
- Hide and lock items.
- Use tools and commands to align shapes and points to each other and the artboard.
- Group and ungroup items.
- Work in Isolation mode.

This lesson takes approximately 45 minutes to complete. Please log in to your account on peachpit.com to download the lesson files for this chapter, or go to the "Getting Started" section at the beginning of this book and follow the instructions under "Accessing the lesson files and Web Edition."

Your Account page is also where you'll find any updates to the chapters or to the lesson files. Look on the Lesson & Update Files tab to access the most current content.

Selecting content in Adobe Illustrator is one of the more important things you'll do. In this lesson, you learn how to locate and select objects using the Selection tools; protect other objects by grouping, hiding, and locking them; align objects to each other and the artboard; and much more.

Starting the lesson

Creating, selecting, and editing artwork is the cornerstone of Adobe Illustrator. In this lesson, you'll learn the fundamentals of selecting, aligning, and grouping artwork using different methods. You'll begin by resetting the preferences in Illustrator and opening the lesson file.

● **Note:** If you have not already downloaded the project files for this lesson to your computer from your Account page, make sure to do so now. See the "Getting Started" section at the beginning of the book.

1 To ensure that the tools function and the defaults are set exactly as described in this lesson, delete or deactivate (by renaming) the Adobe Illustrator CC preferences file. See "Restoring default preferences" in the "Getting Started" section at the beginning of the book.

2 Start Adobe Illustrator CC.

3 Choose File > Open. Locate the file named L2_end.ai, which is in the Lessons > Lesson02 folder that you copied onto your hard disk, and click Open.

This file contains the finished illustration that you'll create in this lesson.

4 Choose File > Open, and open the L2_start.ai file in the Lessons > Lesson02 folder on your hard disk.

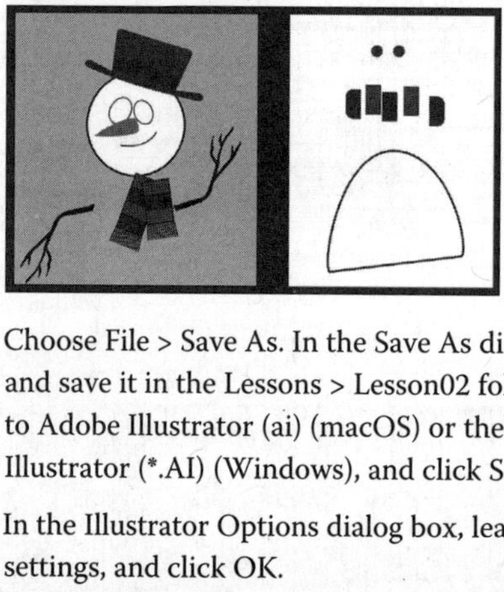

5 Choose File > Save As. In the Save As dialog box, name the file **Snowman.ai**, and save it in the Lessons > Lesson02 folder. Leave the Format option set to Adobe Illustrator (ai) (macOS) or the Save As Type option set to Adobe Illustrator (*.AI) (Windows), and click Save.

6 In the Illustrator Options dialog box, leave the Illustrator options at their default settings, and click OK.

7 Choose View > Fit All In Window.

8 Choose Window > Workspace > Essentials, make sure it's selected, and then choose Window > Workspace > Reset Essentials to reset the workspace.

Selecting objects

Whether you're creating artwork from scratch or editing existing artwork in Illustrator, you will need to become familiar with selecting objects. There are many methods and tools for doing this, and in this section, you'll explore the most widely used, which includes the Selection (▶) and Direct Selection (▷) tools.

Using the Selection tool

The Selection tool (▶) in the Tools panel lets you select, move, rotate, and resize entire objects. In this first section, you'll become familiar with it.

1 Select the Selection tool (▶) in the Tools panel on the left. Move the pointer over the different artwork on the artboards, without clicking.

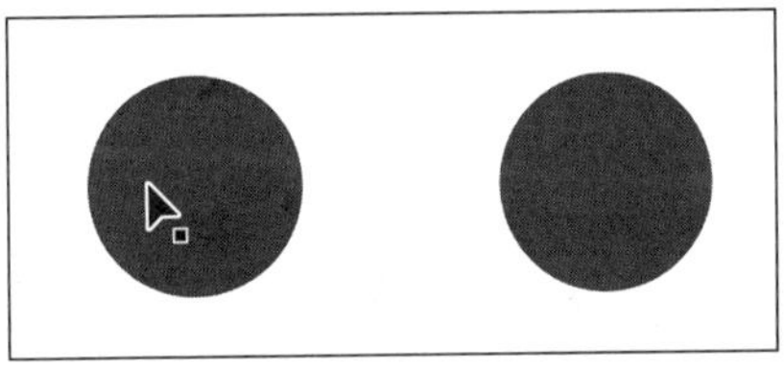

The icon that appears next to the pointer as it passes over objects (▶) indicates that there is artwork that can be selected under the pointer. When you hover over an object, that object is also outlined in a color like blue (in this instance).

2 Select the Zoom tool (🔍) in the Tools panel, and drag across the two blue circles on the artboard on the right, from left to right, to zoom in.

> **Tip:** If you can no longer see both blue circles after zooming, with the Zoom tool selected, drag from *right to left* to zoom out. You can also press the spacebar to temporarily access the Hand tool (✋) and drag in the Document window.

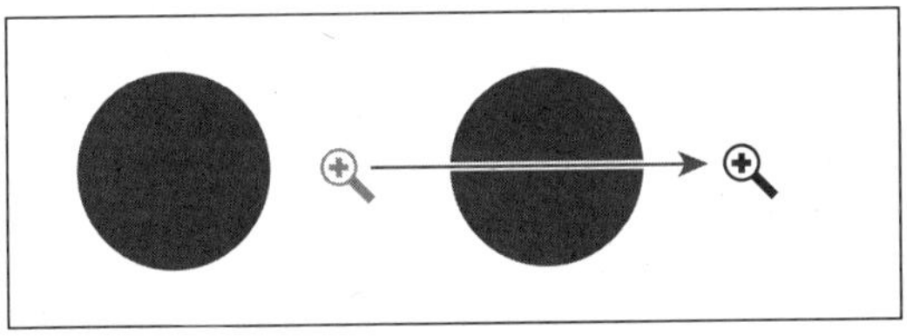

3 Select the Selection tool (▶) in the Tools panel and then position the pointer over the edge of the blue circle on the left.

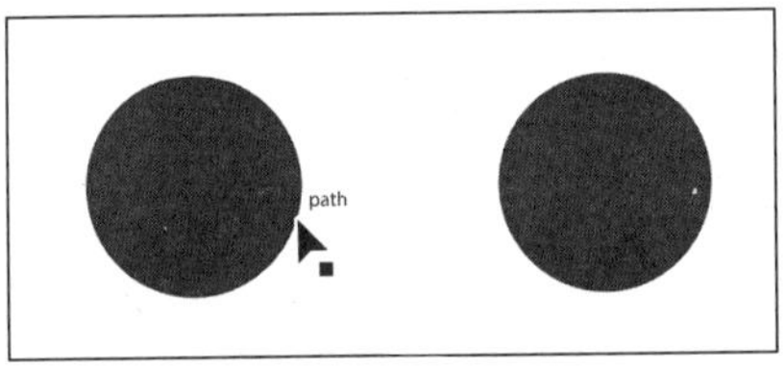

A word such as "path" or "anchor" may appear because Smart Guides are turned on by default. *Smart Guides* are temporary snap-to guides that help you align, edit, and transform objects or artboards.

> **Tip:** You'll learn more about Smart Guides in Lesson 3, "Using Shapes to Create Artwork for a Postcard."

4 Click anywhere inside the blue circle on the left to select it. A bounding box with eight handles appears around the selected circle.

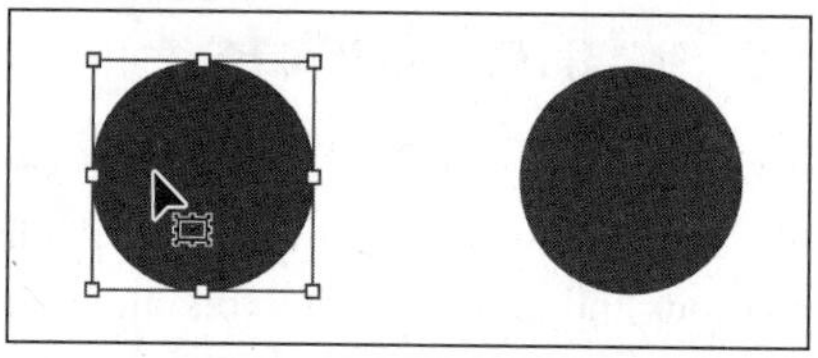

The *bounding box* is used when making changes to artwork (vector or raster), such as resizing or rotating. The bounding box also indicates that an item is selected and ready to be modified, and the color of the bounding box indicates which layer the object is on. Layers are discussed more in Lesson 9, "Organizing Your Artwork with Layers."

Note: To select an item without a fill, you can click the stroke (the edge) or drag across the object.

5 Using the Selection tool, click in the blue circle on the right. Notice that the left blue circle is now deselected and only the right circle is selected.

6 Holding down the Shift key, click the blue circle on the left to add it to the selection and then release the key. Both blue circles are now selected, and a larger bounding box surrounds them.

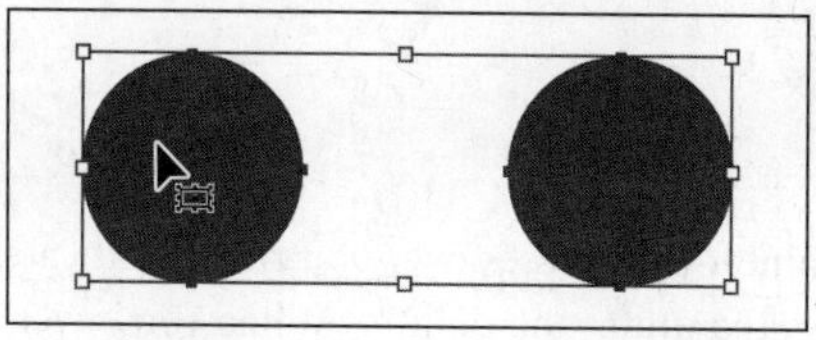

7 Move the circles anywhere in the document by clicking inside either selected circle (in the blue area) and dragging. Because both circles are selected, they move together.

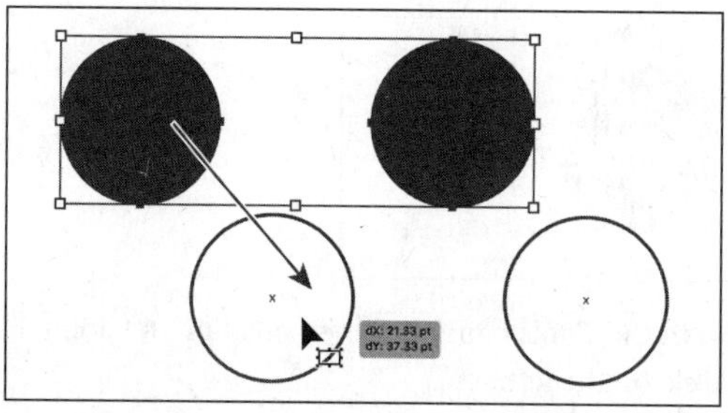

As you drag, you may notice the magenta lines that appear. These are called *alignment guides* and are visible because Smart Guides are turned on (View > Smart Guides). As you drag, the objects align to other objects in the document. Also notice the measurement label (gray box) next to the pointer that shows the object's distance from its original position. Measurement labels also appear because Smart Guides are turned on.

8 Revert to the last saved version of the document by choosing File > Revert. In the dialog box that appears, click Revert.

Using the Direct Selection tool

In Illustrator, as you draw, you create vector paths that are made up of anchor points and paths. Anchor points are used to control the shape of the path and work like pins holding a wire in place. A shape you create, like a square, is composed of at least four anchor points on the corners with paths connecting the anchor points.

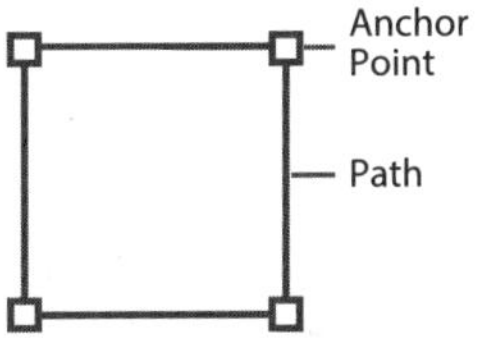

You change the shape of a path or shape by dragging its anchor points (among other things). The Direct Selection tool ( ) lets you select anchor points or paths within an object so that it can be reshaped. Next, you'll become familiar with selecting anchor points using the Direct Selection tool and reshaping a path.

1 Choose View > Fit All In Window.

2 Select the Zoom tool ( ) in the Tools panel, and click several times on the series of red and green shapes below the blue circles to zoom in closely.

3 Select the Direct Selection tool ( ) in the Tools panel on the left. Without clicking, position the pointer over the upper-left corner of one of the green shapes. The word "anchor" should appear next to the pointer.

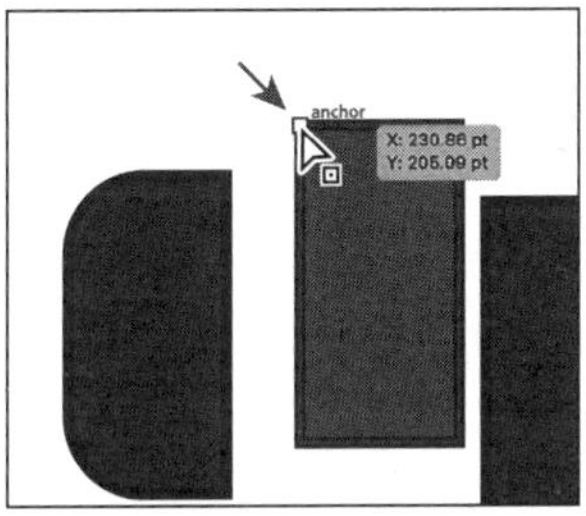

With the Direct Selection tool selected, when the pointer is over an anchor point of a path or object, the word "anchor" appears. The "anchor" label is showing because Smart Guides are turned on (View > Smart Guides). Also notice the little white box to the right of the pointer ( ). The small dot that appears in the center of the white box indicates that the cursor is positioned over an anchor point.

▶ **Tip:** You can also click in the middle of a shape to select it and to see the anchor points around its edge. This can be an easy way to see where the points are, and then you can click a point to select it.

4 Click to select that anchor point and move the pointer away.

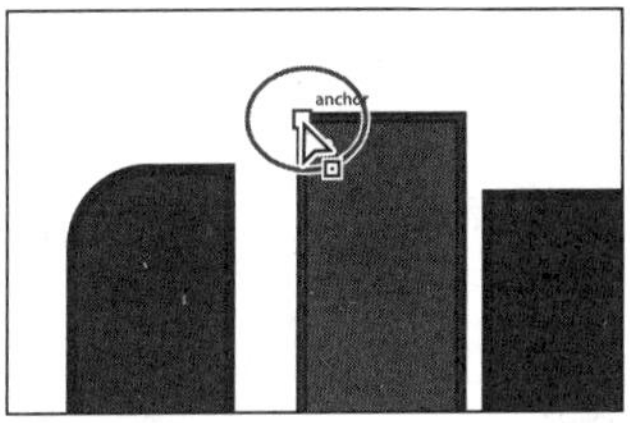

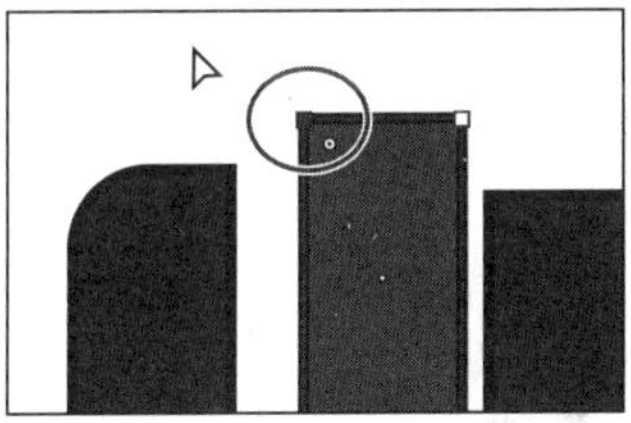

Notice that only the anchor point you selected is solid (filled with blue), indicating that it is selected, and the other anchor points in the shape are hollow (filled with white), indicating that they are not selected.

> **Note:** The gray measurement label that appears as you drag the anchor point has the values dX and dY. *dX* indicates the distance that the pointer has moved along the x-axis (horizontal), and *dY* indicates the distance that the pointer has moved along the y-axis (vertical).

5 With the Direct Selection tool still selected, move the pointer over the selected anchor point and drag it up to edit the shape.

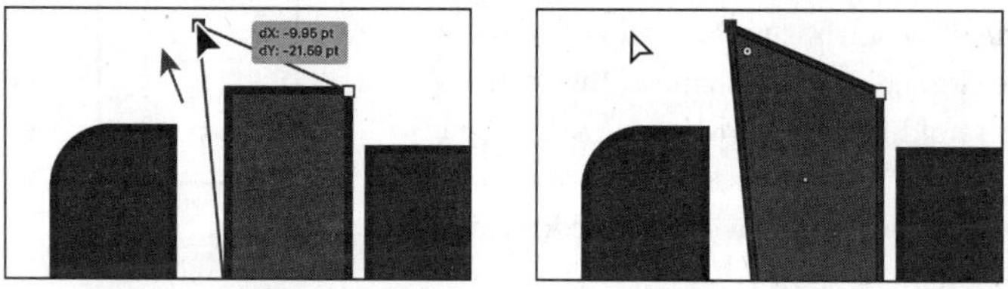

6 Try clicking another point on a corner of the shape, and notice that the previous point is deselected.

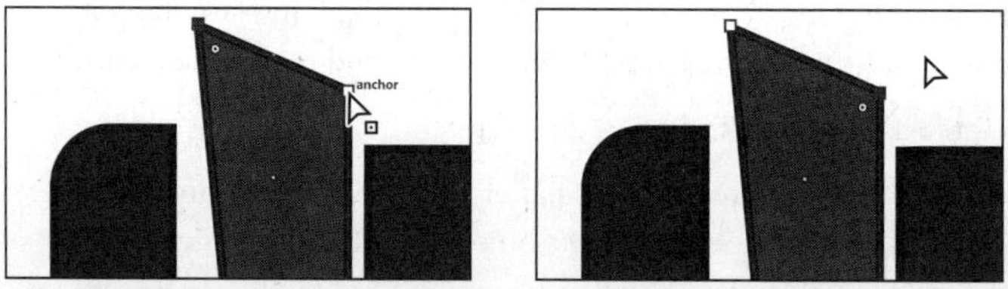

7 Revert to the last saved version of the file by choosing File > Revert. In the dialog box that appears, click Revert.

Creating selections with a marquee

Another way to select content is by dragging across content that you want to select (called a *marquee selection)*, which is what you'll do next.

1 Choose View > Fit All In Window.

2 Select the Zoom tool (🔍) in the Tools panel, and click three times on the blue circles, on the right.

3 Select the Selection tool (▶) in the Tools panel. Position the pointer above and to the left of the leftmost blue circle and then drag downward and to the right to create a marquee that overlaps the tops of both circles. Release the mouse button.

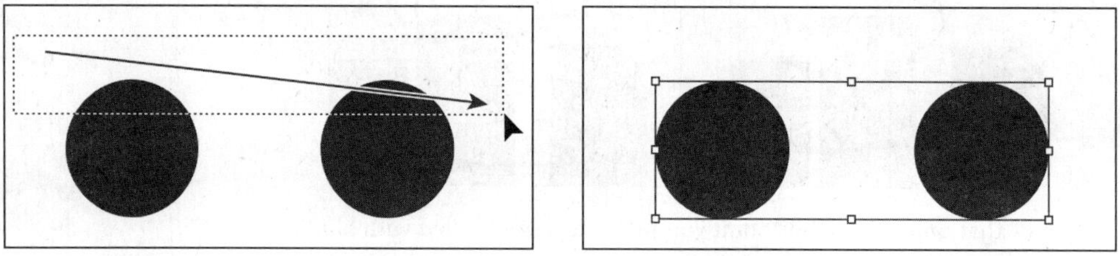

When dragging with the Selection tool (▶), you need to encompass only a small part of an object to select it.

4 Choose Select > Deselect, or click where there are no objects.

Now you'll use the Direct Selection tool to select multiple anchor points in the blue circles by dragging a marquee around anchor points.

5 Select the Direct Selection tool (▷) in the Tools panel. Starting off the top left of the leftmost blue circle (see the following figure), drag across the top edges of the two circles, then release the mouse button. Only the top anchor points become selected.

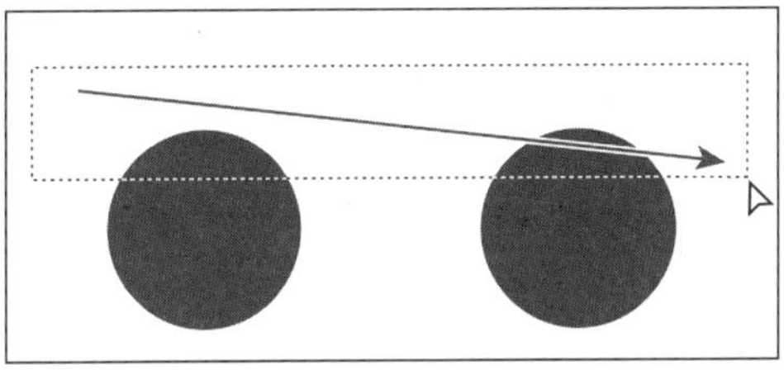

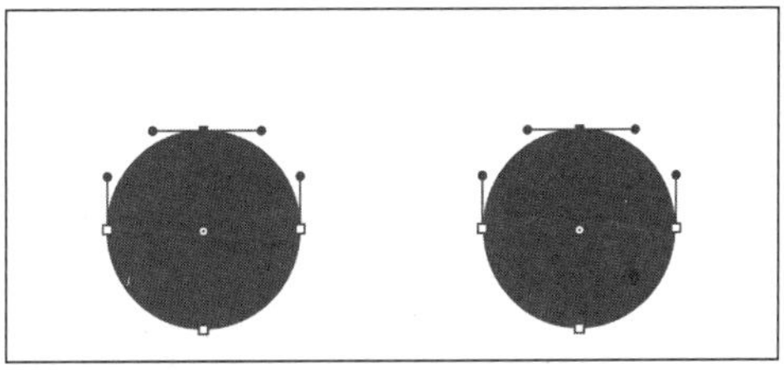

6 Drag one of the selected anchor points to see how they move together.

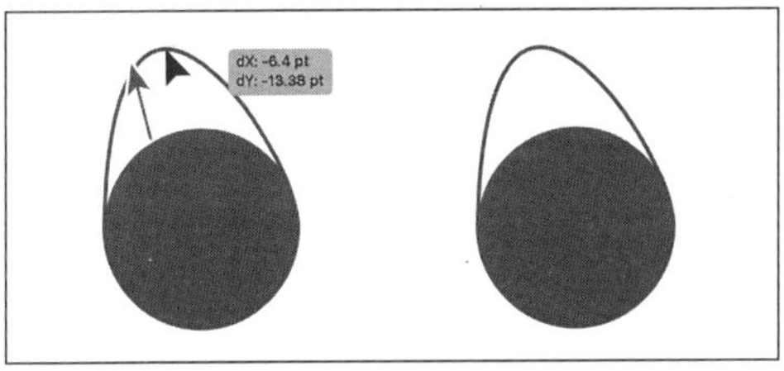

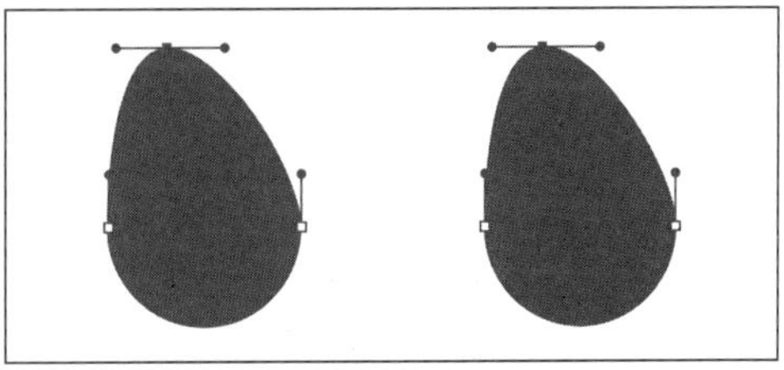

You can use this method when selecting points so that you don't have to click exactly on the anchor point that you want to select.

7 Revert to the last saved version of the file by choosing File > Revert. In the dialog box that appears, click Revert.

Selecting artwork with the Magic Wand tool

You can use the Magic Wand tool (✓) in the Tools panel to select all objects in a document that have the same attributes, like a color fill. The fill is a color applied to the inside of an object. You can customize the Magic Wand tool to select objects based on options, like stroke weight, stroke color, and more, by double-clicking the Magic Wand tool in the Tools panel.

Hiding and locking objects

At times, selecting artwork may be more difficult if there are objects stacked one on another or there are multiple objects in a small area. In this section, you'll learn a common way to make selecting objects easier, by locking and hiding content.

1 Choose View > Fit All In Window.

Next, you'll attempt to drag across artwork to select it.

2 With the Selection tool (▶) selected, move the pointer into the blue area to the left of the snowman (the "x" in the following figure) and drag across the two ellipses that are the eyes of the snowman.

Notice that you drag the large blue shape instead.

3 Choose Edit > Undo Move.

4 With the blue background shape still selected, choose Object > Lock > Selection, or press Command+2 (macOS) or Ctrl+2 (Windows).

Locking objects prevents you from selecting and editing them. You can unlock artwork by choosing Object > Unlock All.

● **Note:** Any artwork within the marquee area will be selected using this method.

5 With the Selection tool (▶), move the pointer into the blue area to the left of the snowman's hat and drag across the head of the snowman to select the whole thing (including the hat). See the following figure.

6 Press the Shift key and click each eye shape, one at a time, to *remove* them from the selection.

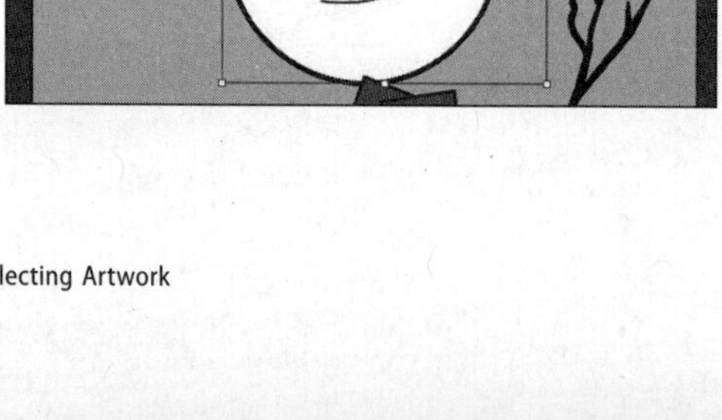

7 Choose Object > Hide > Selection, or press Command+3 (macOS) or Ctrl+3 (Windows).

The selected shapes are temporarily hidden so that you can more easily select other objects.

8 Choose File > Save to save the file.

Selecting similar objects

You can also select artwork based on similar fill color, stroke color, stroke weight, and more, using the Select > Same command. The stroke of an object is the outline (border), and the stroke weight is the width of the stroke. Next, you will select several objects with the same fill and stroke applied.

1 With the Selection tool (▶), click to select one of the blue circles on the right.

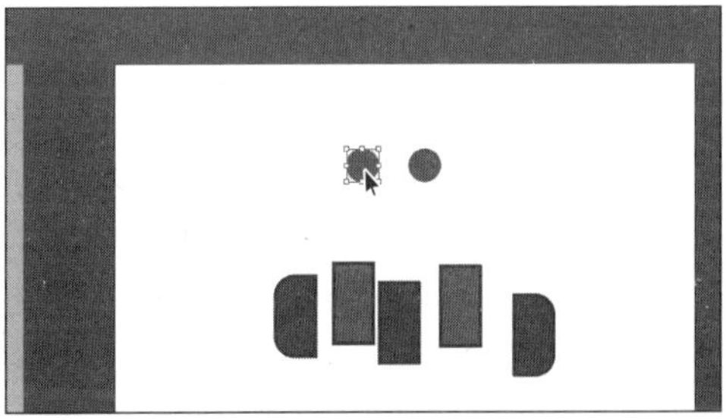

2 Choose Select > Same > Fill Color to select all objects on any artboard with the same fill color (blue) as the selected object.

Notice that the circles with the same blue-colored fill are selected.

3 Click to select one of the red- or green-filled shapes below the blue circles, and then choose Select > Same > Stroke Color.

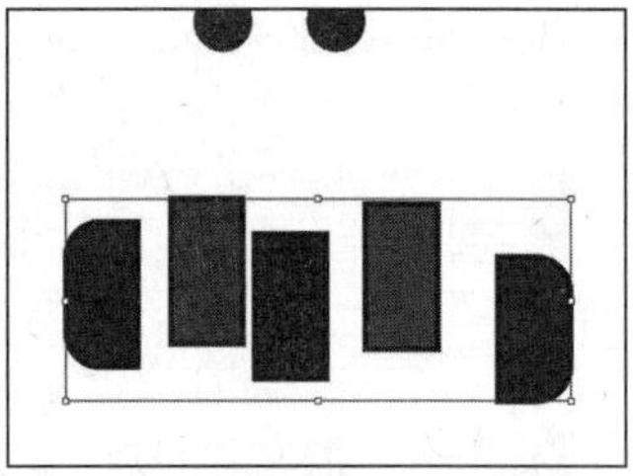

All of the shapes with the same stroke (border) color are now selected. If you know that you may need to reselect a series of objects again, like the selected red and green shapes, you can save a selection. Saved selections are a great way to easily recall a selection later, and are only saved with that document. You'll save the current selection next.

▶ **Tip:** It's helpful to name selections according to use or function. If you name the selection "1 pt stroke," for instance, the name may be misleading if you later change the stroke weight of the artwork.

4 With the shapes still selected, choose Select > Save Selection. Name the selection **Scarf** in the Save Selection dialog box, and click OK so that you'll be able to choose this selection at a later time.

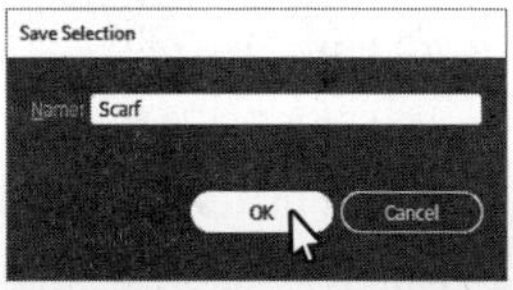

5 Choose Select > Deselect.

Selecting in Outline mode

By default, Adobe Illustrator displays all artwork with their paint attributes, like fill and stroke, showing. However, you can choose to display artwork so that only outlines (or paths) are visible. The next method for selecting involves viewing artwork in Outline mode and can be very useful if you want to select objects within a series of stacked objects.

1 Choose Object > Show All so you can see the artwork you previously hid.

2 With the Selection tool (▶), click within one of the white eye shapes to select it.

Since the shape has a white fill (a color, pattern, or gradient filling the inside of an object), you can click anywhere within the bounds of the object to select it.

3 Choose View > Outline to view artwork as outlines.

▶ **Tip:** In Outline mode, you may see the small x in the center of the shapes. If you click on that x, you can select the shape.

4 With the Selection tool, click in a blank area of the other eye shape.

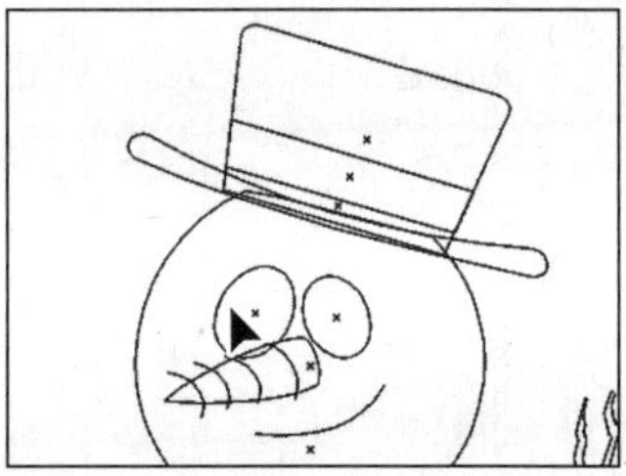

Notice that you cannot select the object by clicking the fill using this method. Outline mode displays artwork as outlines with no fill. To select in Outline mode, you can click the edge of the object or drag a marquee across the shape to select it.

5 With the Selection tool selected, drag across both eye shapes. Press the Up Arrow key several times to move both shapes up a little bit.

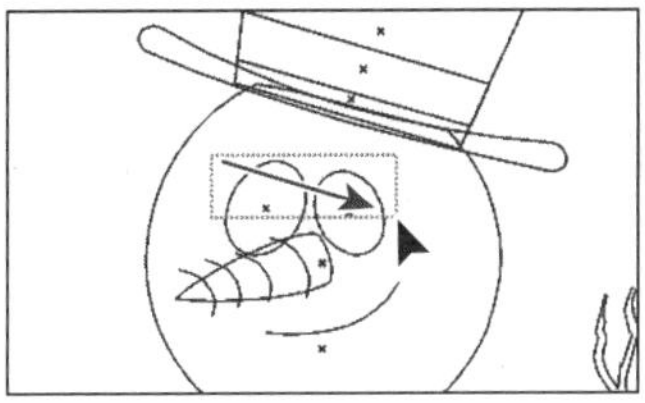

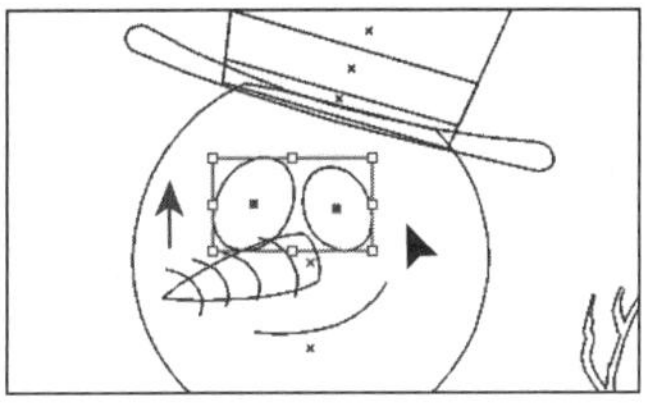

6 Choose View > GPU Preview or View > Preview On CPU (or Preview) if GPU Preview is not available to see the painted artwork.

Aligning objects

Illustrator makes it easy to align or distribute multiple objects relative to each other, the artboard, or a key object. In this section, you'll explore the different options for aligning objects.

Aligning objects to each other

One type of alignment is aligning objects to each other. This can be useful if, for instance, you want to align the top edges of a series of selected shapes to each other. Next, you'll align the red and green shapes to each other.

1 Choose Select > Scarf to reselect the red and green shapes on the right.

2 Click the Next artboard button (▶) in the lower-left corner of the Document window to fit the artboard with the selected red and green shapes in the window.

3 Select the Zoom tool (🔍) in the Tools panel, and drag across (from left to right) the red and green shapes to zoom in.

4 Click the Vertical Align Bottom button (▮) in the Properties panel on the right.

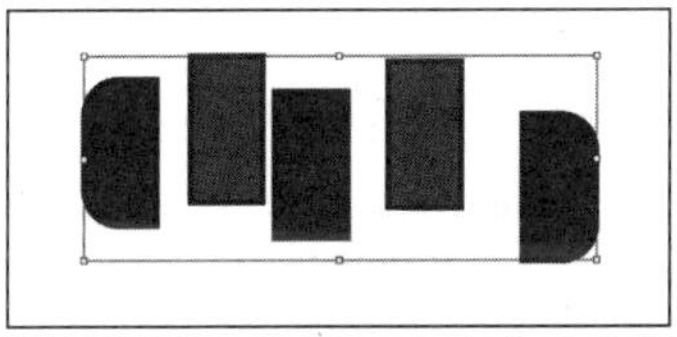

Note: You can also simply click several times to zoom in.

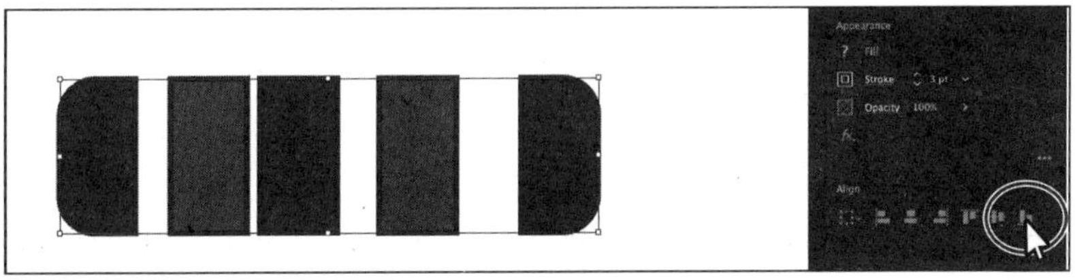

Notice that the bottom edges of all the selected objects move to align with the lowest selected object.

5 Choose Edit > Undo Align to return the objects to their original positions. Leave the objects selected for the next section.

Aligning to a key object

A *key object* is an object that you want other objects to align to. This can be useful when you want to align a series of objects, and maybe one of them is already in the perfect position. You specify a key object by selecting all the objects you want to align, including the key object, and then clicking the key object again. Next, you will align the red and green shapes using a key object.

Note: The key object outline color is determined by the layer color that the object is on.

1 With the shapes still selected, click the leftmost shape with the Selection tool (▶).

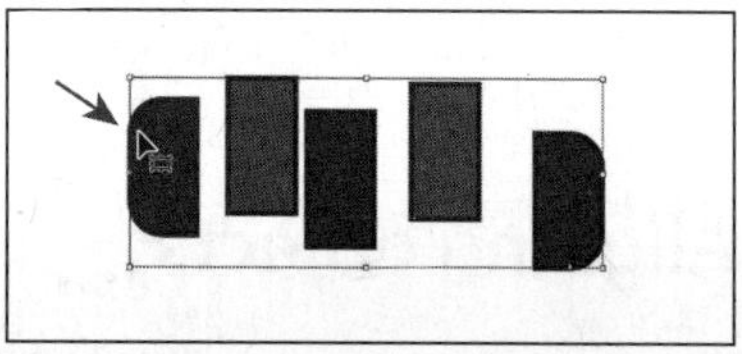

When selected, the key object has a thick outline indicating that other objects will align to it.

Note: To stop aligning and distributing relative to an object, click the object again to remove the blue outline.

2 Click the Vertical Align Top button (▦) in the Properties panel.

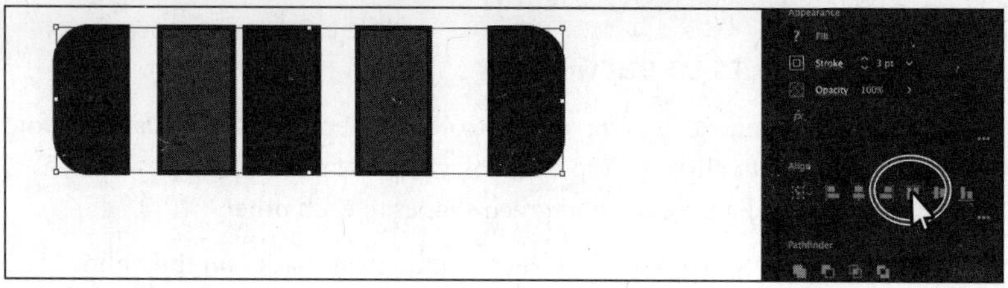

Notice that all of the selected shapes move to align to the top edge of the key object.

3 Choose Select > Deselect.

Aligning anchor points

Next, you'll align two anchor points to each other using the Align options. Like setting a key object in the previous section, you can also set a key anchor point that other anchor points will align to.

1 Choose View > Fit Artboard In Window.

2 Select the Direct Selection tool (▷), and click the lower-left corner point of the white shape at the bottom of the artboard. Shift-click to select the lower-right point of the same shape (see the following figure).

The last selected anchor point is the key anchor point. Other points will align to this point.

3 Click the Vertical Align Top button ( ) in the Properties panel to the right of the document. The first anchor point selected aligns to the second anchor point selected.

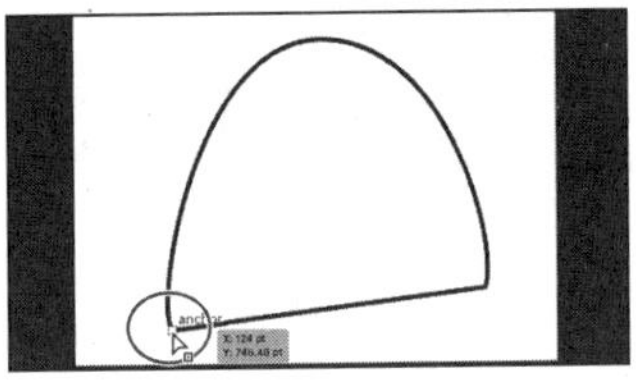

Select the first point.

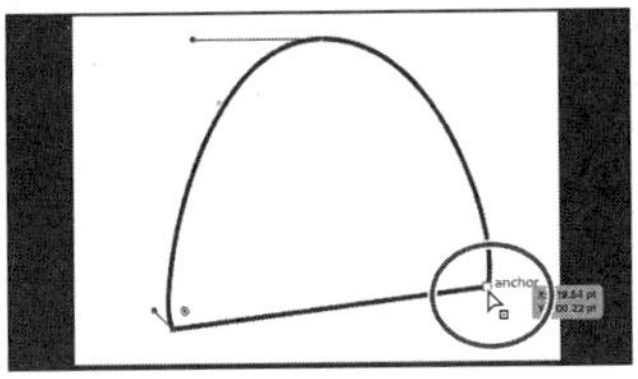

Select the second point.

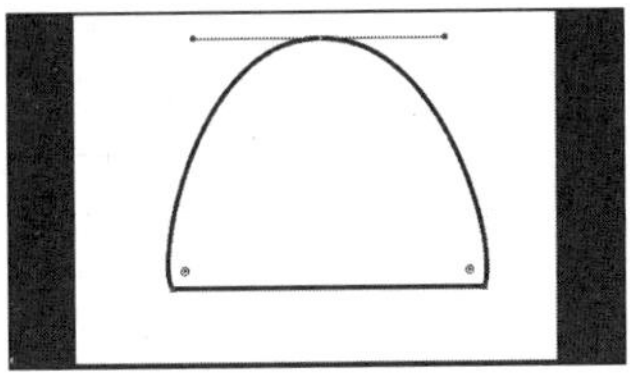

After aligning the points.

4 Choose Select > Deselect.

Distributing objects

Distributing objects using the Align panel enables you to select multiple objects and distribute the spacing between the centers or edges of those objects equally. Next, you will make the spacing between the red and green shapes even.

1 Select the Selection tool ( ) in the Tools panel.

2 Choose Select > Scarf to reselect all of the red and green shapes on the second artboard.

3 Click More Options ( ) in the Align section of the Properties panel (circled in the following figure). Click the Horizontal Distribute Center button ( ) in the panel that appears.

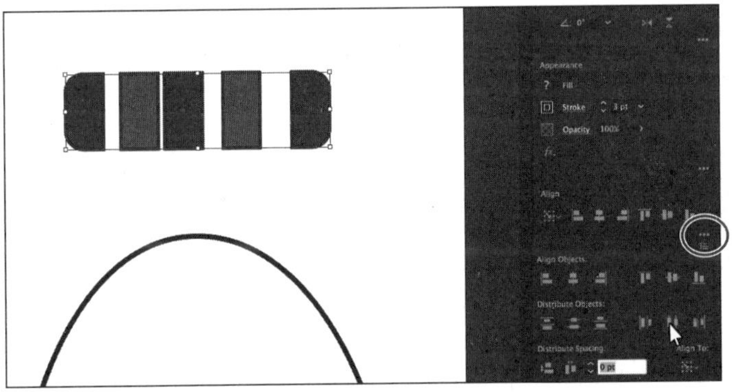

Distributing moves all the selected shapes so that the spacing between the *center* of each of them is equal.

4 Choose Edit > Undo Align.

Note: Using the Horizontal Distribute Center or Vertical Distribute Center button distributes the spacing equally between the *centers* of the objects. If the selected objects are not the same size, unexpected results may occur.

Note: When distributing objects horizontally, make sure that the leftmost and rightmost objects are where you want them and then distribute the objects between them. For vertical distribution, position the topmost and bottommost objects and then distribute the objects between them.

5 With the shapes still selected, click the leftmost shape (red shape) to make it the key object.

You have to define a key object before you are able to enter a value for distribute spacing, next.

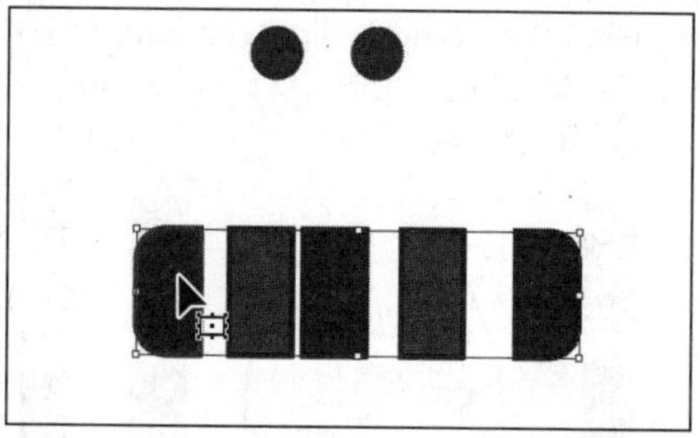

6 Click More Options (■) in the Align section of the Properties panel (circled in the following figure). Ensure that the Distribute Spacing value is 0 (zero) and then click the Horizontal Distribute Space button (■).

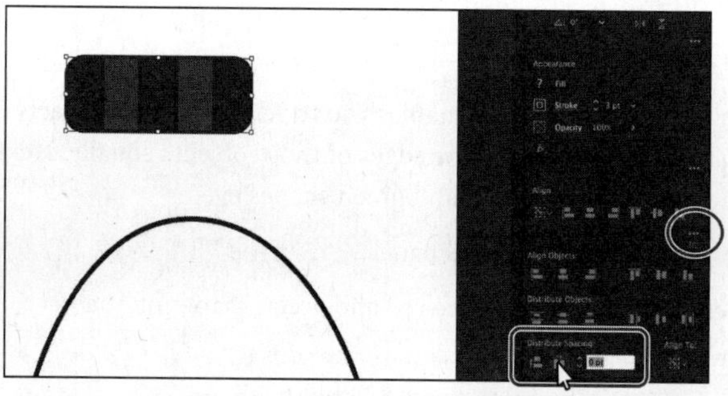

Distribute Spacing distributes the spacing *between* selected objects, whereas the Distribute Objects alignments distribute the spacing between the centers of selected objects. The value you can set is a great way to set a *specific* distance between objects.

7 Choose Select > Deselect.

Aligning to the artboard

You can also align content to the active artboard (page) rather than to a selection or a key object. Aligning to the artboard aligns each selected object separately to the artboard. Next, you'll align the white half-circle shape to the artboard with the snowman.

1 With the Selection tool (▶) selected, click the white half-circle shape at the bottom of the righthand artboard to select it. Choose Edit > Cut.

2 Click the Previous artboard button (■) in the lower-left corner of the Document window to navigate to the first (left) artboard in the document, which contains the snowman.

3 Choose Edit > Paste to paste the white half-circle.

4 Choose Window > Align to open the Align panel.

As of the writing of this book, there is no option in the Properties panel to align a single selected object to the artboard. That is why you are opening the Align panel.

5 Choose Show Options from the Align panel menu (■) (circled in the following figure).

6 Click the Align To Selection button (■) in the Align panel, and choose Align To Artboard in the menu that appears. Any content you align will now align to the artboard.

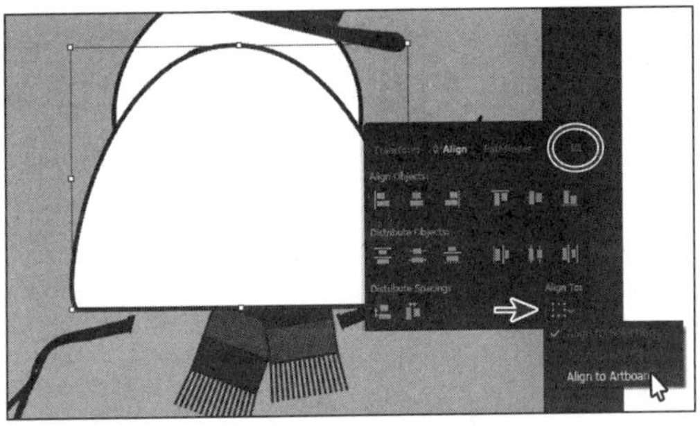

7 Click the Horizontal Align Center button (■) and then click the Vertical Align Bottom button (■) in the Align panel, to align the white half-circle to the horizontal center and vertical bottom of the artboard.

8 Choose Select > Deselect.

9 Click the X at the top of the Align panel group to close it.

Working with groups

You can combine objects into a group so that the objects are treated as a single unit. This way, you can move or transform a number of objects without affecting their individual attributes or positions relative to each other. It can also make selection of artwork easier later.

Grouping items

Next, you'll select multiple objects and create a group from them.

1 Choose View > Fit All In Window to see both artboards.

2 Choose Select > Scarf to select the series of red and green shapes.

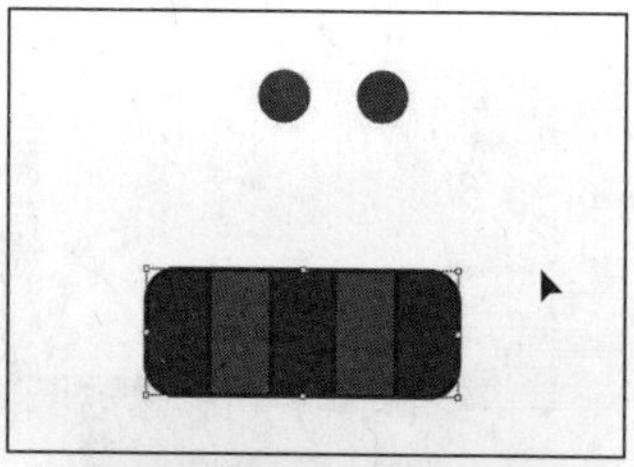

▶ **Tip:** You can also choose Object > Group to group content.

3 Click the Group button in the Quick Actions section of the Properties panel on the right, to group the selected artwork together.

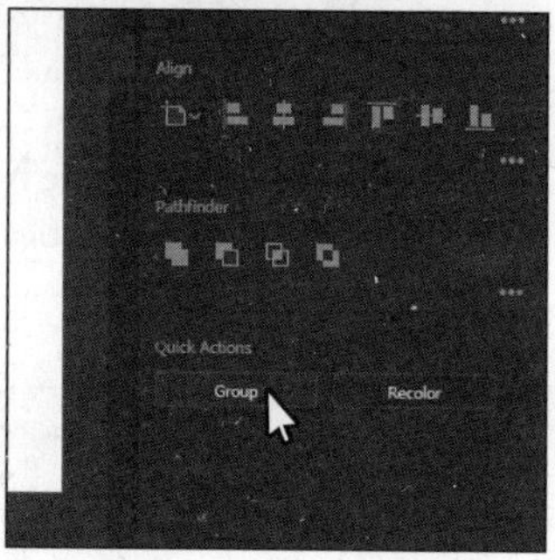

4 Choose Select > Deselect.

5 With the Selection tool (▶) selected, click one of the shapes in the new group.

Because they are grouped together, all are now selected.

6 Drag the group of shapes to just beneath the snowman's head.

This will become part of the snowman's scarf. Right now, the group you dragged onto the snowman is behind other artwork. You'll fix it shortly.

7 Choose Select > Deselect.

Editing a group in Isolation mode

Isolation mode isolates groups (or sublayers) so that you can easily select and edit specific objects or parts of objects without having to ungroup the objects. When in Isolation mode, all objects outside of the isolated group are locked and dimmed so that they aren't affected by the edits you make. Next, you will edit a group using Isolation mode.

1 With the Selection tool (▶), click the snowman's hat.

  You will see that it selects a group of shapes.

2 Double-click a shape in the hat to enter Isolation mode.

  Notice that the rest of the content in the document appears dimmed (you can't select it). At the top of the Document window, a gray bar appears with the words "Layer 1" and "<Group>." This indicates that you have isolated a group of objects that is on Layer 1. You will learn more about layers in Lesson 9, "Organizing Your Artwork with Layers."

3 Click to select the red shape in the hat. Click the Fill color box in the Properties panel on the right, and making sure the Swatches option (▦) is selected in the panel that appears, click to select another color. I chose a green.

● **Note:** You will need to hide the panel to continue, and can do so by pressing the Escape key. I won't always tell you to hide these panels, so it's a good habit to get into.

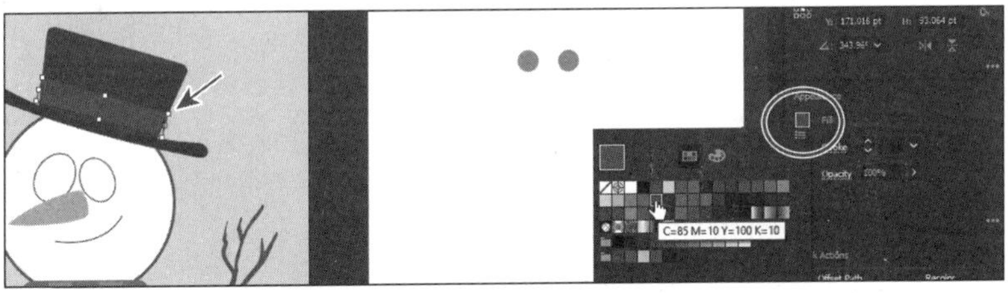

  When you enter Isolation mode, groups are temporarily ungrouped. This enables you to edit objects in the group or to add new content without having to ungroup.

4 Choose Select > Deselect.

5 Double-click outside of the shapes within the group to exit Isolation mode.

6 Click to select the same shape in the hat.

  Notice that it is once again grouped with the rest of the shapes in the hat, and you can also select other objects.

▶ **Tip:** To exit Isolation mode, you can also click the gray arrow in the upper-left corner of the Document window, press the Escape key when in Isolation mode, or double-click a blank area of the Document window.

Creating a nested group

Groups can also be *nested*—grouped within other objects or grouped to form larger groups. Nesting is a common technique used when designing artwork. It's a great way to keep associated content together. In this section, you'll explore how to create a nested group.

1 With the Selection tool (▶), drag a marquee across the hat and head of the snowman. Choose Object > Group.

You have created a *nested group*—a group that is combined with other objects or groups to form a larger group.

After grouping, you may notice that the scarf group is now behind the head shape. This is because of the stacking order of objects, which you will learn about in the next section.

2 Choose Select > Deselect.

3 With the Selection tool, click the hat to select the nested group again.

4 Double-click the hat to enter Isolation mode. Click to select the hat again, and notice that the shapes that make up the hat are still grouped. This is a nested group.

▶ **Tip:** Instead of either ungrouping a group or entering Isolation mode to select the content within, you can select with the Group Selection tool (▷⁺). Nested within the Direct Selection tool (▷) in the Tools panel, the Group Selection tool lets you select an object within a group, a single group within multiple groups, or a set of groups within the artwork.

Select the group. Enter Isolation mode. Select the nested group.

5 Press the Escape key to exit Isolation mode; then click a blank area of the artboard to deselect the objects.

Exploring object arrangement

As you create objects, Illustrator stacks them in order on the artboards, beginning with the first object created. This ordering of objects, called *stacking order*, determines how they display when they overlap. You can change the stacking order of objects in your artwork at any time, using either the Layers panel or Arrange commands.

▶ **Tip:** To learn more about objects and stacking order, see the PDF "Stack_order.pdf" in the Lessons > Lesson_extras folder.

Arranging objects

Next, you will work with the Arrange commands to change how objects are stacked.

1 Choose View > Outline to more easily select artwork.

2 With the Selection tool (▶) selected, drag a marquee across the three parts of the scarf. Drag carefully so as not to select other content.

3 Choose View > GPU Preview or View > Preview On CPU (or Preview) if GPU Preview is not available to display the painted artwork.

4 Shift-click the white half-circle to deselect it, if necessary.

5 Choose Object > Arrange > Bring To Front to bring the scarf shapes in front of the snowman's body shapes.

Selecting objects behind

When you stack objects on top of each other, sometimes it becomes difficult to select objects that are underneath. Next, you'll learn how to select an object through a stack of objects.

1 Drag either of the blue circles on the right artboard, on top of the smaller eye for the snowman. Release the mouse.

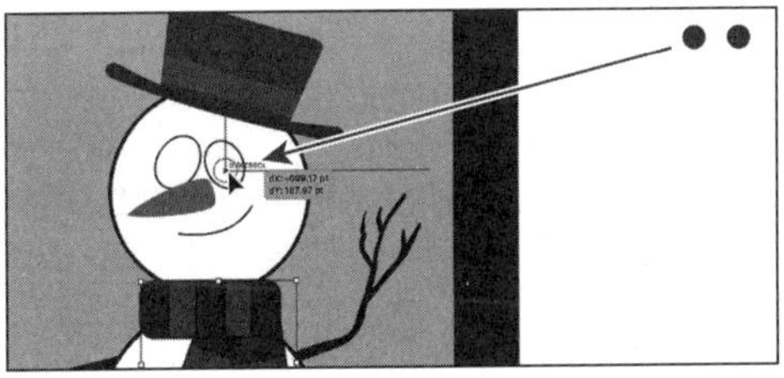

The circle disappears but is still selected. It went behind the ellipse (the eye) because it was created before the eye shape, which means it is lower in the stacking order.

2 With the circle still selected, choose Object > Arrange > Bring To Front. This brings the blue circle to the front of the stack, making it the topmost object.

3 With the Selection tool (▶), select the other blue circle on the right artboard, and drag it onto the larger eye shape on the left artboard.

This circle disappears like the other, but this time, you will deselect the circle and then reselect it using another method.

4 Choose Select > Deselect. Because it is behind the larger eye shape, you can no longer see the blue circle.

● **Note:** To select the hidden blue circle, make sure that you click where the circle and the eye overlap. Otherwise, you won't be able to select the blue circle.

● **Note:** You may see an angle bracket displayed with the pointer ( ).

5 With the pointer positioned over the location of the blue circle you just deselected, the one behind the eye shape, hold down the Command (macOS) or Ctrl (Windows) key, and click until the circle is selected again (this may take several clicks).

6 Choose Object > Arrange > Bring To Front to bring the circle on top of the eye.

7 Choose File > Save and then File > Close.

Review questions

1 How can you select an object that has no fill?

2 Explain how you can select an item in a group without choosing Object > Ungroup.

3 Of the two Selection tools (Selection [▶] and Direct Selection [▷]), which allows you to edit the individual anchor points of an object?

4 What should you do after creating a selection that you are going to use repeatedly?

5 To align objects to the artboard, what do you need to first change in the Properties panel or Align panel before you choose an alignment option?

6 Sometimes you are unable to select an object because it is underneath another object. Explain two ways to get around this issue.

Review answers

1 You can select an object that has no fill by clicking the stroke or by dragging a marquee across any part of the object.

2 You can double-click the group with the Selection tool selected, to enter Isolation mode, edit the shapes as needed, and then exit Isolation mode by pressing the Escape key or by double-clicking outside of the group. Read Lesson 9, "Organizing Your Artwork with Layers," to see how you can use layers to make complex selections. Also, using the Group Selection tool (▷+), you can click once to select an individual item within a group (not discussed in the lesson). Click again to add the next grouped items to the selection.

3 Using the Direct Selection tool (▷), you can select one or more individual anchor points and make changes to the shape of an object.

4 For any selection that you anticipate using again, choose Select > Save Selection. Name the selection so that you can reselect it at any time from the Select menu.

5 To align objects to an artboard, first select the Align To Artboard option.

6 If your access to an object is blocked, you can choose Object > Hide > Selection to hide the blocking object. The object is not deleted. It is just hidden in the same position until you choose Object > Show All. You can also use the Selection tool (▶) to select an object that's behind other objects by pressing the Command (macOS) or Ctrl (Windows) key and then clicking the overlapping objects until the object you want to select is selected.

3 USING SHAPES TO CREATE ARTWORK FOR A POSTCARD

Lesson overview

In this lesson, you'll learn how to do the following:

- Create a document with multiple artboards.
- Use tools and commands to create a variety of shapes.
- Understand Live Shapes.
- Round corners.
- Work with the Shaper tool.
- Work with drawing modes.
- Use Image Trace to create shapes.

This lesson takes approximately 60 minutes to complete. Please log in to your account on peachpit.com to download the lesson files for this chapter, or go to the "Getting Started" section at the beginning of this book and follow the instructions under "Accessing the lesson files and Web Edition."

Your Account page is also where you'll find any updates to the chapters or to the lesson files. Look on the Lesson & Update Files tab to access the most current content.

Basic shapes are at the foundation of creating Illustrator artwork. In this lesson, you'll create a new document and then create and edit a series of shapes using the shape tools for a postcard.

Starting the lesson

In this lesson, you'll explore the different methods for creating artwork using the shape tools and various creation methods to add artwork to a postcard that contains a pirate map.

● **Note:** If you have not already downloaded the project files for this lesson to your computer from your Account page, make sure to do so now. See the "Getting Started" section at the beginning of the book.

1 To ensure that the tools function and the defaults are set exactly as described in this lesson, delete or deactivate (by renaming) the Adobe Illustrator CC preferences file. See "Restoring default preferences" in the "Getting Started" section at the beginning of the book.

2 Start Adobe Illustrator CC.

3 Choose File > Open. Locate the file named L3_end.ai, which is in the Lessons > Lesson03 folder that you copied onto your hard disk, and click Open.

This file contains the finished illustrations that you'll create in this lesson.

4 Choose View > Fit All In Window; leave the file open for reference, or choose File > Close.

Creating a new document

You will now create a document for the postcard that will have two artboards, each with content that you will later combine.

▶ **Tip:** In the New Document dialog box, you will see a series of document presets you can start each project with.

1 Choose File > New to create a new, untitled document. In the New Document dialog box, change the following options:

- Select the Print profile at the top of the dialog box.
- Select the Letter document preset.

On the right, in the Preset Details area, change the following:

- Name: Change it from Untitled-1 to **Postcard**.
- Units: Change the units from Points to **Inches**.
- Width: **6 in** (You don't need to type the **in** for inches.)
- Height: **4.25 in**
- Orientation: **Landscape** ()
- Artboards: **2** (to create two artboards)

You'll learn about the Bleed option shortly. At the bottom of the Preset Details section on the right side of the New Document dialog box, you will also see Advanced Options and More Settings (you may need to scroll to see it).

They contain more settings for document creation that you can explore on your own.

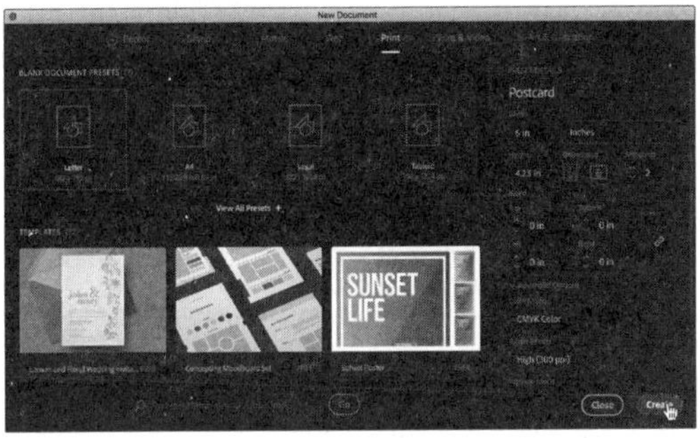

Note: You can set up a document for different kinds of output, such as print, web, video, and more, by choosing a profile. For example, if you are designing a web-page mock-up, you can select the Web profile and select a default document, which automatically displays the page size and units in pixels, changes the color mode to RGB, and changes the raster effects to Screen (72 ppi).

2 Click Create in the New Document dialog box.

3 Choose File > Save As. In the Save As dialog box, ensure that the name of the file is Postcard.ai, and save it in the Lessons > Lesson03 folder. Leave the Format menu set to Adobe Illustrator (ai) (macOS) or the Save As Type option set to Adobe Illustrator (*.AI) (Windows), and click Save.

   Adobe Illustrator (.ai) is called a *native format.* That means it preserves all Illustrator data, including multiple artboards.

4 In the Illustrator Options dialog box, leave the Illustrator options at their default settings, and click OK.

   The Illustrator Options dialog box is full of options for saving the Illustrator document, from specifying a version for saving to embedding any files that are linked to the document.

Tip: If you want to learn more about these options, search for "Save artwork" in Illustrator Help (Help > Illustrator Help).

5 Click the Document Setup button in the Properties panel (Window > Properties).

   The Document Setup dialog box is where you can change document options like units, bleeds, and more, after a document is created.

6 In the Bleed section of the Document Setup dialog box, change the value in the Top field to **0.125 in**, either by clicking the Up Arrow to the left of the field once or by typing the value, and all four fields change. Click OK.

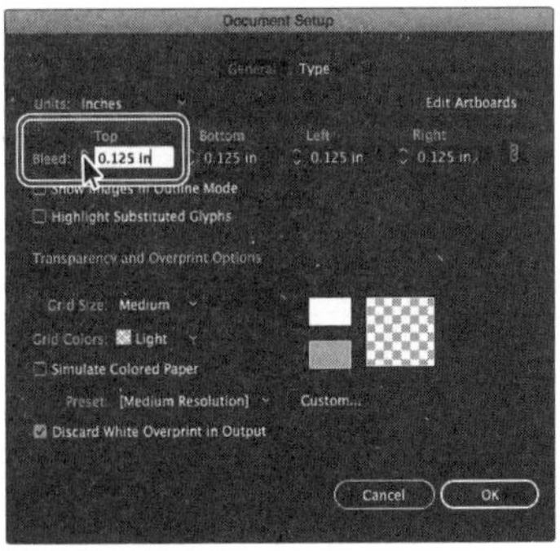

   The red line that appears around both artboards indicates the bleed area. You will typically add bleed to artboards where you want artwork to be printed all the way to the edge of the paper. Bleed is the term used for the area that extends beyond the edge of the printed page, and it ensures that no white edges show up on the final trimmed page.

Note: You could have set up the bleeds when you first set up the document in the New Document dialog box by choosing File > New.

Working with basic shapes

In the first part of this lesson, you'll create a series of basic shapes, such as rectangles, ellipses, rounded rectangles, polygons, and more. Shapes you create are composed of *anchor points* with paths connecting the anchor points. A basic square, for instance, is composed of four anchor points on the corners with paths connecting the anchor points (see the figure at right). A shape is referred to as a *closed path*.

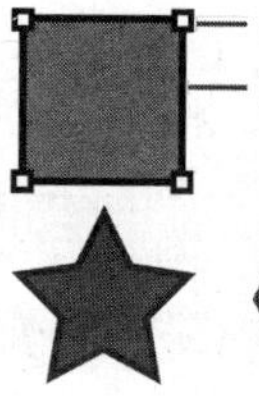

Examples of Closed Paths

A path can be closed, or it can be open with distinct anchor points on each end, called *end points* (see the figure at right). Both open and closed paths can have fills applied to them.

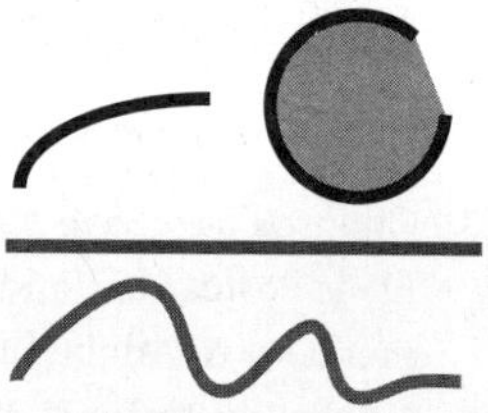
Examples of open paths

You'll begin this exercise by setting up the workspace.

1 Choose Window > Workspace > Essentials (if it's not already selected) and then choose Window > Workspace > Reset Essentials.

2 Choose 2 from the Artboard Navigation menu below the lower-left corner of the Document window.

3 Choose View > Fit Artboard In Window.

Creating and editing rectangles

You'll start this lesson by creating a few rectangles. All of the shape tools, except for the Star tool and Flare tool, create Live Shapes. *Live Shapes* have attributes such as width, height, rotation, and corner radius that are editable later, without having to switch from the drawing tool, and are retained even if you scale or rotate the shape.

1 Select the Rectangle tool (■) in the Tools panel. Move the pointer near the center of the artboard. Press the mouse button and drag down and to the right. Drag until the rectangle is approximately 0.5 inches wide and has a height of 2 inches, as shown in the gray tooltip next to the cursor.

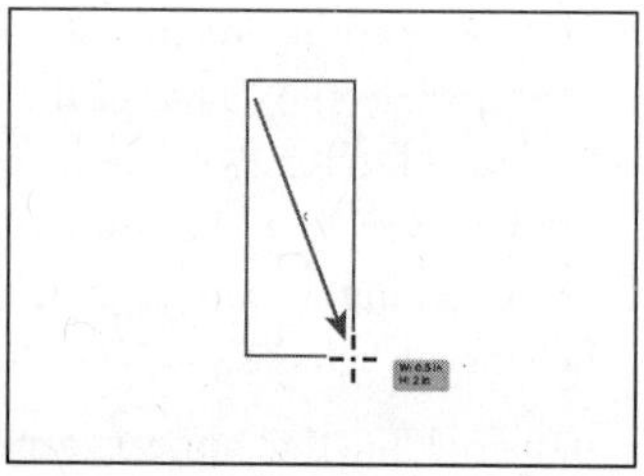

As you drag to create shapes, the tooltip that appears next to the pointer is called the *measurement label* and is part of Smart Guides (View > Smart Guides), which will be discussed throughout this lesson. By default, shapes are filled with a white color and have a black stroke (border). Using any of the shape tools, you can either draw a shape or click the artboard with a shape tool selected to enter values in a dialog box.

▶ **Tip:** Holding down Option (macOS) or Alt (Windows) as you drag with the Rectangle, Rounded Rectangle, or Ellipse tool draws a shape from its center point.

2 With the rectangle selected, move the pointer over the small blue dot in the center of the rectangle (called the *center point widget*). When the pointer changes (▸), drag the shape into the bottom half of the artboard.

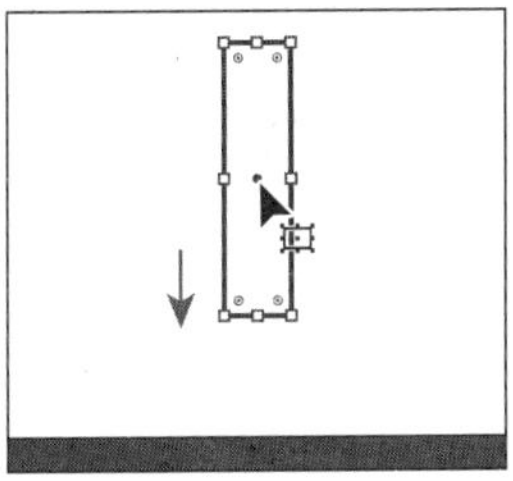

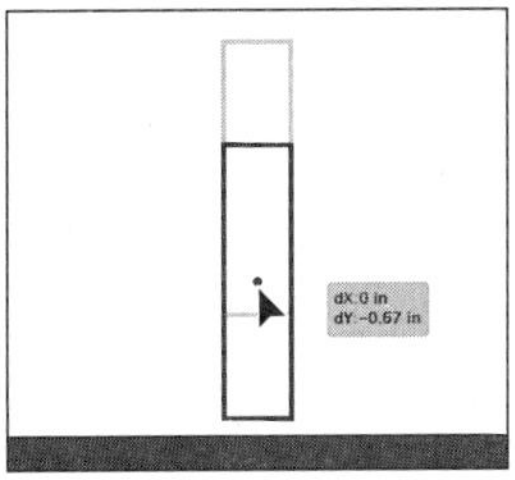

3 Begin dragging the right-middle bounding point of the rectangle to the left to make it narrower. As you drag, press the Option (macOS) or Alt (Windows) key to resize the left and right sides together. When you see a width of approximately 0.3 in the measurement label, release the mouse button and then the key.

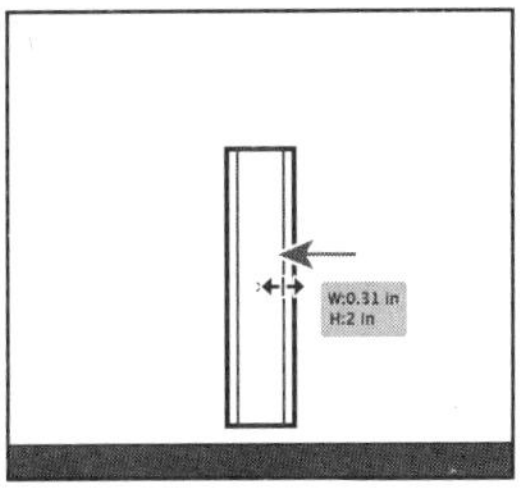

4 Move the pointer just off of a corner on the shape. When you see rotate arrows (↷), press and drag clockwise to rotate the shape. As you drag, press the Shift key to constrain the rotation to 45 degrees. When an angle of 315 shows in the measurement label, release the mouse button and then the key. Leave the shape selected.

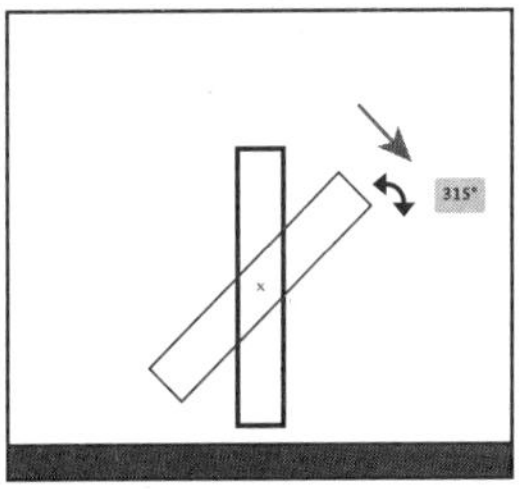

Rounding corners

Rounding the corners of a rectangle can be done using several methods. In this section, you'll learn a few ways to round the corners of rectangles you've already created.

1 With the shape still selected, choose View > Zoom In a few times.

2 Select the Selection tool (▶) in the Tools panel, and drag any of the corner widgets (⊙) in the rectangle toward the center of the rectangle to change the corner radius for all corners without worrying about how much right now.

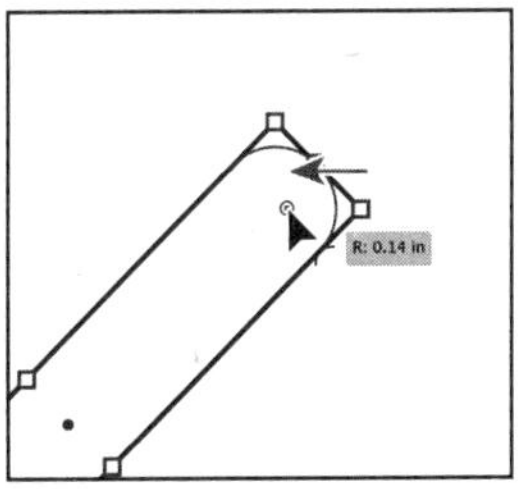

Note: If you drag a corner widget far enough, a red arc appears indicating you've reached the maximum corner radius.

Tip: You can Option-click (macOS) or Alt-click (Windows) a corner widget in a shape to cycle through the different corner types.

Note: You can press the Escape key to hide the panel before moving on.

3 In the Properties panel to the right, click More Options () in the Transform section to show a panel with more options. Ensure that Link Corner Radius Values is on (), and change any of the Radius values to **0.125**. If necessary, click in another field or press the Tab key to see the change to all corners.

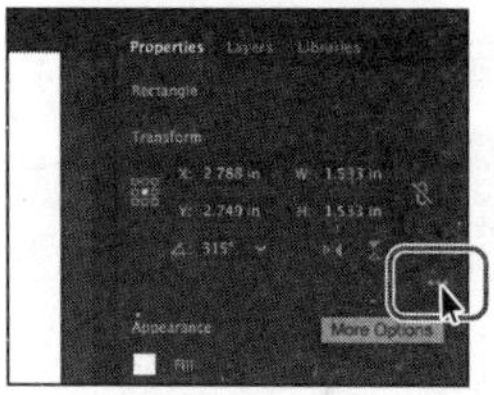

4 Select the Direct Selection tool (). With the shape still selected, double-click the top-corner widget (). In the Corners dialog box, change the radius to **0** (zero), and click OK.

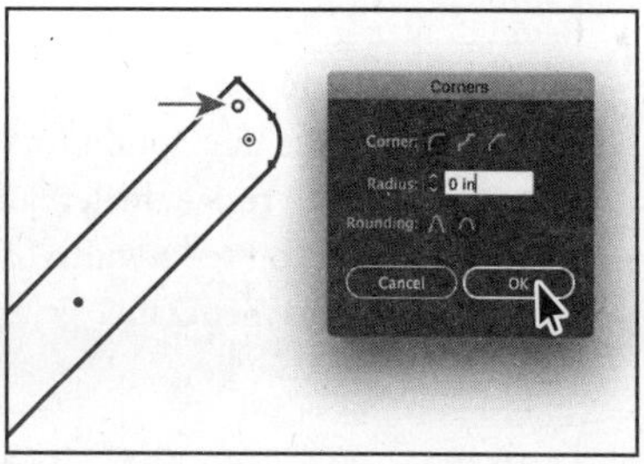

Notice that only that one corner changed. The Corners dialog box allows you to edit the corner type and radius, but it also has an extra option called Rounding for setting absolute versus relative rounding. Absolute means the rounded corner is exactly the radius value. Relative makes the radius value based on the angle of the corner point.

5 Click the bottom-corner widget () to select just that one corner widget. See the first part of the following figure.

6 Drag the bottom-corner widget () away from the center of the shape, until you see 0 in the measurement label. You will need to drag past the corner point.

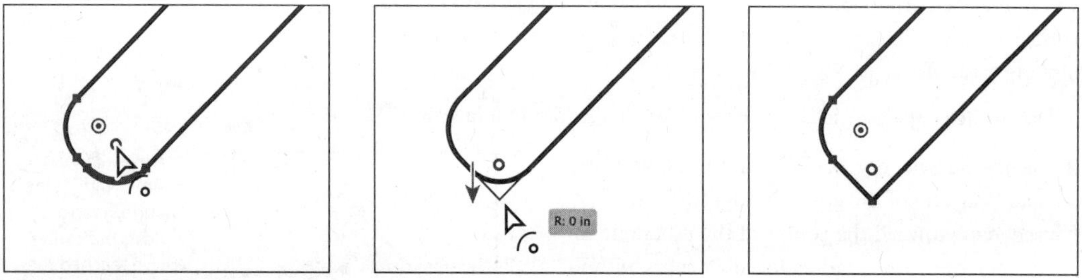

7 Select the Selection tool (▶) in the Tools panel. Click the Fill color box in the Properties panel, and make sure that the Swatches option (▦) is selected in the panel that appears. Select a darker red color to fill the rectangle with red.

8 Click the Stroke color box in the Properties panel, make sure that the Swatches option (▦) is selected, and select None to remove the stroke from the rectangle.

● **Note:** You can press the Escape key to hide the panel before moving on.

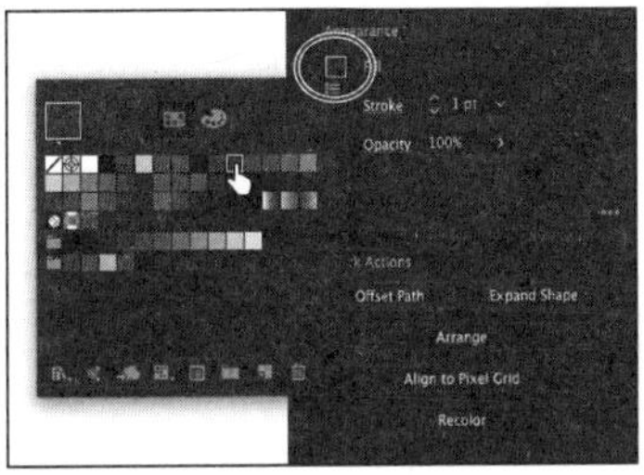

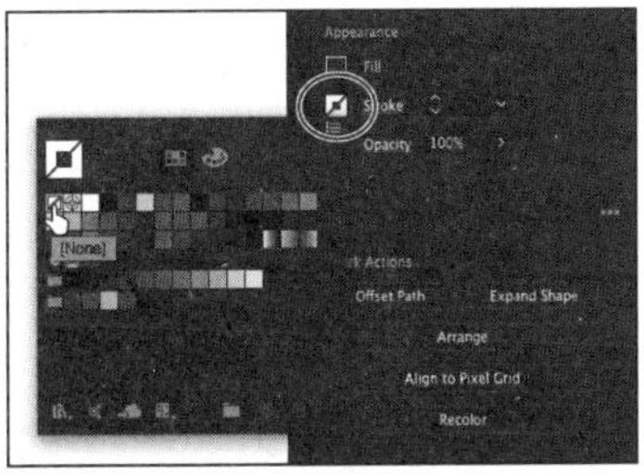

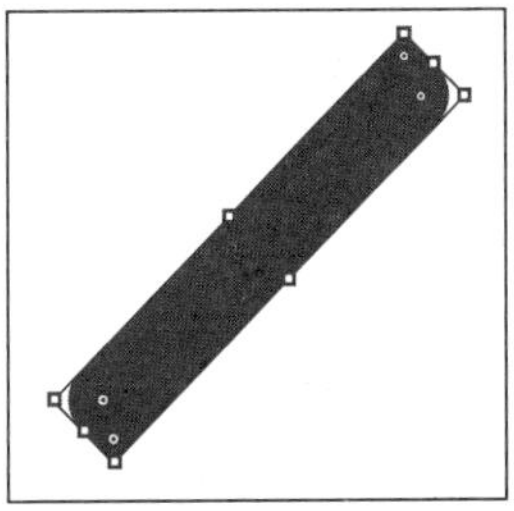

9 Choose Edit > Copy and then choose Edit > Paste In Front to paste a copy of the rectangle right on top of the original.

10 Move the pointer just off of a corner on the shape. When you see rotate arrows (↰), drag counterclockwise to rotate the shape. As you drag, press the Shift key to constrain the rotation to 45 degrees. When an angle of 45 shows in the measurement label, release the mouse button and then the key.

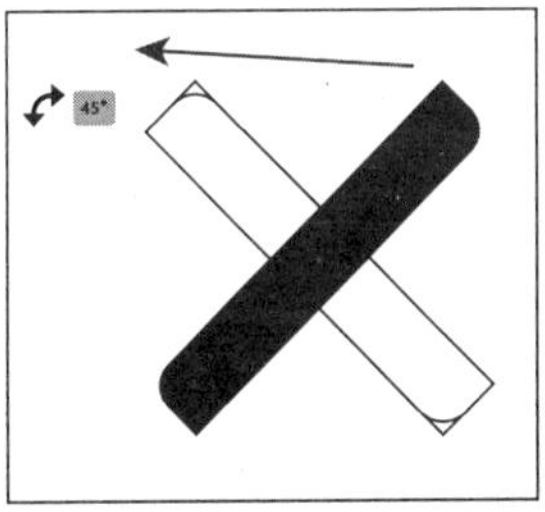

11 Click the Fill color box in the Properties panel, and make sure that the Swatches option (▦) is selected in the panel that appears. Select a lighter red color to fill the rectangle with red.

12 Choose Select > All On Active Artboard to select both shapes. Click the Group button in the Quick Actions section of the Properties panel to the right of the document.

Grouping treats content like a single object which makes it easier to move the currently selected artwork. You'll group other content you create going forward for the same reason.

13 Choose Select > Deselect.

Working with the Rounded Rectangle tool

Next, you'll create a rounded corner rectangle using the Rounded Rectangle tool. Rounded rectangles are also Live Shapes, which means you can edit properties such as the corner radius after the fact. Next, you'll create a shape for the mast of a boat.

1 Choose View > Zoom Out.

2 Click and hold down the mouse button on the Rectangle tool ( ) in the Tools panel, and select the Rounded Rectangle tool ( ).

For the next step, don't release the mouse button until told to do so.

▶ **Tip:** When drawing with the Rounded Rectangle tool, pressing the left arrow key will change the corner radius to 0 (zero), and pressing the right arrow key will set the rounded corner radius at the maximum value for the shape.

3 To the right of the rectangles on the artboard, click and drag to make a rectangle with a width of 0.2 inches and a height of 1.5 inches in the measurement label, but *do not release the mouse button yet.* With the mouse button still held down, press the Down Arrow key several times to see the corner radius become less rounded. Press the Up Arrow key several times to see the corner become more rounded. No matter how rounded the corners are, release the mouse button.

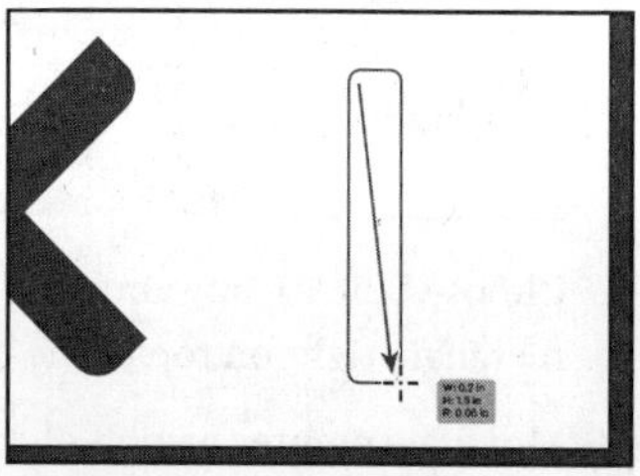

● **Note:** You'll learn a lot more about general transformations in Lesson 5, "Transforming Artwork."

4 In the Properties panel to the right, make sure Constrain Width And Height Proportions to the right of Width (W:) and Height (H:) is deselected (it looks like this:). Select the Width (W:) value and change it to **0.1**. Click in the Height (H:) field, and change the value to **1**. Press Return or Enter. Leave the shape selected.

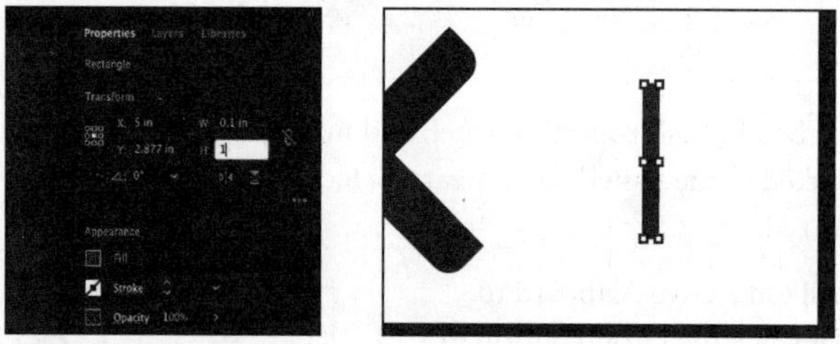

Typing **in** for inches isn't necessary; it is added automatically.

5 Select the Zoom tool ( ) in the Tools panel on the left. Drag across the top part of the selected rounded rectangle to zoom in closely.

● **Note:** Zoom in closer if you don't see the corner widgets after selecting the Selection tool.

6 Select the Selection tool ( ) and, with the rounded rectangle selected, drag any of the corner widgets ( ) toward the top of the shape until the measurement label shows a value of 0.02 in.

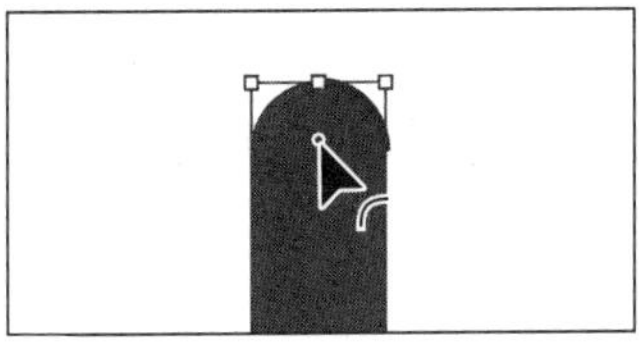

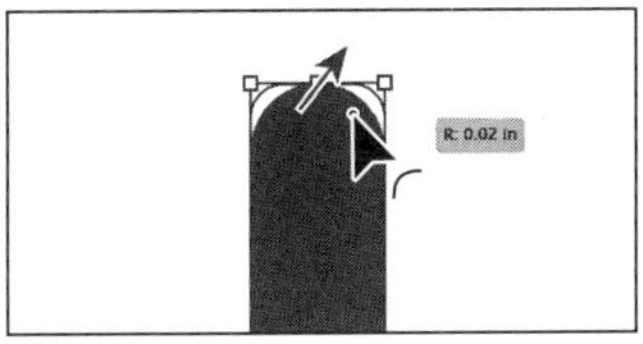

7 Double-click one of the corner widgets (◎) to open the Transform panel. The Transform panel will open, and you should now see corner options. Select Chamfer for the corner type for *the top two corners only* (circled in the following figure).

8 Choose View > Zoom Out until you see the bottom of the shape.

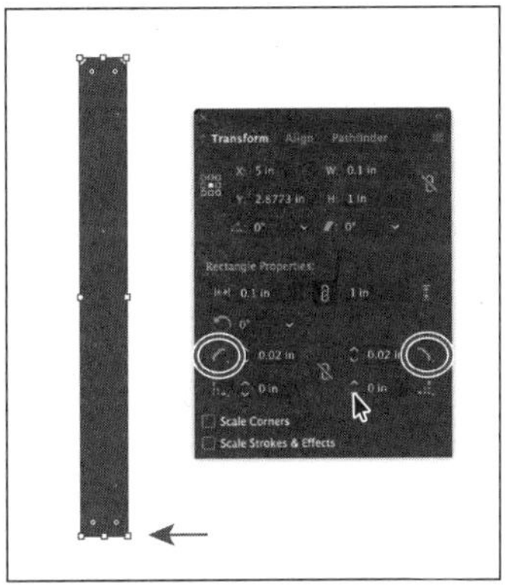

9 Deselect Link Corner Radius Values (so it looks like this [ ]) to change the corners independently. Change the bottom-left and bottom-right corners to **0**.

10 Click the X at the top of the Transform panel group to close it.

11 Click the Fill color box in the Properties panel, and make sure that the Swatches option ( ) is selected in the panel that appears. Select a brown color.

12 Choose Select > Deselect.

Working with the document grid

The document grid allows you to work more precisely by creating a series of nonprinting horizontal and vertical guides behind your artwork in the Document window that objects can snap to. To turn the grid on and use its features, do the following:

- To show the grid or hide the grid, choose View > Show Grid/Hide Grid.
- To snap objects to the gridlines, choose View > Snap To Grid, select the object you want to move, and drag it to the desired location. When the object's boundaries come within 2 pixels of a gridline, it snaps to the point.
- To specify grid properties such as the spacing between gridlines, grid style (lines or dots), grid color, or whether grids appear in the front or back of artwork, choose Illustrator CC > Preferences > Guides & Grid (macOS) or Edit > Preferences > Guides & Grid (Windows).

—From Illustrator Help

Creating and editing ellipses

Next, you'll draw and edit an ellipse with the Ellipse tool () to continue creating a boat. The Ellipse tool can be used to create ellipses and circles.

1 Choose View > Zoom Out a few times.

2 Click and hold down the mouse button on the Rounded Rectangle tool () in the Tools panel, and select the Ellipse tool ().

3 Move the pointer above the brown rectangle. Click and drag to make an ellipse that has a width of 1.5 inches and a height of 0.5 inches.

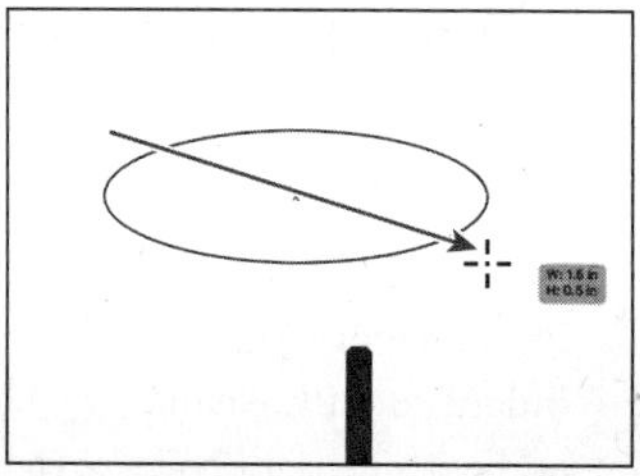

After creating an ellipse, with the Ellipse tool still selected, you can drag the shape from the center widget, transform the shape, and also change the pie angle. Next, you'll create a copy of the ellipse to use later.

4 Select the Selection tool () in the Tools panel. Choose Edit > Copy and then Edit > Paste to paste a copy of the circle you will use later in the lesson. Drag it into a blank area of the artboard, out of the way.

Note: You can also change ellipse properties like pie angle with the Ellipse tool still selected.

Tip: To reset a pie shape back to an ellipse, double-click either pie widget.

5 Click to select the original ellipse. Drag the pie widget (⊙) off the right side of the ellipse, counterclockwise around the top of the ellipse.

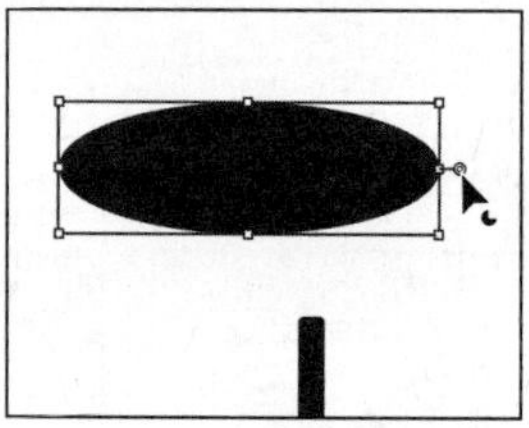

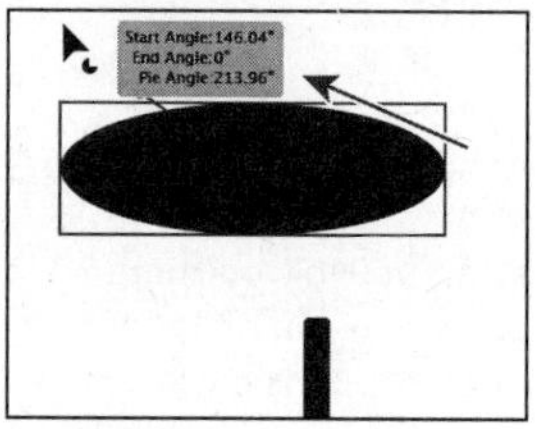

Dragging this widget allows you to create a pie shape. After dragging the widget initially and releasing the mouse button, you will then see a second widget. The widget you dragged controls the start angle. The widget that now appears on the right side of the ellipse controls the end angle.

6 In the Properties panel to the right, click More Options () in the Transform section to show more options. Choose 180° from the Pie Start Angle menu. Press Escape to hide the panel.

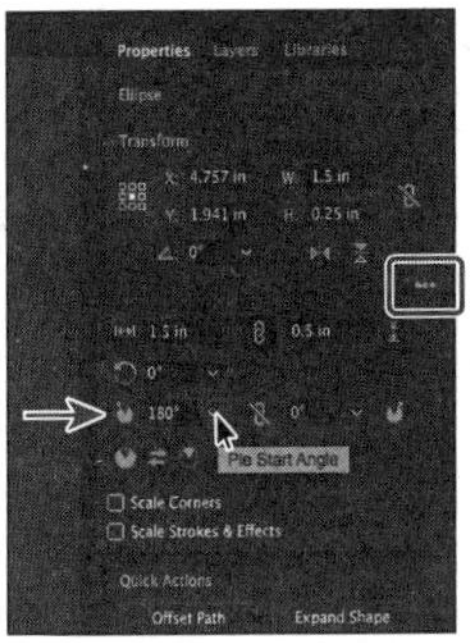

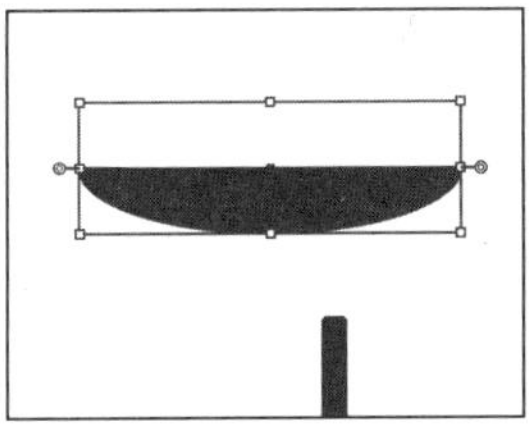

7 Move the pointer over what was the center of the ellipse, and drag the ellipse so it snaps to the bottom edge of the brown rectangle. The word "intersect" will most likely appear when it is snapped.

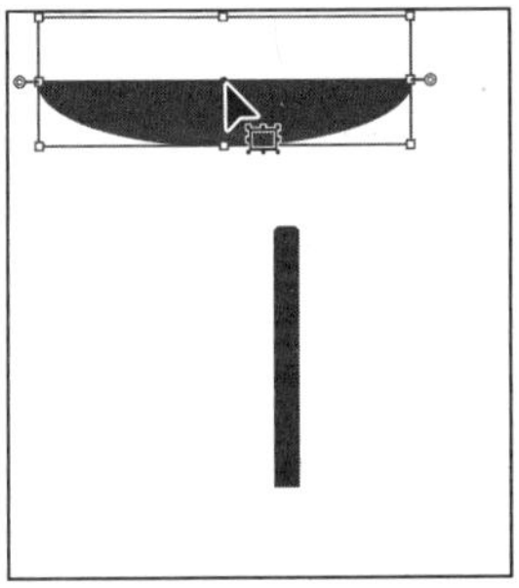
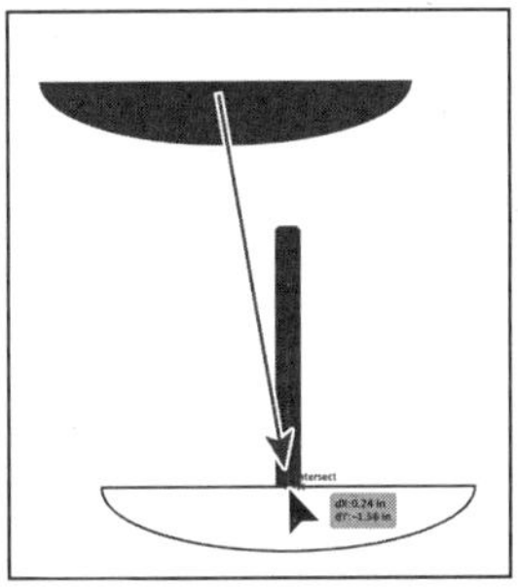

A vertical magenta guide will also show in the center of the brown rectangle to ensure that the ellipse is center-aligned horizontally with the rectangle.

8 Choose Select > Deselect and then choose File > Save.

Changing stroke width and alignment

So far in this lesson, you've mostly edited the fill of shapes but haven't done too much with the strokes (a visible outline or border of an object or path). You can easily change the color of a stroke or the weight of a stroke to make it thinner or thicker, which is what you'll do next.

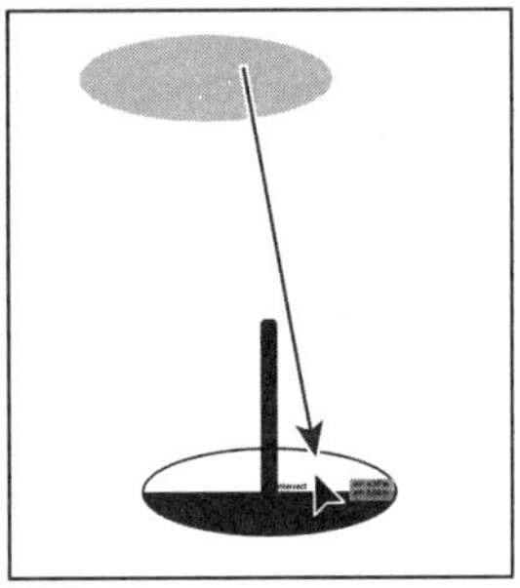

1 With the Selection tool (▶) selected, click the copy of the brown ellipse you made in the last section to select it.

2 Drag it on top of the half ellipse. Magenta smart guides will appear when it's aligned in the center of the half-ellipse.

3 Change the fill color to a darker brown and the stroke color to a lighter brown in the Properties panel.

4 Drag the top-middle point of the ellipse down. As you drag, press the Option key (macOS) or Alt key (Windows) to resize both sides as the same time. When you see a height of 0.1 inch, release the mouse button and then the key.

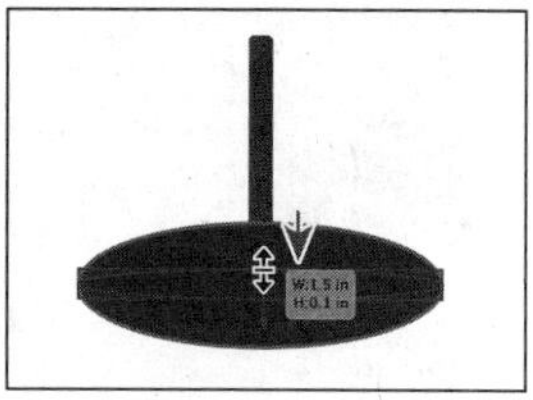

Note: You may notice in the selected artwork that you only see the corner points of the bounding box. It depends on the zoom level of your document.

Note: You can also open the Stroke panel by choosing Window > Stroke, but you may need to choose Show Options from the panel menu ( ).

5 Click the word "Stroke" in the Properties panel to open the Stroke panel. In the Stroke panel, change the stroke weight of the selected rectangle to **2**. Click the Align Stroke To Inside button ( ) to align the stroke to the inside edge of the ellipse.

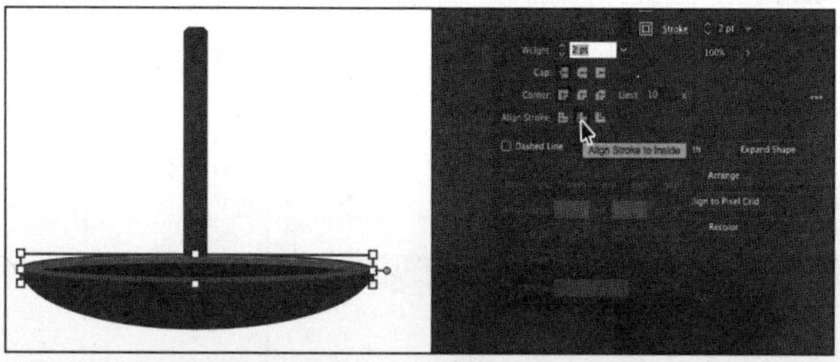

6 Click the brown rectangle and then click the Arrange button in the Properties panel and choose Bring To Front so the rectangle is on top of the ellipses.

7 Choose Select > Deselect.

Creating and editing a circle

Next, you'll draw and edit a perfect circle with the Ellipse tool ( ). Later in the lesson, you'll make a series of copies of the circle you create here for other artwork.

1 Choose View > Fit Artboard In Window to see the whole artboard.

2 Select the Ellipse tool ( ), and move the pointer over a blank area in the upper-left corner of the artboard. Begin dragging down and to the right to begin drawing an ellipse. As you drag, press the Shift key to create a perfect circle. When the width and height are both roughly 1 inch, release the mouse button and then the Shift key.

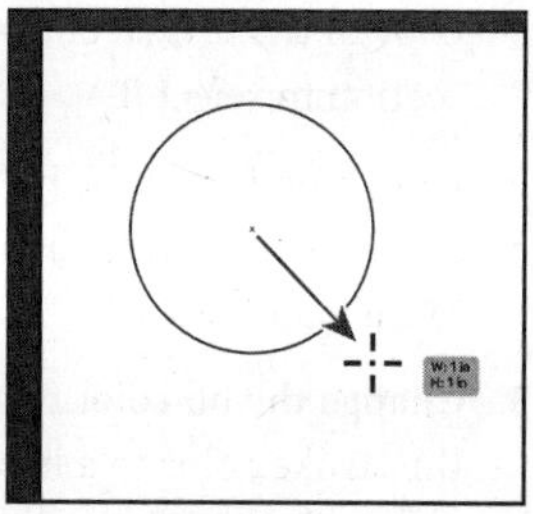

Without switching to the Selection tool, you can reposition and modify an ellipse with the Ellipse tool, which is what you'll do next.

3 With the Ellipse tool selected, position the pointer over the left-middle bounding point of the circle. Click and drag toward the center to make it smaller. As you drag, press Shift+Option (macOS) or Shift+Alt (Windows). Drag until the measurement label shows a width and height of approximately 0.3 inches. Release the mouse button and then the keys.

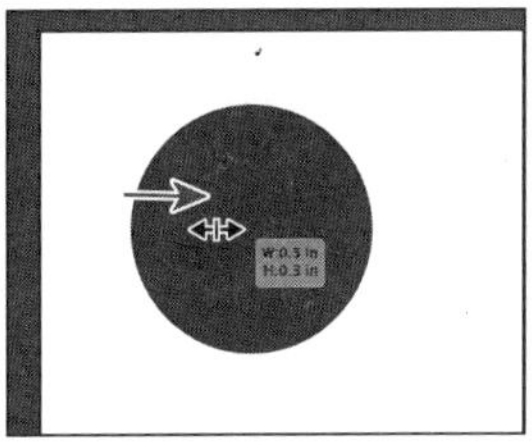

Note: An ellipse is also a Live Shape like a rectangle or rounded rectangle.

4 With the circle selected, click the Fill color in the Properties panel and make sure that the Swatches option ( ) is selected in the panel that appears. Select a light gray color with a tooltip of "C=0 M=0 Y=0 K=10."

Creating polygons

Using the Polygon tool ( ), you can create shapes with multiple straight sides. By default, the Polygon tool draws hexagons (a five-sided shape) and all shapes are drawn from the center. Polygons are also Live Shapes, which means attributes like size, rotation, number of sides, and more are still editable. Now you'll create a triangle to make a diamond gem using the Polygon tool ( ).

1 Click and hold down the mouse button on the Ellipse tool ( ) in the Tools panel, and select the Polygon tool ( ).

2 Choose View > Smart Guides to turn them off.

3 Move the pointer in a blank area of the artboard. Drag to the right to begin drawing a polygon, but *don't release the mouse button yet.* Press the Down Arrow key once to reduce the number of sides on the polygon to five, and don't release the mouse yet. Hold down the Shift key to straighten the shape. Release the mouse button and then the key. Leave the shape selected.

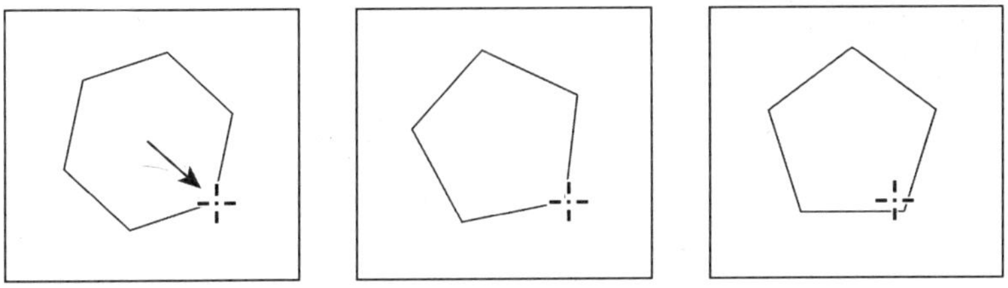

Notice that you didn't see the gray measurement label (the tooltip) since the tooltip is part of the Smart Guides that you turned off. The magenta alignment guides are also not showing since the shape is not snapping to other content on the artboard. Smart Guides can be useful in certain situations, such as when more precision is necessary, and can be toggled on and off when needed.

4 Click the Fill color box in the Properties panel, and make sure that the Swatches option ( ) is selected in the panel that appears. Select a light gray color with a tooltip of "C=0 M=0 Y=0 K=30."

5 Choose View > Smart Guides to turn them back on.

6 With the Polygon tool still selected, drag the side widget on the right side of the bounding box to change the number of sides to three, making a triangle.

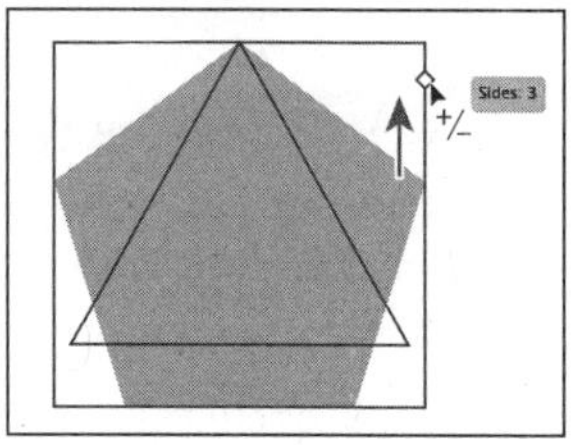

● **Note:** The figure may look different from what you see. Your starting shape may have been bigger or smaller, and that's okay. As long as the resulting size is 1.2 inches in width and 0.8 inches in height.

7 Drag a corner bounding point of the triangle until you see a width of 1.2 inches and a height of 0.8 inches in the measurement label.

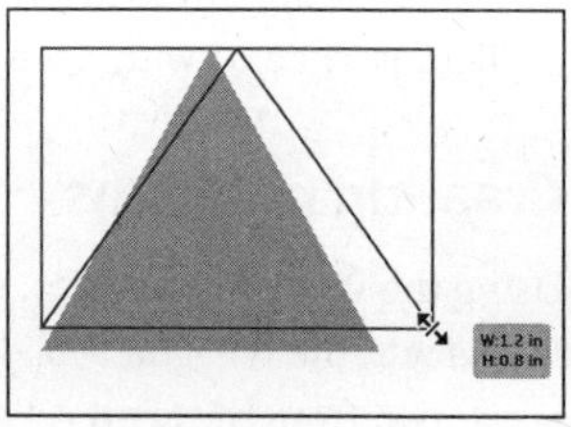

Editing the polygons

Now, you'll make a copy of the polygon and create the rest of the diamond gem.

1 With the triangle still selected, choose Object > Transform > Reflect. In the Reflect dialog box, select Horizontal, and click Copy.

2 Drag the new (top) triangle from the center widget (the blue circle in the center) so its top edge snaps to the bottom edge of the original triangle.

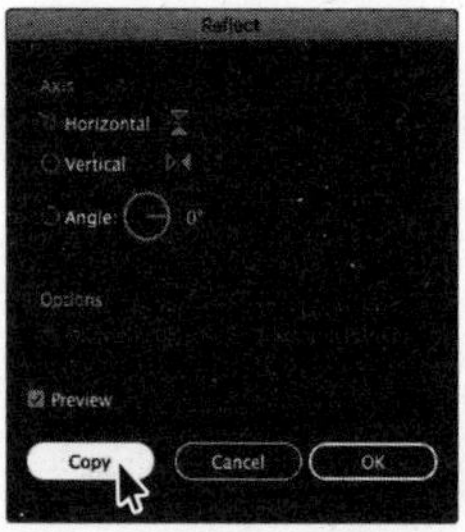

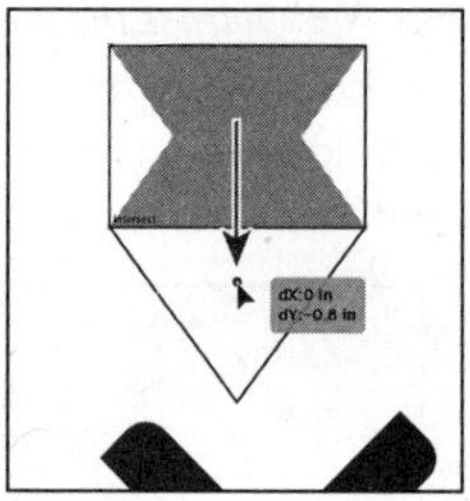

3 Select the Selection tool ( ) in the Tools panel. Click the original (top) triangle.

4 Select the Eraser tool ( ) in the Tools panel. Pressing the Shift key, drag from left to right, across the middle of the triangle. Release the mouse button and then the key.

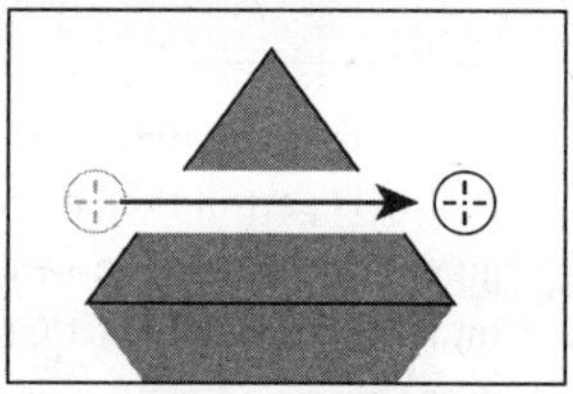

5 Select the Selection tool () and click in a blank area to deselect the artwork. Click the smaller triangle on top and press Backspace or Delete to remove it.

6 Click to select the remaining part of the top triangle, and click the Fill color box in the Properties panel. Make sure that the Swatches option () is selected in the panel that appears, and select a lighter gray color with a tooltip of "C=0 M=0 Y=0 K=5."

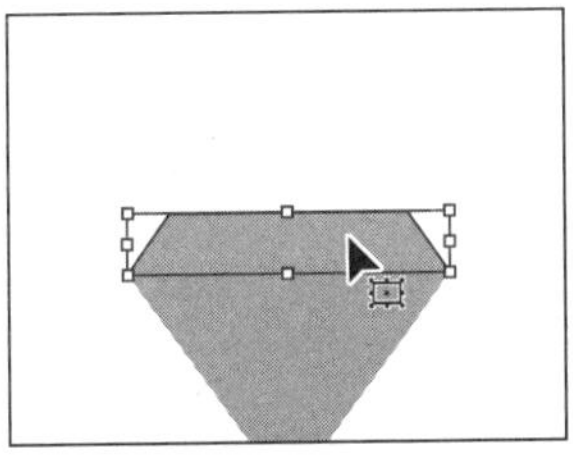

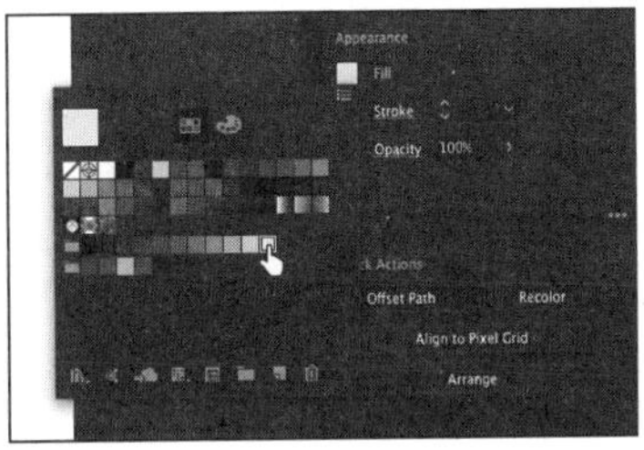

Next, you'll make a copy of the original triangle and make a mountain shape with a rounded corner top.

7 Click the darker gray triangle to select it. Option-drag (macOS) or Alt-drag (Windows) the triangle into the lower-left corner of the artboard to make a copy. Release the mouse button and then the key.

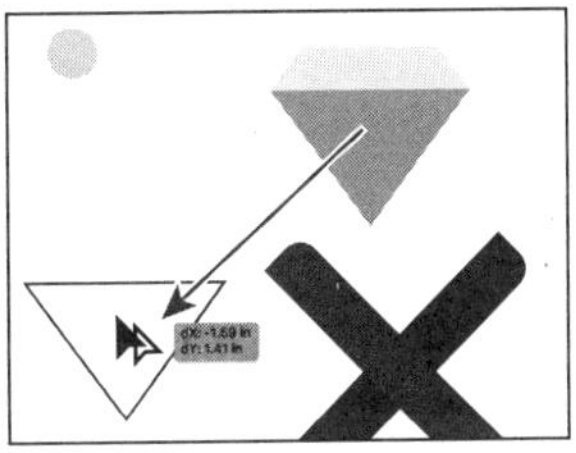

8 Click More Options () in the Transform section of the Properties panel to the right to show more options. To return the triangle to an equal-sided polygon, click the Make Sides Equal button.

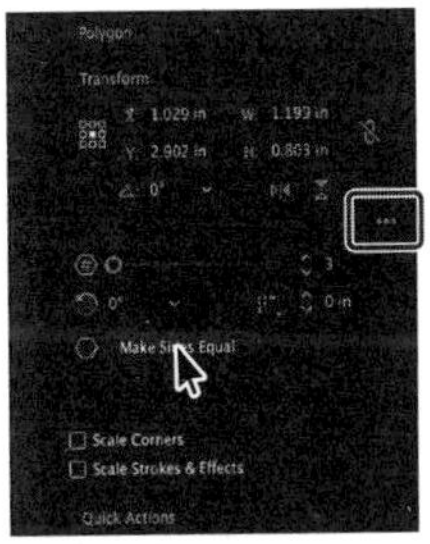

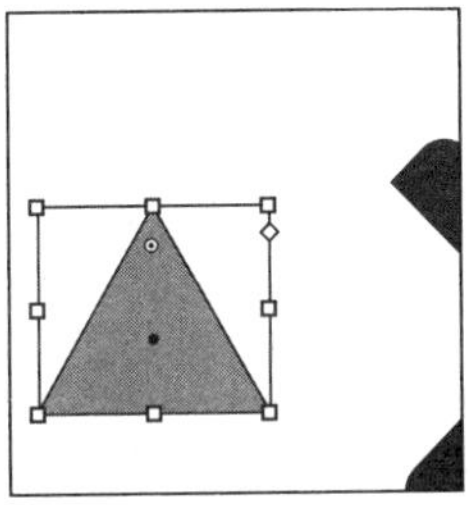

9 Select the Direct Selection tool () in the Tools panel. Click the top-corner widget () of the selected triangle to select it.

10 Drag the top-corner widget toward the center of the shape to round the top corner a little.

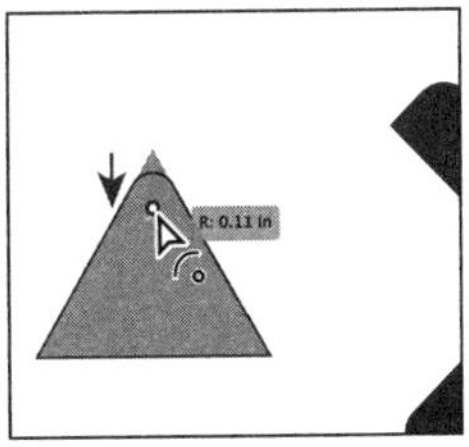

Creating a star

Next, you'll use the Star tool (☆) to create a few stars that will go on the diamond you just created. The Star tool currently doesn't create Live Shapes, which means editing the star after the fact can be more difficult. When drawing with the Star tool, you'll use keyboard modifiers to get the number of points you want and to change the radius of the arms of the star (the length of the arms). Here are the keyboard modifiers you'll use in this section when drawing the star and what each does:

- **Arrow keys:** Pressing the Up Arrow or Down Arrow keys adds or removes arms from the star, respectively, as you draw it.
- **Shift:** This straightens the star (constrains it).
- **Command (macOS) or Ctrl (Windows):** Pressing the key and dragging while creating a star allows you to change the radius of the arms of the star (make the arms longer or shorter).

Next, you'll create a star. This will take a few keyboard commands, so *don't release the mouse button* until you are told.

1 Click and hold down the mouse button on the Polygon tool (⬢) in the Tools panel, and select the Star tool (☆). Move the pointer somewhere on the artboard to the right of the triangle shapes that make up the diamond.

▶ **Tip:** You can also click in the Document window with the Star tool (☆) and edit the options in the Star dialog box instead of drawing it.

2 Click and drag slowly to the right to create a star shape. Notice that as you move the pointer, the star changes size and rotates freely. Drag until the measurement label shows a width of about 1 inch and then stop dragging. *Don't release the mouse button!*

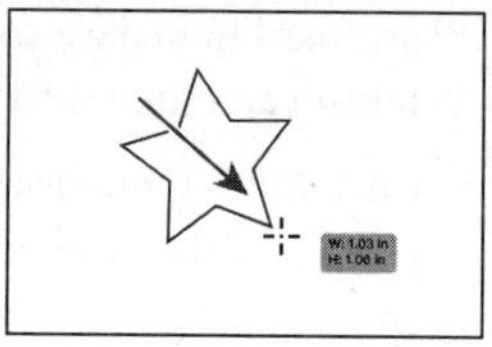

3 Press the Up Arrow key once to increase the number of points on the star to six. *Don't release the mouse button!*

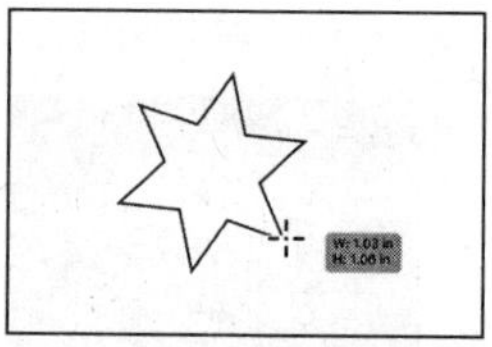

4 Press Command (macOS) or Ctrl (Windows), and continue dragging to the right a little. This keeps the inner radius constant, making the arms longer. Drag until you see a width of approximately 1.5 inches, and stop dragging, without releasing the mouse button. Release Command or Ctrl but *not the mouse button.*

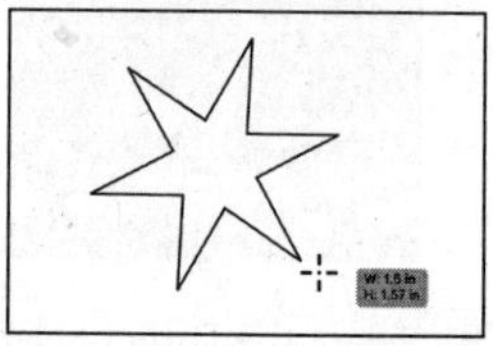

▶ **Tip:** If the stroke color is None (☒), then you don't need to set the stroke weight.

5 Hold down the Shift key. When the star straightens out, release the mouse button and then the Shift key.

6 Change the stroke weight of the star to **0** in the Properties panel.

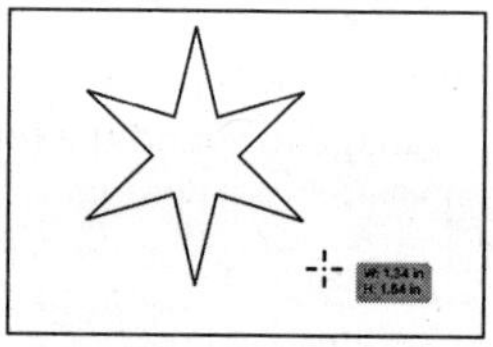

7 Change the fill color in the Properties panel to white.

8 Select the Selection tool (▶), press the Shift key, and drag a corner of star bounding box toward the center. When the star has a width of approximately 0.4 inches, release the mouse button and then the key.

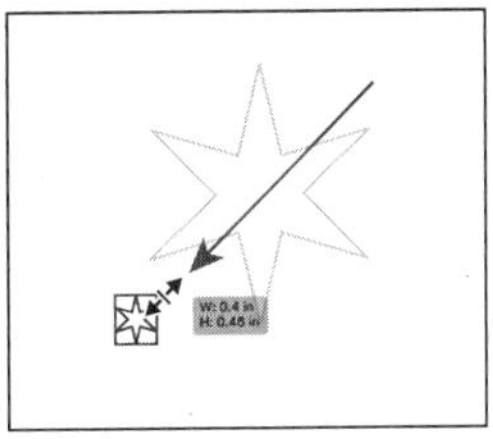

9 Select the Star tool (☆), and draw one more star, a little smaller than the first.

Notice that the new stars have the same basic settings as the first star you drew.

10 Select the Selection tool (▶), and drag the stars on top of the shapes that make up the diamond.

They may be difficult to see since they have a white fill and are on a white artboard. In this case, you could choose View > Outline to more easily see them. Then, after you are finished dragging the shapes by their edges, choose View > GPU Preview (or Preview On CPU if GPU Preview is not supported).

11 Drag across the triangle and star shapes to select them all, and then click the Group button in the Properties panel to group them together.

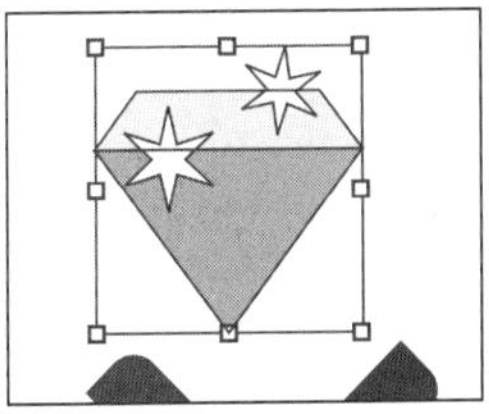

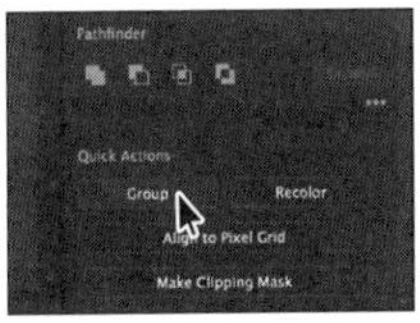

Drawing lines

Next, you'll create lines and line segments, known as *open paths*, with the Line Segment tool to create a few bones. Lines created with the Line Segment tool are Live Lines, and similar to Live Shapes, they have many editable attributes.

1 Select the Line Segment tool (/) in the Tools panel. On the right side of the artboard, above the existing artwork, click and drag to the right. Notice the length and angle in the measurement label next to the pointer as you drag. Drag until the line is around 1.5 inches in length.

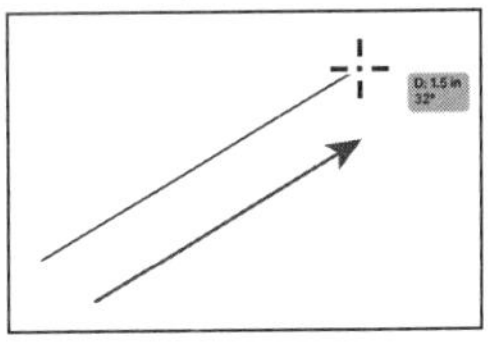

2 With the new line selected, position the pointer just off the right end. When the pointer changes to a rotate arrow (⤸), click and drag (up or down) until you see an angle of 0 (zero) in the measurement label next to the pointer. That will make the line horizontal.

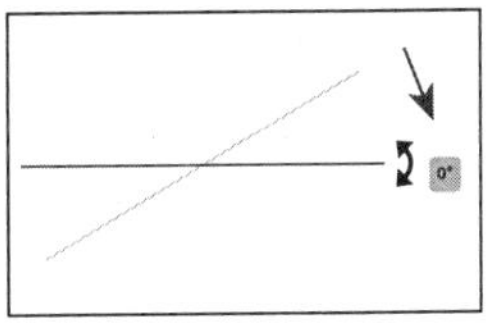

Note: If you drag a line in the same trajectory as the original path, you will see the words "Line Extension" and "on" appear at opposite ends of the line. These are part of Smart Guides and make it easy to drag a line longer or shorter without changing the angle.

Lines rotate around their center point by default. The angle of the line can also be changed in the Properties panel.

3 With the line selected, change the stroke weight to **15 pt** in the Properties panel to the right of the document.

4 Click the Stroke color box in the Properties panel, and make sure that the Swatches option (■) is selected in the panel that appears. Select a lighter gray color with a tooltip of "C=0 M=0 Y=0 K=10."

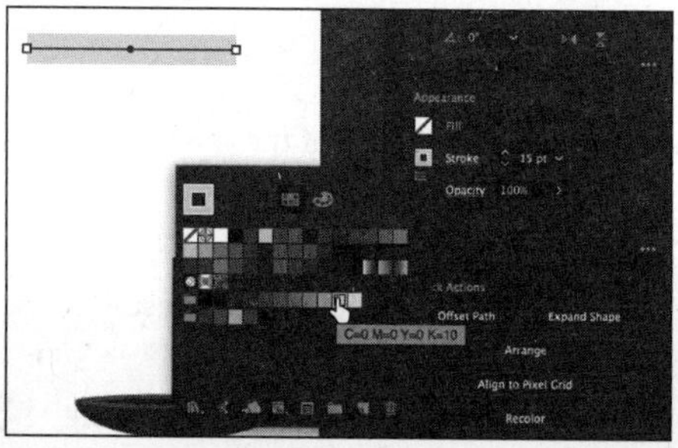

5 Choose Object > Path > Outline Stroke. The line is now a shape with a fill.

6 Select the Selection tool (▶) in the Tools panel, and drag the gray circle in the upper-left corner of the artboard over to the shape.

7 Choose Edit > Copy. Choose Edit > Paste three times to create a total of four circles. Drag the circles onto the shape like you see in the figure to make a bone.

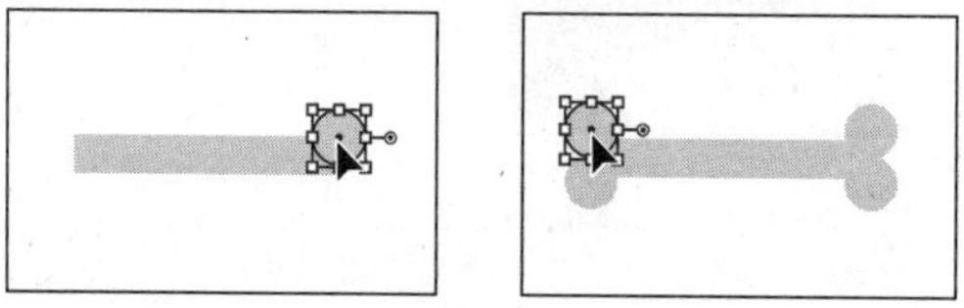

8 Drag across the bone artwork and click the Group button in the Properties panel to keep the artwork together.

9 Move the pointer just off a corner. When the pointer changes to rotate arrows (↰), drag counterclockwise to rotate it until you see approximately 45 degrees in the measurement label.

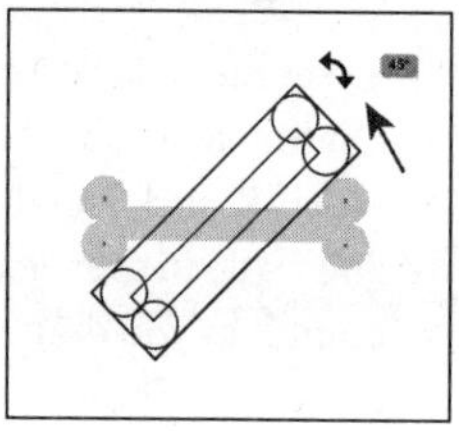

10 Choose Object > Transform > Reflect. In the Reflect dialog box, select Vertical, and click Copy.

11 Drag across the artwork for the bones and click the Group button in the Properties panel to keep the artwork together.

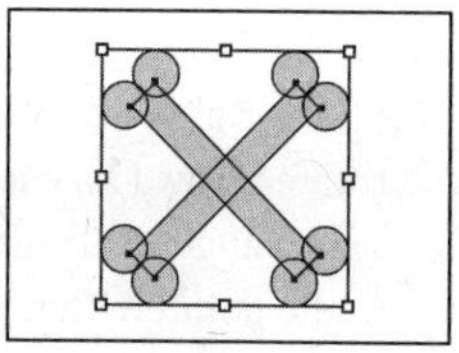

Working with the Shaper tool

Another way to draw and edit shapes in Illustrator involves the Shaper tool ( ). The Shaper tool recognizes natural gestures and produces Live Shapes from those gestures. Without switching tools, you can combine, delete, fill, and transform basic shapes you create. In this section, you'll get a feeling for how the tool works by exploring the most widely used features.

Note: The Shaper tool is present in the Tools panel of the classical workspace. In the Touch Workspace, it is a top-level tool in the toolbar. This tool works best with a stylus on touch surfaces, such as Surface Pro or Wacom Cintiq, or through indirect inputs such as the Wacom Intuos.

Drawing shapes with the Shaper tool

To get started with the Shaper tool, you'll draw a few simple shapes that will eventually become the sail for the boat you made.

1 Choose View > Fit Artboard In Window.

2 Select the Shaper tool ( ) in the Tools panel on the left. Draw a rough representation of a rectangle in a blank area of the artboard, like you would with a pencil on paper. Use the figure as a guide.

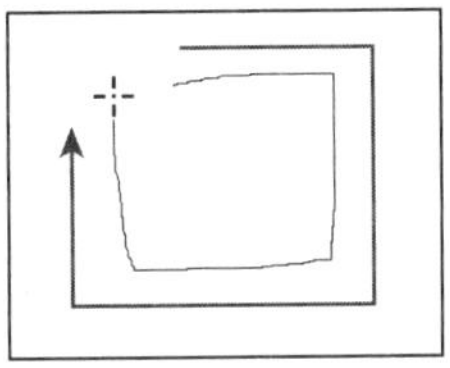

When you finish drawing the shape, the gesture will be converted to a Live Shape with a default gray fill. There are a variety of shapes that can be drawn with the Shaper tool, including (but not limited to) rectangles, squares, ellipses (circles), triangles, hexagons, lines, and more.

3 Draw a scribble over the shape you just drew to delete it.

Note: If you try to draw a scribble, a line may be created instead. Simply scribble across all the shapes to remove them.

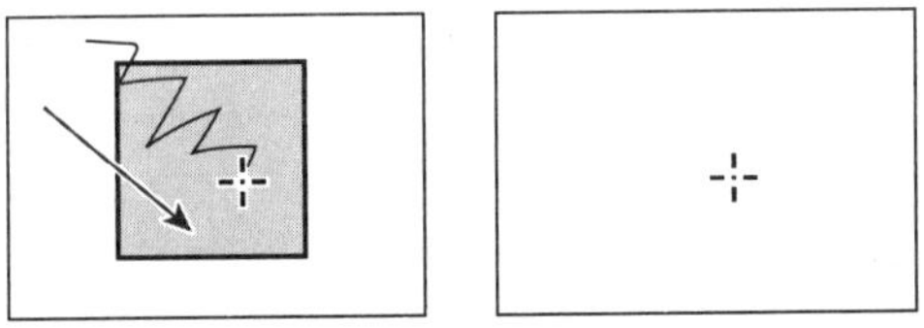

This simple gesture is an easy way to delete shapes. Note that you can scribble across more than one object to remove them, and you simply need to scribble over part of the artwork, not the whole thing to delete it. You can also click within a shape you created to select it and then press Backspace or Delete to remove it.

4 Draw an ellipse in a blank area of the artboard.

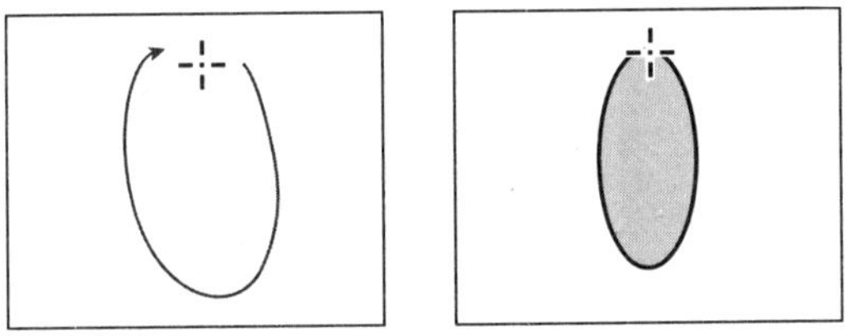

If the shape is not an ellipse, delete it by scribbling across it, and try again.

Once shapes are created, you can also use the Shaper tool to edit those shapes without having to switch tools. Next, you'll edit the ellipse you just created.

5 Click in the ellipse with the Shaper tool to select it.

6 Choose View > Zoom In.

7 Drag a corner of the ellipse to turn it into a circle. When magenta hinting crosshairs (Smart Guides) show in the center, it means the ellipse has become a circle (an ellipse with equal width and height).

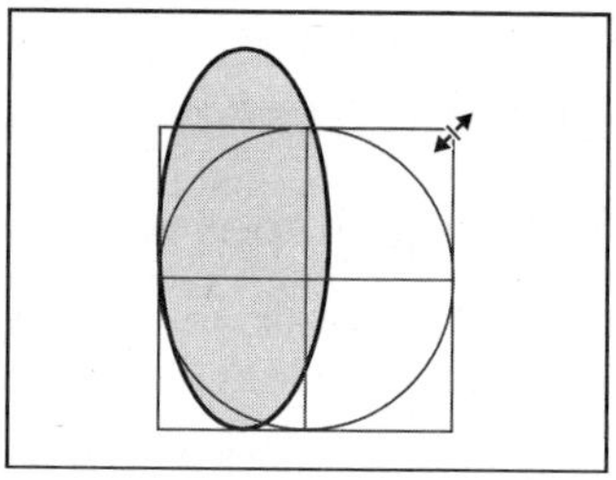

Shapes drawn with the Shaper tool are live and dynamically adjustable, so you can draw and edit intuitively without the extra hassle of switching between tools. Notice that no measurement label appears to indicate the shape size. When transforming shapes with the Shaper tool, measurement labels won't appear, even if Smart Guides are on.

Punching and combining shapes with the Shaper tool

Not only does the Shaper tool let you draw shapes, but you can then combine, subtract, and continuously edit them, all with a single tool. Next, you'll draw a few more shapes and use the Shaper tool to add and subtract them from the original circle, creating a sail for the boat.

Note: Don't worry if the new circle is on or off the edge of the artboard. You'll reposition it all shortly.

1 With the Shaper tool selected, press Shift+Option (macOS) or Shift+Alt (Windows), and drag the circle straight to the left to make a copy. A horizontal magenta alignment guide will show. *Make sure the circles are not touching*, and then release the mouse button and then the keys.

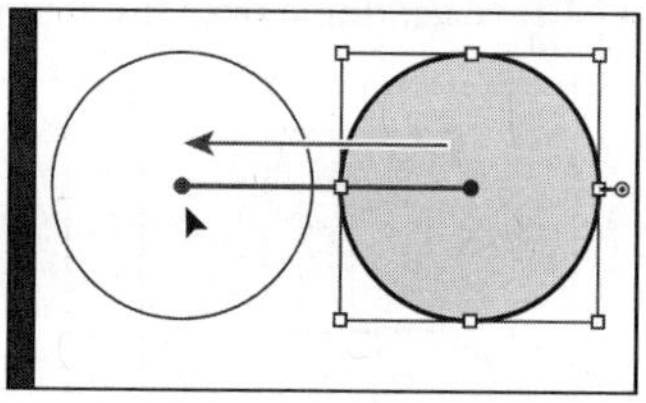

2 Click and hold down the mouse button on the Star tool, and select the Rectangle tool in the Tools panel. Move the pointer over the center top of the circle on the left. When the word "anchor" appears, drag to create a rectangle. Drag to the bottom-center point of the circle on the right.

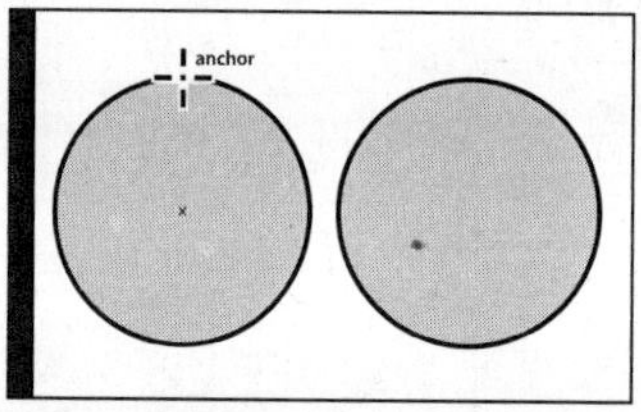

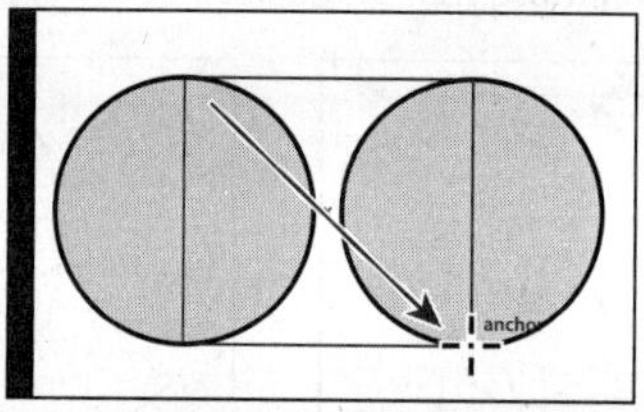

3 Select the Shaper tool ( ) in the Tools panel. Click in a blank area of the artboard to deselect all shapes.

4 Move the pointer to the left of the shapes. Scribble across the circle shape, stopping *just after* the left edge of the rectangle. When you release, the circle on the left will be deleted, and the overlapping area of the shapes will be removed.

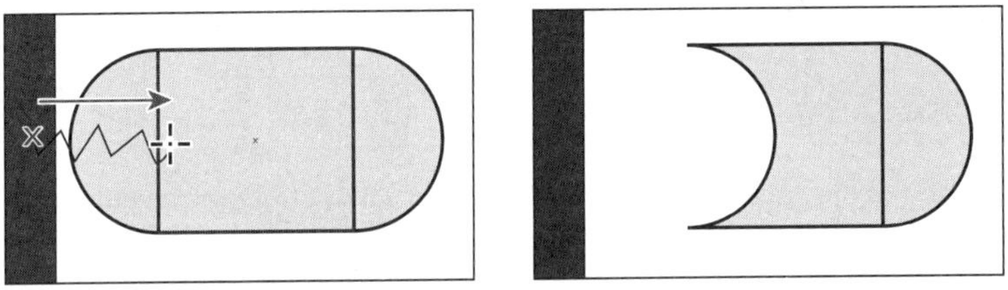

5 Move the pointer *into* the circle on the right, and draw a scribble to the left, into the gray area of the remaining rectangle shape to combine them.

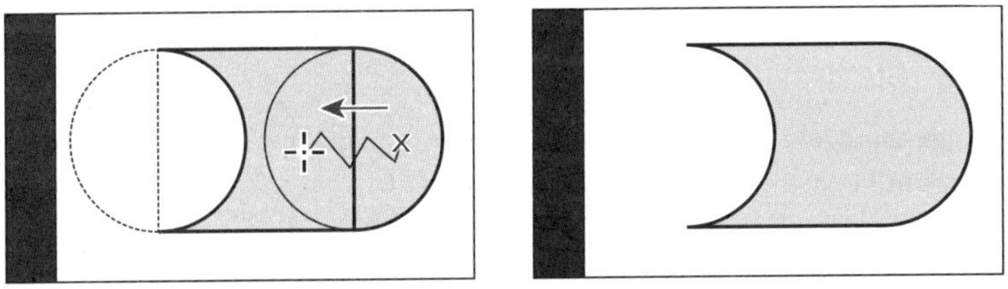

6 Move the pointer over the gray shape to see the outlines of the original shapes, and then click to select the merged group, called a *Shaper Group*. See the first part of the following figure.

7 Click the arrow widget ( ) on the right side of the Shaper Group to be able to select the underlying shapes. After clicking the arrow widget, the Shaper Group is in Construction Mode.

Tip: You can also double-click a Shaper Group to be able to select the underlying shapes.

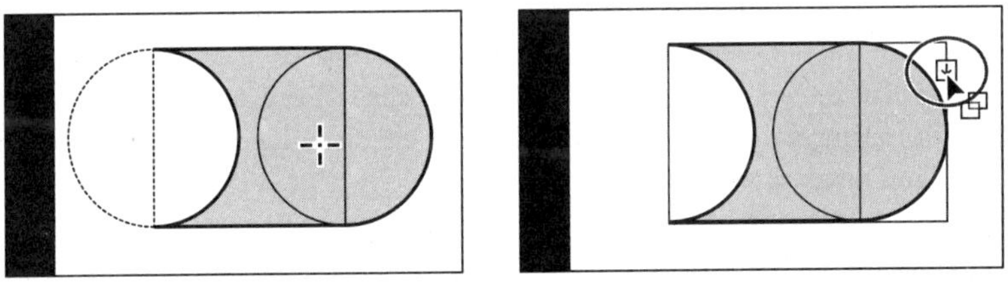

All shapes in a Shaper Group remain editable, even after portions of shapes may have been punched out or merged.

Note: If you attempted to select the shape and you deselected instead, repeat the previous steps. The circle on the left now has no fill, so it cannot be selected by clicking within.

8 Click the *stroke* of the left circle to select it. Press the Option (macOS) or Alt (Windows) key and drag the right-middle bounding point to the left to make the circle a little narrower. Release the mouse button and then the key.

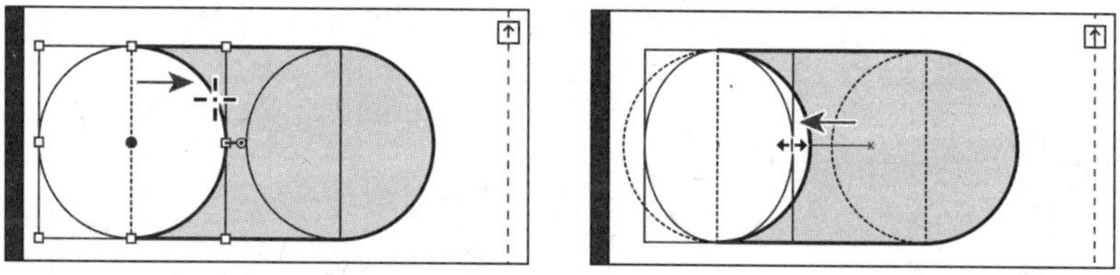

Notice that the circle you dragged is still punched out from the rectangle. Not only can you resize individual shapes in a Shaper Group, but you can also reposition them, rotate them, and more.

9 Press Esc to stop editing the individual shapes, and select the entire Shaper Group.

10 Click the Fill color box in the Properties panel, and make sure that the Swatches option (▦) is selected in the panel that appears. Select a light gray color with a tooltip of "C=0 M=0 Y=0 K=5."

11 Change the stroke weight to **0** in the Properties panel by clicking the down arrow until the stroke is removed.

Note: You can Shift-drag a corner of the sail shape to resize it to fit better with the boat shapes, if needed.

12 Drag the sail shape onto the boat in the lower-right corner. You may need to zoom out.

13 Choose Select > Deselect and then choose File > Save.

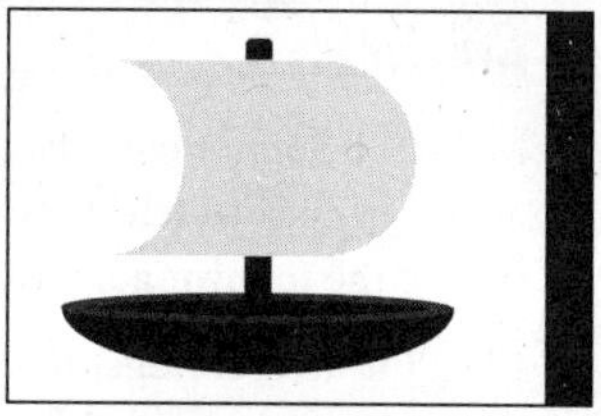

Using Image Trace

Tip: Use Adobe Capture CC on your device to photograph any object, design, or shape and convert it into vector shapes in a few simple steps. Store the resulting vectors in your Creative Cloud libraries, and access them or refine them in Illustrator or Photoshop. Adobe Capture is currently available for iOS (iPhone and iPad) and Android.

In this part of the lesson, you'll learn how to work with the Image Trace command. Image Trace traces existing artwork, like a raster picture from Adobe Photoshop. You can then convert the drawing to vector paths or a Live Paint object. This can be useful for turning a drawing into vector art, tracing raster logos, tracing a pattern or texture, and much more.

1 Click the Previous button (◀) below the document in the status bar to show the artboard to the left in the Document window.

2 Choose File > Place. In the Place dialog box, select the island.png file in the Lessons > Lesson03 folder on your hard disk, leave the options at their defaults, and click Place.

3 Move the pointer over the upper-left corner bleed guide (the red guide off the edge of the artboard), and click to place the image.

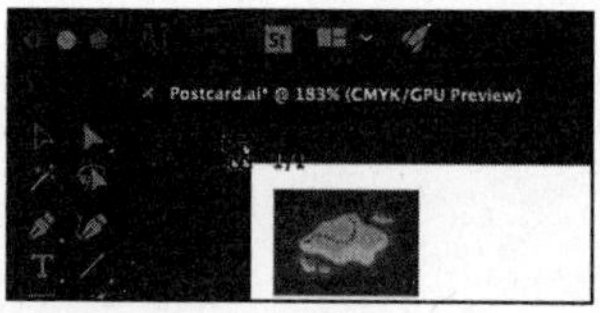

4 With the image selected, click the Image Trace button in the Properties panel to the right of the document, and choose Low Fidelity Photo. The tracing results you see may differ slightly from the figure, and that's okay.

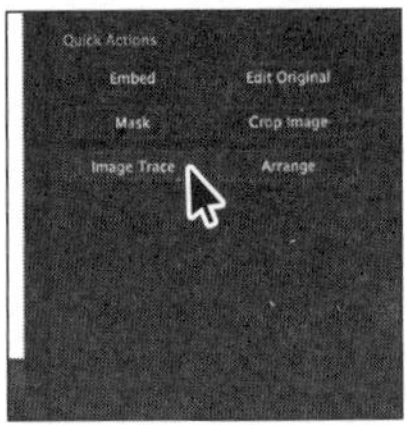

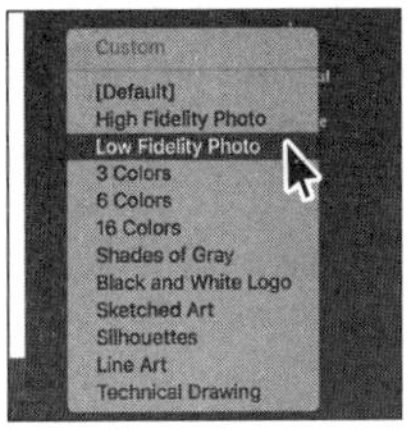

This converts the image into an image tracing object. That means you can't edit the vector content yet, but you can change the tracing settings or even the original placed image and then see the updates.

5 Choose 6 Colors from the Preset menu that's showing in the Properties panel.

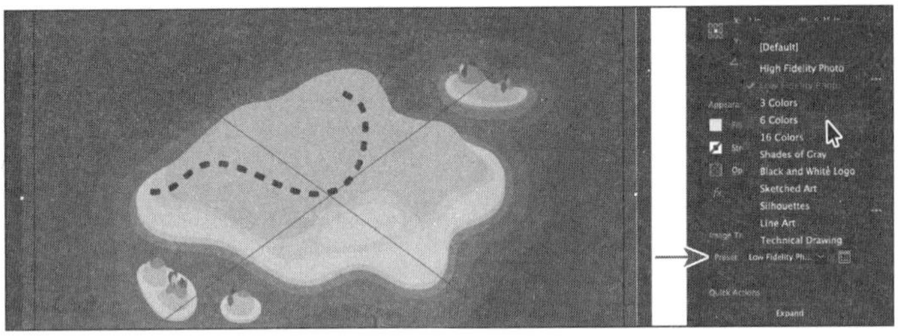

The 6 Colors preset will trace the image, forcing the resulting vector content to use six colors only. In some cases, in an image with a lot of different color, this can apply the same color to a lot of content. An image tracing object is made up of the original source image and the tracing result (which is the vector artwork). By default, only the tracing result is visible. However, you can change the display of both the original image and the tracing result to best suit your needs.

6 Click the Image Trace Panel button (▣) in the Properties panel. In the Image Trace panel, click the Auto-Color button (▣) at the top.

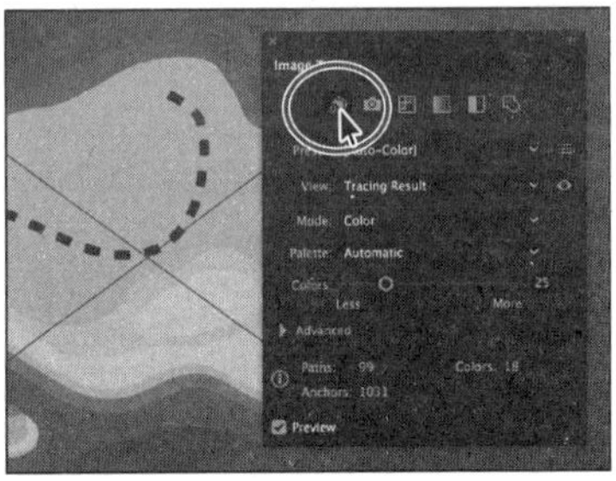

The buttons along the top of the Image Trace panel are saved settings for converting the image to grayscale, black and white, and more. Below the buttons at the top of the Image Trace panel, you will see the Preset option. This is the same option as in the Properties panel. The Mode option allows you to change the color mode of resulting artwork (color, grayscale, or black and white). The Palette option is also useful for limiting the color palette or for assigning colors from a color group.

Note: You can also choose Object > Image Trace > Make, with raster content selected, or begin tracing from the Image Trace panel (Window > Image Trace).

Tip: The Image Trace panel can also be opened by choosing Window > Image Trace.

7 In the Image Trace panel, click the triangle to the left of the Advanced options to reveal them. Change the following options in the Image Trace panel, using the values as a starting point:

- Colors: **20**
- Paths: **50%**
- Corners: **25%**
- Noise: **8 px**

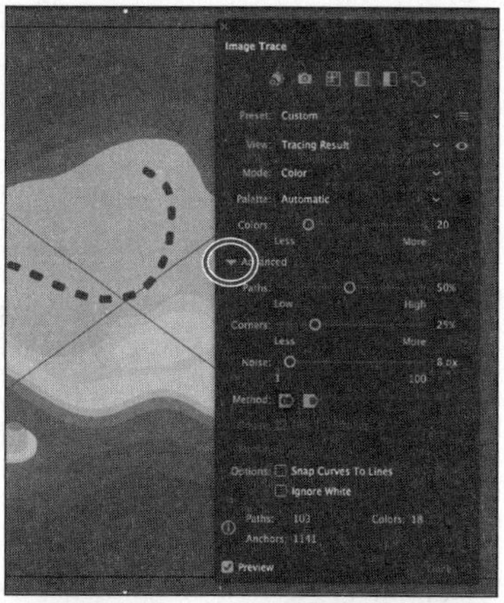

8 Close the Image Trace panel.

9 With the map tracing object still selected, click the Expand button in the Properties panel.

The map is no longer an image tracing object but is composed of shapes and paths that are grouped together.

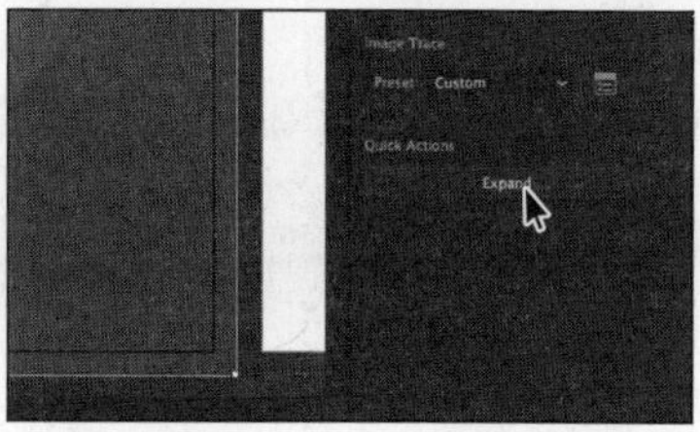

10 Choose Object > Hide > Selection to temporarily hide it.

Working with drawing modes

Note: To learn more about clipping masks, see Lesson 14, "Using Illustrator CC with Other Adobe Applications."

Illustrator has three different drawing modes available that are found at the bottom of the Tools panel: Draw Normal, Draw Behind, and Draw Inside. Drawing modes allow you to draw shapes in different ways. The three drawing modes are as follows:

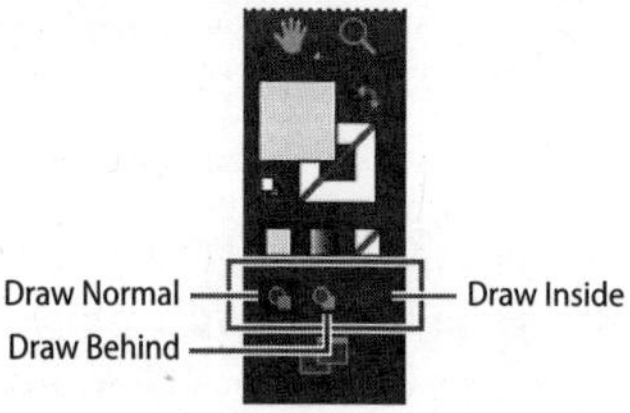

- **Draw Normal mode:** You start every document by drawing shapes in Normal mode, which stacks shapes on top of each other.
- **Draw Behind mode:** This mode allows you to draw behind all artwork on a selected layer if no artwork is selected. If an artwork is selected, the new object is drawn directly beneath the selected object.
- **Draw Inside mode:** This mode lets you draw objects or place images inside other objects, including live text, automatically creating a clipping mask of the selected object.

Using the Draw Inside mode

Next, you will learn how to add artwork inside of a selected shape using the Draw Inside drawing mode. This can be useful if you want to hide (*mask*) part of the artwork.

1 Choose File > Open. In the Open dialog box, select the map_edges.ai file in the Lessons > Lesson03 folder on your hard disk and click Open.

The orange shape you see is just a closed path that was created using the Pencil tool in the Tools panel. You'll copy this shape and paste it back in the Postcard.ai file.

2 Select the Selection tool ( ) in the Tools panel, and click the orange map edges shape to select it. Choose Edit > Copy.

3 Click the Postcard.ai tab to return to the postcard document. Choose Edit > Paste In Place.

4 Click the orange shape to select it, if it isn't, and then click the Draw Inside button ( ), near the bottom of the Tools panel.

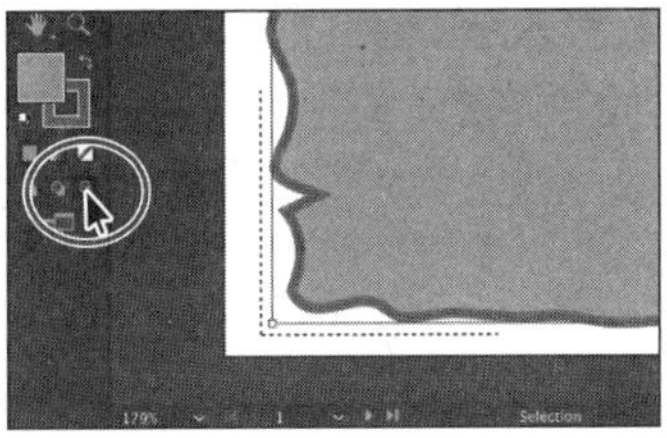

This button is active when a single object is selected (path, compound path, or text), and it allows you to draw within the selected object only. Notice that the orange shape has a dotted open rectangle around it, indicating that, if you draw, paste, or place content, it will be inside the orange shape.

Note: If the Tools panel you see is displayed as a single column, you can click the Drawing Modes button ( ) at the bottom of the Tools panel and choose Draw Inside from the menu that appears.

5 Choose Select > Deselect.

Notice that the orange shape still has the dotted open rectangle around it, indicating that Draw Inside mode is still active. The shape you are about to draw inside of does not need to be selected.

6 Click and hold down the mouse button on the Rectangle tool ( ) in the Tools panel, and select the Ellipse tool ( ). Press the letter D to apply the default white fill and black stroke to the shape you are about to draw. Click and drag to create an ellipse that overlaps the edge of the orange shape.

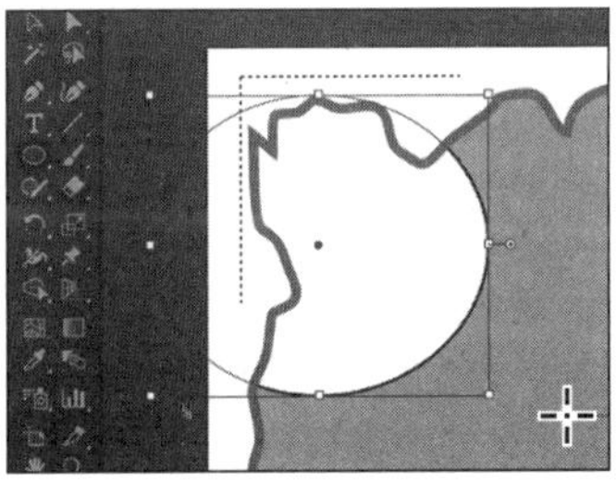

The ellipse you just drew is within the orange shape, and part of it is being hidden.

7 Choose Edit > Undo Ellipse to get rid of the ellipse.

You can also place or paste content into a shape with Draw Inside mode active.

8 Choose Object > Show All to show the island artwork again, which is now behind the orange shape.

9 Select the Selection tool (▶) in the Tools panel, and choose Edit > Cut to cut the selected island artwork from the artboard.

10 Choose Edit > Paste In Place.

The island artwork is placed within the orange shape.

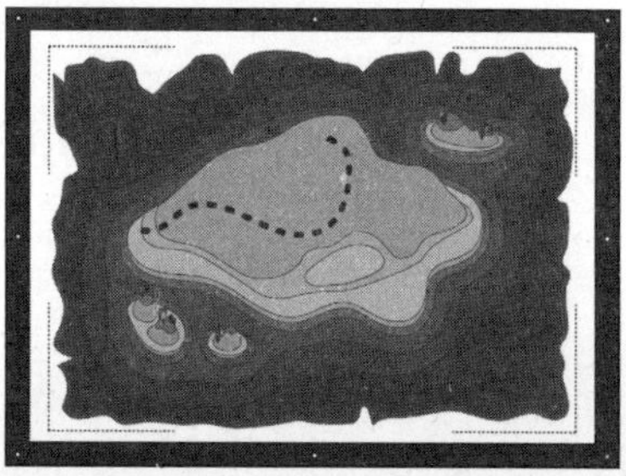

● **Note:** If the Tools panel you see is displayed as a single column, you can click the Drawing Modes button at the bottom of the Tools panel and choose Draw Normal from the menu that appears.

11 Click the Draw Normal button ( ) at the bottom of the Tools panel.

When you are finished adding content inside a shape, you can click the Draw Normal button so that any new content you create will be drawn normally (stacked rather than drawn inside).

12 Choose Select > Deselect.

▶ **Tip:** You can also toggle between the available drawing modes by pressing Shift+D.

Editing content drawn inside

Next, you'll edit the map artwork inside of the shape to see how you can later edit content inside.

▶ **Tip:** You can separate the shapes by choosing Object > Clipping Mask > Release. This would make two objects, stacked one on another.

1 With the Selection tool (▶) selected, click to select the island artwork. Notice that it selects the map edges shape instead.

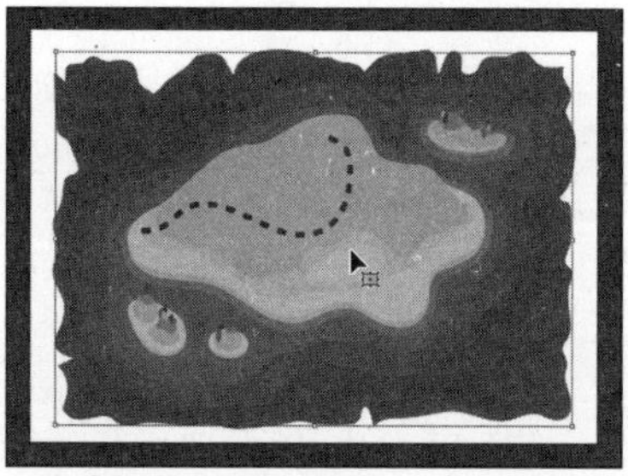

The map edges shape is now a mask, also called a *clipping path.* The island artwork and the map edges shape, together, make a *clip group* and are now treated as a single object. If you look at the top of the Properties panel, you will see Clip Group. Like other groups, if you would like to edit the clipping path (the object that contains the content drawn inside of it) or the content inside, you can double-click the Clip Group object.

2 With the Clip Group selected, click the Isolate Group button in the Properties panel to enter Isolation mode and be able to select the clipping path (map edges shape) or the island artwork within.

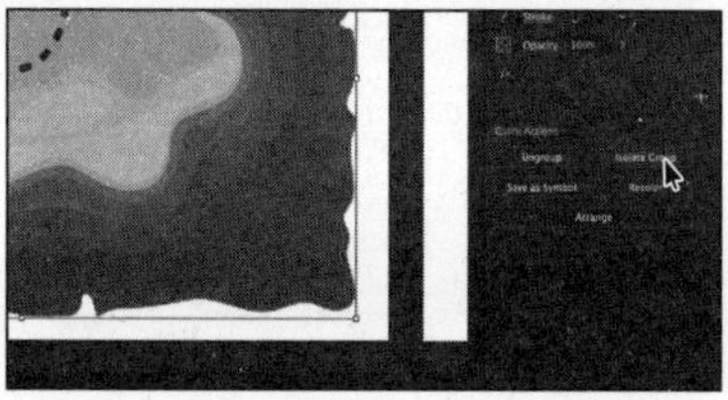

3 Click the map artwork within the map boundaries, and drag it down and to the right a little.

4 Press Esc to exit Isolation mode.

5 Choose Select > Deselect and then choose File > Save.

▶ **Tip:** Sometimes it can be helpful to choose View > Outline to more easily see and select shapes when in Isolation mode.

Working with Draw Behind mode

Throughout this lesson, you've been working in the default Draw Normal mode. Next, you'll draw a rectangle that will cover the artboard and go behind the rest of the content using Draw Behind mode.

1 Click the Draw Behind button ( ) at the bottom of the Tools panel.

As long as this drawing mode is selected, every shape you create using the different methods you've learned will be created behind the other shapes on the page. The Draw Behind mode also affects placed content (File > Place).

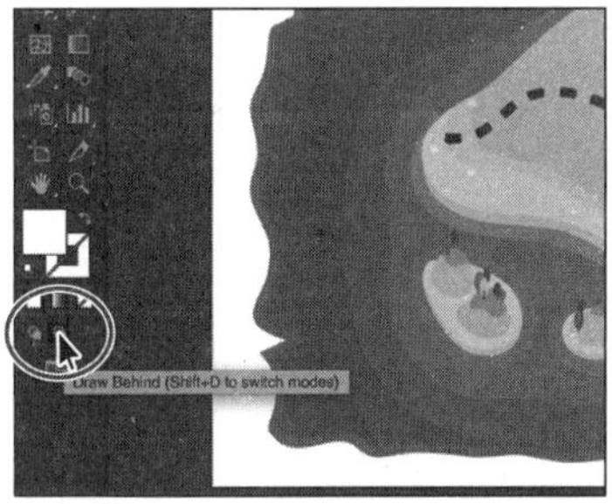

● **Note:** If the Tools panel you see is displayed as a single column, you can click the Drawing Modes button ( ) at the bottom of the Tools panel and choose Draw Behind from the menu that appears.

2 Click and hold down the mouse button on the Ellipse tool ( ) in the Tools panel, and select the Rectangle tool ( ). Position the pointer off the upper-left corner of the artboard where the red bleed guides meet. Click and drag to the lower-right corner of the red bleed guides.

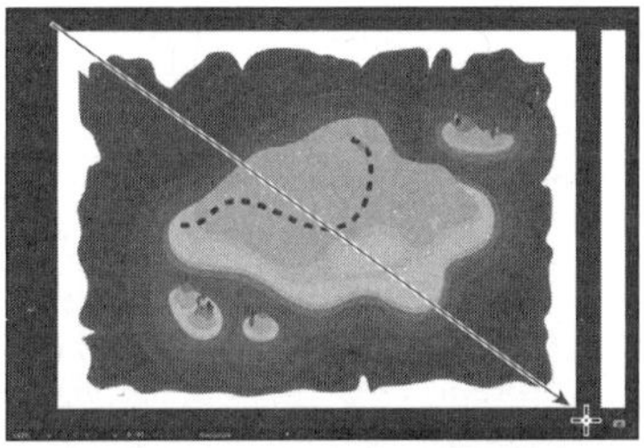

● **Note:** If artwork was selected, clicking the Draw Behind button would allow you to draw artwork behind the selected artwork.

3 With the new rectangle selected, click the Fill color box in the Properties panel. Make sure that the Swatches option ( ) is selected, then change the fill color to a tan color with the tooltip "C=25 M=25 Y=40 K=0." Press the Escape key to hide the panel.

4 Choose Object > Lock > Selection.

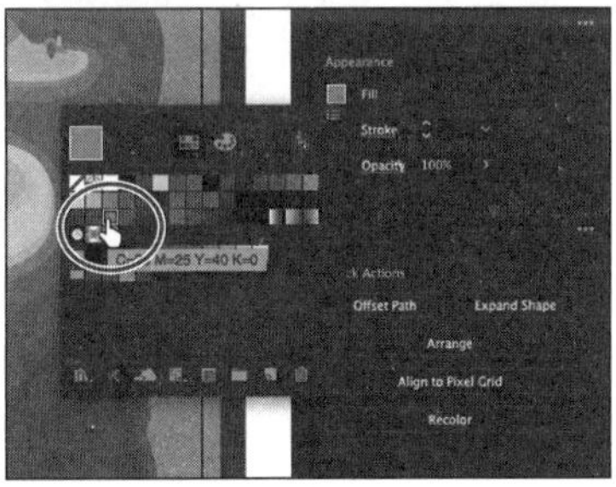

Finishing up

To finish the postcard, you'll bring the artwork onto the artboard with the island artwork on it.

1 Choose View > Fit All In Window to see both artboards.

2 Select the Selection tool (▶), and drag across the ship artwork to select it. Click the Group button in the Properties panel.

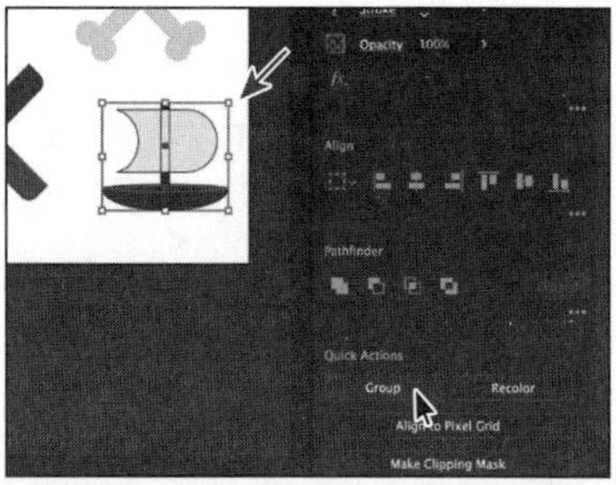

3 Choose Select > All On Active Artboard to select all of the shapes. Choose Object > Arrange > Bring To Front.

You brought the selected artwork to the front because it was created first, which means it would be behind the artwork on the left artboard, which was created after. Next, you'll drag the artwork onto the artboard on the left and resize it.

4 Choose Select > Deselect.

● **Note:** You may want to zoom in to different artwork by choosing View > Zoom In.

5 Drag each group from the right artboard onto the left artboard, one at a time. To resize each group to better fit within the map, you can press the Shift key and drag a corner of the artwork bounding box to scale it. When finished, release the mouse button and then the key.

In the final artwork, I created copies of a few of the objects by choosing Edit > Copy and then Edit > Paste. I also selected copies of the mountain shape and changed the color fill in the Properties panel on the right, for each.

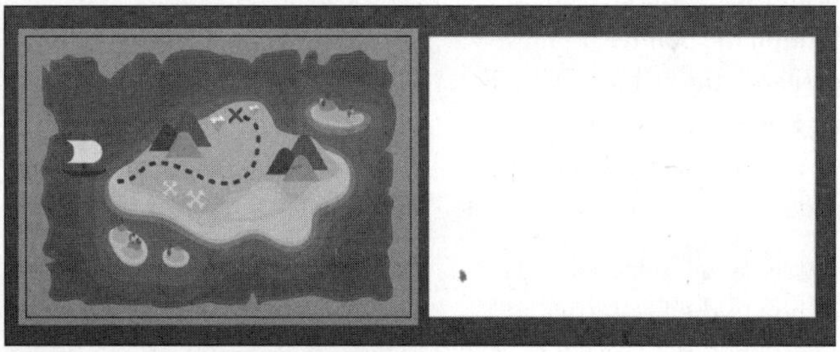

6 Choose File > Save and then File > Close.

Review questions

1 What are the basic tools for creating shapes?

2 What is a Live Shape?

3 How do you select a shape with no fill?

4 What is the Shaper tool?

5 How can you convert a raster image to editable vector shapes?

Review answers

1 There are six shape tools: Rectangle, Rounded Rectangle, Ellipse, Polygon, Star, and Flare (the Flare tool was not covered in the lesson). As explained in Lesson 1, "Getting to Know the Work Area," to tear off a group of tools from the Tools panel, position the pointer over the tool that appears in the Tools panel, and hold down the mouse button until the group of tools appears. Without releasing the mouse button, drag to the triangle on the right side of the group and then release the mouse button to tear off the group.

2 After you draw a rectangle, rounded rectangle, ellipse, or polygon using the shape tool, you can continue to modify its properties such as width, height, rounded corners, corner types, and radii (individually or collectively). This is what is known as a Live Shape. The shape properties such as corner radius are editable later in the Transform panel, in the Properties panel, or directly on the art.

3 Items that have no fill can be selected by clicking the stroke (or edge) or by dragging a selection marquee across the item.

4 Another way to draw and edit shapes in Illustrator involves the Shaper tool. The Shaper tool recognizes natural gestures and produces Live Shapes from those gestures. Without switching tools, you can transform individual shapes you create and even perform operations such as punch and combine.

5 You can convert a raster image to editable vector shapes by selecting it, and then clicking the Image Trace button in the Properties panel. To convert the tracing to paths, click Expand in the Properties panel, or choose Object > Image Trace > Expand. Use this method if you want to work with the components of the traced artwork as individual objects. The resulting paths are grouped.

4 EDITING AND COMBINING SHAPES AND PATHS

Lesson overview

In this lesson, you'll learn how to do the following:

- Cut with the Scissors tool.
- Join paths.
- Work with the Knife tool.
- Outline strokes.
- Work with the Eraser tool.
- Work with the Shape Builder tool.
- Work with Pathfinder commands to create shapes.
- Create a compound path.
- Work with the Reshape tool.
- Edit strokes with the Width tool.

This lesson takes approximately 45 minutes to complete. Please log in to your account on peachpit.com to download the lesson files for this chapter, or go to the "Getting Started" section at the beginning of this book and follow the instructions under "Accessing the lesson files and Web Edition."

Your Account page is also where you'll find any updates to the chapters or to the lesson files. Look on the Lesson & Update Files tab to access the most current content.

Soon after you begin creating simple paths and shapes, you will most likely want to take them further in order to create more complex artwork. In this lesson, you'll explore how to both edit and combine shapes and paths.

Starting the lesson

In Lesson 3, "Using Shapes to Create Artwork for a Postcard," you learned about creating and making edits to basic shapes. In this lesson, you'll take basic shapes and paths and learn how to both edit and combine them to create artwork in order to finish a poster about camping.

Note: If you have not already downloaded the project files for this lesson to your computer from your Account page, make sure to do so now. See the "Getting Started" section at the beginning of the book.

1 To ensure that the tools function and the defaults are set exactly as described in this lesson, delete or deactivate (by renaming) the Adobe Illustrator CC preferences file. See "Restoring default preferences" in the "Getting Started" section at the beginning of the book.

2 Start Adobe Illustrator CC.

3 Choose File > Open. Locate the file named L4_end.ai, which is in the Lessons > Lesson04 folder that you copied onto your hard disk, and click Open. This file contains the finished artwork.

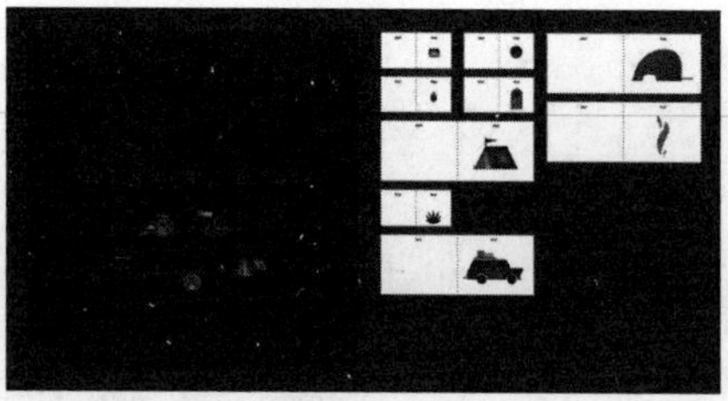

4 Choose View > Fit All In Window; leave the file open for reference, or choose File > Close (I closed it).

5 Choose File > Open. In the Open dialog box, navigate to the Lessons > Lesson04 folder, and select the L4_start.ai file on your hard disk. Click Open.

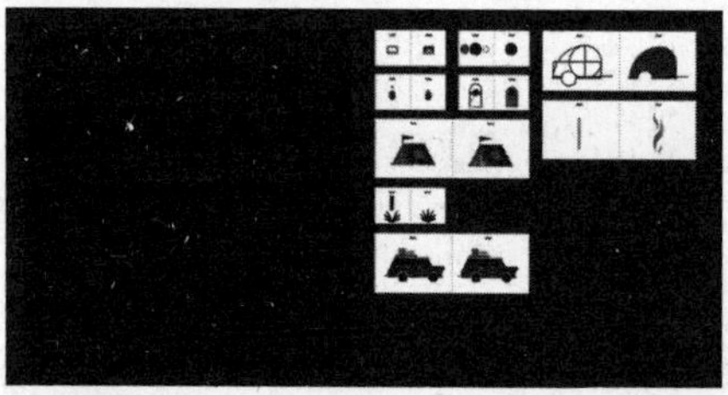

Tip: By default, the .ai extension shows on macOS, but you could add the extension on either platform in the Save As dialog box.

6 Choose File > Save As. In the Save As dialog box, change the name to **HappyCamper.ai** (macOS) or **HappyCamper** (Windows), and choose the Lesson04 folder. Leave the Format option set to Adobe Illustrator (ai) (macOS) or the Save As Type option set to Adobe Illustrator (*.AI) (Windows), and click Save.

7 In the Illustrator Options dialog box, leave the Illustrator options at their default settings, and click OK.

8 Choose Window > Workspace > Reset Essentials.

Note: If you don't see Reset Essentials in the Workspace menu, choose Window > Workspace > Essentials before choosing Window > Workspace > Reset Essentials.

Editing paths and shapes

In Illustrator, you can edit and combine paths and shapes in a variety of ways to achieve the artwork you want. Sometimes, to get the artwork you desire, you start with simpler paths and shapes and use different methods for achieving more complex paths. This includes working with the Scissors tool (✂), the Knife tool (), and the Eraser tool (◆); outlining strokes; joining paths; and more.

● **Note:** You'll explore other methods for transforming artwork in Lesson 5, "Transforming Artwork."

Cutting with the Scissors tool

There are several tools that allow you to cut and divide shapes. You'll start with the Scissors tool (✂), which splits a path at an anchor point or on a line segment and makes an open path. Next, you'll cut a rectangle with the Scissors tool and reshape it to make curtains in a camping trailer illustration.

1 Click the View menu and make sure that the Smart Guides option is selected (a checkmark appears).

2 Choose 2 Window from the Artboard Navigation menu in the lower-left corner of the Document window. Choose View > Fit Artboard In Window.

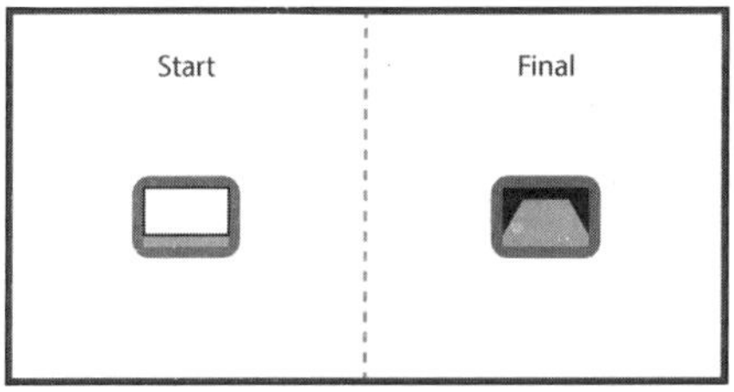

An example of what you will create is labeled "Final" on the right side of the artboard. You will work with the artwork labeled "Start," on the left.

3 Select the Selection tool (▶) in the Tools panel, and click the white shape on the left to select it.

4 Press Command++ (macOS) or Ctrl++ (Windows) a few times to zoom in to the selected artwork.

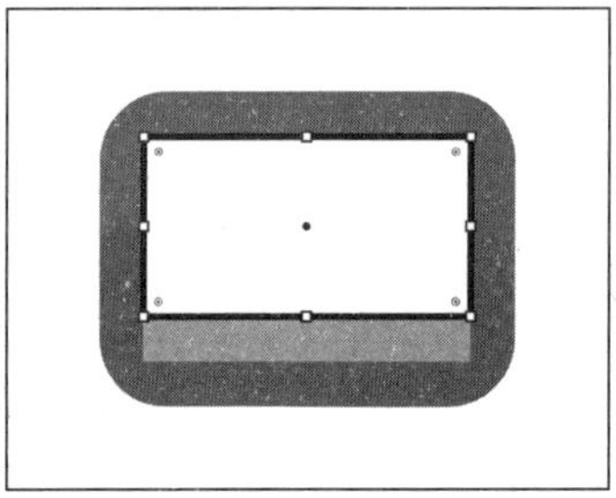

Note: If you don't click directly on a point or path, you will see a warning dialog box. You can simply click OK and try again.

5 With the shape selected, in the Tools panel, click and hold down mouse button on the Eraser tool ( ), and select the Scissors tool ( ). Position the pointer over the bottom edge of the shape (see the figure). When you see the word "path," click to cut the path at that point, and then move the pointer away.

Cuts made with the Scissors tool must be on a line or a curve rather than on an end point of an open path. Clicking the stroke of a shape, the rectangle in this example, with the Scissors tool, the path is cut where you click so that it becomes open (a path with two end points).

6 Select the Direct Selection tool ( ) in the Tools panel. Move the pointer over the selected (blue) anchor point and drag it up.

7 Drag the other anchor point, from where you originally cut the shape with the scissors, up and to the right (see the figure).

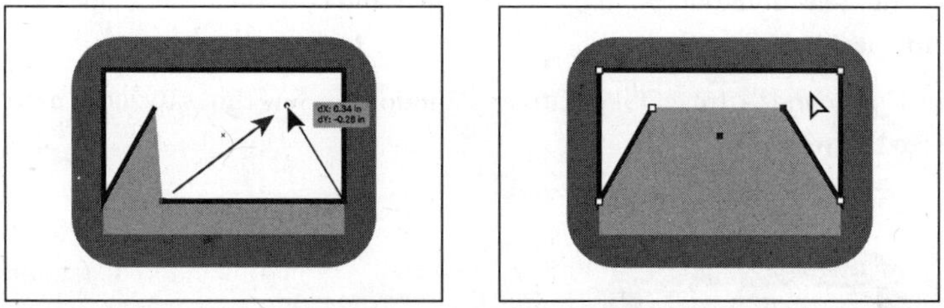

Notice how the stroke (the black border) doesn't go all the way around the white shape. That's because cutting with the Scissors tool makes an open path. If you only want to fill the shape with a color, it doesn't have to be a closed path. It is, however, necessary for a path to be closed if you want a stroke to appear around the entire fill area.

Joining paths

Suppose you draw a "U" shape and later decide you want to close the shape, essentially joining the ends of the "U" with a straight path. If you select the path, you can use the Join command to create a line segment between the end points, closing the path. When more than one open path is selected, you can join them to create a closed path. You can also join the end points of two separate paths. Next, you will join the ends of the white path to create a single closed shape.

1 Select the Selection tool ( ) in the Tools panel. Click away from the white path to deselect it and then click in the white fill to reselect it.

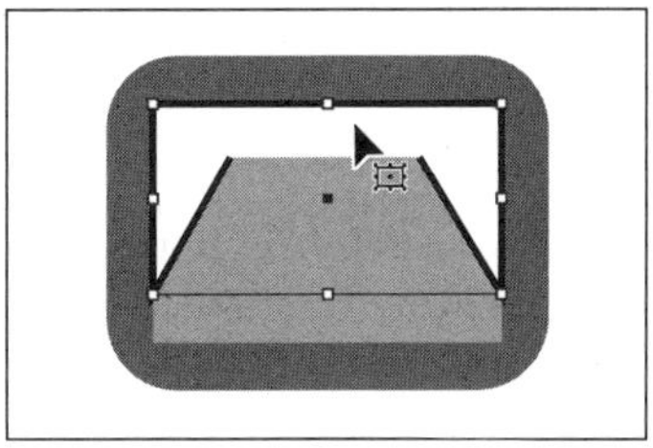

This step is important because only one anchor point was left selected from the previous section. If you were to choose the Join command with only one anchor point selected, an error message would appear. By selecting the whole path, when you apply the Join command, Illustrator simply finds the two ends of the path and connects them with a straight line.

Tip: If you wanted to join specific anchor points from separate paths, select the anchor points, and choose Object > Join > Path or press Command+J (macOS) or Ctrl+J (Windows).

2 Choose Object > Path > Join.

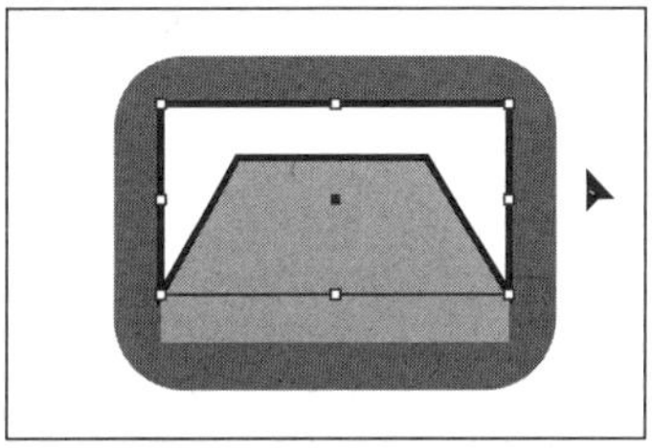

When you apply the Join command to two or more open paths, Illustrator first looks for and joins the paths that have end points stationed closest to each other. This process is repeated every time you apply the Join command until all paths are joined.

Tip: In Lesson 6, "Creating an Illustration with the Drawing Tools," you'll learn about the Join tool ( ), which allows you to join two paths at a corner, keeping the original curve intact.

3 In the Properties panel on the right (Window > Properties), change the stroke to **0** by clicking the down arrow until the stroke is removed.

4 Click the Fill color box (white) in the Properties panel, make sure the Swatches option ( ) is selected in the panel that appears, and click to select the color named Purple3.

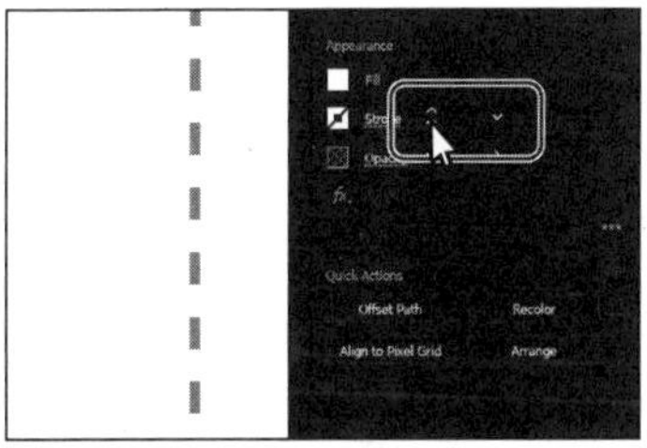

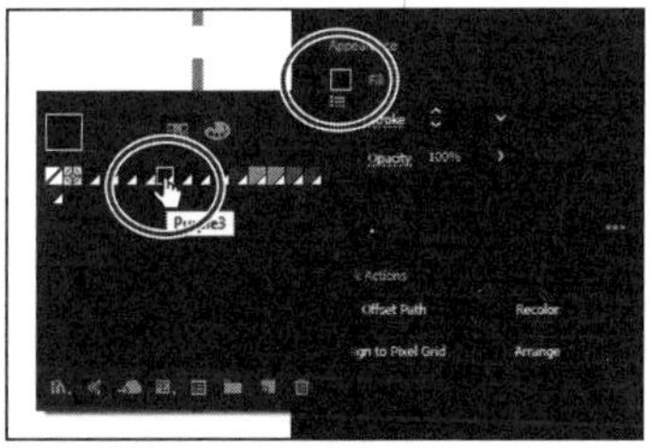

▶ **Tip:** To group selected content, you can also click the Group button in the Quick Actions section of the Properties panel.

5 Drag across the window shapes to select them.

6 Choose Object > Group.

7 Choose Select > Deselect and then choose File > Save.

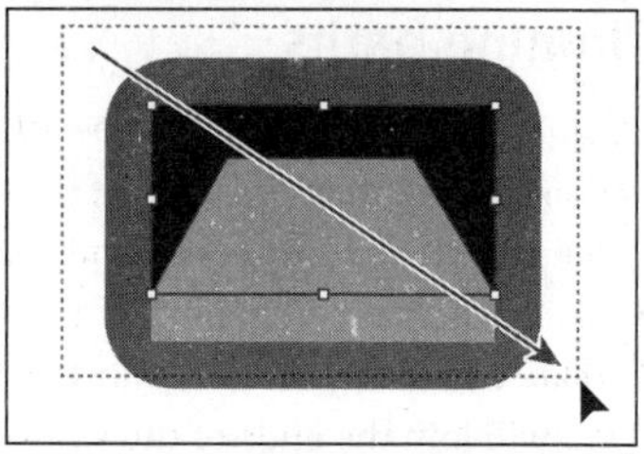

Cutting with the Knife tool

Another way to cut a shape is by using the Knife tool (). To cut with the Knife tool, you drag across a shape, and the result is two closed paths.

1 Choose 3 Tank from the Artboard Navigation menu in the lower-left corner of the Document window.

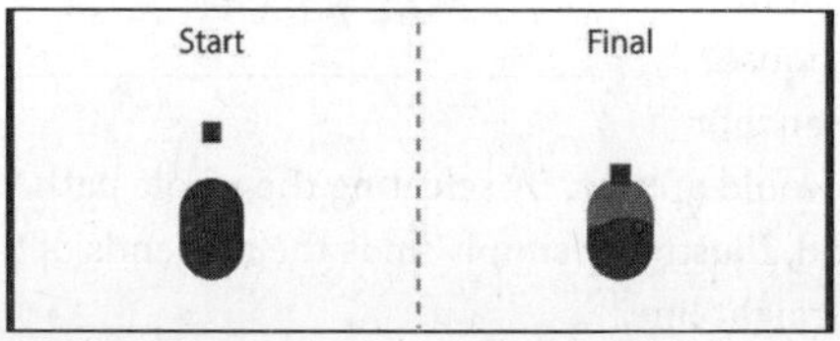

An example of what you will create is labeled "Final" on the right side of the artboard. You will work with the artwork labeled "Start," on the left.

2 Choose View > Fit Artboard In Window to ensure it fits in the Document window.

● **Note:** You can select multiple vector objects and cut them at one time with the Knife tool.

3 Select the Selection tool (), and click the pink oval shape under the artwork labeled "Start."

If an object is selected, the Knife tool will only cut that object. If nothing is selected, it will cut any vector objects it touches.

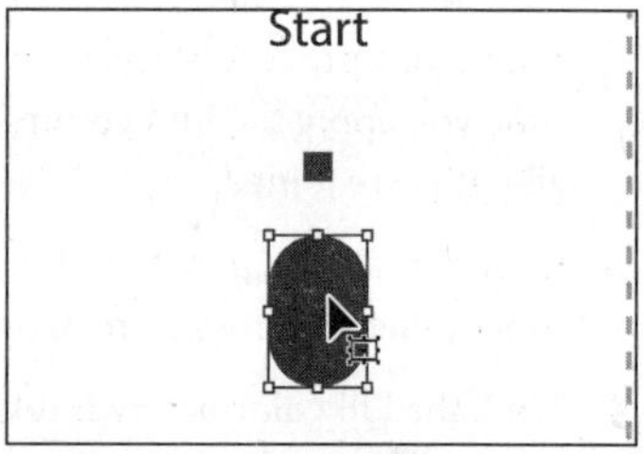

4 Click and hold down the mouse on the Scissors tool (), and select the Knife tool ().

▶ **Tip:** Pressing the Caps Lock key will turn the Knife tool pointer into a more precise cursor (-¦-). This can make it easier to see where the cut will happen.

5 Move the Knife pointer () to the left of the selected shape. Drag across the shape to cut it into two.

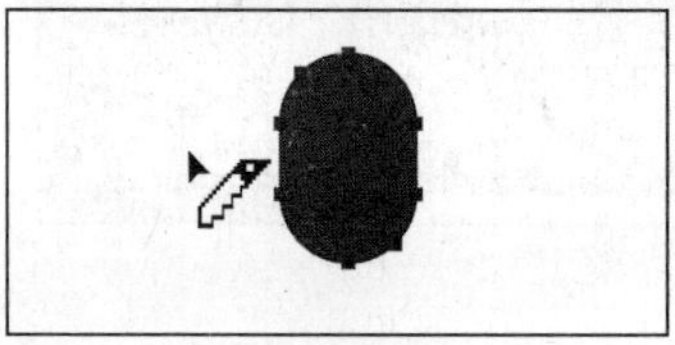

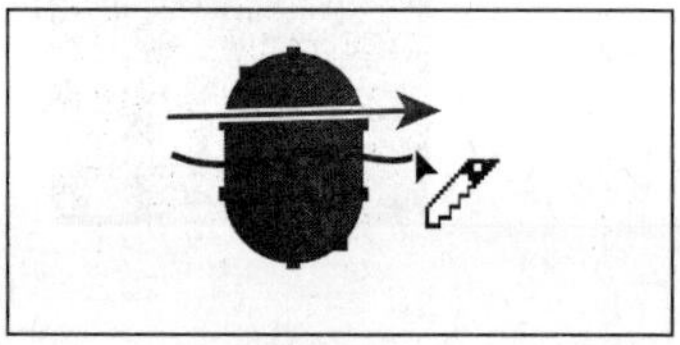

Notice how dragging across a shape with the Knife tool makes a very free-form cut that is not straight at all.

6 Choose Select > Deselect.

7 Select the Selection tool (▶), and click the new, top shape (see the following figure).

8 Click the Fill color box in the Properties panel, make sure the Swatches option (■) is selected in the panel that appears, and click to select the color named Pink.

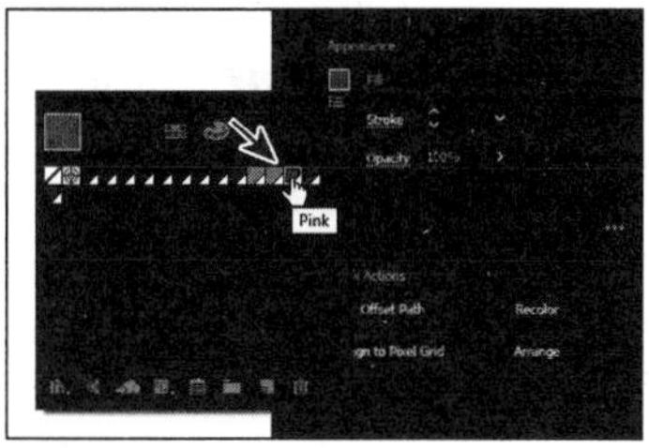

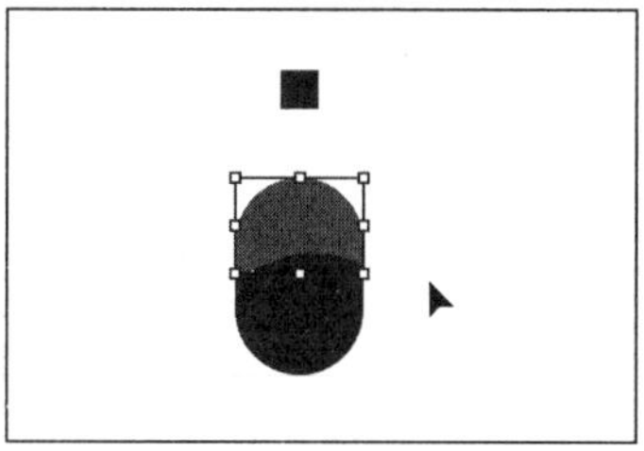

9 Drag the small, red square that is above the shapes, down onto the shapes you cut.

10 Drag across all of the tank shapes labeled "Start," to select them.

11 Choose Object > Group.

12 Choose Select > Deselect.

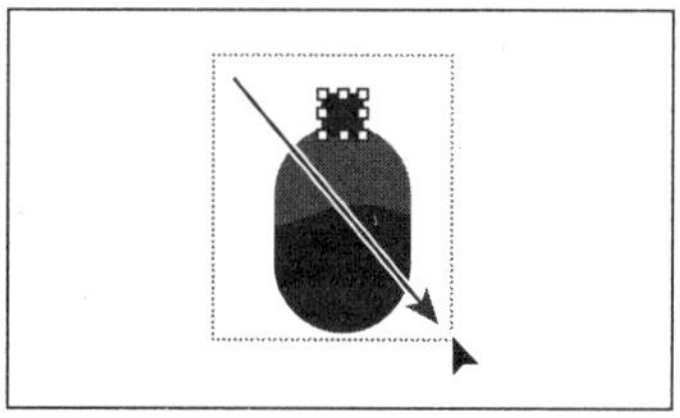

Cutting in a straight line

Next, you'll cut artwork in a straight line with the Knife tool. Pressing the Option (macOS) or Alt (Windows) key allows you to cut in a straight line with the Knife tool. Pressing the Shift key as well constrains the cut to 45 degrees.

1 Choose 4 Tent from the Artboard Navigation menu in the lower-left corner of the Document window.

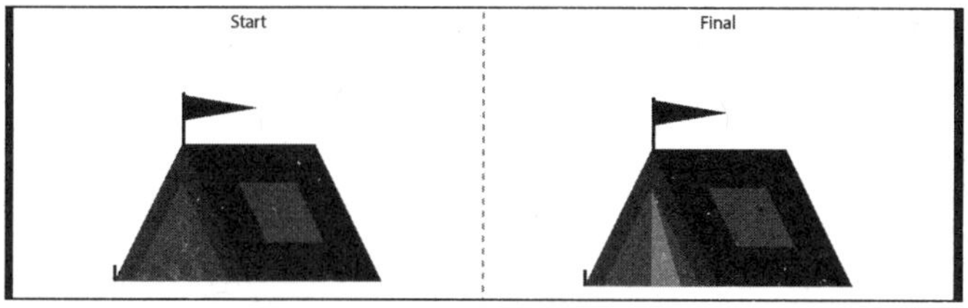

An example of what you will create is labeled "Final" on the right side of the artboard. You will work with the artwork labeled "Start," on the left. You'll cut the tent opening shape into several paths. This requires you to cut in straight lines.

2 Choose View > Fit Artboard In Window.

3 With the Selection tool (▶) selected, click the pink triangle shape under the artwork labeled "Start."

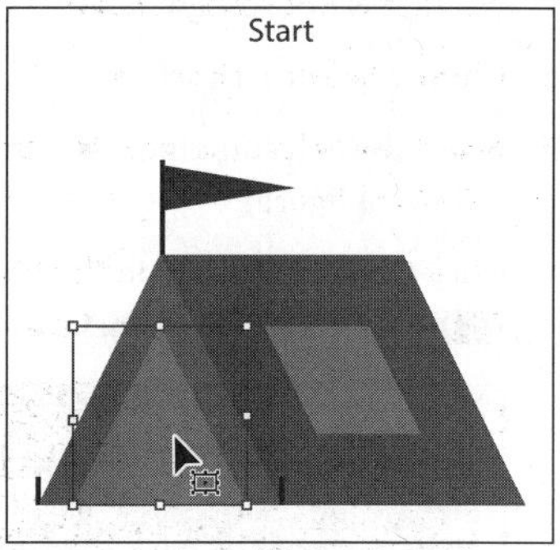

4 Choose View > Zoom In, twice, to zoom in to the artwork.

5 Select the Knife tool (). Position the pointer just above the top point of the selected triangle. Press the Caps Lock key to turn the Knife tool pointer into a precise cursor (-¦-).

The pointer now appears as cross hairs and can make it easier to see exactly where you will begin cutting.

● **Note:** Pressing the Option/Alt key keeps the cut straight, and pressing the Shift key constrains the cutting to a multiple of 45º.

6 Press and hold Option+Shift (macOS) or Alt+Shift (Windows), and drag down, all the way across the shape to cut it into two, in a completely straight line. Release the mouse button and then the keys.

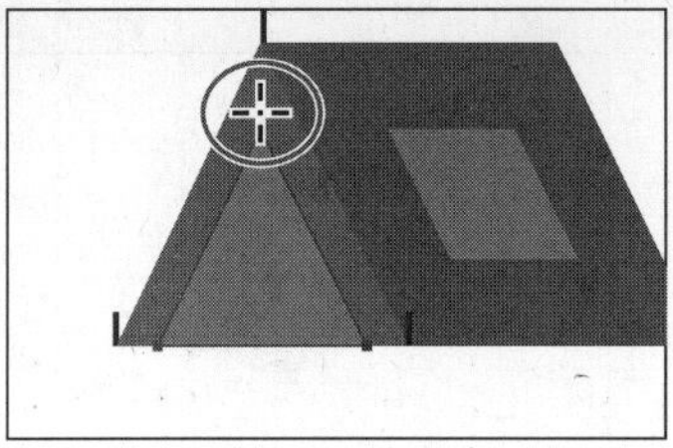

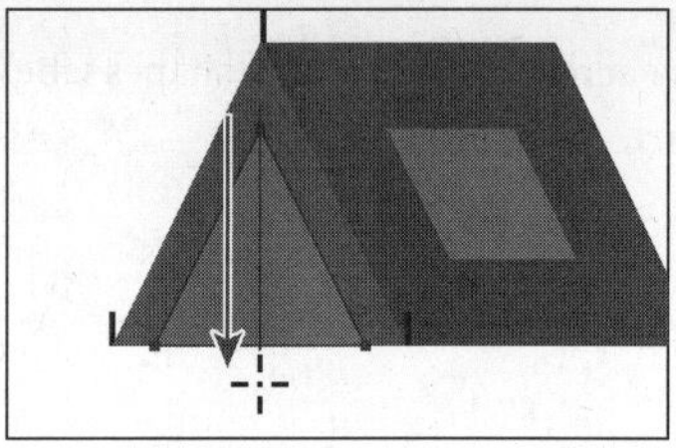

7 Press and hold Option (macOS) or Alt (Windows), and drag from just above the top of the selected triangle, down, at a slight angle, all the way across the shape to cut it into two. Release the mouse button and then the key.

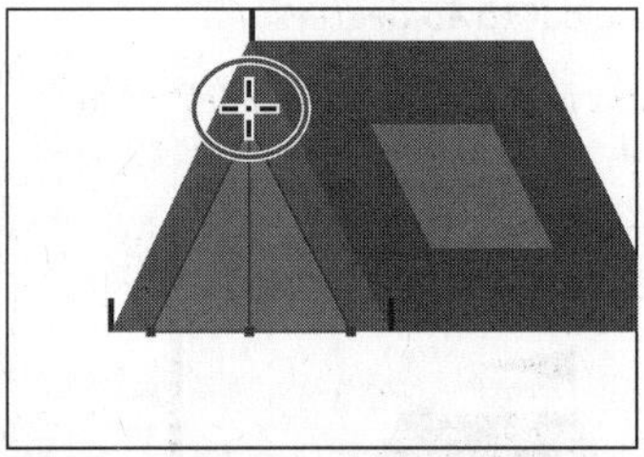

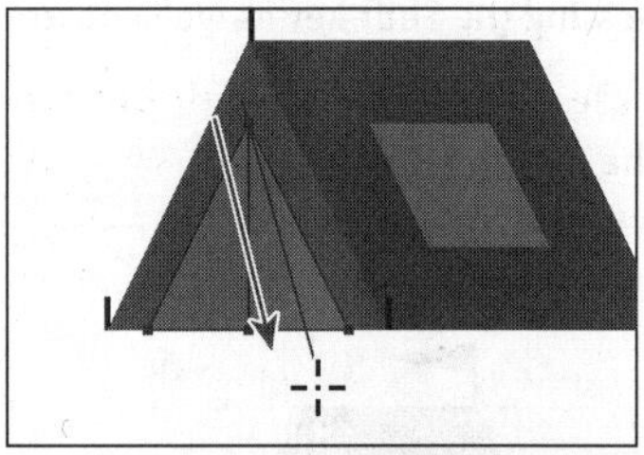

8 Choose Select > Deselect.

9 Select the Selection tool (▶), and click the middle, pink triangle.

10 Click the Fill color box in the Properties panel, make sure the Swatches option (▦) is selected in the panel that appears and click to select the color named Yellow.

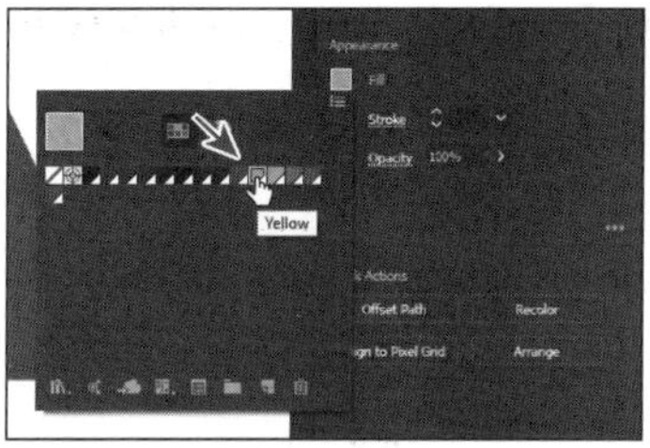

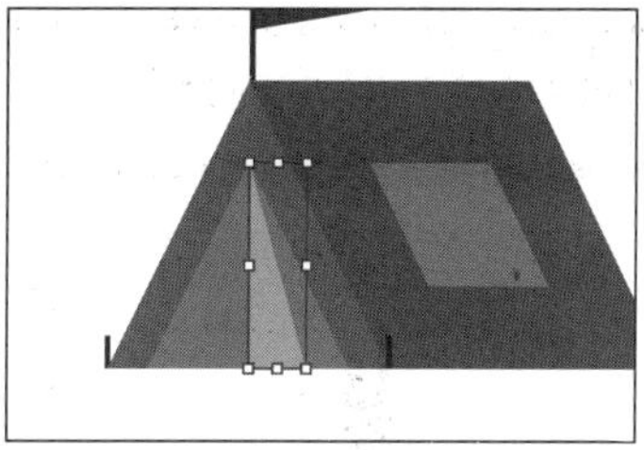

11 Drag across all of the tent shapes labeled "Start," to select them.

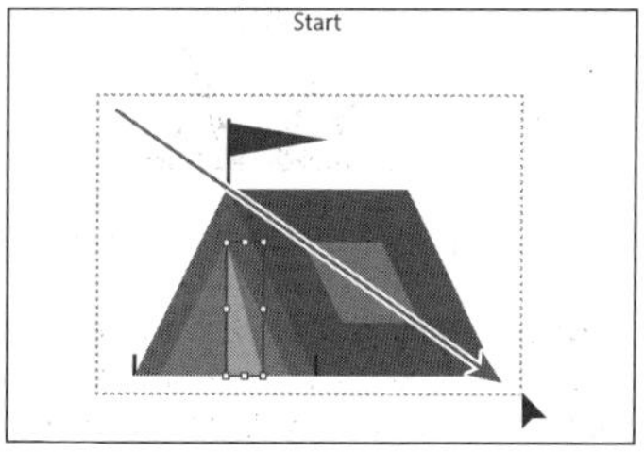

12 Choose Object > Group.

13 Depress the Caps Lock key.

Outlining strokes

Paths, like a line, can show a stroke color but not a fill color by default. If you create a line in Illustrator and want to apply both a stroke and a fill, you can outline the stroke of a path, which converts it into a closed shape (or compound path). Next, you'll outline the stroke of a line so you can erase parts of it in the next section.

1 Choose 5 Plant from the Artboard Navigation menu in the lower-left corner of the Document window.

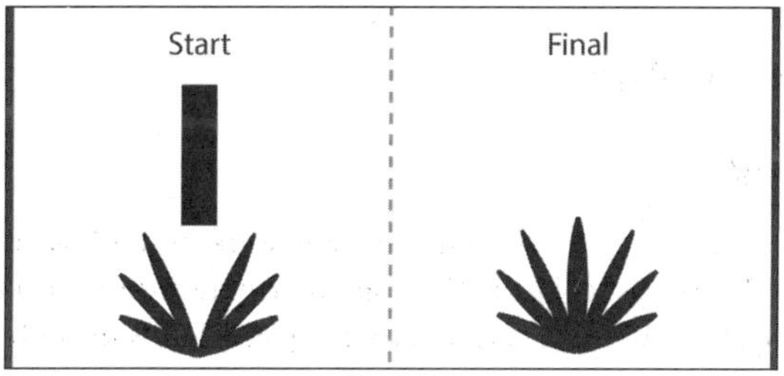

An example of what you will create is labeled "Final" on the right side of the artboard. You'll work with the artwork labeled "Start," on the left.

2 Choose View > Fit Artboard In Window to ensure it fits in the Document window.

3 With the Selection tool (▶), select the purple rectangle labeled "Start."

The rectangle is actually a path. You can tell it's a path with a large stroke. In the Properties panel, you can see that the stroke weight is set to 20. In order to erase part of the path to make it the shape of one of the leaves, it will need to be a shape (rectangle), not a path.

▶ **Tip:** After outlining a stroke, the shape you have may be composed of a lot of anchor points. You can choose Object > Path > Simplify to try to simplify the path, which usually means fewer anchor points.

4 Choose Object > Path > Outline Stroke.

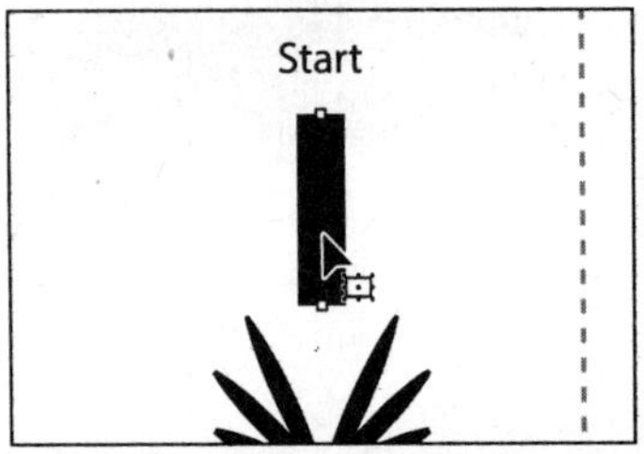

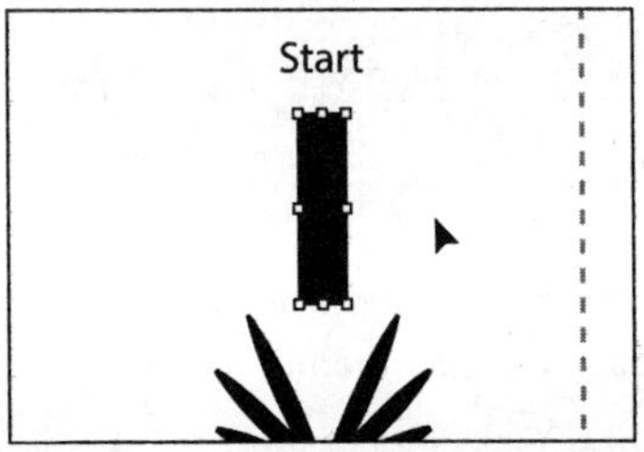

This creates a filled shape that is a closed path.

● **Note:** If you outline the stroke and it shows as "Group" in the Selection Indicator at the top of the Properties panel, then there was a fill set on the line. If the artwork is a group, choose Edit > Undo Outline Stroke, apply a fill of None to the path, and try again.

5 Drag the shape into position like you see in the following figure. Leave the shape selected.

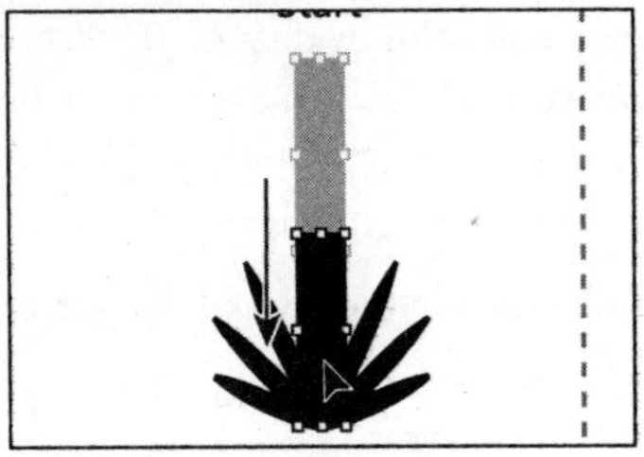

Next, you'll erase parts of the shape.

Using the Eraser tool

● **Note:** You cannot erase raster images, text, symbols, graphs, or gradient mesh objects.

The Eraser tool (◆) lets you erase any area of your vector artwork, regardless of the structure. You can use the Eraser tool on paths, compound paths, paths inside Live Paint groups, and clipping content. Whatever artwork you select is the only artwork you will erase. If you leave all objects deselected, you can erase any object that the tool touches, across all layers. Next, you'll use the Eraser tool to erase part of the selected rectangle so it looks like a leaf.

1 Click and hold down the mouse button on the Knife tool (✐), and select the Eraser tool (◆) in the Tools panel.

2 Double-click the Eraser tool (◆) in the Tools panel to edit the tool properties. In the Eraser Tool Options dialog box, change Size to **20** pt to make the eraser larger. Click OK.

You can change the Eraser tool properties, depending on what your erasing needs are.

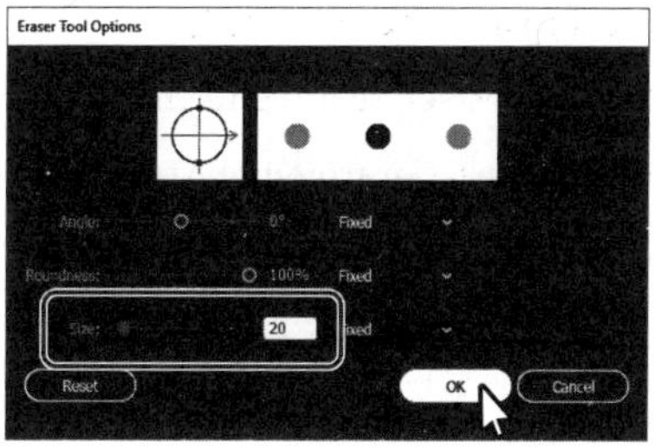

▶ **Tip:** With the Eraser tool selected, you could also click the Tool Options button at the top of the Properties panel to see the options dialog box.

3 Position the pointer above the selected purple shape. Drag down the left side of the shape to erase it.

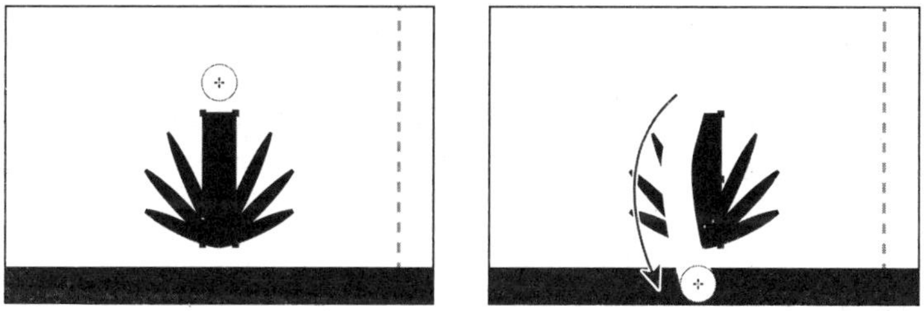

When you release the mouse button, part of the shape is erased, and the shape is still a closed path.

4 Position the pointer above the selected purple shape. Drag down the right side of the shape to erase it.

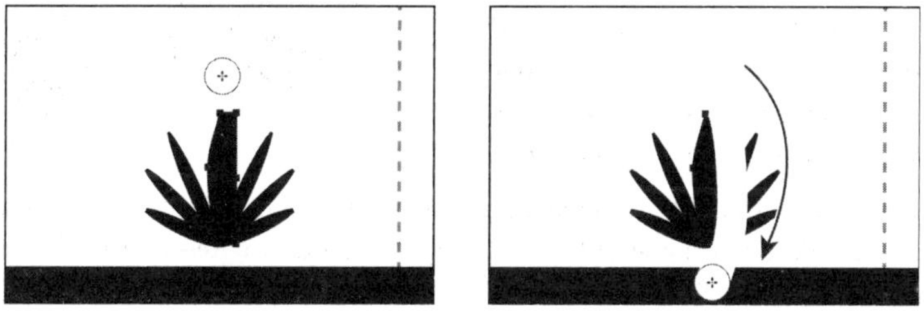

5 Select the Selection tool (▶) and drag across all of the plant shapes labeled "Start," to select them.

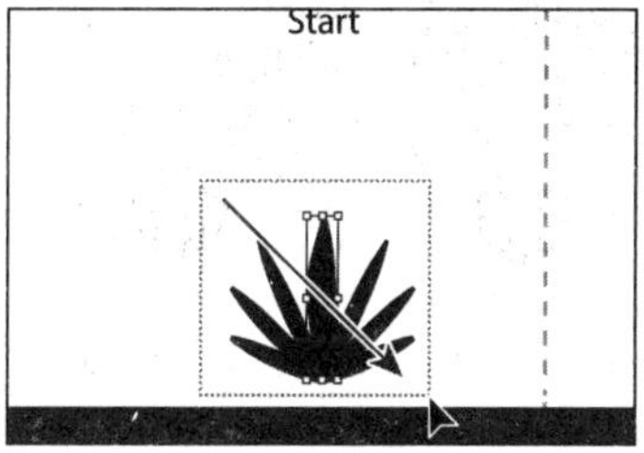

6 Choose Object > Group.

Erasing in a straight line

You can also erase in a straight line, which is what you'll do next.

1 Choose 6 Car from the Artboard Navigation menu in the lower-left corner of the Document window.

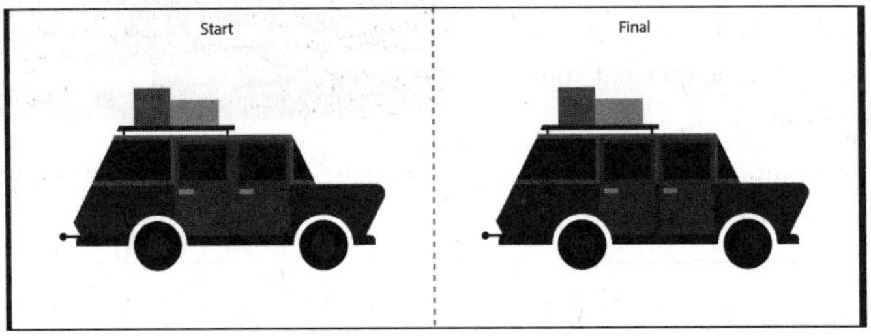

An example of what you will create is labeled "Final" on the right side of the artboard. You will work with the artwork labeled "Start," on the left. You'll select and erase the single door shape to make two doors.

2 Choose View > Fit Artboard In Window to ensure it fits in the Document window.

3 Select the Selection tool (▶), and click to select the door shape labeled "Start."

4 Choose View > Zoom In a few times to zoom in closer.

5 Double-click the Eraser tool (◆) to edit the tool properties. In the Eraser Tool Options dialog box, change Size to **5** pt to make the eraser smaller. Click OK.

▶ **Tip:** If you need to erase a large part of a shape, you can always adjust the eraser size by using the Eraser Tool Options dialog box or by pressing either of the bracket keys ([or]).

6 With the Eraser tool (◆) selected, move the pointer above the middle of the selected shape. Press the Shift key, and drag straight down. Release the mouse button and then the Shift key.

It may look like you erased other parts of the car, but since nothing else was selected, you didn't. The selected door shape is now two separate shapes, both closed paths.

7 Select the Selection tool and drag across all of the car shapes labeled "Start" to select them.

8 Click the Group button in the Quick Actions section of the Properties panel to the right of the document.

9 Choose File > Save.

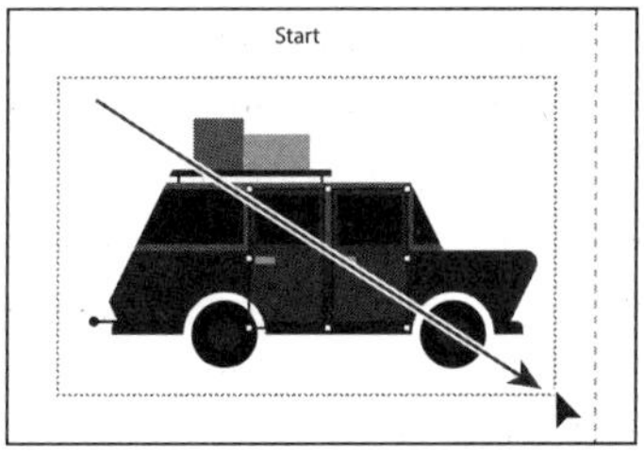

Creating a compound path

Compound paths let you use a vector object to cut a hole in another vector object. Whenever I think of a compound path, I think of a doughnut shape, which can be created from two circles. Holes appear where paths overlap. A compound path is treated like a group, and the individual objects in the compound path can still be edited or released (if you don't want them to be a compound path anymore). Next, you'll create a compound path to create some art for a wheel.

1 Choose 7 Wheel from the Artboard Navigation menu in the lower-left corner of the Document window.

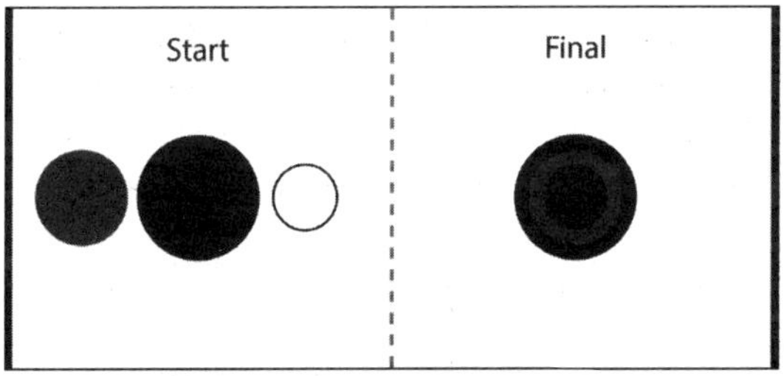

An example of what you will create is labeled "Final" on the right side of the artboard. You will work with the artwork labeled "Start" on the left. You'll create a wheel from the shapes labeled "Start."

2 Choose View > Fit Artboard In Window, if necessary.

3 With the Selection tool (▶) selected, select the gray circle on the left, and drag it so it overlaps the larger dark circle to its right.

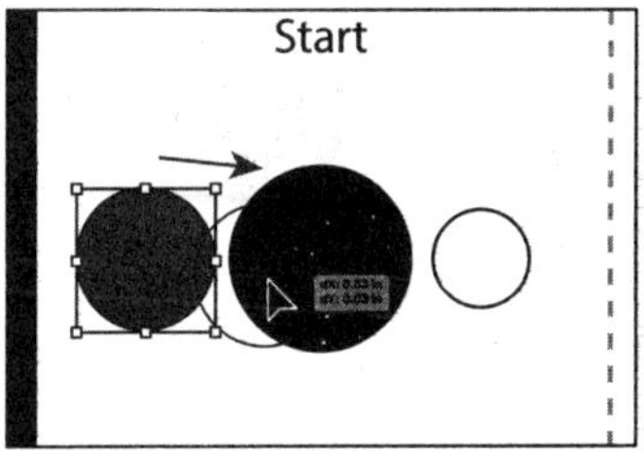

4 Drag the white shape on top of the gray circle and make sure it's centered.

Smart Guides will help you align the circles. You can also select the gray circle and the white circle and align them to each other using the Align options in the Properties panel on the right.

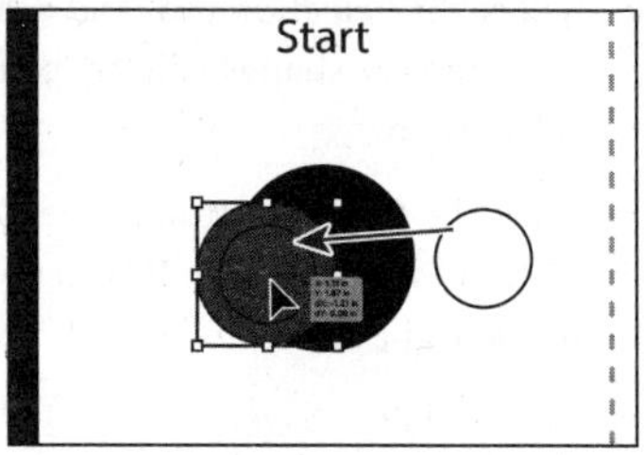

5 Shift-click the gray circle to select it along with the white circle.

▶ **Tip:** You can still edit the original shapes in a compound path like this one. To edit them, select each shape individually with the Direct Selection tool (▶) or double-click the compound path with the Selection tool to enter Isolation mode and select the individual shapes.

● **Note:** When creating a compound path, the appearance attributes of the object lowest in the stacking order determine the appearance of the resulting compound path.

6 Choose Object > Compound Path > Make, and leave the artwork selected.

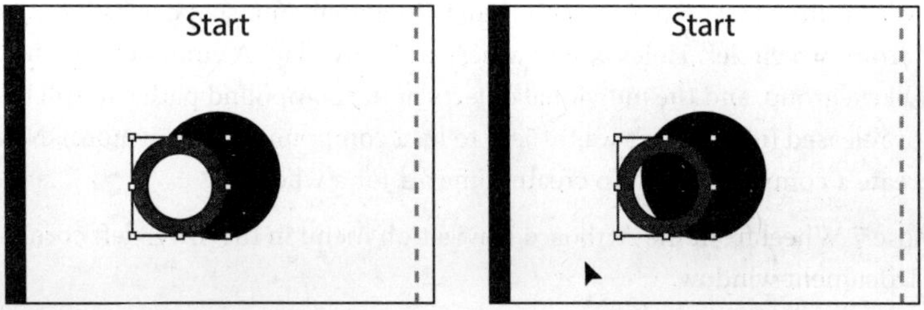

You can now see that the white circle has seemingly disappeared, and you can now see through the shape to the dark color of circle beneath. The white circle was used to "punch" a hole in the gray shape. With the shape still selected, you should see "Compound Path" at the top of the Properties panel to the right.

7 Drag the gray donut shape into the center of the darker circle behind it. The selected shape should be on top. If it isn't, choose Object > Arrange > Bring To Front.

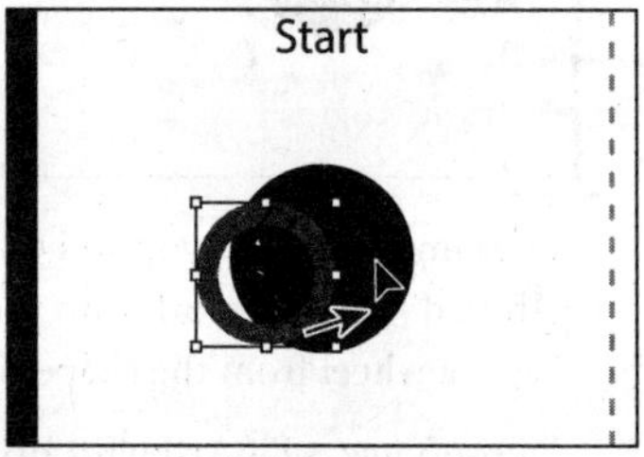

8 Drag across all of the circle shapes labeled "Start" to select them.

9 Choose Object > Group.

10 Choose File > Save.

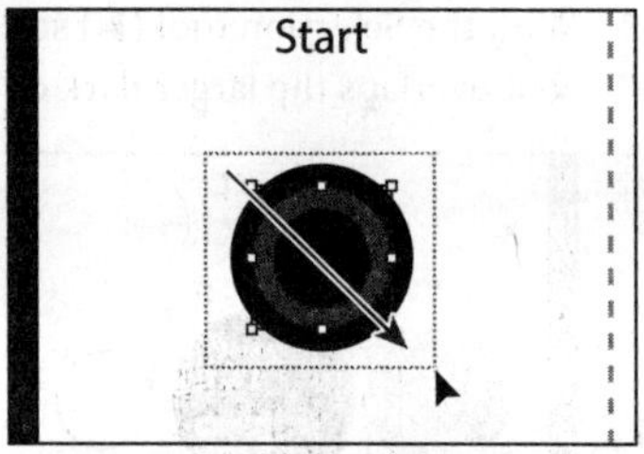

Combining shapes

A lot of the time, creating more complex shapes from simpler shapes can be easier than trying to create them with drawing tools like the Pen tool. In Illustrator, you can combine vector objects in different ways. The resulting paths or shapes differ depending on the method you use to combine the paths. In this section, you'll explore a few of the more widely used methods for combining shapes.

Working with the Shape Builder tool

The first method you'll learn for combining shapes involves working with the Shape Builder tool (). This tool allows you to visually and intuitively merge, delete, fill, and edit overlapping shapes and paths directly in the artwork. Using the Shape Builder tool, you'll create a more complex trailer shape from a series of simpler shapes like circles and squares.

1 Choose 8 Trailer from the Artboard Navigation menu in the lower-left corner of the Document window.

An example of what you will create is labeled "Final" on the right side of the artboard. You will work with the artwork labeled "Start" on the left.

2 Choose View > Fit Artboard In Window to ensure it fits in the Document window.

3 With the Selection tool () selected, drag a marquee selection across the three shapes you see in the figure, labeled "Start," to select the shapes on the artboard. Make sure not to select the white circle.

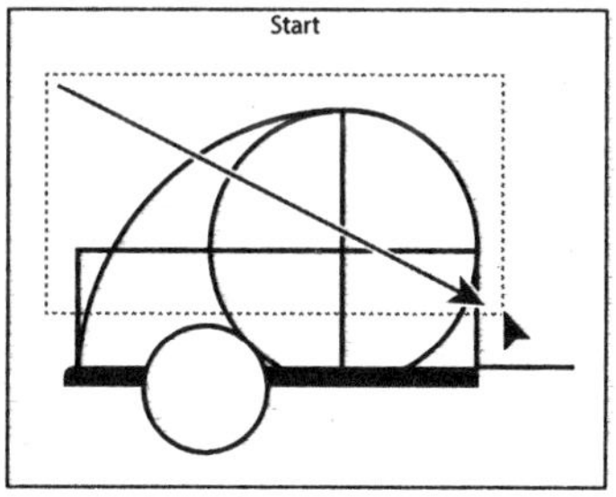

To edit shapes with the Shape Builder tool (), they need to be selected. Using the Shape Builder tool, you will now combine, delete, and paint these simple shapes to create a camper.

▶ **Tip:** You can also press the Shift key and drag a marquee across a series of shapes to combine them. Pressing Shift+Option (macOS) or Shift+Alt (Windows) and dragging a marquee across selected shapes with the Shape Builder tool () selected allows you to delete a series of shapes within the marquee.

4 Select the Shape Builder tool () in the Tools panel. Position the pointer off the upper-left corner of the shapes, and drag from the red X in the figure to the right into the shapes. Release the mouse button to combine the shapes.

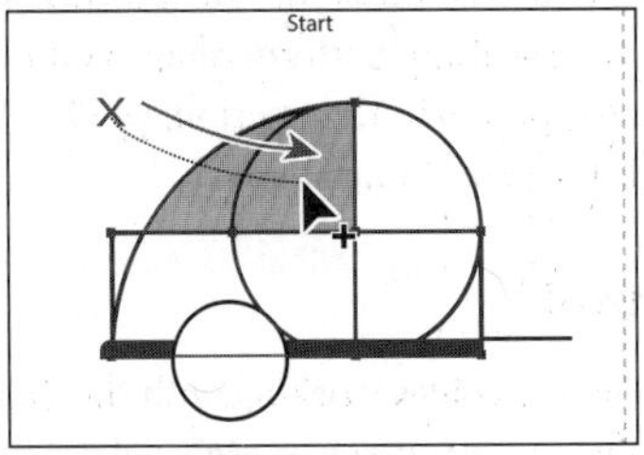

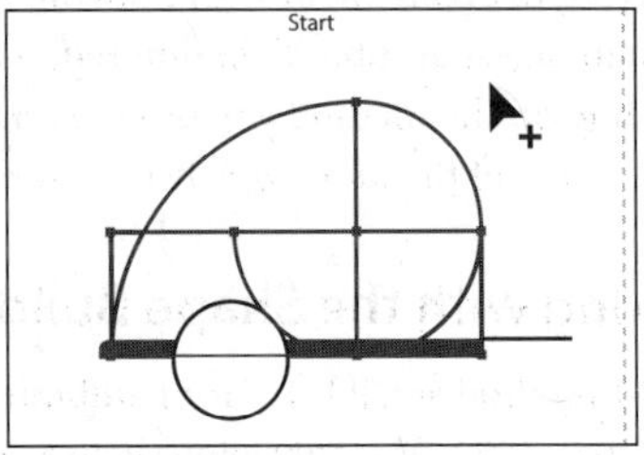

When you select the Shape Builder tool, the overlapping shapes are divided into separate objects temporarily. As you drag from one part to another, a red outline appears, showing you what the final shape will look like when the shapes are merged together, after releasing the mouse button.

● **Note:** Your final combined shapes may have a different stroke and/or fill, and that's okay. You'll change them shortly.

5 Position the pointer off the upper-left corner of the shapes again. Press the Shift key and drag from the red X in the figure, down and to the right. Release the mouse button to combine the shapes.

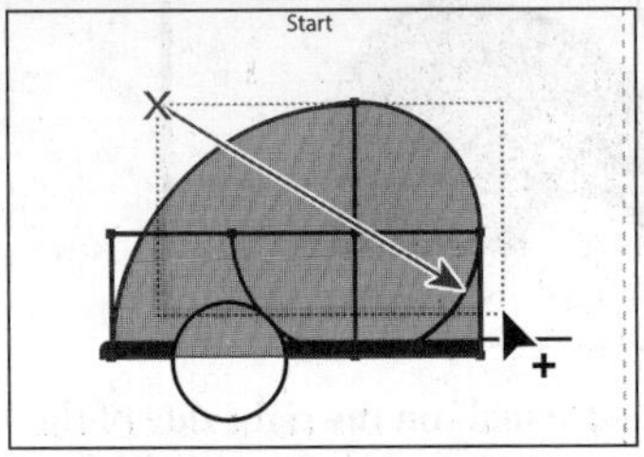

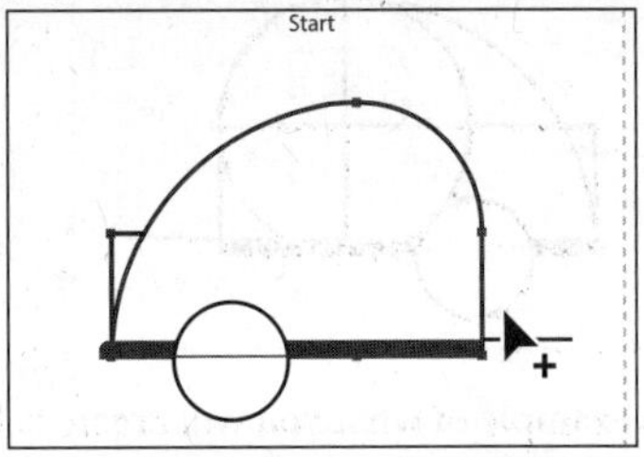

Next, you'll delete a few shapes.

● **Note:** When you position the pointer over the shapes, make sure you see the mesh within those shapes, before clicking to delete.

6 With the shapes still selected, hold down the Option (macOS) or Alt (Windows) key. Notice that, with the modifier key held down, the pointer shows a minus sign (). Click the shape on the far left to delete it. See the figure for which shape to remove.

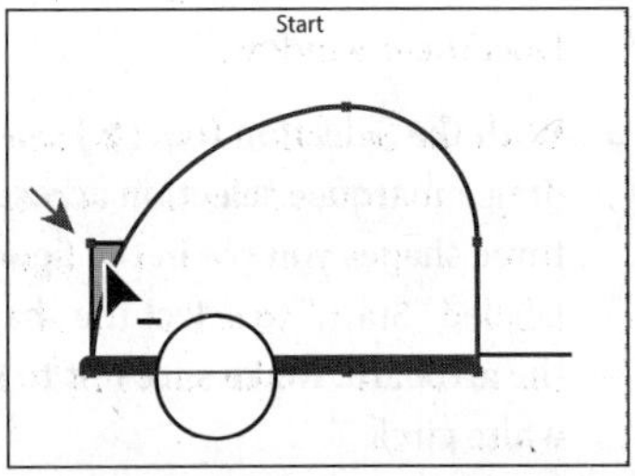

7 Select the Selection tool (). Drag across the larger shape you combined, the purple bar and the white circle to select all three shapes.

8 Select the Shape Builder tool () and move the pointer below the white circle. Hold down the Option (macOS) or Alt (Windows) key and drag through the white circle, stopping before the top of the circle to remove it from the larger shape you combined.

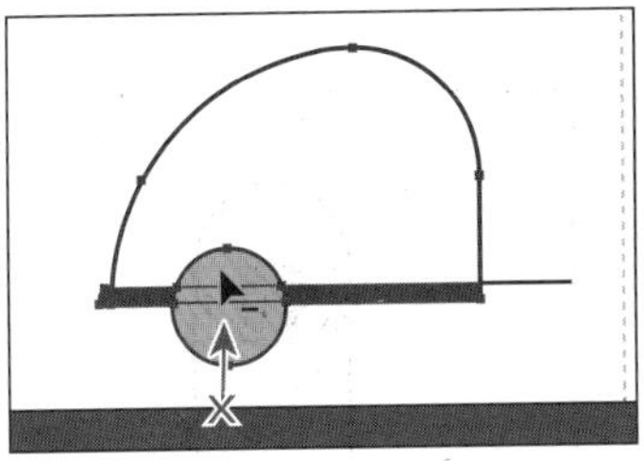

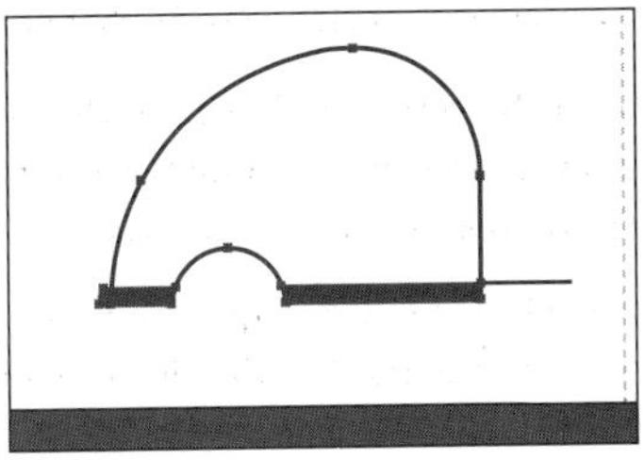

9 Choose Select > Deselect.

10 Select the Selection tool (▶), and click the edge of the larger shape to select it. Change the fill color in the Properties panel to the color named red 1 with the tooltip name that shows as "Red 1." Change the stroke weight to **0**.

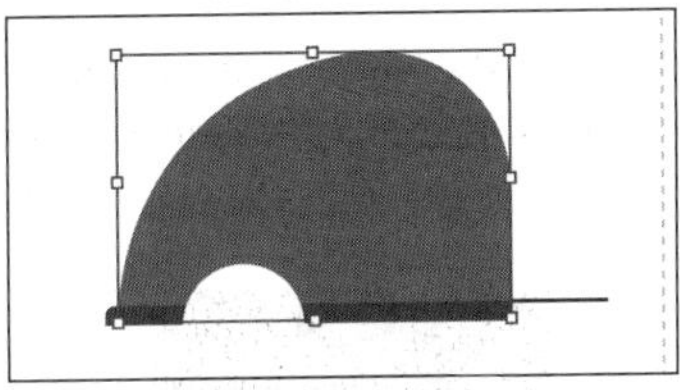

11 Drag across the red shape, purple shape, and black line to select them all.

12 Choose Object > Group.

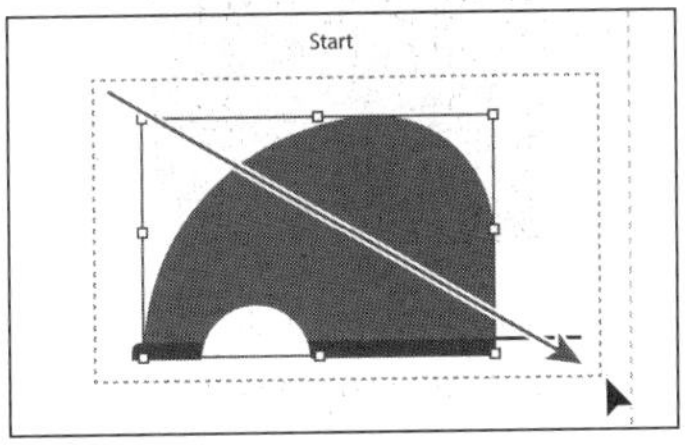

Combining objects using Pathfinder effects

Pathfinder effects, found in the Properties panel or the Pathfinder panel (Window > Pathfinder), are another way to combine shapes in different ways. When a Pathfinder effect such as Unite is applied, the original objects selected are *permanently* transformed.

1 Choose 9 Door from the Artboard Navigation menu in the lower-left corner of the Document window.

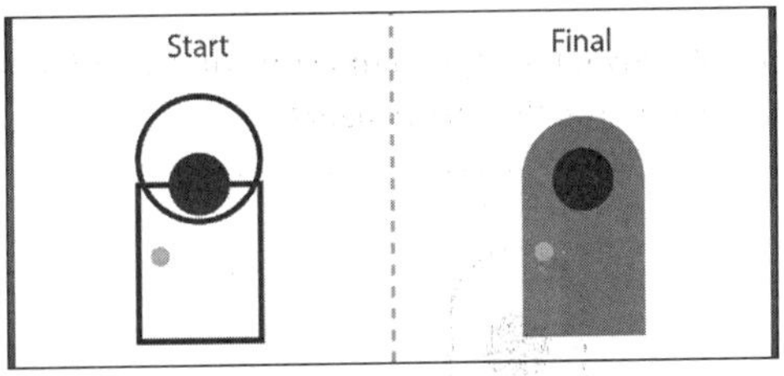

An example of what you will create is labeled "Final" on the right side of the artboard. You will work with the artwork labeled "Start" on the left. You'll combine shapes in different ways to create a single door.

2 Choose View > Fit Artboard In Window.

3 With the Selection tool (▶) selected, drag across the circle and rectangle with the black strokes to select both objects.

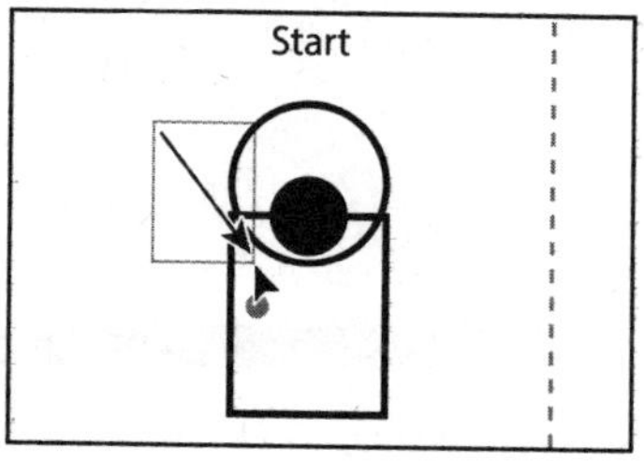

You need to create a shape that looks like the door to the right of the shapes you selected, labeled "Final." You will use the Properties panel and those shapes to create the final artwork.

● **Note:** The Unite button in the Properties panel produces a similar result as the Shape Builder tool, by combining the shapes into one.

▶ **Tip:** Clicking More Options (■) in the Pathfinder section of the Properties panel will reveal the Pathfinder panel, which has more options.

4 With the shapes selected, in the Properties panel on the right, click the Unite button (■) to *permanently* combine the two shapes.

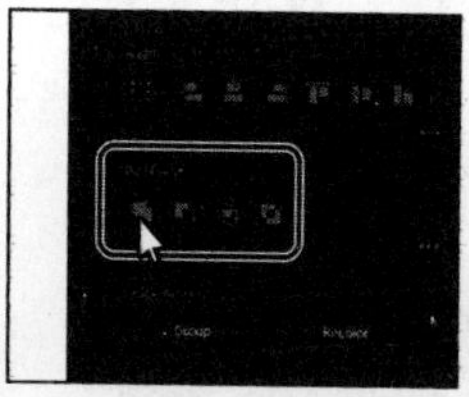

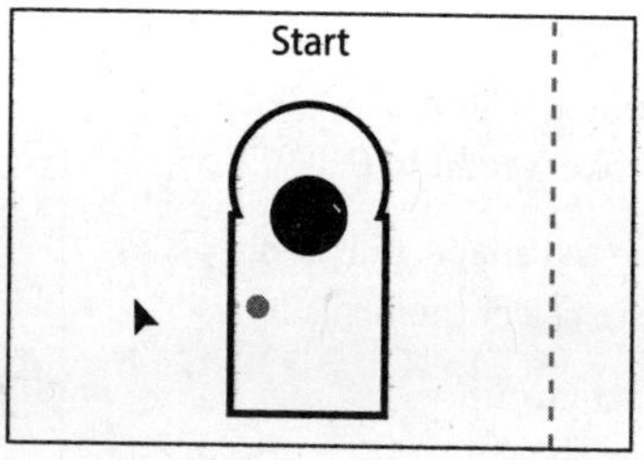

5 Choose Edit > Undo Add to undo the Unite command and bring both shapes back. Leave them selected.

Understanding Shape Modes

In the previous section, the pathfinder effect made a permanent change to the shapes. When several shapes are selected, clicking the Pathfinders that are showing in the Properties panel by default while pressing the Option (macOS) or Alt (Windows) key creates a compound shape rather than a path. The original underlying objects of compound shapes are preserved. As a result, you can still select each original object within a compound shape. Using a shape mode to create a compound shape can be useful if you think that you may want to retrieve the original shapes at a later time.

1 With the shapes still selected, hold down the Option (macOS) or Alt (Windows) key, and click the Unite button (■) in the Properties panel.

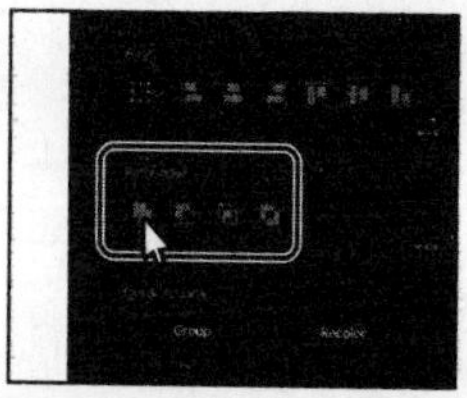

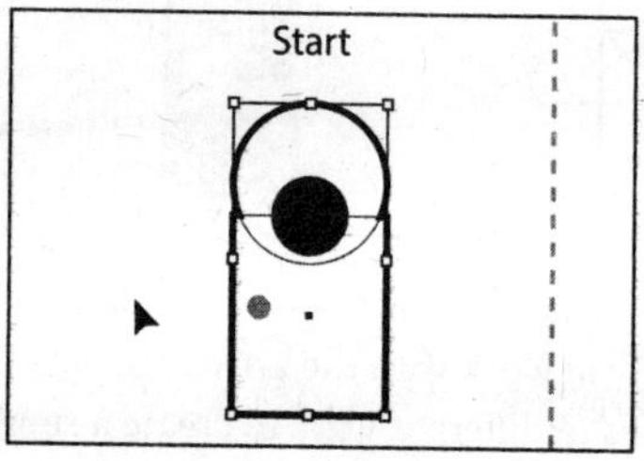

This creates a compound shape that traces the outline of what's left after the shapes are combined. You will still be able to edit both shapes separately.

2 Choose Select > Deselect to see the final shape.

3 With the Selection tool, double-click the black stroke of the newly combined shape to enter Isolation mode.

4 Click the edge of the circle at the top or drag across the path to select it.

5 Drag the selected circle from the blue dot in the center, straight down. As you drag, press the Shift key. Drag down until you see that a horizontal Smart Guide appears and the center of the circle is aligned with the top edge of the rectangle. When in position, release the mouse button and then the Shift key.

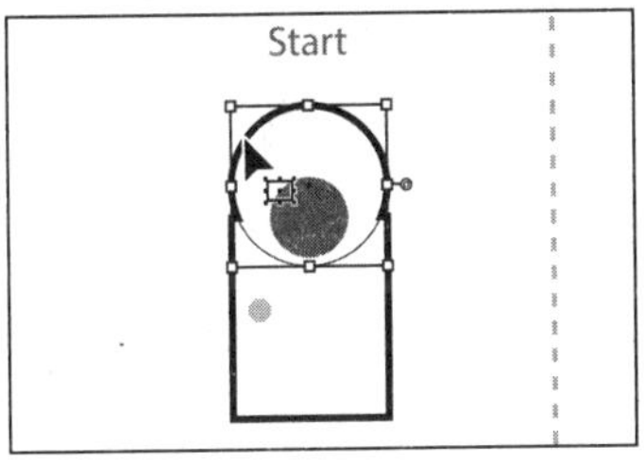

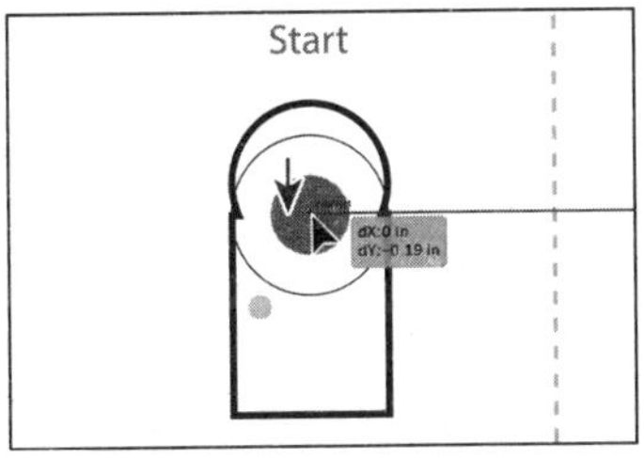

6 Press the Escape key to exit Isolation mode.

You will now expand the shape. Expanding a compound shape maintains the shape of the compound object, but you can no longer select or edit the original objects. You will typically expand an object when you want to modify the appearance attributes and other properties of specific elements within it.

7 Click away from the shape to deselect it and then click to select it again.

8 Click the Expand button in the Properties panel.

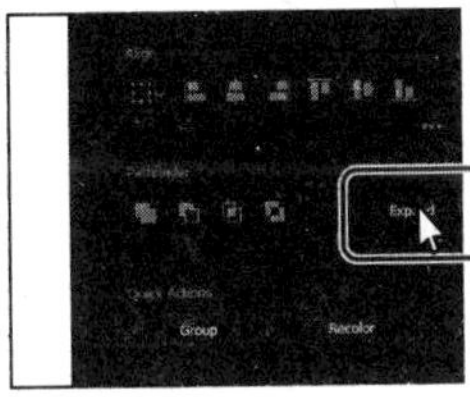

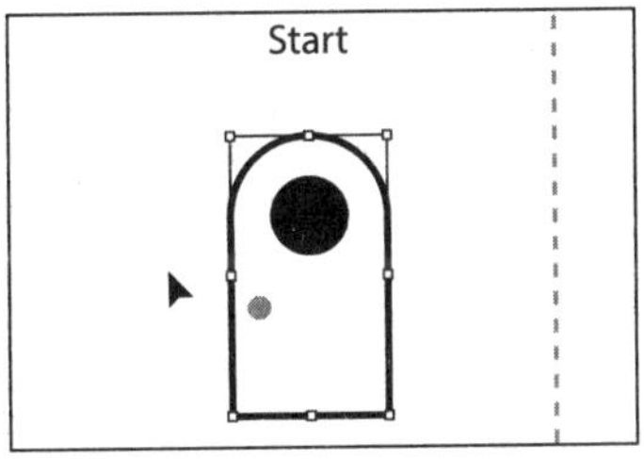

9 Change the fill color in the Properties panel to the color named Pink. Change the stroke weight to **0**.

10 Drag across the shapes that make up the door to select them all.

11 Click the Group button toward the bottom of the Properties panel to group the content together.

Tip: To edit the original shapes in a compound shape like this one, you can also select them individually with the Direct Selection tool (▶).

Note: You can also press the arrow keys to move the shape if you find it difficult to drag.

Creating the trailer

In this short section, you'll drag all of the pieces for the trailer together and group them.

1 Choose View > Zoom Out several times.

2 Press the spacebar to access the Hand tool and drag in the Document window to see the wheel, door, window, and tank artboards.

● **Note:** You may find that with the Smart Guides on, it is difficult to position the content on the trailer. You can always turn off the Smart Guides (View > Smart Guides), then turn them on when you are finished dragging the artwork.

3 With the Selection tool selected, drag the wheel, door, window, and tank artwork you created onto the trailer artwork labeled "Start." Position them like you see in the figure.

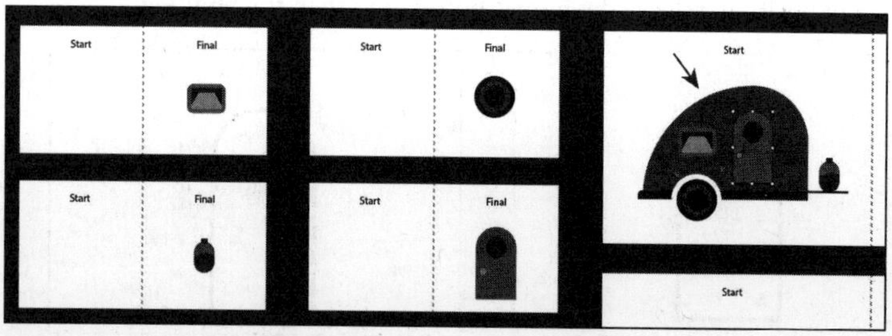

4 Drag across the trailer artwork and choose Object > Group.

Reshaping a path

In Lesson 3, "Using Shapes to Create Artwork for a Postcard," you learned about creating shapes and paths (lines). You can use the Reshape tool to stretch parts of a path without distorting its overall shape. In this section, you'll change the shape of a line, giving it a bit of curve, so you can turn it into a flame.

1 Choose 10 Flame from the Artboard Navigation menu in the lower-left corner of the Document window.

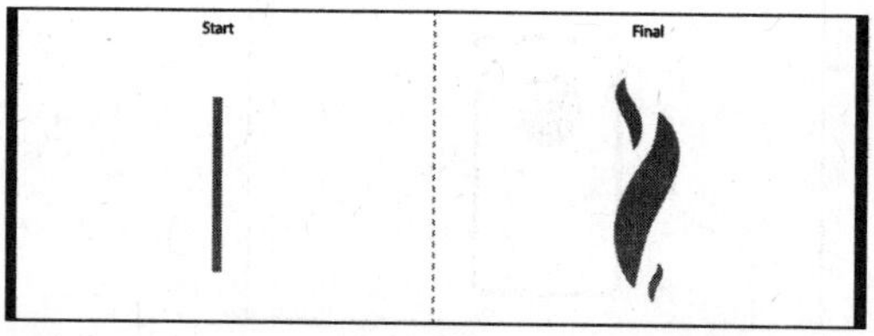

An example of what you will create is labeled "Final" on the right side of the artboard. You will work with the artwork labeled "Start" on the left. You'll reshape the straight line on the left to start.

2 Select the Selection tool (▶) and click the line labeled "Start."

3 Click and hold down the mouse button on the Scale tool (⧉) and select the Reshape tool (✓) from the tool menu.

4 Move the pointer over the path. When the pointer changes (), drag away from the path to add an anchor point and reshape the path. Move the pointer farther down the path and drag the path to the left. You can look at the flame shape labeled "Final," to the right, for guidance.

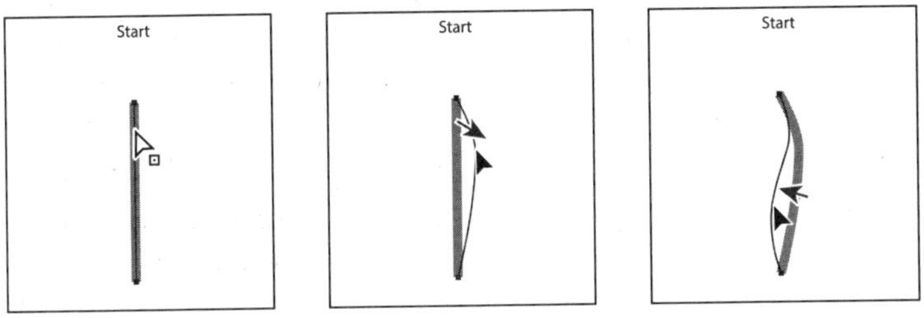

The Reshape tool can be used to drag an existing anchor point or path segment. If you drag from an existing path segment, an anchor point is created.

5 Move the pointer over the top anchor point of the path and drag it to the right a little. Leave the path selected.

All of the anchor points were selected in the path, which means the Reshape tool will adjust the entire path.

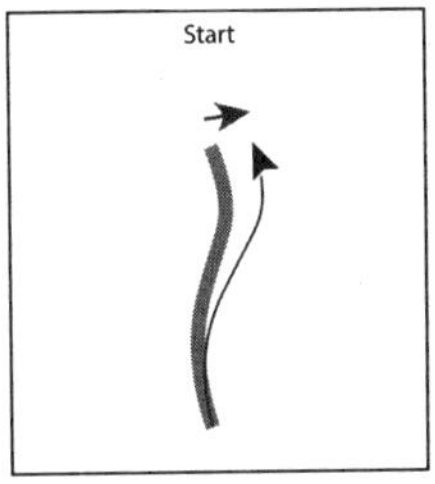

● **Note:** You can use the Reshape path on a closed path, like a square or circle, but if the entire path is selected, the Reshape tool will add anchor points and reshape the path.

● **Note:** Only selected anchor points will be adjusted when dragging with the Reshape tool.

Using the Width tool

Not only can you adjust the weight of a stroke, like you did in Lesson 3, but you can alter regular stroke widths either by using the Width tool () or by applying width profiles to the stroke. This allows you to create a variable width along the stroke of a path. Next, you will use the Width tool to adjust the path you just reshaped to look like a flame.

1 Select the Width tool () in the Tools panel. Position the pointer over the middle of the path you just reshaped, and notice that the pointer has a plus symbol next to it () when over the path. If you were to drag, you would edit the width of the stroke. Drag away from the line, to the right. Notice that, as you drag, you are stretching the stroke to the left and right equally. Release the mouse when the measurement label shows Side 1 and Side 2 at *approximately* 0.2 in.

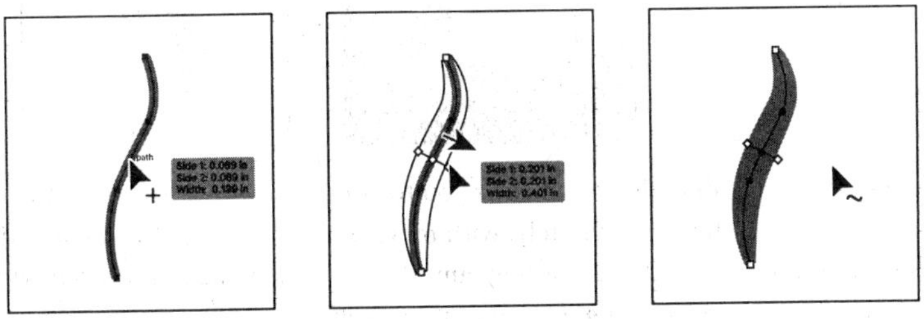

▶ **Tip:** You can drag one width point on top of another width point to create a discontinuous width point. If you double-click a discontinuous width point, the Width Point Edit dialog box allows you to edit both width points.

You just created a variable stroke on a path, not a shape with a fill. The new point on the original path that's filled with blue is called the *width point*. The lines extending from the width point are the *handles*.

2 Click in a blank area of the artboard to deselect the point.

> ▶ **Tip:** If you select a width point by clicking it, you can press Delete to remove it. If there was only one width point on a stroke, removing that point would remove the width completely.

3 Position the pointer anywhere over the path, and the new width point you just created will appear (an arrow is pointing to it in the first part of the figure below). The width point you see on the path next to the pointer is where a new point would be created if you were to click.

4 Position the pointer over the original width point, and when you see lines extending from it and the pointer changes (▶~), click and drag it up and down to see the effect on the path.

> ● **Note:** You don't have to position the pointer over the center of the line and drag to create another width point. You can drag from anywhere in the stroke area.

5 Choose Edit > Undo Width Point Change to return the width point to its original position on the path.

Aside from dragging to add a width point to a path, you can also double-click and enter values in a dialog box. That's what you'll do next.

> ▶ **Tip:** You can move the pointer over a width point, press the Option (macOS) or Alt (Windows) key, and drag to duplicate it.

6 Move the pointer over the top anchor point of the path, and notice that the pointer has a wavy line next to it (▶~) and the word "anchor" appears (see the first part of the following figure). Double-click the point to create a new width point and to open the Width Point Edit dialog box.

7 In the Width Point Edit dialog box, change the Total Width to **0 in**, and click OK.

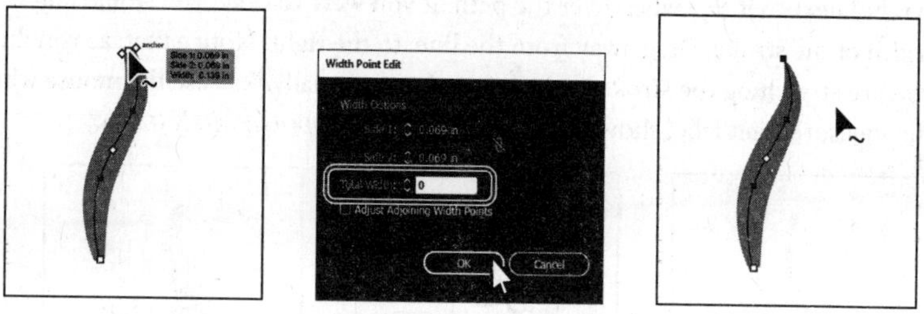

The Width Point Edit dialog box allows you to adjust the length of the width point handles together or separately, with more precision. Also, if you select the Adjust Adjoining Width Points option, any changes you make to the selected width point affect neighboring width points as well.

8 Move the pointer over the bottom anchor point of the path, and double-click. In the Width Point Edit dialog box, change the Total Width to **0 in**, and click OK.

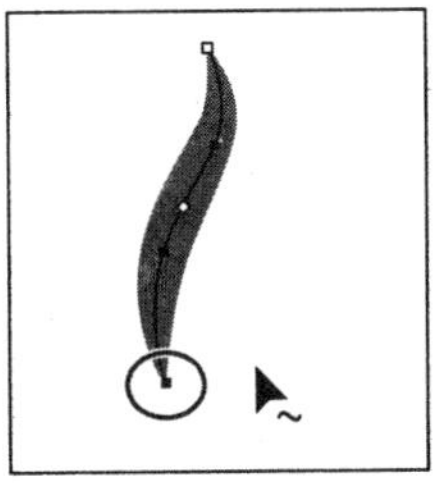

9 Move the pointer over the original width point. When the width point handles appear, drag one of them away from the center of the path to make it a little wider. Leave the path selected for the next section.

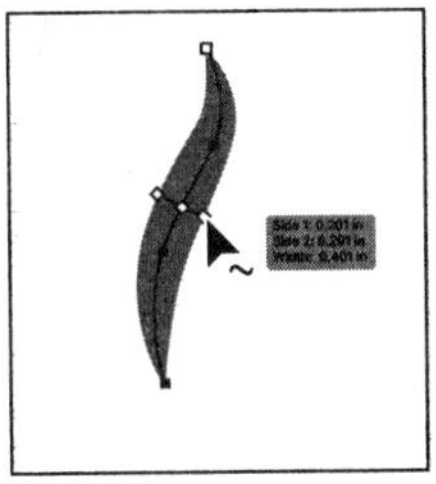

▶ **Tip:** You can select a width point and Option-drag (macOS) or Alt-drag (Windows) one of the width point handles to change one side of the stroke width.

▶ **Tip:** After defining the stroke width, you can save the variable width as a *profile* that you can reuse later, from the Stroke panel or the Control panel. To learn more about variable width profiles, search for "Painting with fills and strokes" in Illustrator Help (Help > Illustrator Help).

Finishing up the illustration

To finish the illustration, you will drag the artwork you grouped on each artboard into the main illustration on the left.

1 Select the Selection tool (▶) and, with the path selected, choose Edit > Copy and then Edit > Paste to paste a copy.

2 With the copy selected, choose Object > Path > Outline Stroke so you can more easily scale the shape without having to adjust a stroke weight.

3 Shift-drag the corner of the path to make it smaller. Release the mouse button and then the key. Drag it into position like you see in the figure.

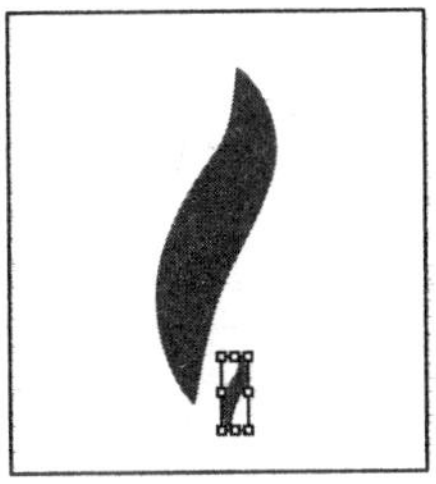

4 With the smaller copy selected, choose Edit > Copy and then Edit > Paste, scale the new copy larger, and position it like you see in the figure.

5 With the shape still selected, click the Flip Along Horizontal Axis option ( ) in the Properties panel. Drag the shape into position like you see in the figure.

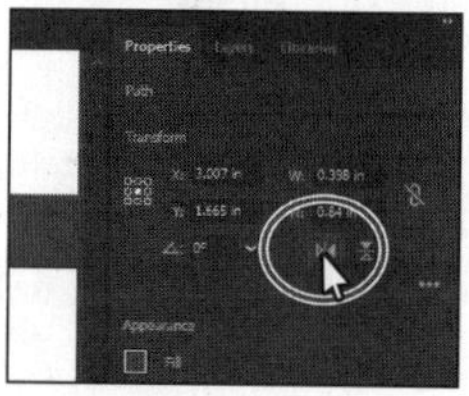
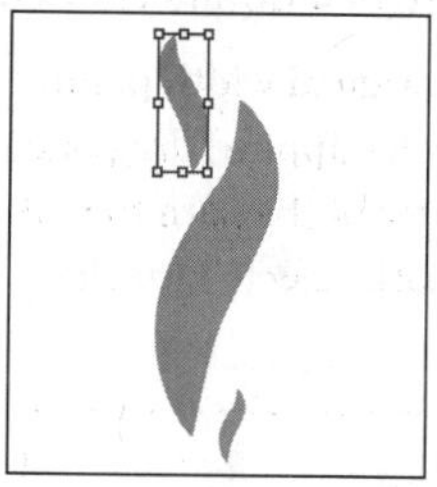

6 Drag across the three flame shapes to select them all. Choose Object > Group.

7 Choose View > Zoom Out a few times so you can see the campfire artwork to the right of the artboard. Drag the group of flames onto the fire artwork to the right of the artboard.

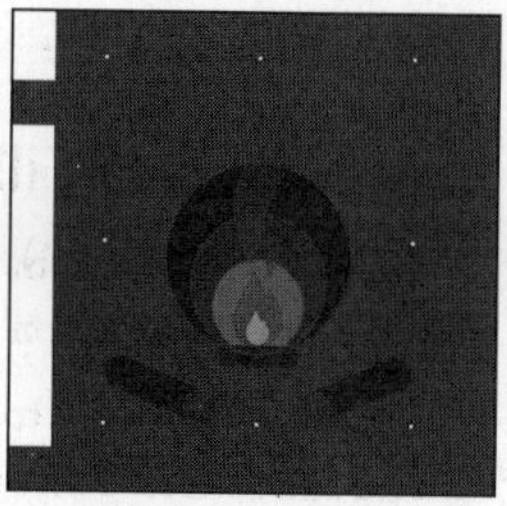

8 Drag across all of the campfire shapes to select them. Choose Object > Group.

9 Choose View > Fit All In Window.

10 Choose View > Smart Guides to turn them off.

11 Drag each of the artwork groups you created, into the main illustration like you see in the figure.

You may want to adjust the size of each group so they fit within the existing artwork better. With the Selection tool, you can hold down the Shift key and drag a corner point to resize artwork proportionally. When finished resizing, release the mouse button and then the Shift key.

12 Choose View > Smart Guides to turn them on for the next lesson.

13 Choose File > Save and then choose File > Close.

Review questions

1 Name two ways you can combine several shapes into one.

2 What is the difference between the Scissors tool (✂) and the Knife tool (✐)?

3 How can you erase with the Eraser tool (◆) in a straight line?

4 What is the main difference between shape modes and Pathfinder effects in the Properties panel or Pathfinder panel?

5 Why would you outline strokes?

Review answers

1 Using the Shape Builder tool (⊕), you can visually and intuitively merge, delete, fill, and edit overlapping shapes and paths directly in the artwork. You can also use the Pathfinder effects, which can be found in the Properties panel, the Effects menu, or the Pathfinder panel, to create new shapes out of overlapping objects. As you saw in Lesson 3, "Using Shapes to Create Artwork for a Postcard," shapes can also be combined using the Shaper tool.

2 The Scissors tool (✂) is meant to split a path, graphics frame, or empty text frame at an anchor point or along a segment. The Knife tool (✐) cuts objects along a path you draw with the tool, dividing objects. When you cut a shape with the Scissors tool, it becomes an open path. When you cut a shape with the Knife tool, they become closed paths.

3 To erase in a straight line with the Eraser tool (◆), you need to press and hold the Shift key before you begin dragging with the Eraser tool.

4 In the Properties panel, when a shape mode (such as Unite) is applied, the original objects selected are permanently transformed, but you can hold down the Option (macOS) or Alt (Windows) key, and the original underlying objects are preserved. When a Pathfinder effect (such as Merge) is applied, the original objects selected are permanently transformed.

5 Paths, like a line, can show a stroke color but not a fill color by default. If you create a line in Illustrator and want to apply both a stroke and a fill, you can outline the stroke, which converts the line into a closed shape (or compound path).

5 TRANSFORMING ARTWORK

Lesson overview

In this lesson, you'll learn how to do the following:

- Add, edit, rename, and reorder artboards in an existing document.
- Navigate artboards.
- Work with rulers and guides.
- Position and align content with Smart Guides.
- Position objects with precision.
- Move, scale, rotate, reflect, and shear objects using a variety of methods.
- Use the Free Transform tool to distort an object.
- Work with the Puppet Warp tool.

This lesson takes approximately 60 minutes to complete. Please log in to your account on peachpit.com to download the lesson files for this chapter, or go to the "Getting Started" section at the beginning of this book and follow the instructions under "Accessing the lesson files and Web Edition."

Your Account page is also where you'll find any updates to the chapters or to the lesson files. Look on the Lesson & Update Files tab to access the most current content.

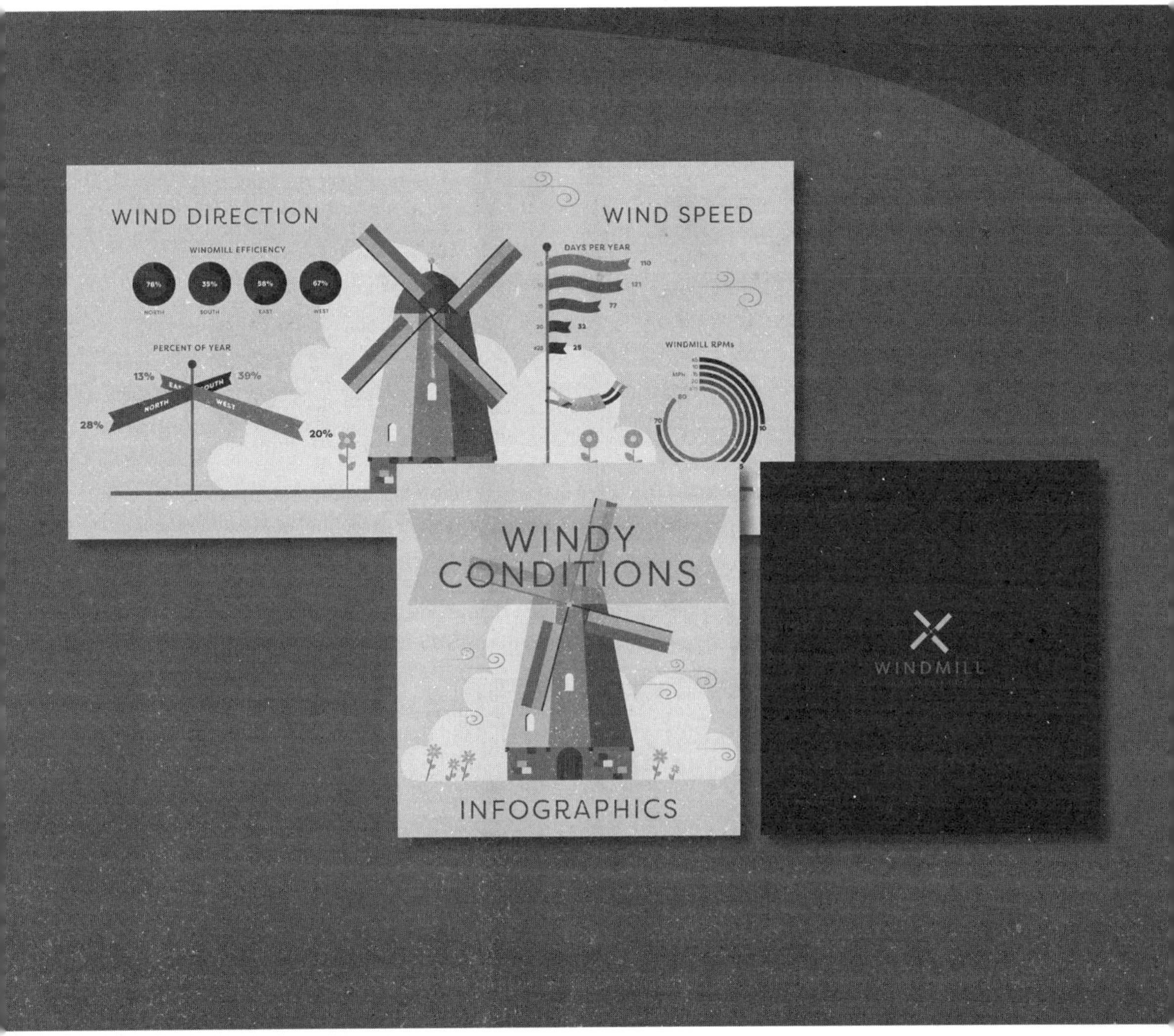

You can modify objects in many ways as you create artwork, by quickly and precisely controlling their size, shape, and orientation. In this lesson, you'll explore creating and editing artboards, the various Transform commands, and specialized tools, while creating several pieces of artwork.

Starting the lesson

In this lesson, you'll transform artwork and use it to complete an infographic. Before you begin, you'll restore the default preferences for Adobe Illustrator, and then open a file containing the finished artwork to see what you'll create.

● **Note:** If you have not already downloaded the project files for this lesson to your computer from your Account page, make sure to do so now. See the "Getting Started" section at the beginning of the book.

1 To ensure that the tools function and the defaults are set exactly as described in this lesson, delete or deactivate (by renaming) the Adobe Illustrator CC preferences file. See "Restoring default preferences" in the "Getting Started" section at the beginning of the book.

2 Start Adobe Illustrator CC.

3 Choose File > Open, and open the L5_end.ai file in the Lessons > Lesson05 folder on your hard disk.

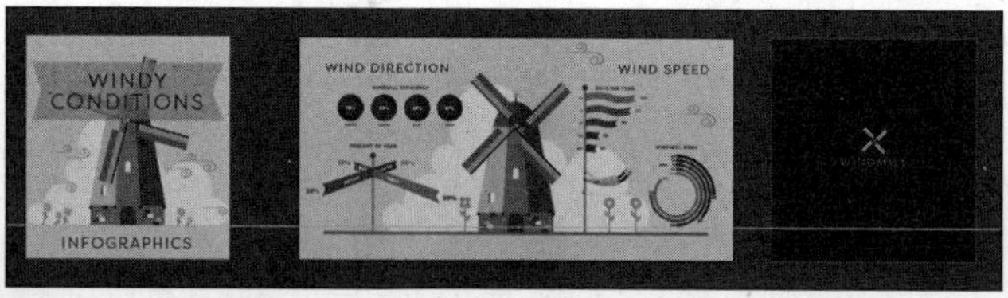

This file contains the three artboards that make up the front, back cover, and center for an infographic pamphlet. Any data presented is purely fictitious.

4 Choose View > Fit All In Window, and leave the artwork onscreen as you work.

5 Choose File > Open. In the Open dialog box, navigate to the Lessons > Lesson05 folder, and select the L5_start.ai file on your hard disk. Click Open.

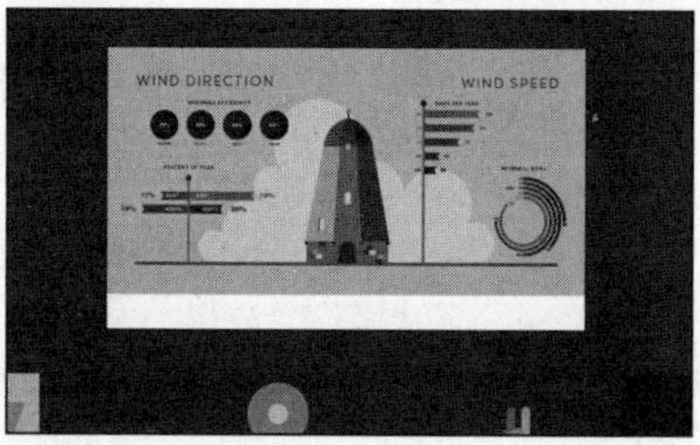

● **Note:** If you don't see Reset Essentials in the Workspace menu, choose Window > Workspace > Essentials before choosing Window > Workspace > Reset Essentials.

6 Choose File > Save As. In the Save As dialog box, name the file **Infographic.ai**, and navigate to the Lesson05 folder. Leave the Format option set to Adobe Illustrator (ai) (macOS) or the Save As Type option set to Adobe Illustrator (*.AI) (Windows) and then click Save.

7 In the Illustrator Options dialog box, leave the Illustrator options at their default settings and then click OK.

8 Choose Window > Workspace > Reset Essentials.

Working with artboards

Artboards represent the regions that can contain printable or exportable artwork, similar to pages in Adobe InDesign or artboards in Adobe Photoshop or Adobe Experience Design. You can use artboards for creating a variety of things, such as multiple-page PDF files, printed pages with different sizes or different elements, independent elements for websites or apps, or video storyboards, for instance.

Adding artboards to a document

You can add and remove artboards at any time while working in a document. You can create artboards in different sizes, resize them in Artboard Editing mode, and position them anywhere in the Document window. All artboards are numbered and can have a name assigned to them. Next, you'll add a few artboards to the Infographic.ai document.

1 Choose View > Fit Artboard In Window and then press Command+– (macOS) or Ctrl+– (Windows) twice to zoom out.

2 Press the spacebar to temporarily access the Hand tool (✋). Drag the artboard to the left to see more of the darker canvas to the right of the artboard.

3 Click the Edit Artboards button in the Properties panel on the right to enter Artboard Editing mode and to select the Artboard tool in the Tools panel.

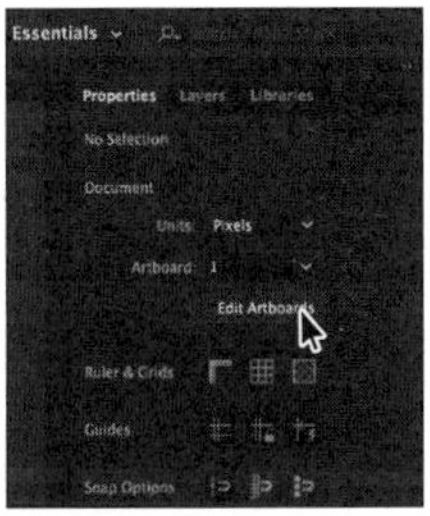

Note: You can also simply select the Artboard tool (⊡) in the Tools panel to enter Artboard Editing mode.

4 Move the pointer to the right of the existing artboard and drag down and to the right. When the measurement label next to the pointer shows an approximate width of 800 pixels and height of 800 pixels, release the mouse button.

Note: If a message appears after drawing the artboard, click Okay to close it.

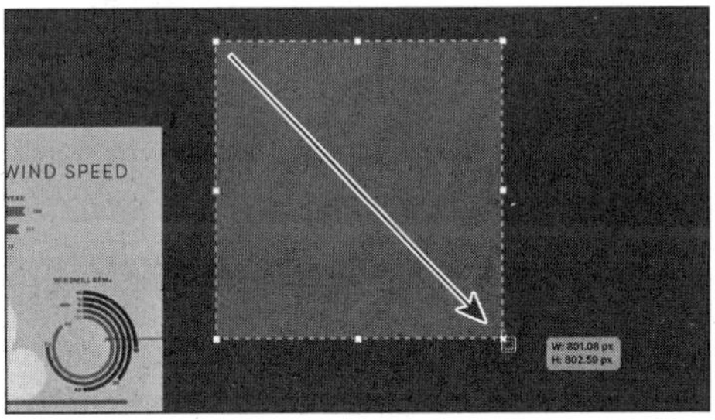

The new artboard should be selected. You can tell it's selected because of the dashed bounding box surrounding it. In the Properties panel on the right, you'll see properties for the selected artboard like position (X, Y) and size (width and height), name, and more.

5 In the Properties panel on the right, select the width value and type **800**. Select the height value and type **850** then press Return or Enter to accept the height.

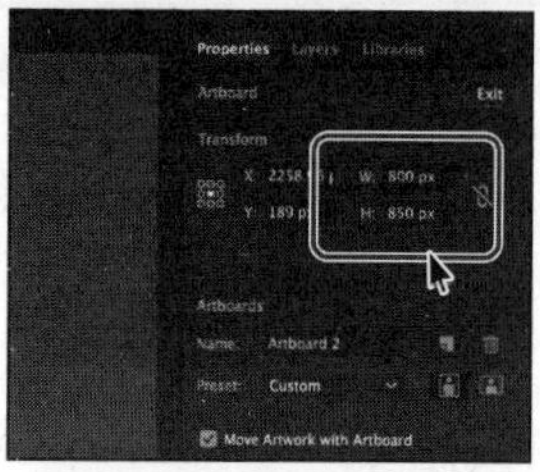

6 Change the name to **Back** in the Artboards section of the Properties panel. Press Return or Enter to make the change.

Next, you'll create another artboard that's the same size.

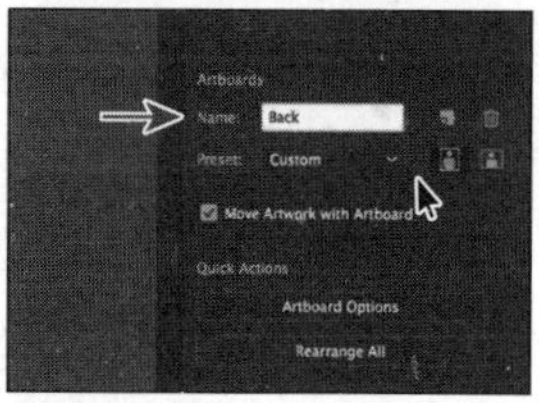

7 Click the New Artboard button ( ), in the Properties panel on the right, to create a new artboard that is the same size as the selected artboard (Back) and added just to the right of the Back artboard.

8 Change the name of the new artboard to **Front** in the Properties panel.

When editing artboards, in Artboard Editing mode, you can see the name of each artboard in the upper-left corner of the artboard.

Editing artboards

After creating artboards, you can edit or delete artboards by using the Artboard tool ( ), menu commands, Properties panel, or the Artboards panel. Next, you'll reposition and change the size of an artboard.

1 Choose View > Fit All In Window to see all of your artboards.

2 Press Command+– (macOS) or Ctrl+– (Windows) twice to zoom out.

3 While still in Artboard Editing mode, and with the Artboard tool ( ) still selected in the Tools panel, drag the artboard named Front to the left of the original artboard. Don't worry about its exact position yet, but make sure it doesn't cover any artwork.

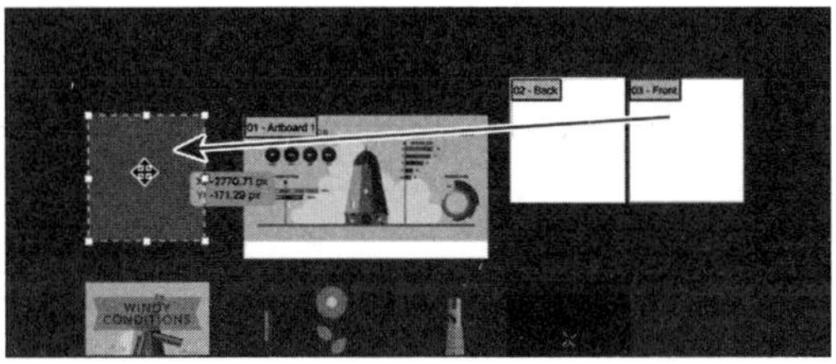

In the Properties panel on the right, in Artboard Editing mode, you'll see lots of options for editing the selected artboard. When an artboard is selected, the Preset menu lets you change the artboard to a set size. The sizes in the Preset menu include typical print, video, tablet, and web sizes. You can also switch orientation, rename, or delete the artboard.

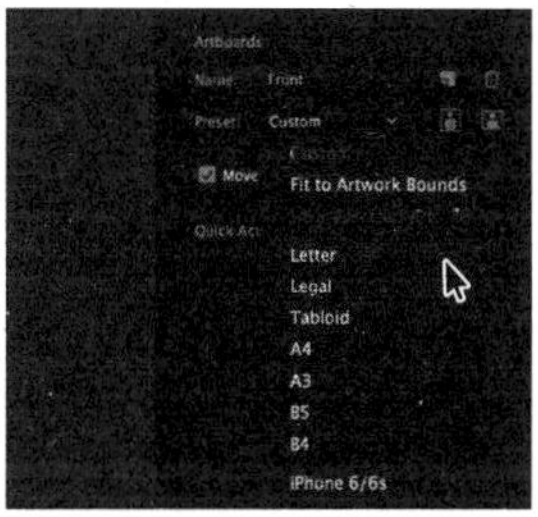

▶ **Tip:** To delete an artboard, select the artboard with the Artboard tool ( ), and either press Delete or click the Delete Artboard button ( ) in the Properties panel. You can delete all but one artboard.

4 Click in the larger, original artboard in the center and choose View > Fit Artboard In Window to fit that artboard in the Document window.

Commands such as View > Fit Artboard In Window typically apply to the selected or *active* artboard.

5 Drag the bottom-middle point of the artboard up to resize it. When the point snaps to the bottom of the blue shape, release the mouse button.

▶ **Tip:** You can also transform multiple selected artboards at one time.

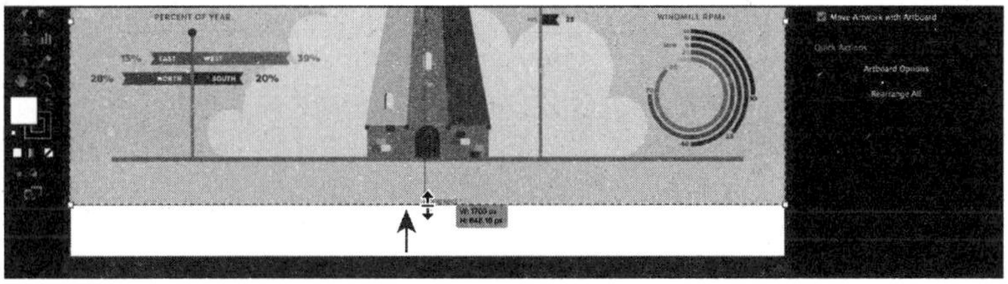

Tip: To exit Artboard Editing mode, you can also select another tool in the Tools panel besides the Artboard tool () or press Esc.

6 Click the Exit button at the top of the Properties panel to exit Artboard Editing mode.

Exiting Artboard Editing mode will deselect all artboards and also select the Selection tool () in the Tools panel on the left.

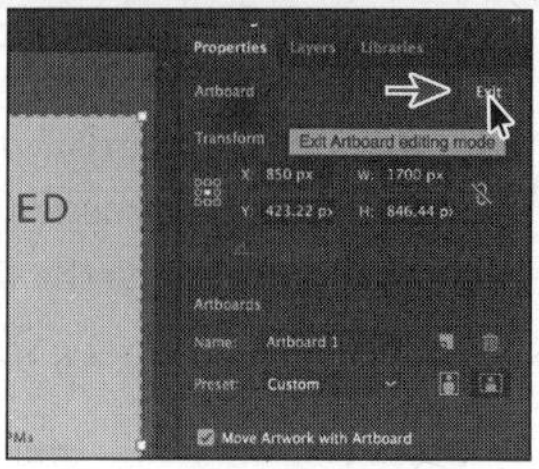

7 Choose View > Fit All In Window to fit all of the artboards in the Document window.

Aligning artboards

In order to organize the artboards in your document, maybe to keep similar artboards next to each other, you can move and align artboards to suit your working style. Next, you'll select all of the artboards and align them.

1 Select the Artboard tool () in the Tools panel on the left.

This is another way to enter Artboard Editing mode and can be useful when artwork is selected since you can't see the Edit Artboards button in the Properties panel with artwork selected.

Tip: With the Artboard tool () selected, you can press the Shift key and drag across a series of artboards to select them.

2 Click in the leftmost artboard labeled 03-Front to select it. Press the Shift key, and click in the other two artboards to the right, one at a time, to select all three.

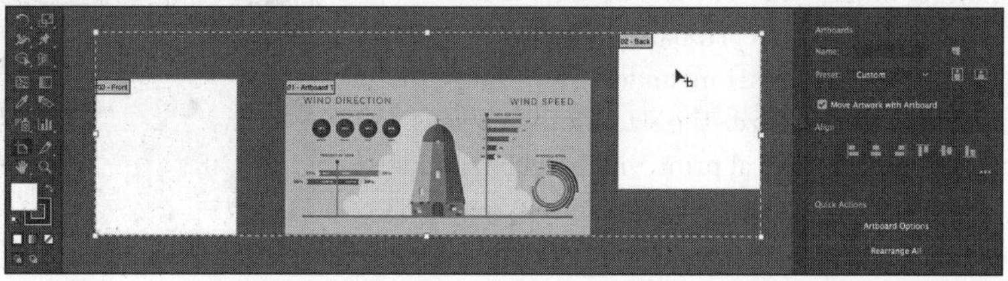

The Shift key allows you to add artboards to the selection, rather than draw an artboard, when the Artboard tool is selected.

3 Click the Vertical Align Center option () in the Properties panel on the right to align the artboards to each other. Leave the artboards selected.

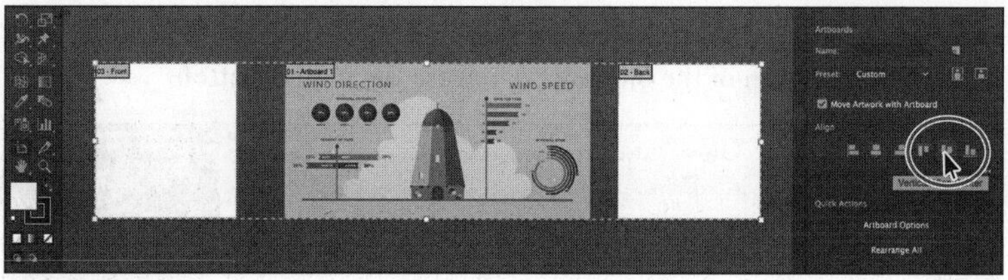

Renaming artboards

By default, artboards are assigned a number and a name, as you've seen. When you navigate the artboards in a document, it can be helpful to name them. Next, you're going to rename artboards so that the names are more useful.

1 While still in Artboard Editing mode, click to select the middle (largest) artboard. Click the Artboard Options button in the Properties panel.

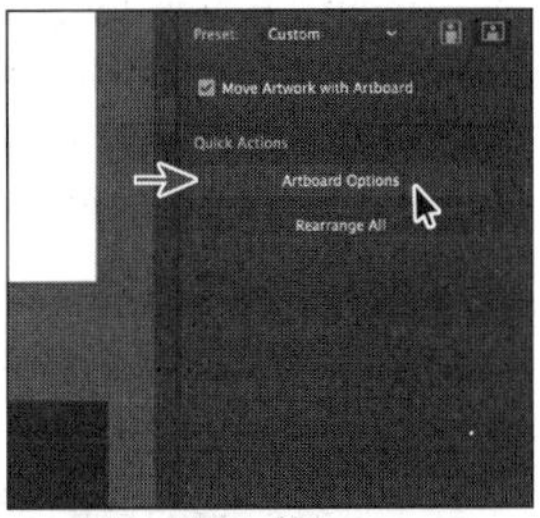

2 In the Artboard Options dialog box, change the name to **Inside**, and click OK.

The Artboard Options dialog box has a lot of extra options for artboards, as well as a few you've already seen, like width and height.

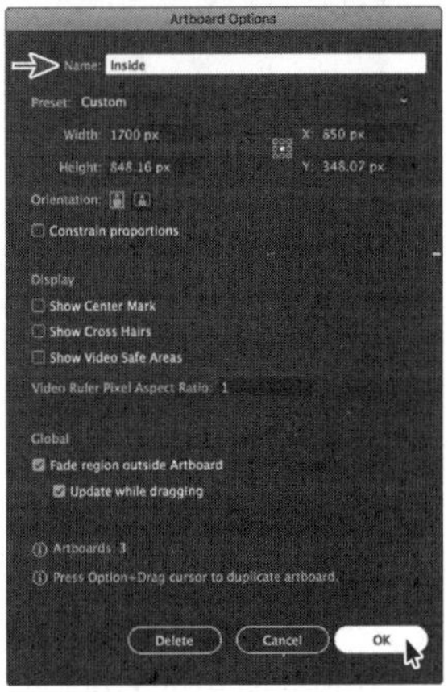

3 Choose Window > Artboards to open the Artboards panel.

The Artboards panel allows you to see a list of all of the artboards in the document. It also allows you to reorder, rename, add, and delete artboards and to choose many other options related to artboards without being in Artboard Editing mode.

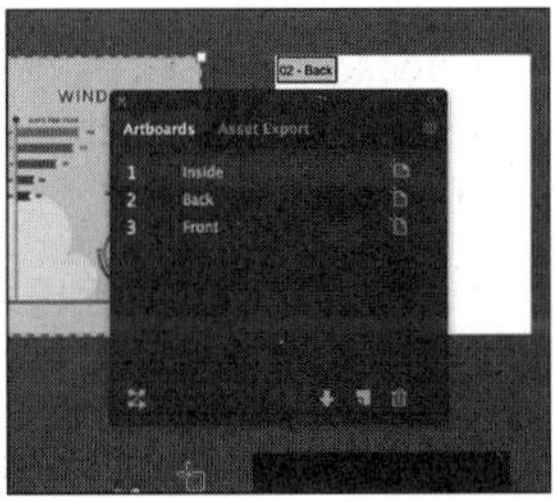

4 Choose File > Save, and keep the Artboards panel showing for the next steps.

Reordering artboards

You can navigate between artboards in your document using the Next artboard (▶) and Previous artboard (◀) buttons in the Properties panel with the Selection tool selected, nothing selected, and not in Artboard Editing mode, or below the Document window. By default, artboards are ordered according to the order in which they are created, but you can change that order. Next, you'll reorder the artboards in the Artboards panel so that if you use the Next or Previous artboard buttons, you navigate in an artboard order you determine.

1 With the Artboards panel open, double-click the number 2 to the left of the name "Back," and then double-click the number 1 to the left of the name "Inside" in the Artboards panel.

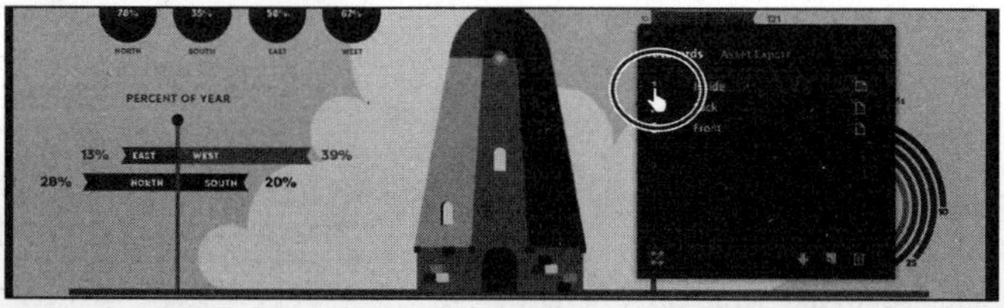

Double-clicking the number to the left of an artboard name that isn't selected in the Artboards panel makes that artboard the *active* artboard and fits it in the Document window.

▶ **Tip:** You can also reorder the artboards by selecting an artboard in the Artboards panel and clicking the Move Up (⬆) or Move Down (⬇) button at the bottom of the panel.

▶ **Tip:** The Artboard Options icon (▣) appears to the right of the name of each artboard in the Artboards panel. It not only allows access to the artboard options for each artboard but also indicates the orientation (vertical or horizontal) of the artboard.

2 Drag the "Front" artboard name up until a line appears above the artboard named "Inside." Release the mouse button.

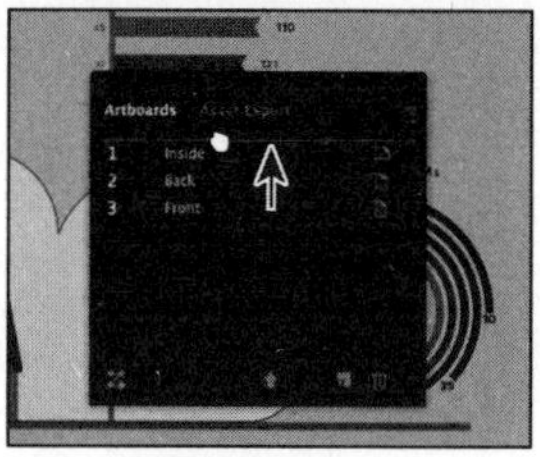

This makes the Front artboard the first artboard in the list.

3 Choose View > Fit Artboard In Window to fit the Front artboard in the Document window, if necessary.

4 Click the Exit button in the Properties panel to exit Artboard Editing mode.

5 Click the Next artboard button (▶) in the Properties panel.

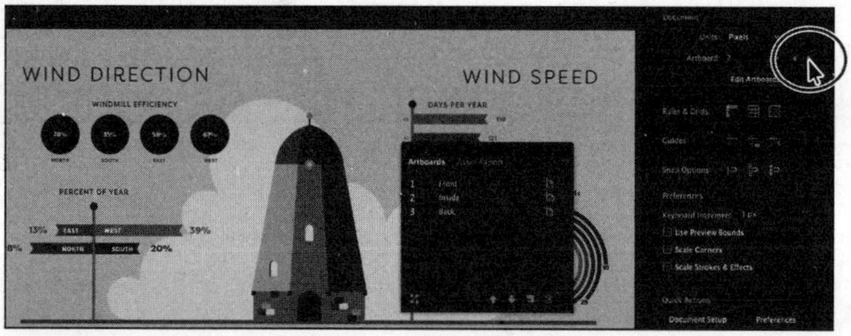

This fits the next artboard in the Artboards panel list, named "Inside," in the Document window. If you hadn't changed the order of the artboards in the Artboards panel, the Next artboard button in the previous step would have been dimmed (you couldn't select it) because the Front artboard was the last artboard in the Artboards panel list.

6 Click the X at the top of the Artboards panel group to close it.

Now that the artboards are set up, you will concentrate on transforming artwork to create the content for your project.

Rearranging artboards

In Artboard Editing mode (with the Artboard tool selected in the Tools panel), you can click the Rearrange All button in the Properties panel to open the Rearrange All Artboards dialog box.

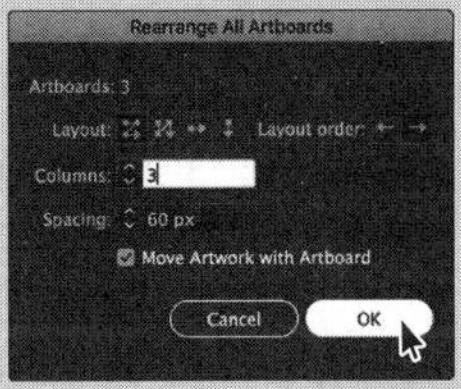

In the Rearrange All Artboards dialog box, you can arrange your artboards in columns and set the spacing between each artboard to a set amount. For instance, if you had a document with six artboards and set the columns to 3, the artboards would be arranged in two rows (or two columns) of three artboards.

You can also click the Rearrange All Artboards button at the bottom of the Artboards panel (Window > Artboards) or choose Object > Artboards > Rearrange All Artboards.

Working with rulers and guides

With the artboards set up, next you'll learn about aligning and measuring content using rulers and guides. *Rulers* help you accurately place and measure objects and distances. They appear at the top and left in the Document window and can be shown and hidden. There are two types of rulers in Illustrator: *artboard rulers* and *global rulers*. The point on each ruler (horizontal and vertical) where the 0 (zero) appears is called the *ruler origin*. Artboard rulers, which are the default rulers, set the ruler origin to the upper-left corner of the *active* artboard. Global rulers set the ruler origin to the upper-left corner of the *first* artboard, or the artboard that is at the top of the list in the Artboards panel, no matter which artboard is active. By default, rulers are set to artboard rulers, which means the origin is in the upper-left corner of the active artboard.

● **Note:** You could switch between the artboard and global rulers by choosing View > Rulers > and selecting Change To Global Rulers or Change To Artboard Rulers (depending on which option is currently chosen), but don't do that now.

Creating guides

Guides are nonprinting lines created from the rulers that help you align objects. Next, you'll create a guide so later you could more accurately align content on an artboard.

▶ **Tip:** You can also choose View > Rulers > Show Rulers.

1 With nothing selected and the Selection tool (▶) selected, click the Show Rulers button in the Properties panel to the right to show the page rulers.

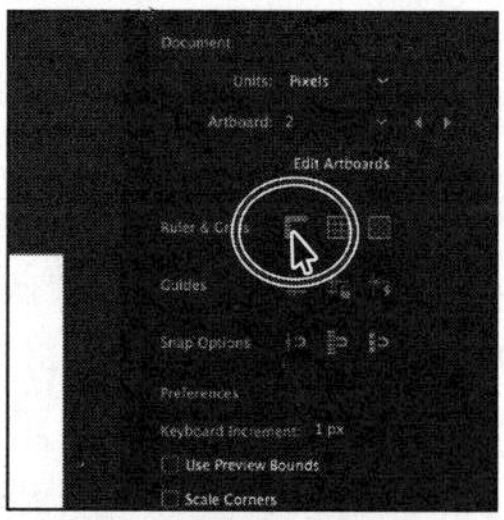

2 Choose View > Fit All In Window.

3 Click each of the artboards, and as you do, look at the horizontal and vertical rulers (along the top and left sides of the Document window).

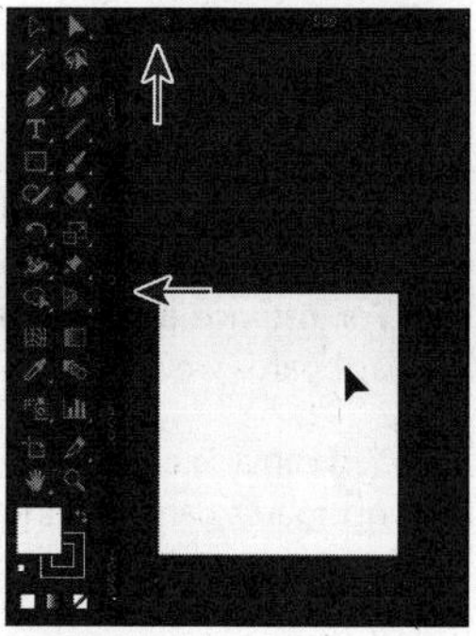

Notice that 0 (zero) for each ruler is always in the upper-left corner of the active (selected) artboard (the last artboard you clicked in). The point on each ruler (horizontal and vertical) where the 0 appears is called the *ruler origin*. By default, the ruler origin is in the upper-left corner of the *active* (selected) artboard. As you can see, the 0 point on both rulers corresponds to the edges of the active artboard.

4 With the Selection tool, click in the leftmost artboard, called "Front."

Notice the *very* subtle black outline around the Front artboard, with "1" showing in the Artboard Navigation menu (below the Document window) and in the Document section of the Properties panel to the right of the document, all of which indicate that the Front artboard is the currently active artboard. There can be only one active artboard at a time. Commands such as View > Fit Artboard In Window apply to the active artboard.

5 Choose View > Fit Artboard In Window.

That fits the active artboard in the window and the ruler origin (0,0) is in the upper-left corner of that same artboard. Next you'll create a guide on the active artboard.

6 Drag from the top ruler down, into the artboard. When the guide reaches 600 pixels on the ruler, release the mouse button. The units for this document are set at pixels.

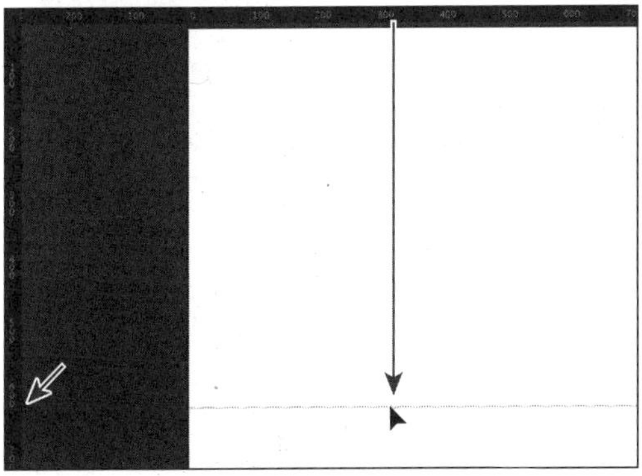

> **Tip:** Dragging from a ruler with the Shift key pressed "snaps" a guide to the measurements on the ruler.

> **Tip:** You can double-click the horizontal or vertical ruler to add a new guide.

After creating a guide, it's selected, and when selected, its color matches the color of the layer that it's associated with (darker blue in this case) when you move the pointer away from it.

7 With the guide still selected (in this case, it will be blue if selected), change the Y value in the Properties panel to **600**, and press Return or Enter.

8 Click away from the guide to deselect it.

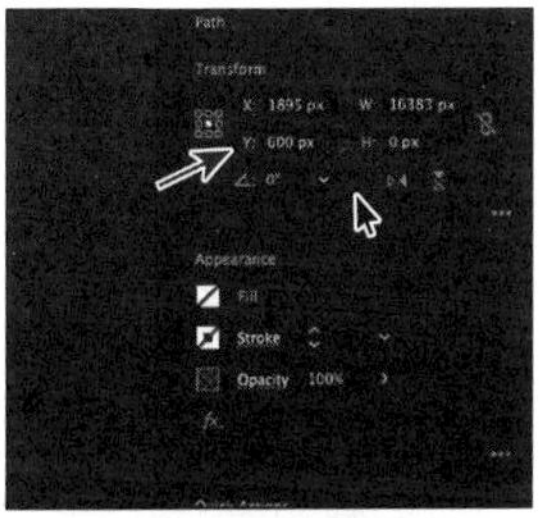

9 Click the Units menu in the Properties panel, and choose Inches to change the units for the entire document. You can now see that the rulers show inches instead of pixels.

10 Choose File > Save.

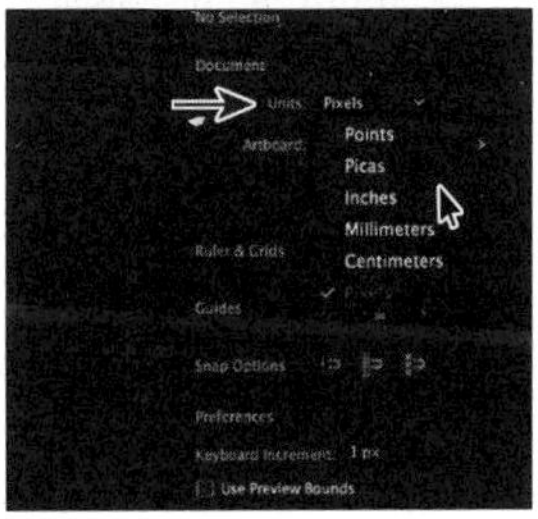

> **Tip:** To change the units for a document (inches, points, etc.), you can also right-click either ruler and choose the new units.

Editing the ruler origin

On the horizontal ruler, measurements to the right of 0 (zero) are positive and to the left are negative. On the vertical ruler, measurements below 0 (zero) are positive and above are negative. You can move the ruler origin to start the horizontal and/or vertical measurements at another location, and that's what you'll do next.

1 Choose View > Zoom Out.

2 Drag from the upper-left corner of the Document window, where the rulers intersect (■), to the lower-left corner of the Front artboard.

This sets the ruler origin (0,0) to the lower-left corner of the artboard. In other words, the measurements start in the lower-left corner of the artboard.

3 With the Selection tool (▶) selected, click on the guide to select it.

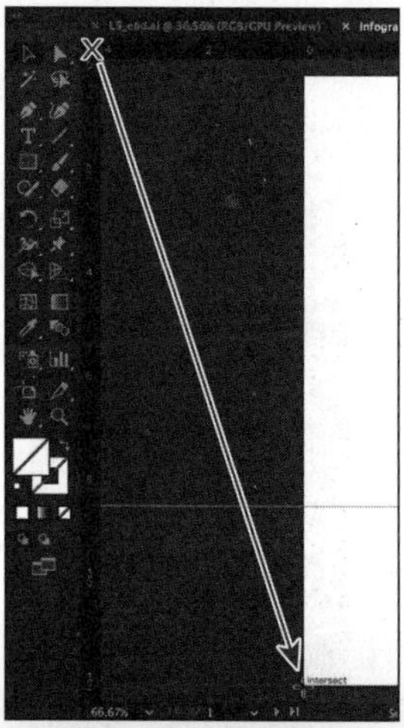

4 Look in the Properties panel on the right to see the Y value. Right now, because you moved the ruler origin (0,0), the Y shows the vertical distance from the bottom of the artboard. Change the Y value to **–1.75** (inches), and press Return or Enter.

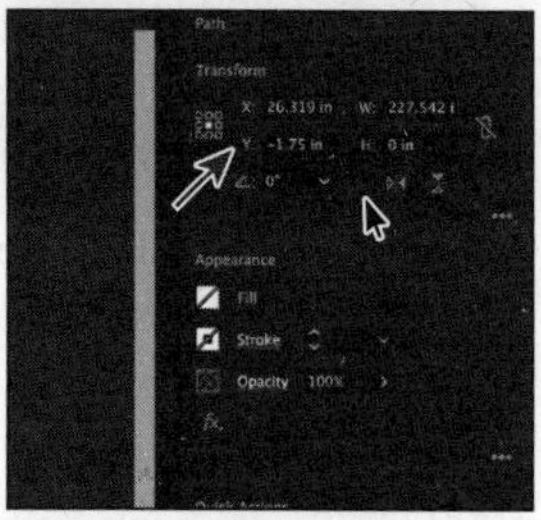

5 Position the pointer in the upper-left corner of the Document window, where the rulers intersect (■), and *double-click* to reset the ruler origin to the upper-left corner of the artboard.

6 Choose Select > Deselect to deselect the guide.

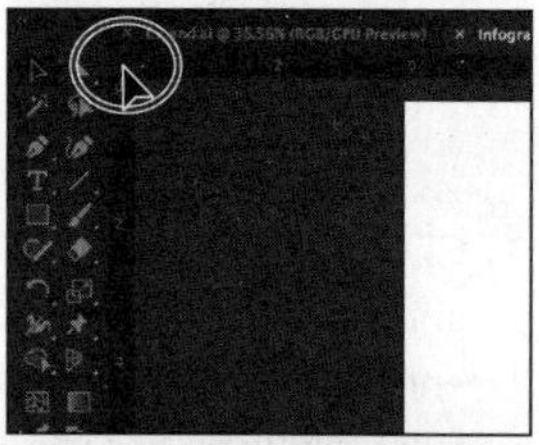

▶ **Tip:** You can also lock guides by choosing View > Guides > Lock Guides. You can hide guides by clicking the Hide Guides button in the Properties panel or pressing Command+; (macOS) or Ctrl+; (Windows).

7 Click the Lock Guides button in the Properties panel to lock all guides and prevent them from being selected.

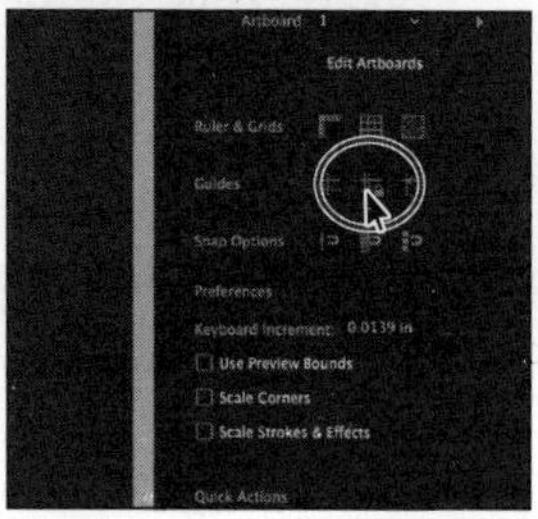

Transforming content

In Lesson 4, "Editing and Combining Shapes and Paths," you learned how to take simple paths and shapes and create more complex artwork by editing and combining that content. That was a form of transforming artwork. In this lesson, you'll learn how to scale, rotate, and transform content in other ways, using a variety of tools and methods.

Working with the Bounding Box

As you've seen in this lesson and previous lessons, a bounding box appears around selected content. You can transform content using the bounding box, but you can also turn it off. This makes it so you can't resize content by dragging anywhere on the bounding box with the Selection tool.

1 With the Front artboard showing, choose View > Zoom Out until you see the group of artwork that contains the text headline "WINDY CONDITIONS" beneath the artboards.

2 With the Selection tool (▶) selected, click to select the group. Move the pointer over the upper-left corner of the selected group. If you were to drag right now, you would resize the content.

3 Choose View > Hide Bounding Box.

This command hides the bounding box around the group and makes it so you can't resize the group by dragging anywhere on the bounding box with the Selection tool.

4 Move the pointer over the upper-left point of the group again, and drag it onto the upper-left corner of the Front artboard. You'll find that being zoomed out can make it more difficult to be precise with placement.

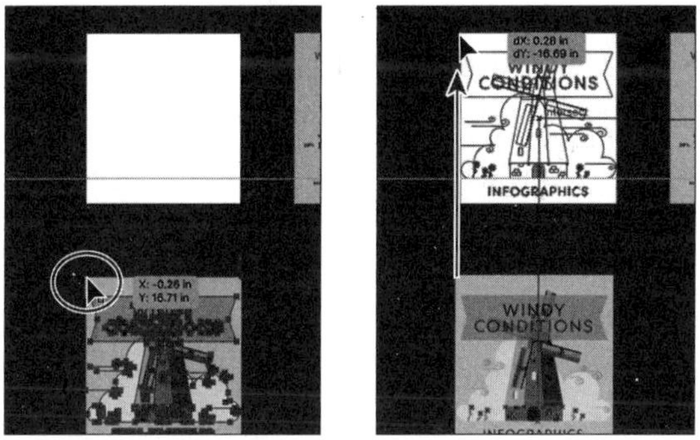

5 Choose View > Show Bounding Box.

Positioning artwork using the Properties panel

At times, you may want to position objects more precisely—relative either to other objects or to the artboard. You could use the alignment options, like you saw in Lesson 2, "Techniques for Selecting Artwork," but you can also use Smart Guides and Transform options in the Properties panel to move objects to exact coordinates on the x- and y-axes and to control the position of objects in relation to the edge of the artboard. Next, you'll add content to the background of an artboard and position that content precisely.

1 Choose View > Fit All In Window to see all of the artboards. Click in the blank artboard that's farthest to the right to make it the active artboard.

   Transformation commands, like you are about to learn, apply to the active artboard.

▶ **Tip:** You could have also aligned the content to the artboard using the alignment options available. You'll find there are at least a few ways to accomplish most tasks in Illustrator.

2 Click to select the blue shape with the WINDMILL logo on top, beneath the artboards. In the Transform section of the Properties panel, click the upper-left point of the reference point locator (). Change the X value to **0** and the Y value to **0**, and press Return or Enter.

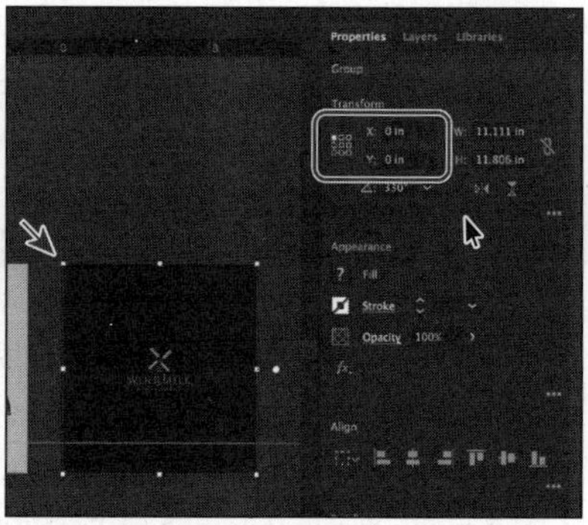

   The group of content is moved into the upper-left corner of the active artboard. The points in the Reference Point locator map to the points of the bounding box for the selected content. For instance, the upper-left reference point refers to the upper-left point of the bounding box.

3 Choose Select > Deselect and then choose File > Save.

Scaling objects

So far in this book, you've scaled most content with the selection tools. In this part of the lesson, you'll use several other methods for scaling artwork.

1 Press Command+– (macOS) or Ctrl+– (Windows) (or View > Zoom Out), if you need, to see the person in the raincoat off the bottom edge of the artboards.

2 With the Selection tool () selected, click the artwork of the person in the yellow raincoat.

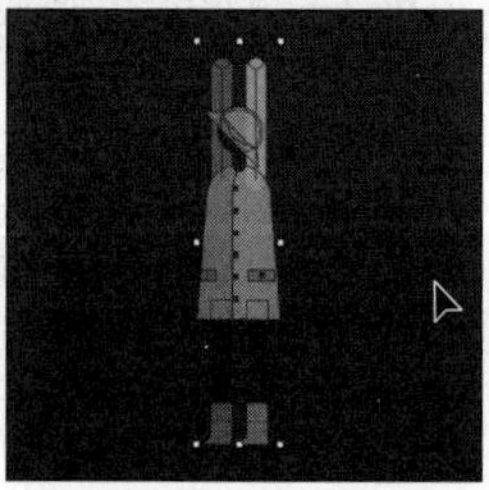

3 Press Command++ (macOS) or Ctrl++ (Windows) a few times to zoom in.

4 In the Properties panel, click the center reference point of the reference point locator ( ), if it's not selected, to resize from the center. Ensure that Constrain Width And Height Proportions is set ( ), type **30%** in the Width (W) field, and then press Enter or Return to decrease the size of the artwork.

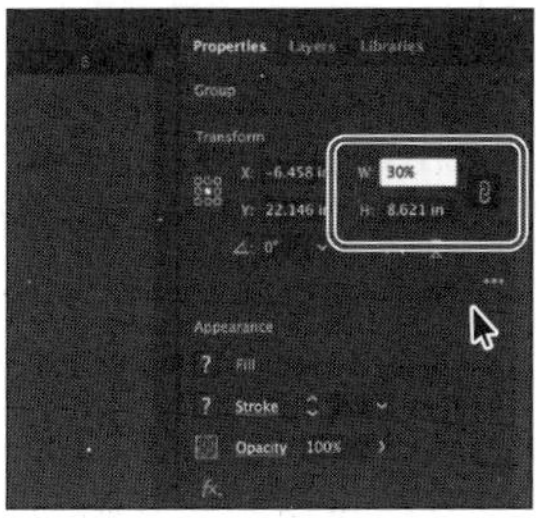

▶ **Tip:** When typing values to transform content, you can type different units such as percent (%) or pixels (px), and they will be converted to the default unit, which is inches (in) in this case.

5 Choose View > Hide Edges so you hide the inside edges.

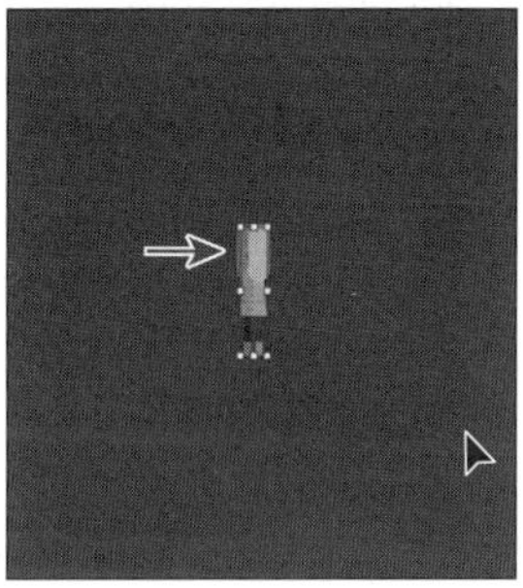

Notice that the artwork is smaller, but the arms of the person are still the same width. That's because they are a path with a stroke applied. By default, strokes and effects, like drop shadows, are *not* scaled along with objects. For instance, if you enlarge a circle with a 1-pt stroke, the stroke remains 1 pt. By selecting Scale Strokes & Effects before you scale—and then scaling the object—that 1-pt stroke would scale (change) relative to the amount of scaling applied to the object.

6 Choose View > Show Edges so you show the inside edges again.

7 Choose Edit > Undo Scale.

8 In the Properties panel, click Show More ( ) in the Transform section to see more options. Select Scale Strokes & Effects. Type **30%** in the Width (W) field and then press Enter or Return to decrease the size of the artwork.

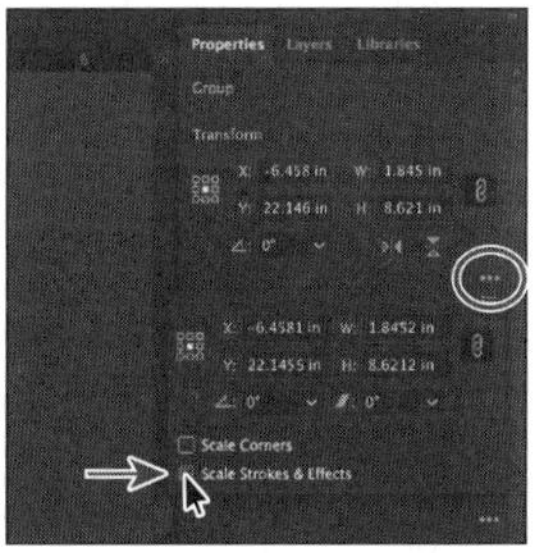

● **Note:** The figure shows selecting the Scale Strokes & Effects option only.

Now, the stroke applied to the paths that make up the arms, are scaled as well.

9 Press the spacebar to select the Hand tool, and drag to the right so you can see the flower to the left of the person.

10 With the Selection tool ( ) selected, click to select the flower artwork.

In the Tools panel on the left, you should see the Scale tool ( ). The Scale tool is used to scale content by dragging. For a lot of the transform tools, like the Scale tool, you can also double-click the tool to edit selected content in a dialog box. This is similar to choosing Object > Transform > Scale.

▶ **Tip:** You could also choose Object > Transform > Scale to access the Scale dialog box.

11 Double-click the Scale tool (⧉) in the Tools panel. In the Scale dialog box, change Uniform to **20%**, and select Scale Strokes & Effects, if it isn't already selected. Toggle Preview on and off to see the change in size. Click OK.

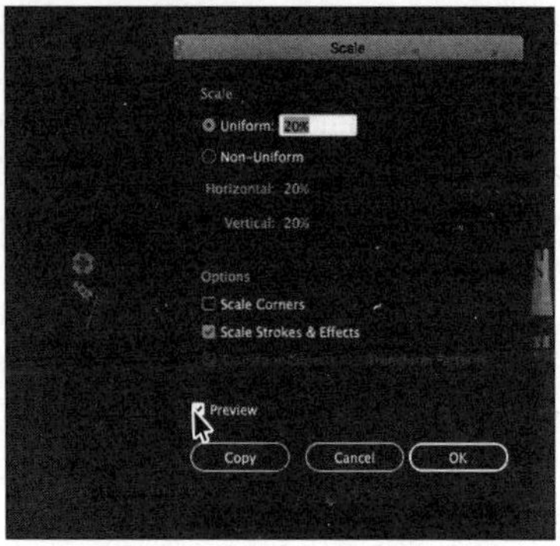

This method of scaling artwork may be useful, for instance, if there is a lot of overlapping artwork, when precision matters, you need to scale content non-uniformly, and more.

12 Select the Selection tool, and drag the flower up onto the artboard, just above the gray line that the windmill and other artwork is sitting on. You may need to zoom out.

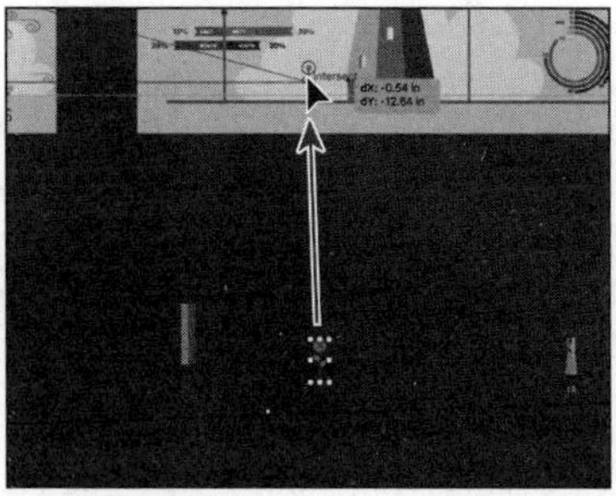

13 Choose View > Fit Artboard In Window.

14 Press the Option key (macOS) or Alt key (Windows), and drag the flower to the right. Release the mouse button and then the key to make a copy. Do this several times to place copies along the line on the artboard.

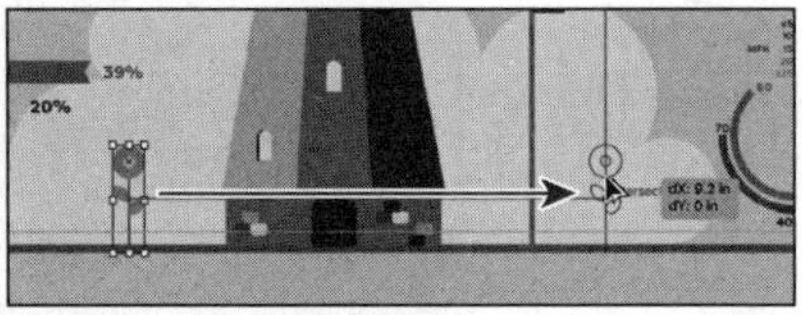

Reflecting objects

▶ **Tip:** You could also choose Object > Transform > Reflect to access the Reflect dialog box.

When you *reflect* an object, Illustrator flips the object across an invisible vertical or horizontal axis. In a similar way to scaling and rotating, when you reflect an object, you either designate the reference point or use the object's center point, by default. Next, you'll copy artwork and use the Reflect tool (▷◀) to flip artwork 90° across an axis.

1 Choose View > Fit All In Window.

2 Select the Zoom tool (🔍) in the Tools panel, and drag from left to right across the curly green shape below the artboards to zoom in.

3 Select the Selection tool (▶), and click to select the curly green shape.

4 Choose Edit > Copy and then choose Edit > Paste In Place to create a copy on top of the selected shape.

5 Select the Reflect tool (▷◀), which is nested within the Rotate tool (↺) in the Tools panel. Click the straight part of the path to set the invisible axis that the shape will reflect around, rather than the center, which is the default.

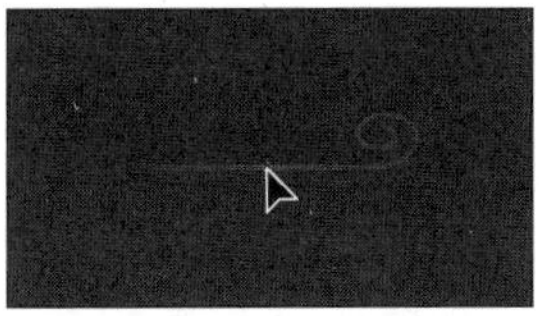

6 With the artwork still selected, position the pointer off the right edge and drag clockwise. As you drag, press the Shift key to constrain the rotation to 45° as the artwork is reflected. When the artwork looks like the figure, release the mouse button and then release the modifier key.

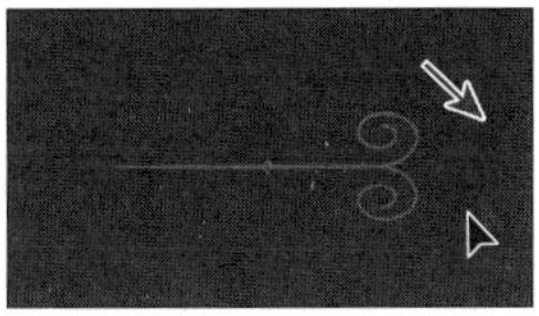

7 Select the Selection tool (▶) in the Tools panel, and with the shape still selected, click More Options (•••) in the Transform area of the Properties panel and make sure Scale Strokes & Effects is *not* selected.

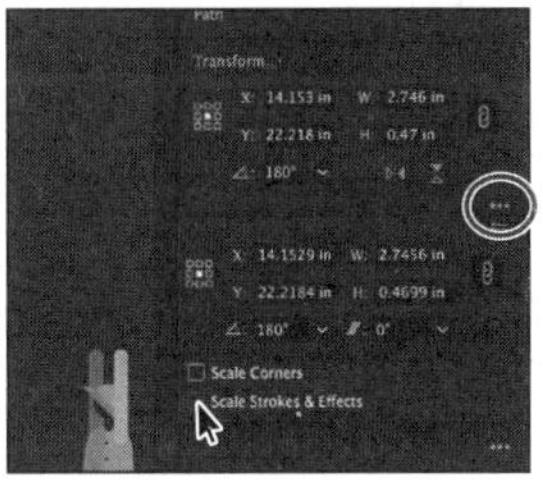

8 Drag the lower-right point of the bounding box away from the center to make the shape larger.

9 Drag across the two curly shapes and choose Object > Group to keep them together.

10 Choose View > Fit All In Window.

11 Drag the group onto the middle artboard.

12 Press the Option key (macOS) or Alt key (Windows) and drag the group to another area of the artboard. Release the mouse button and then the key to make a copy. You can do this several times to place copies around the artboard, if you like.

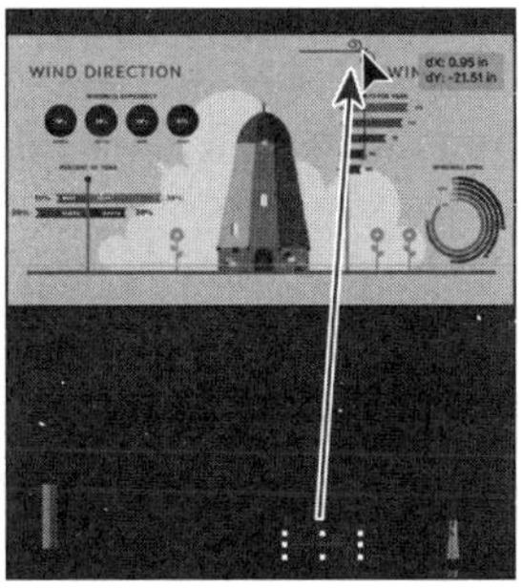

▶ **Tip:** If all you want to do is flip content in place, you can also click either the Flip Along Horizontal Axis button or Flip Along Vertical Axis button in the Properties panel.

▶ **Tip:** You can set the reference point, reflect, and even copy in one step. With the Reflect tool (▷◀) selected, Option-click (macOS) or Alt-click (Windows) to set the reference point and to open the Reflect dialog box, where you can set options and copy.

▶ **Tip:** If you want to copy artwork and reflect artwork as you drag, begin dragging artwork with the Reflect tool. As you drag, hold down the Option (macOS) or Alt (Windows) key. When the artwork is where you want it, release the mouse button and then the keys. Pressing Shift+Option (macOS) or Shift+Alt (Windows) will copy the reflected artwork and constrain the reflection angle to 45 degrees.

Rotating objects

There are lots of ways to rotate artwork, including methods that range from more precise to more freeform rotation. In previous lessons, you learned that you can rotate selected content with the Selection tool. By default, objects are rotated around a designated reference point in the center of content. In this part of the lesson, you'll learn about the Rotate tool and the Rotate command.

1 Choose View > Fit All In Window.

2 With the Selection tool (▶) selected, click to select the artwork of the person in the yellow raincoat. Press Command++ (macOS) or Ctrl++ (Windows) a few times to zoom in.

3 Move the pointer off of one of the corners of the bounding box, and when the rotate arrow (↰) appears, click and drag counterclockwise to rotate it. As you drag, press the Shift key to constrain the rotation to 45 degrees. When you see 90 degrees in the measurement label next to the pointer, release the mouse button and then the key.

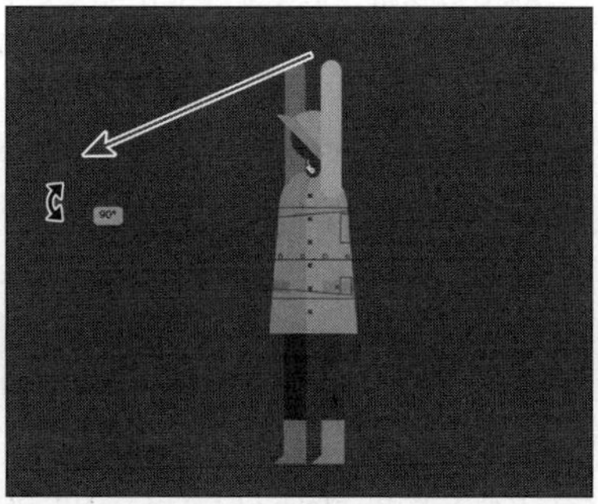

The Selection tool rotates content around the center, by default. Next, you'll use the Rotate tool, which allows you to rotate around a different point.

4 Press the spacebar to access the Hand tool, and drag to the right to see the group to the far left of the person (see the following figure).

5 With the Selection tool selected, click to select the group.

6 Select the Rotate tool (↺) in the Tools panel (it's under the Reflect tool [▷◀]). Position the pointer on the bottom edge of the selected artwork, and click to set the reference point (where it will rotate around). Look at the figure for where to click.

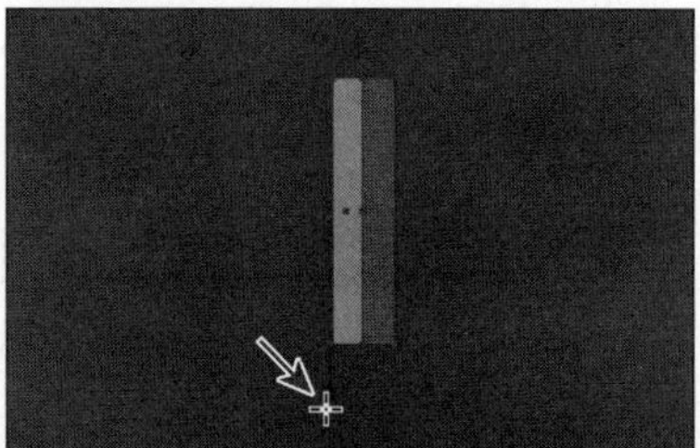

By default, the rotate-around point is in the center of selected artwork. The Rotate tool allows you to rotate content around a different reference point.

7 Move the pointer off the right side of the selected artwork and begin dragging clockwise. As you drag, press Option+Shift (macOS) or Alt+Shift (Windows) to copy the artwork as you rotate it, and constrain the rotation to 45 degrees. Release the mouse button and then the keys when you see –90 degrees in the measurement label.

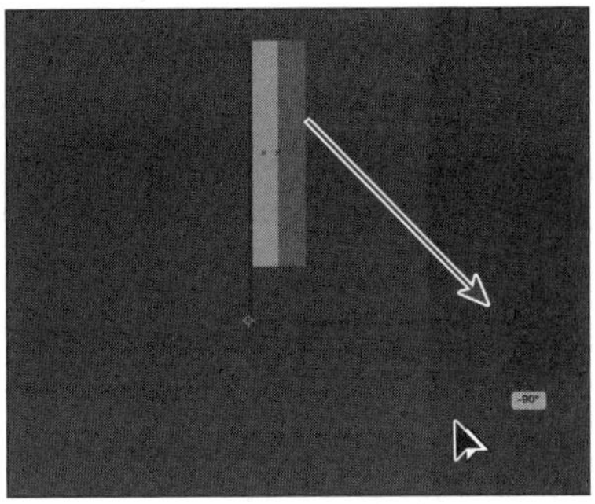

The Properties panel (or Control panel or Transform panel) is another place to rotate artwork precisely. In the Transform panel, you can always see the angle of rotation and change it later for individual objects.

● **Note:** The measurement label you see may look different than the figure, and that's okay.

8 Choose Object > Transform > Transform Again, *twice*, to repeat the previous transformations on the selected shape.

9 Select the Selection tool (▶), and drag across all four groups to select them.

10 Choose Object > Group.

11 With the group still selected, double-click the Rotate tool in the Tools panel. In the Rotate dialog box that appears, change the Angle value to **45°**, and click OK.

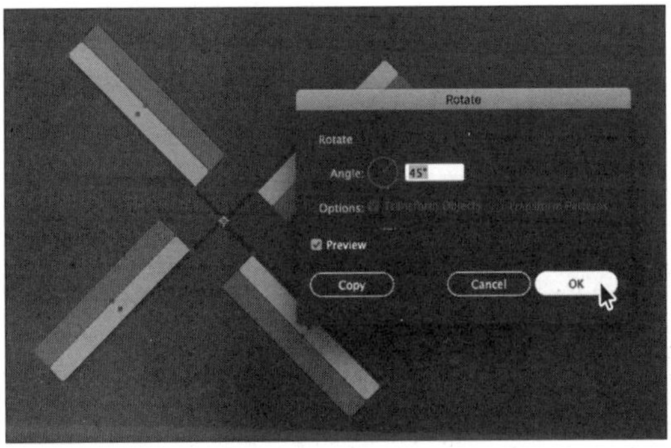

▶ **Tip:** After transforming content using various methods, including rotation, you will notice that the bounding box may be rotated. You can choose Object > Transform > Reset Bounding Box to reset the bounding box around the artwork again.

12 Choose View > Fit All In Window.

13 With the Selection tool (▶) selected, drag the selected group up, on top of the windmill artwork.

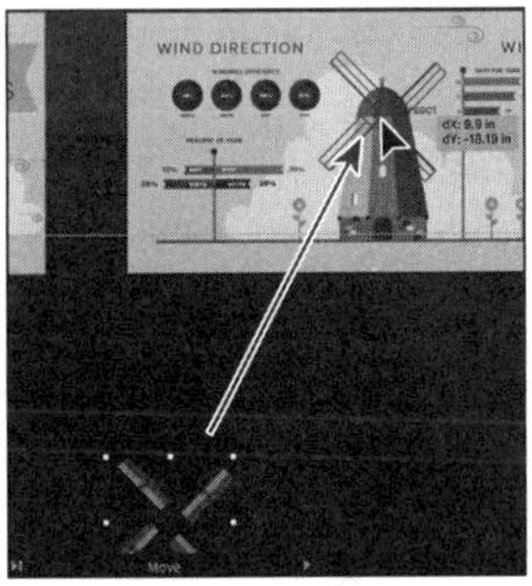

Distorting objects with effects

● **Note:** To learn more about effects, see Lesson 12, "Exploring Creative Uses of Effects and Graphic Styles."

You can distort the original shapes of objects in different ways, using various tools. Now you'll distort part of the flower and other artwork using effects. These are different types of transformations because they are applied as effects, which means you could ultimately edit the effect later or remove it in the Appearance panel.

1 Select the Selection tool (▶), and click one of the flowers. Press Command++ (macOS) or Ctrl++ (Windows) several times to zoom in closely.

2 Double-click the flower group to enter isolation mode; then click to select the larger orange circle.

3 Click the Effect button (fx) in the Properties panel.

4 Choose Distort & Transform > Pucker & Bloat in the menu that appears.

5 In the Pucker & Bloat dialog box, select Preview, and drag the slider to the right to change the value to roughly 35%, which distorts the shape. Click OK.

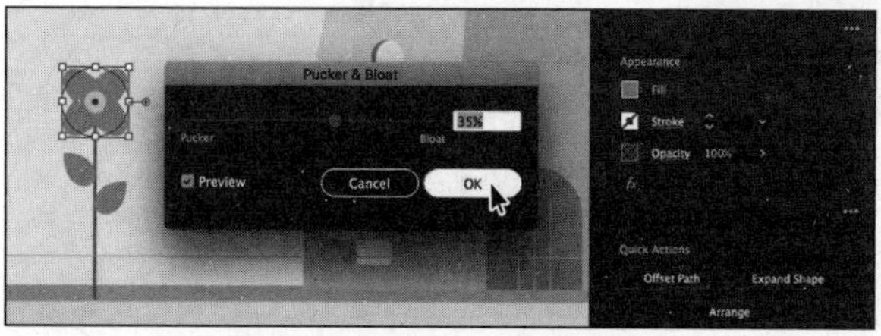

Effects you apply to shapes are live, which means they can be edited or removed at any time. You can access the effect(s) applied to selected artwork in the Appearance panel (Window > Appearance).

6 Press Esc to exit Isolation mode.

7 Press the spacebar, and drag to the left to see the DAYS PER YEAR flags.

8 Click to select the top flag shape. You may need to zoom out.

9 Click the Effect button (fx) in the Properties panel, and choose Distort & Transform > Twist.

10 In the Twist dialog box, change Angle to **20**, select Preview to see the effect, and then click OK.

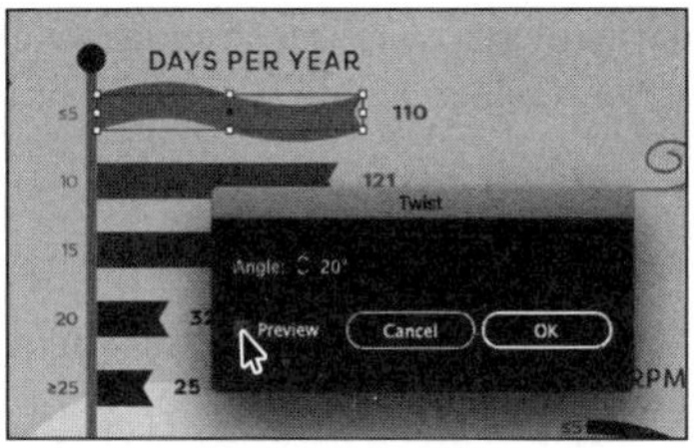

11 Click the banner below the selected banner; then press the Shift key, and click the remaining three banner shapes to select them all.

12 Choose Effect > Apply Twist.

Choosing Apply Twist applies the last applied effect with the same options. If you were to choose Effect > Twist, the last applied effect would be applied, but the dialog box would open so you could set options.

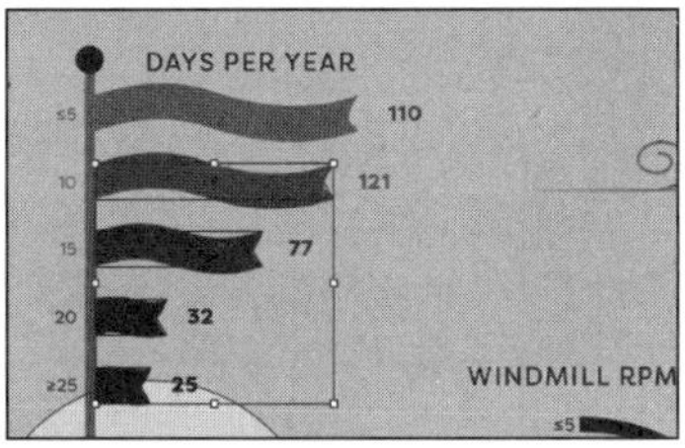

Transforming with the Free Transform tool

The Free Transform tool (![]) is a multipurpose tool that allows you to distort an object, combining functions like moving, scaling, shearing, rotating, and distorting (perspective or free). The Free Transform tool is also touch-enabled, which means you can control transformation using touch controls on certain devices.

● **Note:** To learn more about touch controls, search for "Touch Workspace" in Adobe Help (Help > Illustrator Help).

1 Press the spacebar to select the Hand tool, and drag in the Document window until you see the "PERCENT OF YEAR" text to the left of the windmill.

2 With the Selection tool (▶) selected, click to select the shape labeled "EAST WEST."

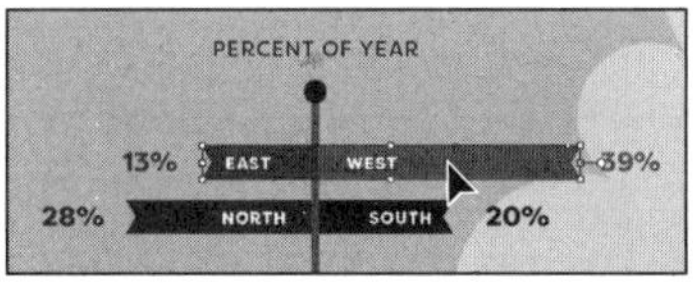

3 Click and hold down on the Puppet Warp tool (✱), and select the Free Transform tool (![]) in the Tools panel.

With the Free Transform tool selected, the Free Transform widget appears in the Document window. This widget, which is free-floating and can be repositioned, contains options to change how the Free Transform tool works. By default, the Free Transform tool allows you to move, shear, rotate, and scale objects. By selecting other options, like Perspective Distort, you can change how the tool works.

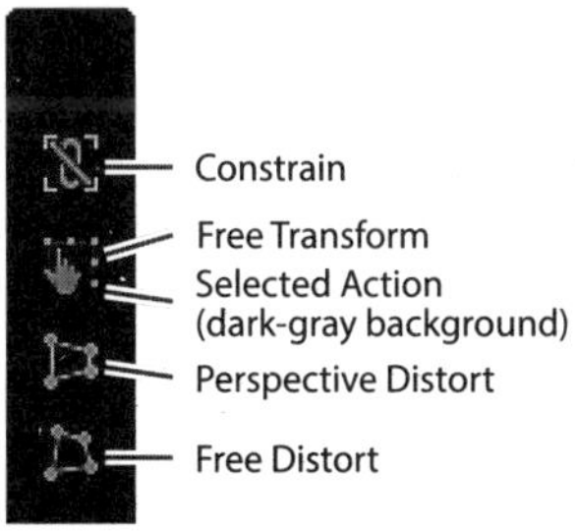

● **Note:** To learn more about the options for the Free Transform tool, search for "Free Transform" in Adobe Help (Help > Illustrator Help).

4 With the Free Transform tool selected, click the Perspective Distort option ( ) in the Free Transform widget (circled in the following figure).

5 Choose View > Smart Guides to temporarily turn them off.

With the Smart Guides off, you can adjust the artwork without it snapping to everything else in the document.

6 Position the pointer over the lower-right corner of the bounding box, and the pointer changes in appearance ( ). Drag down a little, until it looks something like the figure.

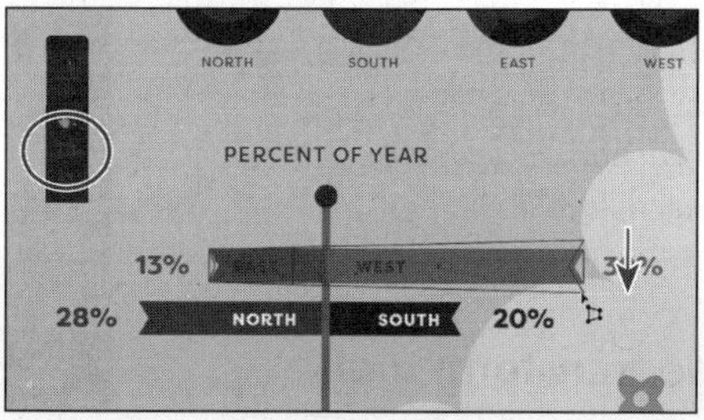

7 Press the Command key (macOS) or Ctrl key (Windows) to temporarily select the Selection tool and click to select the shape labeled "NORTH SOUTH." Release the key to return to the Free Transform tool.

8 With the Perspective Distort option ( ) in the Free Transform widget still selected, drag the lower-left point down a little, until it looks like the figure. Leave the group selected.

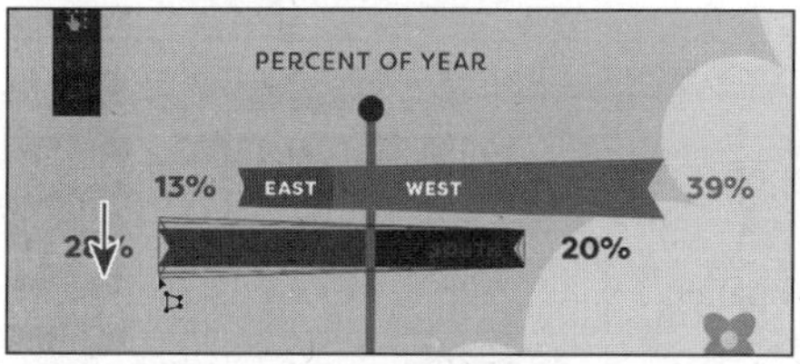

9 Choose View > Smart Guides to turn them back on.

10 Choose File > Save.

Shearing objects

Shearing an object slants, or skews, the sides of the object along the axis you specify, keeping opposite sides parallel and making the object asymmetrical. Next, you'll apply shear to the selected sign artwork.

1 With the group labeled "NORTH SOUTH" still selected, select the Shear tool ( ), nested within the Scale tool ( ) in the Tools panel.

2 Move the pointer off the right side of the group, press the Shift key to constrain the artwork to its original width, and drag up. Release the mouse button and then the Shift key when you see a shear angle (S) of *approximately* –20.

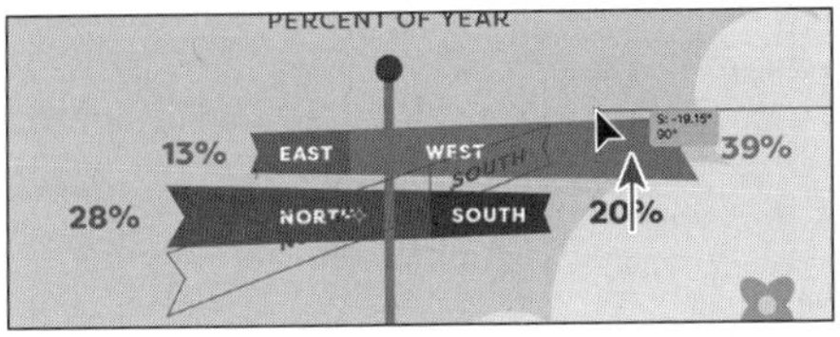

3 Press the Command key (macOS) or Ctrl key (Windows) to temporarily select the Selection tool. Click to select the shape labeled "EAST WEST." Release the key to return to the Shear tool.

4 Press the Shift key to constrain the artwork to its original width, and drag from off the right side of the group, down. Release the mouse button and then the Shift key when you see a shear angle (S) of *approximately* –160.

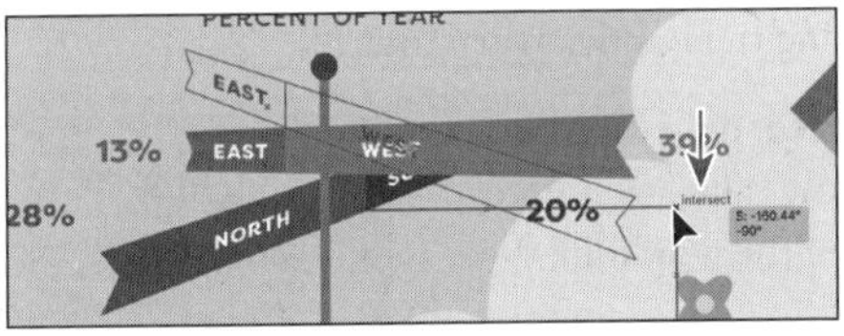

5 Select the Selection tool ( ), and drag the "NORTH SOUTH" group and then the "EAST WEST" group so they are each aligned with the sign pole like you see in the following figure.

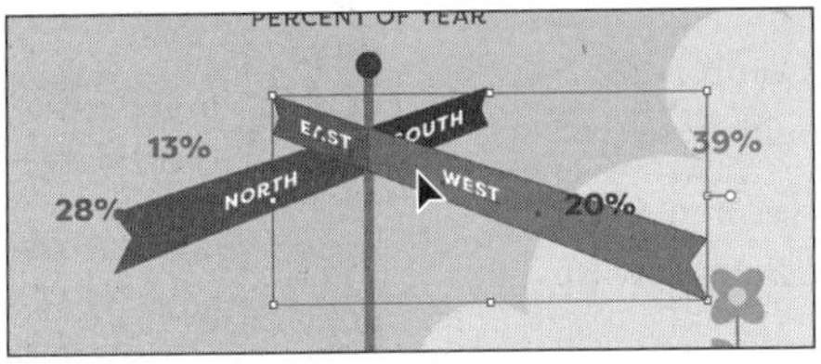

6 Click the NORTH SOUTH group to select it. Click the Ungroup button in the Properties panel to the right.

7 Choose Select > Deselect.

Tip: You can set a reference point, shear, and even copy in one step. With the Shear tool ( ) selected, Option-click (macOS) or Alt-click (Windows) to set the reference point and to open the Shear dialog box, where you can set options and even copy if necessary.

8 Click the NORTH text to select that group.

9 Choose Object > Arrange > Bring To Front.

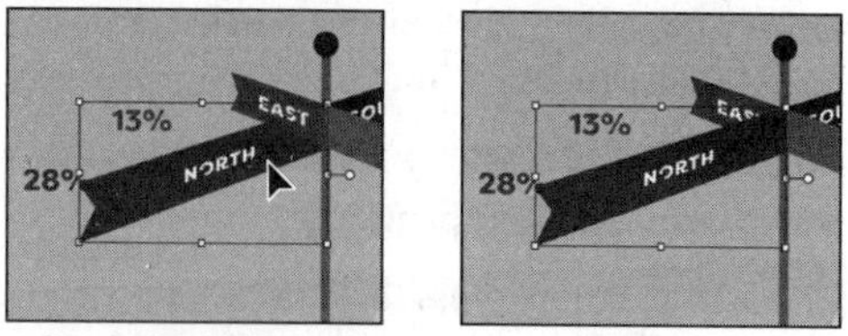

10 Drag each of the numbers with percent (%) next to the ends of the signs. I moved the flower to the right as well.

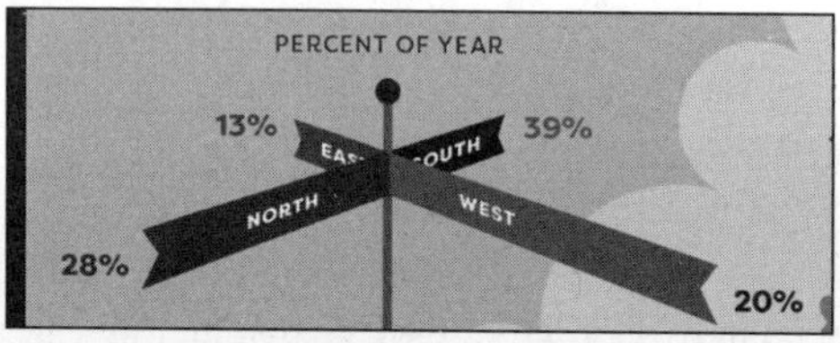

11 Choose View > Fit All In Window and then choose File > Save.

Using Puppet Warp

In Illustrator, you can easily twist and distort artwork naturally, into different positions, using the Puppet Warp tool. In this section, you'll warp the artwork of the person in the yellow raincoat using the Puppet Warp tool.

● **Note:** It's difficult to see exactly where to drag the person in the figure. If you look at the figures on the next page, you may get a better idea of what I mean by "Make sure the hands of the person are directly on the flagpole."

1 With the Selection tool (▶) selected, drag the artwork of the person in the yellow rain jacket onto the artboard above, to the right of the windmill, like you see in the figure.

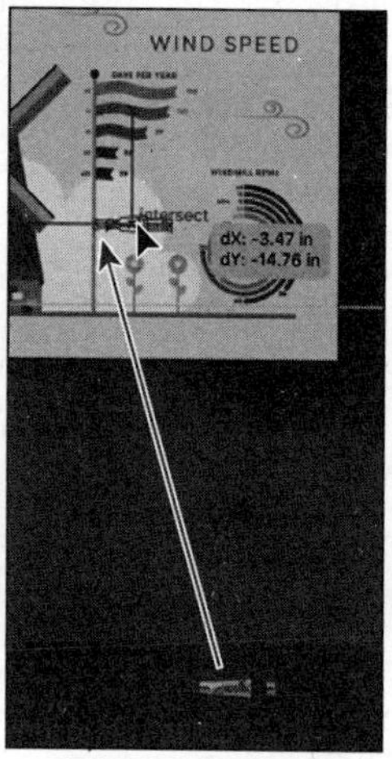

Make sure the hands of the person are directly on the flagpole. The idea is to have the person appear to be holding on to the DAYS PER YEAR flag pole, as the wind blows them to the right.

2 Press Command++ (macOS) or Control++ (Windows) several times to zoom in closely.

3 Press and hold on the Free Transform tool (⛶) in the Tools panel, and select the Puppet Warp tool (📌).

Using the Puppet Warp tool, you'll start by bending the arm of the person. To do that, you'll need to set pins. Pins are a way to hold part of the selected artwork to the artboard. You can rotate the artwork around a pin, reposition pins to move artwork, and more.

4 Move the pointer over the top hand of the person, and when the pointer shows a plus (+) next to it, click to add a pin. On the same arm, click roughly halfway down the arm, where the elbow might be. Finally, click to set a pin in the middle of the raincoat.

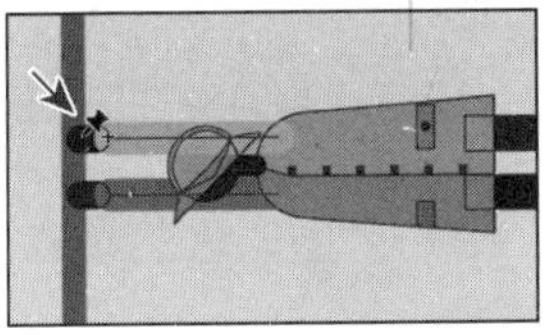
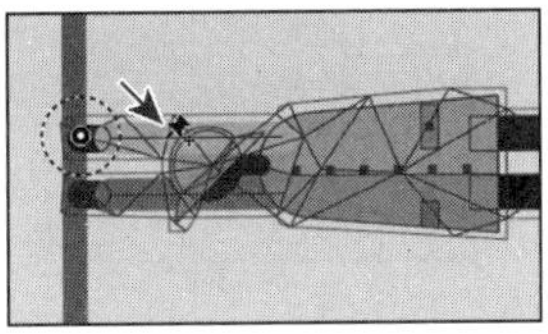
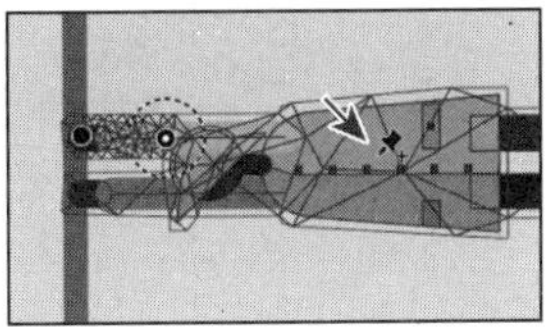

As you add pins, you can see a mesh showing on the artwork.

5 In the Properties panel on the right, you should see Puppet Warp options. Deselect Show Mesh. That will make it easier to see the pins and provide a clearer view of transformations you make.

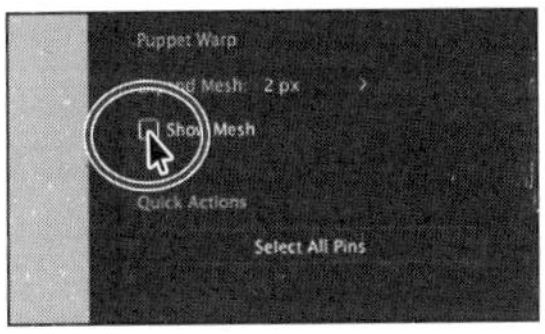

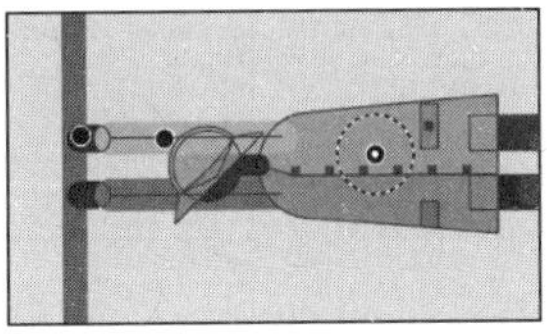

6 Click the pin you added to the hand to select it. You can tell that a pin is selected because it has a white dot in the center. Drag the selected pin up to move the hand and not the rest of the artwork.

▶ **Tip:** You can press the Shift key and click multiple pins to select them or click the Select All Pins button in the Properties panel to select all of the pins.

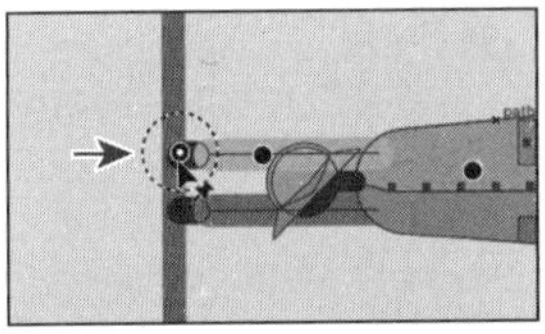
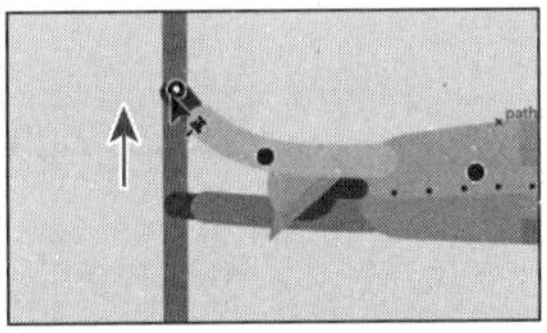

You set the pin on the hand so you could move it. The pin farther down the arm, near the "elbow," was for a pivot point or to ensure that only from that point to the hand moved. The third pin on the body was to keep the body in place without moving it. Setting at least three pins like this usually achieves a better result.

7 With the hand pin still selected, move the pointer over the dotted circle and drag counterclockwise a little to rotate around the pin.

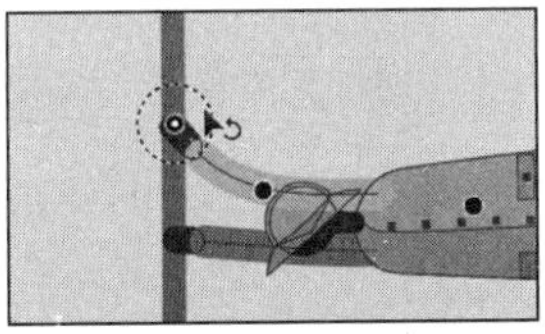
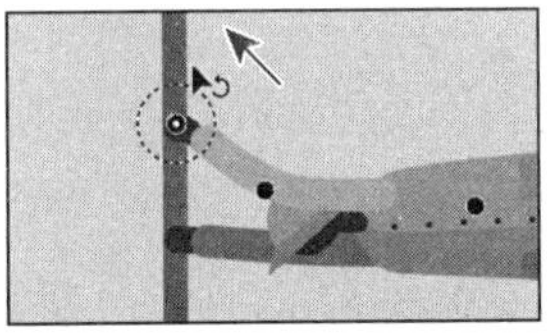

8 Click between the feet to set a pin. Press the Shift key and click the pin in the body to select the pin at the feet and in the body. Drag either pin down a little to bend the body.

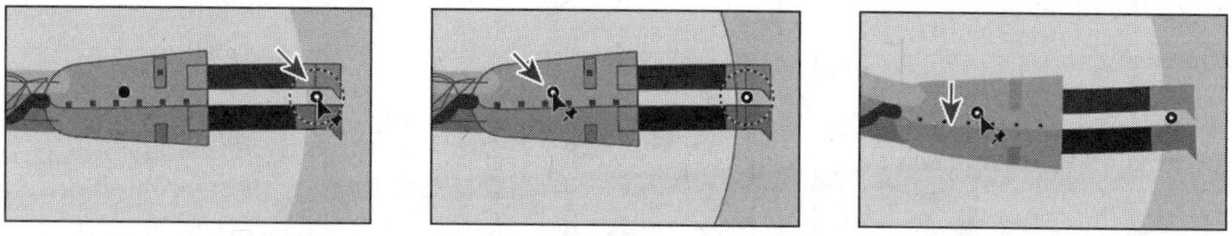

9 Click the pin at the feet to select only that pin. *Make sure it's the only pin selected.* Remember that selected pins have a white dot in the center. If the pin in the body is still selected, click the pin at the feet *again*. Drag the selected pin at the feet, up.

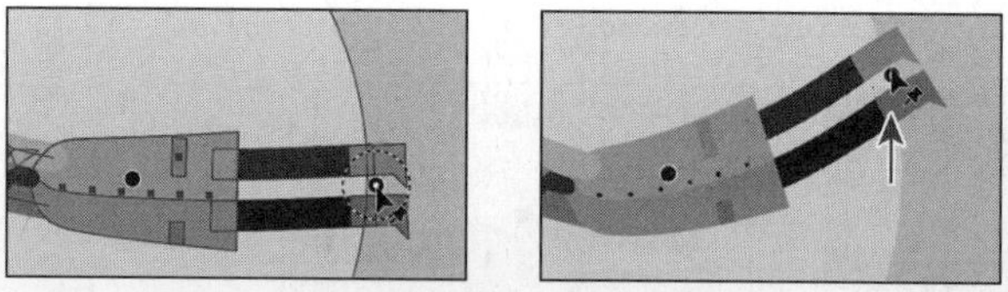

10 Move the pointer over the dotted circle of the selected pin, and drag counter-clockwise a little to rotate around the pin.

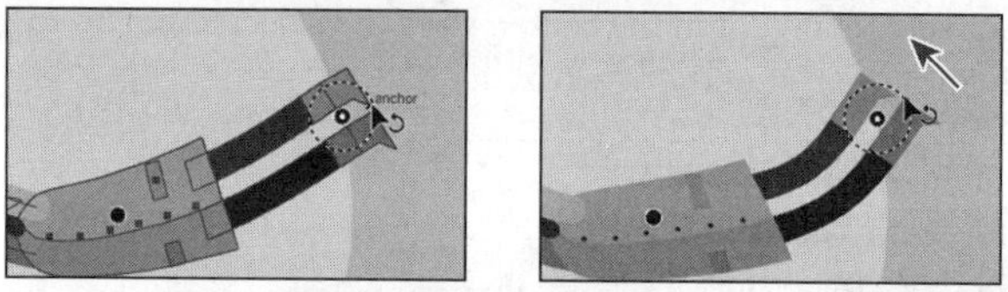

11 Choose Select > Deselect and then choose View > Fit All In Window.

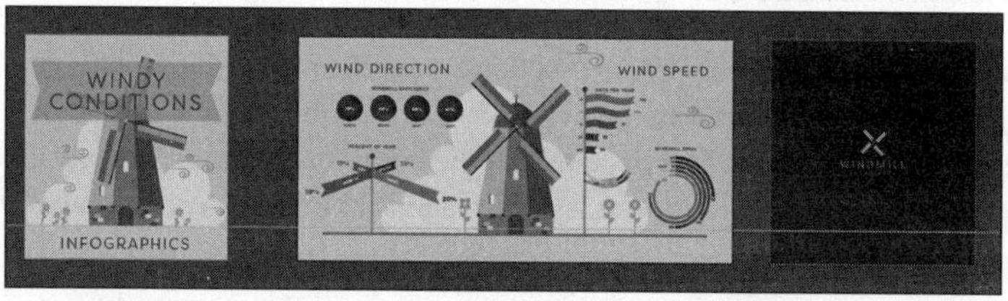

12 Choose File > Save and then File > Close.

Review questions

1 Name three ways to change the size of an existing active artboard.

2 What is the *ruler origin*?

3 What is the difference between *artboard rulers* and *global rulers*?

4 Briefly describe what the Scale Strokes & Effects option in the Properties panel or Transform panel does.

5 Briefly describe what the Puppet Warp tool does.

Review answers

1 To change the size of an existing artboard, you can do the following:

- Double-click the Artboard tool (), and edit the dimensions of the active artboard in the Artboard Options dialog box.
- With nothing selected and the Selection tool selected, click the Edit Artboards button to enter Artboard Editing mode. With the Artboard tool selected, position the pointer over an edge or corner of the artboard, and drag to resize.
- With nothing selected and the Selection tool selected, click the Edit Artboards button to enter Artboard Editing mode. With the Artboard tool selected, click in an artboard in the Document window, and change the dimensions in the Properties panel.

2 The ruler origin is the point where 0 (zero) appears on each ruler. By default, the ruler origin is set to be 0 (zero) in the top-left corner of the active artboard.

3 There are two types of rulers in Illustrator: artboard rulers and global rulers. Artboard rulers, which are the default rulers, set the ruler origin at the upper-left corner of the active artboard. Global rulers set the ruler origin at the upper-left corner of the first artboard, no matter which artboard is active.

4 The Scale Strokes & Effects option, which can be accessed from the Properties panel or the Transform panel, scales any strokes and effects as the object is scaled. This option can be turned on and off, depending on the current need.

5 In Illustrator, you can easily twist and distort artwork naturally, into different positions, using the Puppet Warp tool.

6 CREATING AN ILLUSTRATION WITH THE DRAWING TOOLS

Lesson overview

In this lesson, you'll learn how to do the following:

- Understand paths and anchor points.
- Draw curved and straight lines with the Pen tool.
- Edit curved and straight lines.
- Add and delete anchor points.
- Draw with the Curvature tool.
- Delete and add anchor points.
- Convert between smooth points and corner points.
- Create dashed lines and add arrowheads.
- Draw and edit with the Pencil tool.
- Work with the Join tool.

This lesson takes approximately 90 minutes to complete. Please log in to your account on peachpit.com to download the lesson files for this chapter, or go to the "Getting Started" section at the beginning of this book and follow the instructions under "Accessing the lesson files and Web Edition."

Your Account page is also where you'll find any updates to the chapters or to the lesson files. Look on the Lesson & Update Files tab to access the most current content.

Aside from creating artwork using shapes like in previous lessons, you can also create artwork using drawing tools such as the Pencil tool, Pen tool, and Curvature tool. With these tools, you can draw precisely, including drawing straight lines, curves, and complex shapes. You'll start with the Pen tool and use all of these tools and more to create an illustration.

Starting the lesson

In the first part of this lesson, you'll come to understand paths and ease into drawing with the Pen tool after lots of practice.

● **Note:** If you have not already downloaded the project files for this lesson to your computer from your Account page, make sure to do so now. See the "Getting Started" section at the beginning of the book.

1 To ensure that the tools function and the defaults are set exactly as described in this lesson, delete or deactivate (by renaming) the Adobe Illustrator CC preferences file. See "Restoring default preferences" in the "Getting Started" section at the beginning of the book.

2 Start Adobe Illustrator CC.

3 Choose File > Open, and open the L6_practice.ai file in the Lessons > Lesson06 folder on your hard disk.

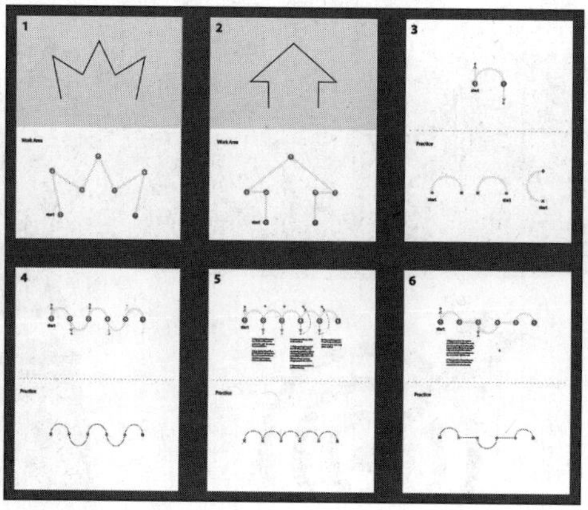

The document is made up of six artboards, numbered 1 through 6. As you progress through the first part of this lesson, you will be asked to move between artboards.

4 Choose File > Save As. In the Save As dialog box, navigate to the Lesson06 folder, and open it. Rename the file to **PenPractice.ai**. Choose Adobe Illustrator (ai) from the Format menu (macOS), or choose Adobe Illustrator (*.AI) from the Save As Type menu (Windows). Click Save.

5 In the Illustrator Options dialog box, leave the default settings, and then click OK.

6 Choose Window > Workspace > Reset Essentials.

● **Note:** If you don't see Reset Essentials in the menu, choose Window > Workspace > Essentials before choosing Window > Workspace > Reset Essentials.

An intro to drawing with the Pen tool

The Pen tool (✒) is one of the main drawing tools in Illustrator that's used to create both freeform and more precise artwork and also plays a role in editing existing vector artwork. It's important to have an understanding of a tool like the Pen tool (or Curvature tool) when working with Illustrator. *Just know that it takes plenty of practice to feel comfortable with the Pen tool!*

▶ **Tip:** Adobe has created a simple game for learning the Pen tool. Check it out here: https://helpx.adobe.com/illustrator/how-to/pen-tool-game.html.

In this first section, you'll begin to explore the Pen tool, and later in the lesson, you'll create artwork using the Pen tool and other tools and commands.

1 Choose 1 from the Artboard Navigation menu in the lower-left corner of the Document window.

2 Choose View > Fit Artboard In Window.

3 Select the Zoom tool (🔍) in the Tools panel, and click twice in the bottom half of the artboard to zoom in.

4 Choose View > Smart Guides to turn off the Smart Guides. Smart Guides can be useful when you draw, but you won't need them now.

5 In the Properties panel to the right of the document, click the Fill color box, make sure the Swatches option (▦) is selected, and choose None (☒). Then, click the stroke color, and make sure that the Black swatch is selected. Make sure the stroke weight is also **1 pt** in the Properties panel.

   When you begin drawing with the Pen tool, it's usually best to have no fill on the path you create because the fill can cover parts of the path you are trying to create. You can add a fill later, if necessary.

6 Select the Pen tool (✒) in the Tools panel. Position the pointer in the area labeled "Work Area" in the artboard, and notice the asterisk next to the Pen icon (✒*), indicating that you'll create a new path if you begin drawing.

● **Note:** If you see ✕ instead of the Pen icon (✒*), the Caps Lock key is active. Caps Lock turns the Pen tool icon into ✕ for increased precision. After you begin drawing, with the Caps Lock key active, the Pen tool icon looks like this: -¦-.

7 In the area labeled "Work Area," click and release on the orange point labeled 1, where you see "start," to set the first anchor point.

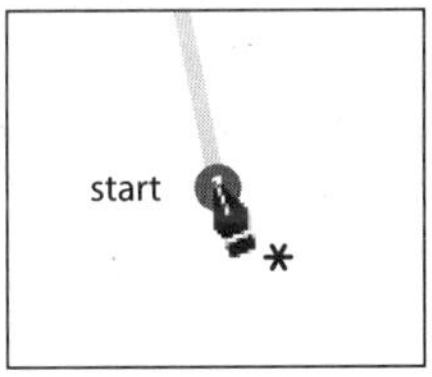

8 Move the pointer away from the point you just created, and you'll see a line connecting the first point and the pointer, no matter where you move the pointer.

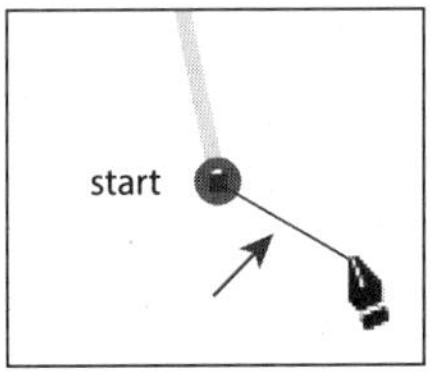

   That line is called the Pen tool preview (or Rubber Band). Later, as you create curved paths, it will make drawing them easier because it is a preview of what the path will look like. Also notice that the asterisk has disappeared from next to the pointer, indicating that you are now drawing a path.

● **Note:** If the path looks curved, you have accidentally dragged with the Pen tool; choose Edit > Undo Pen and then click again without dragging.

9 Position the pointer over the gray dot labeled 2. Click and release to create another anchor point.

You just created a path. A simple path is composed of two anchor points and a line segment connecting the anchor points. You use the anchor points to control the direction, length, and curve of the line segment.

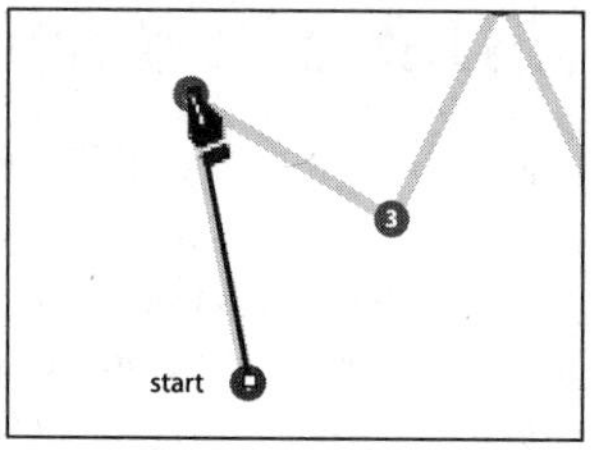

▶ **Tip:** You can toggle the Pen tool preview by choosing Illustrator CC > Preferences > Selection & Anchor Display (macOS) or Edit > Preferences > Selection & Anchor Display (Windows) to open the Preferences dialog box. In the dialog box, with the Selection & Anchor Display category options showing, deselect Enable Rubber Band For: Pen Tool.

10 Continue clicking points 3 through 7, releasing the mouse button every time you click to create an anchor point.

Notice that only the last anchor point is filled (not hollow like the rest of the anchor points), indicating that it is selected.

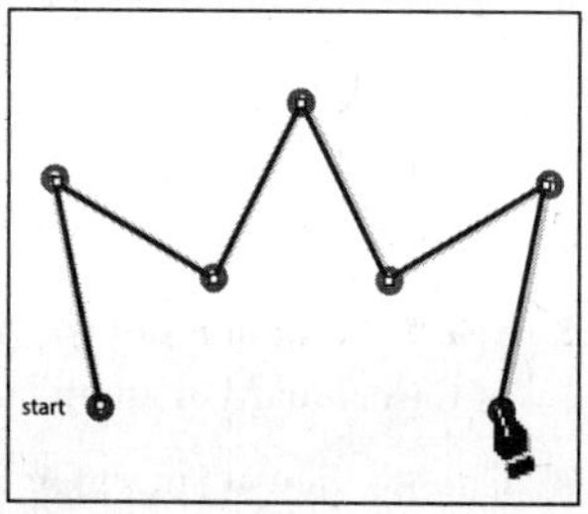

11 Choose Select > Deselect.

Selecting paths

The type of anchor point you created in the previous section is called a corner point. *Corner points* are not smooth like a curve; rather, they create an angle where the anchor point is. Now that you can create corner points, you will move on to adding other types of points such as smooth points to create curves in a path. But first, you'll learn a few more techniques for selecting paths.

In Lesson 2, "Techniques for Selecting Artwork," you were introduced to selecting content with the Selection and Direct Selection tools. Next, you'll explore a few more options for selecting artwork with those same Selection tools.

▶ **Tip:** You can also drag across a path to select it with the Selection tool.

1 Select the Selection tool (▶) in the Tools panel, and position the pointer over a straight line in the path you just created. When the pointer shows a solid black box (▶) next to it, click.

This selects the entire path and all of the anchor points.

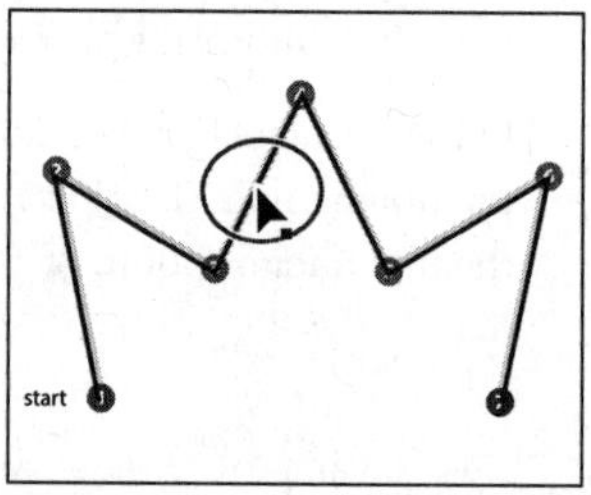

2 Position the pointer over one of the straight lines in the path. When the pointer changes appearance (▶), drag the path to a new location anywhere on the artboard.

All the anchor points travel together, maintaining the shape of the path.

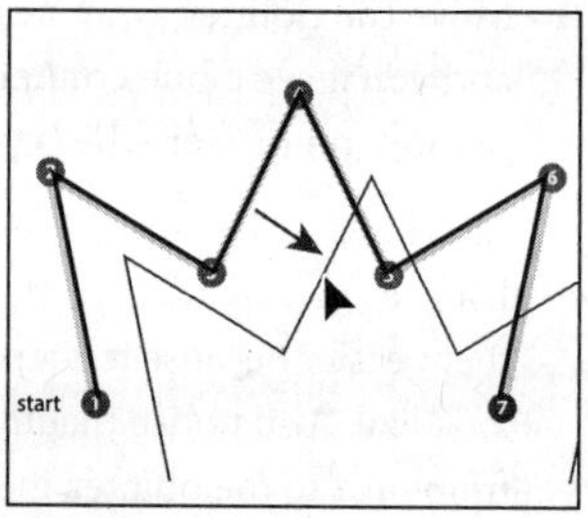

3 Choose Edit > Undo Move to move the path back to its original position.

4 With the Selection tool selected, click an empty area of the artboard to deselect the path.

Tip: If the Pen tool ( ) were still selected, you could Command-click (macOS) or Ctrl-click (Windows) in a blank area of the artboard to deselect the path. This temporarily selects the Direct Selection tool. When you release the Ctrl or Command key, the Pen tool is selected again.

5 Select the Direct Selection tool ( ) in the Tools panel. Move the pointer anywhere over the path between anchor points. When the pointer changes ( ), click the path to reveal all of the anchor points.

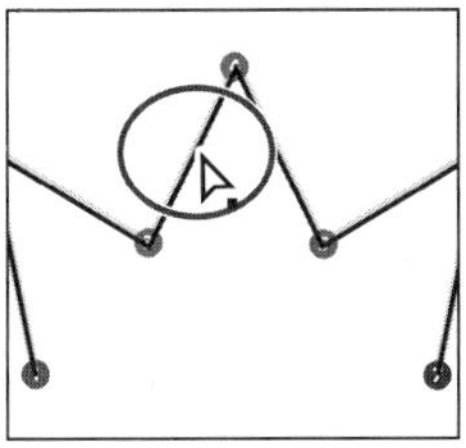

You just selected a line segment (path). If you were to press Backspace or Delete (*don't*), only that part of the path between two anchor points would be removed.

6 Move the pointer over the anchor point labeled 4; the anchor point will become a little larger than the others, and the pointer will show a small box with a dot in the center ( ) next to it (the figure shows this). Both of these indicate that if you click, you will select the anchor point. Click to select the anchor point, and the selected anchor point is filled (looks solid), whereas the other anchor points are still hollow (deselected).

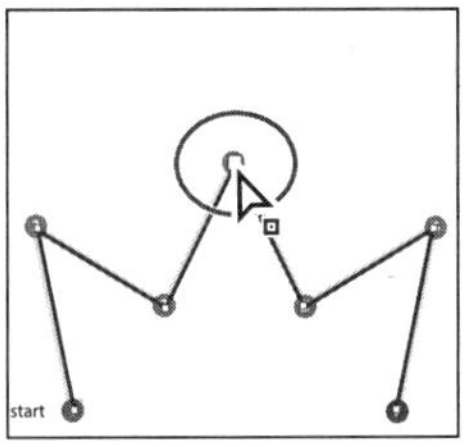

Note: When you position the pointer over a line segment that is not already selected, a black, solid square appears next to the Direct Selection tool pointer, indicating that you will select a line segment.

7 Drag the selected anchor point up to reposition it.

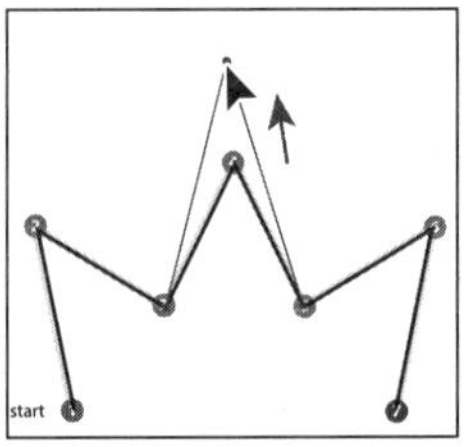

The anchor point moves, but the others remain stationary. This is one method for editing a path, like you saw in Lesson 2, "Techniques for Selecting Artwork."

8 Click in a blank area of the artboard to deselect.

9 Position the Direct Selection pointer over the path between points 5 and 6. When the pointer changes ( ), click to select. Choose Edit > Cut.

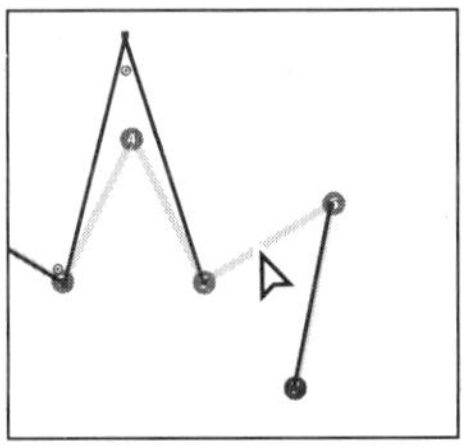

Note: If the entire path disappears, choose Edit > Undo Cut, and try again.

This removes the selected segment between anchor points 5 and 6. Next, you'll learn how to connect the paths again.

10 Select the Pen tool ( ), and move the pointer onto the blue anchor point labeled 5. Notice that the Pen tool shows a forward slash ( ), indicating that if you click, you will continue drawing from that anchor point. Click the point.

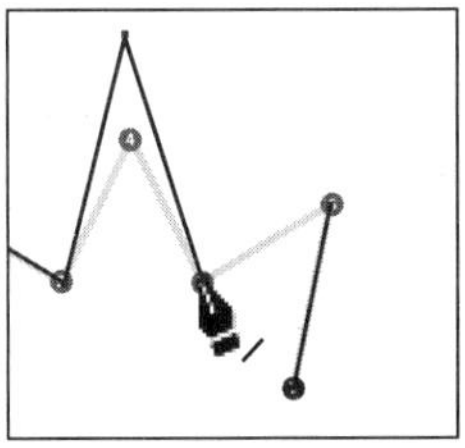

11 Position the pointer over the other anchor point (point 6) that was connected to the cut line segment. The pointer now shows a merge symbol next to it (), indicating that you are connecting to another path. Click the point to reconnect the paths.

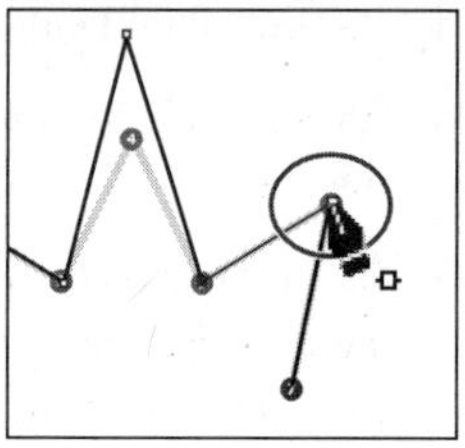

12 Choose File > Save.

Drawing straight lines with the Pen tool

In previous lessons, you learned that using the Shift key as well as Smart Guides in combination with shape tools constrains the shape of objects. The Shift key and Smart Guides can also constrain paths drawn with the Pen tool to create straight paths in angles of 45°. Next, you'll learn how to draw straight lines and constrain angles as you draw.

1 Choose 2 from the Artboard Navigation menu in the lower-left corner of the Document window.

2 Select the Zoom tool () in the Tools panel, and click twice in the bottom half of the artboard to zoom in.

3 Choose View > Smart Guides to turn on the Smart Guides.

4 With the Pen tool () selected, in the area labeled "Work Area," click on the point labeled 1, where you see "start," to set the first anchor point.

   The Smart Guides most likely are attempting to "snap" the anchor point you create to other content on the artboard, possibly making it difficult to add an anchor point exactly where you want it. This is expected behavior and is sometimes why you might turn off the Smart Guides when drawing.

5 Move the pointer above the original anchor point to the point labeled 2. When you see 1.5 inches in the gray measurement label that appears next to the pointer, click to set another anchor point.

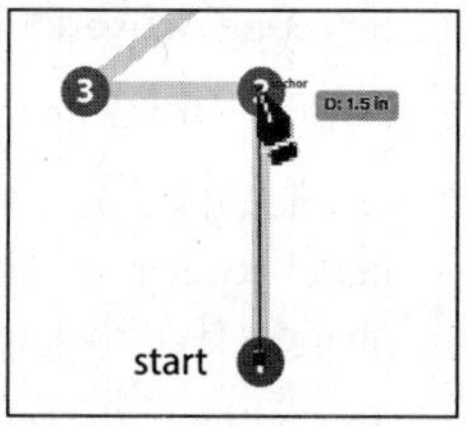

   As you've learned in previous lessons, the measurement label and alignment guides are part of the Smart Guides. The measurement labels showing distance can be useful at times when drawing with the Pen tool.

6 Choose View > Smart Guides to turn *off* the Smart Guides.

   Without Smart Guides on, to align points, you will need to press the Shift key, which is what you'll do next.

7 Press the Shift key, and click in the point labeled 3. Release the Shift key.

With Smart Guides turned off, there is no measurement label, and the point is only aligning with the previous point because you are holding down the Shift key.

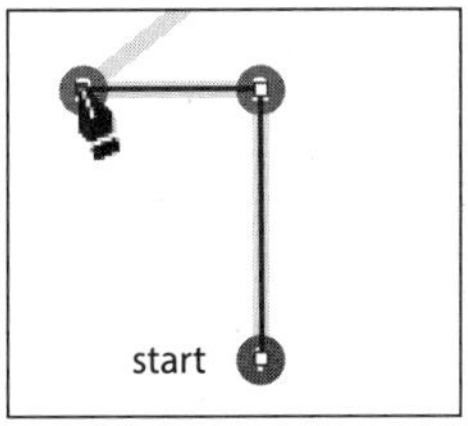

● **Note:** The points you set don't have to be in exactly the same position as the path at the top of the artboard.

8 Click to set point 4 and then click to set point 5.

Like you've already seen, without holding the Shift key, you can set an anchor point anywhere. The path is not constrained to angles of 45°.

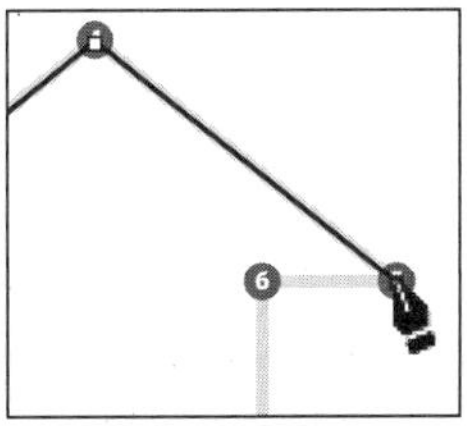

9 Press the Shift key, and click to set points 6 and 7.

10 Choose Select > Deselect.

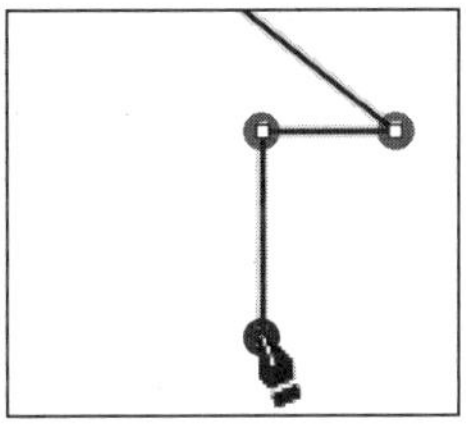

Introducing curved paths

In this part of the lesson, you'll learn how to draw curved lines with the Pen tool. In vector drawing applications such as Illustrator, you can draw a curve, called a Bezier curve. Paths can have two kinds of anchor points: *corner points* and *smooth points*. At a corner point, a path abruptly changes direction. At a smooth point, path segments are connected as a continuous curve. By setting anchor points and dragging direction handles, you can define the shape of the curve. This type of anchor point, with direction handles, is called a *smooth point*.

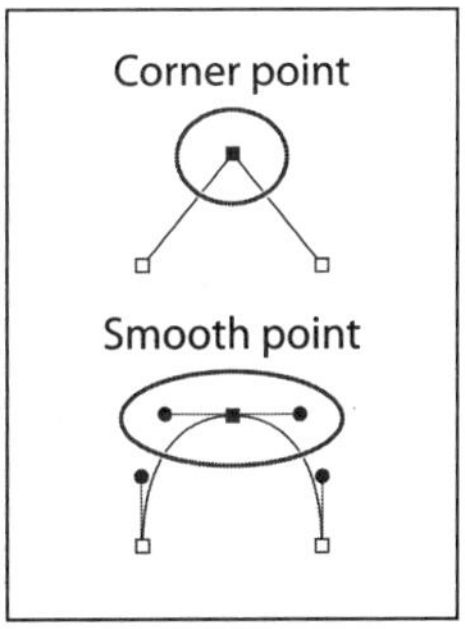

Although drawing curves this way can take some time to learn, it gives you some of the greatest control and flexibility in creating paths. The goal for this exercise is not to create anything specific but to get accustomed to the feel of creating Bezier curves. First, you'll just get the feel for how to create a curved path.

1 Choose 3 from the Artboard Navigation menu in the lower-left corner of the Document window. You will draw in the area labeled "Practice."

2 Select the Zoom tool (🔍) in the Tools panel, and click twice in the bottom half of the artboard to zoom in.

3 Select the Pen tool ( ) in the Tools panel. In the Properties panel, make sure that the fill color is None ( ) and the stroke color is Black. Also, make sure the stroke weight is still **1 pt** in the Properties panel.

4 With the Pen tool selected, click in a blank area of the artboard to create a starting anchor point. Move the pointer away after releasing the mouse button.

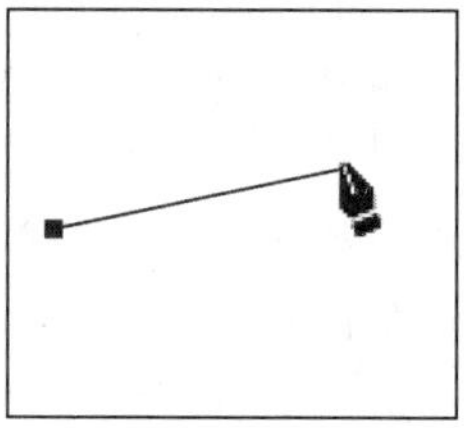

5 Click and drag to create a curved path.

As you drag away from the point, direction handles appear. *Direction handles* consist of direction lines that end in round direction points. The angle and length of the direction handles determine the shape and size of the curve. Direction handles do not print.

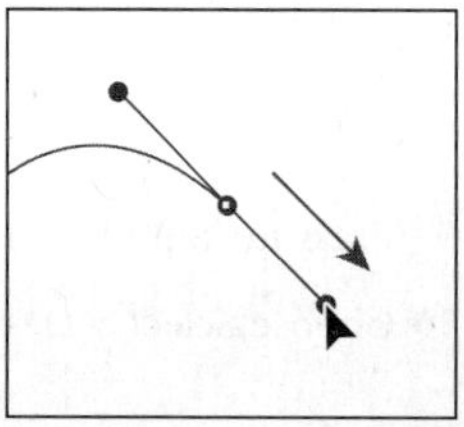

6 Move the pointer away from the anchor point you just created to see the rubber banding. Move the pointer around a bit to see how it changes.

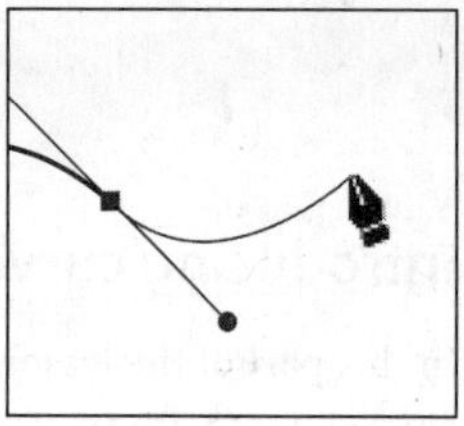

7 Continue clicking and dragging in different areas to create a series of points.

8 Choose Select > Deselect. Leave the file open for the next section.

Components of a path

As you draw, you create a line called a path. A path is made up of one or more straight or curved *segments*. The beginning and end of each segment is marked by *anchor points*, which work like pins holding a wire in place. A path can be closed (for example, a circle) or open, with distinct endpoints (for example, a wavy line). You change the shape of a path by dragging its anchor points, the *direction points* at the end of *direction lines* that appear at anchor points, or the path segment itself.

—From Illustrator Help

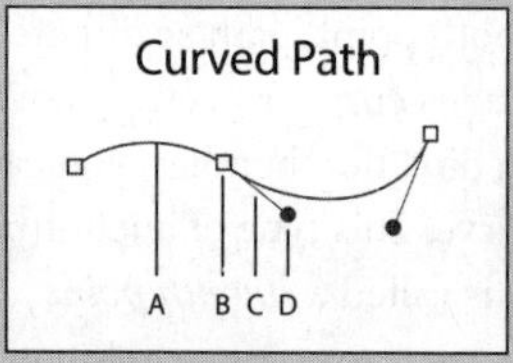

A. Line Segment
B. Anchor Point
C. Direction Line
D. Direction Point

Drawing a curve with the Pen tool

In this part of the lesson, you'll use what you just learned about drawing curves to trace a curved shape with the Pen tool.

1 Press the spacebar to temporarily select the Hand tool (✋), and drag down until you see the curve at the top of the current artboard (on Artboard 3).

2 With the Pen tool (✒) selected, click and drag from the point labeled 1, up to the red dot, and then release the mouse button.

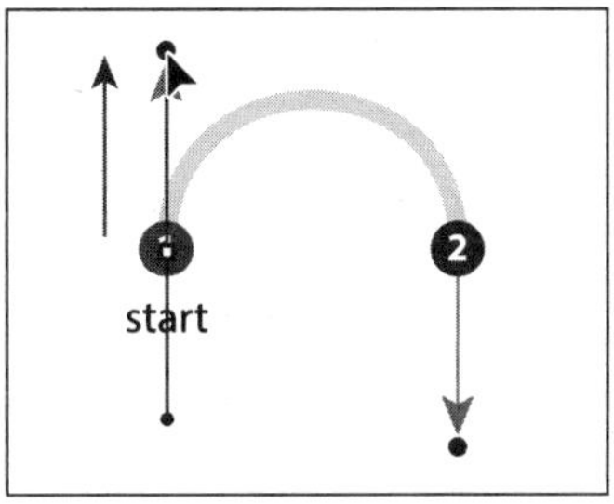

This creates a direction line going in the same general direction as the path. Up to this point, you've started your paths by simply clicking to create an anchor point, not dragging, like you did in this step. To create a more "curved" path, dragging out direction lines on the very first anchor point can be helpful.

● **Note:** The artboard may scroll as you drag. If you lose visibility of the curve, choose View > Zoom Out until you see the curve and anchor point. Pressing the spacebar allows you to use the Hand tool to reposition the artwork.

3 Click point 2 and drag down. Release the mouse button when the pointer reaches the red dot and the path you are creating follows the gray arc.

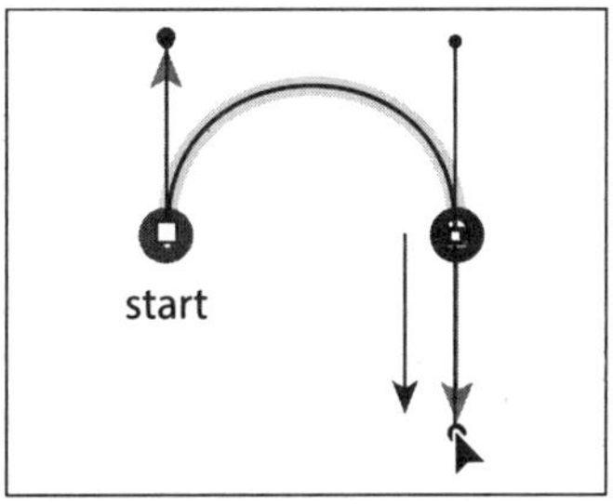

If the path you created is not aligned exactly with the template, select the Direct Selection tool (▶), and select the anchor points one at a time to show the direction handles. You can then drag the ends of the direction handles (called *direction points*) until your path follows the template more accurately.

● **Note:** Pulling the direction handle longer makes a steeper curve; when the direction handle is shorter, the curve is flatter.

4 Select the Selection tool (▶), and click the artboard in an area with no objects, or choose Select > Deselect.

Deselecting the first path allows you to create a new path. If you click somewhere on the artboard with the Pen tool while the path is still selected, the path connects to the next point you draw.

▶ **Tip:** While drawing with the Pen tool, to deselect objects, you can press the Command (macOS) or Ctrl (Windows) key to temporarily switch to the Direct Selection tool and then click the artboard where there are no objects. Another way to end a path is to press the Escape key when you are finished drawing.

If you want to try drawing the curve for more practice, scroll down to the Practice area in the same artboard and trace the different curves.

Drawing a series of curves with the Pen tool

Now that you've experimented with drawing a curve, you will draw a shape that contains several continuous curves.

1 Choose 4 from the Artboard Navigation menu in the lower-left corner of the Document window. Select the Zoom tool (🔍), and click several times in the *top* half of the artboard to zoom in.

2 In the Properties panel to the right of the document, make sure that the fill color is None (⧄), the stroke color is Black, and the stroke weight is still **1 pt**.

3 Select the Pen tool (✒). Click and drag up on point 1, labeled "start," in the direction of the arc, stopping at the red dot.

4 Position the pointer over the point labeled 2 (to the right), and drag down to the red dot, adjusting the first arc (between points 1 and 2) with the direction handle before you release the mouse button.

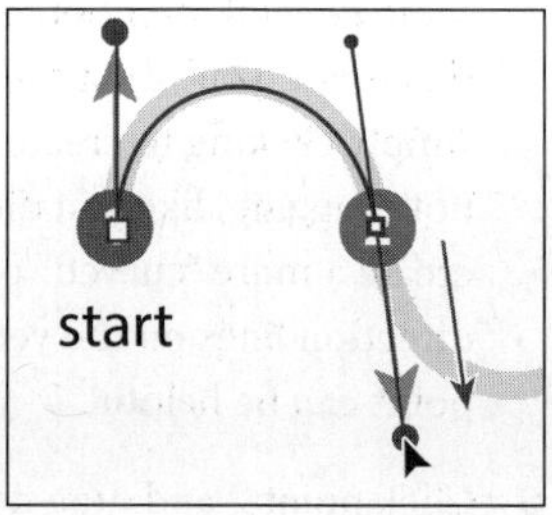

When it comes to smooth points (curved), you'll find that you spend a lot of time focusing on the path segment *behind* (before) the current anchor point you are creating. Remember, by default there are two direction lines for an anchor point. The previous direction line controls the shape of the previous segment.

● **Note:** Don't worry if the path you draw is not exact. You can correct the line with the Direct Selection tool (▷) when the path is complete.

▶ **Tip:** As you drag out the direction handles for an anchor point, you can press and hold the spacebar to reposition the anchor point. When the anchor point is where you want it, release the spacebar.

5 Continue along the path, alternating between dragging up and down. Put anchor points only where there are numbers and finish with the point labeled 6.

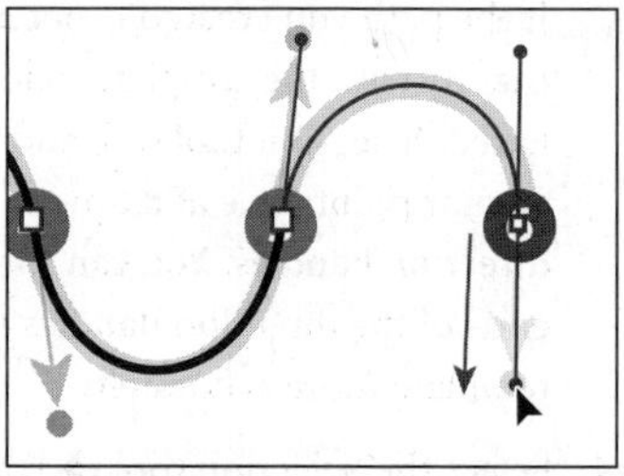

If you make a mistake as you draw, you can undo your work by choosing Edit > Undo Pen and then draw the last point again. Note that your direction lines may not match the figures, and that's okay.

6 When the path is complete, select the Direct Selection tool (▷), and click to select any anchor point in the path.

When an anchor point is selected, the direction handles appear, and you can readjust the curve of the path if necessary. With a curve selected, you can also change the stroke and fill of the curve. When you do this, the next line you draw will have the same attributes. If you want to try drawing the shape again for more practice, scroll down to the bottom half of the same artboard (labeled Practice), and trace the shape down there.

● **Note:** For more information about these attributes, see Lesson 7, "Using Color to Enhance Signage."

7 Choose Select > Deselect and then choose File > Save.

Converting smooth points to corner points

When creating curves, the direction handles help to determine the shape and size of the curved segments, as you've already seen. Removing the direction lines from an anchor point can convert a smooth point into a corner point. In this next part of the lesson, you'll practice converting between smooth points and corner points.

1 Choose 5 from the Artboard Navigation menu in the lower-left corner of the Document window.

   On the top of the artboard, you can see the path that you will trace. You'll use the top artboard as a template for the exercise, creating your paths directly on top of those. Use the Practice section at the bottom of the artboard for additional practice on your own.

2 Select the Zoom tool ( ), and click several times in the top part of the artboard to zoom in.

3 In the Properties panel, make sure that the fill color is None ( ), the stroke color is Black, and the stroke weight is still **1 pt**.

4 Select the Pen tool ( ). Pressing the Shift key, click and drag up from point 1, labeled "start," in the direction of the arc, stopping at the red dot. Release the mouse button and then release the Shift key.

   Pressing the Shift key when dragging constrains the direction handles to multiples of 45°.

5 Click point 2 (to the right), and begin dragging down to the gold dot. As you drag, press and hold the Shift key. When the curve looks correct, release the mouse button and then release the Shift key. Leave the path selected.

   Now you need the curve to switch directions and create another arc. You will *split* the direction lines to convert a smooth point to a corner point.

6 Press the Option (macOS) or Alt (Windows) key, and position the pointer over the last *anchor point* you created. When a convert-point icon (^) appears next to the Pen tool pointer ( ), click and drag a direction line up to the red dot above. Release the mouse button and then release the modifier key. If you do not see the caret (^), you might end up creating an additional loop.

Note: The Option (macOS) or Alt (Windows) key essentially allows you to create a new direction line that is independent of the other for that anchor point. If you don't hold down the Option (macOS) or Alt (Windows) key, the direction handles would not be split, so it would stay a smooth point.

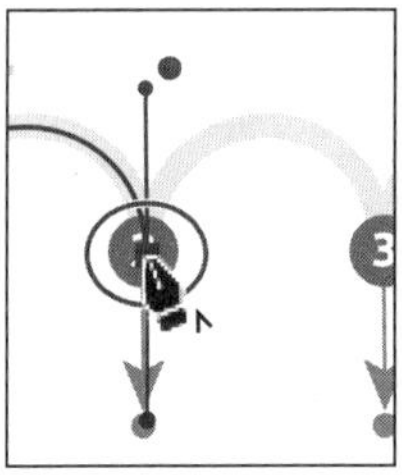

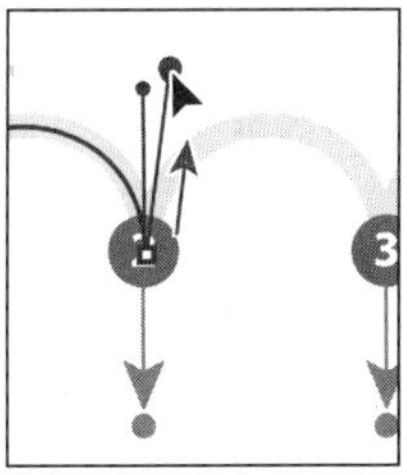

▶ **Tip:** After you draw a path, you can also select single or multiple anchor points and click the Convert Selected Anchor Points To Corner button ( ) or Convert Selected Anchor Points To Smooth button ( ) in the Properties panel.

You can also Option-drag (macOS) or Alt-drag (Windows) the end of the direction handle (called the *direction point*). An arrow is pointing to it in the first part of the figure. Either method "splits" the direction handles so they can go in different directions.

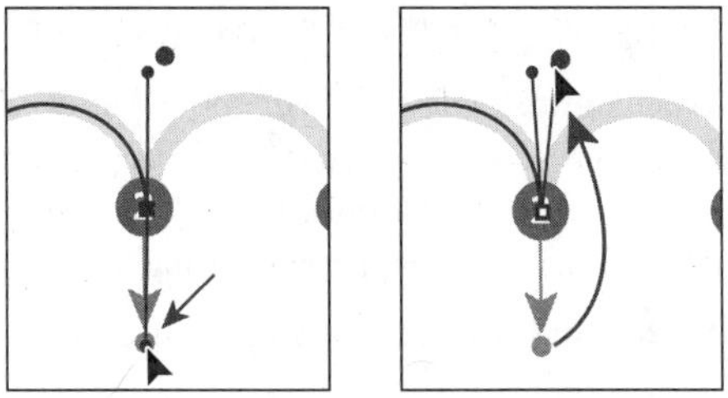

7 Move the Pen tool pointer over point 3 to the right on the template path, and drag down to the gold dot. Release the mouse button when the path looks similar to the template path.

8 Press the Option (macOS) or Alt (Windows) key, and move the pointer over the last anchor point you created. When a convert-point icon (^) appears next to the Pen tool pointer ( ), click and drag a direction line up to the red dot above. Release the mouse button and then release the modifier key.

For the next point, you will not release the mouse button to split the direction handles, so pay close attention.

9 For anchor point 4, click and drag down to the gold dot until the path looks correct. This time, *do not release the mouse button*. Press the Option (macOS) or Alt (Windows) key, and drag up to the red dot for the next curve. Release the mouse button and then release the modifier key.

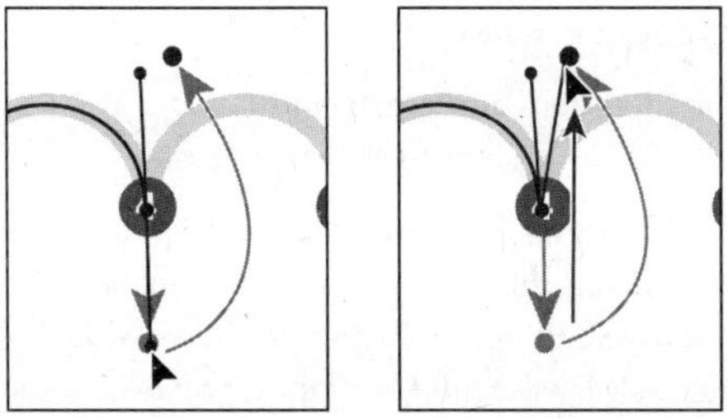

10 Continue this process using the Option (macOS) or Alt (Windows) key to create corner points until the path is completed.

11 Use the Direct Selection tool to fine-tune the path and then deselect the path.

If you want to try drawing the same shape for more practice, scroll down to the Practice area in the same artboard, and trace the shape down there.

Combining curves and straight lines

Of course in the real world, when you draw with the Pen tool, you won't just create either curves or straight lines. In this next section, you'll learn how to go from curves to straight lines and from straight lines to curves.

1 Choose 6 from the Artboard Navigation menu in the lower-left corner of the Document window. Select the Zoom tool (), and click several times in the top half of the artboard to zoom in.

2 Select the Pen tool (). Click point 1, labeled "start," and drag up, stopping at the red dot. Release the mouse button.

   Up to this point, you've been dragging to a gold or red dot in the templates. In the real world those obviously won't be there, so for the next point you will drag to create a point without much template guidance. Don't worry, you can always choose Edit > Undo Pen and try again!

3 Click and drag down from point 2, and release the mouse button when the path roughly matches the template.

   This method of creating a curve should be familiar to you by now.

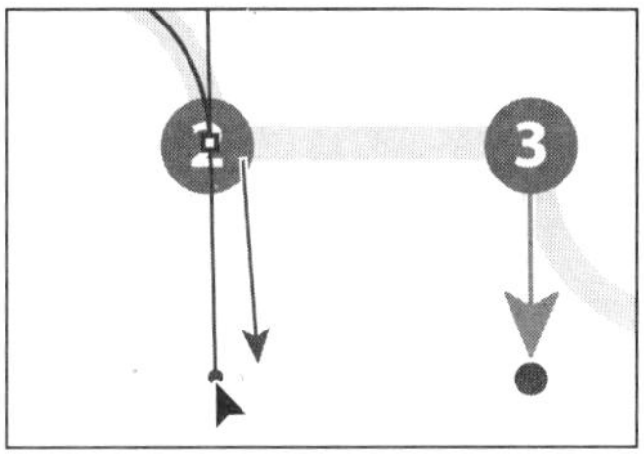

   If you were to click point 3 (*don't*), even pressing the Shift key (to produce a straight line), the path would be curved. The last point you created is a smooth anchor point and has a leading direction handle. The figure to the right shows what the path would look like if you clicked with the Pen tool on the next point.

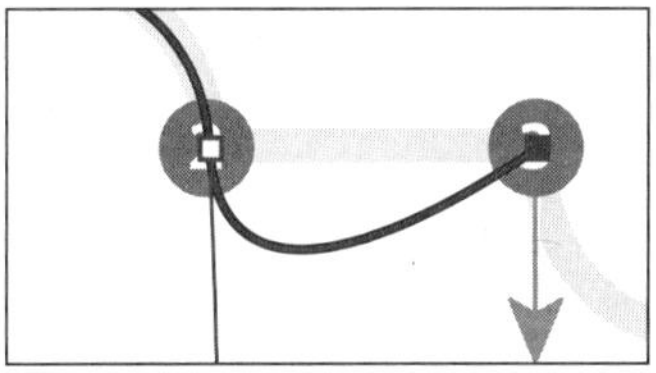

   You will now continue the path as a straight line by removing the leading direction handle.

4 Position the pointer over the last point created (point 2). When the convert-point icon appears (), click. This deletes the *leading* direction handle from the anchor point (not the trailing direction handle), as shown in the second part of the following figure.

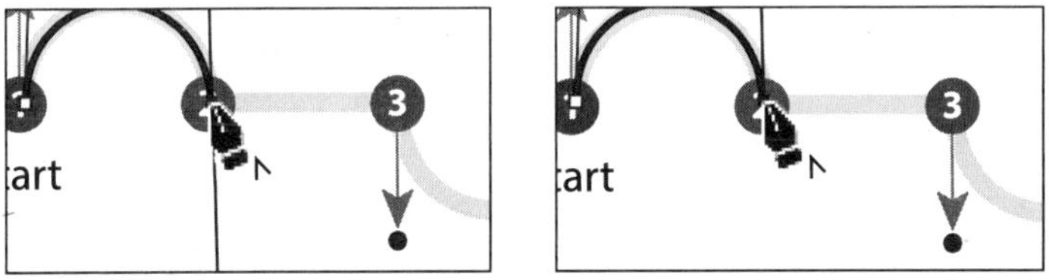

5 Press the Shift key, and click point 3 in the template path to the right to set the next point, creating a straight segment.

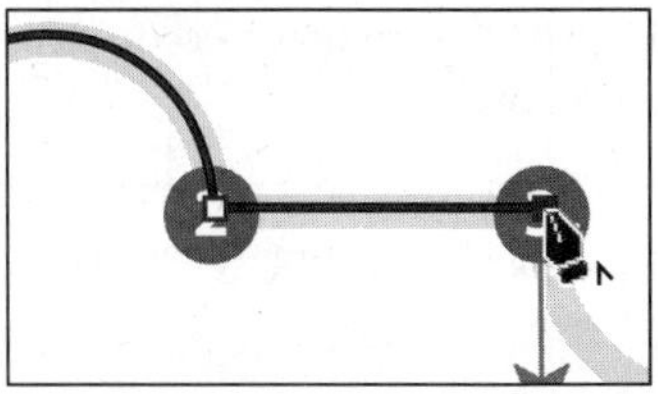

6 For the next arc, position the pointer over the last point created. When the convert-point icon appears (), click and drag down from that point to the red dot. This creates a new, independent direction line.

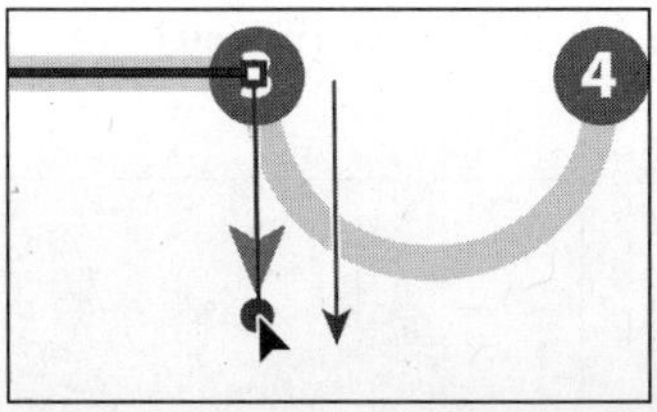

For the rest of this section, I'm going to ask you to complete the path, following the remaining part of the template. I don't include any figures, so go through the figures in the previous steps if you need guidance.

7 Click to create the next point (point 4), and drag up to complete the arc.

8 Click the last anchor point you just created to remove the direction line.

9 Shift-click the next point to create the second straight segment.

10 Click and drag up from the last point created to create a direction line.

11 Click and drag down on the end point (point 6) to create the final arc.

If you want to try drawing the same shape for more practice, scroll down to the Practice area in the same artboard, and trace the shape down there. Make sure you deselect the previous artwork first.

12 Choose File > Save and then choose File > Close.

Remember, you can always go back and work on those Pen tool templates in the L6_practice.ai file as many times as you need. Take it as slow as you need and *practice, practice, practice.*

Creating artwork with the Pen tool

Next, you'll take what you've learned and create some artwork to be used in your project. To start, you'll draw a coffee cup, which combines curves and corners. Just take your time as you practice with this shape, and use the template guides provided to assist you in drawing it.

▶ **Tip:** Don't forget, you can always undo a point you've drawn (Edit > Undo Pen) and then try again.

1 Choose File > Open, and open the L6_end.ai file in the Lessons > Lesson06 folder.

2 Choose View > Fit All In Window to see the finished artwork. (Use the Hand tool [✋] to move the artwork to where you want it.) If you don't want to leave the artwork open, choose File > Close.

3 Choose File > Open. In the Open dialog box, navigate to the Lessons > Lesson06 folder, and select the L6_start.ai file on your hard disk. Click Open to open the file.

4 Choose View > Fit All In Window.

5 Choose File > Save As, name the file **CoffeeShop.ai**, and select the Lesson06 folder in the Save As dialog box. Choose Adobe Illustrator (ai) from the Format menu (macOS) or choose Adobe Illustrator (*.AI) from the Save As Type menu (Windows), and click Save. In the Illustrator Options dialog box, leave the options set at the defaults and then click OK.

6 Choose 1 Main from the Artboard Navigation menu in the lower-left corner of the Document window, if it's not already chosen.

7 Choose View > Fit Artboard In Window.

8 Select the Zoom tool (🔍), and zoom in to the cup in the bottom half of the artboard.

9 In the Layers panel (Window > Layers), click to select the layer named "Artwork."

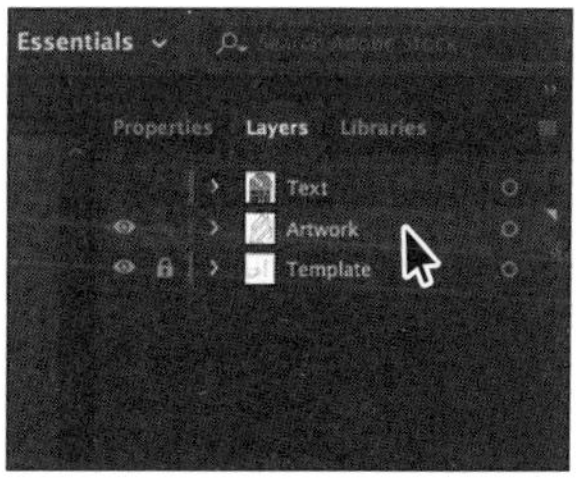

10 In the Properties panel (Window > Properties), make sure that the fill color is None (☐) and the stroke color is Black. Also make sure the stroke weight is 1 pt in the Properties panel.

Drawing a coffee cup

Now that you have the file open and ready, you're going to put to use some of the Pen tool practice you did in previous sections, by drawing a coffee cup. This next section has more than the average number of steps, so take your time.

Note: You do not have to start at the blue square (point A) to draw this shape. You can set anchor points for a path with the Pen tool in a clockwise or counterclockwise direction.

1 Select the Pen tool ( ) in the Tools panel. Drag from the blue square labeled "A" to the red dot above it to set the starting anchor point and direction of the first curve.

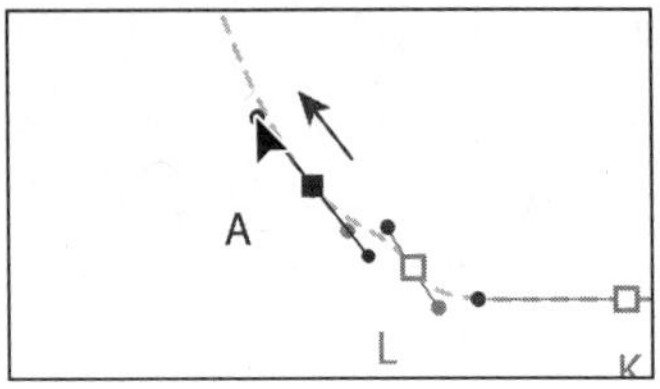

2 Drag from point B to the red dot to create the first curve.

The next point you create will be a simple corner point.

3 Position the pointer over the point C, and click (*don't drag*) to set a corner point.

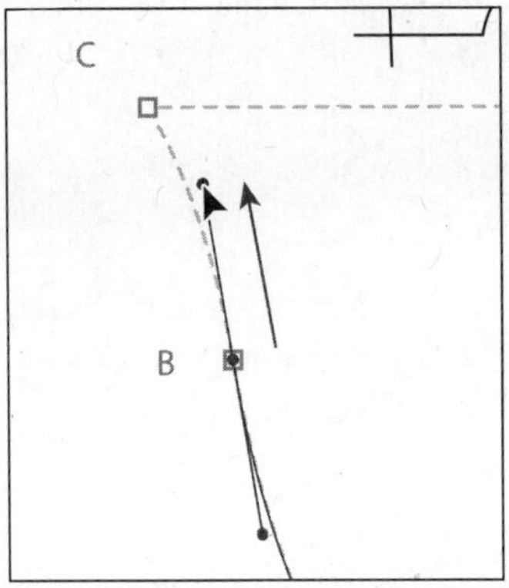

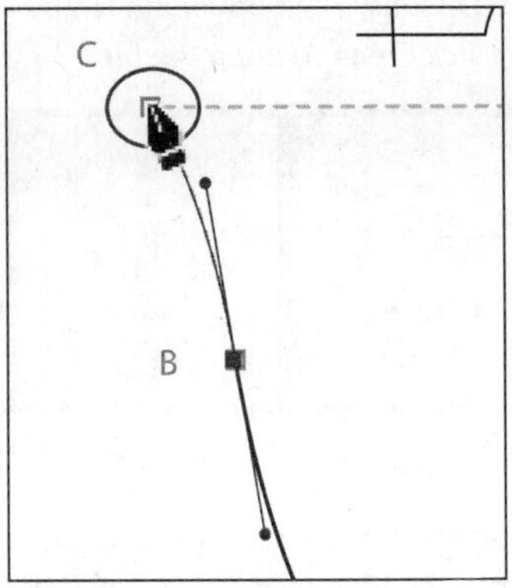

Note: If you find that the path you are drawing has a fill of white, part of the template may be hidden. You can always change the fill to None (☐) for the path you are drawing.

4 Press the Shift key, and click point D to create a straight line; then release the key.

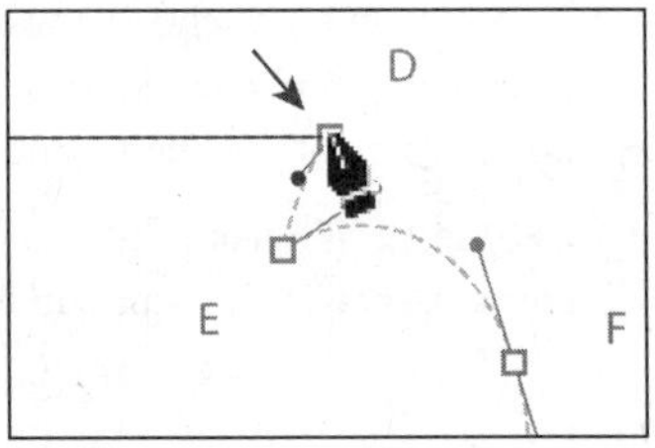

5 Position the Pen tool pointer over point D again. When the convert-point icon appears ( ) next to the pointer, drag down from point D to the red dot. This creates a new direction line.

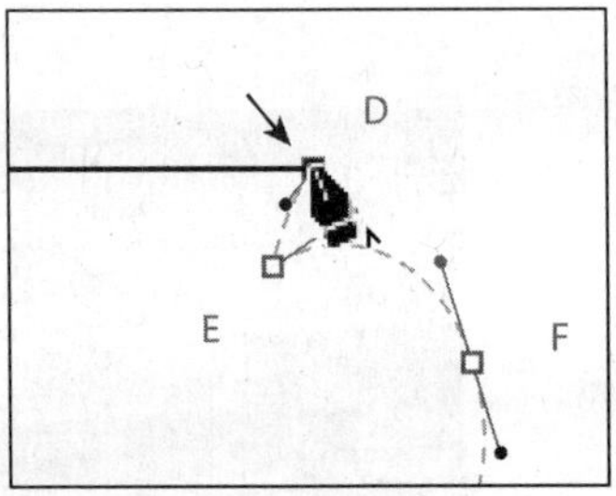

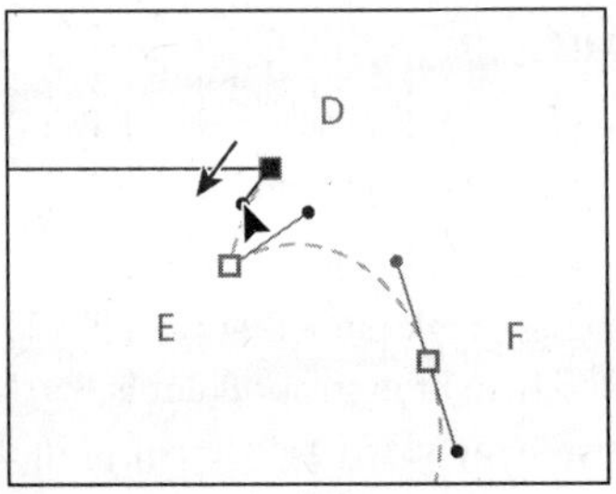

As you draw with the Pen tool, you may want to edit a curve you previously drew without ending the path you are drawing. Pressing a modifier key with the Pen tool selected, you can position the pointer over a previous path segment and drag to modify it, which is what you'll do next.

6 Position the pointer over the path between points C and D. Press the Option (macOS) or Alt (Windows) key. The pointer changes appearance (). Drag the path down to make the path curved, like you see in the figure. Release the mouse button and then the key. Now, you can continue drawing the path.

Tip: You can also press the Option+Shift (macOS) or Alt+Shift (Windows) keys to constrain the handles to a perpendicular direction, which ensures that the handles are the same length.

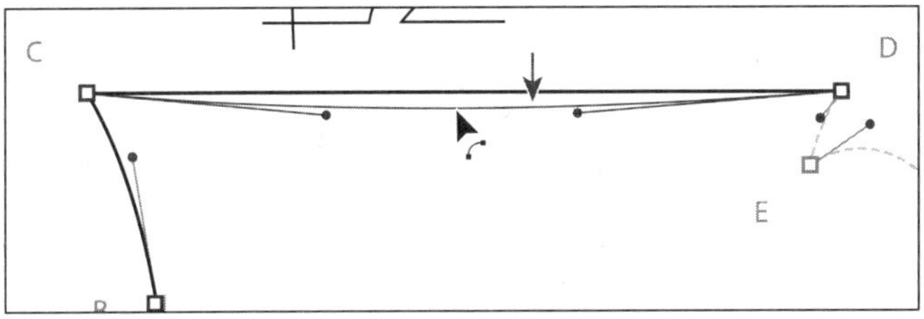

This adds direction handles to the top anchor points.

7 Position the pointer over point E. Notice that as you move the pointer, you can see the Pen tool rubber banding, which means you are still drawing the path. Click point E to create a corner point, and release the mouse button.

8 With the Pen tool pointer over point E, click and drag up and to the right from that point to the red dot.

Note: After releasing the mouse button in the previous step, if you move the pointer away and then bring it back to point E, the convert-point icon [^] will appear next to the pointer.

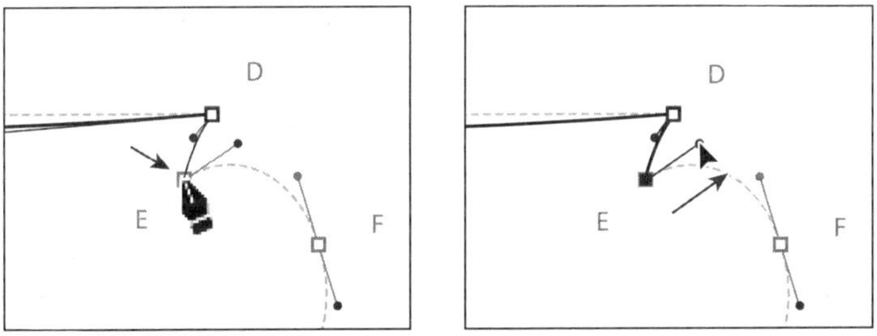

This creates a new leading direction handle and sets up the next path to be a curve.

9 Continue drawing by dragging from the anchor point at F to the red dot.

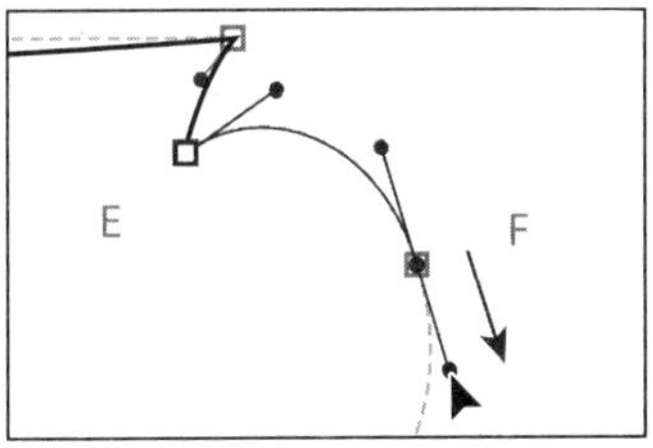

For the next point, G, you will create another smooth point, but you will edit the direction handles independently using a modifier key as you draw. For the next step, don't release the mouse button until you are told.

● **Note:** You could also create the point in this step by dragging and releasing the mouse button when the pointer reaches the gold dot. You could then position the Pen tool icon over the anchor point. When the convert-point icon (^) appears next to the pointer, you could drag out a new direction handle.

10 Begin dragging from point G to the gold dot. When the pointer reaches the gold dot, *without releasing the mouse button yet*, press the Option (macOS) or Alt (Windows) key, and continue dragging from the gold dot to the red dot to make the *leading* direction handle longer. When the pointer reaches the red dot, release the mouse button and then release the key.

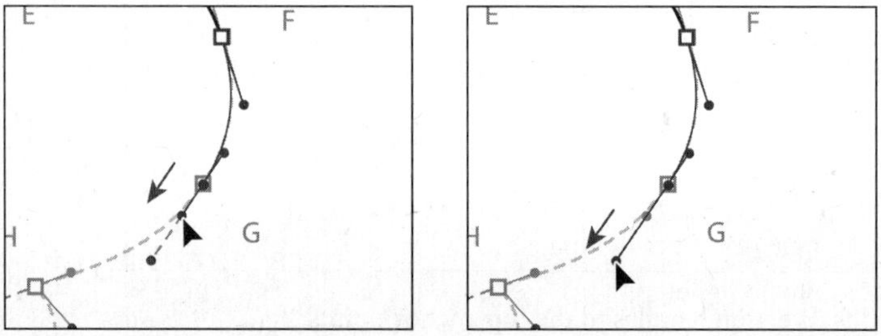

Next, you'll create a smooth point and split the direction handles.

11 Continue drawing the point at H by first dragging from the anchor point to the gold dot. *Without releasing the mouse button,* press the Option (macOS) or Alt (Windows) key and drag from the gold dot to the red dot.

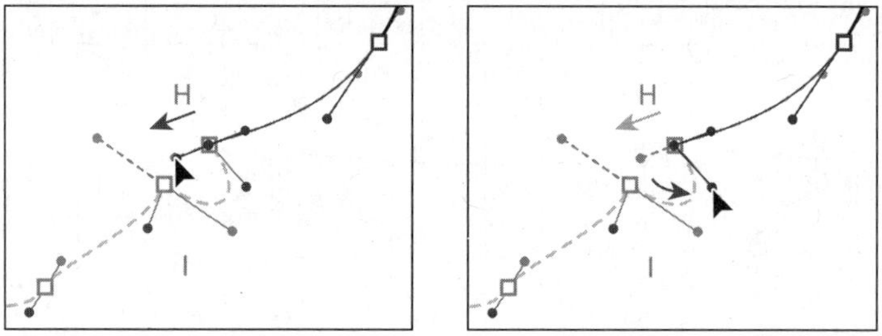

12 Continue drawing the point at I by first dragging from the anchor point to the gold dot. *Without releasing the mouse button,* press the Option (macOS) or Alt (Windows) key and continue dragging from the gold dot to the red dot.

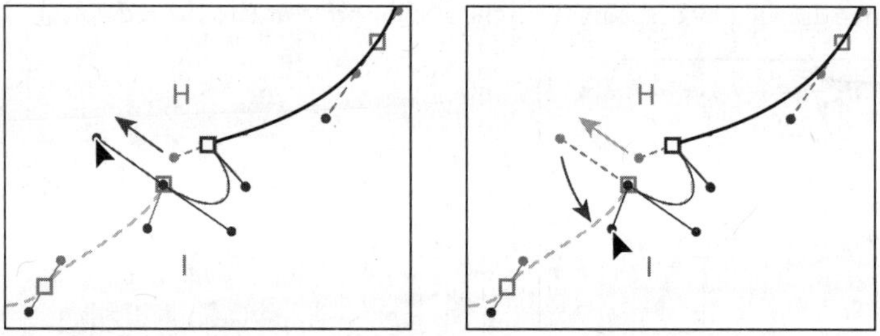

13 Continue drawing the point at J by dragging from the anchor point to the red dot.

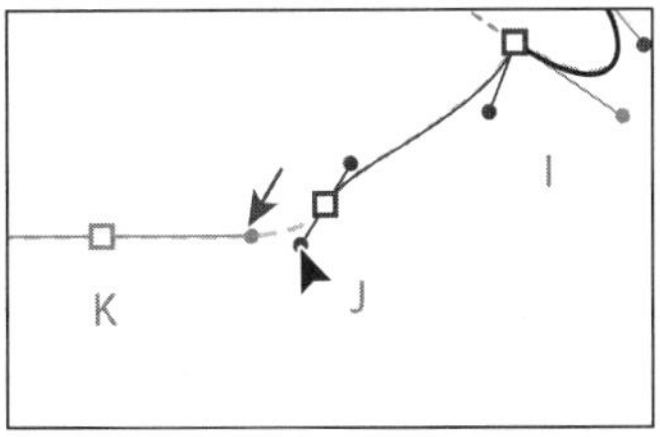

14 Begin dragging from point K to the red dot. As you drag, press the Shift key to constrain the direction handles. When you reach the red dot, release the mouse button and then the key.

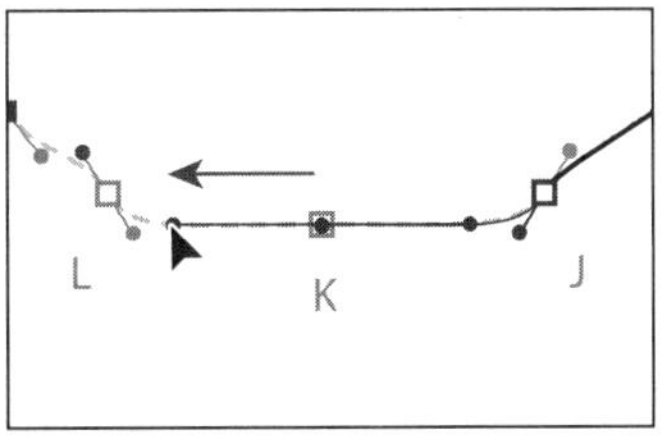

Note: If you press and hold the Shift key before you click and drag from a point, the point will be aligned with the previous point. That's not what you want in this case.

15 Continue drawing by clicking and dragging from the point at L to the red dot.

Next, you'll complete the drawing of the coffee cup by closing the path.

16 Position the Pen tool over the starting point A without clicking.

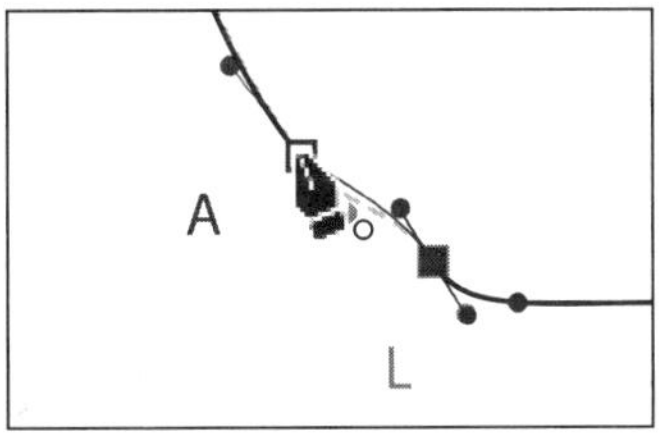

Notice that an open circle appears next to the Pen tool pointer ( ), indicating that the path will close if you were to click the anchor point (don't click yet). If you were to click and drag, the direction handles on either side of the point would move as a single straight line. You need to extend one of the direction handles to match the template.

17 Press the Option (macOS) or Alt (Windows) key with the pointer still over point A. Click and drag up and to the left. Notice that a direction handle shows but is going in the opposite direction (it's going down and to the right). Drag until the curve looks right. Release the mouse button and then the key.

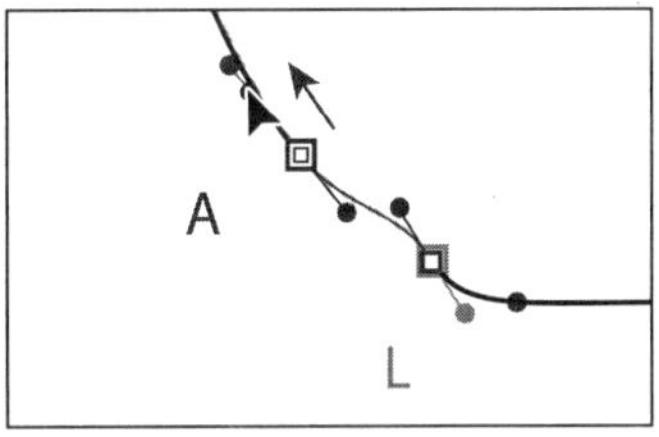

Tip: When creating a closing anchor point, you can press the spacebar to move the point as you create it.

Normally, as you drag away from a point, direction lines appear before and after the point. Without the modifier key, as you drag away from closing point, you are reshaping the path before *and* after the anchor point. Pressing the Option (macOS) or Alt (Windows) modifier key on the closing point allows you to edit the previous direction handle independently.

18 Command-click (macOS) or Ctrl-click (Windows) away from the path to deselect it and then choose File > Save.

Note: This is a shortcut method for deselecting a path while keeping the Pen tool selected. You could also choose Select > Deselect, among other methods.

Drawing with the Curvature tool

With the Curvature tool (), you can draw and edit paths quickly and visually to create paths with smooth refined curves and straight lines, without editing direction lines. Using the Curvature tool, you can also edit paths while drawing or after the path is complete using the same tool. The paths it creates are composed of anchor points and can be edited with any of the drawing or selecting tools. In this section, you'll explore the Curvature tool while creating a spoon.

1 Choose 3 Spoon from the Artboard Navigation menu in the lower-left corner of the Document window.

2 Choose View > Fit Artboard In Window (if necessary).

● **Note:** You may want to zoom in to the spoon template in this section.

Looking at the template path, you'll see a vertical guide running through points A and I. After you draw half of the spoon, you will copy and reflect it around the guide and then join the two halves together.

3 Select the Curvature tool () in the Tools panel. Click the blue square at point A to set the starting anchor point and release the mouse button. See the first part of the following figure.

● **Note:** Like the Pen tool, you don't have to start at the blue square (point A) to draw this shape. You can set anchor points for a path with the Curvature tool in a clockwise or counterclockwise direction.

4 Click point B to create a point. After clicking, release the mouse button, and move the pointer away from point B. Notice the preview of the curve before and after point B.

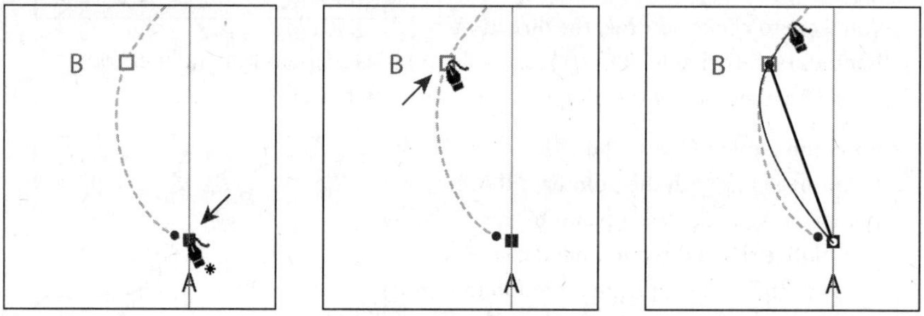

The Curvature tool works by creating anchor points where you click. The drawing curve will "flex" around the points dynamically. Direction handles are created when necessary to curve the path for you.

5 Click point C and then click point D, releasing the mouse button. Move the pointer away from point D.

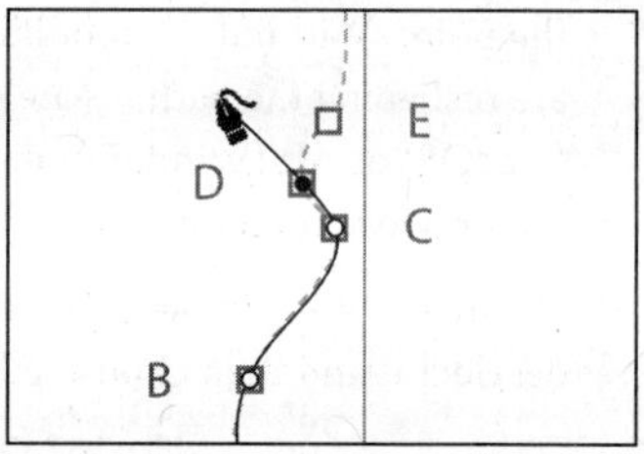

At this point, the path between points A and B will no longer be affected by new points (E, F, etc.), but the path is not following the template. While drawing with the Curvature tool, you can go back and edit points as well as add points.

6 Hover the pointer over the path segment between points A and B. When a plus sign (+) appears next to the pointer, click to create a new point. Drag the new point to the red dot in the template, repositioning it to match the shape of the dotted template.

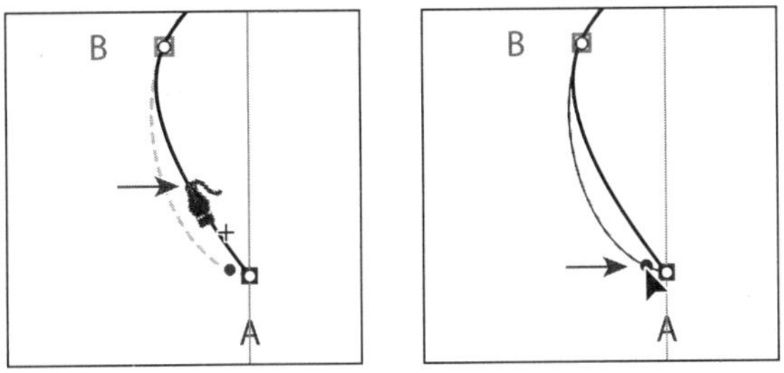

Note: The points you create with the Curvature tool can have three appearances, indicating its current state: selected (●), corner point (not selected [⊙]), and smooth point (not selected [○]).

7 Click point E and then click point F.

8 Shift-click to add point G.

Pressing the Shift key while clicking with the Curvature tool aligns the new point vertically (in this case) or horizontally with the previous point. Notice that the path segments before and after point F are curved, but they need to be straight to follow the template. To convert a default smooth point to a corner point, you can double-click a point you've made with the Curvature tool.

9 Hover the pointer over the anchor point at F. When the pointer changes (⊙), double-click to convert the point to a corner point.

Double-clicking a point, which converts it to a corner point, has the effect of splitting the direction handles for the point.

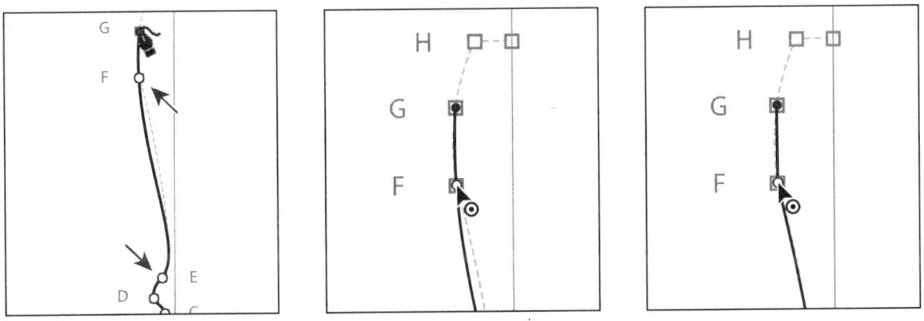

Next, you'll add a new point and convert it to a corner point in one step.

10 Option-click (macOS) or Alt-click (Windows) point H.

By Option-clicking (macOS) or Alt-clicking (Windows) when you create a point with the Curvature tool, you create a corner point instead of the default smooth point.

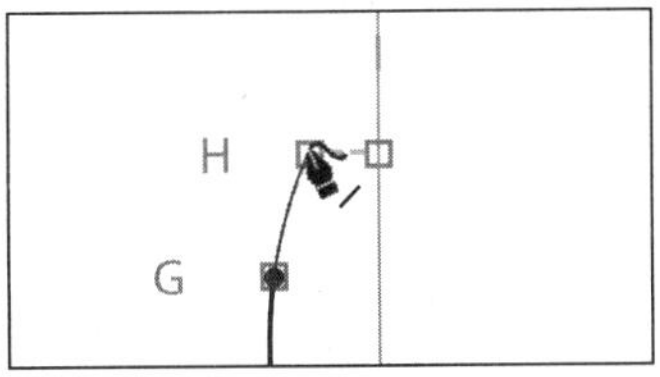

Tip: To close a path with the Curvature tool, hover the pointer over the first point you created in the path, and a circle appears next to the pointer. Click to close the path.

11 Shift-click point I.

12 Press the Escape key to stop drawing and then choose Select > Deselect.

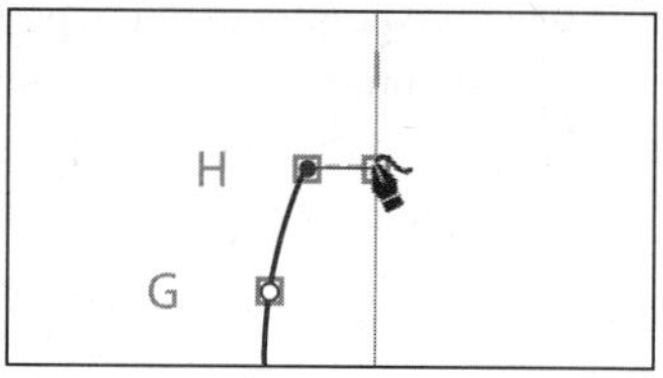

Editing curves

In this part of the lesson, you'll adjust curves you've drawn using several methods learned previously and a few new ones.

Reflecting the spoon shape

Since the spoon you are creating is symmetrical, you drew only half of it. Now you'll copy, reflect, and join the spoon path to create a whole spoon.

1 Choose View > Smart Guides to turn them on.

2 Select the Selection tool, and click to select the spoon path.

3 In the Layers panel, click the visibility column (eye icon) for the layer named "Template" to hide the contents.

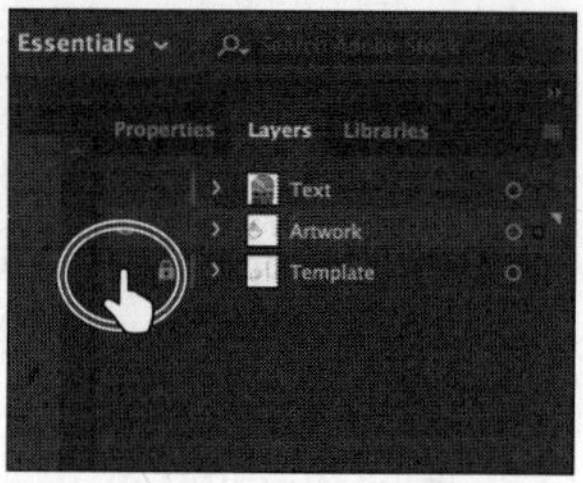

4 Click and hold down the mouse button on the Rotate tool in the Tools panel, and select the Reflect tool.

5 While holding down the Option (macOS) or Alt (Windows) key, position the pointer over point I (see the first part of the following figure). When you see the word "anchor" appear, click with the modifier key held down.

6 In the Reflect dialog box, select Vertical if necessary, and click Preview. Click Copy to copy the shape and reflect it in one step.

7 Select the Selection tool and Shift-click the original path to select both and press Cmd+J (macOS) or Ctrl+J (Windows) *twice* to join the paths together.

8 Choose Select > Deselect.

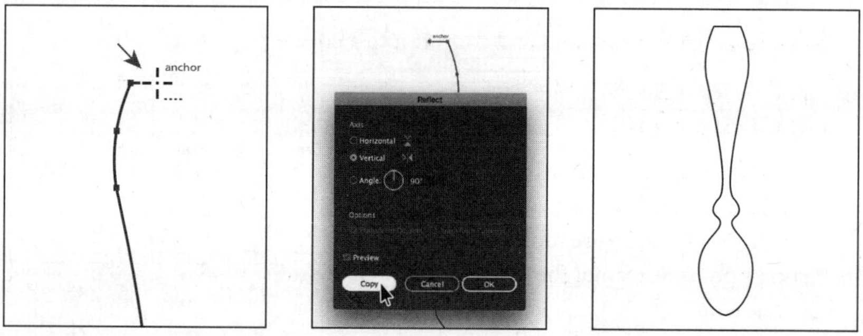

Rounding corner points

In Lesson 3, "Using Shapes to Create Artwork for a Postcard," you learned about Live Shapes and the ability to round corners. You can also round corner points on paths, which is what you'll do next.

1 Select the Zoom tool (), and click a few times on the top of the spoon to zoom in.

2 Select the Direct Selection tool (), and drag across the two points shown in the first part of the following figure to select them.

   Notice that a Live Corners widget () shows next to each of the anchor points. With both points selected, you can edit the radius of both by dragging one of the Live Corners widgets or double-clicking one of them.

3 Drag either Live Corner widget toward the center of the spoon just a bit to make the corners round. When the measurement label shows a radius of roughly 0.1 in, release the mouse button.

4 Choose Select > Deselect.

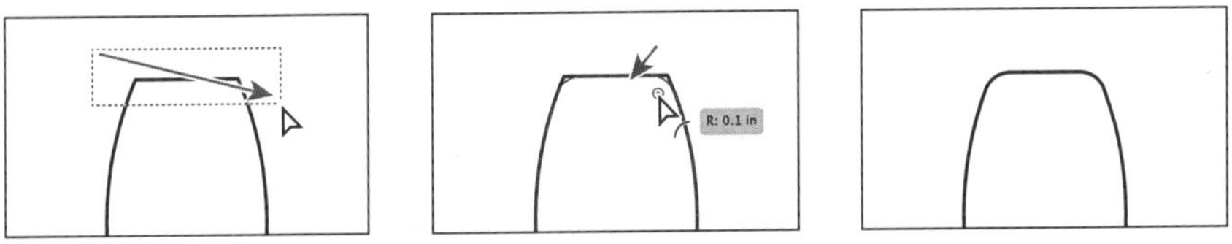

5 Choose View > Smart Guides to turn off the Smart Guides.

6 Select the Selection tool (), and click to select the spoon path.

7 Choose Edit > Copy.

8 Choose 1 Main from the Artboard Navigation menu in the lower-left corner of the Document window.

9 Click in a blank area of the artboard to ensure that it's the active artboard. Choose Edit > Paste to paste the spoon. Drag it off to the side for the moment.

Note: You will need to select the spoon by its stroke since it doesn't have a fill.

Editing paths and points

Next, you'll edit a few of the paths and points for the coffee cup you created earlier.

1 Select the Direct Selection tool (), and starting at the red X you see in the figure, drag across the "handle" of the coffee cup to select just that part of the path.

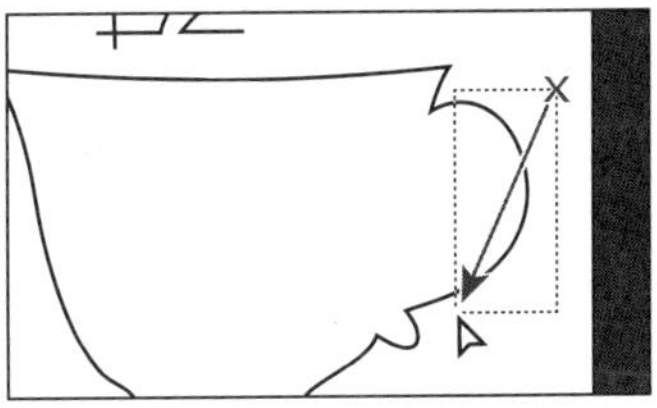

   Selecting with the Direct Selection tool in this way selects only the path segments and anchor points contained within the marquee selection. Clicking with the Selection tool () selects the entire path.

2 Choose Edit > Copy and then Edit > Paste In Front.

3 Press Command+J (macOS) or Ctrl+J (Windows) to close the path.

4 Select the Selection tool, and Shift-drag the right-middle bounding point to the left to make it smaller. Release the mouse button and then the key.

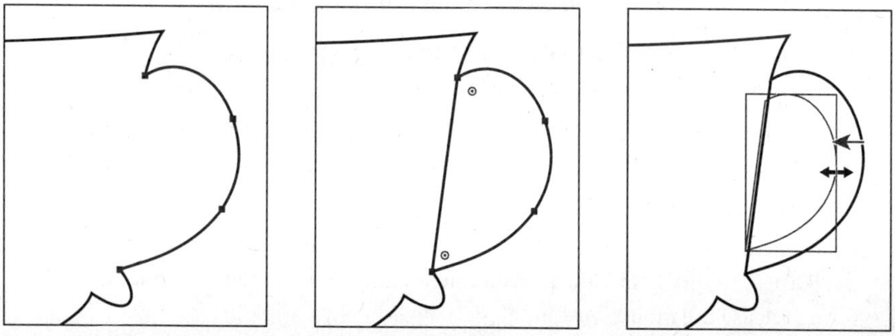

5 Select the Direct Selection tool, and click the anchor point you see in the figure to select it. Drag the anchor point to the right just a bit so it roughly matches the figure.

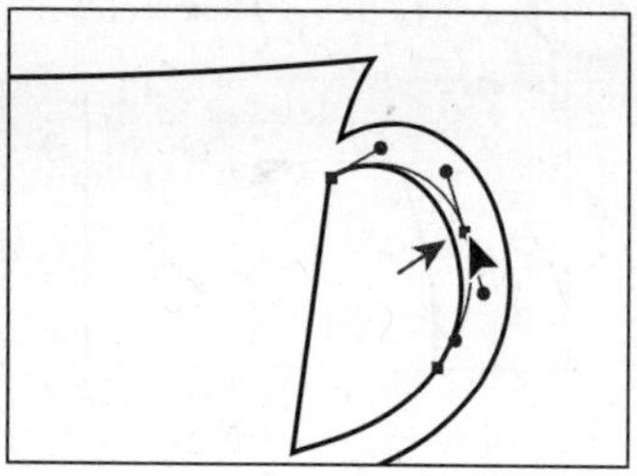

6 Position the pointer over the part of the path you see in the figure below, and click to select the path.

Notice that the pointer changes appearance () with the pointer over the path. This indicates that you can drag the path, which will adjust the anchor points and direction handles as you drag.

Tip: As you are dragging a path with the Direct Selection tool, you can also press the Shift key to constrain the handles to a perpendicular direction, which ensures that the handles are the same length.

7 Drag the path up and to the left to make the curve a little less rounded. This is an easy way to make edits to a path.

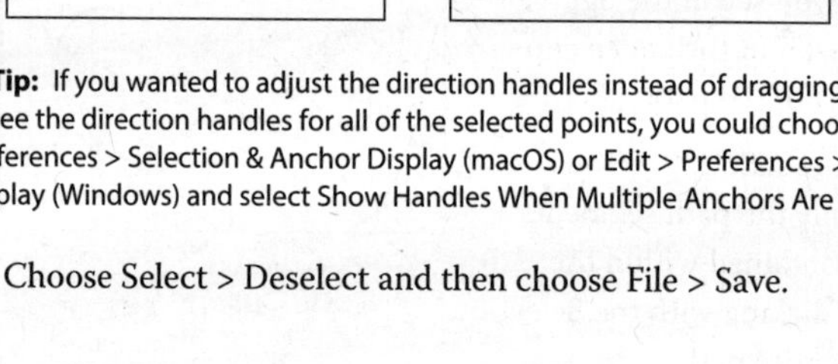

Tip: If you wanted to adjust the direction handles instead of dragging the path and wanted to see the direction handles for all of the selected points, you could choose Illustrator CC > Preferences > Selection & Anchor Display (macOS) or Edit > Preferences > Selection & Anchor Display (Windows) and select Show Handles When Multiple Anchors Are Selected.

8 Choose Select > Deselect and then choose File > Save.

Deleting and adding anchor points

Most of the time, the goal of drawing paths with a tool like the Pen tool or Curvature tool is to avoid adding more anchor points than necessary. You can reduce a path's complexity or change its overall shape by deleting unnecessary points (and therefore gain more control over the shape), or you can extend a path by adding points to it. Next, you'll delete and add anchor points to the coffee cup path so that it has a flatter bottom.

1 Select the Zoom tool ( ) in the Tools panel, and click twice, *slowly*, on the bottom of the cup to zoom in.

2 With the Direct Selection tool ( ) selected, click the coffee cup path to select it.

3 Select the Pen tool ( ) in the Tools panel, and position the pointer over the anchor point at the bottom center of the cup (see the figure). When a minus sign (–) appears to the right of the Pen tool pointer ( ), click to remove the anchor point.

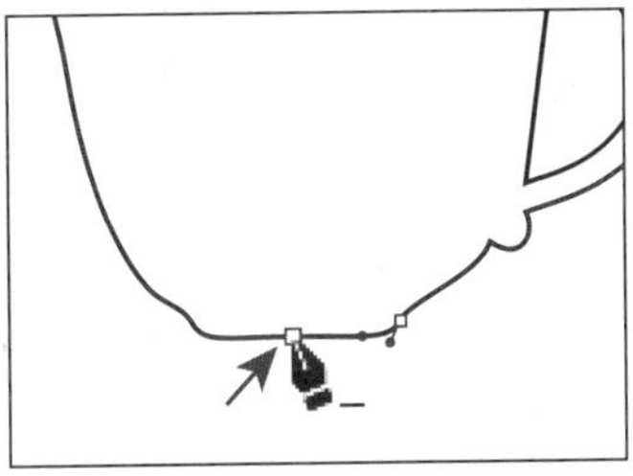

Tip: With an anchor point selected, you can also click Remove Selected Anchor Points ( ) in the Properties panel to delete the anchor point.

4 Position the Pen tool pointer over the bottom of the cup shape again. Look at the first part of the following figure for where to position the pointer. This time, when a plus sign (+) appears to the right of the Pen tool pointer ( ), click to add an anchor point.

5 Move the pointer over to the right a bit, and click the path to add another point. Leave this last point selected.

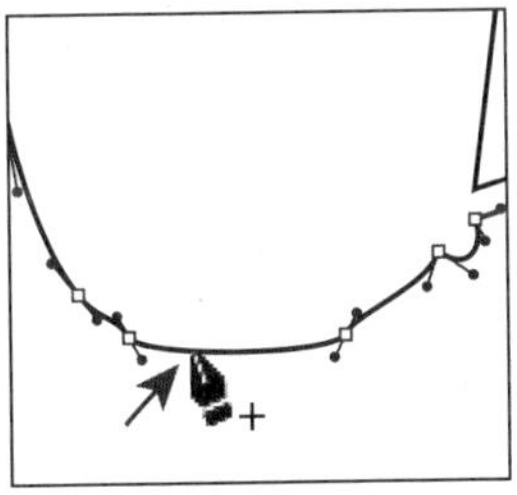

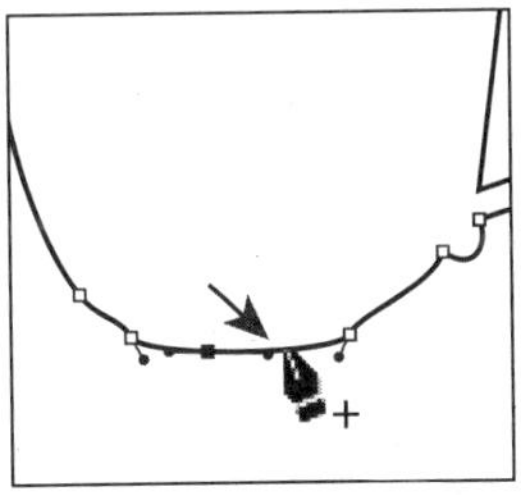

Adding points to a curved path means that the anchor points will most likely have direction lines and be considered smooth points.

Converting between smooth points and corner points

To more precisely control the path you create, you can convert points from smooth points to corner points and from corner points to smooth points, using several methods.

> **Tip:** You could also convert between corner and smooth points by double-clicking an anchor point (or Option-clicking [macOS] or Alt-clicking [Windows]) with the Curvature tool, like you saw earlier.

1 Select the Direct Selection tool ( ), and with the last point still selected, Shift-click the other point you added to the left. In the second part of the following figure, arrows are pointing to the anchor points to select. Click the Convert Selected Anchor Points To Corner button ( ) in the Properties panel.

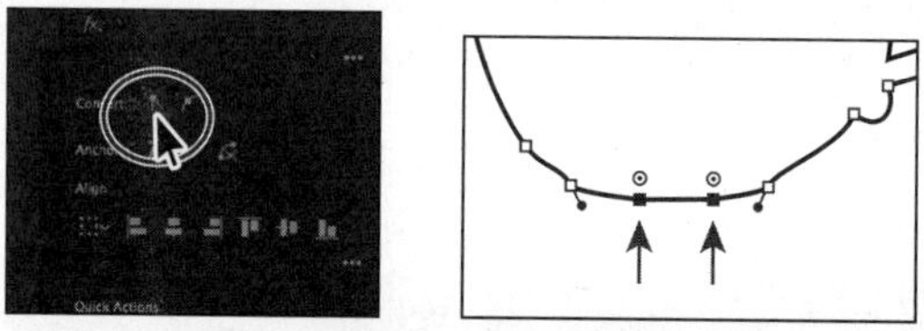

> **Note:** If the points align to the artboard after clicking the align button, try again. Make sure that Align To Key Object is selected in the Properties panel first.

2 With both points selected, click the Vertical Align Bottom button ( ) in the Properties panel to align one point to the other.

As you saw in Lesson 2, "Techniques for Selecting Artwork," selected anchor points align to the last selected anchor point, which is known as the *key anchor.*

3 Press the Down arrow *five times* to move both points down.

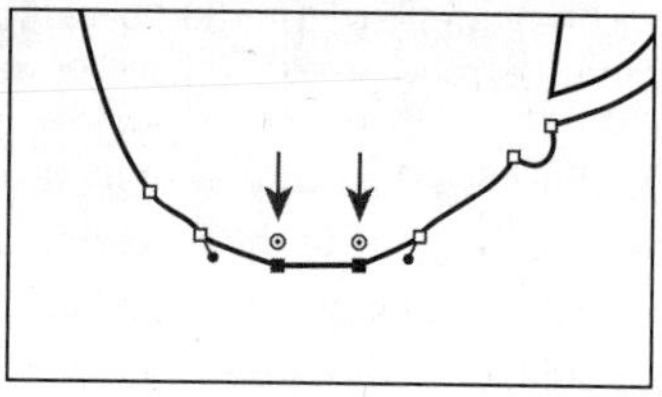

4 Choose Select > Deselect.

> **Note:** If you find it difficult to select the second anchor point, you can also drag a marquee across the bottom of the coffee cup to select the two anchor points or enter Outline mode (View > Outline).

5 With the Direct Selection tool, click the coffee cup path to show all of the anchor points. Click the anchor point labeled 1 in the figure first and then Shift-click the anchor point labeled 2. Click the Horizontal Align Left button ( ) in the Properties panel to align them.

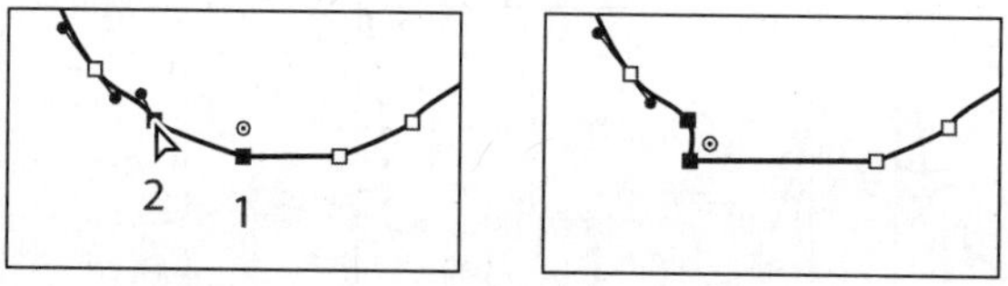

6 Click the anchor point labeled 3 in the figure first and then Shift-click the anchor point labeled 4. Click the Horizontal Align Right button ( ) to align them. Leave the path (and points) selected.

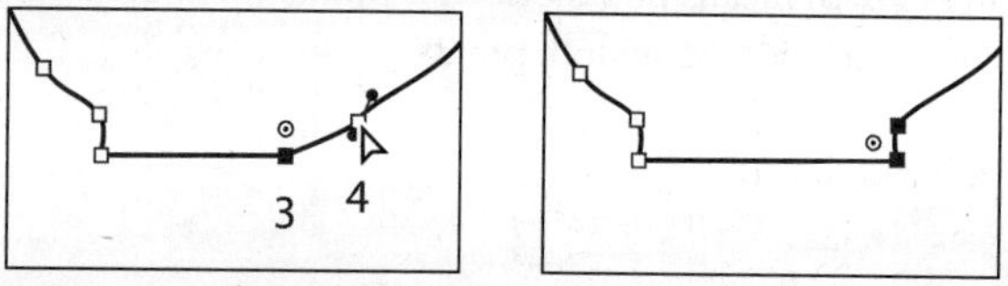

Working with the Anchor Point tool

Another way to convert anchor points between smooth and corner points is using the Anchor Point tool. Next, you'll convert anchor points using the Anchor Point tool ( ).

1 Position the pointer over the Pen tool ( ) in the Tools panel, and click and hold down the mouse button to reveal more tools. Select the Anchor Point tool ( ).

   You will also see the Add Anchor Point tool ( ) and the Delete Anchor Point tool ( ), which are specifically for adding or removing anchor points.

2 Position the pointer over the point with an arrow pointing to it in the figure. Click to convert the point from a smooth point (with direction handles) to a corner point.

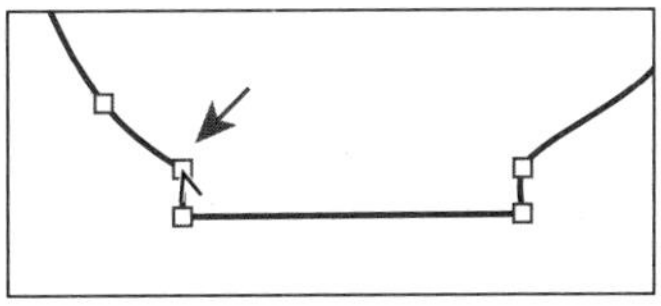

3 Position the pointer over the anchor point below the point you just converted. Click and drag up when the pointer looks like this: . As you drag, press the Shift key. Drag up until you reach the anchor point above it. Release the mouse button and then release the key.

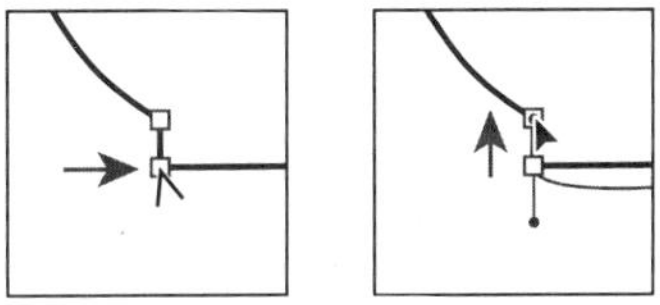

Tip: If you position the Anchor Point tool pointer over the end of a direction handle that is split, you can press the Option (macOS) or Alt (Windows) key and, when the pointer changes ( ), click to make the direction handles a single straight line again (not split).

Note: Don't drag if the pointer looks like this: . This means that the pointer is not over the anchor point, and if you drag, you will reshape the curve.

   With the Anchor Point tool, you can perform tasks such as converting between smooth and corner points, splitting direction handles, and more. Next, you'll do the same thing to the right side of the bottom of the coffee cup.

4 Position the pointer over the point with an arrow pointing to it in the figure. Click to convert the point from a smooth point (with direction handles) to a corner point.

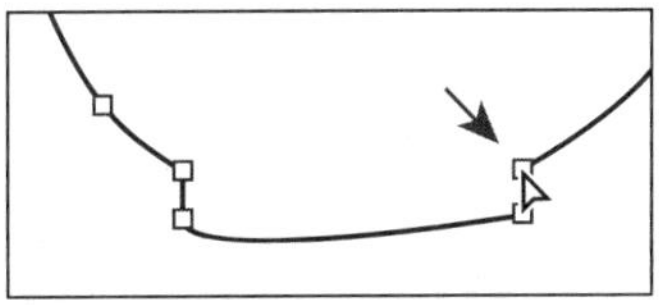

5 Position the pointer over the anchor point below the point you just converted. Click and drag down when the pointer looks like this: . As you drag, press the Shift key. Drag down until the end of the opposite direction handle reaches the point above. Release the mouse button and then release the key.

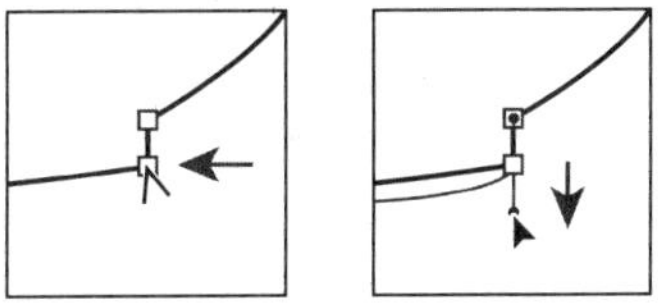

6 Choose Select > Deselect and then choose File > Save.

Creating a dashed line

Dashed lines apply to the stroke of an object and can be added to a closed path or an open path. Dashes are created by specifying a sequence of dash lengths and the gaps between them. Next, you will add a dash to a line.

1 Choose View > Fit Artboard In Window.

2 In the Layers panel, click the visibility column for the layer named "Text" to show the layer contents.

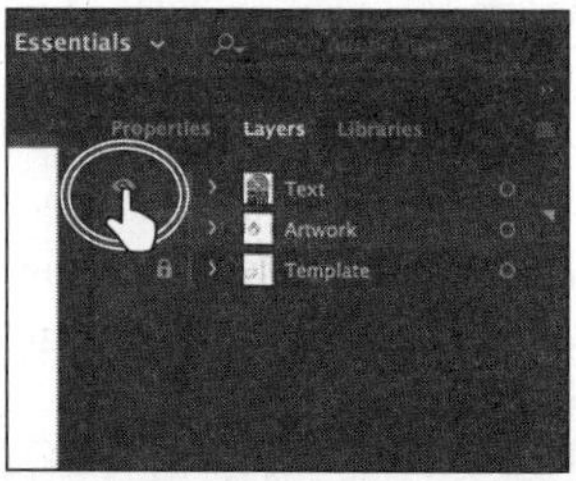

3 Select the Zoom tool (🔍), and click twice to zoom in to the red circles that are now showing.

4 Select the Selection tool (▶) in the Tools panel, and click the dark gray path in the center of the red circles.

▶ **Tip:** The Preserves Exact Dash And Gap Lengths button (▭) allows you to retain the appearance of the dashes without aligning to the corners or the dash ends.

5 Click the Properties panel tab to show the panel. Click the word "Stroke" in the Properties panel to show the Stroke panel. Change the following options in the Stroke panel:

- Weight: **8 pt**
- Dashed Line: **Selected**
- First Dash value: **4 pt** (This creates a 4-pt dash, 4-pt gap repeating pattern.)
- First Gap value: **2 pt** (This creates a 4-pt dash, 2-pt gap repeating pattern.)
- Aligns Dashes To Corners And Path Ends (▭): Selected

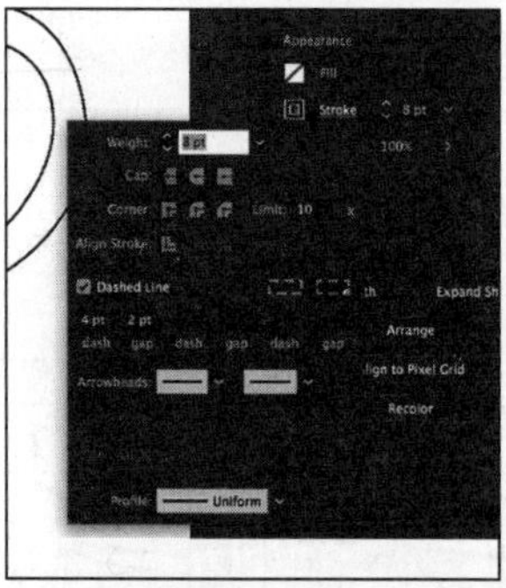

6 Press the Escape key to hide the Stroke panel.

● **Note:** Be careful about pressing the Escape key when you change a value in a panel, like you just did. Sometimes the value may not be accepted. You can press Enter or Return to both accept the last value in a panel and hide the panel.

7 Choose File > Save, and leave the line selected.

Adding arrowheads to a path

You can add arrowheads to both ends of a path using the Stroke panel. There are many different arrowhead styles to choose from in Illustrator, as well as arrowhead editing options. Next, you'll apply different arrowheads to the dashed path.

1 With the dashed line still selected, click the word "Stroke" again in the Properties panel to open the Stroke panel (or choose Window > Stroke). In the Stroke panel, change only the following options:

- Choose Arrow 21 from the menu directly to the right of the word "Arrowheads." This adds an arrowhead to the start (right end) of the line.
- Scale (*beneath where you chose Arrow 21*): **30%**
- Choose Arrow 17 from the arrowheads menu to the far right of the word "Arrowheads." This adds an arrowhead to the end of the line.
- Scale (*beneath where you chose Arrow 17*): **50%**
- Click the Extend Arrow Tip Beyond End Of Path button ().

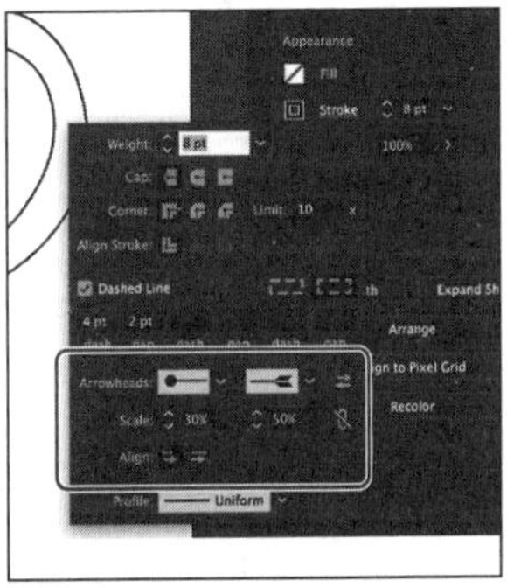

2 Click the edge of the coffee cup path, and change the fill color to White.

3 Click the spoon shape, and change the fill color to a light gray (I chose the color with the tooltip that shows "C=0 M=0 Y=0 K=10").

● **Note:** You may need to zoom out to see your spoon.

4 With the spoon selected, choose Object > Transform > Rotate, change the Angle to **90**, select Preview, and then click OK.

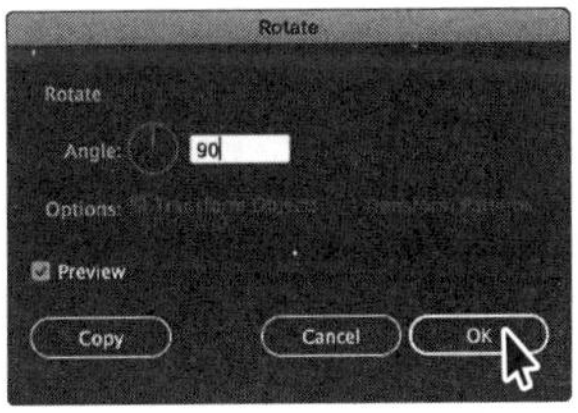

● **Note:** If the spoon is behind the coffee cup in the stacking order, you can choose Object > Arrange > Bring To Front with the spoon selected.

5 Drag the spoon into the position you see in the following figure.

Working with the Pencil tool

The Pencil tool (✎) lets you draw freeform open and closed paths that contain curves and straight lines. As you draw with the Pencil tool, anchor points are created on the path where necessary and according to the Pencil tool options you set. The path can easily be adjusted when the path is complete.

Drawing freeform paths with the Pencil tool

Next, you'll draw and edit a simple path using the Pencil tool.

1 Choose 2 Coffee Bean from the Artboard Navigation menu in the lower-left corner of the Document window.

2 Choose View > Fit Artboard In Window, if necessary.

3 In the Layers panel, click the visibility column for the layer named "Template" to show the layer contents.

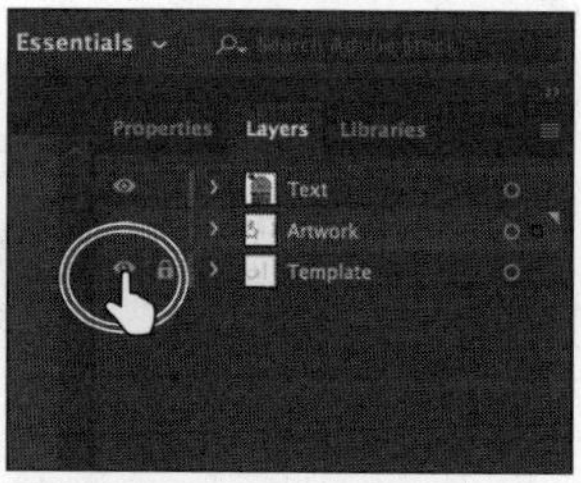

4 Select the Zoom tool (🔍) in the Tools panel, and click a few times, slowly, on the top of the artboard to zoom in where you see "A."

5 Choose Select > Deselect.

6 In the Properties panel, make sure that the fill color is None (☒) and the stroke color is Black. Also make sure the stroke weight is 1 pt in the Properties panel.

▶ **Tip:** When it comes to the Fidelity value, dragging the slider closer to Accurate usually creates more anchor points and more accurately reflects the path you've drawn. Dragging the slider toward Smooth makes fewer anchor points and a smoother, less complex path.

7 Click and hold down on the Shaper tool (✓) in the Tools panel to select the Pencil tool (✎). Double-click the Pencil tool. In the Pencil Tool Options dialog box, set the following options, leaving the rest at their default settings:

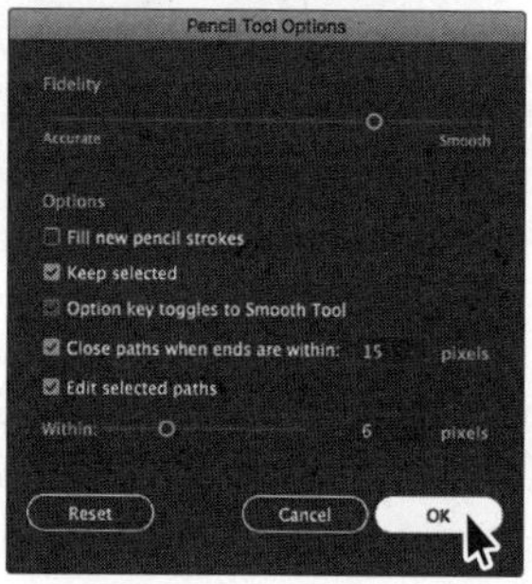

- Drag the Fidelity slider to the right, one position closer to Smooth. This will reduce the number of points on a path drawn with the Pencil tool and make the path smoother.
- Keep Selected: **Selected** (the default setting)
- Option Key (Alt Key on Windows) Toggles To Smooth Tool: **Selected** (The Smooth tool is used to smooth the path after it is drawn.)
- Close Paths When Ends Are Within: **Selected** (the default setting)

8 Click OK.

The asterisk (*) that appears next to the Pencil tool pointer indicates that you are about to create a new path. If you don't see the asterisk, it means that you are about to redraw a shape that the pointer is near.

9 Starting at the red X in the template, click and drag around the dashed template path. When the pointer gets close to the start of the path (at the red X), a small circle displays next to it (✎) to indicate that if you release the mouse button, the path will close. When you see the circle, release the mouse button to close the path.

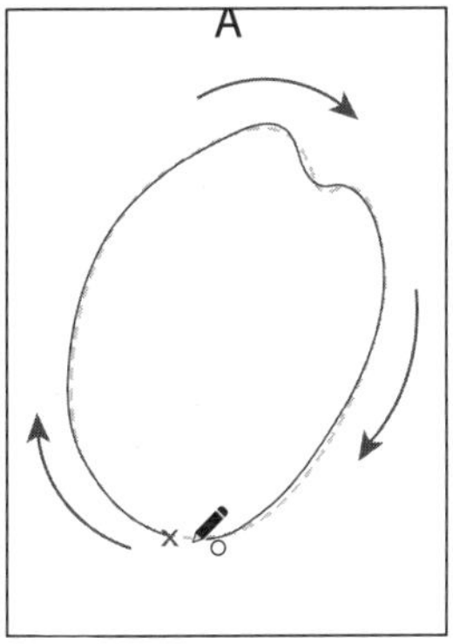

Notice that as you are drawing, the path may not look perfectly smooth. After releasing the mouse button, the path is smoothed based on the Fidelity value that you set in the Pencil Tool Options dialog box.

10 Position the Pencil tool on or near the path to redraw it. When the asterisk disappears from the pointer, click and drag to reshape the path. Make sure you wind up back on the original path. Think of it as redrawing parts of the path.

Note: If you see an X (×) instead of the Pencil icon (✎), the Caps Lock key is active. Caps Lock turns the Pencil tool icon into an X for increased precision.

Note: When editing a path with the Pencil tool, you may find that a new path is created instead of editing the original shape. You can always undo and make sure that you finish back on the original path (or at least close to it).

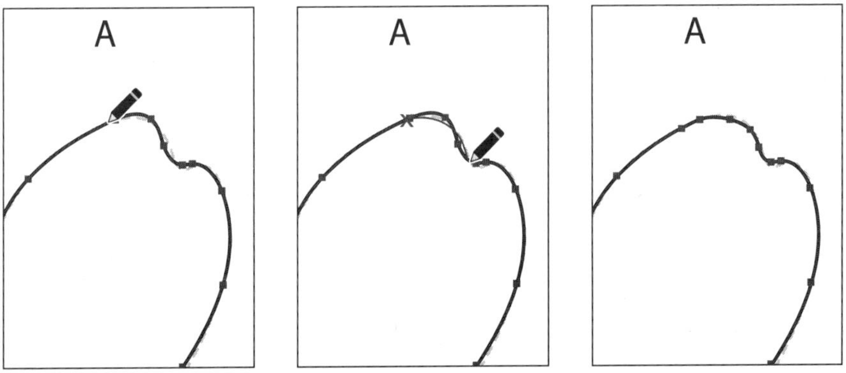

Tip: If you wanted to "smooth" parts of the path you drew, you could press the Option key (macOS) or Alt key (Windows) and drag along the path. This can simplify the path and remove anchor points. This is possible because you selected Option Key (Alt Key on Windows) Toggles To Smooth Tool in the Pencil Tool Options dialog box earlier.

Drawing straight segments with the Pencil tool

Aside from drawing more freeform paths, you can also create straight lines that can be constrained to 45° angles with the Pencil tool. That's what you'll do next.

1 Scroll down the artboard to see the template shapes labeled "B" and "C," if you can't see them.

2 Position the pointer over the red X at the bottom of the path labeled "B." Click and drag around the left side of the shape and stop at the green X, but *don't release the mouse button yet.*

● **Note:** When drawing the path, after reaching the green X, you could have released the mouse button to stop drawing and then just started drawing from the same place later. You can tell you are continuing a path with the Pencil tool when a line appears next to the Pencil tool pointer (✎), with the pointer positioned over the end of a path.

3 With the mouse button still down, press Option (macOS) or Alt (Windows), and drag a straight line that follows the flat edge of the shape. When you reach the red X again and a small circle displays next to the Pencil tool pointer (✎), release the mouse button and then the key to close the path.

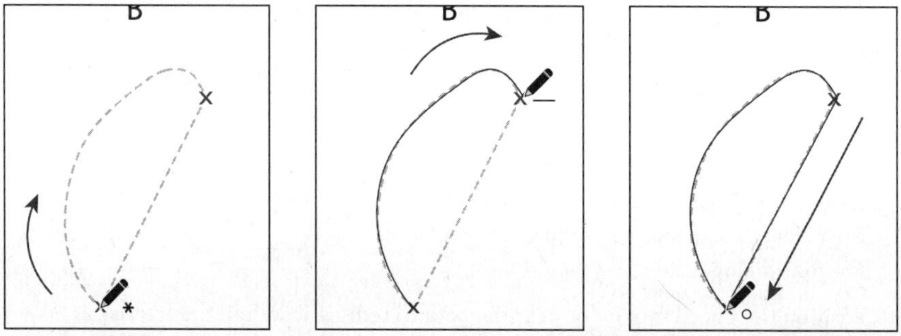

4 Position the pointer over the red X at the top of the path labeled "C" (it's below "B"). Click and drag down around the right side of the shape and stop at the green X, but *don't release the mouse button yet.*

5 With the mouse button still down, press the Shift key, and drag a straight line that follows the flat edge of the shape. When you reach the red X again and a small circle displays next to the Pencil tool pointer (✎), release the mouse button and then the key to close the path.

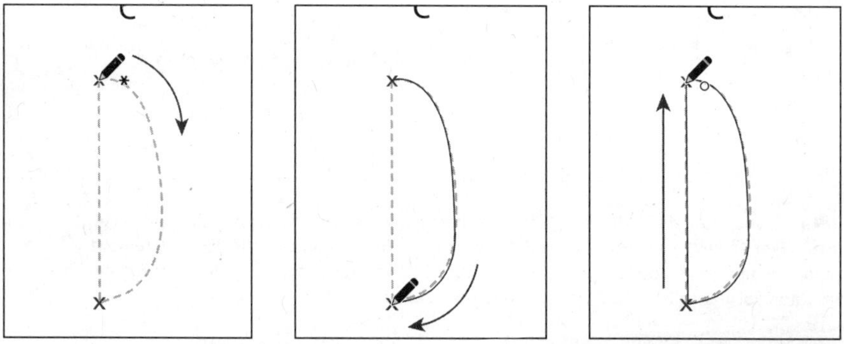

6 With shape "C" selected, choose Object > Transform > Rotate. In the Rotate dialog box, change Angle to **-25°**, select Preview, and then click OK.

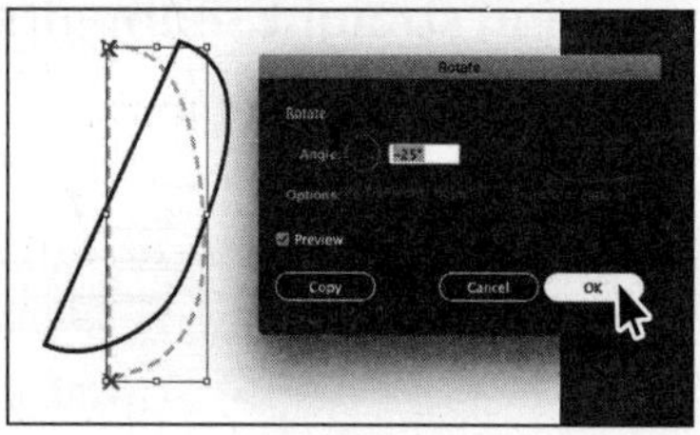

Finishing the coffee bean

In this last part of the section, you'll take the shapes you created with the Pencil tool, bring them together to create a coffee bean, then add it to the final artwork.

1 Choose View > Fit Artboard In Window.

2 Select the Selection tool (▶), and click to select the top shape labeled "A." Change the fill color to the swatch named "CoffeeBean" in the Properties panel.

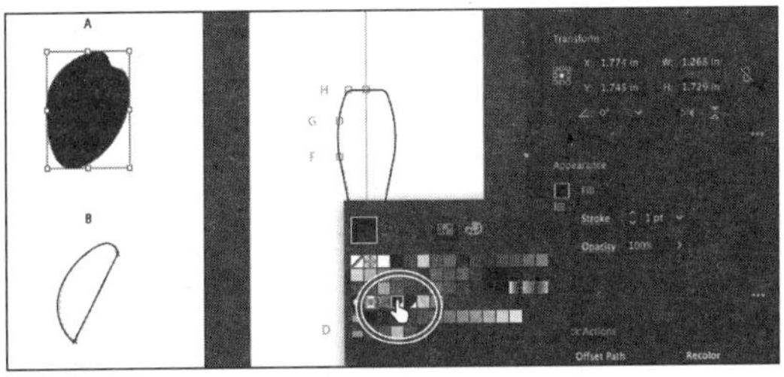

3 Click to select shape B, and then Shift-click to select shape C. Change the fill color for both to the swatch named "CoffeeBean2" in the Properties panel.

4 Choose Select > Deselect.

5 Drag shape B and then shape C onto shape A, something like you see in the figure.

   Feel free to adjust the individual shapes using any of the methods you've learned so far (I did).

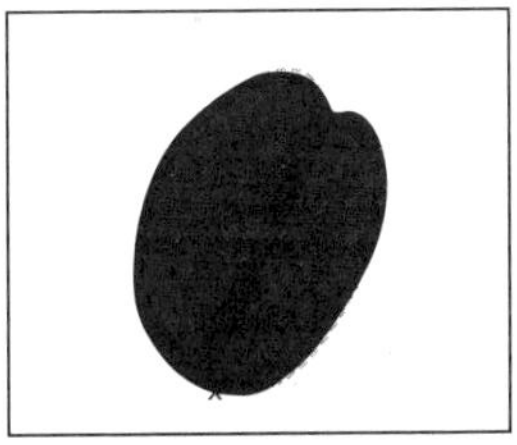

6 Drag across all three shapes to select them, and choose Object > Group.

7 Choose View > Fit All In Window.

8 Drag the coffee bean group on front of the coffee cup and spoon. You may want to resize the coffee bean group a little.

9 Choose Select > Deselect.

Joining with the Join tool

In this lesson and earlier lessons, you've used the Join command (Object > Path > Join) to join as well as close paths. Using the Join tool (✂), you can easily join paths that cross, overlap, or have open ends using scrubbing gestures.

1 Choose View > Steam. This command will zoom in to the shapes above the coffee cup and also hide the layer named "Template."

2 Click and hold down the mouse on the Pencil tool (✎), and select the Join tool (✂).

Unlike the Join command (Object > Path > Join) you learned about in Lesson 3, "Using Shapes to Create Artwork for a Postcard," the Join tool can trim overlapping paths as it joins, and it doesn't simply create a straight line between the anchor points you are joining. The angle created by the two paths to be joined are taken into account.

Note: If you were to instead join the ends of the open path by pressing Cmd+J (macOS) or Ctrl+J (Windows), a straight line would connect the ends.

3 With the Join tool selected, drag across the two ends of the path on the right (see the figure for which paths to drag across).

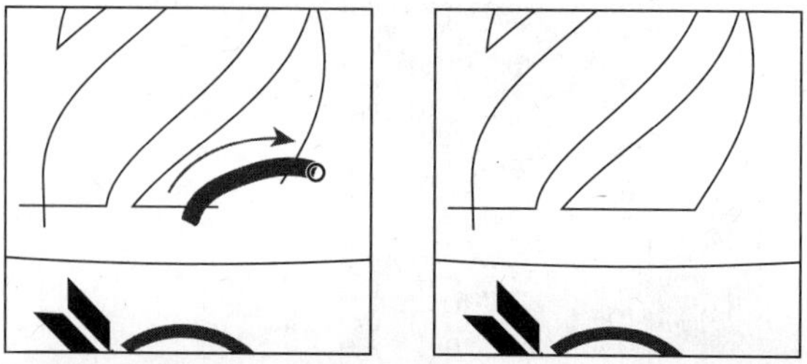

When dragging (also called *scrubbing*) across paths, they will be either "extended and joined" or "trimmed and joined." In this example, the paths were extended and joined. The Join tool works on paths that are selected or not, but the result of joining is not selected to continue working on more paths.

4 Drag across (or scrub) the excess part of the paths on the shape to the left to remove them and close the path. In this case, the path was "trimmed and joined."

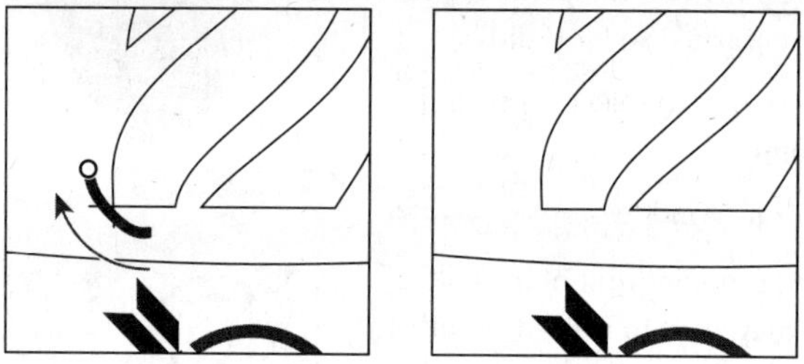

5 Choose View > Fit Artboard In Window.

6 Select the Selection tool, and drag across the "steam" shapes above the cup to select them.

7 Change the Fill color to the swatch named "Steam" and the stroke weight to **0** in the Properties panel.

8 Choose Object > Group, and drag the group down like the following figure.

9 Choose Select > Deselect, and take a step back to admire all that you've accomplished!

10 Choose File > Save and then choose File > Close.

Review questions

1 Describe how to draw straight vertical, horizontal, or diagonal lines using the Pen tool ( ).

2 How do you draw a curved line using the Pen tool?

3 Name two ways to convert a smooth point on a curve to a corner point.

4 Which tool would you use to edit a segment on a curved line?

5 How can you change the way the Pencil tool ( ) works?

6 How is the Join tool different from the Join command (Object > Path > Join)?

Review answers

1 To draw a straight line, click with the Pen tool ( ) and then move the pointer and click again. The first click sets the starting anchor point, and the second click sets the ending anchor point of the line. To constrain the straight line vertically, horizontally, or along a 45° diagonal, press the Shift key as you click to create the second anchor point with the Pen tool.

2 To draw a curved line with the Pen tool, click to create the starting anchor point, drag to set the direction of the curve, and then click to end the curve.

3 To convert a smooth point on a curve to a corner point, use the Direct Selection tool ( ) to select the anchor point and then use the Anchor Point tool ( ) to drag a direction handle to change the direction. Another method is to choose a point or points with the Direct Selection tool and then click the Convert Selected Anchor Points To Corner button ( ) in the Properties panel.

4 To edit a segment on a curved line, select the Direct Selection tool, and drag the segment to move it; or drag a direction handle on an anchor point to adjust the length and shape of the segment. Dragging a path segment with the Direct Selection tool or pressing the Option (macOS) or Alt (Windows) key and dragging a path segment with the Pen tool is another way to reshape a path.

5 To change the way the Pencil tool ( ) works, double-click the Pencil tool in the Tools panel to open the Pencil Tool Options dialog box. There you can change the fidelity and other options.

6 Unlike the Join command, the Join tool can trim overlapping paths as it joins, and it doesn't simply create a straight line between the anchor points you are joining. The angle created by the two paths to be joined are taken into account.

7 USING COLOR TO ENHANCE SIGNAGE

Lesson overview

In this lesson, you'll learn how to do the following:

- Understand color modes and the main color controls.
- Create, edit, and paint with colors using a variety of methods.
- Name and save colors, and build a color palette.
- Work with color groups.
- Use the Color Guide panel.
- Explore the Edit Colors/Recolor Artwork features.
- Copy and paint appearance attributes from one object to another.
- Work with Live Paint.

This lesson takes approximately 90 minutes to complete. Please log in to your account on peachpit.com to download the lesson files for this chapter, or go to the "Getting Started" section at the beginning of this book and follow the instructions under "Accessing the lesson files and Web Edition."

Your Account page is also where you'll find any updates to the chapters or to the lesson files. Look on the Lesson & Update Files tab to access the most current content.

Spice up your illustrations with colors by taking advantage of color controls in Adobe Illustrator CC. In this information-packed lesson, you'll discover how to create and paint fills and strokes, use the Color Guide panel for inspiration, work with color groups, recolor artwork, and more.

Starting the lesson

In this lesson, you'll learn about the fundamentals of color by creating and editing colors for an art store sign and logo, using the Color panel, Swatches panel, and more.

● **Note:** If you have not already downloaded the project files for this lesson to your computer from your Account page, make sure to do so now. See the "Getting Started" section at the beginning of the book.

1 To ensure that the tools function and the defaults are set exactly as described in this lesson, delete or deactivate (by renaming) the Adobe Illustrator CC preferences file. See "Restoring default preferences" in the "Getting Started" section at the beginning of the book.

2 Start Adobe Illustrator CC.

3 Choose File > Open, and open the L7_end.ai file in the Lessons > Lesson07 folder to view a final version of the artwork.

4 Choose View > Fit All In Window. You can leave the file open for reference or choose File > Close to close it.

5 Choose File > Open. In the Open dialog box, navigate to the Lessons > Lesson07 folder, and select the L7_start.ai file on your hard disk. Click Open to open the file. This file has all the pieces already in it; they just need to be painted.

6 Choose View > Fit All In Window.

7 Choose File > Save As. In the Save As dialog box, navigate to the Lesson07 folder, and name it **ArtSign.ai**. Leave the Format option set to Adobe Illustrator (ai) (macOS) or the Save As Type option set to Adobe Illustrator (*.AI) (Windows), and click Save.

8 In the Illustrator Options dialog box, leave the options at their default settings and then click OK.

9 Choose Window > Workspace > Reset Essentials.

● **Note:** If you don't see Reset Essentials in the menu, choose Window > Workspace > Essentials before choosing Window > Workspace > Reset Essentials.

Exploring color modes

There are many ways to experiment with and apply color to your artwork in Adobe Illustrator CC. As you work with color, it's important to keep in mind the medium in which the artwork will be published, such as a print piece or a website. The colors you create need to be described in the correct way for the medium. This usually requires that you use the correct color mode and color definitions for your colors. The first part, color modes, will be described next.

Before starting a new document, you should decide which color mode the artwork should use, *CMYK* or *RGB*.

- **CMYK**—Cyan, magenta, yellow, and black are the colors used in four-color process printing. These four colors are combined and overlapped in a screen pattern to create a multitude of other colors.
- **RGB**—Red, green, and blue light are added together in various ways to create an array of colors. Select this mode if you are using images for onscreen presentations, the Internet, or mobile apps.

When creating a new document by choosing File > New, each profile has a specific color mode. For instance, the Print profile uses the CMYK color mode. You can easily change the color mode by making a selection in the Color Mode menu.

Tip: To learn more about color and graphics, search for "About color" in Illustrator Help (Help > Illustrator Help).

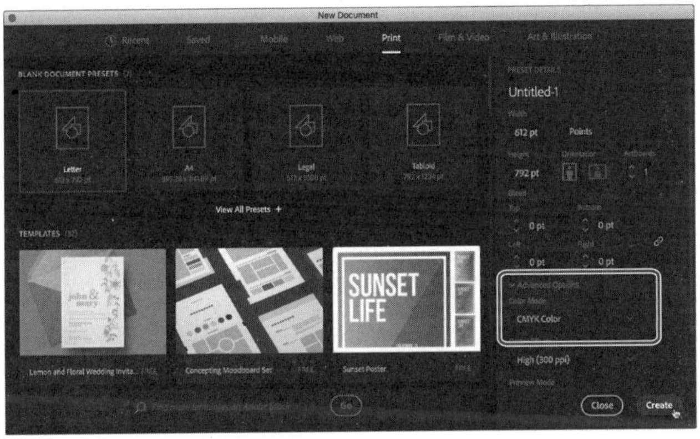

When a color mode is selected, colors in the document are displayed in the selected color mode. You can change the color mode of a document, after a file is created, by choosing File > Document Color Mode and then choosing either CMYK Color or RGB Color in the menu.

Working with color

In this lesson, you'll learn about the traditional methods of coloring (also called *painting*) objects in Illustrator using a combination of panels and tools, such as the Properties panel, Swatches panel, Color Guide panel, Color Picker, and the paint options in the Tools panel.

● **Note:** The Tools panel you see may be a single column, and that just depends on the resolution of your screen.

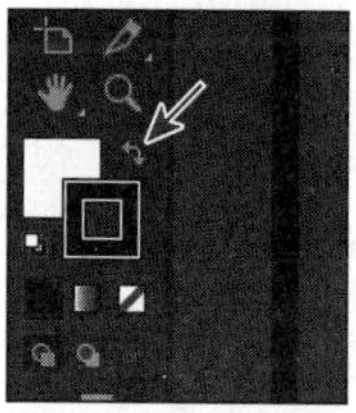

In previous lessons, you learned that objects in Illustrator can have a fill, a stroke, or both. At the bottom of the Tools panel (on the left), notice the Fill and Stroke boxes. The Fill box is white (in this case), and the Stroke box is Black. If you click those boxes one at a time, you'll see that whichever is clicked is brought in front of the other (it's selected). When a color is chosen, it is applied to the fill or stroke, whichever is selected. As you explore more of Illustrator, you'll see these fill and stroke boxes in lots of other places like the Properties panel, Swatches panel, and more.

As you will see in this section, Illustrator provides a lot of ways to arrive at the color you need. You'll start by applying an existing color to a shape and then work your way through the most widely used methods for creating and applying color.

Applying an existing color

● **Note:** Throughout this lesson, you'll be working on a document with a color mode that was set to CMYK when the document was created, which means that the majority of colors you create will, by default, be composed of cyan, magenta, yellow, and black.

Every new document in Illustrator has a series of default colors available for you to use in your artwork in the form of swatches in the Swatches panel. The first method of working with color you'll explore is to paint a shape with an existing color.

1 Click the ArtSign.ai document tab at the top of the Document window, if you did not close the L7_end.ai document.

2 Choose 1 Art Sign from the Artboard Navigation menu in the lower-left corner of the Document window (if it's not chosen already) and then choose View > Fit Artboard In Window.

3 With the Selection tool (▶), click to select the large red shape in the background.

4 Click the Fill box in the Properties panel (■) on the right to reveal a panel. Click the Swatches option (■) in the panel, if it isn't already selected, to show the saved default swatches. Position the pointer over a swatch in the list to reveal a tooltip with the swatch name. Click to apply the blue swatch named "Sign Bg" to change the color of the fill for the selected artwork.

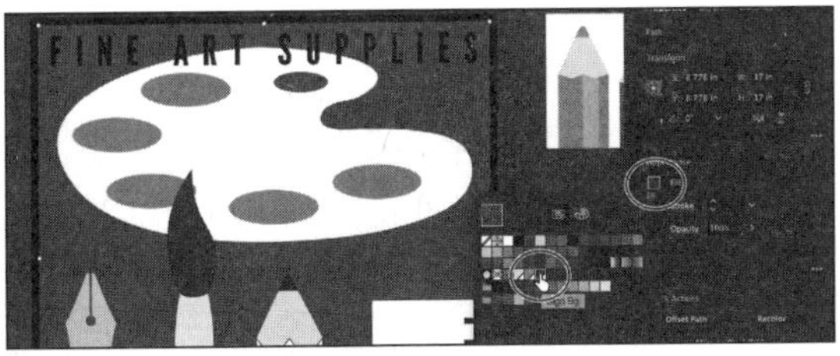

5 Press the Escape key to hide the panel.

Creating a custom color

There are lots of ways to create your own custom colors in Illustrator. Using the Color panel (Window > Color) or Color Mixer, you can apply color to an object's fill and stroke and also edit and mix colors using different color models (CMYK, for example). The Color panel and Color Mixer display the current fill and stroke of the selected content, and you can either visually select a color from the color spectrum bar at the bottom of the panel or mix your own colors, changing the color values in various ways. Next, you'll create a custom color using the Color Mixer.

1 With the Selection tool ( ), click the gray ellipse below the word "ART," toward the top of the artboard.

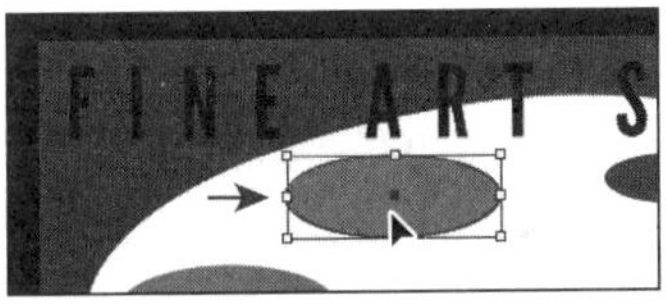

2 Click the Fill box in the Properties panel ( ) on the right, to reveal a panel. Select the Color Mixer option ( ) in the panel that appears.

3 Click in the light-green part of the color spectrum to sample a light-green color and apply it to the fill.

Since the spectrum bar is so small, you most likely won't achieve the same color as I did. That's okay, because you'll edit it shortly to match.

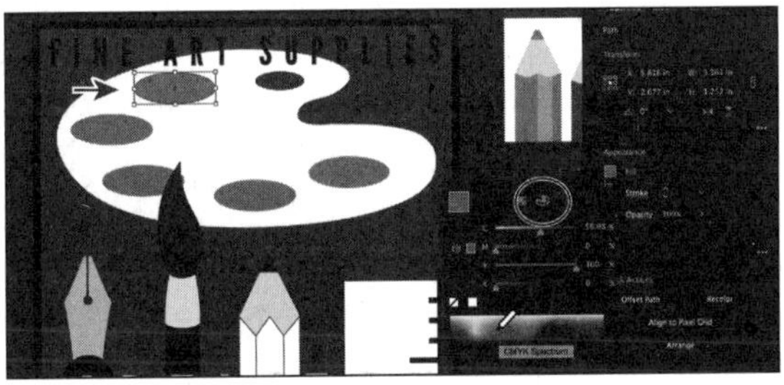

If artwork is selected when you create a color this way, the color is automatically applied.

▶ **Tip:** Each CMYK value is a percentage of 100.

4 In the Color Mixer panel, type the following values in the CMYK fields: C=**52**, M=**0**, Y=**100**, K=**0**. This ensures that we are all using the same green.

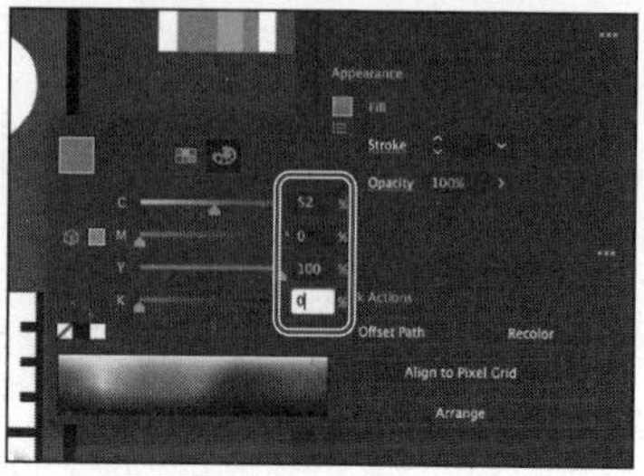

Colors created in the Color Mixer panel are not saved anywhere except for in the fill or stroke of the selected artwork. If you want to easily reuse the color you just created elsewhere in this document, you can save it as a swatch in the Swatches panel. All documents start with a default number of swatches, as mentioned earlier. Any colors you save or edit in the Swatches panel are available to the current document only (by default) since each document has its own defined swatches.

Saving a color as a swatch

You can name and save different types of colors, gradients, and patterns in the document as swatches so that you can apply and edit them later. Swatches are listed in the Swatches panel in the order in which they were created, but you can reorder or organize the swatches into groups to suit your needs.

Next, you'll save the green color you just created as a swatch so you can easily reuse it.

1 Click the Fill box in the Properties panel (■) on the right to reveal a panel. Click the Swatches button at the top of the panel to see the swatches. Click the New Swatch button (■) at the bottom of the panel to create a swatch from the fill color of the selected artwork.

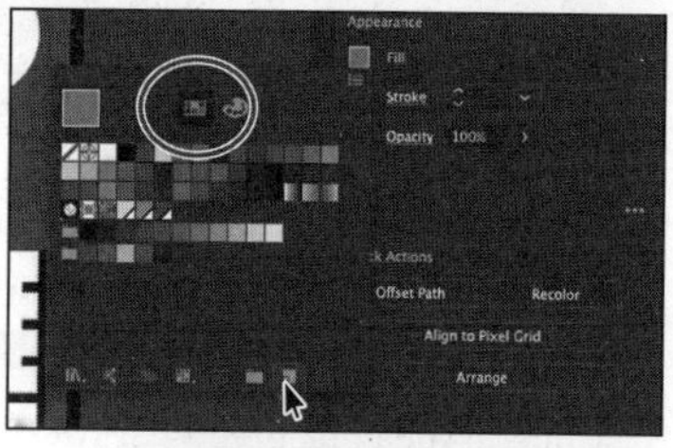

▶ **Tip:** Naming colors can be an art form. You can name them according to their value (C=45, ...), appearance (Light Green), or description like "text header," among other attributes.

2 In the New Swatch dialog box that appears, change the following options:

- Swatch Name: **Light Green**
- Add To My Library: **Deselected** (In Lesson 13, "Creating Artwork for a T-Shirt," you'll learn all about Libraries.)

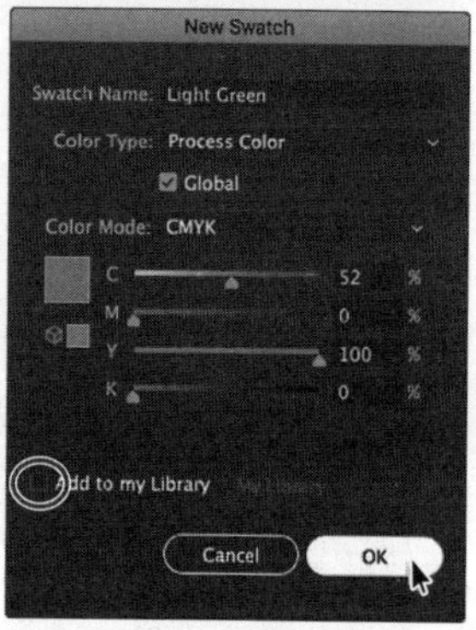

Notice the "Global" option that is selected by default. New swatches you create are global by default. That means, if you later edit this swatch, everywhere it is applied, regardless of whether or not the artwork is selected, is updated.

3 Click OK to save the swatch.

Notice that the new Light Green swatch is highlighted in the Swatches panel (it has a white border around it). That's because it is applied to the selected shape automatically. Also notice the little white triangle in the lower-right corner of the swatch. This indicates that it's a global swatch.

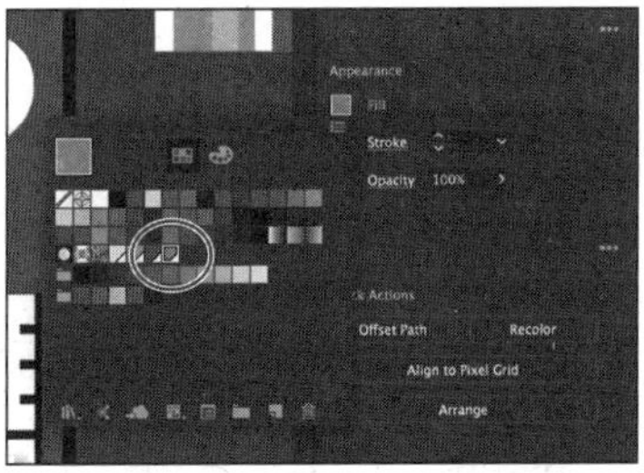

● **Note:** If the panel is hidden, click the Fill box in the Properties panel.

4 Leave the Light Green filled shape selected for the next section.

Creating a copy of a swatch

One of the easiest ways to create and save a color as a swatch is to make a copy of a swatch and edit the copy. Next, you'll create another swatch by copying and editing the Light Green swatch.

1 With the shape still selected, click the Fill box in the Properties panel (■) on the right to reveal a panel. Click the Swatches button at the top of the panel to see the swatches, if they aren't showing. Once again, you should see that the Light Green swatch is highlighted because it's applied to the shape.

2 Choose Duplicate Swatch from the panel menu (☰).

   This creates a new swatch from the fill color of the selected artwork (the Light Green swatch) that is now applied to the selected shape.

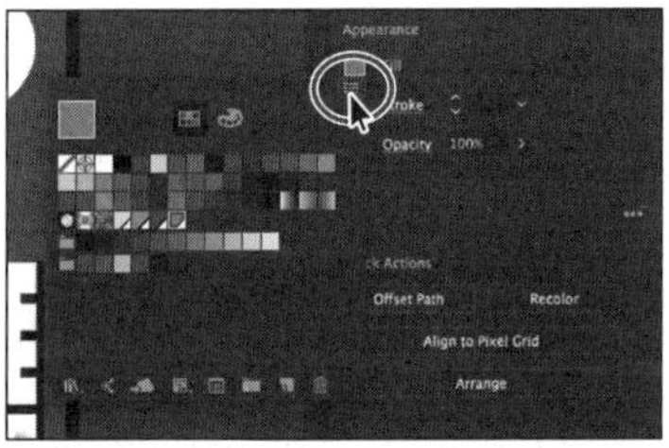

● **Note:** The figure shows where to click to show the panel menu.

3 Click to apply the *original* Light Green swatch to the selected shape.

4 With the Selection tool (▶), click the gray ellipse below the word "FINE" to select it.

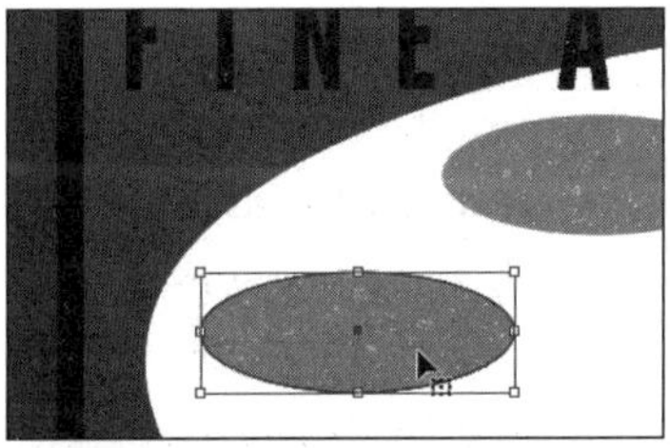

5 Click the Fill box in the Properties panel, and double-click the green swatch *copy* to both apply it to the selected artwork and edit the color settings.

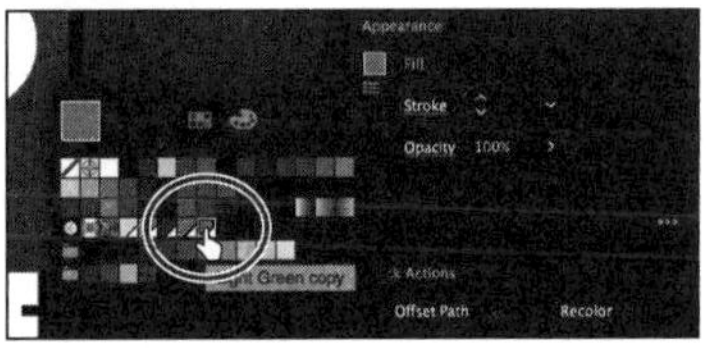

▶ Tip: In the Swatch Options dialog box, the Color Mode menu lets you change the color mode of a specific color to RGB, CMYK, Grayscale, or another mode when you create it.

6 In the Swatch Options dialog box, change the name to **Orange**; change the values to C=**6**, M=**51**, Y=**89**, K=**0**; and make sure that Add To My Library is deselected. Select Preview and then click OK.

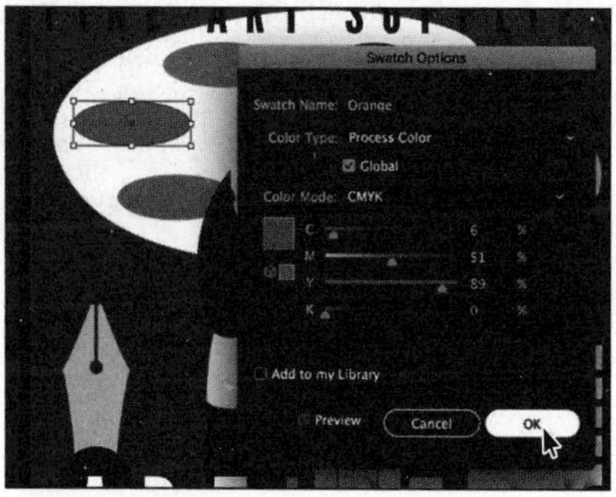

Make sure the new Orange swatch is applied to the selected shape.

Editing a global swatch

Next, you'll save a color as a swatch and learn about *global color*. When you edit a global color, all artwork with that swatch applied, regardless of whether it's selected, is updated.

1 With the Selection tool (▶), click to select the gray ellipse below the orange ellipse you just applied the Orange swatch to.

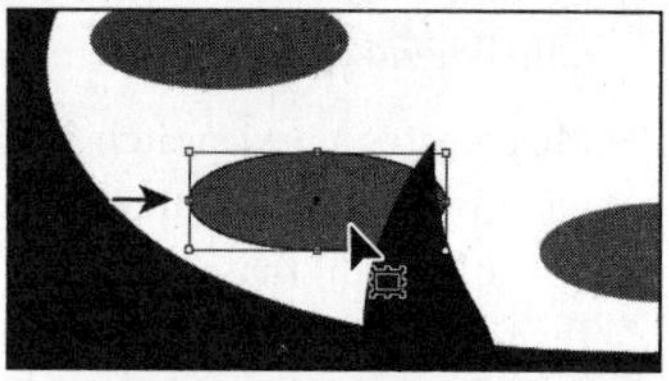

2 Click the Fill box (■) in the Properties panel, and click the New Swatch button (■) at the bottom of the panel.

3 In the New Swatch dialog box, change the following options:

- Swatch Name: **Pink**
- Global: **Selected** (the default setting)
- Change the CMYK values to C=**5**, M=**100**, Y=**60**, K=**0**
- Add To My Library: **Deselected**

4 Click OK.

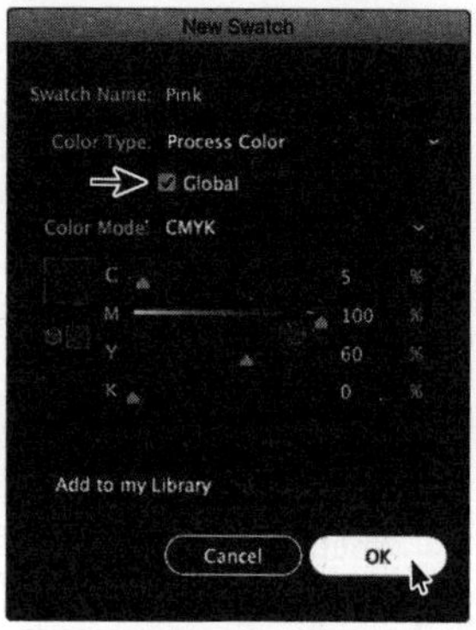

Notice that the new swatch is in the same row as the gray color swatches. When you selected the shape, it was filled with a gray swatch, which was selected in the Swatches panel. When you click the New Swatch button to make a new color, it duplicates the selected swatch and puts the new swatch next to the original in the Swatches panel.

Note: If the panel is hidden, click the Fill box in the Properties panel.

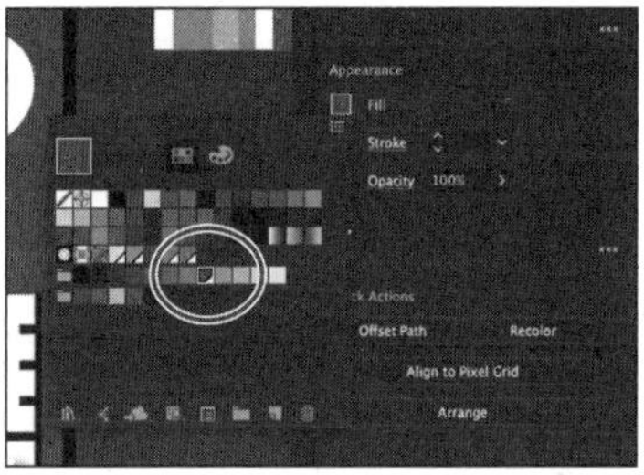

5 Drag the Pink swatch to the right of the Orange swatch to keep them together.

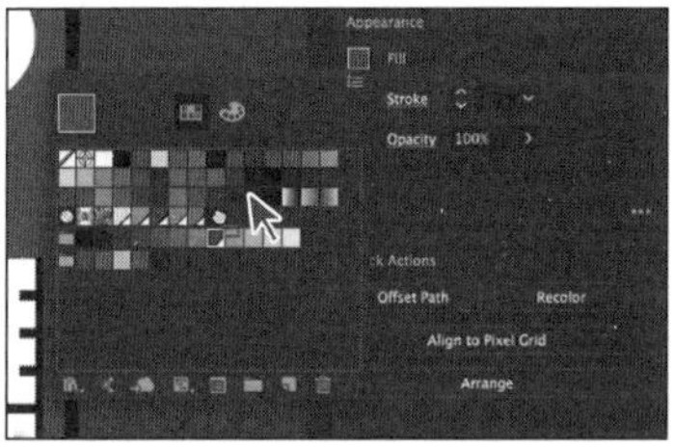

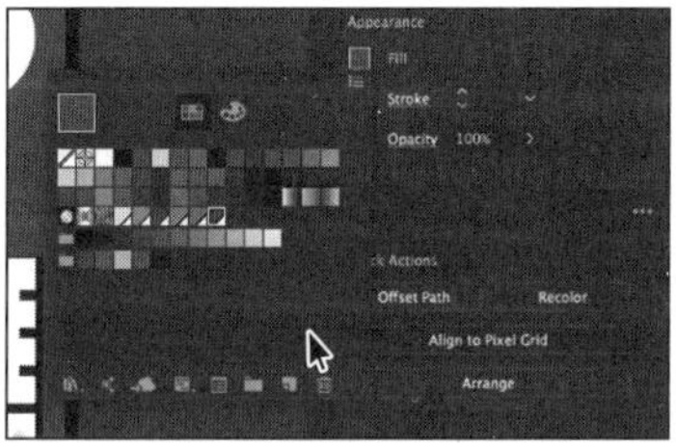

6 With the Selection tool, click the ruler shape at the bottom of the artboard. Click the Fill box in the Properties panel, and select the new swatch named "Pink."

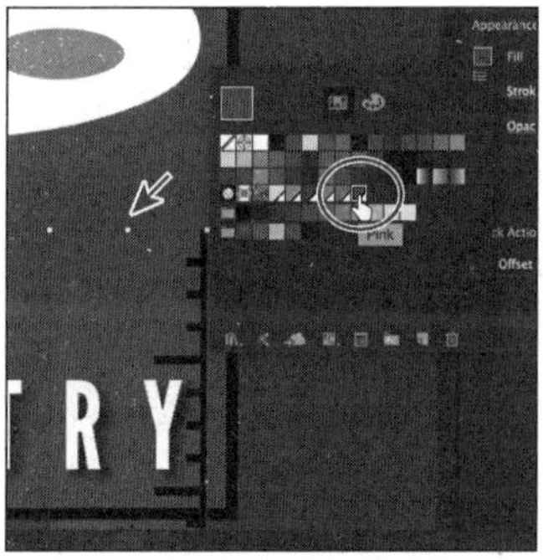

7 With the ruler shape still selected, click the Fill box (■) in the Properties panel. Double-click the swatch named “Pink.” In the Swatch Options dialog box, change the Y value (Yellow) to **30**, select Preview to see the changes (you may need to click in another field to see the change), and then click OK.

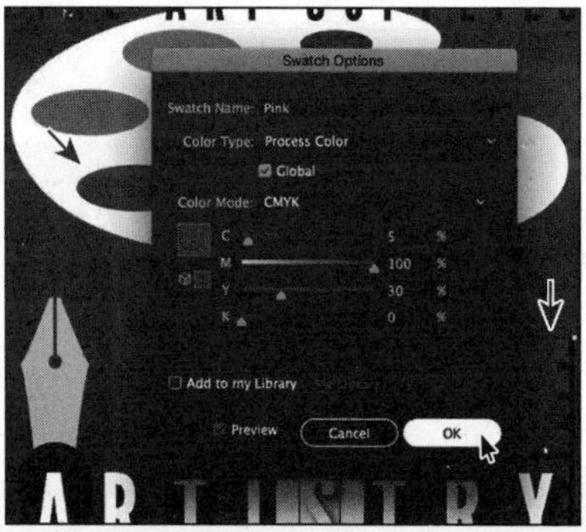

All of the shapes with the global swatch applied are updated, even if they weren’t selected.

Editing a non-global swatch

The default colors that comes with Illustrator are not saved as global swatches by default. That means that editing one of those color swatches will not update artwork that uses the color, unless that artwork is selected. Next, you’ll apply and edit a swatch that was not saved as a global swatch.

1 With the Selection tool (▶) selected, click to select the large blue shape in the background that you first applied a fill color to.

2 Click the Fill box (■) in the Properties panel and then click the green color swatch with the tooltip that shows as “C=75 M=0 Y=75 K=0” to apply it.

You can tell that the green color swatch you applied is *not* a global swatch because it doesn’t have the small white triangle in the lower-right corner of the swatch in the Swatches panel.

3 Choose Select > Deselect.

4 Choose Window > Swatches to open the Swatches panel as a separate panel. Double-click the swatch you just applied to edit it.

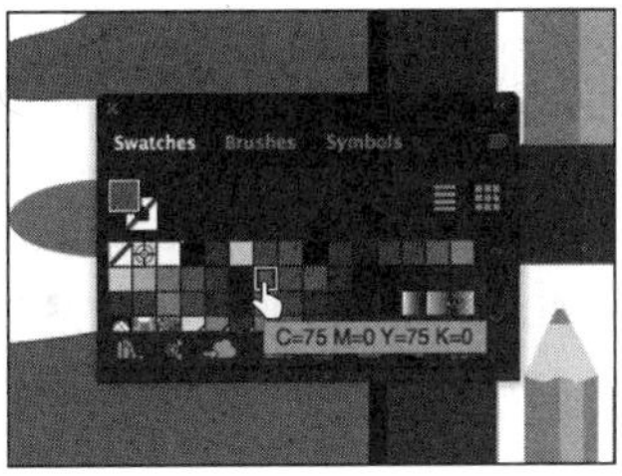

Most of the formatting options you find in the Properties panel can also be found in a separate panel in the Window menu. Opening the Swatches panel, for instance, can be a useful way to work with colors without having to select artwork.

5 In the Swatch Options dialog box, change the name to **Background** and the values to C=**80**, M=**10**, Y=**45**, K=**2**, and select Preview.

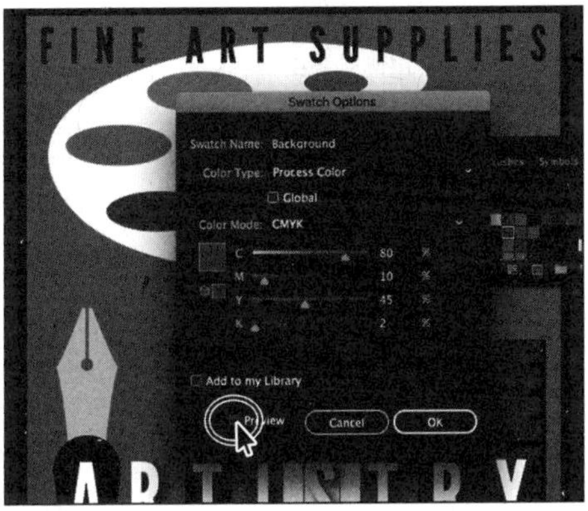

Notice that the color of the background shape doesn't change. That's because the swatch is not a global swatch (global is not selected in the Swatch Options dialog box for the swatch). Only selected shapes with the swatch applied will change if you edit a non-global swatch.

6 Click OK. Click the X at the top of the Swatches panel group to close it.

7 Click to select the background shape. Click the Fill box (■) in the Properties panel, and notice that the green color swatch is no longer applied.

8 Click the green Background swatch you just edited to apply it again.

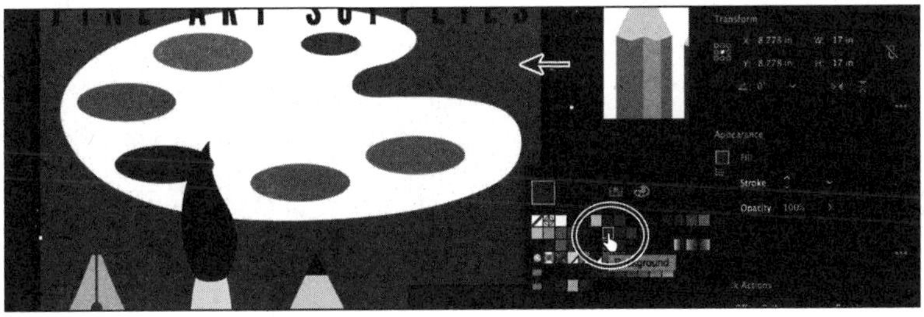

Note: You can change an existing swatch into a global swatch, but it requires a bit more effort. You either need to select all of the shapes with that swatch applied before you edit the swatch and make it global, or you edit the swatch to make it global and then reapply the swatch to the content.

Using the Color Picker to create color

Another method for creating color is to use the Color Picker. The Color Picker lets you select a color in a color field and in a spectrum either by defining colors numerically or by clicking a swatch, and it is found in other Adobe applications like InDesign and Photoshop. Next, you will create a color using the Color Picker and then save that color as a swatch in the Swatches panel.

1 With the Selection tool (▶), click the gray ellipse to the right of the brown end of the paintbrush.

2 Double-click the gray Fill box at the bottom of the Tools panel, to the left of the document, to open the Color Picker.

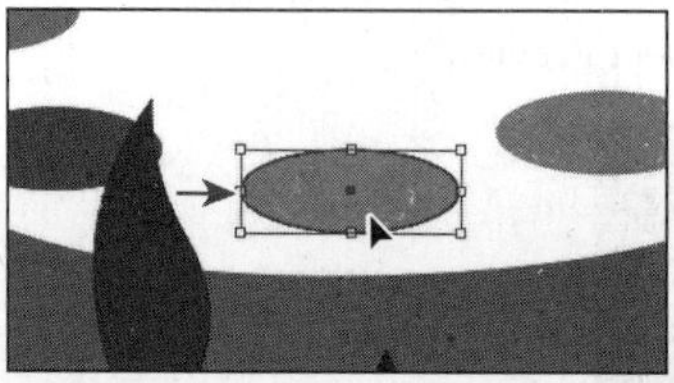

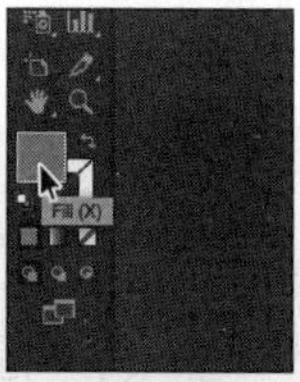

In the Color Picker dialog box, the larger color field shows saturation (horizontally) and brightness (vertically). The color spectrum bar to the right of the color field shows the hue.

3 In the Color Picker dialog box, click and drag up and down in the color spectrum bar (labeled "B" in the following figure) to change the color range. Make sure that you wind up with the triangles in a blue color (it doesn't have to be exact).

▶ **Tip:** You can also change the color spectrum you see by selecting H, S, B, R, G, or B.

4 Click and drag in the color field (labeled "A" in the following figure). As you drag right and left, you adjust the saturation, and as you drag up and down, you adjust the brightness. The color you create when you click OK (don't yet) appears in the New color rectangle, labeled "C" in the figure. Don't worry about matching the color in the figure yet.

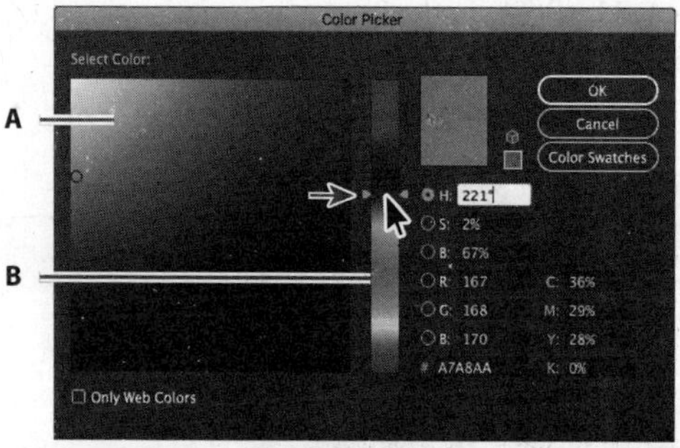

Drag in the color spectrum bar.

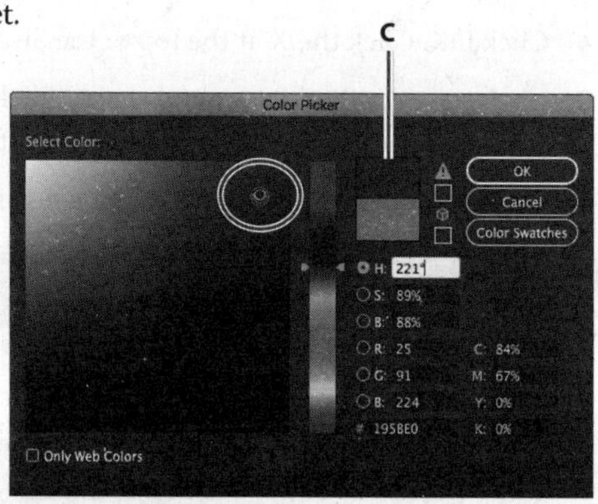

Drag in the color field.

5 In the CMYK fields, change the values to C=**90**, M=**15**, Y=**0**, and K=**0**.

6 Click OK, and you should see that the blue is applied to the fill of the shape.

7 Click the Fill box ( ) in the Properties panel to show the swatches. Click the New Swatch button ( ) at the bottom of the panel, and change the following options in the New Swatch dialog box:

- Swatch Name: **Blue**
- Global: **Selected** (the default setting)
- Add To My Library: **Deselected**

8 Click OK to see the color appear as a swatch in the Swatches panel.

9 Choose Select > Deselect and then choose File > Save.

● **Note:** The Color Swatches button in the Color Picker shows you the swatches in the Swatches panel and the default color books (the sets of swatches that come with Illustrator), and it lets you select a color from one. You can return to the color spectrum by clicking the Color Models button and then editing the swatch color values, if necessary.

Using Illustrator swatch libraries

Swatch libraries are collections of preset colors, such as Pantone and TOYO, and thematic libraries, such as Earthtone and Ice Cream. Illustrator has default swatch libraries that appear as separate panels when you open them, and these cannot be edited. When you apply color from a library to artwork, the color in the library becomes a swatch that is saved in that document only and appears in the Swatches panel. Libraries are a great starting point for creating colors.

Next, you will create a spot color using a Pantone Plus library, which prints using a spot ink. You will then apply that color to artwork. When color is defined in Illustrator and later printed, the appearance of the color may vary. This is why most printers and designers rely on a color-matching system, like the PANTONE system, to help maintain color consistency and, in some cases, to give a wider range of colors.

● **Note:** Sometimes it's practical to use process (typically CMYK) and spot inks (PANTONE, for instance) in the same job. For example, you might use one spot ink to print the exact color of a company logo on the same pages of an annual report where photographs are reproduced using process color. You can also use a spot-color printing plate to apply a varnish over areas of a process color job. In both cases, your print job would use a total of five inks—four process inks and one spot ink or varnish.

Adding a spot color

In this section, you'll see how to open a color library, such as the PANTONE color system, and how to add a PANTONE MATCHING SYSTEM (PMS) color to the Swatches panel.

1 Choose Window > Swatch Libraries > Color Books > PANTONE+ Solid Coated.

The PANTONE+ Solid Coated library appears in its own panel.

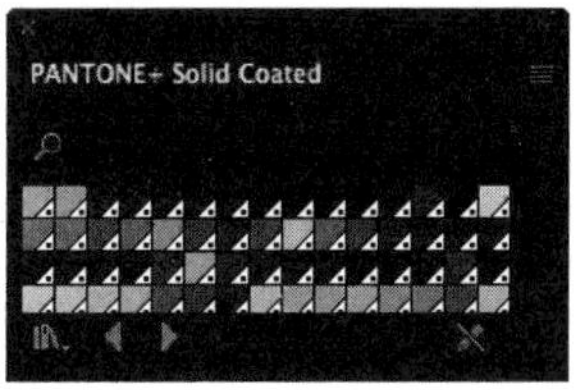

2 Type **137** in the Find field. As you type, the list is filtered, showing a smaller and smaller range of swatches.

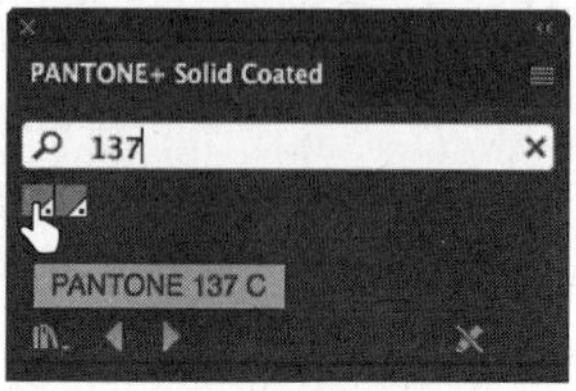

3 Click the swatch PANTONE 137 C, beneath the search field to add it to the Swatches panel for this document. Click the X to the right of the search field to stop the filtering.

4 Close the PANTONE+ Solid Coated panel.

● **Note:** If you exit Illustrator with the PANTONE library panel still open and then relaunch Illustrator, the panel does not reopen. To automatically open the panel whenever Illustrator opens, choose Persistent from the PANTONE+ Solid Coated panel menu (☰).

5 With the Selection tool (▶), Shift-click the three white pencil shapes under the letter "S" in "ARTISTRY."

6 Click the Fill box (□) in the Properties panel to show the swatches and select the PANTONE 137 C swatch to fill the shapes.

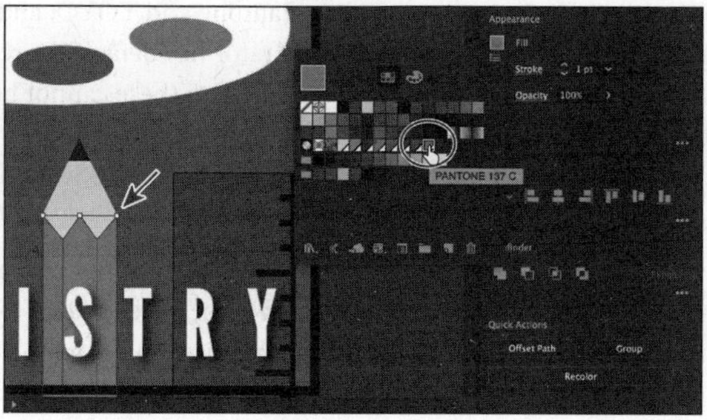

7 Choose Select > Deselect and then choose File > Save.

PANTONE swatches vs. other swatches in the Swatches panel

In the Swatches panel, you can identify spot-color swatches by the spot-color icon (◙) when the panel is in List view or by the dot in the lower corner (◪) when the panel is in Thumbnail view. Process colors do not have a spot-color icon or a dot.

Creating and saving a tint of a color

A *tint* is a mixture of a color with white to make the color lighter. You can create a tint from a global process color, like CMYK, or from a spot color. Next, you'll create a tint of the Pantone swatch you added to the document.

1 With the Selection tool ( ), click the middle, yellow pencil shape.

2 Click the Fill box in the Properties panel ( ) on the right. Click the Color Mixer button ( ) at the top of the panel that appears.

   In the section "Creating a custom color," you created a custom color using the Color Mixer sliders. In that section, you were creating a custom color from scratch—that's why there were CMYK sliders. Now you will see a single slider labeled "T" for tint. When using the color mixer for a *global* swatch, you will create a tint instead of mixing CMYK values.

3 Drag the tint slider to the left to change the tint value to **70%**.

4 Click the Swatches option ( ) at the top of the panel to show the swatches. Click the New Swatch button ( ) at the bottom of the panel to save the tint.

5 Position the pointer over the swatch icon to see its name, which is PANTONE 137 C 70%.

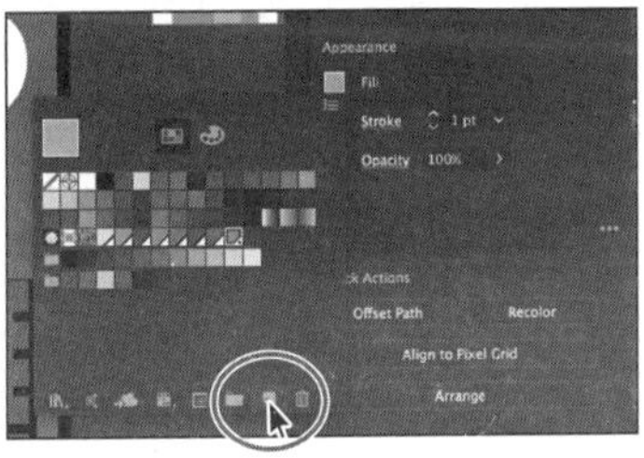

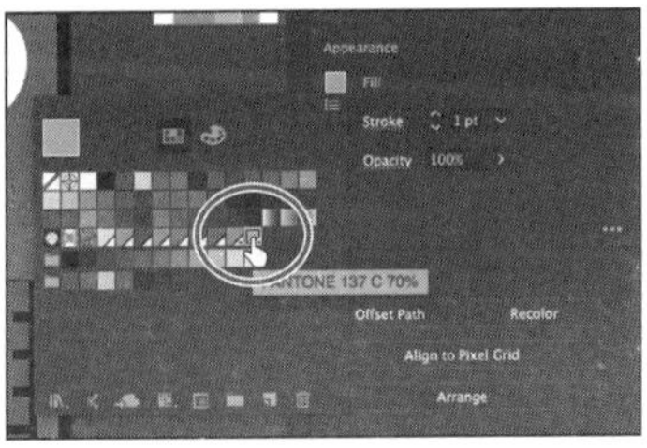

6 Choose Select > Deselect and then choose File > Save.

Converting colors

When working with colors, Illustrator offers Edit Colors commands (Edit > Edit Colors) that allow you to convert colors between color modes, blend colors, invert colors, and much more, for selected artwork. Next, you'll change the pencil with the PANTONE 137 C color applied to use CMYK colors instead of Pantone.

1 Choose Select > All On Active Artboard to select all artwork on the artboard, including the shapes with the Pantone color and tint applied.

2 Choose Edit > Edit Colors > Convert To CMYK.

Any colors in the selected shapes that had Pantone applied as a spot color are now composed of CMYK. Using this method for converting to CMYK does *not* affect Pantone color swatches (PANTONE 137 C and the tint, in this case) in the Swatches panel. It simply converts the selected *artwork* colors to CMYK. The swatches in the Swatches panel are no longer applied to the artwork.

Note: Currently, Convert to RGB in the Edit Color menu is dimmed (you cannot select it). That's because the Document Color Mode is CMYK. To convert selected content color to RGB using this method, first choose File > Document Color Mode > RGB Color.

Copying appearance attributes

At times you may want to simply copy appearance attributes, such as text formatting, fill, and stroke, from one object to another. This can be done with the Eyedropper tool ( ) and can really speed up your creative process.

1 Choose Select > Deselect.

2 Using the Selection tool ( ), select the last gray ellipse.

3 Select the Eyedropper tool ( ) in the Tools panel on the left. Click the yellow/orange of the pencil (not the tint). See the figure.

The gray ellipse has the attributes from the pencil shape applied, including a 1-pt black stroke.

4 Click the Stroke color ( ) in the Properties panel, and change the color to None ( ).

5 Select the Selection tool ( ) in the Tools panel.

6 Choose Select > Deselect and then choose File > Save.

Tip: You can double-click the Eyedropper tool in the Tools panel, before sampling, to change the attributes that the Eyedropper picks up and applies.

Creating a color group

In Illustrator, you can save colors in color groups, which consist of related color swatches in the Swatches panel. Organizing colors by their use, such as grouping all colors for a logo, can be helpful for organization and more, as you'll soon see. Color groups cannot contain patterns, gradients, the None color, or Registration color.

Next, you'll create a color group of some of the swatches you've created to keep them organized.

1 Choose Window > Swatches to open the Swatches panel. In the Swatches panel, click the swatch named "Sign Bg" to select it. Holding down the Shift key, click the swatch named "Blue" to the right to select five color swatches.

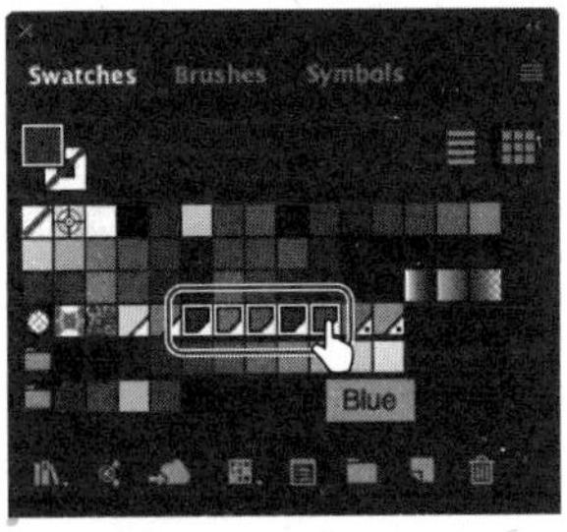

▶ **Tip:** You may want to drag the bottom of the Swatches panel down to see more of the content.

2 Click the New Color Group button (■) at the bottom of the Swatches panel. Change Name to **Palette Colors** in the New Color Group dialog box, and click OK to save the group.

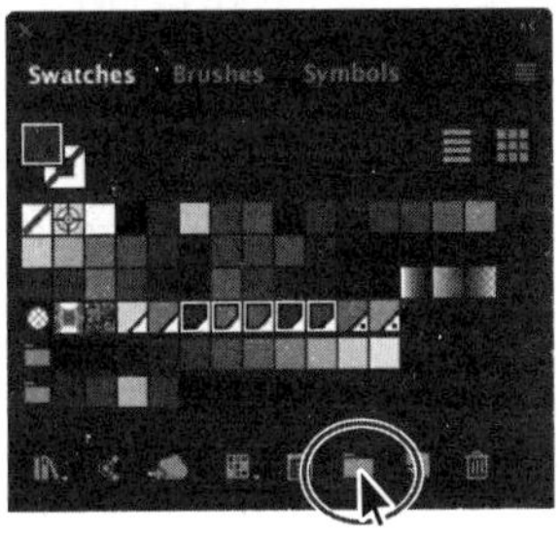

● **Note:** If objects are selected when you click the New Color Group button, an expanded New Color Group dialog box appears. In this dialog box, you can create a color group from the colors in the artwork and convert the colors to global colors.

3 With the Selection tool (▶) selected, click a blank area of the Swatches panel to deselect all in the panel.

Each swatch in a color group can still be edited independently by double-clicking a swatch in the group and editing the values in the Swatch Options dialog box.

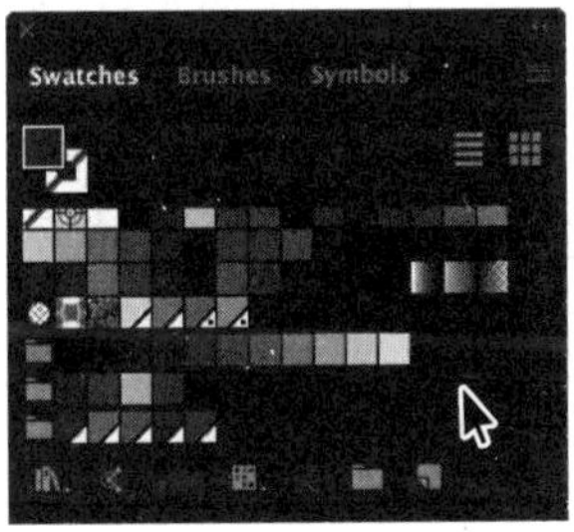

4 Click and drag the swatch named "Sign Bg" in the color group to the right of the PANTONE 137 C 70% swatch. Leave the Swatches panel open.

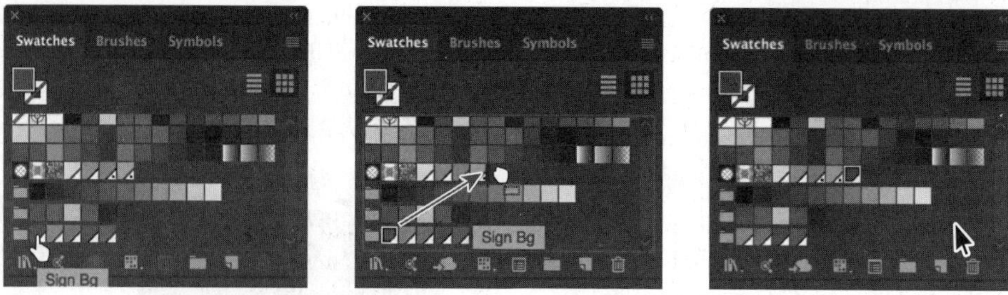

▶ **Tip:** Aside from dragging colors in or out of a color group, you can rename a color group, reorder the colors in the group, and more.

You can drag colors into or out of a color group. When dragging into a color group, make sure that you see a line appear on the right edge of a swatch within the group. Otherwise, you may drag the swatch to the wrong place. You can always choose Edit > Undo Move Swatches and try again.

Creative inspiration with the Color Guide panel

The Color Guide panel can provide you with color inspiration as you create your artwork. You can use it to pick color tints, analogous colors, and much more, and then apply them directly to artwork, edit them using several methods, or save them as a group in the Swatches panel. Next, you'll use the Color Guide panel to select different colors for a few pencils that will become part of a logo, and then you'll save those colors as a color group in the Swatches panel.

1 Choose 2 Pencils 1 from the Artboard Navigation menu in the lower-left corner of the Document window.

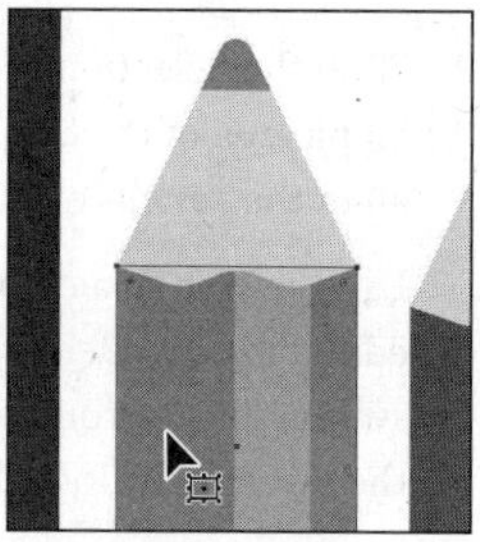

2 With the Selection tool (▶), click the darker green pencil body. Make sure that the Fill box is selected in the Tools panel or Swatches panel.

3 Choose Window > Color Guide to open the panel. Click the Set Base Color To The Current Color button (▣) (see the following figure).

This allows the Color Guide panel to suggest colors based on the color showing in the Set Base Color To The Current Color button. The colors you see in the Color Guide panel may differ from what you see in the figure. That's okay.

▶ **Tip:** You can also choose a different color variation (different from the default Tints/Shades), such as Show Warm/Cool, by clicking the Color Guide panel menu icon (▤) and choosing one.

Next, you'll experiment with colors using Harmony Rules.

4 Choose Analogous from the Harmony Rules menu (circled in the following figure) in the Color Guide panel.

A base group of colors is created to the right of the base color (darker green), and a series of tints and shades of those colors appears in the body of the panel. There are lots of harmony rules to choose from, each instantly generating a color scheme based on any color you want. The base color you set (green) is the basis for generating the colors in the color scheme.

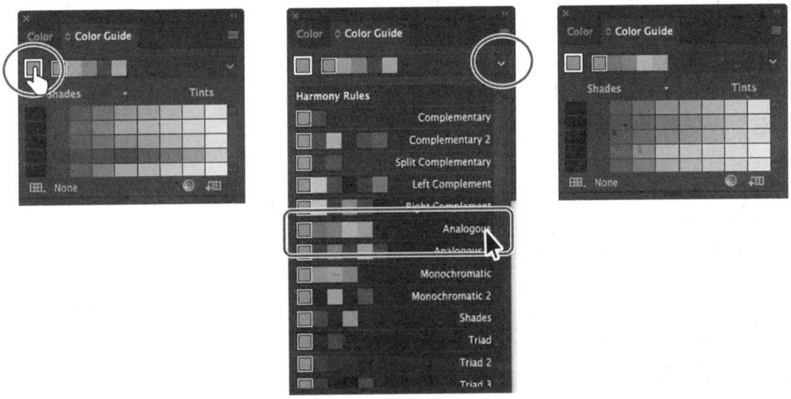

5 Click the Save Color Group To Swatch Panel button (▣) at the bottom of the Color Guide panel to save the base colors (the five colors at the top) in the Swatches panel as a group. Leave the panel open.

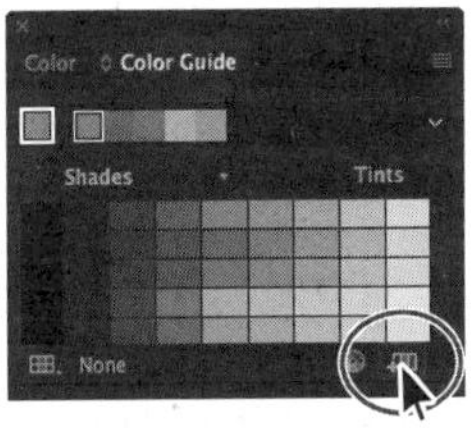

6 Choose Select > Deselect.

In the Swatches panel you should see the new group added. You may need to scroll down in the panel.

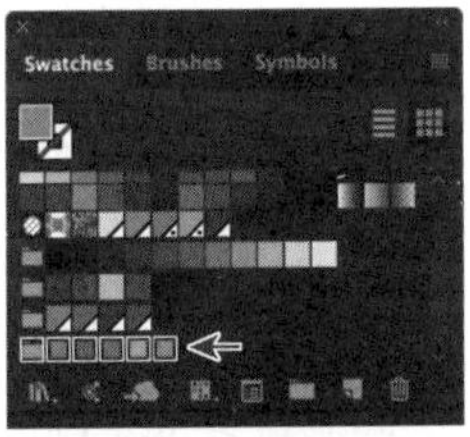

Next, you'll experiment with the colors in the color group that you just created to create an alternate group of colors.

7 In the list of swatches in the Color Guide panel, select the fifth color from the left in the fourth row (see the figure). If the pencil body were still selected, it would now be filled with a yellow/green.

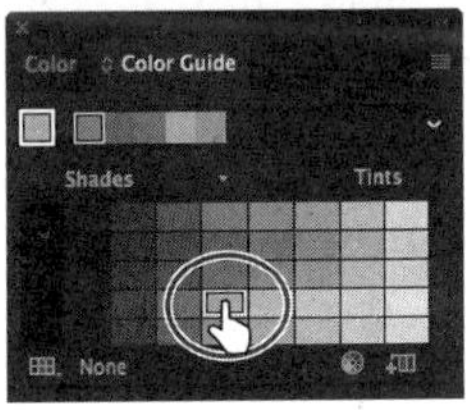

Note: If you choose a different color variation than the one suggested, your color will differ from those in the rest of this section.

8 Click the Set Base Color To The Current Color button ( ) (circled in the following figure) to ensure that all colors that the panel creates are based on that same yellow/green.

9 Choose Triad 2 from the Harmony Rules menu.

10 Click the Save Color Group To Swatch Panel button ( ) to save the colors as a group in the Swatches panel.

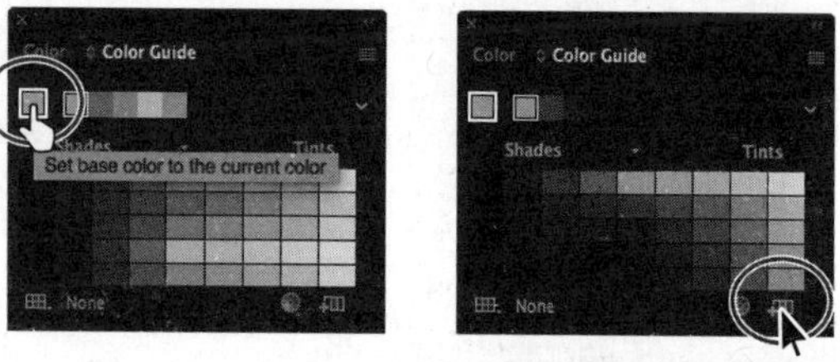

Editing a color group in the Edit Colors dialog box

When you create color groups in the Swatches panel or in the Color Guide panel, you can edit the swatches in the group either individually (by double-clicking each in the Swatches panel) or together. In this section, you'll learn how to edit the colors of a color group saved in the Swatches panel using the Edit Colors dialog box. Later, you will apply those colors to artwork.

1 Choose Select > Deselect (if it's available).

Deselecting right now is important! If artwork is selected when you edit the color group, the edits can apply to the selected artwork.

2 In the Swatches panel, click the Color Group icon ( ) to the left of the colors in the *bottom* color group (the one you just saved) to ensure that it's selected. It's circled in the figure.

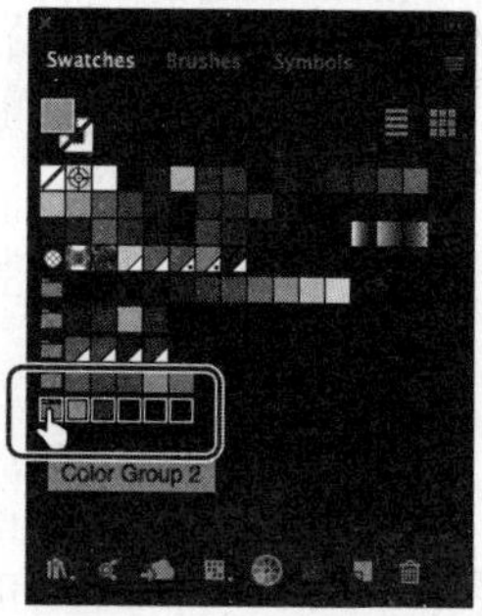

Tip: With no artwork selected, you could also double-click the Color Group icon (the folder) to open the Edit Colors dialog box.

3 Click the Edit Color Group button ( ) at the bottom of the Swatches panel to open the Edit Colors dialog box.

The Edit Color Group button ( ) appears in multiple locations, like the Swatches and Color Guide panels. The Edit Colors dialog box allows you to edit a group of colors in various ways or even to create new color groups. On the right side of the Edit Colors dialog box, under the Color Groups section, all of the existing color groups in the Swatches panel are listed.

4 Select the name "Color Group 2" in the field above the Color Groups section if not already selected (circled in the figure), and rename the group **Pencil Colors**. This is one way you can rename a color group.

Next, you'll make a few changes to the colors in the Pencil Colors group. On the left side of the Edit Colors dialog box, you can edit the colors of each color group, either individually or together, and edit them visually or precisely using specific color values. In the color wheel, you'll see markers (circles) that represent each color in the selected group.

5 In the color wheel on the left side of the dialog box, drag the blue circle, called a *marker*, in the lower-left section of the color wheel down and to the left just a little bit.

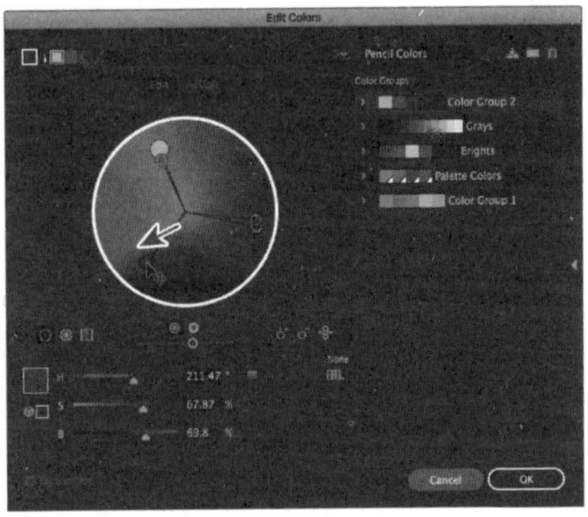

Moving the color markers away from the center of the color wheel increases saturation, and moving them toward the center decreases saturation. Moving a color marker around the color wheel (clockwise or counterclockwise) edits the hue.

Tip: You'll notice that all of the colors in the group move and change together. This is because they are linked together by default.

Note: The largest yellow/green marker is the base color of the color group that you set in the Color Guide panel initially.

6 Drag the Adjust Brightness slider below the color wheel to the right to brighten all the colors at once.

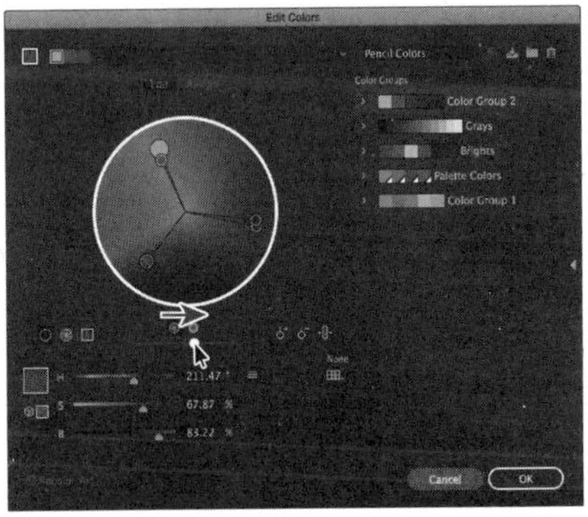

Next, you will edit the colors in the group independently and then save the colors as a new named group.

7 Click the Unlink Harmony Colors button ( ) so it looks like this ( ) in the Edit Colors dialog box to edit the colors independently.

Note: You can match the H, S, B (hue, saturation, brightness) values below the color wheel in the Edit Colors dialog box to mimic what you see in the figure, if you want to match exactly the color I achieved.

The lines between the color markers (circles) and the center of the color wheel become dotted, indicating that you can edit the colors independently. Next, you'll edit just one of the colors, since they are now unlinked. You will edit that color by using specific color values rather than by dragging the color in the color wheel.

8 Click the Color Mode icon ( ) to the right of the H, S, B values below the color wheel, and choose CMYK from the menu, if the CMYK sliders are not already visible.

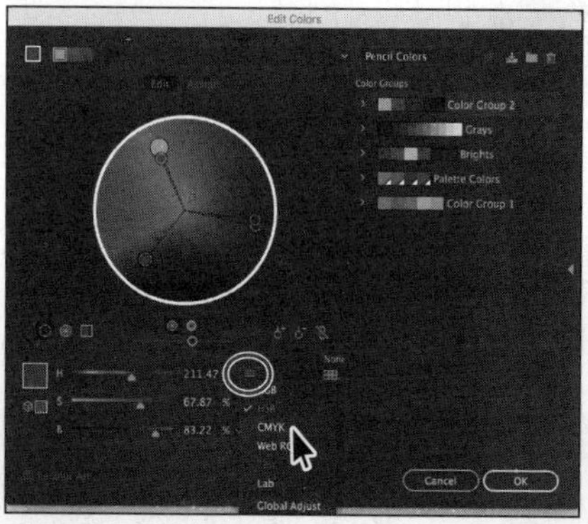

● **Note:** The figure shows the result of changing the CMYK values.

● **Note:** It's okay if the color markers in your Edit Colors dialog box are different from those shown in the figure.

9 Click to select the top red/purple marker on the right side of the color wheel. Change the CMYK values to C=**29**, M=**80**, Y=**100**, and K=**28**.

Notice that the marker has moved in the color wheel, and it's the only one that moved. That's because you clicked the Unlink Harmony Colors button. Leave the dialog box open.

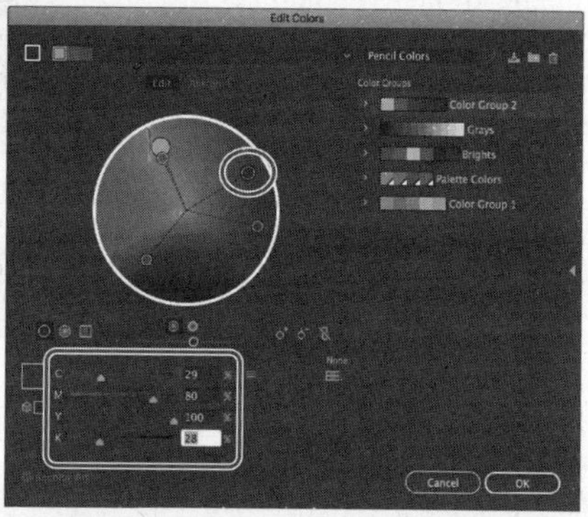

10 Click the Save Changes To Color Group button ( ) in the upper-right corner of the Edit Colors dialog box to save the changes to the color group.

If you decide to make changes to colors in another color group, you can select the color group you want to edit on the right side of the Edit Colors dialog box and edit the colors on the left side.

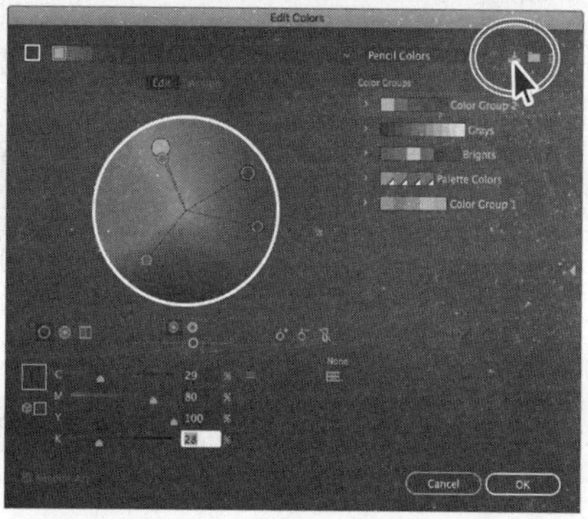

You can then save the changes to the group by clicking the Save Changes To Color Group button (icon) in the upper-right corner of the dialog box.

11 Click OK to close the Edit Colors dialog box.

The changes to the colors in the group should show in the Swatches panel. Don't worry if the colors you see don't exactly match the figure.

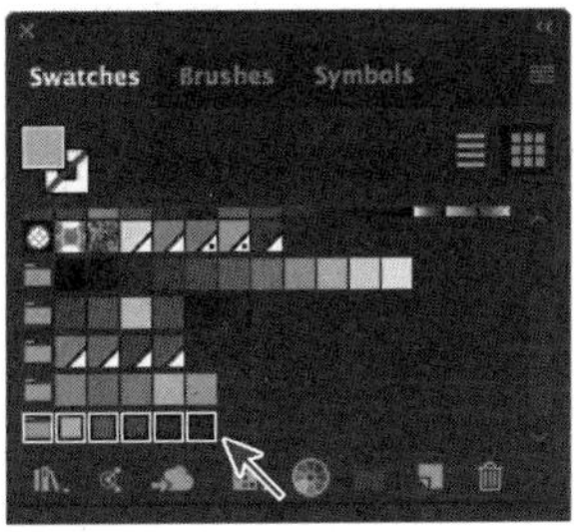

12 Choose File > Save.

Note: If a dialog box appears after clicking OK, click Yes to save the changes to the color group in the Swatches panel.

Editing colors in artwork

You can also edit the colors in selected artwork using the Recolor Artwork command. It's really useful when global swatches weren't used in the artwork. Without using global colors in your artwork, updating a series of colors in selected artwork may take a lot of time. Next, you will edit the colors for pencil artwork that was created with some colors that were not global swatches.

1 Choose Select > All On Active Artboard to select all of the artwork.

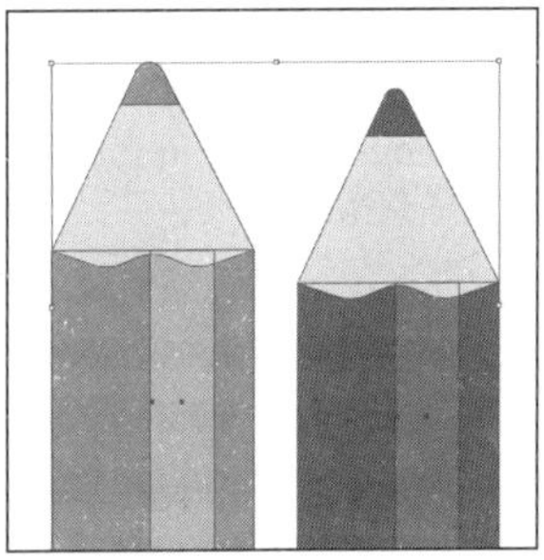

2 Click the Recolor button in the Properties panel to open the Recolor Artwork dialog box.

The options in the Recolor Artwork dialog box allow you to edit, reassign, or reduce the colors in your *selected* artwork and to create and edit color groups. You'll probably notice that it looks an awful lot like the Edit Colors dialog box. The big difference is that instead of editing color and color groups, as well as creating color groups to apply later, you are dynamically editing colors in the currently selected artwork.

Tip: You can also choose Edit > Edit Colors > Recolor Artwork.

3 In the Recolor Artwork dialog box, click the Hide Color Group Storage icon (icon) on the right side of the dialog box (circled in the following figure) to hide the color groups temporarily.

Like in the Edit Colors dialog box, all of the color groups in the Swatches panel appear on the right side of the Recolor Artwork dialog box (in the Color Groups storage area). In the Recolor Artwork dialog box, you can apply colors from these color groups to the selected artwork. In this part of the lesson, you just need to edit the colors found in the selected artwork.

4 Click the Get Colors From Selected Art icon () in the upper-right corner of the Recolor Artwork dialog box, to make sure that the colors from the selected artwork are showing in the Recolor Artwork dialog box.

5 Click the Edit tab to edit the colors in the artwork using the color wheel.

6 Make sure that the Link Harmony Colors icon is disabled so that you can edit all of the colors independently. The Link Harmony Colors icon should look like this: , not like this: .

The lines between the color markers (circles) and the center of the color wheel should be dotted. When you created a color group, you worked with the color wheel and the CMYK sliders to edit color. This time, you will adjust color using a different method.

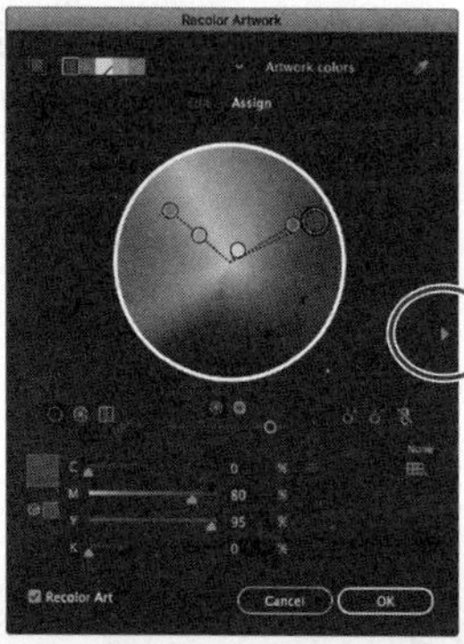

7 Click the Display Color Bars button () to show the colors in the selected artwork as bars.

8 Click the darker orange color bar to select it.

9 At the bottom of the dialog box, change the M value (Magenta) to **100**. If the Recolor Artwork dialog box isn't in the way, you should see the artwork changing.

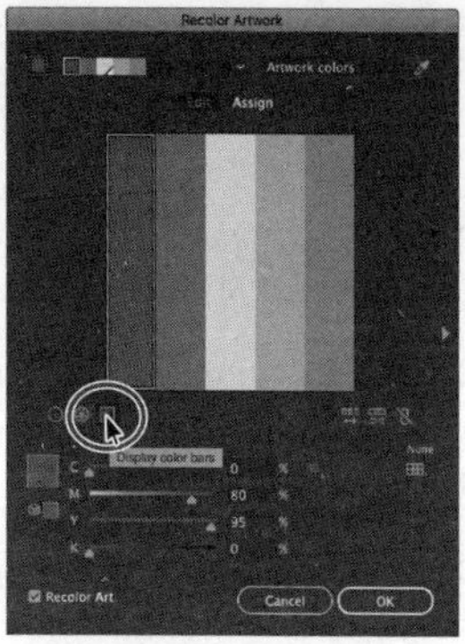

Tip: If you want to return to the original logo colors, click the Get Colors From Selected Art button ().

Note: If you don't see the CMYK sliders, choose CMYK from the menu () to the right of the sliders in the Recolor Artwork dialog box.

10 Click the light orange color bar to the right of the currently selected color bar. With the pointer over the light orange color bar, right-click and choose Select Shade from the menu that appears. Click in the shade picker, and drag to change the color of the color bar. Click away from the shade menu to close it.

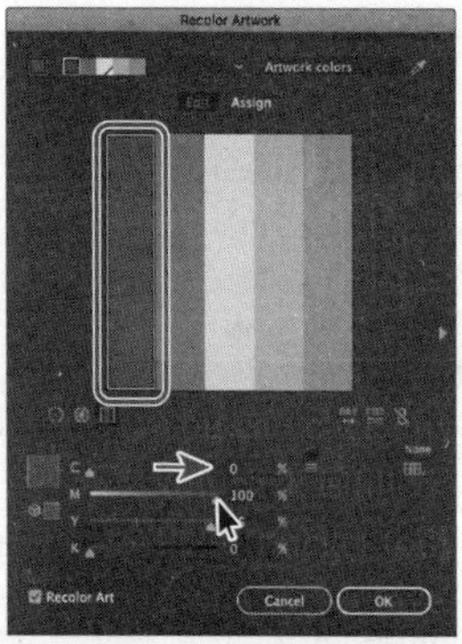

Click the dark orange color bar and edit it.

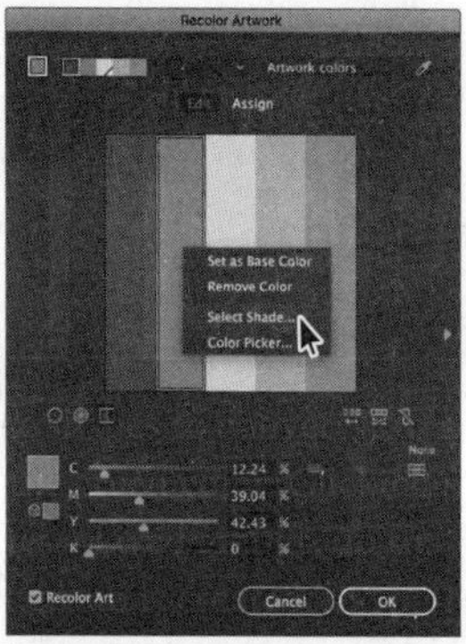

Choose Select Shade with the light orange color bar selected.

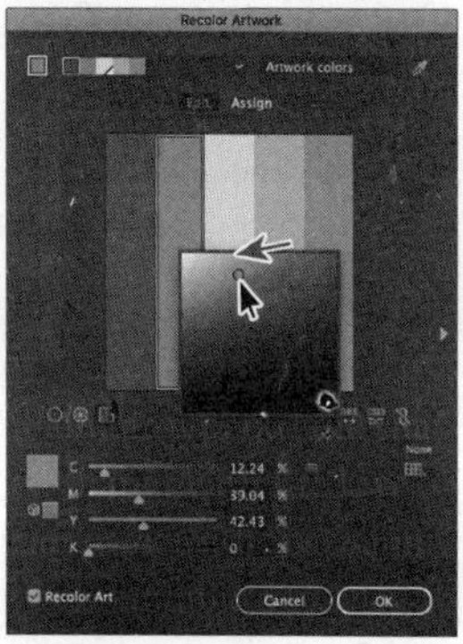

Change the shade.

Editing the colors as bars is just another way to view and edit the colors, and there are so many options for editing. To learn more about these options, search for "Color groups (harmonies)" in Illustrator Help (Help > Illustrator Help).

Tip: You can save the edited colors as a color group by clicking the Show Color Group Storage icon (▶) on the right side of the dialog box and then clicking the New Color Group button (▬).

11 Click OK in the Recolor Artwork dialog box.

12 Choose Select > Deselect and then choose File > Save.

Note: For more information about working with the Color Themes panel, search for "Color themes" in Illustrator Help (Help > Illustrator Help).

Working with Adobe Color Themes

The Adobe Color Themes panel (Window > Color Themes) displays color themes you have created and synced with your account on the Adobe Color CC website (https://color.adobe.com/). The Adobe ID used in Illustrator CC is automatically used to sign in to the Adobe Color CC website, and the Adobe Color Themes panel is refreshed with your Adobe color themes.

Assigning colors to your artwork

In the previous section, you learned that you can edit colors in existing selected artwork in the Recolor Artwork dialog box. You can also "assign" colors from an existing color group to your artwork in the Recolor Artwork dialog box. Next, you'll assign a color group to other artwork.

1 Choose 3 Pencils 2 from the Artboard Navigation menu in the lower-left corner of the Document window.

2 Choose Select > All On Active Artboard to select the colored pencil artwork.

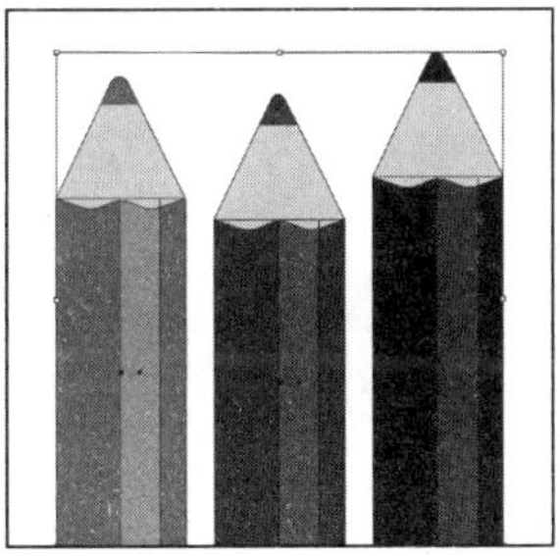

3 Click the Recolor button in the Properties panel to open the Recolor Artwork dialog box.

Tip: You can also choose Edit > Edit Colors > Recolor Artwork.

4 Click the Show Color Group Storage icon (▶) on the right side of the dialog box to show the color groups, if they aren't already showing. Make sure that, in the top left of the dialog box, the Assign button is selected.

On the left side of the Recolor Artwork dialog box, notice that the colors from the selected pencil artwork are listed in the Current Colors (7) column, in what is called *hue-forward* sorting. That means they are arranged, from top to bottom, in the ordering of the color wheel: red, orange, yellow, green, blue, indigo, and violet.

● **Note:** If the artwork colors do not change, make sure that Recolor Art is selected in the lower-left corner of the Recolor Artwork dialog box.

5 Under Color Groups in the Recolor Artwork dialog box, select the Pencil Colors color group you created earlier. The selected artwork on the artboard should change in color.

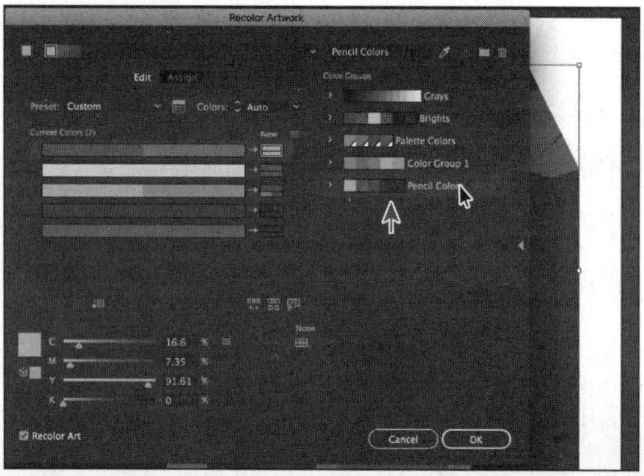

On the left side of the Recolor Artwork dialog box, notice that the colors from the Pencil Colors color group are *assigned* to the colors in the pencil artwork. The Current Colors column shows what the color originally was in the pencil artwork, and an arrow to the right of each of those colors points to the New column, which contains what the color has become (or has been *reassigned to*).

● **Note:** White, black, and grays are typically preserved, or unchanged, when you assign a color group.

6 Click the Hide Color Group Storage icon (◀) to hide the color groups. Drag the dialog box by the title bar at the top so that you can see the artwork.

7 Click the small arrow to the right of the cream-colored bar in the Current Colors column (see the following figure).

This tells Illustrator *not* to change that color in the selected artwork (the pencil artwork). You can see that reflected in the artwork on the artboard.

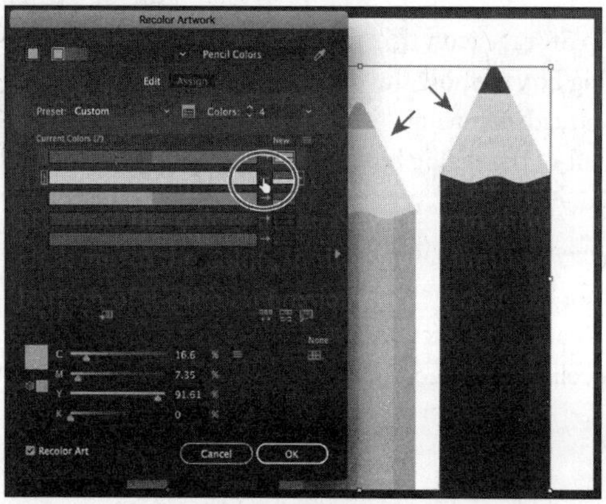

You also might not like how the colors in the Pencil Colors group were assigned to your artwork. You can edit the colors in the New column in different ways, even reassigning current colors. That's what you'll do next.

8 Drag the lighter blue bar up, on top of the darker blue bar in the Current Colors column.

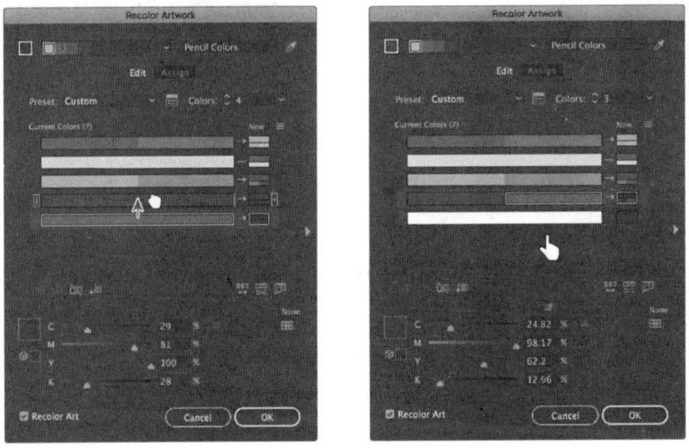

Essentially, you just told Illustrator to replace the darker blue *and* the lighter blue with the magenta (red) color in the New column. Illustrator assigns both colors using the same tint values as the original colors.

9 In the New column, drag the top yellow color box in the column down on top of the blue color and release the mouse button.

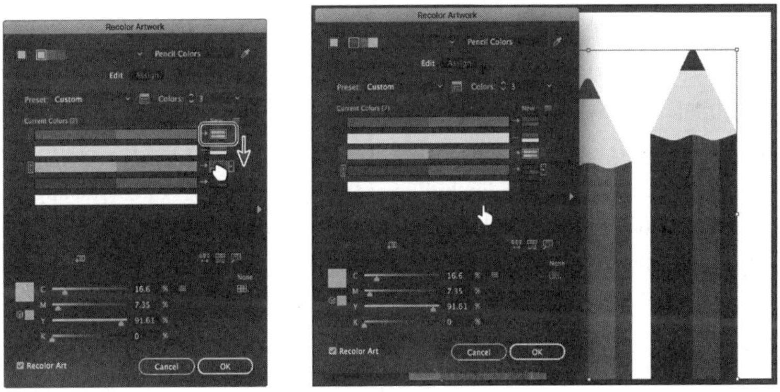

This is one way that you can reassign the group colors to the colors in the artwork. The colors in the New column show what you see in the artwork. If you click one of the colors in the New column, notice that the CMYK sliders at the bottom of the dialog box let you edit that one color.

▶ **Tip:** You can also double-click a color in the New column to edit it in the Color Picker.

10 Click the burgundy (red) color box in the New column (circled in the figure). Change the Y value (Yellow) to **100**, if necessary.

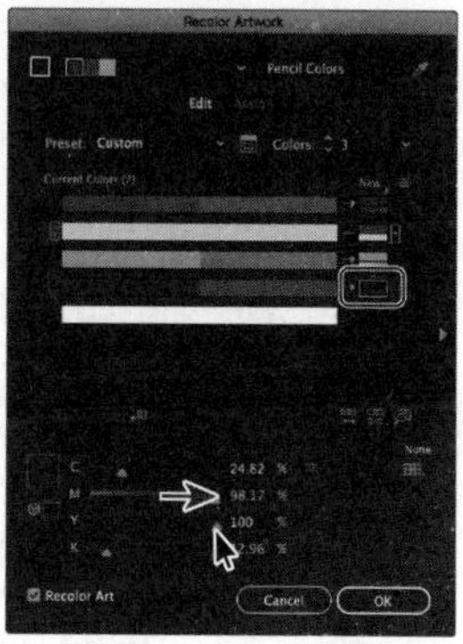

11 Click the Show Color Group Storage icon (▶) on the right side of the dialog box to show the color groups.

12 Click the Save Changes To Color Group button (![]) in the upper-right corner of the Recolor Artwork dialog box to save the changes to the color group without closing the dialog box.

13 Click OK to close the Recolor Artwork dialog box. The color changes that you just made to the color group are saved in the Swatches panel.

● **Note:** To learn more, search for "Working with color groups" in Illustrator Help (Help > Illustrator Help).

14 Choose Select > Deselect and then choose File > Save.

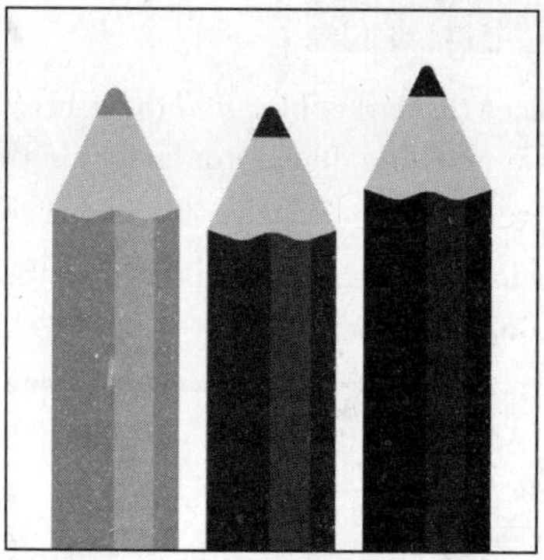

There are many kinds of color edits that can be made to selected artwork in the Recolor Artwork dialog box, including reducing the number of colors, applying other colors (like Pantone colors), and much more. You can close the Color Guide panel group and the Swatches panel group.

Working with Live Paint

Live Paint lets you paint vector graphics intuitively, by automatically detecting and correcting gaps that might otherwise affect the application of fills and strokes. Paths divide the drawing surface into areas that can be colored, whether the area is bounded by a single path or by segments of multiple paths. Painting objects with Live Paint is like coloring in a coloring book or using watercolors to paint a sketch, and the underlying shapes are not edited.

Note: To learn more about Live Paint and all that it can do, search for "Live Paint groups" in Illustrator Help (Help > Illustrator Help).

Creating a Live Paint group

Next, you will paint artwork using the Live Paint Bucket tool.

1 Choose 4 Live Paint from the Artboard Navigation menu in the lower-left corner of the Document window.

2 With the Selection tool ( ) selected, drag across the artwork at the top of the artboard to select it.

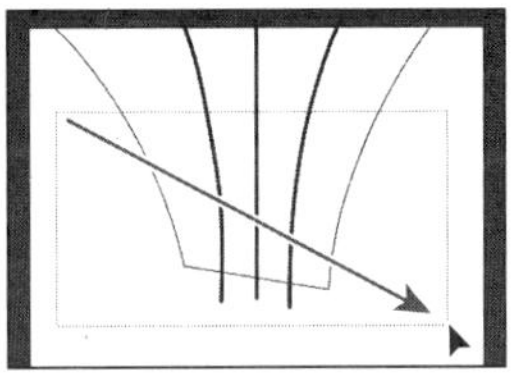

The artwork is composed of a shape and three lines that were drawn on top of the shape.

3 Select the Live Paint Bucket tool ( ) from the Shape Builder tool ( ) group in the Tools panel.

4 Click the Fill box in the Properties panel on the right to reveal a panel. Click the Swatches option at the top of the panel to see the swatches. Click to select the green swatch named "Light Green" in the original Palette Colors color group.

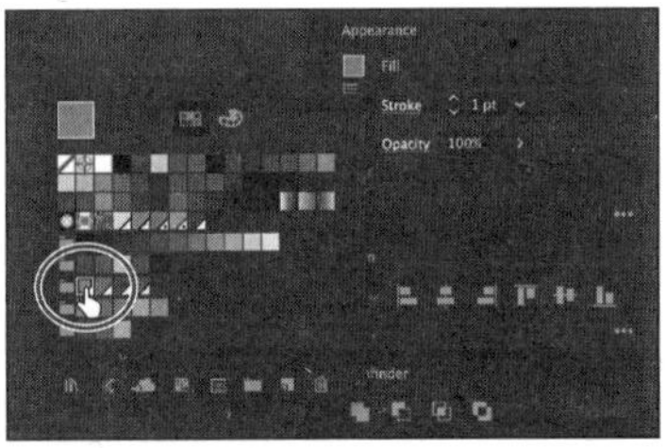

Note: You may need to Press Esc to hide the panel.

5 Position the pointer over the first part of the shape (on the left), and click to convert the selected shapes to a Live Paint group.

Tip: You can convert selected artwork to a Live Paint group by choosing Object > Live Paint > Make.

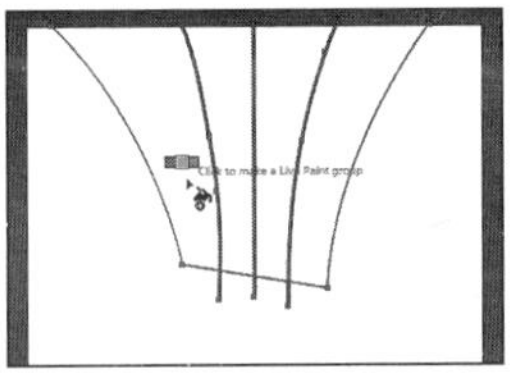

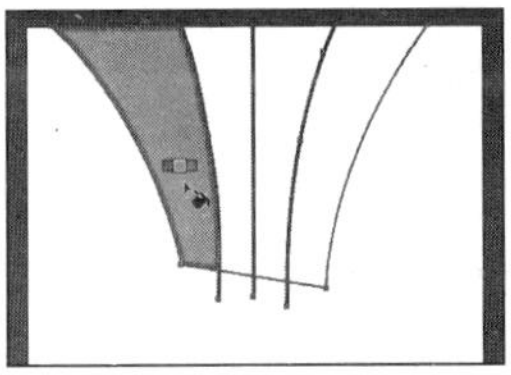

You can click any of the shapes to convert it to a Live Paint group, but the shape you click is filled with the green color. Clicking selected shapes with the Live Paint Bucket tool creates a Live Paint group that you can paint with that same tool. Once a Live Paint group is created, the paths are fully editable, but they are treated like a group. Colors are automatically reapplied to new regions created when you move or adjust a path's shape.

Painting with the Live Paint Bucket tool

After objects are converted to a Live Paint group, you can paint them using several methods, which is what you'll do next.

1 Position the pointer over the area to the right of the green area, in the Live Paint group.

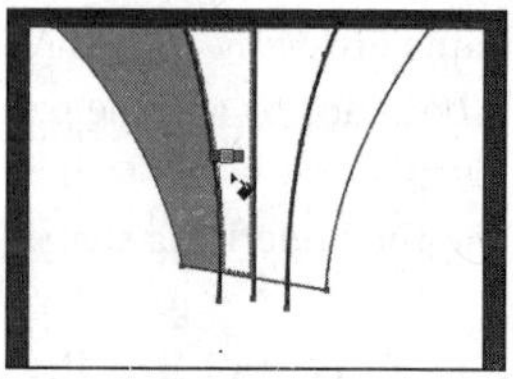

A red highlight appears around the shape that will be painted, and three color swatches appear above the pointer. The selected color (light green) is in the middle, and the two adjacent colors in the Swatches panel are on either side.

● **Note:** As you press the arrow key to change colors, notice, in the Swatches panel, that the color is highlighted. You can press the up or down arrow key, along with right or left arrow keys to select a new swatch to paint with.

2 Press the right arrow key once to select the orange swatch (shown in the three swatches above the pointer). Click to apply the orange color to the shape.

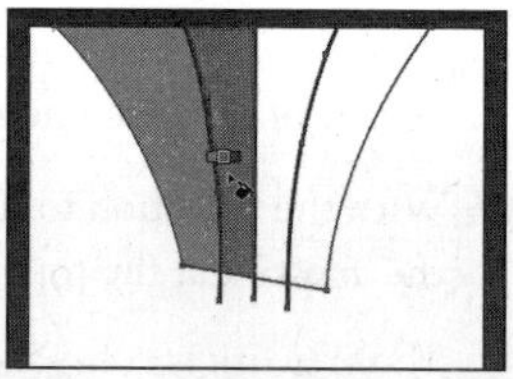

3 Click the Fill box in the Properties panel on the right and click to select the swatch named "Pink." Click in the area to the right of the orange area. See the following figure.

4 Click the Fill box in the Properties panel on the right and click to select the swatch named "Blue," and then click in the area to the right of the pink area.

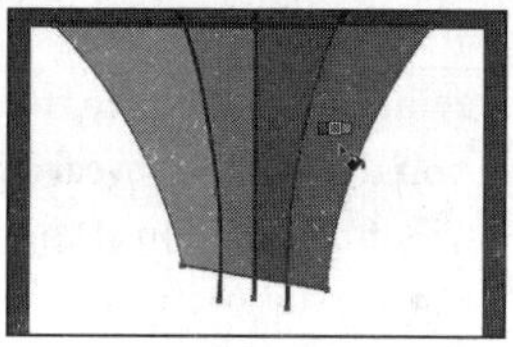

By default, you can only paint fills with the Live Paint Bucket tool. Next, you'll see how to enable painting of strokes with the Live Paint Bucket tool.

▶ **Tip:** With the live Paint Bucket tool selected in the Tools panel, you can also click the Tool Options button at the top of the Properties panel to open the tool options dialog box.

5 Double-click the Live Paint Bucket tool (![]) in the Tools panel. This opens the Live Paint Bucket Options dialog box. Select the Paint Strokes option and then click OK.

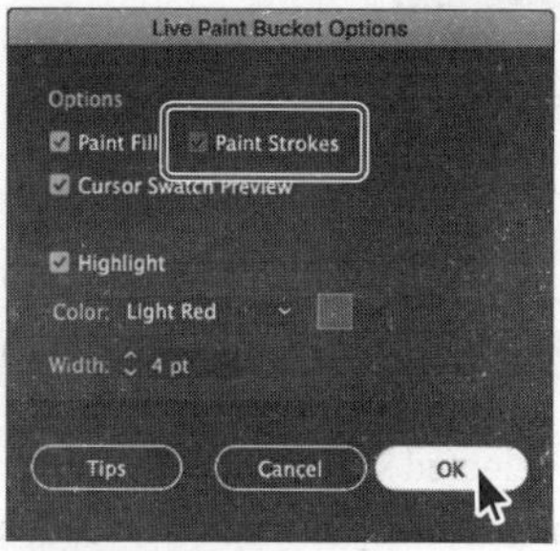

6 Click the Stroke box in the Properties panel (![]) on the right, and select None (![]) for the stroke color. Press the Escape key to hide the panel.

7 Position the pointer directly over the path extending beyond the colored areas, as shown in the figure. When the pointer changes to a paintbrush (), click the stroke to remove the stroke color (by applying the None swatch). Do the same for the two other strokes extending out.

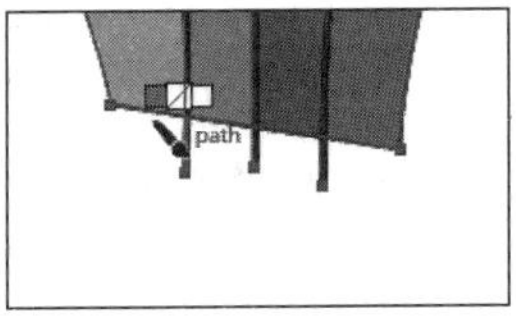

8 Choose Select > Deselect and then choose File > Save.

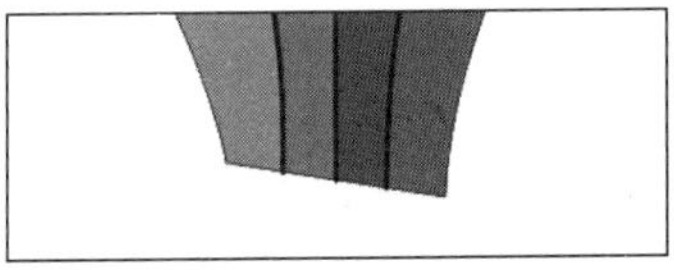

Modifying a Live Paint group

When you make a Live Paint group, each path remains editable. When you move or adjust a path, the colors that were previously applied don't just stay where they were, like they do in natural media paintings or with image-editing software. Instead, the colors are automatically reapplied to the new regions that are formed by the intersecting paths. Next, you will edit paths in a Live Paint group.

1 Select the Selection tool (), and drag across the gray rectangle and brown handle at the bottom of the artboard. See the first part of the following figure.

2 Choose Object > Live Paint > Make.

3 Drag the selected group straight up so that the group and the white rectangle above it overlap.

4 With the Selection tool, Shift-click the white rectangle to select both objects.

5 Choose Object > Live Paint > Merge to add the new white shape to the Live Paint group.

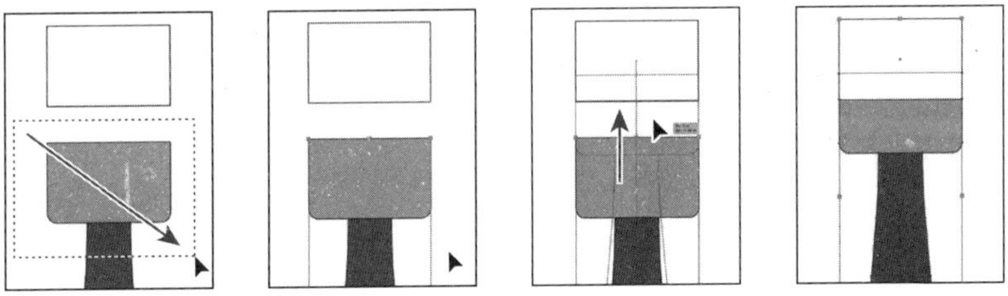

6 Select the Live Paint Bucket tool () in the Tools panel. Click the Fill color in the Properties panel and select a lighter gray color. Click to paint the top part of the paintbrush. Click to select a darker gray color for the fill color in the Properties panel and click the overlapping area.

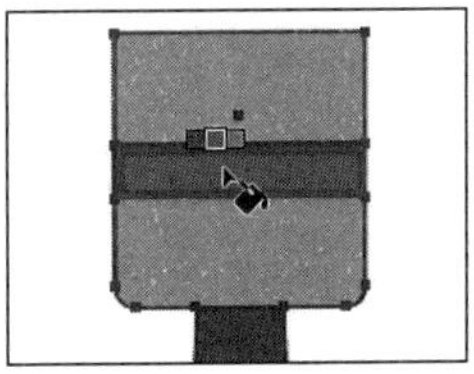

7 Select the Selection tool, and with the Live Paint object selected, double-click the Live Paint object to enter Isolation mode.

▶ **Tip:** You could also edit the anchor points of the selected artwork using the Direct Selection tool (▷), for instance. The paths are still editable, and the colors are reapplied to the new regions that are formed by edited paths.

8 Click the bottom gray shape (right above the brown "handle"). Drag the top-middle bounding point up to resize it.

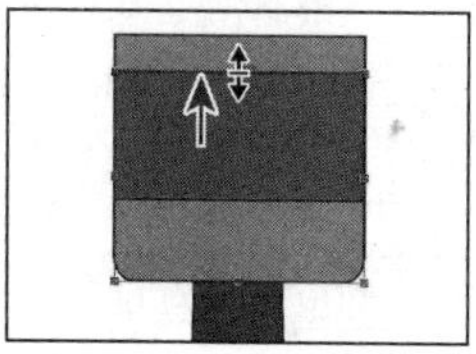

Notice how the color fill and stroke changes every time you release the mouse button.

9 Choose Select > Deselect and then press the Escape key to exit Isolation mode.

10 Choose Object > Show All to show the end of the paintbrush that I hid in the file. An arrow is pointing to it in the following figure.

11 Choose View > Fit All In Window.

12 Choose File > Save and then choose File > Close.

Review questions

1 Describe what a *global color* is.

2 How can you save a color?

3 Describe what a *tint* is.

4 How can you choose color harmonies for color inspiration?

5 Name two things that the Recolor Artwork dialog box allows you to do.

6 Explain what Live Paint allows you to do.

Review answers

1 A global color is a color swatch that, when you edit it, automatically updates all artwork to which it is applied. All spot colors are global; however, process colors you save as swatches are global by default, but they can be either global or local.

2 You can save a color for painting other objects in your artwork by adding it to the Swatches panel by doing one of the following:

- Drag the color from a Fill box, and drop it over the Swatches panel.
- Click the New Swatch button (■) at the bottom of the Swatches panel.
- Choose New Swatch from the Swatches panel menu (■).
- Choose Create New Swatch from the Color panel menu (■).

3 A *tint* is a mixture of a color with white to make the color lighter. You can create a tint from a global process color, like CMYK, or from a spot color.

4 You can choose color harmonies from the Color Guide panel. Color harmonies are used to generate a color scheme based on a single color.

5 You use the Recolor Artwork dialog box to change the colors used in selected artwork, create and edit color groups, or reassign or reduce the colors in your artwork, among other functions.

6 Live Paint lets you paint vector graphics intuitively by automatically detecting and correcting gaps that might otherwise affect the application of fills and strokes. Paths divide the drawing surface into areas, any of which can be colored, regardless of whether the area is bounded by a single path or by segments of multiple paths.

8 ADDING TYPE TO A POSTER

Lesson overview

In this lesson, you'll learn how to do the following:

- Create and edit area and point type.
- Import text.
- Change text attributes.
- Fix missing fonts.
- Work with Glyphs.
- Modify text with the Touch Type tool.
- Create columns of text.
- Create and edit paragraph and character styles.
- Wrap type around an object.
- Reshape text with a warp.
- Create type on a path and on shapes.
- Create text outlines.

This lesson takes approximately 75 minutes to complete. Please log in to your account on peachpit.com to download the lesson files for this chapter, or go to the "Getting Started" section at the beginning of this book and follow the instructions under "Accessing the lesson files and Web Edition."

Your Account page is also where you'll find any updates to the chapters or to the lesson files. Look on the Lesson & Update Files tab to access the most current content.

Text as a design element plays a major role in your illustrations. Like other objects, type can be painted, scaled, rotated, and more. In this lesson, you'll discover how to create basic text and interesting text effects.

Starting the lesson

You'll be adding type to a poster during this lesson, but before you begin, restore the default preferences for Adobe Illustrator CC. Then open the finished art file for this lesson to see the illustration.

Note: If you have not already downloaded the project files for this lesson to your computer from your Account page, make sure to do so now. See the "Getting Started" section at the beginning of the book.

1. To ensure that the tools function and the defaults are set exactly as described in this lesson, delete or deactivate (by renaming) the Adobe Illustrator CC preferences file. See "Restoring default preferences" in the "Getting Started" section at the beginning of the book.
2. Start Adobe Illustrator CC.
3. Choose File > Open. Locate the file named L8_end.ai in the Lessons > Lesson08 folder. Click Open.

   You will most likely see a Missing Fonts dialog box since the file is using a specific Typekit font. Simply click Close in the Missing Fonts dialog box. You will learn all about Typekit fonts later in this lesson.

   Leave the file open for reference later in the lesson, if you like. I closed it.
4. Choose File > Open. In the Open dialog box, navigate to the Lessons > Lesson08 folder, and select the L8_start.ai file on your hard disk. Click Open to open the file.

   This file already has nontext components in it. You will add all of the text elements to complete the poster (front and back).
5. Choose File > Save As. In the Save As dialog box, navigate to the Lesson08 folder, and name the file **FoodTruck.ai**. Leave the Format option set to Adobe Illustrator (ai) (macOS) or the Save As Type option set to Adobe Illustrator (*.AI) (Windows) and then click Save.

   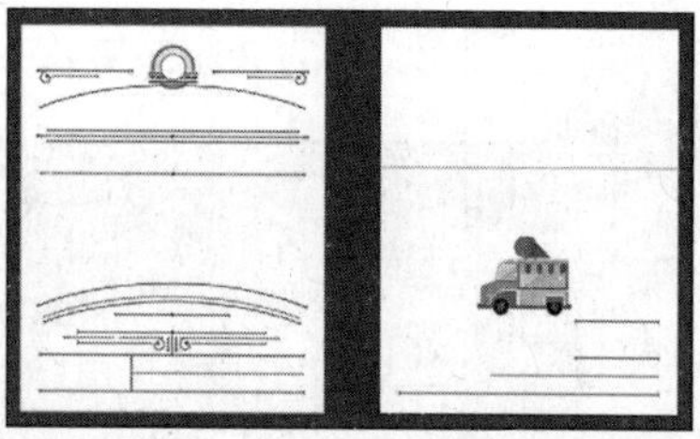
6. In the Illustrator Options dialog box, leave the Illustrator options at their default settings and then click OK.
7. Choose Window > Workspace > Reset Essentials.

Note: If you don't see Reset Essentials in the Workspace menu, choose Window > Workspace > Essentials before choosing Window > Workspace > Reset Essentials.

Adding type to the poster

Type features are some of the most powerful tools in Illustrator. You can add a single line of type to your artwork, create columns and rows of text like you do in Adobe InDesign, place text, flow text into a shape or along a path, and work with letterforms as graphic objects. In Illustrator, you can create text in three main ways: as point type, area type, and type on a path.

Adding text at a point

Point type is a horizontal or vertical line of text that begins where you click and expands as you enter characters. Each line of text is independent—the line expands or shrinks as you edit it but doesn't wrap to the next line unless you add a paragraph return or a soft return. Entering text this way is useful for adding a headline or a few words to your artwork. Next, you will add some text to the poster as point type.

1 Ensure that 1 Poster 1 is chosen in the Artboard Navigation menu in the lower-left corner of the Document window.

2 Choose View > Fit Artboard In Window and then press Command++ (macOS) or Ctrl++ (Windows) three or so times to zoom in.

3 Choose Window > Layers to show the Layers panel. Select the layer named "Text," if it's not already selected.

4 Click the Properties panel tab to show it.

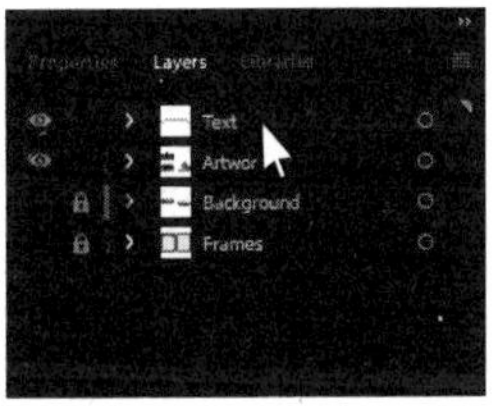

Note: Selecting a layer means any content you create going forward will be on that layer. You'll learn all about layers and how to use them in Lesson 9, "Organizing Your Artwork with Layers."

5 Select the Type tool (**T**) in the Tools panel on the left. Click (*don't drag*) in a blank space on the artboard. Some selected placeholder text, "Lorem ipsum," is now on the artboard. Type **Pie Oh Pie • 123 Cheese • Plus Many More!**.

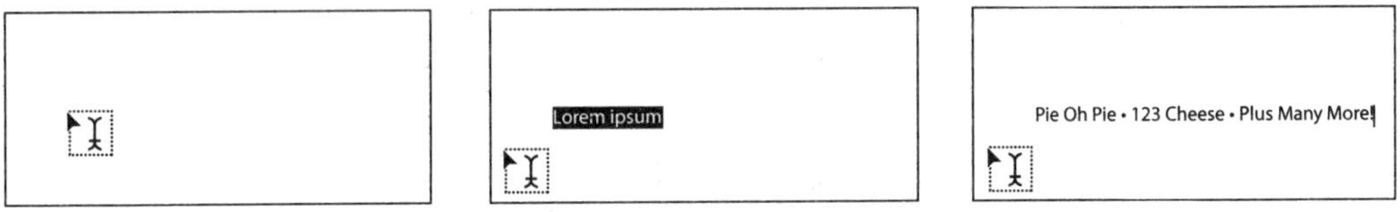

To add the bullet points between the words, you can choose Type > Insert Special Character > Symbols > Bullet. You can also simply add a hyphen (-) or other character.

● **Note:** Scaling point type this way will stretch the text if you drag any bounding point. This may result in a font size that is not a round number (12.93 pt, for instance).

6 Select the Selection tool (▶) in the Tools panel, and drag the lower-right bounding point of the text down and to the left.

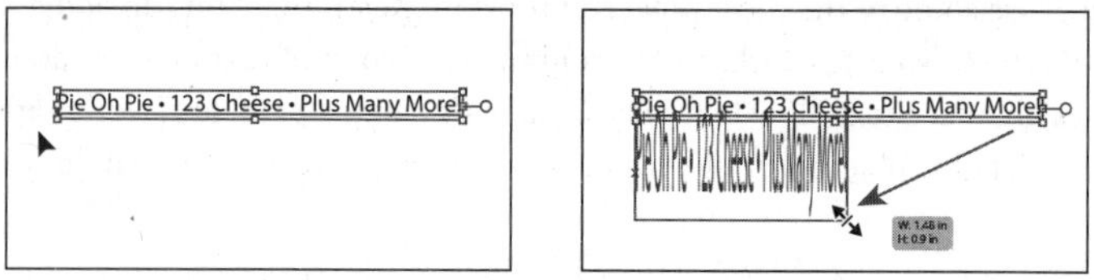

7 Choose Edit > Undo Scale.

8 Choose View > Fit Artboard In Window.

Adding area type

Area type uses the boundaries of an object (like a rectangle) to control the flow of characters, either horizontally or vertically. When the text reaches a boundary, it automatically wraps to fit inside the defined area. Entering text in this way is useful when you want to create one or more paragraphs, such as for a poster or a brochure.

To create area type, you click with the Type tool (T) where you want the text and drag to create an area type object (also called a *text area, text object*, or *type object*). You can also convert an existing shape or object to a type object by clicking the edge of an object (or inside the object) with the Type tool. When the cursor appears, you can type. Next, you'll create a type object and enter more text.

1 Select the Zoom tool (🔍) and drag from left to right, across the lower-left corner of the same artboard to zoom in.

2 Select the Type tool (T). Move the pointer into a blank area of the artboard. Click and drag down and to the right to create a text area that is about an inch in width; the height should roughly match the following figure.

▶ **Tip:** Filling type objects with placeholder text is a preference you can change. Choose Illustrator CC > Preferences (macOS) or Edit > Preferences (Windows), select the Type category, and deselect "Fill New Type Objects With Placeholder Text" to turn the option off.

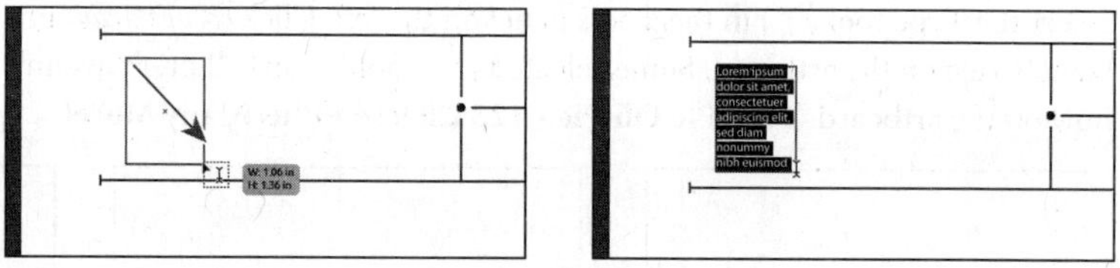

By default, type objects are filled with selected placeholder text that you can replace with your own.

3 With the placeholder text selected, type **Sat/Sun 2pm Highview Park**.

Notice how the text wraps horizontally to fit within the type area.

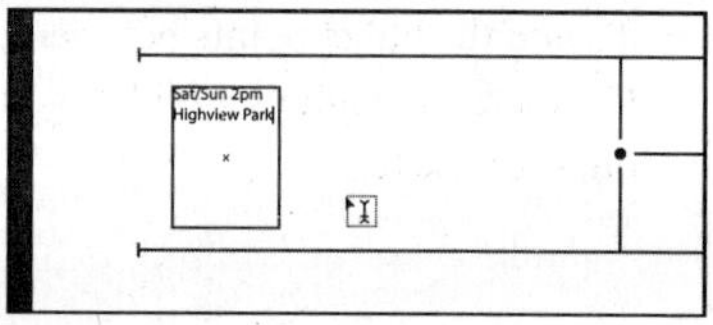

4 Select the Selection tool (▶), and drag the lower-right bounding point to the left and then back to the right to see how the text wraps within.

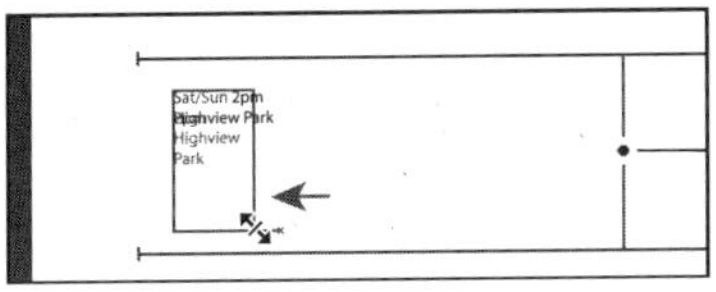

You can drag any of the eight bounding points on the text area to resize it, not just the lower right.

Before you continue, make sure that the text looks like you see in the figure.

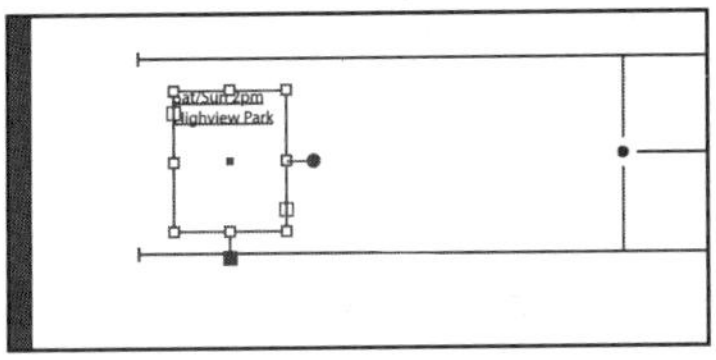

Working with Auto Sizing

By default, when you create area type by dragging with the Type tool, the type area will not resize to fit the text within (similar to how InDesign treats text frames by default). If there is too much text, the text that doesn't fit will not be visible and will be considered overset. For each type area, you can enable a feature called *Auto Sizing* so that area type will resize to fit the text within, and that's what you'll do next.

1 With the text area selected, look at the bottom-middle bounding point and you'll see a widget (⇣) indicating that the type area is *not* set to auto size. Hover the pointer over the box at the end of the widget (the pointer will change [▶]), and double-click.

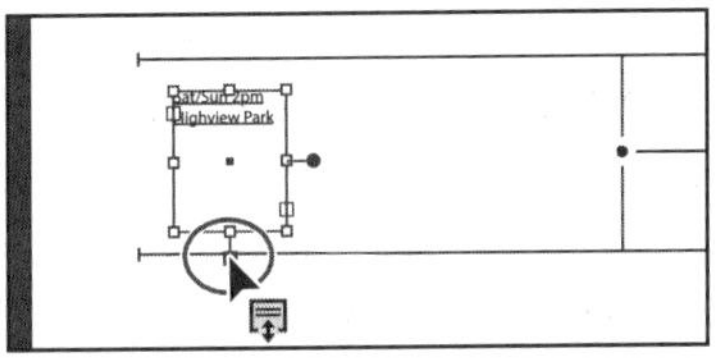

● **Note:** The figure shows just before double-clicking.

By double-clicking the widget, you turn Auto Sizing on. As the text is edited and re-edited, the frame shrinks and grows vertically (only) to accommodate the changing amount of copy and eliminates overset text (text that won't fit) without manually sizing and resizing frames.

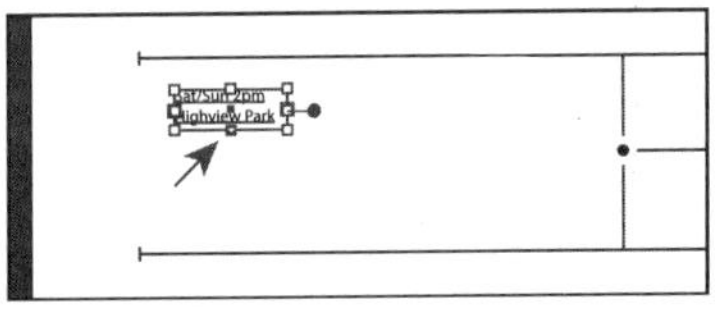

▶ **Tip:** If Auto Sizing is enabled for a selected type area, dragging one of the bottom bounding points on the type area down disables Auto Sizing for the type area.

2 Select the Type tool (**T**), and position the pointer *immediately after* the word "Park." Make sure you see this pointer (I), not this pointer ([I]). Click to insert the cursor. Press Return or Enter, and type **Raleigh, North Carolina**.

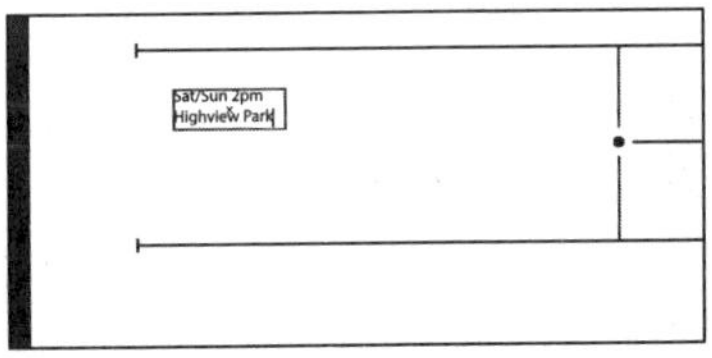

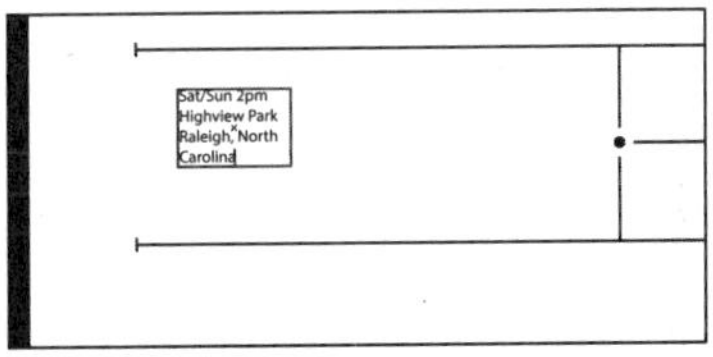

▶ **Tip:** If you double-click text with the Selection tool (▶) or Direct Selection tool (▷), the Type tool becomes selected.

● **Note:** In this instance, clicking when you see this pointer ([I]) will create a new point type area.

The type area will expand vertically to fit the new text. If you were to double-click the Auto Sizing widget, Auto Sizing would be turned off for the area type. The type area would remain the current size no matter how much text was added.

● **Note:** You could have also chosen Edit > Undo Typing to remove the text. In this lesson, I just want to give you more practice selecting text.

3 Select and delete the Raleigh, North Carolina text.

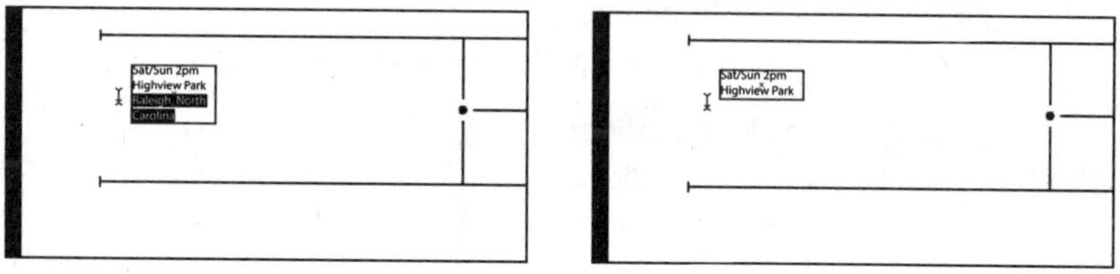

Notice that the type object shrank vertically to fit around the text because Auto Sizing is on for the type object.

Converting between area type and point type

You can easily convert between area type objects and point type objects. This can be useful if you type a headline by clicking (creating point type) but later want to resize and add more text without stretching the text inside. This method is also useful if you paste text from InDesign into Illustrator because text pasted from InDesign into Illustrator (with nothing selected) is pasted as point type. Most of the time, it would be better suited as an area type object so that you could flow the text within. Next, you will convert a type object from area type to point type.

1 With the Selection tool selected, press the Option (macOS) or Alt (Windows) key, and drag the type object you created in the previous section over to the right side of the artboard. Release the mouse button and then the key to make a copy.

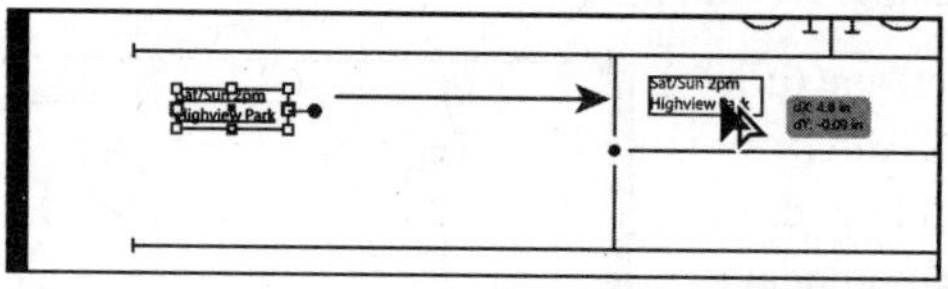

▶ **Tip:** Clicking once in text inserts the cursor. Clicking twice in text selects a word. Clicking three times selects the entire paragraph in Illustrator.

▶ **Tip:** To see the soft return, you can show hidden characters by choosing Type > Show Hidden Characters.

2 Move the pointer over the type area to the left, and double-click to insert the cursor and switch to the Type tool. Press Command+A (macOS) or Ctrl+A (Windows) to select all of the text in the type area; then type **AUG 19th/20th**.

3 Click right before the "1" in "19th." Press Backspace or Delete to remove the space between "AUG" and "19th."

4 Press Shift+Enter (Shift+Return) to add a soft return.

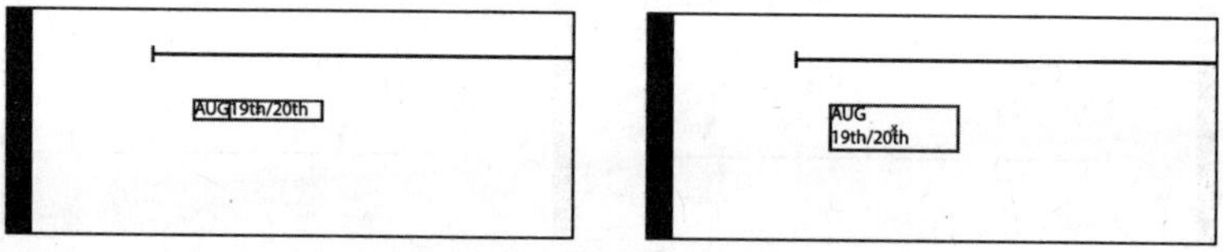

5 Press Esc to select the Selection tool (▶).

6 Move the pointer over the annotator (—●) off the right edge of the type object. A filled end on the annotator indicates that it's area type. When the pointer changes (▶T), click once to see the message "Double-click to convert to Point Type." Double-click the annotator to convert the area type to point type.

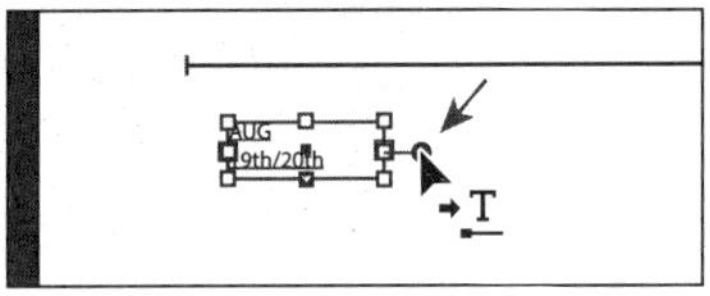

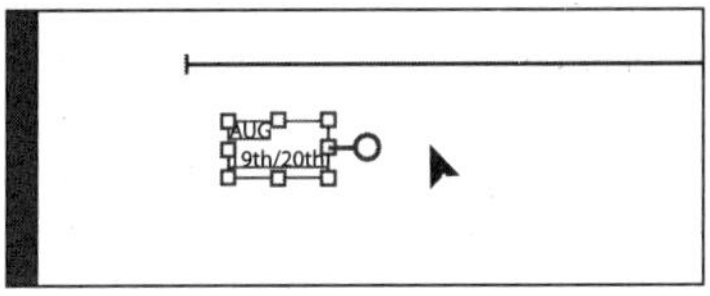

The annotator end should now be hollow (—○), indicating that it is a point type object. If you were to resize the bounding box, the text would scale as well.

7 Press the Shift key, and drag the lower-right bounding point down and to the right until the text just fits between the line above and the line below. Release the mouse button and then the key.

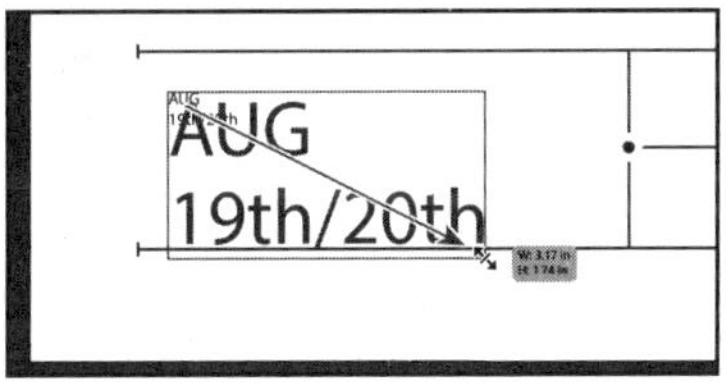

Because the text is point type, it stretches when the type area is resized. Pressing the Shift key is very important because otherwise the text would most likely be distorted.

8 Choose File > Save.

▶ **Tip:** With a type object selected, you can also choose Type > Convert To Point Type or Convert To Area Type, depending on what the selected text area is.

Importing a plain-text file

You can import text into artwork from a file that was created in another application. As of the writing of this book, Illustrator supports DOC, DOCX, RTF, Plain text (ASCII) with ANSI, Unicode, Shift JIS, GB2312, Chinese Big 5, Cyrillic, GB18030, Greek, Turkish, Baltic, and Central European encoding. One of the advantages of importing text from a file, rather than copying and pasting it, is that imported text retains its character and paragraph formatting (by default). For example, text from an RTF file retains its font and style specifications in Illustrator, unless you choose to remove formatting when you import the text. In this section, you'll place text from a plain-text file into your design.

1 Choose 2 Poster 2 from the Artboard Navigation menu in the lower-left corner of the Document window.

▶ **Tip:** You can add placeholder text to your document if you don't have the final text ready yet. With the cursor in a type object or in text on a path, choose Type > Fill With Placeholder Text.

2 Choose File > Place. In the Lessons > Lesson08 folder, select the L8_text.txt file. In the Place dialog box on macOS, click the Options button to see the import options, if necessary. Select Show Import Options, and click Place.

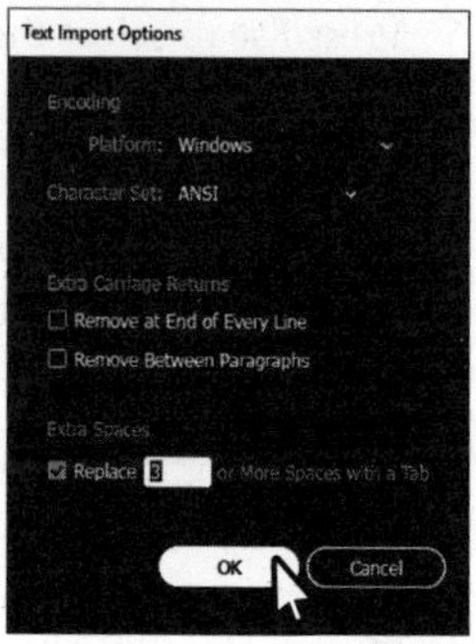

In the Text Import Options dialog box that appears, you can set some options prior to importing text.

▶ **Tip:** You can place text into an existing type area as well.

3 Leave the default settings and then click OK.

4 Move the loaded text icon onto the aqua guide. When the word "Guide" appears, click and drag down and to the right and then release the mouse button. Use the figure as a guide.

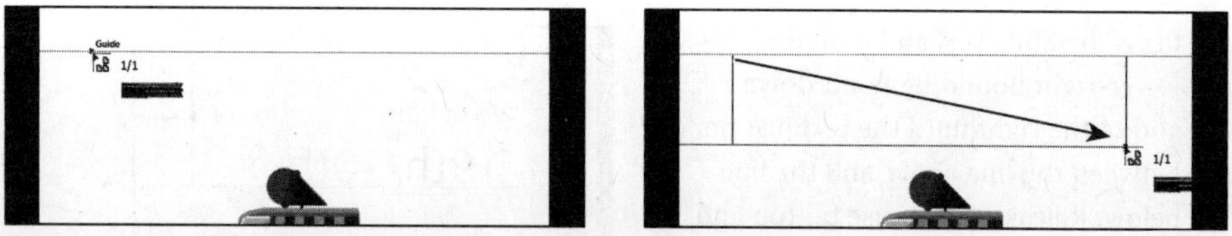

If you were to simply click with the loaded text pointer, a type object would be created that was smaller than the size of the artboard.

▶ **Tip:** When you place (File > Place) RTF (Rich Text Format) or Word documents (DOC or DOCX) in Illustrator, the Microsoft Word Options dialog box appears. In the Microsoft Word Options dialog box, you can select to keep the generated table of contents, footnotes and endnotes, and index text, and you can even choose to remove the formatting of the text before you place it (the styles and formatting are brought in from Word by default).

5 With the Selection tool (▶), drag the bottom bounding point of the type object up until you see an overset text icon (⊞) in the out port. I didn't need to.

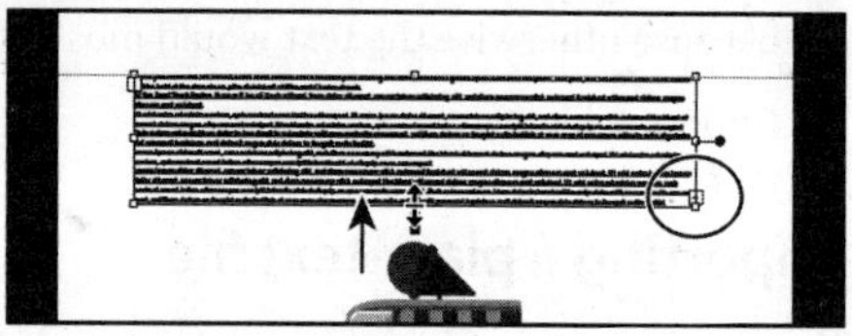

Threading text

When working with area type (*not* point type), each area type object contains an *in port* and an *out port*. The ports enable you to link type objects and flow text between them.

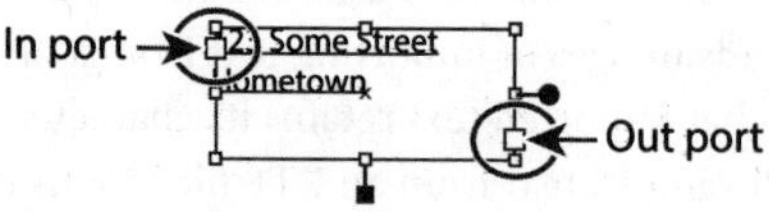

An empty out port indicates that all the text is visible and that the type object isn't linked. An arrow in a port indicates that the type object is linked to another type object. A red plus sign (⊞) in an out port indicates that the object contains additional text, which is called *overflow text*. To show all of the overflow text, you can thread the text to another type object, resize the type object, or adjust the text. To *thread*, or continue, text from one object to the next, you have to link the objects. Linked type objects can be of any shape; however, the text must be entered in an object or along a path, not as point type (by simply clicking to create text).

Next, you will thread text between two type objects.

1 With the Selection tool ( ), click the out port (larger box) in the lower-right corner of the type object that has the red plus sign in it ( ).

The pointer changes to a loaded text icon ( ) when you move it away.

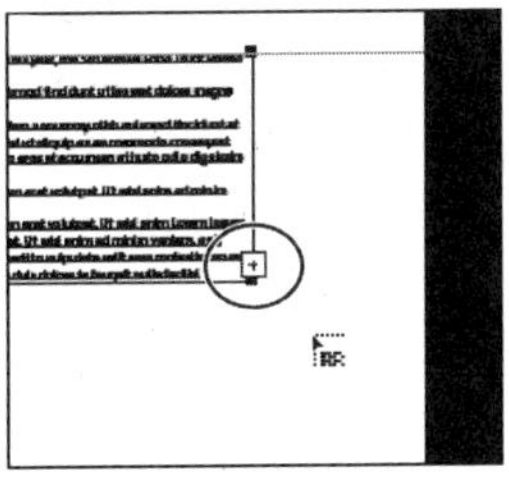

● **Note:** It may be difficult to click the out port because of the guides. You can always zoom in, remembering to zoom out again for the next steps.

● **Note:** If you double-click an out port, a new type object appears. If this happens, you can either drag the new object where you would like it to be positioned or choose Edit > Undo Link Threaded Text, and the loaded text icon reappears.

2 Position the pointer in the lower-left area of the artboard and click. An area type object is created that is the same size as the original.

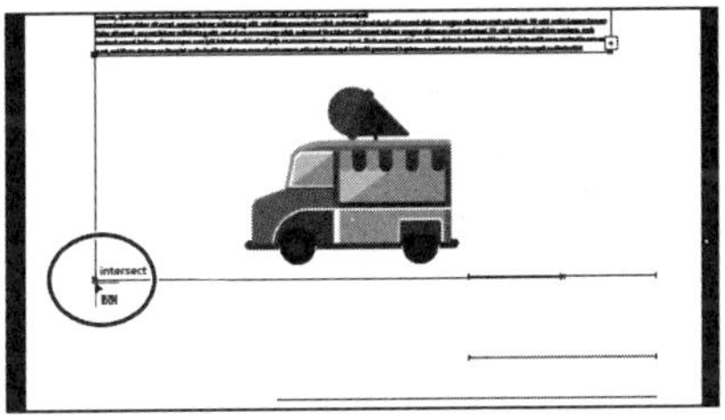

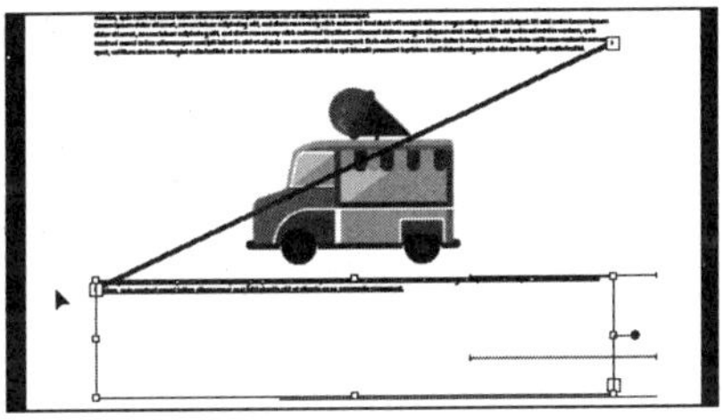

With the second type object still selected, notice the line connecting the two type objects. This line is the *thread* that tells you that the two objects are connected. If you don't see this thread (line), choose View > Show Text Threads.

The out port ( ) of the top type object on the artboard and the in port ( ) of the bottom type object on the artboard have small arrows in them indicating how the text is flowing from one to the other.

▶ **Tip:** Another way to thread text between objects is to select an area type object, select the object (or objects) you want to link to, and then choose Type > Threaded Text > Create.

3 Click the top type object, and drag the bottom-middle point up to make it shorter.

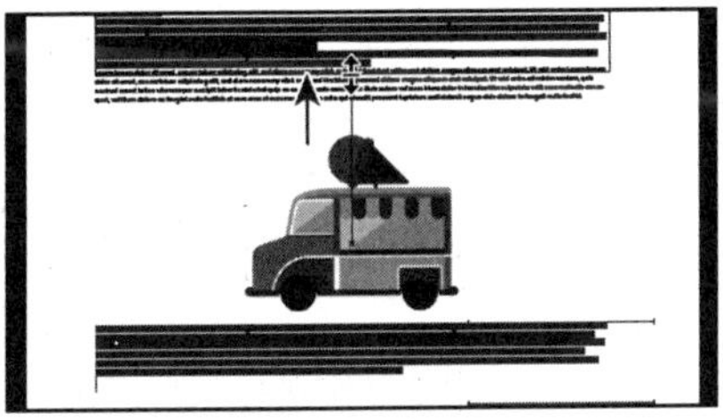

The text will flow between the type objects. If you delete the second type object, the text is pulled back into the original object as overflow text. Although not visible, the overflow text is not deleted.

▶ **Tip:** You can split the threaded text so that each type area is no longer connected to the next by selecting one of the threaded text areas (but the text remains) by choosing Type > Threaded Text > Remove Threading. Choosing Type > Threaded Text > Release Selection will break the thread to the selected type area and remove the text.

Formatting type

You can format text using character and paragraph formatting, apply fill and stroke attributes to it, and change its transparency. You can apply these changes to one character, a range of characters, or all characters in a type object that you select. As you'll soon see, selecting the type object, rather than selecting the text inside, lets you apply formatting options to all of the text in the object, including options from the Character and Paragraph panels, fill and stroke attributes, and transparency settings.

In this section, you'll discover how to change text attributes, such as size and font, and later learn how to save that formatting as text styles.

Changing font family and font style

Note: The Creative Cloud desktop application must be installed on your computer, and you must have an Internet connection to initially sync fonts. The Creative Cloud desktop application is installed when you install your first Creative Cloud application, like Illustrator.

In this section, you'll apply a font to text. Aside from applying local fonts to text from your machine, Creative Cloud subscribers can apply Typekit fonts that have been synced with their computer. Typekit is a subscription service offering access to a library of fonts for use in desktop applications such as InDesign or Microsoft Word and on websites. A Typekit Portfolio plan is included with your Creative Cloud subscription, and trial Creative Cloud members have access to a selection of fonts from Typekit for web and desktop use. The fonts appear alongside other locally installed fonts in the fonts list in Illustrator, as you'll soon see. By default, Typekit is turned on in the Creative Cloud desktop application (version 1.9 and later) so that it can sync fonts and make them available in your desktop applications.

Note: For questions about Typekit font licensing, visit https://helpx.adobe.com/typekit/using/font-licensing.html. For more information on working with Typekit fonts, visit https://helpx.adobe.com/creative-cloud/help/add-fonts-typekit.html.

Sync Typekit fonts

Next, you'll select and sync Typekit fonts to your machine so that you can use them in Illustrator.

1 Ensure that the Creative Cloud for desktop application is launched and you are signed in with your Adobe ID (*this requires an Internet connection*).

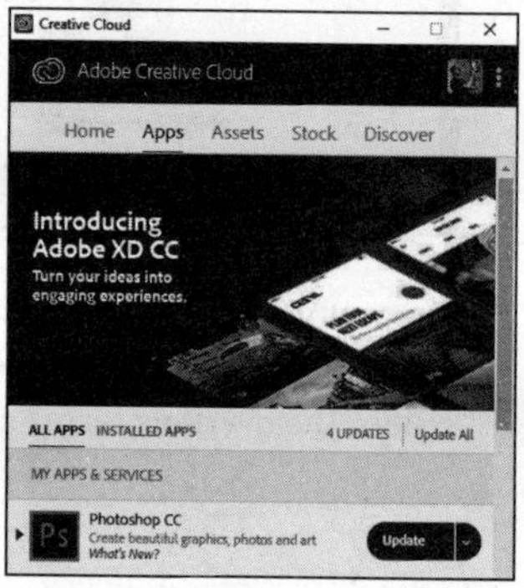

Note: To learn about the Creative Cloud for desktop application, visit https://www.adobe.com/creativecloud/desktop-app.html.

2 In Illustrator, choose Select > Deselect.

3 Press Command++ (macOS) or Ctrl++ (Windows) a few times to zoom in to the text in the center of the artboard.

4 Select the Type tool (T) in the Tools panel, move the pointer over the text and click to insert the cursor in either threaded type object. Choose Select > All or press Command+A (macOS) or Ctrl+A (Windows) to select all of the text in both threaded type objects.

5 In the Properties panel to the right of the document, click the arrow to the right of the Font Family menu in the Properties panel, and notice the fonts that appear in the menu. These fonts are those that are installed locally.

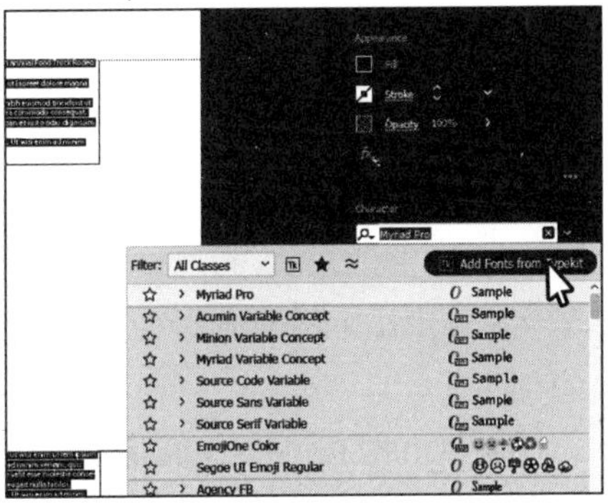

In the font menu, an icon appears to the right of the font names in the list indicating what type of font it is (Tk is Typekit, *O* is OpenType, TT is TrueType, and a is Adobe Postscript).

6 Click the Add Fonts From Typekit button.

A browser will open and should open the Typekit.com website and log you in using your Adobe ID. If you do not have an Internet connection, you can choose any other font in the font menu in Illustrator instead.

Note: If you are taken to the Typekit.com home page, you can simply click the Browse option on the page.

7 Once the Typekit.com website is open in your browser, click the Show Filters button if you don't see the Classification options on the right side of the page. Click the Sans Serif option in the Classification options to sort the fonts.

8 Hover over any font. If you wanted to use that font, you would click to explore which styles (bold, italic, etc.) you would sync.

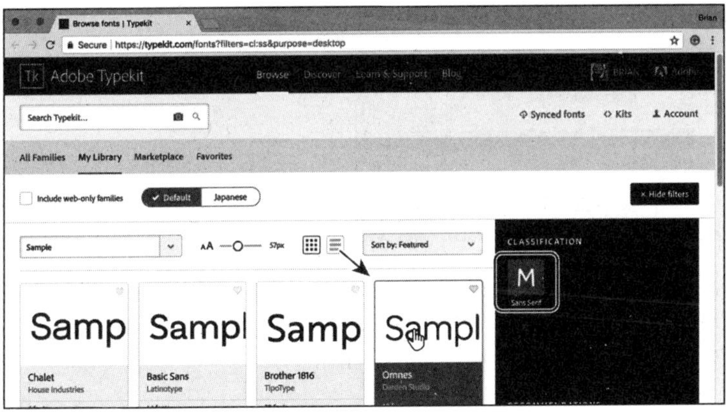

Note: Click the search glass (🔍) or press Enter or Return to search the site for the Roboto font if the results menu doesn't appear, and select Roboto on the page that opens.

9 Type **Roboto** in the Search Typekit field toward the top of the page. Choose Roboto from the results menu that appears.

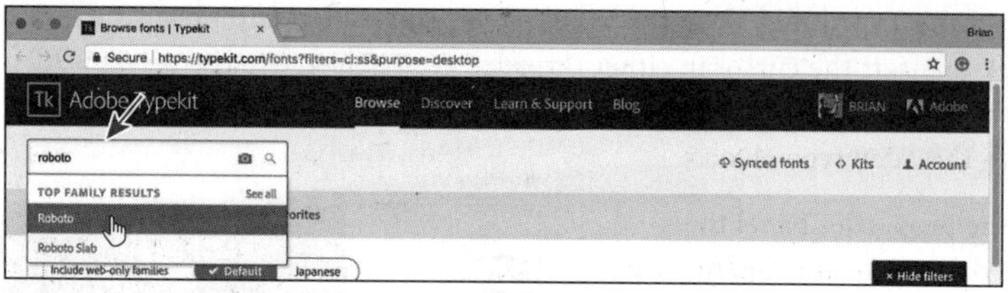

Tip: The fonts are synced to all computers where you've installed the Creative Cloud application and logged in. To view fonts, open the Creative Cloud desktop application, and click the Assets > Fonts panel.

10 In the page that appears, click the Sync button to the right of Roboto Light, Roboto Italic, Roboto Bold, and Roboto Condensed Regular.

11 After syncing the Roboto font styles, follow the same process by searching for the font named Colt at the top of the page showing. When the Colt page opens, click the Sync button for Colt Bold. You can close the browser and return to Illustrator. Once the fonts are synced to your computer (be patient, it may take some time), you may begin to use them.

Apply fonts to text in Illustrator

Now that the Typekit fonts are synced with your machine, you can use them in any application, and that's what you'll do next.

1 Back in Illustrator, with the threaded text still selected, click the arrow to the right of the Font Family menu in the Properties panel to the right of the document. Click the Apply Typekit Filter button (Tk) to filter the font list and show only the Typekit fonts you just synced.

Note: You may see other Typekit fonts in your menu (aside from the Roboto and Colt fonts), and that's okay.

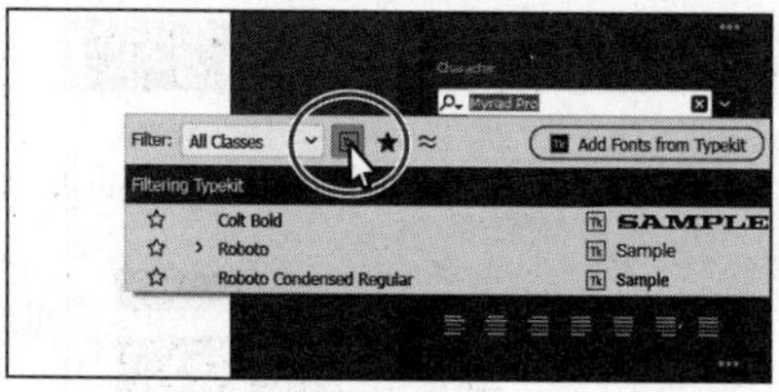

Tip: You could also use the arrow keys (Up and Down) to navigate the list of fonts. When the font you want is chosen, you can press Enter or Return to apply it.

2 Move the pointer over the fonts in the menu, and you should see a preview of the font the pointer is over, applied to the selected text. Click the arrow to the left of Roboto in the menu, and choose Light.

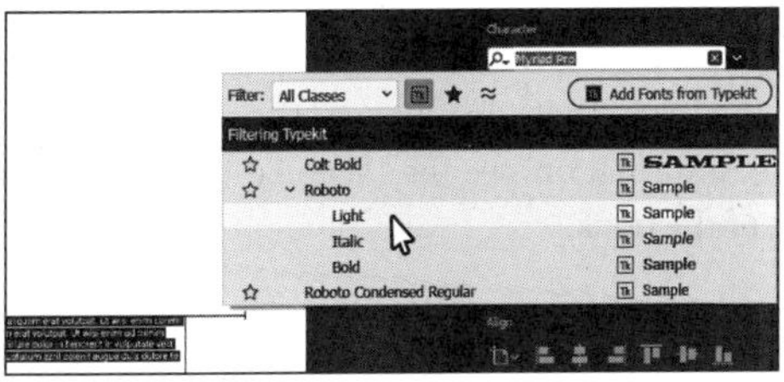

3 Choose 1 Poster 1 from the Artboard Navigation menu in the lower-left corner of the Document window.

4 With the Selection tool (▶) selected, click the "AUG 19th/20th" text toward the bottom of the artboard to select the type object. Press the Shift key and click the type object to the right to select both.

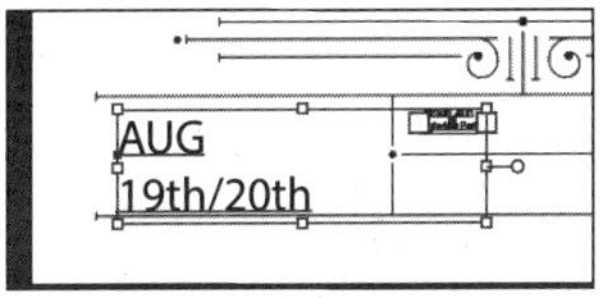

If you want to apply the same font to all of the text in a point type or area type object, you can simply select the object, not the text, and then apply the font.

5 With the type objects selected, click the font name in the Properties panel (I see Myriad Pro). Begin typing the letters **col**.

▶ **Tip:** With the cursor in the font name field, you can also click the X on the right side of the Font Family field to remove the current font shown.

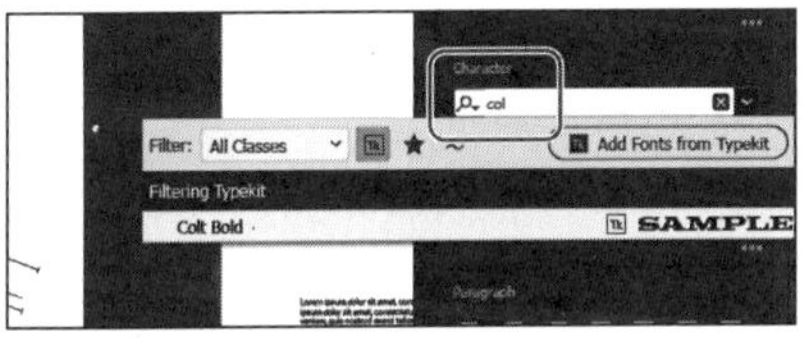

A menu appears beneath where you are typing. Illustrator filters through the list of fonts and displays the font names that contain "col," regardless of where "col" is in the font name and regardless of whether it's capitalized. The Typekit font filter is still turned on from before, so you will turn it off next.

6 Click the Clear Filter button (▣) in the menu that is showing to see all of the available fonts, not just Typekit fonts. In the menu that appears beneath where you are typing, move the pointer over the fonts in the list. Illustrator shows a live font preview of the text. Click to select Colt Bold to apply the font.

▶ **Tip:** You can click the Eyeglass icon (🔍) to the left of the Font Name field and choose to search the first word only. You can also open the Character panel (Window > Type > Character) and search for a font by typing the name.

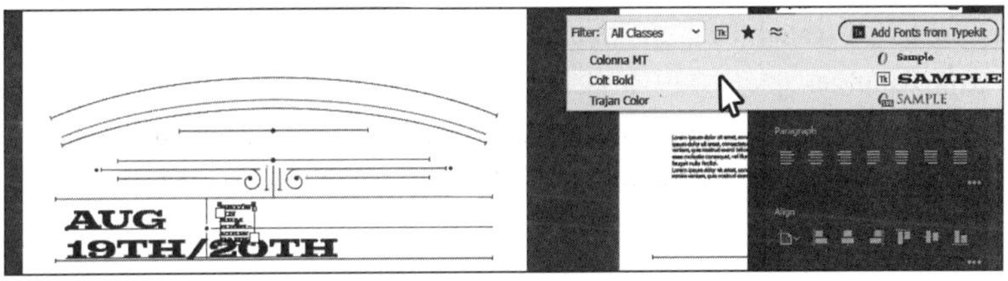

7 Click away from the content, in a blank area, to deselect all.

Fixing missing fonts

To learn how to fix missing fonts, check out the video *Fixing Missing Fonts* that is a part of the Web Edition. For more information, see the "Web Edition" section of "Getting Started" at the beginning of the book.

Changing font size

By default, typeface size is measured in points (a point equals 1/72 of an inch). In this section, you will change the font size of text and also see what happens to point type that is scaled.

1 Click to select the type object that contains the text "SAT/SUN..."

> **Tip:** You can dynamically change the font size of selected text using keyboard shortcuts. To increase the font size in increments of 2 points, press Command+Shift+> (macOS) or Ctrl+Shift+> (Windows). To reduce the font size, press Command+Shift+< (macOS) or Ctrl+Shift+< (Windows).

2 Choose 36 pt from the Font Size menu in the Properties panel.

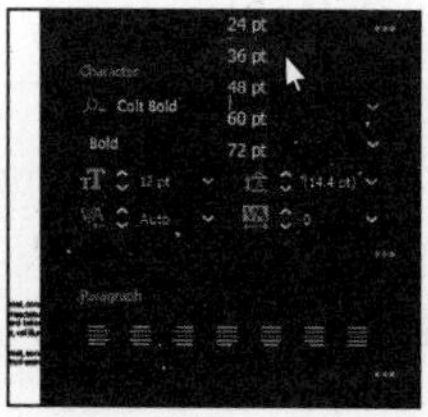

3 Click the Down arrow to the left of font size field in the Properties panel twice to make the font size 34.

4 Choose View > Zoom In to see all of the text in the selected type object.

5 Drag the lower-right corner of the type object to make it bigger. See the figure.

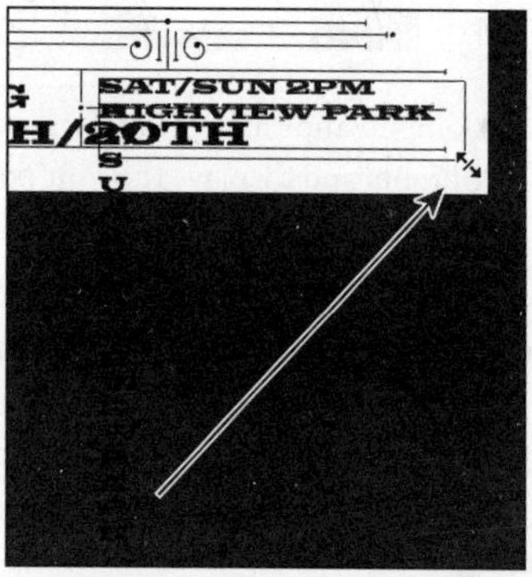

6 Choose View > Fit Artboard In Window.

7 Double-click in the "AUG 19th/20th" text to switch to the Type tool and insert the cursor; then drag across the "19th/20th" text to select it.

Looking in the Character section of the Properties panel, you'll see that the font size is not a whole number. That's because you scaled the point type earlier by dragging.

> **Note:** If you need, change the font size so the "19th/20th" text is as wide as the "AUG" text.

8 Select the value in the Font Size field, and type **20**. The idea is to make the "19th/20th" text as wide as the "AUG" text. Press Enter or Return.

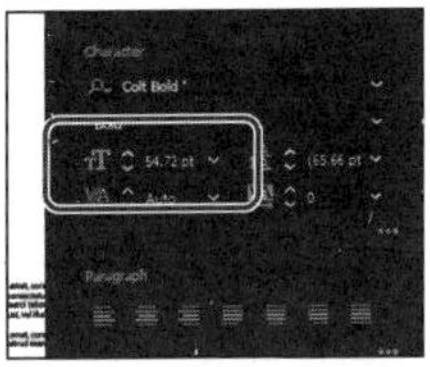

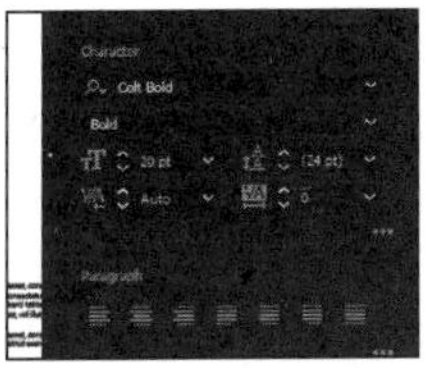

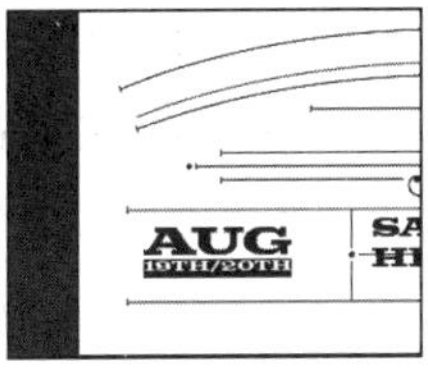

9 Select the Selection tool, and pressing the Shift key, drag a corner of the AUG type object to make it (and the text within) larger. Drag it into position like you see in the figure.

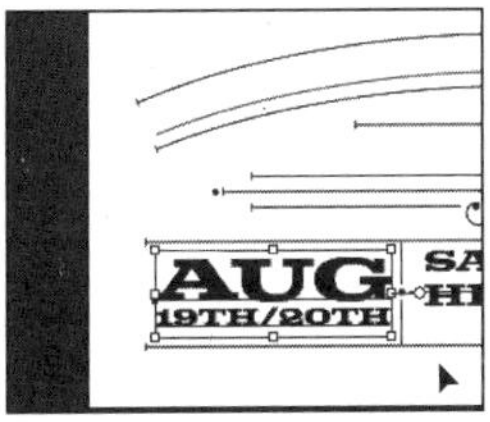

Changing font color

You can change the appearance of text by applying fills, strokes, and more. In this section, you'll simply change the fill of selected text by selecting type objects. Know that you can also select text with the Type tool to apply different color fills and strokes to text.

1 With the Selection tool (▶) selected and with the AUG 19th/20th type object still selected, press the Shift key, and click the text to the right that begins with "SAT/SUN...."

2 Click the Fill color box in the Properties panel. With the Swatches option (■) selected in the panel that appears, select the swatch named "Pink."

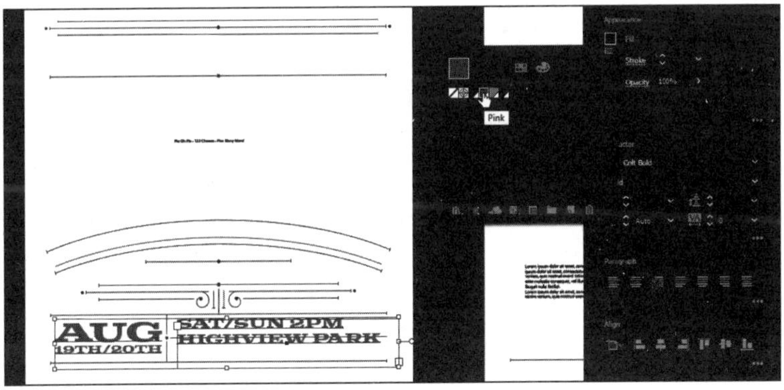

3 Choose Select > Deselect.

4 Choose File > Save.

Changing additional character formatting

In Illustrator you can change a lot of text attributes besides font, font size, and color. Like in InDesign, text attributes are split between character and paragraph formatting and can be found in the Properties panel, Control panel, and two main panels: the Character panel and the Paragraph panel.

The Character panel, which you can access by clicking More Options ( ) in the Character section of the Properties panel or by choosing Window > Type > Character, contains formatting for selected text such as font, font size, kerning, and more. In this section, you will apply some of the many possible attributes to experiment with the different ways you can format text.

1 With the Selection tool ( ) selected, click the SAT/SUN type object.

2 In the Properties panel, change Leading ( ) to **63 pt**.

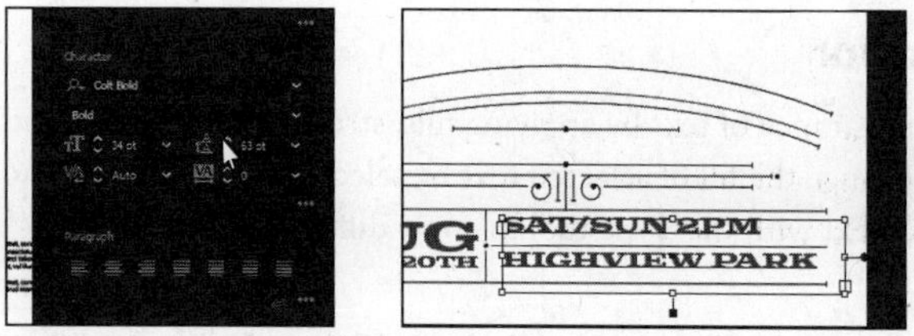

Leading is the vertical space between lines of text. Adjusting the leading can be useful for fitting text into a text area. In this case, it adds space between the lines of text so the text fits better in the decorative lines on the artboard.

3 Drag both type objects into position like you see in the following figure.

4 Select the Type tool and drag across the word "PM" in "2 PM" to select it.

● **Note:** If the text wraps differently in the type object, select the Selection tool and drag the right, middle point of the type object left or right to match the figure.

5 With the text selected, click More Options ( ) in the Character section of the Properties panel to show the Character panel (circled in the following figure). Click the Superscript button ( ) to superscript the word.

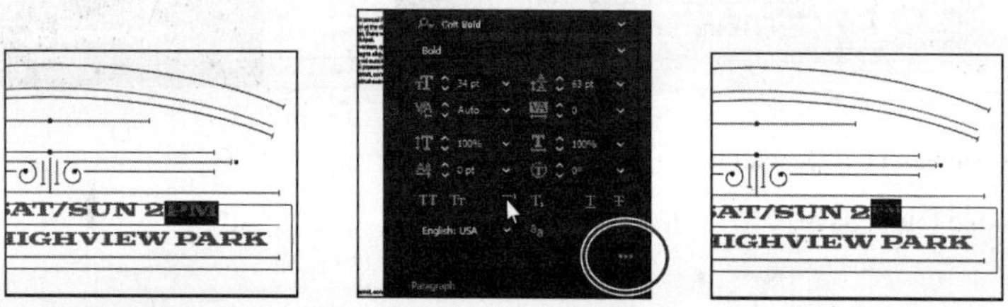

6 Select the Selection tool (▶), and click the type object that contains the "AUG 19th/20th" text.

7 Choose Edit > Copy and then Edit > Paste to paste a copy.

8 Double-click the text to insert the cursor. Press Command+A (macOS) or Ctrl+A (Windows) to select all of the text. Type **CORRAL** in capital letters.

   You'll use this text later in the lesson when you modify text with the Touch Type tool.

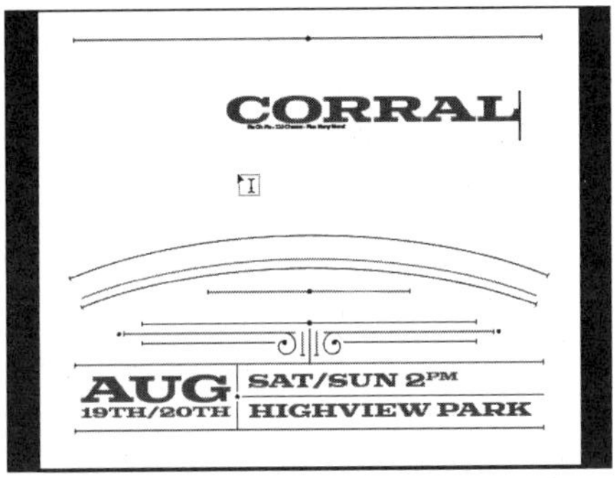

Changing paragraph formatting

As with character formatting, you can set paragraph formatting, such as alignment or indenting, before you enter new type or change the appearance of existing type. Paragraph formatting applies to entire paragraphs rather than just selected content. Most of this type of formatting can be done in the Properties panel, Control panel, or Paragraph panel. You can access the Paragraph panel by clicking More Options (•••) in the Paragraph section of the Properties panel or by choosing Window > Type > Paragraph.

1 Choose 2 Poster 2 from the Artboard Navigation menu in the lower-left corner of the Document window.

2 With the Type tool (T) selected, click in the threaded text. Press Command+A (macOS) or Ctrl+A (Windows) to select all of the text between the two type objects.

3 Click the Justify With Last Line Aligned Right button (≡) in the Paragraph section of the Properties panel to align the text to the right.

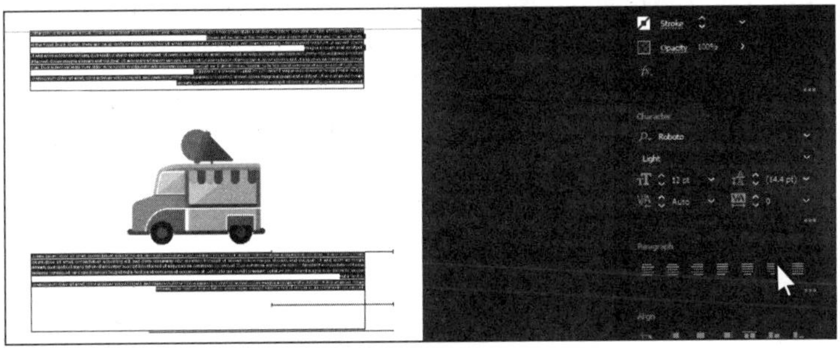

4 With the text selected, click More Options (•••) in the Paragraph section of the Properties panel to show the Paragraph panel.

5 Change Space After Paragraph () to **6 pt** in the Paragraph panel.

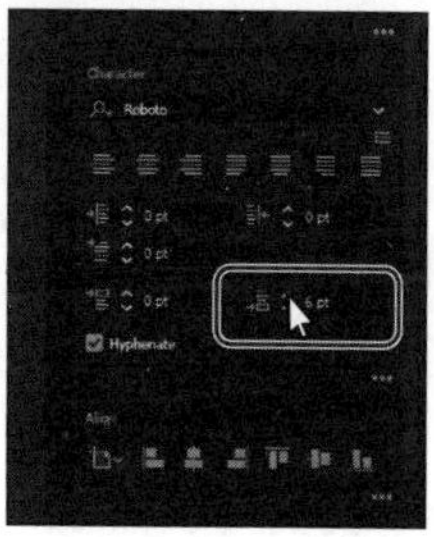

Setting a spacing value after paragraphs, rather than pressing the Enter or Return key, is useful for maintaining consistency and ease of editing later.

6 Press the Esc key to hide the Paragraph panel.

7 Choose 18 pt from the Font Size menu in the Properties panel.

8 Choose Select > Deselect and then choose File > Save.

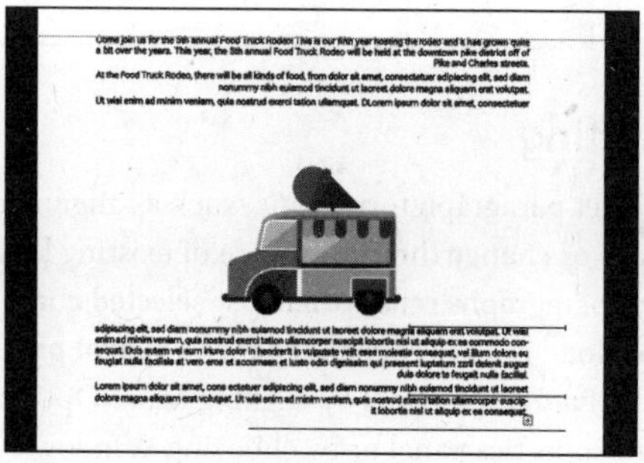

Working with Glyphs

To learn about working with the Glyphs panel, check out the video *Working with the Glyphs Panel* that is part of the Web Edition. For more information, see the "Web Edition" section of "Getting Started" at the beginning of the book.

Modifying text with the Touch Type tool

Using the Touch Type tool (), you can modify the properties of a character, such as size, scale, and rotation, using a mouse cursor or touch controls. This is a very visual (and personally more fun) way of applying the character formatting properties: baseline shift, horizontal and vertical scale, rotation, and kerning.

1 Choose 1 Poster 1 from the Artboard Navigation menu in the lower-left corner of the Document window.

2 Click the Layers panel tab to show the Layers panel. Click the visibility column to the left of the layer named "Background."

3 Click the Properties panel tab to show that panel again.

4 With the Selection tool (▶), click to select the "CORRAL" type object you created earlier and change the font size to **118 pt** in the Properties panel to the right. Drag it into position like you see in the following figure.

5 Choose View > Zoom In a few times.

6 Select the Touch Type tool (⌶) by pressing and holding down on the Type tool (**T**) in the Tools panel and then selecting the Touch Type tool.

After selecting the Touch Type tool, a message briefly appears at the top of the Document window telling you to click a character to select it.

7 Click the first letter "R" in "CORRAL" to select it.

A box with a dot above it appears around the letter after you select it. The different points around the box allow you to adjust the character in different ways.

8 Click and drag the upper-right corner of the box away from the center to make the letter a little larger. Stop dragging when you see roughly 105% for H. Scale and V. Scale in the measurement label.

Notice that width and height change proportionally together. You just adjusted the horizontal scale and the vertical scale for the letter "R." If you were to look in the Character panel (Window > Type > Character), you would see that the Horizontal Scale and Vertical Scale values are roughly 105%.

9 Position the pointer over the rotate handle (the little circle above the letter "R"). When the pointer changes (↜), drag clockwise until you see approximately -17° in the measurement label.

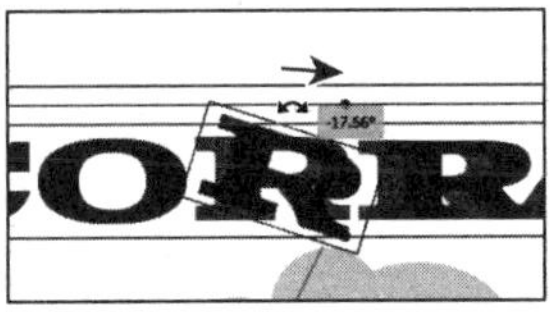

▶ **Tip:** You can also nudge a selected letter with the arrow keys or press Shift+arrow key to move the letter in bigger increments.

● **Note:** There are limits to how far you can drag in any direction. Those limits are based on the kerning and baseline shift value limits.

10 Drag the selected letter "R" down and to the left a little.

By dragging a letter up or down, you are adjusting the baseline shift. Make sure the letter covers the brown path below it.

11 Click to select the second letter "R" to the right. Drag the letter from its center to the left a little to close the gap between the two Rs.

Resizing and reshaping type objects

You can create unique type object shapes by reshaping them using a variety of methods, including adding columns to area type objects or reshaping type objects using the Direct Selection tool. To start this section, you'll copy some of the text at the bottom of the first artboard to the second artboard so you have more text to work with.

1 Choose View > Fit All In Window.

2 Select the Selection tool (▶). Press the Option (macOS) or Alt (Windows) key and drag a copy of the type object that contains the text "AUG 19th/20th" anywhere onto the artboard on the right. Release the mouse button and then the key.

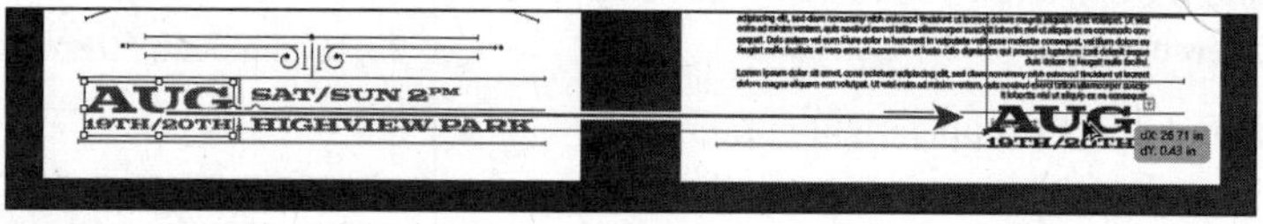

3 Press the Option (macOS) or Alt (Windows) key, and drag the type object that contains the text "SAT/SUN..." anywhere onto the artboard on the right. Release the mouse button and then the key.

4 Drag the type objects into position like you see in the following figure.

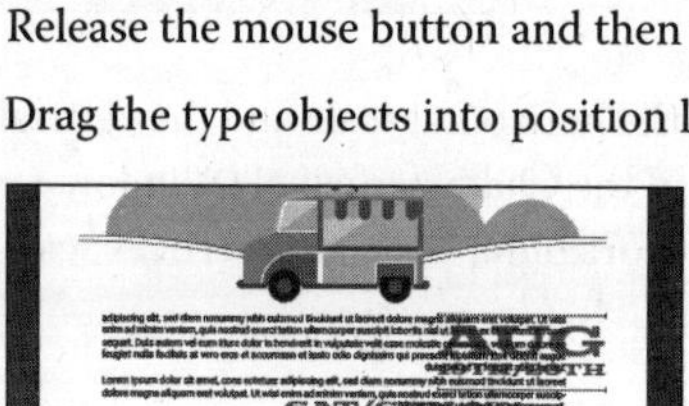

The threaded text will overlap the text. You'll fix that shortly.

Creating columns of text

You can easily create columns and rows of text by using the Type > Area Type Options command. This can be useful for creating a single type object with multiple columns or for organizing text, such as a table or simple chart, for instance. Next, you'll add a few columns to a type object.

1 Choose View > Fit Artboard In Window.

2 With the Selection tool (▶) selected, click the text above the truck to select the top type object.

▶ **Tip:** To learn more about the large number of options in the Area Type Options dialog box, search for "Creating Text" in Illustrator Help (Help > Illustrator Help).

3 Choose Type > Area Type Options. In the Area Type Options dialog box, change Number to **2** in the Columns section, and select Preview. Click OK.

The text in the top type object is now flowing between two columns.

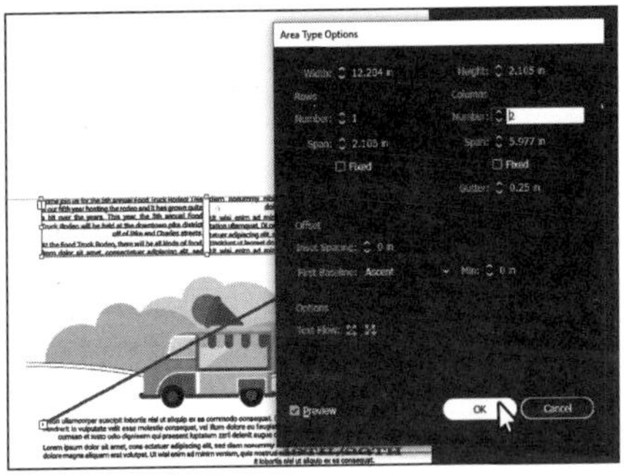

4 Drag the bottom-middle bounding point up and down to see the text flow between the columns and the threaded text below it. Drag so that the text overlaps the truck artwork.

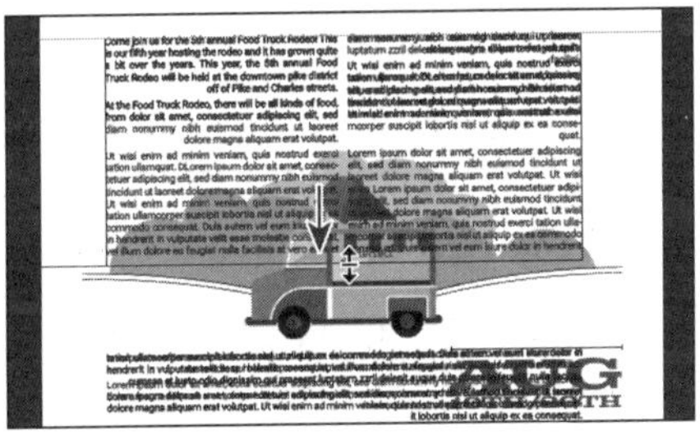

Reshaping type objects

In this next section, you'll reshape and resize a type object to better fit text.

1 With the Selection tool (▶) selected, click the text in the type object at the bottom of the artboard. Drag the right-middle handle to the left. Stop dragging when the right edge of the type object is aligned with the rear of the truck.

2 Press Command++ (macOS) or Ctrl++ (Windows) a few times to zoom in to the selected type object.

3 Select the Direct Selection tool (▶). Click the lower-right corner of the type object to select the anchor point.

4 Drag that point to the left to adjust the shape of the path so the text goes around the “SAT/SUN...” text. As you drag, press the Shift key. Release the mouse button and then the Shift key when finished.

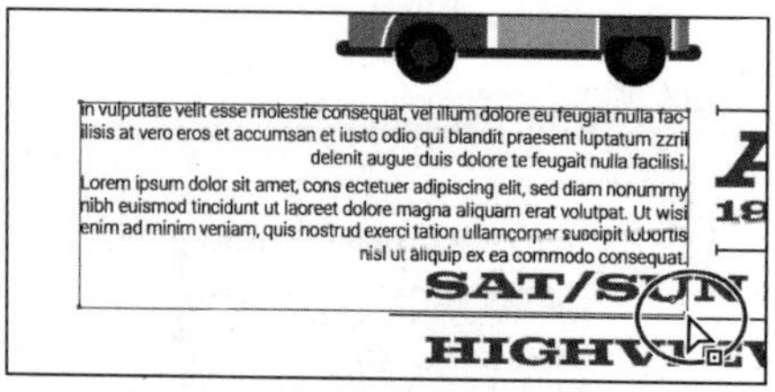

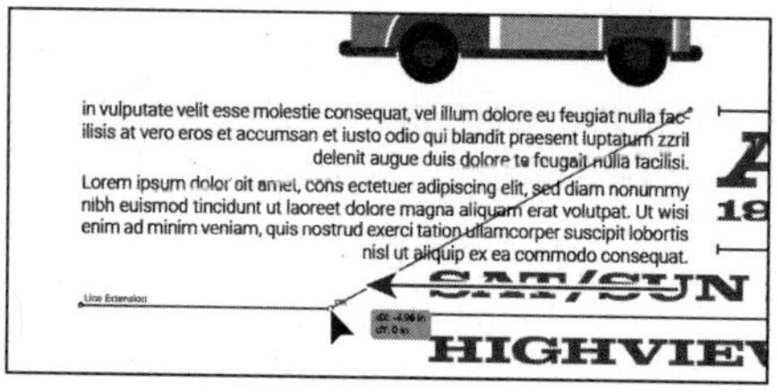

Creating and applying text styles

● **Note:** If you place a Microsoft Word document and choose to keep the formatting, the styles used in the Word document may be brought into the Illustrator document and may appear in the Paragraph Styles panel.

Styles allow you to format text consistently and are helpful when text attributes need to be updated globally. Once a style is created, you only need to edit the saved style, and then all text formatted with that style is updated. Illustrator provides two types of text styles.

- **Paragraph**—Retains character and paragraph attributes and applies them to an entire paragraph.
- **Character**—Retains character attributes and applies them to selected text.

Creating and applying a paragraph style

You’ll start by creating a paragraph style for the body copy.

1 Choose View > Fit All In Window.

2 Select the Type tool (T) by pressing and holding down on the Touch Type tool (T) in the Tools panel and then selecting the Type tool. Insert the cursor anywhere in the threaded text.

By inserting the cursor in text when you create a paragraph style, the formatting attributes from the paragraph that the cursor is in are saved.

3 Choose Window > Type > Paragraph Styles, and click the Create New Style button (■) at the bottom of the Paragraph Styles panel.

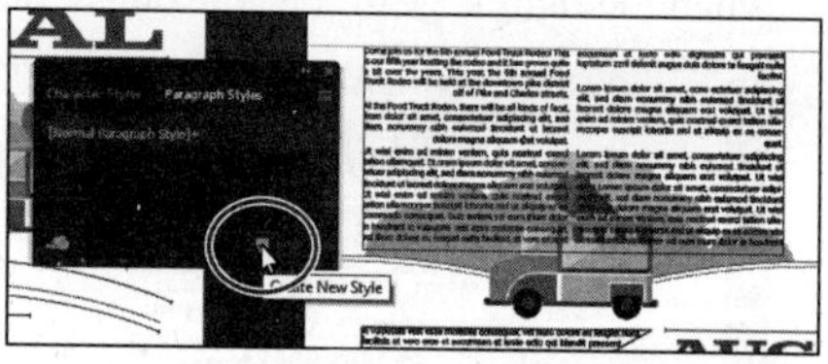

This creates a new paragraph style in the panel, called “Paragraph Style 1.” The character and paragraph formatting from the paragraph with the cursor in it has been “captured” and saved in this new style.

4 Double-click directly on the style name "Paragraph Style 1" in the list of styles. Change the name of the style to **Body**, and press Enter or Return to edit the name inline.

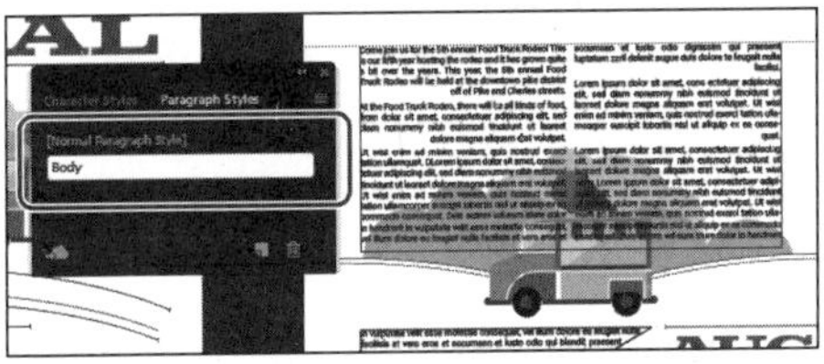

By double-clicking the style to edit the name, you are also applying the new style to the paragraph (where the cursor is). This means that if you edit the Body paragraph style, this paragraph will update as well.

5 With the cursor in the text, choose Select > All to select all of the text.

6 Click the Body style in the Paragraph Styles panel to apply the style to the text.

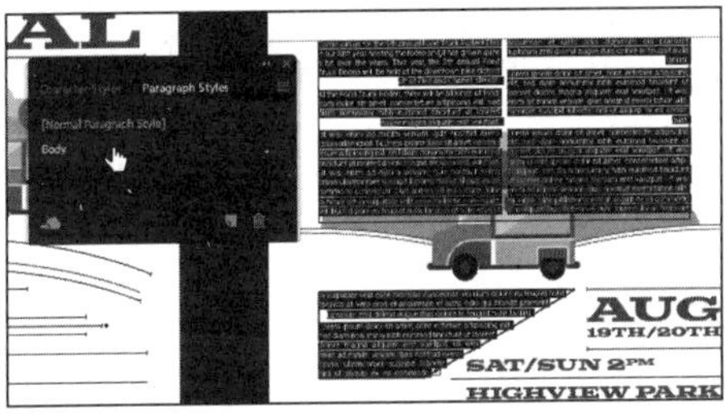

The text should not change in appearance since the formatting for all of the text is currently the same.

Note: As you saw after this step, the text did not change in appearance. Right now, you are simply doing a little extra work to allow you to work faster later. If you decide to change the "Body" style formatting later, all of the text that is currently selected will update to match the style.

7 Select the Selection tool (▶), and click the text on the first artboard that begins with "Pie Oh Pie...." Click the Body style in the Paragraph Styles panel to apply the style to the text.

8 With the "Pie Oh Pie..." type object selected, change the font size to **24** in the Properties panel. Click the Fill color box, make sure the Swatches options is selected in the panel that appears, and select the Pink color.

9 Drag the text down into position on the artboard, like you see in the figure.

Editing a paragraph style

After creating a paragraph style, you can easily edit the style formatting. Then anywhere the style has been applied, the formatting will be updated automatically. Next, you'll edit the Body style to see firsthand why paragraph styles can save you time and maintain consistency.

1 Choose View > Fit All In Window. With the Selection tool selected, click one of the threaded type objects.

▶ **Tip:** There are many more options for working with paragraph styles, most of which are found in the Paragraph Styles panel menu, including duplicating, deleting, and editing paragraph styles. To learn more about these options, search for "paragraph styles" in Illustrator Help (Help > Illustrator Help).

2 Double-click to the right of the style name "Body" in the Paragraph Styles panel list to open the Paragraph Style Options dialog box, select the Indents And Spacing category on the left side of the dialog box, and change the following:

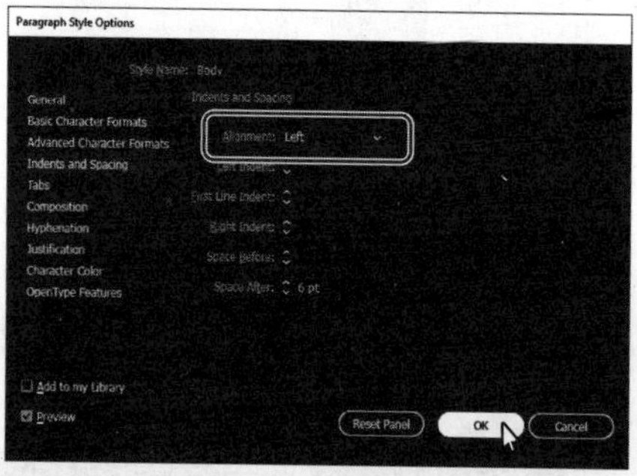

- Alignment: **Left**

Since Preview is selected by default, you can move the dialog box out of the way to see the text change everywhere that the Body style is applied.

3 Click OK.

4 Leave the type object selected and choose File > Save.

Creating and applying a character style

Character styles, unlike paragraph styles, can be applied only to selected text and can contain only character formatting. Next, you will create a character style from text styling within the columns of text.

1 Choose View > Zoom In to zoom in to the selected type object.

2 Using the Type tool (**T**), in the first column, select "Food Truck Rodeo."

3 Click the Fill color box in the Properties panel, and select the swatch named Brown. Choose Italic from the Font Style menu.

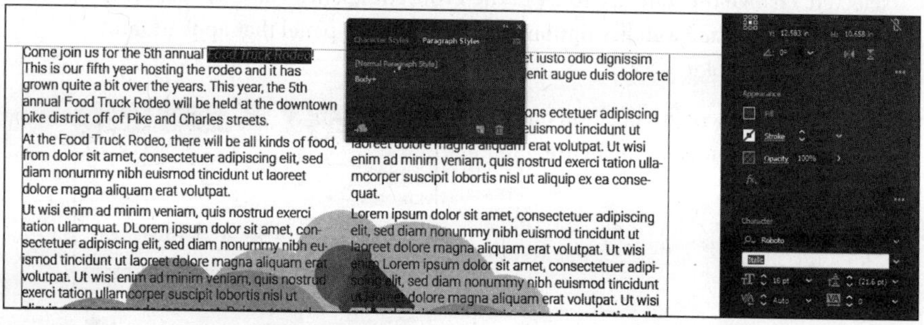

4 In the Paragraph Styles panel group, click the Character Styles panel tab.

5 In the Character Styles panel, Option-click (macOS) or Alt-click (Windows) the Create New Style button (■) at the bottom of the Character Styles panel.

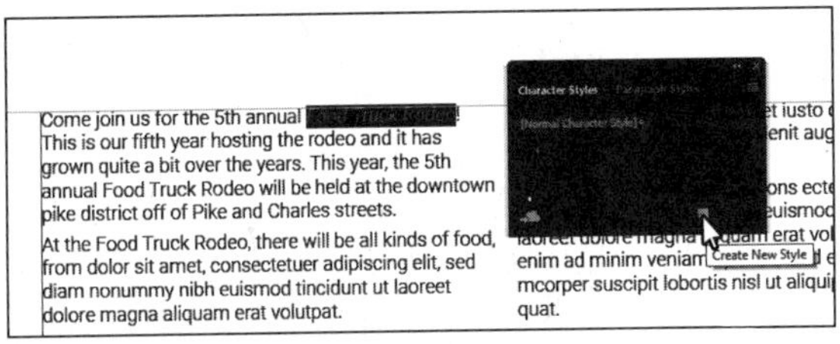

Option-clicking (macOS) or Alt-clicking (Windows) the Create New Style button in a Styles panel lets you edit the style options before it is added to the panel.

6 In the dialog box that opens, change the following options:

- Style Name: **EventName**
- Add To My Library: **Deselected**

7 Click OK.

The style records the attributes applied to your selected text.

8 With the text still selected, click the style named "EventName" in the Character Styles panel to assign the style to that text so that it will update if the style formatting changes.

Note: If you apply the character style and a plus appears next to the style name, you can Option-click (macOS) or Alt-click (Windows) the style name to apply it.

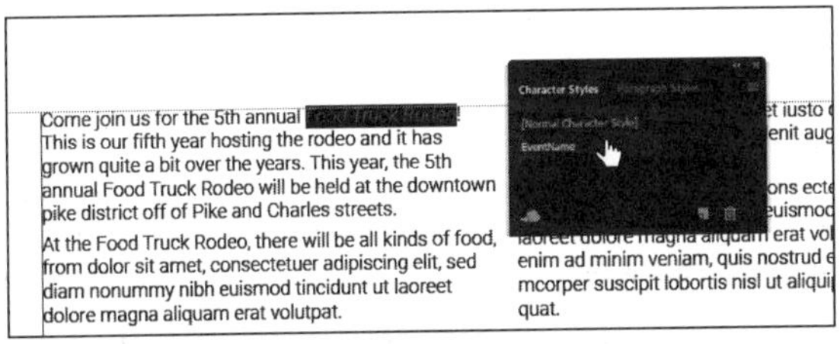

9 In the rest of the text, anytime you see the text "Food Truck Rodeo," select it, and click the EventName style in the Character Styles panel to apply it.

Note: You must select the entire phrase "Food Truck Rodeo," rather than just placing the cursor in the text.

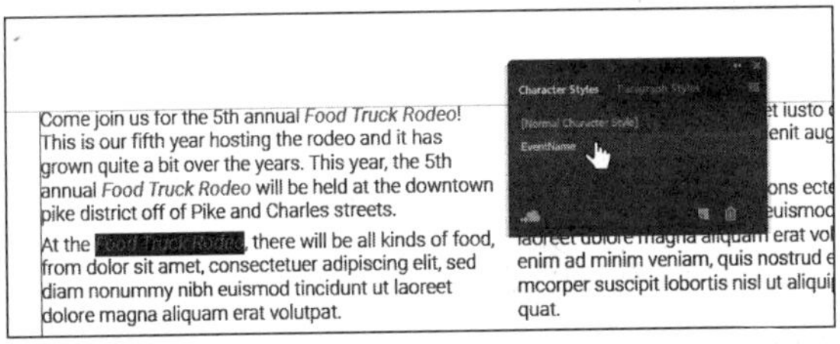

10 Choose Select > Deselect.

Editing a character style

After creating a character style, you can easily edit the style formatting, and, anywhere that style is applied, the formatting will be updated automatically.

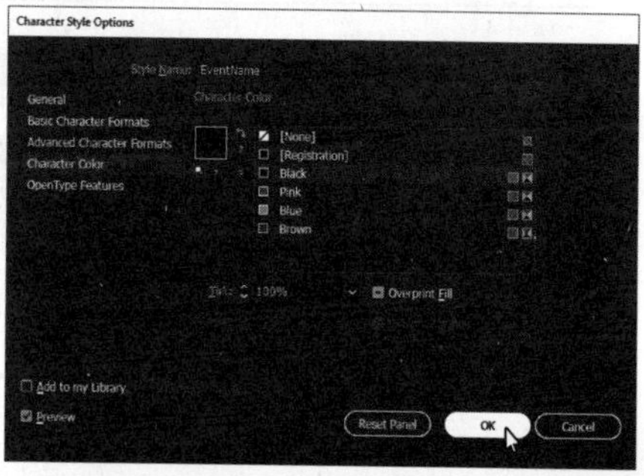

1 Double-click to the right of the EventName style name in the Character Styles panel (not the style name itself). In the Character Style Options dialog box, click the Character Color category on the left side of the dialog box, and change the following:
  - Character Color: **Black**
  - Add To My Library: **Deselected**
  - Preview: **Selected**

2 Click OK.

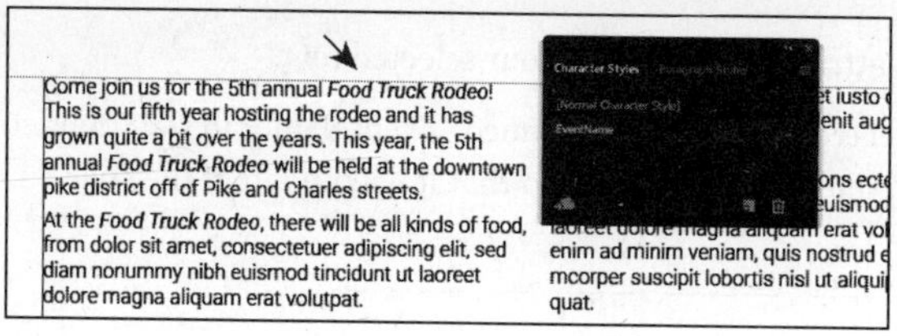

Sampling text formatting

Using the Eyedropper tool (), you can quickly sample type attributes and copy them to text without having to create a type style.

1 Choose 1 Poster 1 from the Artboard Navigation menu in the lower-left corner of the Document window.

2 With the Type tool (**T**) selected, click in the blank area above the "CORRAL" text. Type **FOOD TRUCK RODEO**.

3 Click the new text three times to select it.

The text you type may be italic, which means the character style named EventName is applied.

4 Select the Eyedropper tool (🖉) in the Tools panel, and click the "C" in the "CORRAL" text. Be careful not to click either letter "R" because all of the text modifications you applied with the touch Type tool would also be sampled.

This applies the formatting from the "CORRAL" text to the selected text.

5 Change the font size to **55** in the Properties panel to the right of the document.

6 Choose Select > Deselect.

You'll work with the "FOOD TRUCK..." text shortly.

Wrapping text

In Illustrator, you can easily wrap text around objects, such as type objects, imported images, and vector artwork, to avoid text running over those objects or to create interesting design effects. Next, you'll wrap text around part of the artwork. In Illustrator, like InDesign, you apply text wrap to the content that the text will wrap around.

1 Choose 2 Poster 2 from the Artboard Navigation menu in the lower-left corner of the Document window.

2 Select the Selection tool (▶), and click the ice cream truck artwork.

3 Choose Object > Text Wrap > Make. Click OK if a dialog box appears.

To wrap text around an object, that object must be in the same layer as the text that will wrap around it, and the object must also be located above the text in the layer hierarchy.

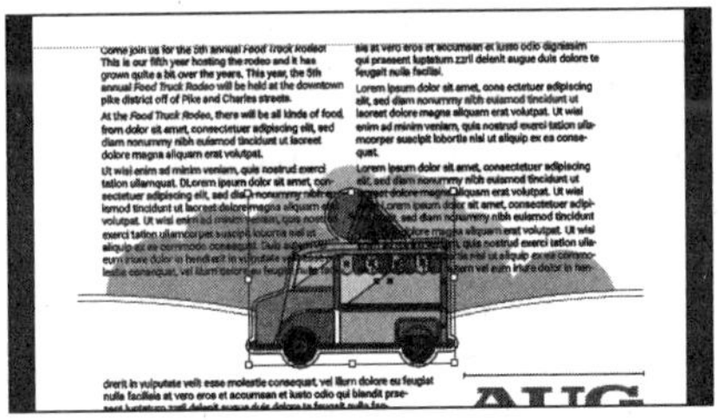

4 With the truck selected, choose Object > Arrange > Bring To Front.

The truck should now be on top of the text in the stacking order and the text is wrapping around the ice cream truck artwork.

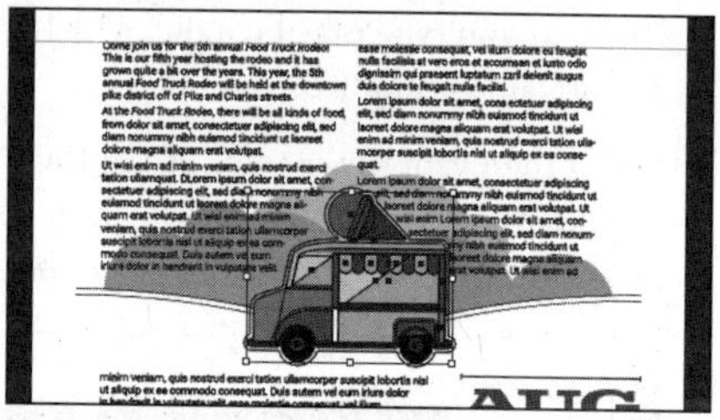

● **Note:** Your text may wrap differently, and that's okay.

5 Choose Object > Text Wrap > Text Wrap Options. In the Text Wrap Options dialog box, change Offset to **20 pt**, and select Preview to see the change. Click OK.

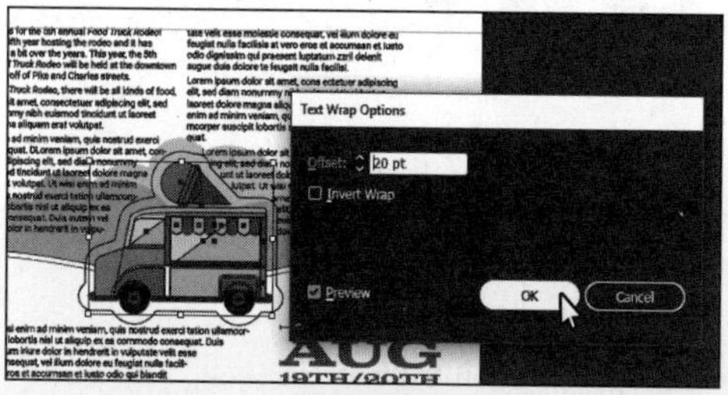

You may see a red plus in the bottom type object now. The text is flowing around the truck artwork, and some was pushed into the bottom type object. In the real world, you would need to "copyfit" the text by changing appearance properties like font size and leading or editing the text.

Warping text

You can create some great design effects by warping text into different shapes using envelopes. You can make an envelope out of an object on your artboard, or you can use a preset warp shape or a mesh grid as an envelope. As you explore warping with envelopes, you'll also discover that you can use envelopes on any object except graphs, guides, or linked objects.

Reshaping text with a preset envelope warp

● **Note:** For more information about envelopes, see "Reshape using envelopes" in Illustrator Help (Help > Illustrator Help).

Illustrator comes with a series of preset warp shapes that you can warp text with. Next, you'll apply one of the preset warp shapes that Illustrator provides.

1 Choose 1 Poster 1 from the Artboard Navigation menu in the lower-left corner of the Document window.

2 Click the "FOOD TRUCK RODEO" type object with the Selection tool to select it.

3 Choose Object > Envelope Distort > Make With Warp.

4 In the Warp Options dialog box that appears, select Preview. The text appears as an arc, by default. Make sure Arc Upper is chosen in the Style menu. Drag the Bend, Horizontal, and Vertical Distortion sliders to see the effect on the text. When you are finished experimenting, drag both Distortion sliders to **0%**, make sure that Bend is **30%**, and then click OK.

Editing the envelope warp

If you want to make any changes, you can edit the text and shape that make up the envelope warp object separately. Next, you will edit the text and then the warp shape.

1 With the envelope object still selected, click the Edit Contents button (▣) at the top of the Properties panel.

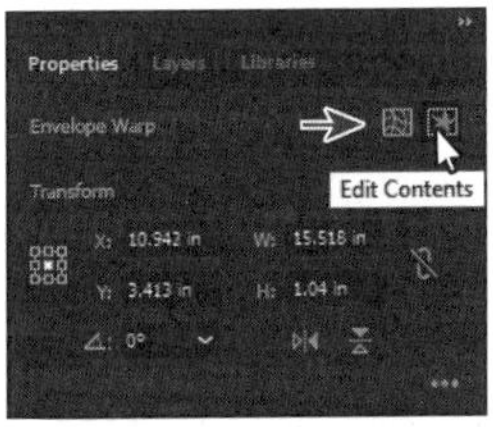

2 Select the Type tool (**T**), and move the pointer over the warped text. Notice that the unwarped text appears in blue. Double-click the word "RODEO" to select it. Press Delete or Backspace twice to remove the "RODEO" text and the space before it.

▶ **Tip:** If you double-click with the Selection tool instead of with the Type tool, you enter Isolation mode. This is another way to edit the text within the envelope warp object. Press the Escape key to exit Isolation mode if that is the case.

You can also edit the preset shape, which is what you'll do next.

3 Select the Selection tool (▶), and make sure that the envelope object is still selected. Click the Edit Envelope button (▣) at the top of the Properties panel.

▶ **Tip:** To take the text out of the warped shape, select the text with the Selection tool, and choose Object > Envelope Distort > Release. This gives you two objects: the type object and an arc upper shape.

Note: The warp object will most likely scale smaller when you edit the Warp Options. That's due to editing the text within.

4 Click the Warp Options button in the Properties panel to show the same Warp Options dialog box you saw when you first applied the warp. Change the Bend to **20%**, make sure that H (horizontal) Distortion is 0 and V (vertical) Distortion is 0, and click OK.

5 With the Selection tool, Shift-drag a corner to make envelope object (warped text) larger. Drag it into the approximate center of the poster, making sure to closely match the position you see in the figure.

Working with type on a path

In addition to having text in point and type areas, you can have type along a path. Text can flow along the edge of an open or closed path and can lead to some really creative ways to display text.

Creating type on a path

In this section, you'll add some text to an open path.

1 With the Selection tool (▶), select the brown curved path below the two trucks.

2 Press Command++ (macOS) or Ctrl++ (Windows) a few times to zoom in to it.

3 Select the Type tool (**T**) and position the cursor over the middle of the path to see an insertion point with an intersecting wavy path (⌶) (see the figure). Click when this cursor appears.

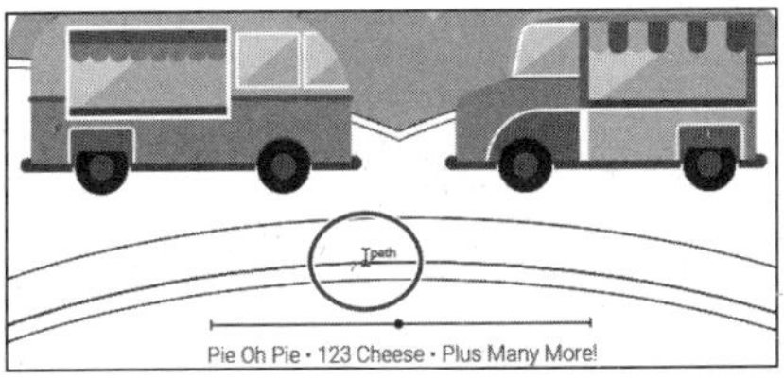

Placeholder text is added to the path, and it starts where you clicked. Your text may have different formatting than you see in the previous figure and that's okay. Also, the stroke attributes of the path change to None.

4 Choose Window > Type > Paragraph Styles to open the Paragraph Styles panel. Click the [Normal Paragraph Style] to apply the style. Close the panel.

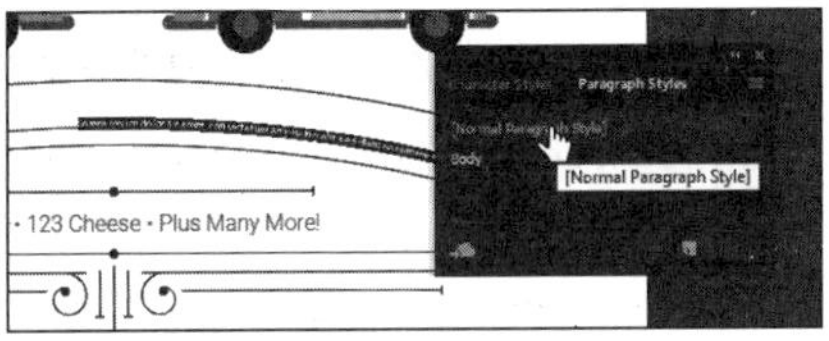

Note: You may see less text on the path and that's okay.

5 Type **Over 30 Local food truck vendors**. The new text follows the path.

6 Press Command+A (macOS) or Ctrl+A (Windows) to select all of the text.

7 In the Properties panel to the right of the document, change the following formatting options:

- Fill color: **Pink**
- Font Family: **Roboto**
- Font Style: **Bold**
- Font Size: **40 pt**

8 Choose Type > Change Case > Upper Case.

9 Press Command++ (macOS) or Ctrl++ (Windows) to zoom in further.

10 Select the Selection tool, and position the pointer over the line on the left edge of the text (just to the left of the "O" in "Over"). When you see this cursor (), click and drag to the left, trying to center the text as best you can on the path. Use the following figure as a guide.

Tip: With the path or the text on the path selected, you can choose Type > Type On A Path > Type On A Path Options to set more options.

From where you click a path to the end of the path is where the text can flow. If you align the text left, center, or right, it's aligned within that area on the path.

11 Choose Select > Deselect and then choose File > Save.

Creating type on a closed path

Next, you'll add text around a circle and explore some of the text on a path options available.

1 Press Command+0 (macOS) or Ctrl+0 (Windows) to fit the artboard in the Document window.

2 Select the Zoom tool (🔍) in the Tools panel, and zoom in to the white circle toward the top of the artboard (above the "FOOD TRUCK" text).

3 Select the Type tool (**T**), and position the pointer over the top edge of the white circle. The Type cursor (⌶) changes to a Type cursor with a circle (⌶). This indicates that if you click (*don't click*), text will be placed *inside* of the circle, creating a type object in the shape of a circle.

Instead of adding text to the inside of a shape, you want to add text to the path, which is what you'll do next.

● **Note:** Instead of pressing the Option (macOS) or Alt (Windows) key to allow the Type tool to type on a path, you can select the Type On A Path tool (⌶) by holding down the Type tool in the Tools panel.

4 While pressing the Option (macOS) or Alt (Windows) key, position the pointer over the top of the white circle (use the figure as a guide). The insertion point with an intersecting wavy path (⌶) appears. Click and placeholder text that is selected, appears.

5 Type **CELEBRATING LOCAL** in all caps.

6 Click three times on the text to select it. Change the font size to **16 pt** and the font to Roboto Bold (if it isn't already).

Next, you'll edit the type on a path options for the text.

7 Select the Selection tool ( ) in the Tools panel. With the path type object selected, choose Type > Type On A Path > Type On A Path Options. In the Type On A Path Options dialog box, select Preview, and change Spacing to **20 pt**.

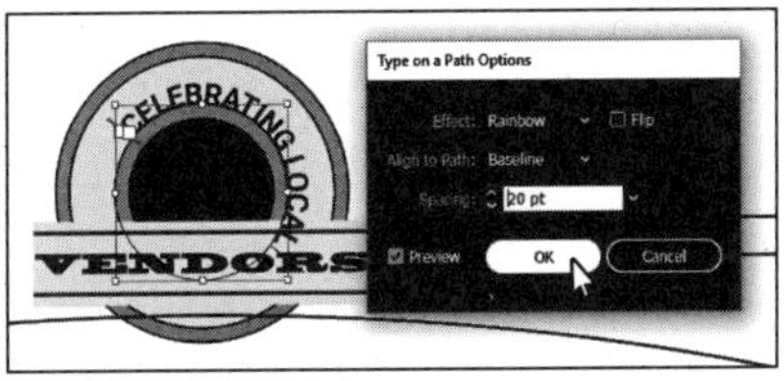

8 Click OK.

9 Move the pointer over the line on the left end of the word "CELEBRATING." That line you see is called a *bracket*. When you see this cursor ( ), with an arrow pointing to the ***left***, drag down and to the left around the circle in a counterclockwise fashion. That moves the *end* of the text, giving you room to move the beginning. See the first two parts of the following figure.

10 Move the pointer over the line on the left end of the word "CELEBRATING" again. When you see this cursor ( ), with an arrow pointing to the ***right***, drag down and to the left around the circle just a little in a counterclockwise fashion. That moves the *beginning* of the text. See the last part of the following figure.

● **Note:** To learn about the Type On A Path options like "Flip," search for "Creating type on a path" in Illustrator Help (Help > Illustrator Help).

● **Note:** Brackets appear at the beginning of the type, at the end of the path, and at the midpoint between the start and end brackets. All of these brackets can be adjusted to reposition the text in the path.

Creating text outlines

Converting text to outlines means converting text into *vector* shapes that you can edit and manipulate as you would any other graphic object. Text outlines are useful for changing the look of large display type, but they are rarely useful for body text or other type at small sizes. The file recipient doesn't need to have your fonts installed to open and view the file correctly if you convert all text to outlines.

When you create outlines from text, you should consider that text is no longer editable. Also, bitmap fonts and outline-protected fonts cannot be converted to outlines, and outlining text that is less than 10 points in size is not recommended. When type is converted to outlines, the type loses its *hints*—instructions built into outline fonts to adjust their shape to display or print optimally at many sizes. You must also convert all type in a selection to outlines; you cannot convert a single letter within a type object. Next, you will convert the main heading to outlines.

1 Choose View > Fit All In Window.

2 Click the Layers panel tab to show the panel. Click the visibility column to the left of the layer named "Frames" to show it. Click the Properties panel tab to show it again.

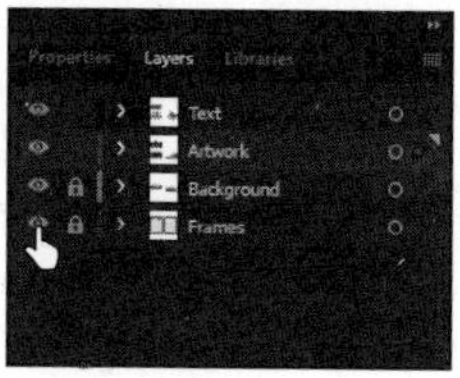

● **Note:** The original text is still there; it's just hidden. This way, you can always choose Object > Show All to see the original text if you need to make changes.

3 With the Selection tool (▶) selected, click the heading text "CORRAL" on the artboard on the left to select it.

4 Choose Edit > Copy and then choose Object > Hide > Selection.

5 Choose Edit > Paste In Front.

6 Choose Type > Create Outlines.

The text is no longer linked to a particular font. Instead, it is now artwork, much like any other vector art in your illustration.

7 Choose View > Guides > Hide Guides and then choose Select > Deselect.

Finishing up

There are a few things left to finish the poster on the right, and that's what you'll do next.

1 With the Selection tool (▶), click to select the "FOOD TRUCK" text. Press the Shift key and click one of the lines around it to select the group of lines, and the "CORRAL" text to select all of that content.

2 Click the Group button in the Properties panel to group the content.

3 Choose Edit > Copy.

4 Choose 2 Poster 2 from the Artboard Navigation menu in the lower-left corner of the Document window.

5 Choose Edit > Paste In Place. Drag the pasted group up into the blank area.

6 Choose Select > Deselect.

7 Choose View > Fit All In Window to see everything.

8 Choose File > Save and then choose File > Close.

Review questions

1 Name a few methods for creating text in Adobe Illustrator.

2 What does the Touch Type tool (⌶) let you do?

3 What is *overflow text*?

4 What is *text threading*?

5 What is the difference between a *character style* and a *paragraph style*?

6 What is the advantage of converting text to outlines?

Review answers

1 The following methods can be used for creating text:

- With the Type tool (T), click the artboard and start typing when the cursor appears. A point type object is created to accommodate the text.
- With the Type tool, drag to create a text area. Type when a cursor appears.
- With the Type tool, click a path or closed shape to convert it to text on a path, or click in a text area. Option-clicking (macOS) or Alt-clicking (Windows) when crossing over the stroke of a closed path creates text around the shape.

2 The Touch Type tool (⌶) allows you to visually edit certain character formatting options for individual characters in text. You can edit the character rotation, kerning, baseline shift, and horizontal and vertical scale of text and the text remains editable.

3 Overflow text is text that does not fit within an area type object or path. A red plus sign (⊞) in an out port indicates that the object contains additional text.

4 Text threading allows you to flow text from one object to another by linking type objects. Linked type objects can be of any shape; however, the text must be entered in an area or along a path (not at a point).

5 A character style can be applied to selected text only. A paragraph style is applied to an entire paragraph. Paragraph styles are best for indents, margins, and line spacing.

6 Converting text to outlines eliminates the need to send the fonts along with the Illustrator file when sharing with others and makes it possible to add effects to type that aren't possible when the type is still editable (live).

9 ORGANIZING YOUR ARTWORK WITH LAYERS

Lesson overview

In this lesson, you'll learn how to do the following:

- Work with the Layers panel.
- Create, rearrange, and lock layers and sublayers.
- Move objects between layers.
- Merge layers into a single layer.
- Locate objects in the Layers panel.
- Isolate content in a layer.
- Copy and paste objects and their layers from one file to another.
- Make a layer clipping mask.
- Apply an appearance attribute to objects and layers.

This lesson takes approximately 45 minutes to complete. Please log in to your account on peachpit.com to download the lesson files for this chapter, or go to the "Getting Started" section at the beginning of this book and follow the instructions under "Accessing the lesson files and Web Edition."

Your Account page is also where you'll find any updates to the chapters or to the lesson files. Look on the Lesson & Update Files tab to access the most current content.

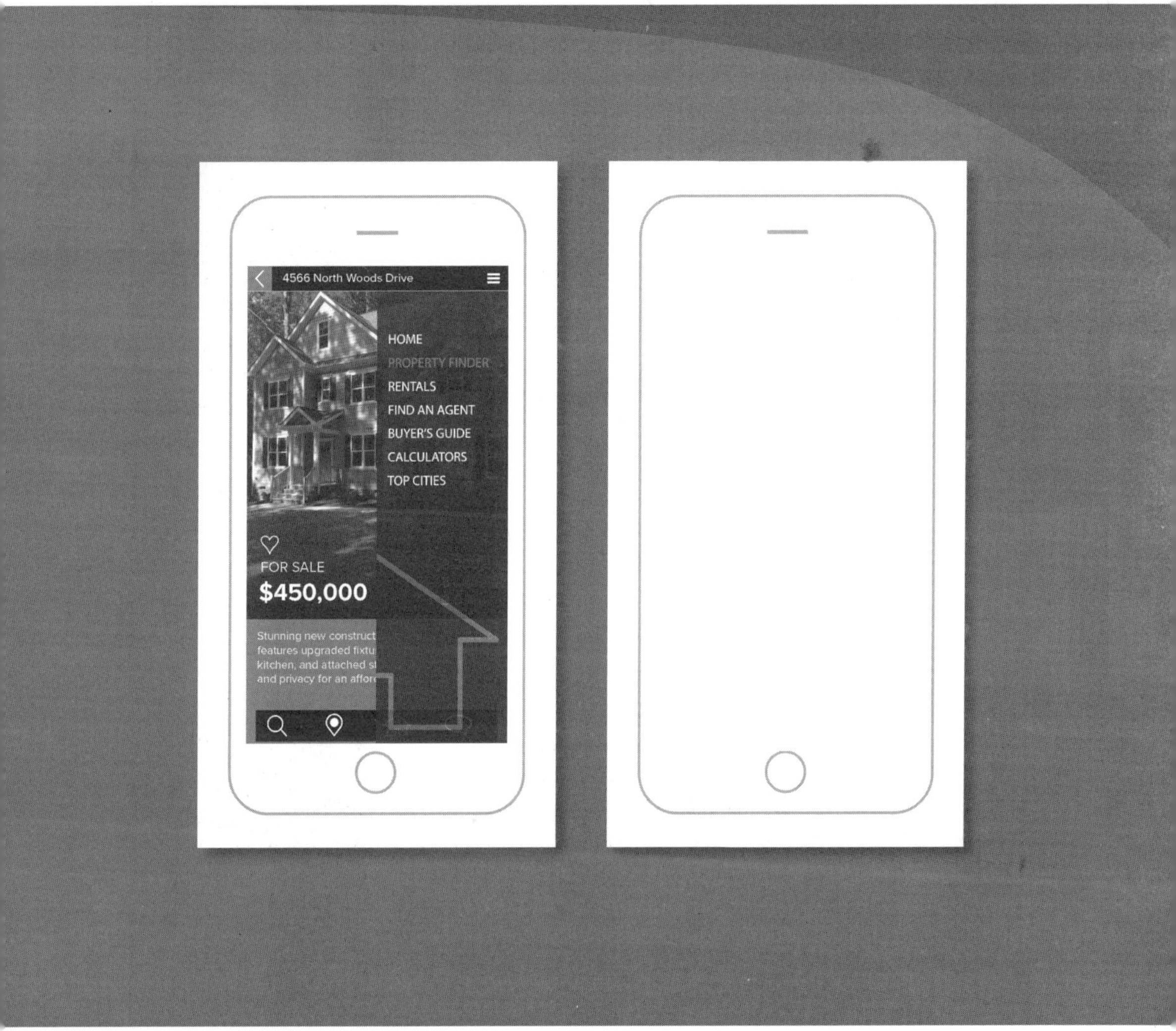

Layers let you organize your work into distinct levels that can be edited and viewed individually or together. Every Adobe Illustrator CC document has at least one layer. Creating multiple layers in your artwork lets you easily control how artwork is printed, displayed, selected, and edited.

Starting the lesson

In this lesson, you'll organize the artwork for a real estate app design as you explore the various ways to use the Layers panel.

Note: If you have not already downloaded the project files for this lesson to your computer from your Account page, make sure to do so now. See the "Getting Started" section at the beginning of the book.

1 To ensure that the tools function and the defaults are set exactly as described in this lesson, delete or deactivate (by renaming) the Adobe Illustrator CC preferences file. See "Restoring default preferences" in the "Getting Started" section at the beginning of the book.

2 Start Adobe Illustrator CC.

3 Choose File > Open, and open the L9_end.ai file in the Lessons > Lesson09 folder, located on your hard disk.

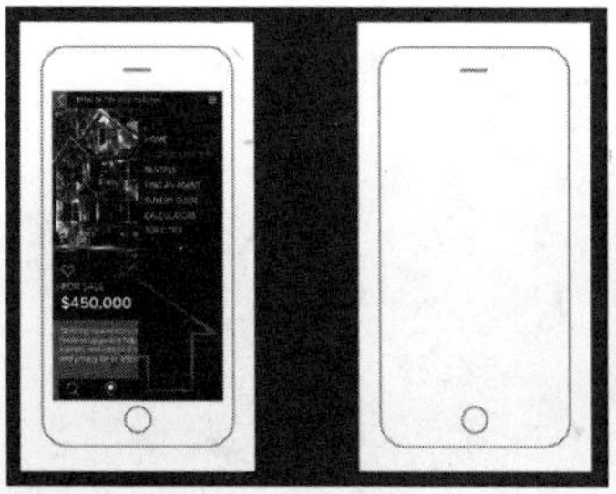

4 Choose View > Fit All In Window.

5 Choose Window > Workspace > Reset Essentials.

Note: If you don't see Reset Essentials in the Workspace menu, choose Window > Workspace > Essentials before choosing Window > Workspace > Reset Essentials.

6 Choose File > Open. In the Open dialog box, navigate to the Lessons > Lesson09 folder, and select the L9_start.ai file on your hard disk. Click Open.

The Missing Fonts dialog box *may* appear, indicating that a font (ProximaNova) was used in the file that Illustrator can't find on your machine. The file uses a Typekit font that you most likely don't have synced with your machine, so you will fix the missing font before moving on.

Note: If the font is unable to sync, you may not have an Internet connection or you may need to launch the Creative Cloud desktop application, sign in with your Adobe ID, choose Assets > Fonts, and click Turn Typekit On. If you went through Lesson 8, "Adding Type to a Poster," you would have this already turned on. For more information, visit http://helpx.adobe.com/creative-cloud/help/add-fonts-typekit.html.

7 In the Missing Fonts dialog box, ensure that Sync is selected for each font in the Sync column, and click Sync Fonts. After some time, the font should be synced with your machine, and you should see a success message in the Missing Fonts dialog box. Click Close.

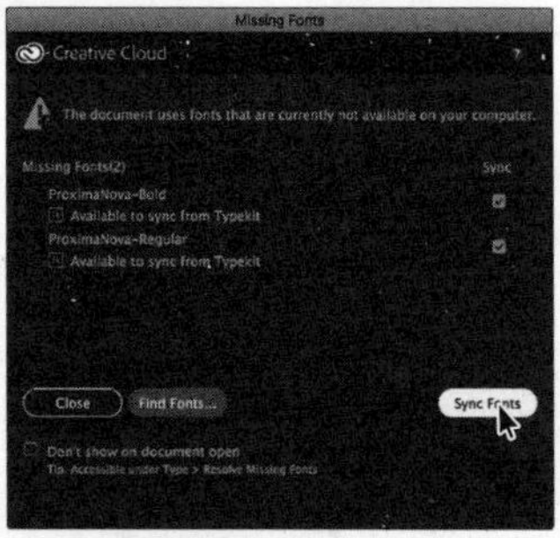

This will sync the Typekit font to your computer and ensure that the font shows as intended in Illustrator.

Note: If you see a warning message in the Missing Fonts dialog box or cannot select Sync, you can click Find Fonts to replace the font with a local font. In the Find Font dialog box, make sure that Proxima Nova is selected in the Fonts in Document section, and choose System from the Replace With Font From menu. This shows all the local fonts that are available to Illustrator. Select a font from the Fonts In System section, and click Change All to replace the font. Do the same for Proxima Nova Bold. Click Done.

8 Choose File > Save As, name the file **RealEstateApp.ai**, and select the Lesson09 folder. Leave the Format option set to Adobe Illustrator (ai) (macOS) or the Save As Type option set to Adobe Illustrator (*.AI) (Windows) and then click Save. In the Illustrator Options dialog box, leave the Illustrator options at their default settings and then click OK.

9 Choose Select > Deselect (if available).

10 Choose View > Fit All In Window.

Understanding layers

Layers are like invisible folders to help you hold and manage all of the items (some of which can be difficult to select or track) that make up your artwork. If you shuffle those folders, you change the stacking order of the items in your artwork. (You learned about stacking order in Lesson 2, "Techniques for Selecting Artwork.")

The structure of layers in your document can be as simple or as complex as you want. When you create a new Illustrator document, all of the content you create is organized in a single layer. However, you can create new layers and sublayers (like subfolders) to organize your artwork, as you'll learn about in this lesson.

1 Click the L9_end.ai tab at the top of the document window to show that document.

2 Click the Layers panel tab on the right side of the workspace, or choose Window > Layers.

In addition to organizing content, the Layers panel offers an easy way to select, hide, lock, and change your artwork's appearance attributes. In the following figure, the Layers panel is showing the content for the L9_end.ai file and won't match what you see in the RealEstateApp.ai file. You can refer to this figure as you progress through the lesson.

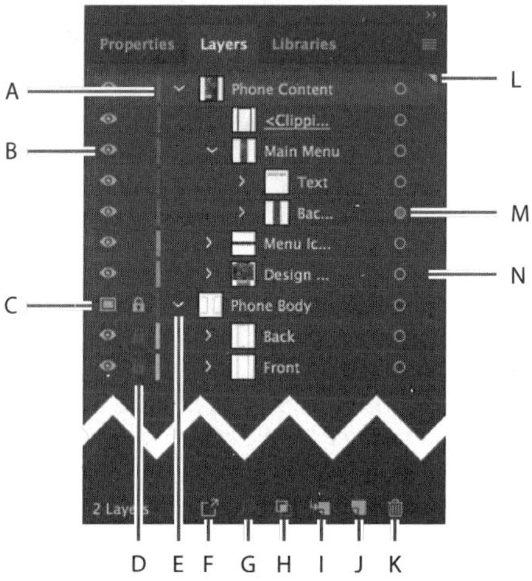

A. Layer Color
B. Visibility Column (eye icon)
C. Template Layer icon
D. Edit Column (lock/unlock)
E. Disclosure Triangle (expand/collapse)
F. Collect For Export
G. Locate Object
H. Make/Release Clipping Mask
I. Create New Sublayer
J. Create New Layer
K. Delete Selection
L. Current Layer Indicator (the triangle)
M. Target Column
N. Selection Column

Note: The figure shows the top and bottom of the Layers panel. The Layers panel in the Essentials workspace is very tall, which is why the figure shows a split in the panel.

Creating layers and sublayers

By default, every document begins with one layer, named "Layer 1." As you create artwork, you can rename and add layers and sublayers at any time. Placing objects on separate layers lets you more easily select and edit them. For example, by placing type on a separate layer, you can focus on the type without affecting the rest of the artwork.

Creating new layers

● **Note:** How many layers you create, what you name them, and how content is organized within those layers varies depending on the project you are working on. For this lesson, I thought about what would make sense for layer organization, so you're creating layers based on that. There is no "wrong" layer structure, but, as you gain more experience with layers, you'll see what makes more sense for you.

Next, you'll change the default layer name and then create new layers using different methods. The idea for this project is to organize the artwork so you can more easily work with it later. In a real-world situation, you'll set up layers before you begin working on the artwork or as you create your artwork. In this lesson, you'll organize artwork with layers *after* the artwork is created, which can be a bit more challenging.

1 Click the RealEstateApp.ai tab at the top of the document window.

2 If the Layers panel isn't visible, click the Layers panel tab on the right side of the workspace, or choose Window > Layers. Layer 1 (the default name for the first layer) is highlighted, indicating that it is active.

3 In the Layers panel, double-click directly on the layer name "Layer 1" to edit it inline. Type **Phone Body** and then press Enter or Return.

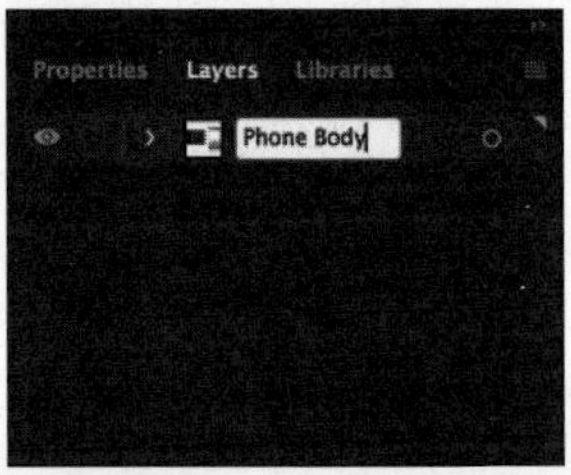

Instead of keeping all the content on one single layer, you'll create several layers and sublayers to better organize the content and to make it easier to select content later.

▶ **Tip:** You can easily delete a layer by selecting the layer or sublayer and clicking the Delete Selection button (🗑) at the bottom of the Layers panel. This deletes the layer or sublayer and all content on it.

4 Click the Create New Layer button (■) at the bottom of the Layers panel.

Layers and sublayers that aren't named are numbered in sequence. For example, the new layer is named Layer 2. When a layer or sublayer in the Layers panel contains other items, a disclosure triangle (▶) appears to the left of the layer or sublayer name. You can click the disclosure triangle to show or hide the contents. If no triangle appears, the layer has no content on it.

5 Double-click the layer thumbnail for Layer 2 (the white box) or to the right of the layer name "Layer 2" in the Layers panel to open the Layer Options dialog box. Change the name to **Phone Content**, and notice all the other options available. Click OK.

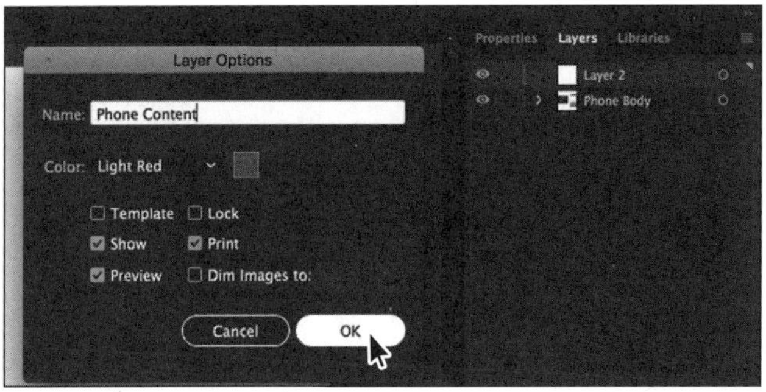

● **Note:** The Layer Options dialog box has a lot of the options you've already worked with, including naming layers, Preview or Outline mode, locking layers, and showing and hiding layers. You can also deselect the Print option in the Layer Options dialog box, and any content on that layer will not print.

By default, the new layer is added above the currently selected layer (Phone Body, in this case) in the Layers panel and becomes active. Notice that the new layer has a different layer color (a light red) to the left of the layer name. This will become more important later, as you select content. Next, you will create a new layer and name it in one step, using a modifier key.

6 Option-click (macOS) or Alt-click (Windows) the Create New Layer button ( ) at the bottom of the Layers panel. In the Layer Options dialog box, change the name to **Menu Icons** and then click OK.

▶ **Tip:** Choosing New Layer from the Layers panel menu ( ) will also create a new layer and open the Layer Options dialog box.

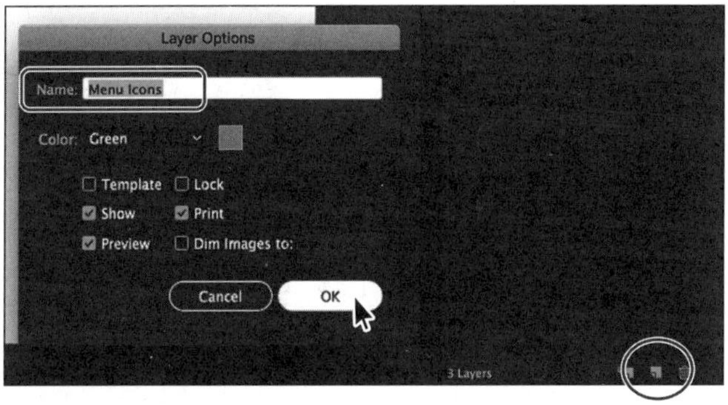

● **Note:** The layer copy has the same layer color as the original layer (Menu Icons). In this lesson, that's okay, but in the real world you may want to make the layer color different for each layer. This can be helpful when selecting artwork later.

7 With the "Menu Icons" layer selected in the Layers panel, click the Layers panel menu ( ) and choose Duplicate "Menu Icons" to create a copy of the layer.

8 Double-click directly on the new layer name in the panel, and change it to **Design Content**. Press Enter or Return to accept the change.

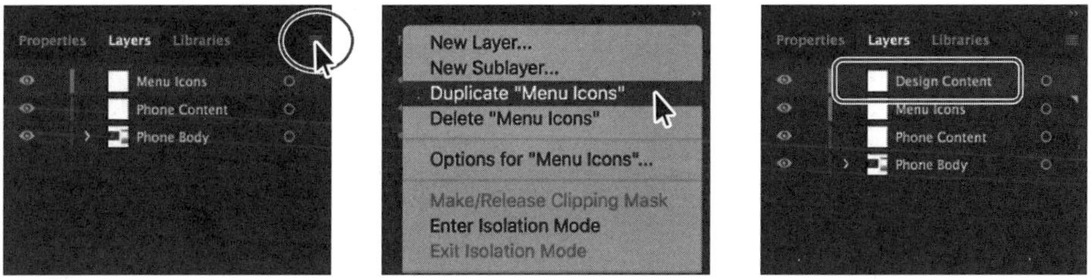

Creating sublayers

Next, you'll create a sublayer, which is a layer nested within a layer. Sublayers can be useful for organizing content within a layer without grouping or ungrouping content.

● **Note:** To create a new sublayer and name it in one step, Option-click (macOS) or Alt-click (Windows) the Create New Sublayer button or choose New Sublayer from the Layers panel menu to open the Layer Options dialog box.

1 Click the layer named "Phone Content" to select it and then click the Create New Sublayer button ( ) at the bottom of the Layers panel.

A new sublayer is created on the Phone Content layer and is selected. You can think of this new sublayer as a "child" of the "parent" layer named "Phone Content."

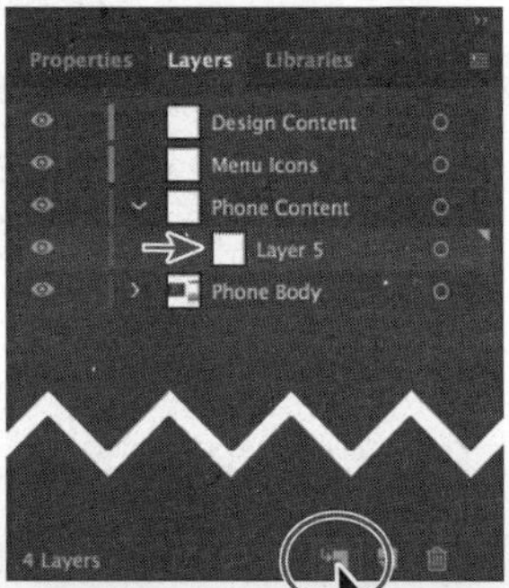

2 Double-click the new sublayer name (Layer 5, in my case), change the name to **Main Menu**, and then press Enter or Return.

Creating a new sublayer opens the selected layer to show existing sublayers and content.

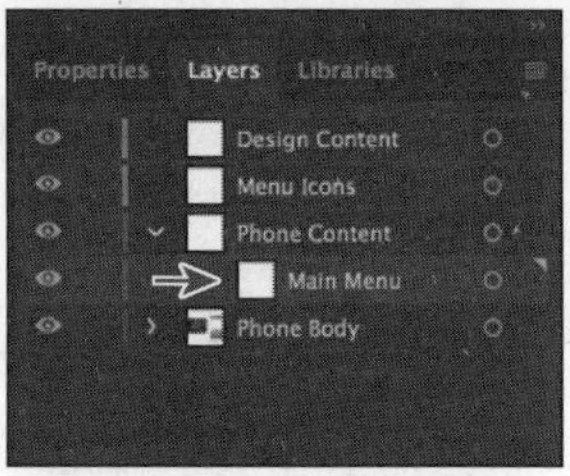

3 Click the disclosure triangle ( ) to the left of the Phone Content layer to hide the content of the layer.

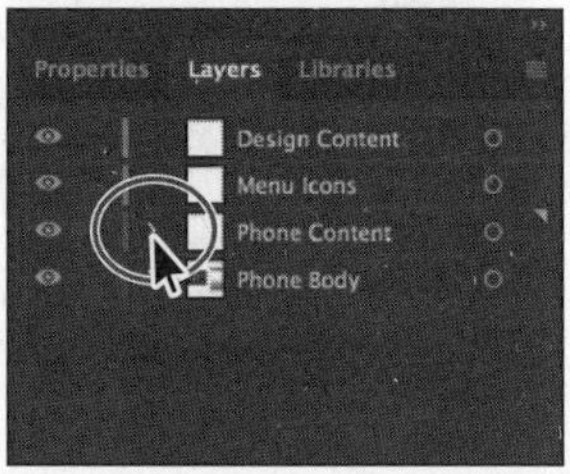

4 Drag the left edge of the Layers panel to the left to make it wider.

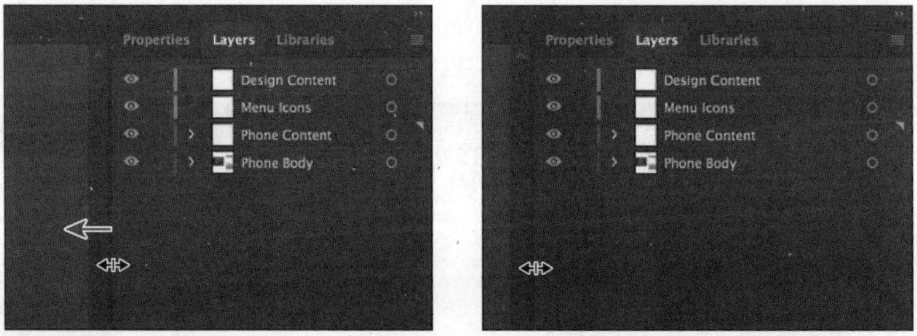

Editing layers and objects

By rearranging the layers in the Layers panel, you can change the stacking order of objects in your artwork. On an artboard, objects in layers that are higher in the Layers panel list are in front of objects located on layers lower in the list, and each layer has its own stacking order as well. Layers are useful for a variety of reasons, including the ability to move objects between layers and sublayers to organize and more easily select your artwork.

Locating layers

When working in artwork, there may be times when you select content on the artboard and then want to locate that same content in the Layers panel. This can help you to determine how content is organized.

1 With the Selection tool (▶), click to select the green rectangle with text on it toward the bottom of the left artboard. Click the Locate Object button (🔍) at the bottom of the Layers panel to reveal the group of objects within the Layers panel.

Clicking the Locate Object button will open the layer that the layer content is on, and the Layers panel will scroll, if necessary, to reveal the selected content.

In the Layers panel, you'll see a selection indicator (■) to the far right of the layer that the selected content is on, the <Group> object, as well as the objects in the group.

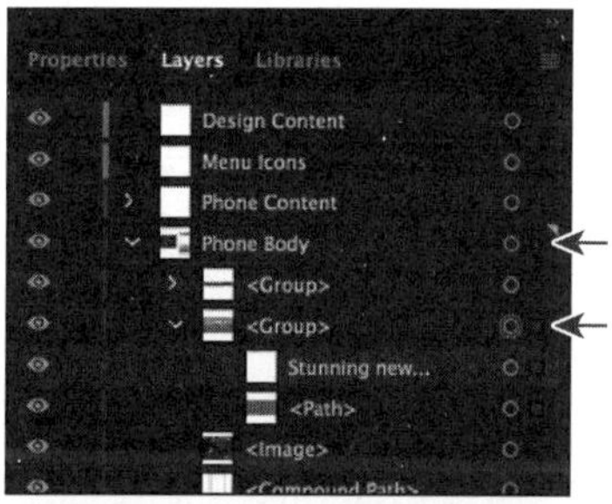

2 In the Layers panel, double-click the <Group> text, and rename it **Description**.

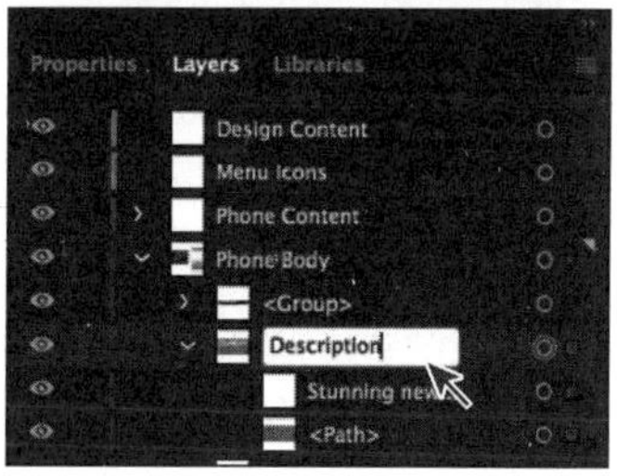

When content is grouped, a group object (<Group>) is created that contains the grouped content. Look at the top of the Properties panel to see the word "Group" in the Selection Indicator. Renaming a group doesn't change the fact that it's a group, but it can make it easier to find in the Layers panel.

3 Choose Select > Deselect.

4 Click the disclosure triangle (⌄) to the left of the Description group to collapse the group and then click the disclosure triangle (⌄) to the left of the Phone Body layer name to collapse the layer and hide the contents of the entire layer.

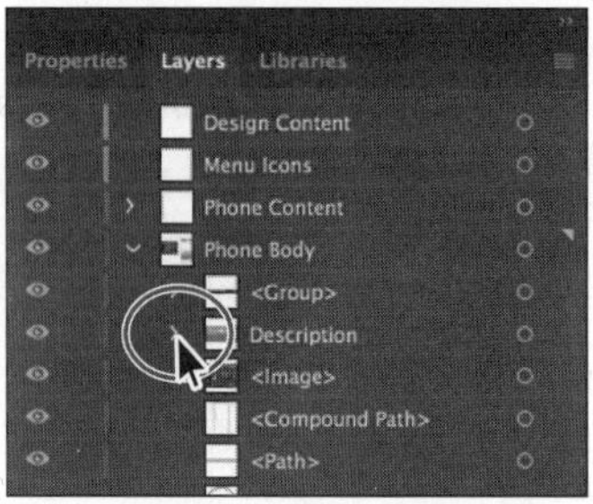

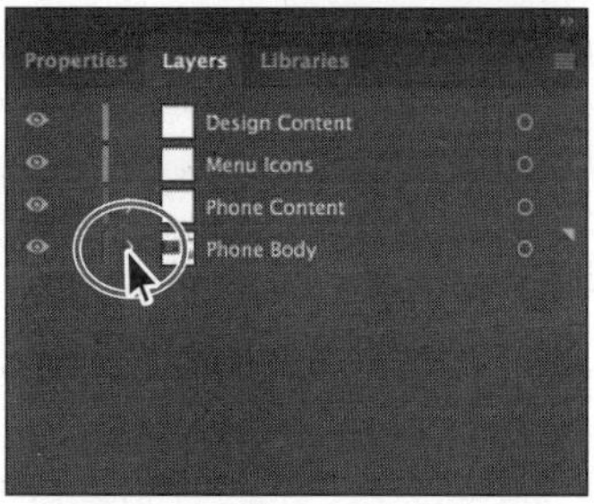

Keeping layers, sublayers, and groups collapsed is a great way to make the Layers panel less visually cluttered. The Phone Content layer and Phone Body layer are the only layers with a disclosure triangle because they're the only layers with content on them.

Moving content between layers

Next, you'll move the artwork to the different layers to take advantage of the layers and sublayers you've created.

1 In the artwork, using the Selection tool (▶), click the text "FOR SALE $450,000" to select a group of content.

In the Layers panel, notice that the Phone Body layer name has the selected-art indicator (the color square); it's circled in the figure.

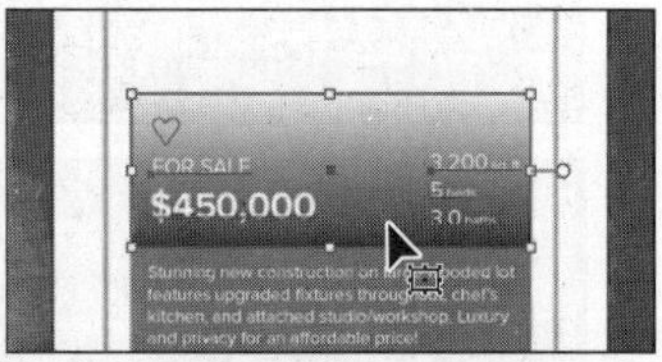

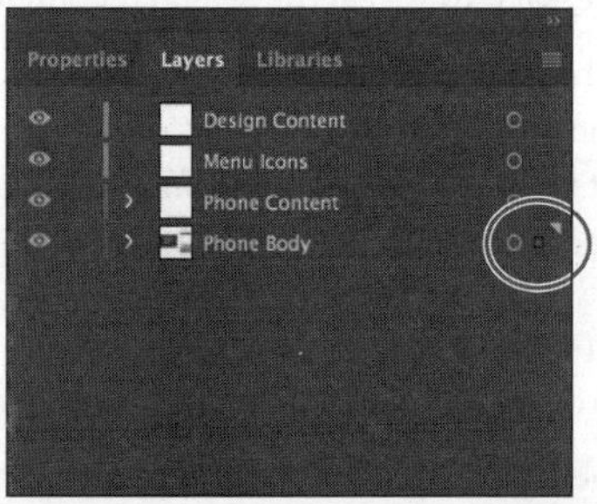

Also notice that the color of the bounding box, paths, and anchor points of the selected artwork matches the color of the layer.

If you want to move selected artwork from one layer to another, you can either drag the selected-art indicator to the right of each sublayer or drag the selected-art indicator to the right of the layer name. That's what you'll do next.

2 Drag the selected-art indicator (the little blue box) from the far right of the Phone Body layer name straight up to the right of the target icon (◙) on the Design Content layer.

This action moves all of the selected artwork to the Design Content layer. The color of the bounding box, paths, and anchor points in the artwork changes to the color of the Design Content layer, which is green (in my case).

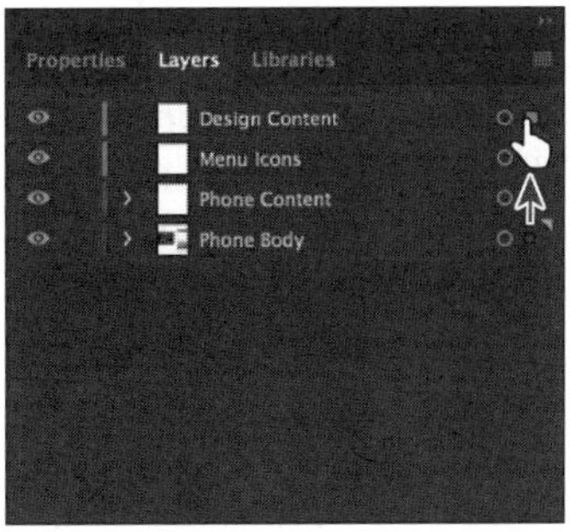

▶ **Tip:** You can also press Option (macOS) or Alt (Windows) and drag the selected-art indicator to another layer to duplicate the content. Remember to release the mouse button and then the key.

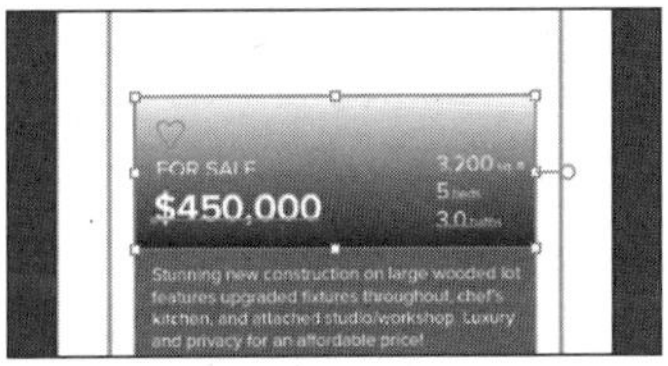

3 Choose Select > Deselect.

4 Click the disclosure triangle (▸) to the left of the Phone Body layer to show the layer content.

5 Click the top <Group> object that contains the top navigation artwork. Press the Shift key and click the <Image> object to select the <Group>, Description, and <Image> layers without selecting the artwork on the artboard.

6 Drag any of the selected objects to the Design Content layer at the top of the list. When the Design Content layer shows a highlight, release the mouse button.

● **Note:** This is another way to move artwork between layers. Any content that is dragged to another layer is automatically at the top of the layer stack on that layer.

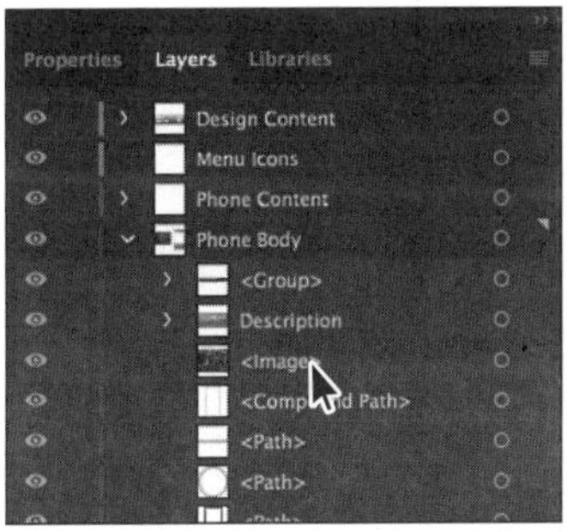

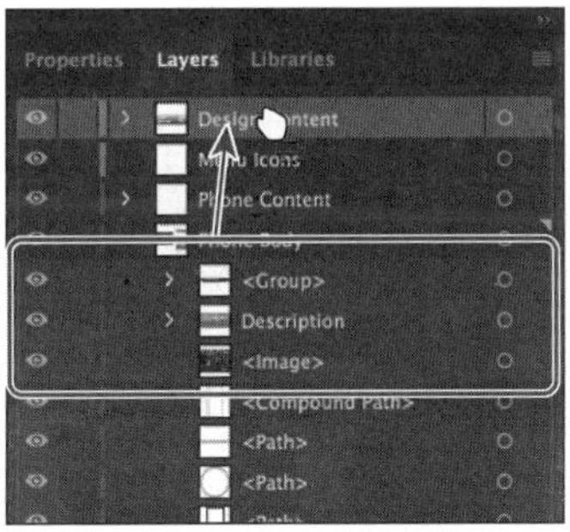

7 Click the disclosure triangle (▾) to the left of the Phone Body layer to hide the layer contents.

Viewing layers

The Layers panel lets you hide layers, sublayers, or individual objects from view. When a layer is hidden, the content on the layer is also locked and cannot be selected or printed. You can also use the Layers panel to display layers or objects individually, in either Preview or Outline mode. In this section, you'll learn how to view layers in Outline mode to make artwork potentially easier to select.

1 Choose View > Outline. This displays the artwork so that only its outlines (or paths) are visible. You should be able to see the menu icons that are hidden beneath the green shape. An arrow is pointing to them in the figure.

Notice the eye icons ( ) in the Layers panel now. They indicate that the content on that layer is in Outline mode.

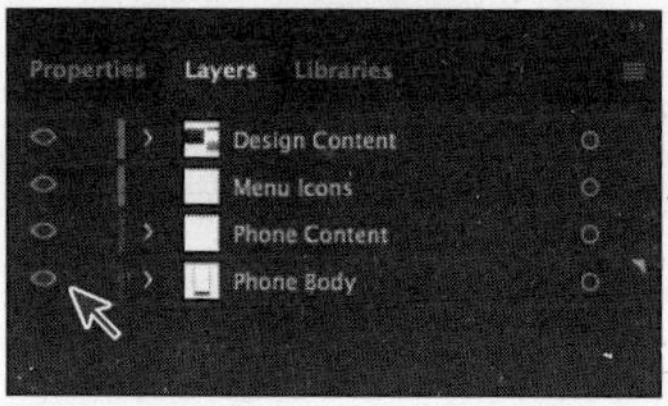

2 Choose View > GPU Preview or View > Preview On CPU (or Preview) if GPU Preview is not available to see the painted artwork.

Sometimes, you may want to view part of the artwork in outline mode while retaining the strokes and fills for the rest of the artwork. This can be useful if you need to see all artwork in a given layer, sublayer, or group.

3 In the Layers panel, click the disclosure triangle ( ) for the Design Content layer to reveal the layer content. Command-click (macOS) or Ctrl-click (Windows) the eye icon ( ) to the left of the Design Content layer name to show the content for *only that layer* in Outline mode.

▶ **Tip:** To view layer artwork in Outline mode, you can also double-click either the layer thumbnail or just to the right of the layer name to open the Layer Options dialog box. You can then deselect Preview and click OK.

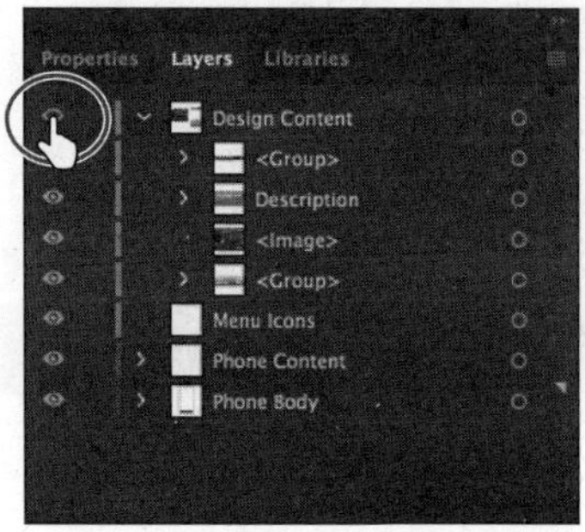

Displaying a layer in Outline mode is also useful for selecting the anchor points or center points on objects.

4 Select the Selection tool ( ), and click one of the mobile icons to select the group.

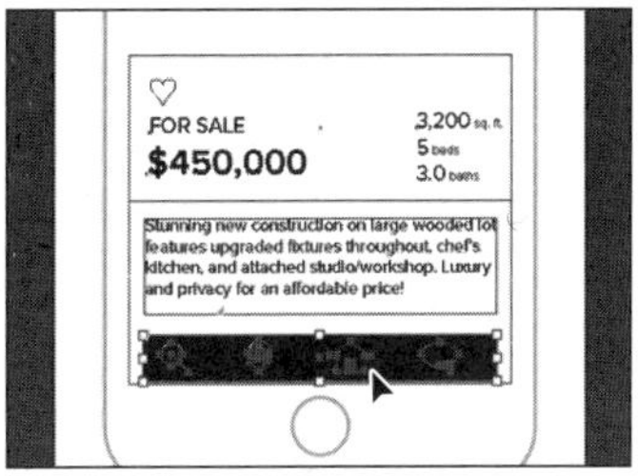

5 Click the Locate Object ( ) button at the bottom of the Layers panel to see where the selected group is in the Layers panel.

6 Choose Edit > Cut to cut the mobile icon group from the document.

Cutting content or deleting content will remove it from the Layers panel.

7 Click the disclosure triangle ( ) to the left of the Design Content layer and the Phone Body layer to hide the layer content for each.

8 Click to select the Menu Icons layer, and choose Edit > Paste In Place to paste the group into that layer.

● **Note:** In the figure, all of the layers are toggled closed. Yours may look different, and that's okay.

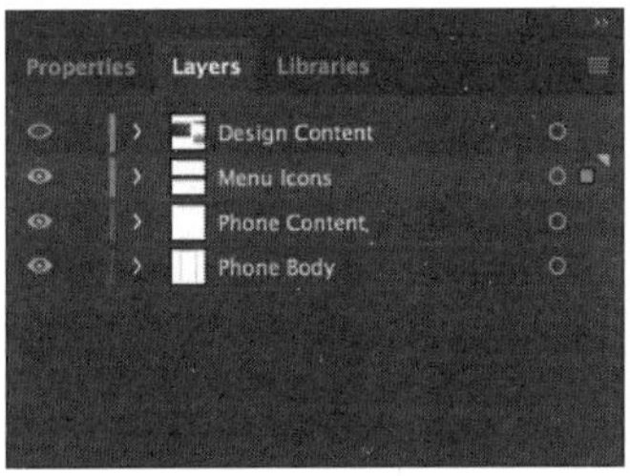

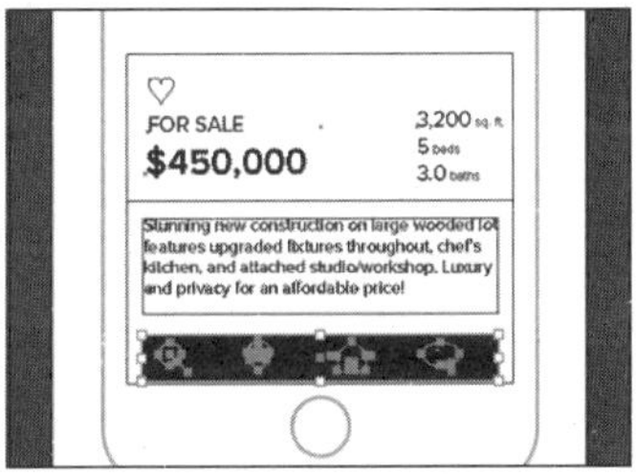

Selecting a layer before you create or paste content is something you will be doing a lot of in Illustrator. This way, you can organize content, keeping it on the layer you think is best, as you go.

● **Note:** The Paste In Place and Paste on All Artboards commands paste artwork on the active artboard at the same position as the artboard from where the artwork is copied.

9 Command-click (macOS) or Ctrl-click (Windows) the eye icon ( ) to the left of the Design Content layer name to show the content for that layer in Preview mode again.

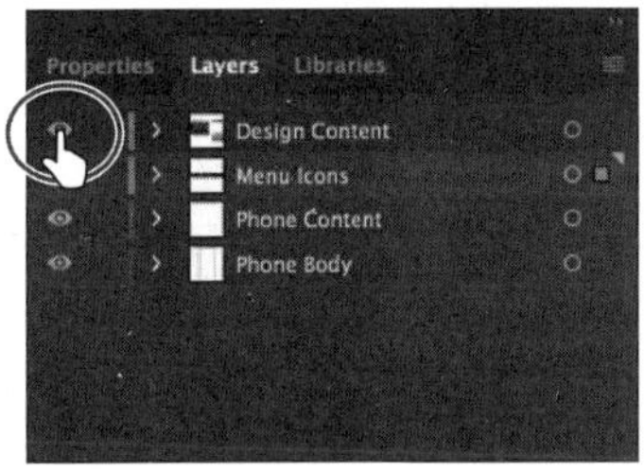

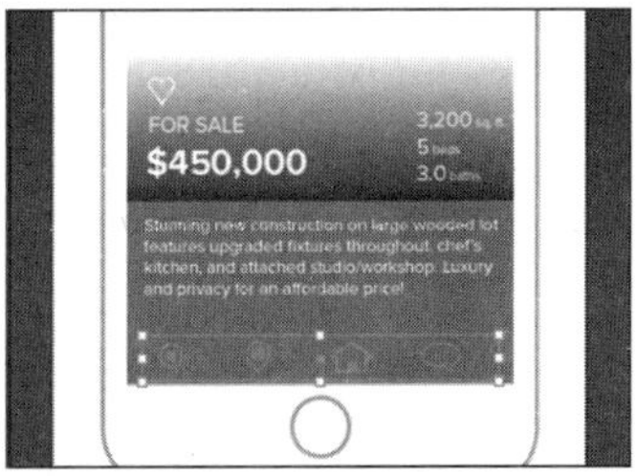

The menu icons will be behind the design content now since the Menu Icons layer is beneath the Design Content layer in the Layers panel. You'll fix that next.

Reordering layers

In earlier lessons, you learned that objects have a stacking order, depending on when and how they were created. That stacking order applies to each of the layers in the Layers panel. By creating multiple layers in your artwork, you can control how overlapping objects are displayed. Next, you'll reorder layers to achieve a different stacking order.

1 Click the disclosure triangle (▶) to the left of the Design Content layer to show the layer content.

2 Option-click (macOS) or Alt-click (Windows) the eye icon (👁) to the left of the Design Content layer to hide the *other* layers.

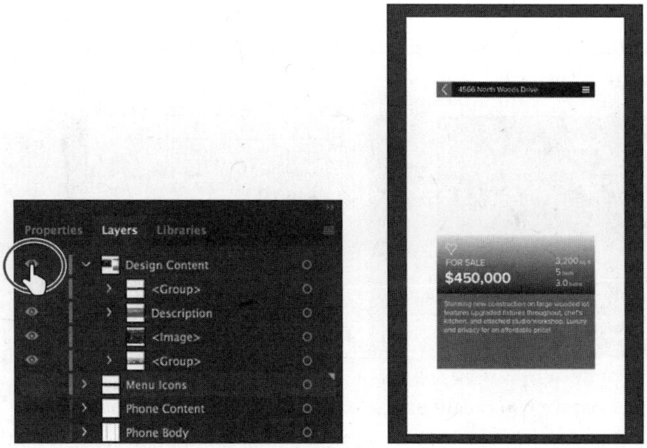

Hiding all layers except those that you want to work with can be very useful so you can focus on the content at hand.

3 With the Selection tool (▶) selected, click in a blank area, away from artwork to deselect, if necessary. Shift-drag the image off the left edge of the artboard into the approximate center of the artboard. Release the mouse button and then the Shift key.

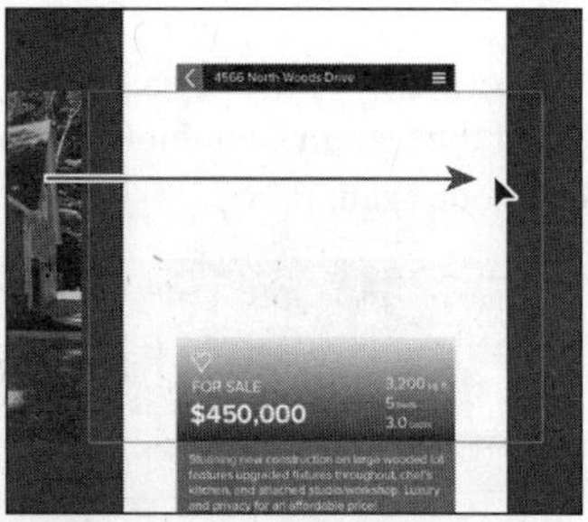

Notice the <Image> object in the Design Content layer in the Layers panel.

4 Choose Object > Arrange > Send To Back.

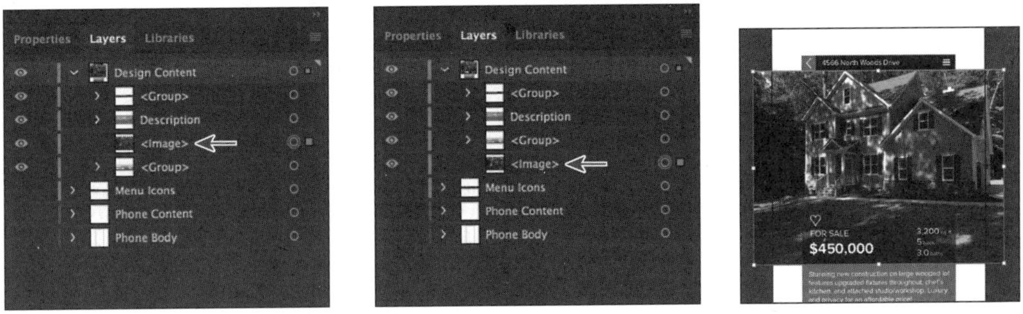

▶ **Tip:** You can also drag the <Image> object down below the <Group> object beneath it in the Layers panel. When a highlight line appears, release the mouse button to reorder the layers. The Arrange commands work within the layer that the selected content is on.

5 Choose Select > Deselect.

6 Click the disclosure triangle (▾) to the left of the Design Content layer to hide the layer content.

It's a good idea to get in the practice of collapsing layers in my opinion so you can more easily find content and work with layers in the Layers panel later.

7 Choose Show All Layers from the Layers panel menu (≡) or Option-click (macOS) or Alt-click (Windows) the eye icon (👁) to the left of the Design Content layer to show all layers again.

8 Click the Design Content layer to select it in the Layers panel, if necessary. Shift-click the Menu Icons layer to select both.

9 Drag either layer down on top of the Phone Content layer. When the layer is highlighted, release the mouse button to move the layers into the Phone Content layer. They are now sublayers of the parent Phone Content layer.

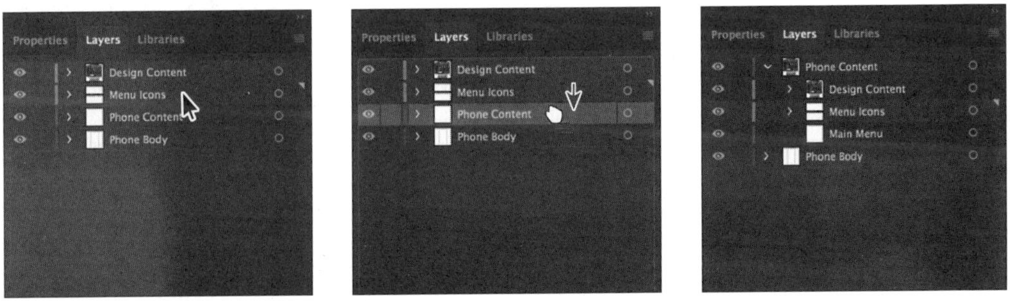

Collecting into a new layer

To streamline your artwork, you can merge layers, sublayers, content, or groups to combine the contents into one layer or sublayer. Note that items will be merged into the layer or group that you selected last. Next, you will merge content into a new layer and then merge a few sublayers into one.

1 Click the disclosure triangle ( ) to the left of the Phone Content layer to hide the layer content. Click the disclosure triangle ( ) to the left of the Phone Body layer to show the layer content.

2 Press the Option (macOS) or Alt (Windows) key, and click the <Path> object that has a circle in the thumbnail to select the content on the artboard.

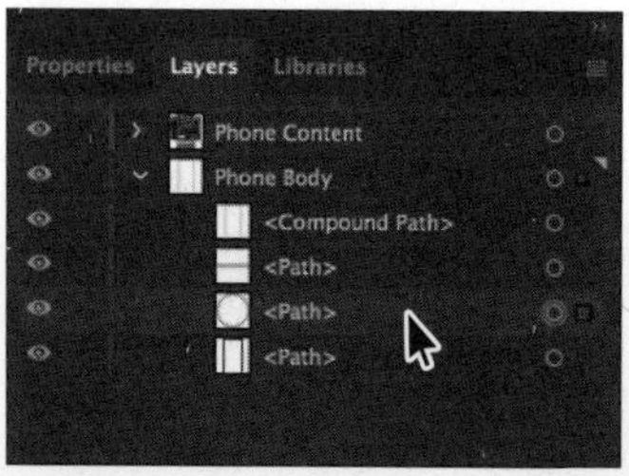

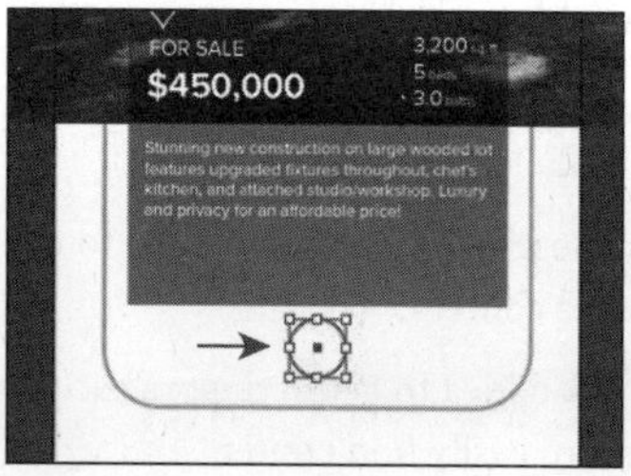

This can be helpful if you are looking at content in the Layers panel and need to select it or, in the least, see where it is in your document. You could also click the Selection column (where the selection indicator appears) to select content without selecting the layer.

▶ **Tip:** You can also Command-click (macOS) or Ctrl-click (Windows) layers or sublayers in the Layers panel to select multiple, nonsequential layers.

3 In the content for the Phone Body layer, with the <Path> layer selected, Shift-click the <Path> object above it to select both objects. See the figure.

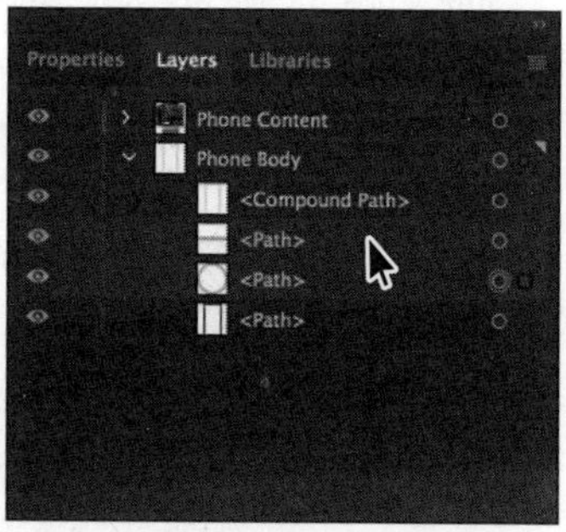

4 Click the Layers panel menu icon ( ), and choose Collect In New Layer to create a new sublayer (in this case) and put the selected content in it.

The objects in the new sublayer retain their original stacking order.

▶ **Tip:** Choose Merge Selected from the Layers panel menu to merge selected content into a single layer. The last layer you select determines the name and color of the merged layer. Layers can only merge with other layers that are on the same hierarchical level in the Layers panel. Likewise, sublayers can only merge with other sublayers that are in the same layer and on the same hierarchical level. Objects can't be merged with other objects.

5 Double-click the new sublayer name (mine is Layer 6), and change the name to **Front**. Press Enter or Return. The layer color you see may be different from what you see in the figure and that's okay.

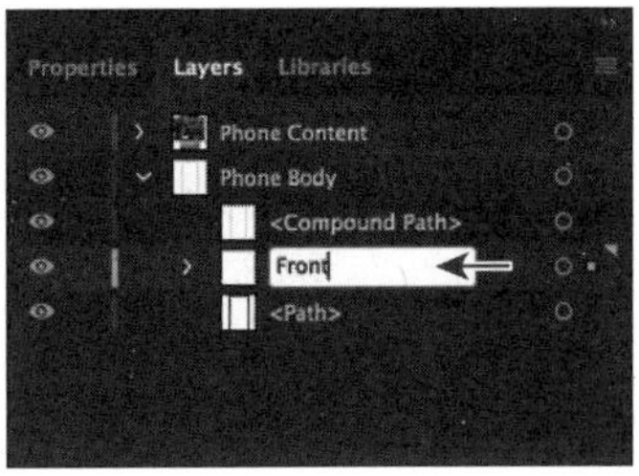

6 Choose Select > Deselect.

7 Choose File > Save.

Duplicating layer content

You can also use the Layers panel as another method for duplicating layers and other content. Next, you'll duplicate the Front sublayer, then move the content onto the right-hand artboard, and finally duplicate content between layers.

1 Drag the Front sublayer down to the Create New Layer button (■) to make a copy of the layer. Double-click the new layer name (Front copy) and name it **Back**.

The <Compound Path> object at the top of the Phone Body layer also needs to be in the Front sublayer and the Back sublayer. Next, you'll drag a copy into the Back sublayer and then drag the original into the Front sublayer.

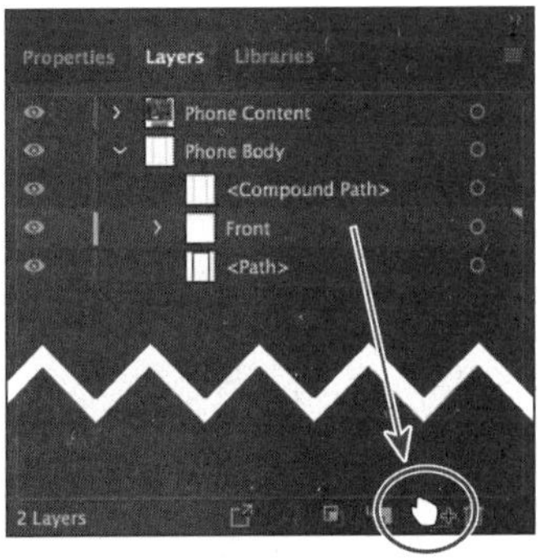

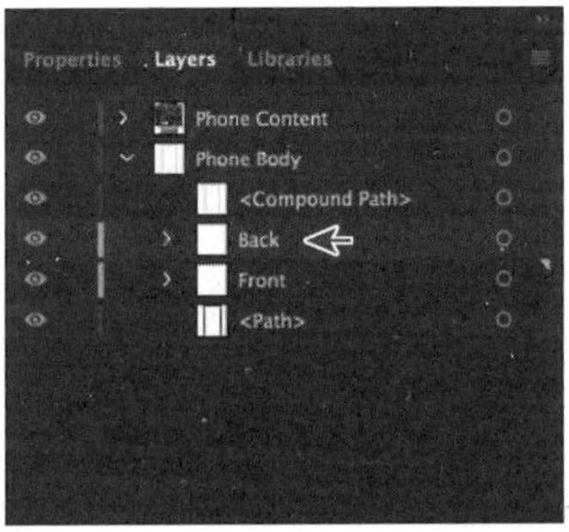

2 Click to select the <Compound Path> object. Pressing Option (macOS) or Alt (Windows), drag the object onto to the Back sublayer. When the layer is highlighted, release the mouse button and then the key.

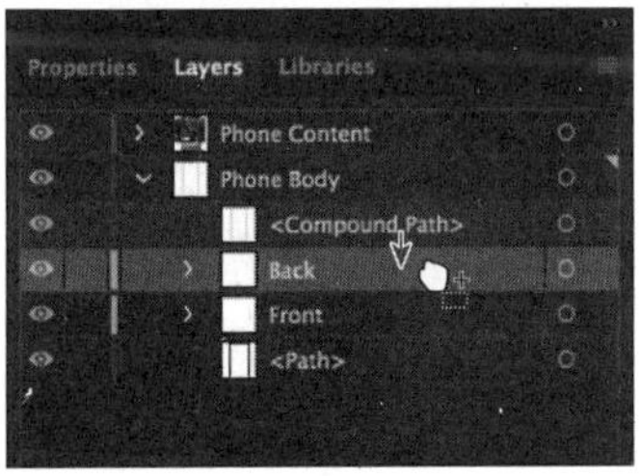

This copies the <Compound Path> content (the shape of the phone) onto the Back sublayer. Dragging with the modifier key copies the selected content. This is the same as selecting the content on the artboard, choosing Edit > Copy, selecting the Back sublayer in the Layers panel, and then choosing Edit > Paste In Place.

▶ **Tip:** You can also Option-drag (macOS) or Alt-drag (Windows) the selected-art indicator to duplicate content. You can also select the <Compound Path> row in the Layers panel and choose Duplicate "<Compound Path>" from the Layers panel menu to create a copy of the same content.

Next, you'll move the Back sublayer content onto the artboard on the right.

3 Click the Selection column to the far right of the Back layer name. Even if you already see a color box, click it again to select *all* content on the layer.

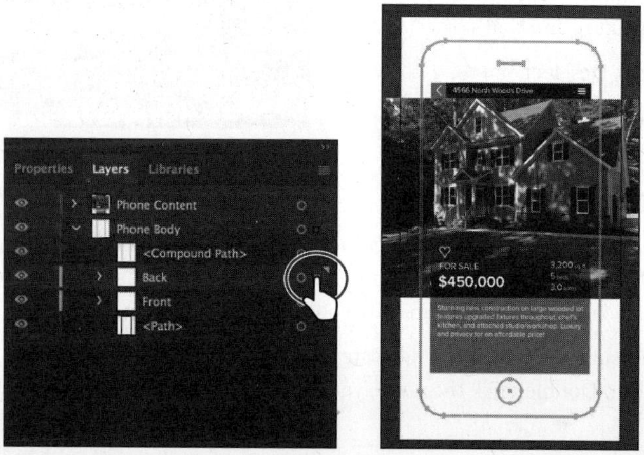

4 Choose 2 Phone Back from the Artboard Navigation menu in the lower-left corner of the Document window to center that artboard in the window and select it.

5 Click the Properties panel tab to open the Properties panel. Choose Align To Artboard from the Align To Selection menu in the Properties panel. Then click the Horizontal Align Center button (▪) to align the contents of the Back sublayer to the horizontal center of the 2 Phone Back artboard.

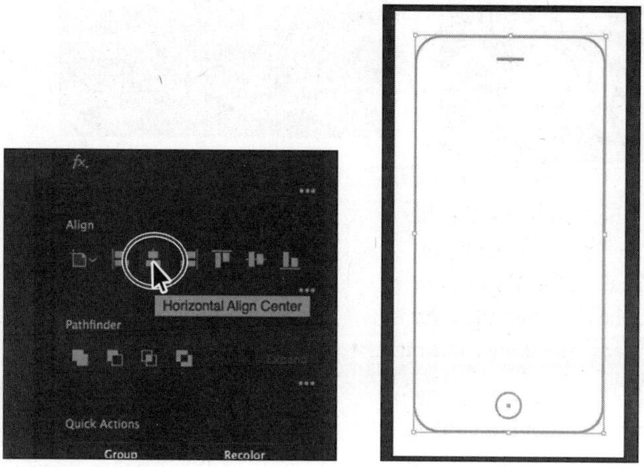

6 Click the Layers panel tab to show the Layers panel again. Click to select the original <Compound Path> object in the Layers panel. Drag it onto to the Front sublayer to move it onto that sublayer.

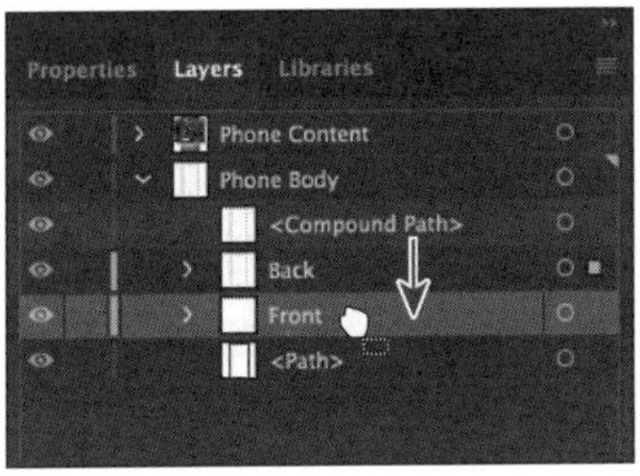

● **Note:** I dragged the left edge of the Layers panel to the left to see more of the layer names.

7 Click the disclosure triangle ( ) to the left of the Phone Body layer to hide the contents.

8 Choose View > Fit All In Window.

9 Choose Select > Deselect and then choose File > Save.

Pasting layers

To complete the app design, you'll copy and paste the remaining pieces of artwork from another file. You can paste a layered file into another file and even keep the layers intact. In this section, you'll also learn a few new things, including how to apply appearance attributes to layers and how to reorder layers.

1 Choose Window > Workspace > Reset Essentials.

2 Choose File > Open. Open the Menu.ai file in the Lessons > Lesson09 folder on your hard disk.

3 Choose View > Fit Artboard In Window.

4 Click the Layers panel tab to show the panel. To see how the objects in each layer are organized, Option-click (macOS) or Alt-click (Windows) the eye icon ( ) for one layer at a time in the Layers panel to show one layer and hide the others. You can also click the disclosure triangle ( ) to the left of each layer name to expand and collapse the layers for further inspection. When you're finished, make sure that both layers are showing and that they are collapsed.

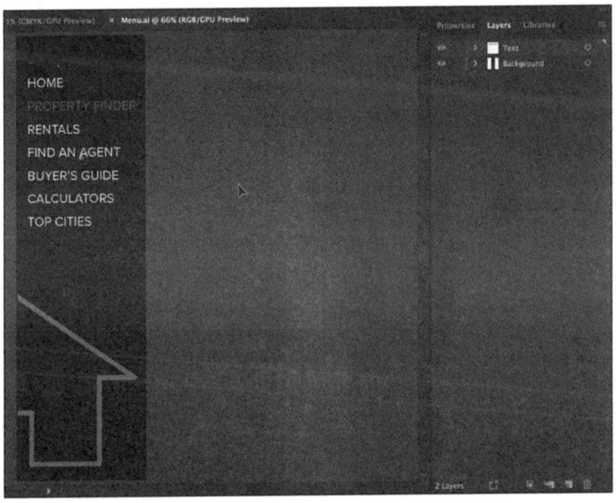

5 Choose Select > All and then choose Edit > Copy to select and copy the content to the clipboard.

6 Choose File > Close to close the Menu.ai file without saving any changes. If a warning dialog box appears, click No (Windows) or Don't Save (macOS).

Note: If the target document has a layer of the same name, Illustrator combines the pasted content into a layer of the same name.

7 In the RealEstateApp.ai file, choose Paste Remembers Layers from the Layers panel menu ( ). A checkmark next to the option indicates that it's selected.

When Paste Remembers Layers is selected, artwork is pasted into the layer(s) from which it was copied, regardless of which layer is active in the Layers panel. If the option is not selected, all objects are pasted into the active layer, and the layers from the original file are not pasted in.

8 Choose Edit > Paste to paste the content into the center of the Document window.

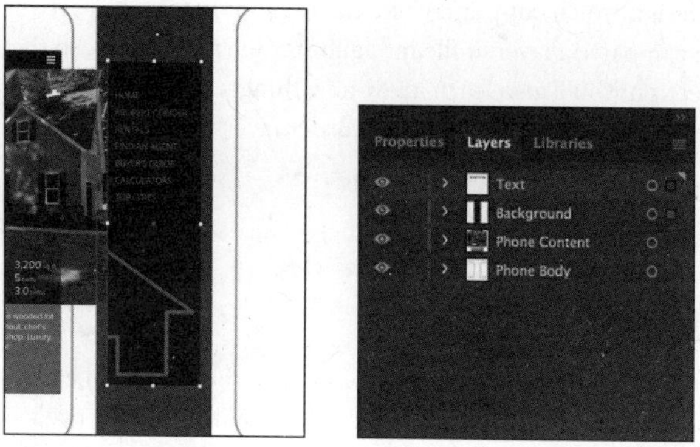

The Paste Remembers Layers option causes the Menu.ai layers to be pasted as two separate layers at the top of the Layers panel (Text and Background). Now you'll move the newly pasted layers into the Main Menu sublayer of the Phone Content layer and then change the ordering of the layers.

9 Select the Text layer (if it's not already selected), and Shift-click the Background layer name in the Layers panel to select both layers.

10 Click the disclosure triangle ( ) to the left of the Phone Content layer to show the layer contents.

11 Drag either of the selected layers (Text or Background) down on top of the Main Menu sublayer to move the content to the new layer.

The two pasted layers become sublayers of the Main Menu sublayer. Notice that they keep their individual layer colors.

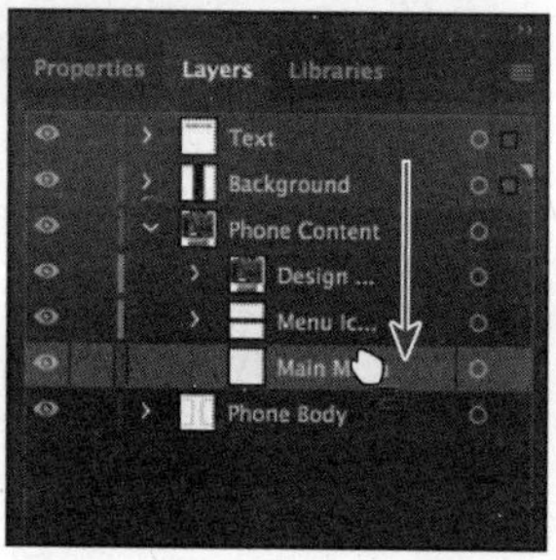

12 Choose Select > Deselect.

Changing layer order

As you've seen, you can easily drag layers, sublayers, groups, and other content in the Layers panel to reorganize the layer ordering. There are also several Layers panel options for commands such as reversing layer ordering and more that can make reorganizing layers easier.

1 Click the disclosure triangle ( ) to the left of the Main Menu sublayer to hide the contents.

2 Click the Design Content sublayer, and Shift-click the Main Menu sublayer name to select all three layers (Design Content, Menu Icons, and Main Menu).

3 Choose Reverse Order from the Layers panel menu ( ) to reverse the layer ordering.

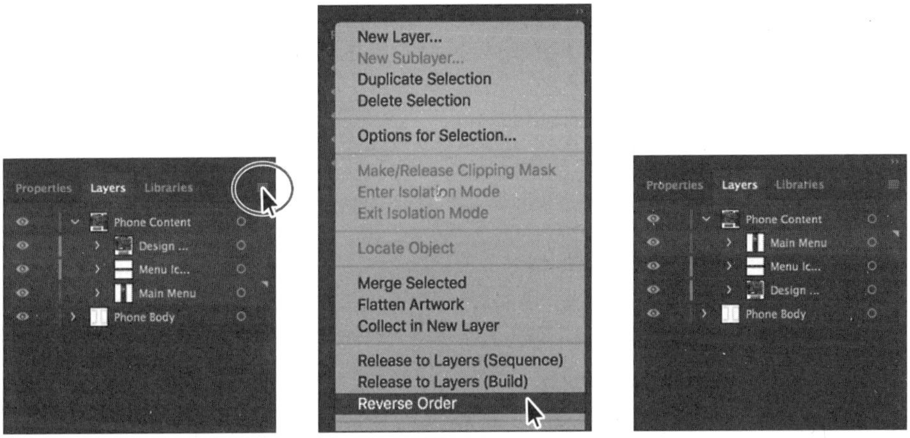

4 Click the Selection column to the far right of the Main Menu layer name to select the layer content.

5 With the Selection tool selected, drag the content onto the artboard on the left.

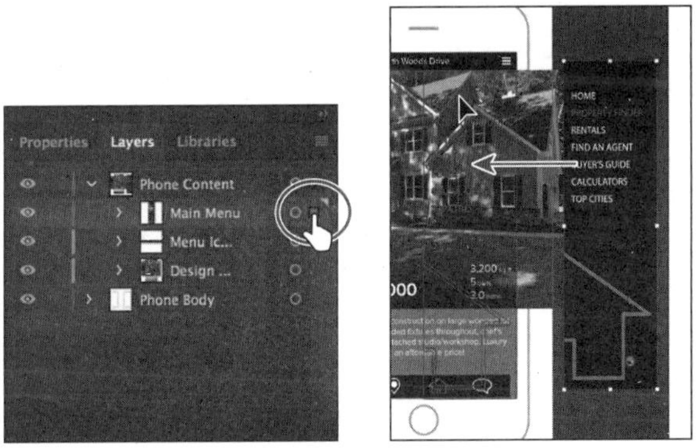

6 Choose Select > Deselect (if available).

Applying appearance attributes to layers

● **Note:** To learn more about working with appearance attributes, see Lesson 12, "Exploring Creative Uses of Effects and Graphic Styles."

● **Note:** I dragged the left edge of the Layers panel to the left to make it easier to see the names.

You can apply appearance attributes, such as styles, effects, and transparency, to layers, groups, and objects, using the Layers panel. When an appearance attribute is applied to a layer, any object on that layer takes on that attribute. If an appearance attribute is applied only to a specific object on a layer, it affects only that object, not the entire layer. Next, you'll apply an effect to artwork on one layer.

1 Click the disclosure triangle ( ) to the left of the Main Menu sublayer to show the layer contents, if necessary. Click the target icon ( ) to the right of the Background sublayer in the target column.

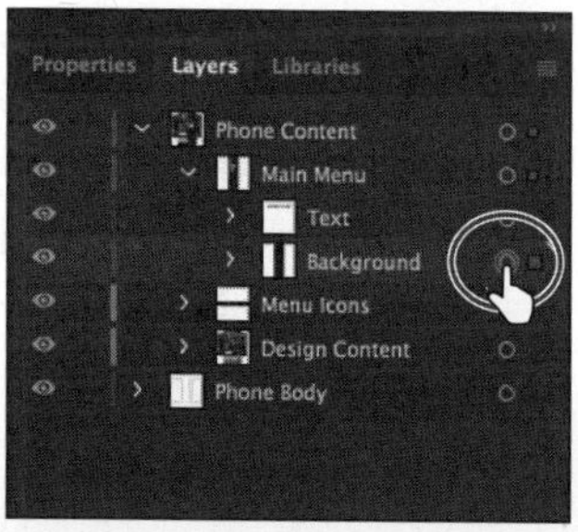

● **Note:** Clicking the target icon also selects the object(s) on the artboard. You could simply select the content on the artboard to apply an effect.

Clicking the target icon indicates that you want to apply an effect, style, or transparency change to that layer, sublayer, group, or object. In other words, the layer, sublayer, group, or object is *targeted*. The content is also selected in the Document window. When the target button appears as a double-ring icon (either or), the item is targeted; a single-ring icon indicates that the item is not targeted.

2 Click the Properties panel tab to show the Properties panel. Change the Opacity to **75** in the Properties panel.

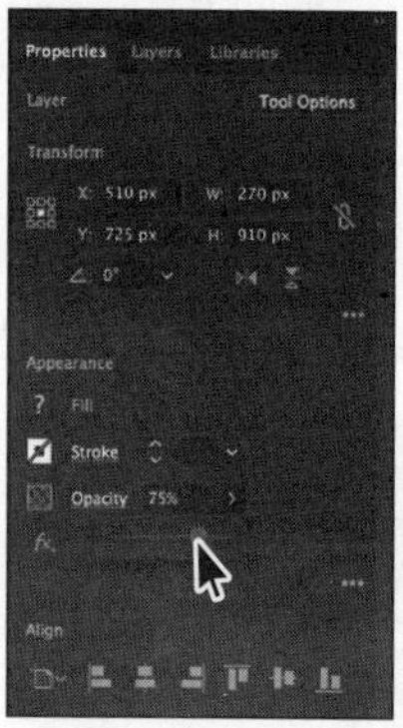

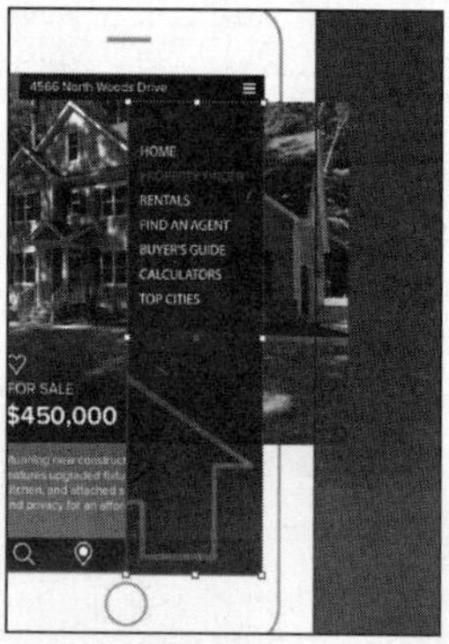

The target icon ( ) for the Background layer in the Layers panel is now shaded, indicating that the layer has at least one appearance attribute (an opacity change) applied to it. All content on the layer has the opacity change applied.

3 Choose Select > Deselect.

Creating a clipping mask

The Layers panel lets you create clipping masks to control whether artwork on a layer (or in a group) is hidden or revealed. A *clipping mask* is an object or group of objects that masks (with its shape) artwork below it in the same layer or sublayer so that only artwork within the shape is visible. In Lesson 14, "Using Illustrator CC with Other Adobe Applications," you will learn about creating clipping masks that are independent of the Layers panel. Now you'll create a clipping mask for the phone content.

Note: Once again, collapsing the Phone Content layer will keep the Layers panel a little neater.

1 Click the Layers panel tab to show the Layers panel. Click the disclosure triangle (▸) to the left of the Phone Body layer to show its contents, and click the disclosure triangle (▾) to the left of the Phone Content layer to hide its contents.

2 Drag the layer named <Path> onto the Phone Content layer to move it to that layer.

This path will be used as the clipping mask for all of the content on the layer.

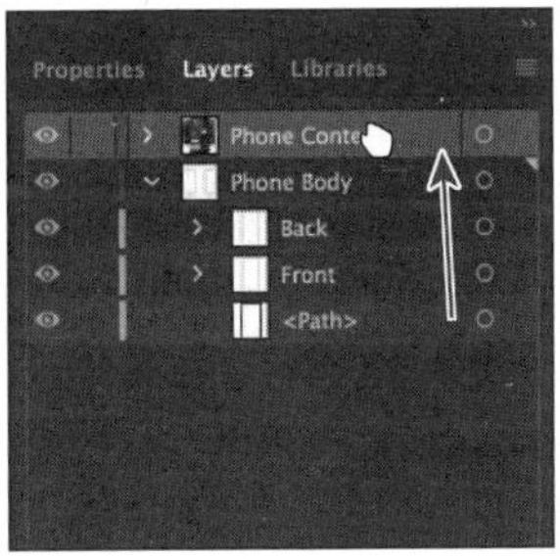

3 Click the disclosure triangle (▸) to the left of the Phone Content layer to show the layer content.

In the Layers panel, a masking object must be above the objects it masks. In the case of a layer mask, the masking object must be the topmost object on the layer. You can create a clipping mask for an entire layer, a sublayer, or a group of objects. You want to mask all of the content in the Phone Content layer, so the clipping object needs to be at the top of the Phone Content layer, which is what you just did.

4 Press the Option (macOS) or Alt (Windows) key, and click the <Path> object at the top of the Phone Content layer to select the content on the artboard.

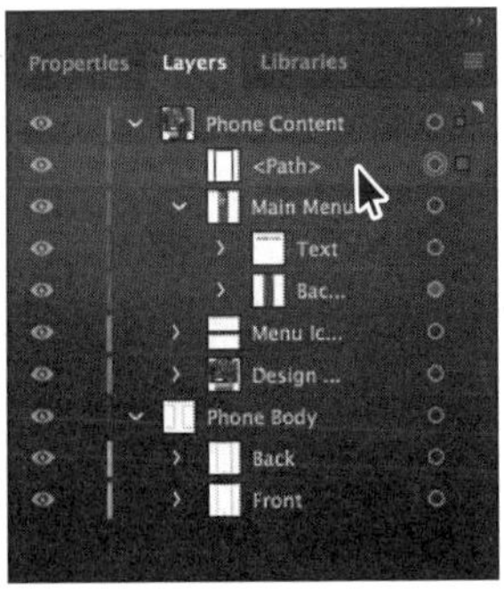

You don't need to select the shape to make a mask. I really just wanted you to see how big it was and see where it was positioned.

5 Choose Select > Deselect.

▶ **Tip:** To release the clipping mask, you can select the Phone Content layer again and click the same Make/Release Clipping Mask button (▣).

6 Select the Phone Content layer to highlight it in the Layers panel. Click the Make/Release Clipping Mask button (▣) at the bottom of the Layers panel.

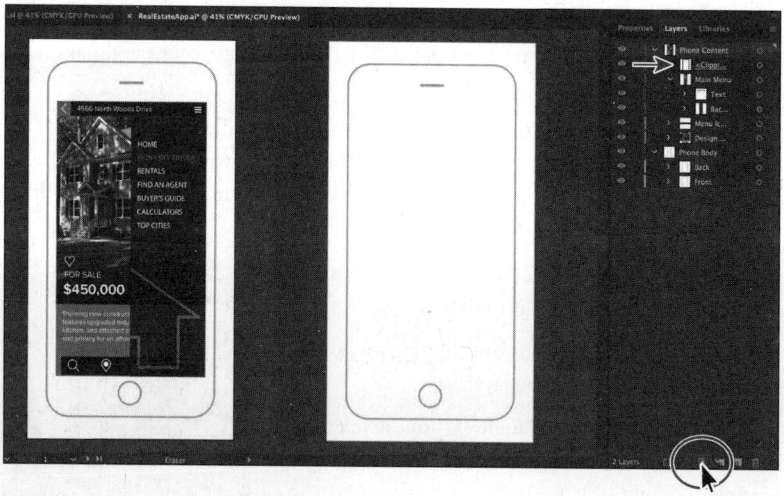

The name of the <Path> sublayer is underlined to indicate that it is the masking shape, and it has been renamed to "Clipping Path." On the artboard, the <Path> sublayer has hidden the parts of the phone content that extended outside of the shape.

Now that the artwork is complete, you may want to combine all the layers into a single layer and then delete the empty layers. This is called *flattening* artwork. Delivering finished artwork in a single-layer file can prevent accidents, such as hiding layers or omitting parts of the artwork during printing. To flatten specific layers without deleting hidden layers, you can select the layers you want to flatten and then choose Merge Selected from the Layers panel menu (☰).

● **Note:** For a complete list of shortcuts that you can use with the Layers panel, see "Keyboard shortcuts" in Illustrator Help (Help > Illustrator Help).

7 Choose File > Save and then choose File > Close.

Review questions

1 Name at least two benefits of using layers when creating artwork.

2 Describe how to reorder layers in a file.

3 What is the purpose of changing the color for a layer?

4 What happens if you paste a layered file into another file? Why is the Paste Remembers Layers option useful?

5 How do you create a layer clipping mask?

Review answers

1 The benefits of using layers when creating artwork include organizing content, selecting content more easily, protecting artwork that you don't want to change, hiding artwork that you aren't working with so that it's not distracting, and controlling what prints.

2 You reorder layers by selecting a layer name in the Layers panel and dragging the layer to its new location. The order of layers in the Layers panel controls the document's layer order—topmost in the panel is frontmost in the artwork.

3 The color for a layer controls how selected anchor points and direction lines are displayed on a layer and helps you identify which layer an object resides on in your document.

4 The paste commands paste layered files or objects copied from different layers into the active layer by default. The Paste Remembers Layers option keeps the original layers intact when the objects are pasted.

5 Create a clipping mask on a layer by selecting the layer and clicking the Make/Release Clipping Mask button (◘) in the Layers panel. The topmost object in the layer becomes the clipping mask.

10 GRADIENTS, BLENDS, AND PATTERNS

Lesson overview

In this lesson, you'll learn how to do the following:

- Create and save a gradient fill.
- Apply and edit a gradient on a stroke.
- Apply and edit a radial gradient.
- Add colors to a gradient.
- Adjust the direction of a gradient.
- Adjust the opacity of color in a gradient.
- Blend the shapes of objects in intermediate steps.
- Create smooth color blends between objects.
- Modify a blend and its path, shape, and color.
- Create and paint with patterns.

This lesson takes approximately 60 minutes to complete. Please log in to your account on peachpit.com to download the lesson files for this chapter, or go to the "Getting Started" section at the beginning of this book and follow the instructions under "Accessing the lesson files and Web Edition."

Your Account page is also where you'll find any updates to the chapters or to the lesson files. Look on the Lesson & Update Files tab to access the most current content.

To add texture and interest to your artwork in Illustrator, you can apply gradient fills, which are graduated blends of two or more colors, patterns, and blends of shapes and colors. In this lesson, you'll explore how to work with each of these to complete a project.

Starting the lesson

In this lesson, you'll explore various ways to work with gradients, blend shapes and colors, and create and apply patterns. Before you begin, you'll restore the default preferences for Adobe Illustrator CC. Then you'll open the finished art file for this lesson to see what you'll create.

● **Note:** If you have not already downloaded the project files for this lesson to your computer from your Account page, make sure to do so now. See the "Getting Started" section at the beginning of the book.

1 To ensure that the tools function and the defaults are set exactly as described in this lesson, delete or deactivate (by renaming) the Adobe Illustrator CC preferences file. See "Restoring default preferences" in the "Getting Started" section at the beginning of the book.

2 Start Adobe Illustrator CC.

3 Choose File > Open, and open the L10_end.ai file in the Lessons > Lesson10 folder on your hard disk.

4 Choose View > Fit All In Window. If you don't want to leave the document open as you work, choose File > Close.

To begin working, you'll open an art file that you need to finish.

5 Choose File > Open. In the Open dialog box, navigate to the Lessons > Lesson10 folder, and select the L10_start.ai file on your hard disk. Click Open to open the file.

6 Choose View > Fit All In Window.

7 Choose File > Save As, name the file **Cake.ai**, and select the Lessons > Lesson10 folder in the Save As menu. Leave the Format option set to Adobe Illustrator (ai) (macOS) or the Save As Type option set to Adobe Illustrator (*.AI) (Windows) and then click Save.

8 In the Illustrator Options dialog box, leave the Illustrator options at their default settings and then click OK.

9 Choose Reset Essentials from the workspace switcher in the Application bar.

● **Note:** If you don't see Reset Essentials in the workspace switcher menu, choose Window > Workspace > Essentials before choosing Window > Workspace > Reset Essentials.

Working with gradients

A *gradient fill* is a graduated blend of two or more colors, and it always includes a starting color and an ending color. You can create different types of gradient fills in Illustrator, including *linear*, in which the beginning color blends into the ending color along a line, and *radial*, in which the beginning color radiates outward, from the center point to the ending color. You can use the gradients provided with Adobe Illustrator CC or create your own gradients and save them as swatches for later use.

You can use the Properties panel to access the Gradient panel (Window > Gradient) or the Gradient tool (■) to apply, create, and modify gradients. In the Gradient panel, the Gradient Fill box or Stroke box displays the current gradient colors and gradient type applied to the fill or stroke of an object.

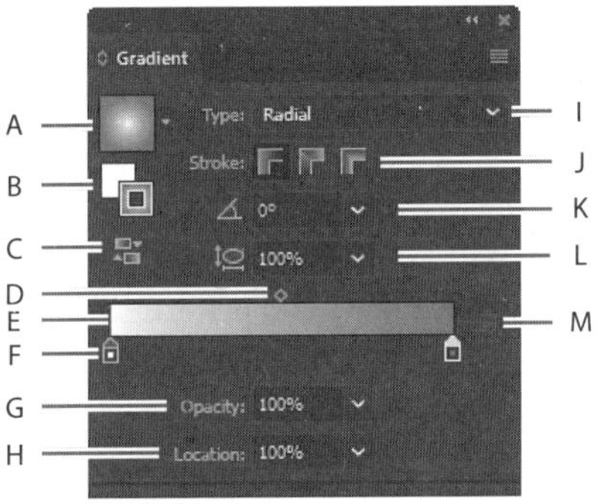

A. Gradient
B. Fill box/ Stroke box
C. Reverse Gradient
D. Gradient midpoint
E. Gradient slider
F. Color stop
G. Opacity
H. Location
I. Gradient type
J. Stroke gradient type
K. Angle
L. Aspect ratio
M. Delete Stop

Note: The Gradient panel you see won't match the figure, and that's okay.

In the Gradient panel under the gradient slider (labeled "E" in the previous figure), the leftmost gradient stop (labeled "F") is called a color stop. This marks the starting color; the right gradient stop marks the ending color. A *color stop* is the point at which a gradient changes from one color to the next. You can add more color stops by clicking below the gradient slider, and double-clicking a color stop opens a panel where you can choose a color from swatches, or color sliders.

Applying a linear gradient to a fill

With the simplest, two-color linear gradient, the starting color (leftmost color stop) blends into the ending color (rightmost color stop) along a straight line. To begin the lesson, you'll apply a gradient fill that comes with Illustrator to the green background shape.

1 Using the Selection tool (▶), click to select the large green rectangle in the background of the artboard on the left.

2 Click the Fill color in the Properties panel, select the Swatches option, and select the gradient swatch named "White, Black." Leave the swatches showing.

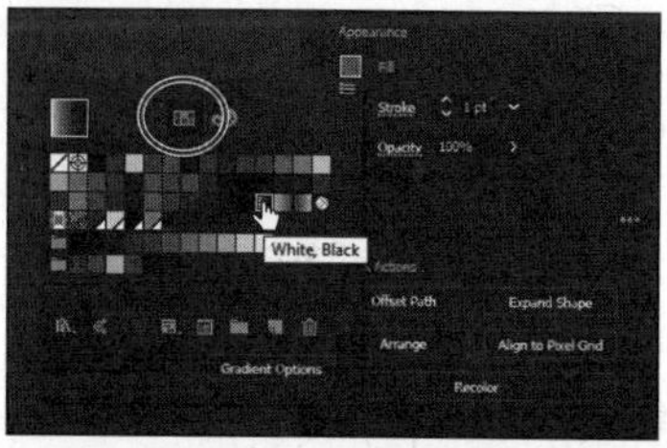

The default black-and-white gradient is applied to the fill of the selected shape.

Editing a gradient

Next, you'll edit the colors in the default black and white gradient you applied.

1 Click the Fill color in the Properties panel again to show the swatches, if it's not still showing. Click the Gradient Options button in the Swatches panel that appears to open the Gradient panel (Window > Gradient), and perform the following:

- Make sure that the Fill box is selected (circled in the figure).
- Double-click the white, leftmost gradient stop to select the starting color of the gradient (an arrow is pointing to it in the figure).
- Click the Swatches button in the panel that appears.
- Click to select the light brown swatch named "BG 10%."

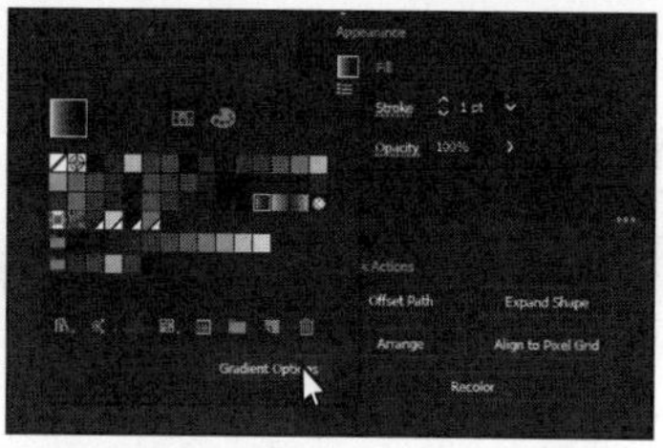

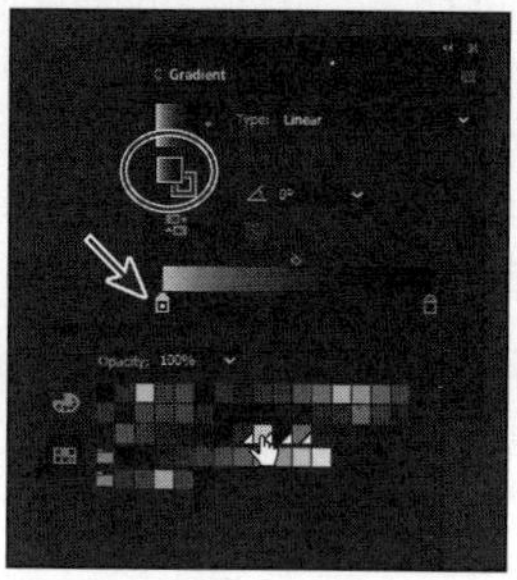

2 Click in a blank area of the Gradient panel to hide the Swatches panel.

3 In the Gradient panel, perform the following:

- Double-click the black color stop on the right side of the gradient slider to edit the color in the Gradient panel (circled in the figure). In the panel that appears, click the Color button ( ) to open the Color panel.
- Click the menu icon ( ), and choose CMYK from the menu, if CMYK values aren't showing.
- Change the CMYK values to C=**25**, M=**25**, Y=**25**, and K=**0**.
- After entering the last value, click in a blank area of the Gradient panel.

> **Tip:** To move between text fields, press the Tab key. Press Enter or Return to apply the last value typed.

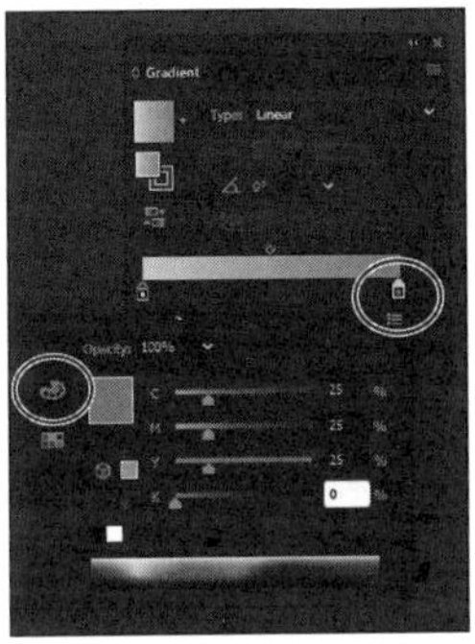

Saving a gradient

Next, you'll save the gradient you just edited as a swatch, in the Swatches panel. Saving a gradient is a great way to be able to apply it to other artwork easily and maintain consistency in the gradient appearance.

1 In the Gradient panel, click the Gradient menu arrow ( ) to the left of the word "Type," and click the Add To Swatches button ( ) at the bottom of the panel that appears.

The Gradient menu you just saw lists all the default and saved gradients that you can apply.

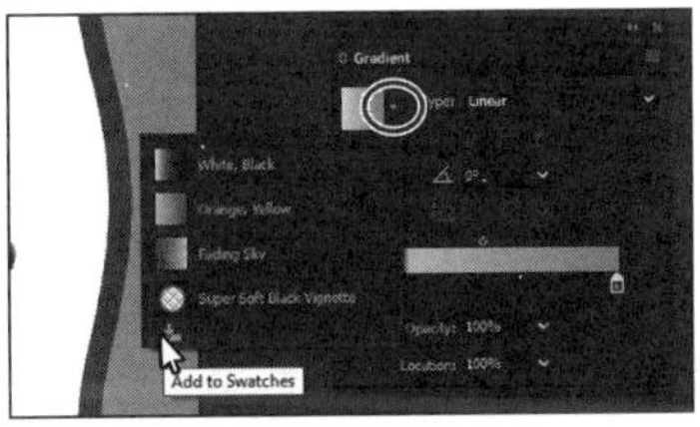

> **Tip:** Like most things in Illustrator, there is more than one method for saving a gradient swatch. You can also save a gradient by selecting an object with a gradient fill or stroke, clicking the Fill box or Stroke box in the Swatches panel (whichever the gradient is applied to), and then clicking the New Swatch button ( ) at the bottom of the Swatches panel.

2 Click the X at the top of the Gradient panel to close it.

3 With the background shape still selected, click the Fill color box in the Properties panel. With the Swatches option ( ) selected, double-click the "New Gradient Swatch 1" thumbnail to open the Swatch Options dialog box.

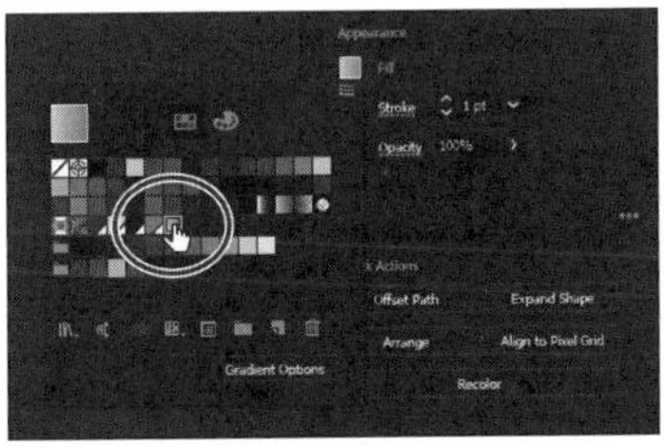

4 In the Swatch Options dialog box, type **Background** in the Swatch Name field and then click OK.

5 Click the Show Swatch Kinds Menu button (▦) at the bottom of the Swatches panel, and choose Show Gradient Swatches from the menu to display only gradient swatches in the Swatches panel.

The Swatches panel lets you sort colors based on type, like gradient swatches.

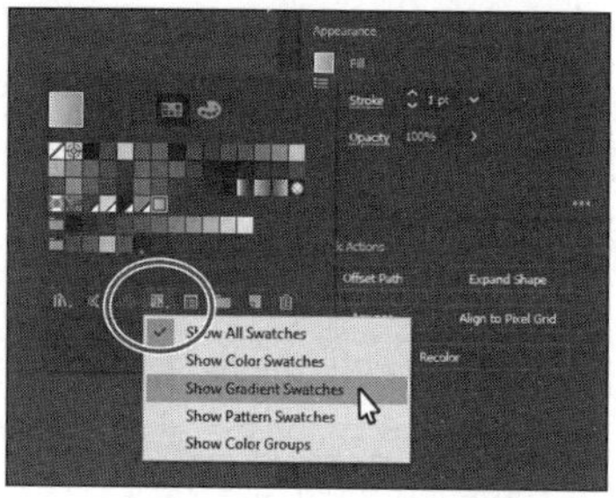

6 With the rectangle still selected on the artboard, apply some of the different gradients to the shape fill by selecting them in the Swatches panel.

7 Click the gradient named "Background" (the one you just saved) in the Swatches panel to make sure it's applied before continuing to the next step.

8 Click the Show Swatch Kinds Menu button (▦) at the bottom of the Swatches panel, and choose Show All Swatches from the menu.

9 Choose File > Save, and leave the rectangle selected.

Adjusting a linear gradient fill

Once you have painted an object with a gradient, you can adjust the direction, the origin, and the beginning and end points of the gradient applied to the artwork, using the Gradient tool. Now you'll adjust the gradient fill in the background shape.

1 With the Selection tool (▶) selected, double-click the background shape to isolate it.

This is a great way to enter Isolation mode for a single shape so you can focus on it without the other content (in this case) on top of it.

2 Choose View > Zoom Out.

3 Select the Gradient tool (▦) in the Tools panel.

With the Gradient tool, you can apply a gradient to the fill of an object or edit an existing gradient fill. Notice the horizontal gradient annotator (bar) that appears in the middle of the rectangle, which indicates the direction of the gradient. The larger circle on the left shows the starting point of the gradient (the first color stop), and the smaller square on the right is the ending point (the last color stop).

▶ **Tip:** You can hide the gradient annotator (bar) by choosing View > Hide Gradient Annotator. To show it again, choose View > Show Gradient Annotator.

4 Move the pointer over the bar in the gradient annotator.

The bar turns into the gradient slider, much like the one found in the Gradient panel. You can use the gradient slider on the art to edit the gradient without opening the Gradient panel.

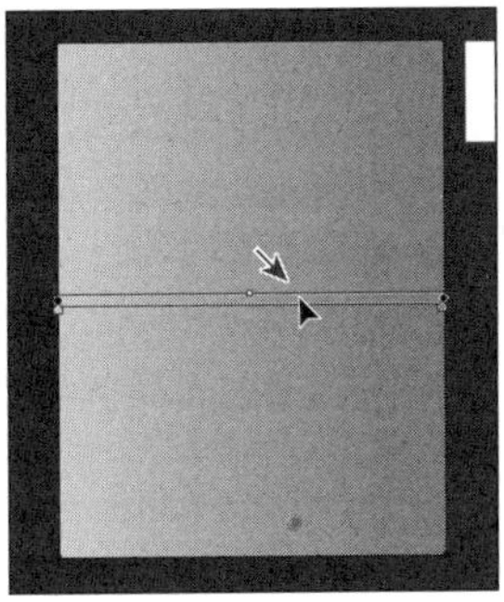

● **Note:** If you move the pointer to different areas of the gradient slider, the appearance of the pointer may change. This indicates that different functionality has been activated.

● **Note:** Holding down the Shift key constrains the gradient to 45-degree angles.

5 With the Gradient tool selected, pressing the Shift key, drag from the top of the artboard down to the bottom of the artboard to change the position and direction of the starting and ending colors of the gradient in the rectangle. Release the mouse button and then release the key.

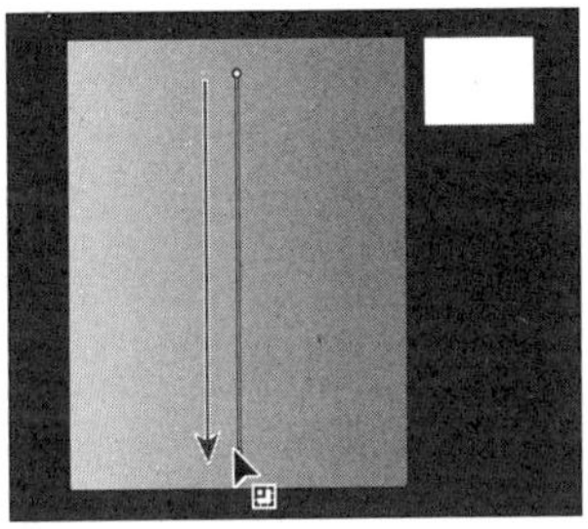

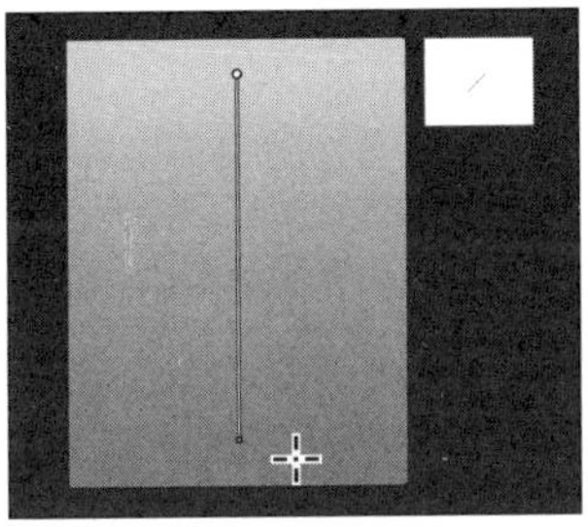

6 With the Gradient tool, move the pointer just off the small white square at the *bottom* of the gradient annotator. A rotation icon (⟲) appears. Drag to the right to rotate the gradient in the rectangle and then release the mouse button.

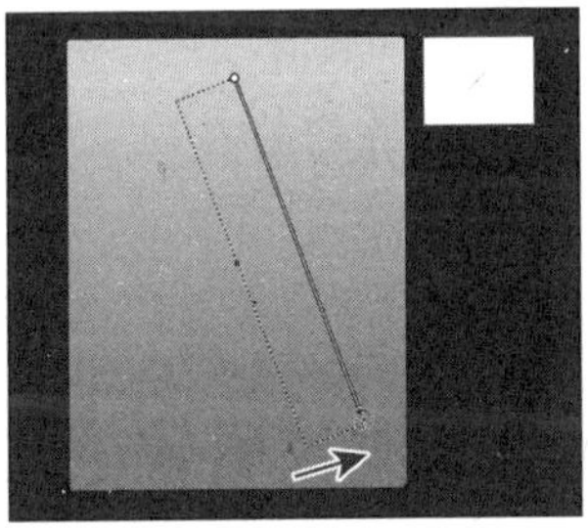

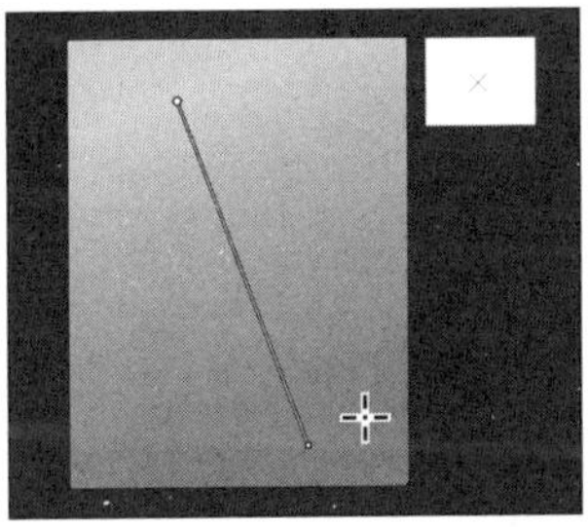

7 Double-click the Gradient tool in the Tools panel to open the Gradient panel. Ensure that the Fill box is selected in the panel (circled in the figure) and then choose **–60** from the Angle menu.

8 Choose Object > Lock > Selection to lock the rectangle so you don't accidentally move it later and to make selecting other artwork easier.

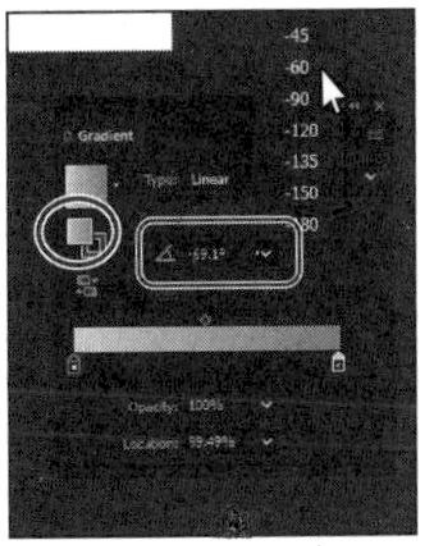

● **Note:** Entering the gradient rotation in the Gradient panel, rather than adjusting it directly on the artboard, is useful when you want to achieve consistency and precision.

9 Select the Selection tool, and press Esc to exit Isolation mode. You should see all of the artwork again.

10 Choose File > Save.

Applying a linear gradient to a stroke

You can also apply a gradient blend to the stroke of an object. Unlike a gradient applied to the fill of an object, you cannot use the Gradient tool to edit a gradient on the stroke of an object. A gradient on a stroke, however, has more options available in the Gradient panel than a gradient fill. Next, you will add a series of colors to a stroke gradient to create a frame for the artwork.

1 With the Selection tool ( ) selected, click the red stroke of the shape around the cake to select that shape.

● **Note:** Depending on the resolution of your screen, you may see a single-column Tools panel.

● **Note:** The Color panel group may open. If it does, you can close it.

2 Click the Stroke box at the bottom of the Tools panel, and click the Gradient box below the Fill box to apply the last used gradient.

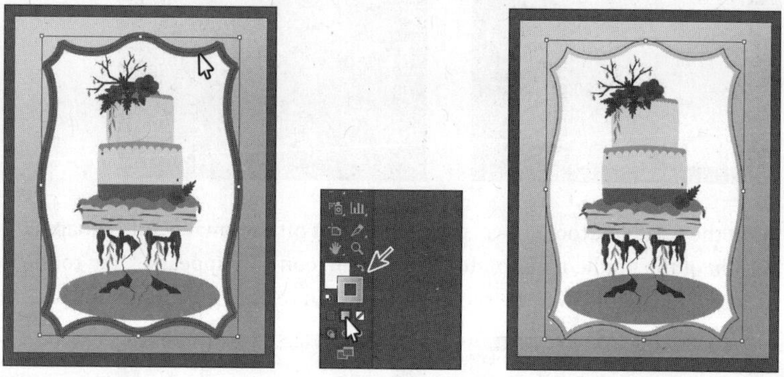

3 Select the Zoom tool ( ) in the Tools panel, and drag across the stroke of the selected shape to zoom in to it. Select the Selection tool.

Editing a gradient on a stroke

For a gradient on a stroke, you can choose how to align the gradient to the stroke: within, along, or across. In this section, you'll explore how to align a gradient to the stroke and also edit the colors of the gradient.

● **Note:** You can apply a gradient to a stroke in three ways: within a stroke (default) ( ), along a stroke ( ), and across a stroke ( ).

1 In the Gradient panel, click the Stroke box (if not already selected; it's circled in the figure) to edit the gradient applied to the stroke. Leave Type as Linear, and click the Apply Gradient Across Stroke button ( ) to change the gradient type.

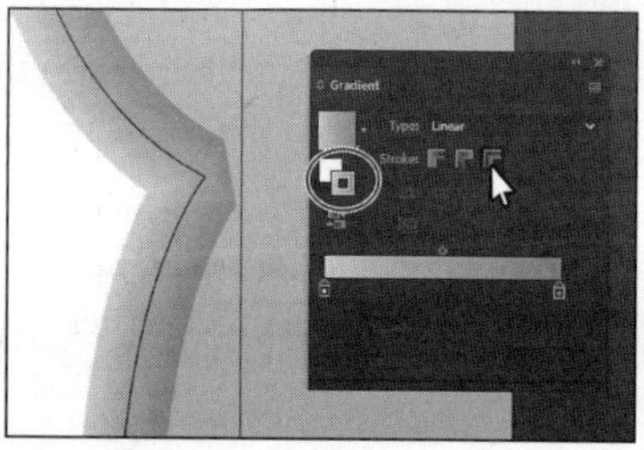

Next, you'll add colors to the gradient using a few methods.

2 Position the pointer below the gradient slider, between the two color stops. When the pointer with a plus sign (▷+) appears, click to add another color stop like you see in the middle part of the following figure.

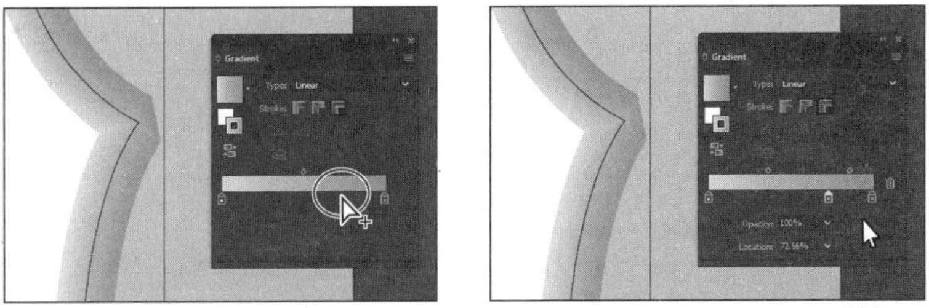

3 Double-click that new color stop and, with the swatches selected (▦), click the swatch named "BG 10%." Press the Escape key to hide the swatches and return to the Gradient panel.

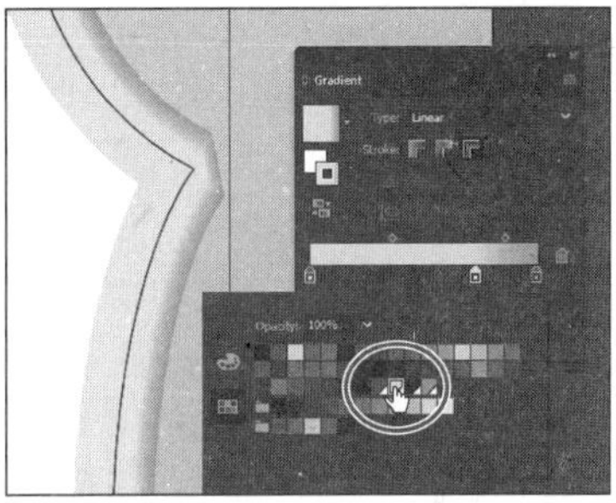

4 With the color stop still selected, change Location to 50%.

For the next few steps, you'll discover how to add a new color to the gradient by dragging to create a copy of a color stop in the Gradient panel.

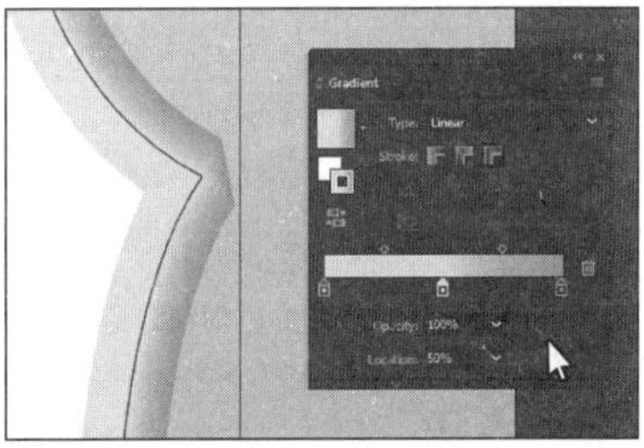

5 Pressing the Option (macOS) or Alt (Windows) key, drag the color stop on the far right to the left; release the mouse button when you see *roughly* 25% in the Location value and then release the modifier key.

There are now four color stops. Next you'll see how to remove a color stop.

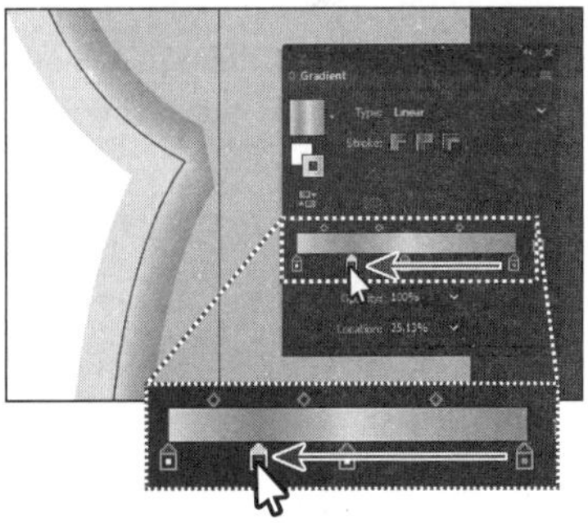

6 Drag the color stop on the far left down, away from the gradient slider. When you see that it's gone from the slider, release the mouse to remove it.

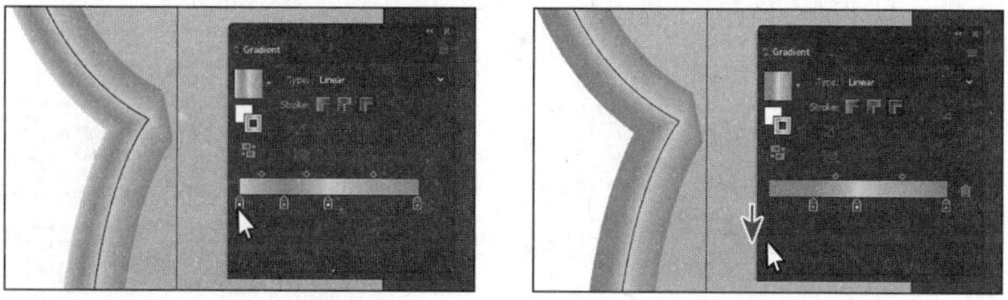

7 Click the X at the top of the Gradient panel to close it.

Applying a radial gradient to artwork

As previously noted, with a *radial gradient*, the starting color (leftmost color stop) of the gradient defines the center point of the fill, which radiates outward to the ending color (rightmost color stop). Next, you'll create and apply a radial gradient fill to a shape to make a shadow underneath the cake.

1 Choose View > Fit Artboard In Window.

2 With the Selection tool (▶) selected, click the orange ellipse.

3 Press Command++ (macOS) or Ctrl++ (Windows) a few times to zoom in.

4 Change the fill color to the White, Black gradient in the Properties panel. Leave the Swatches panel showing.

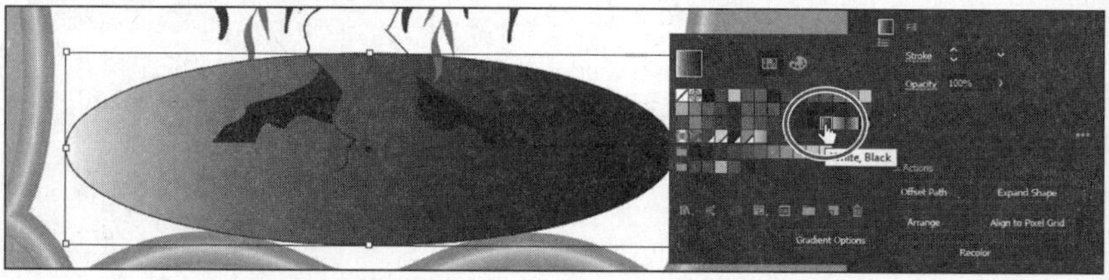

5 Click the Gradient Options button in the Swatches panel to open the Gradient panel. In the Gradient panel, make sure the Fill box is selected. Choose Radial from the Type menu to convert the linear gradient to a radial gradient.

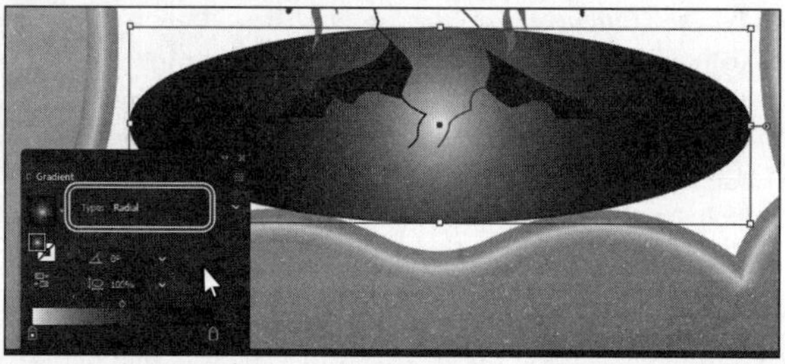

Editing the colors in the radial gradient

Previously in this lesson, you edited gradient colors in the Gradient panel. You can also edit the colors in a gradient using the Gradient tool, which is what you'll do next.

1 In the Gradient panel, with the ellipse still selected, click the Reverse Gradient button (▣) to swap the white and black colors in the gradient.

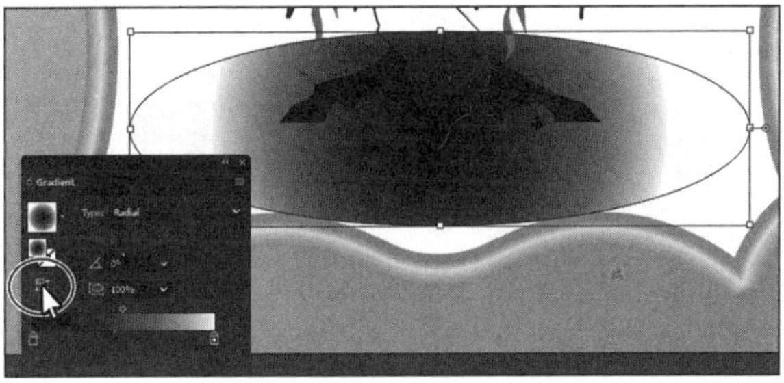

2 Select the Gradient tool (▣) in the Tools panel.

3 Position the pointer over the gradient annotator (bar) in the ellipse to reveal the gradient slider, and perform the following:

- Double-click the black color stop in the center of the ellipse to edit the color.
- In the panel that appears, click the Swatches button (▣), if it's not already selected.
- Select the swatch named "Radial 1."

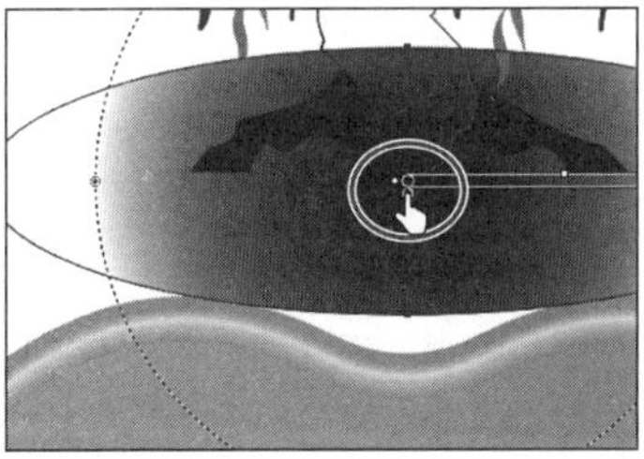

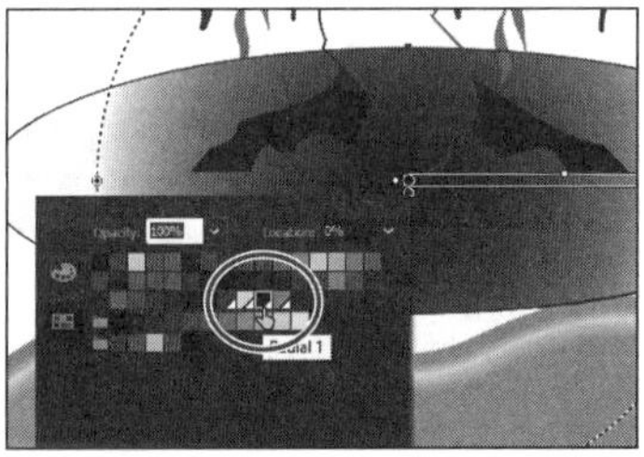

Notice that the gradient annotator starts from the center of the ellipse and points to the right. The dashed circle around the gradient annotator when the pointer is over it indicates that it is a radial gradient. You can set additional options for radial gradients, as you'll soon see.

4 Press Escape to hide the panel.

5 Position the pointer beneath the gradient slider, in the middle. When the pointer with a plus sign (▷₊) appears, click to add another color to the gradient (see the first part of the following figure).

> **Tip:** When you edit a color stop that has a swatch applied, you can easily see which swatch is applied because it is highlighted in the panel.

6 Double-click the new color stop. In the panel that appears, click the Swatches button (▦), and select the swatch named "Radial 2." Change Location to **45%**. Press Enter or Return to change the value and hide the panel.

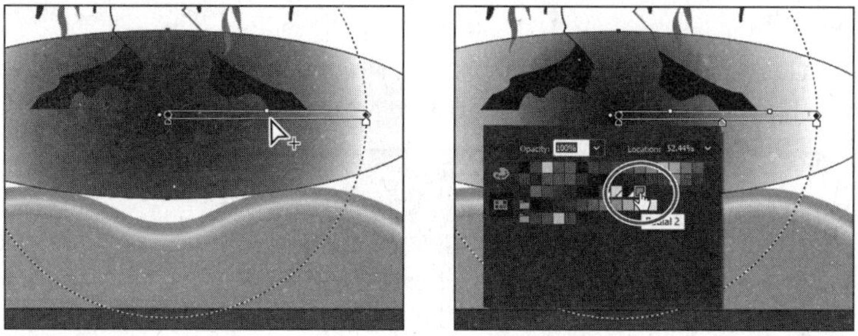

7 Choose File > Save.

Adjusting the radial gradient

Next, you'll change the aspect ratio of the radial gradient and change the radius and the origin of the radial gradient.

> **Note:** You may not see the dotted circle as you drag the end of the gradient annotator. That's okay. It appears if you position the pointer over the gradient annotator bar first, before dragging the right end point.

1 With the Gradient tool (■) selected and the ellipse still selected, move the pointer over the right end of the gradient annotator (see the first part of the following figure). When the pointer changes (▸), drag to the right, stopping at the right edge of the ellipse shape, and release the mouse button to lengthen the gradient.

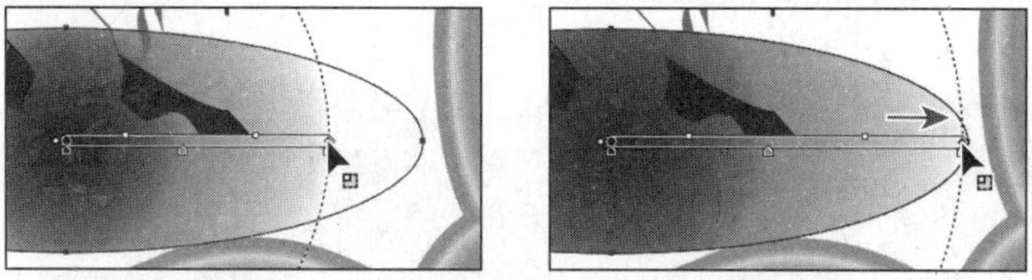

> **Tip:** You can also drag the gradient slider to reposition the gradient in the ellipse.

> **Tip:** You can drag the small white dot to the left of the larger white dot to reposition the center of the gradient without moving the entire gradient bar. This also changes the radius of the gradient.

2 In the Gradient panel, ensure that the Fill box is selected and then change the Aspect Ratio (▣) to **30%** by selecting it from the menu. Leave the panel open.

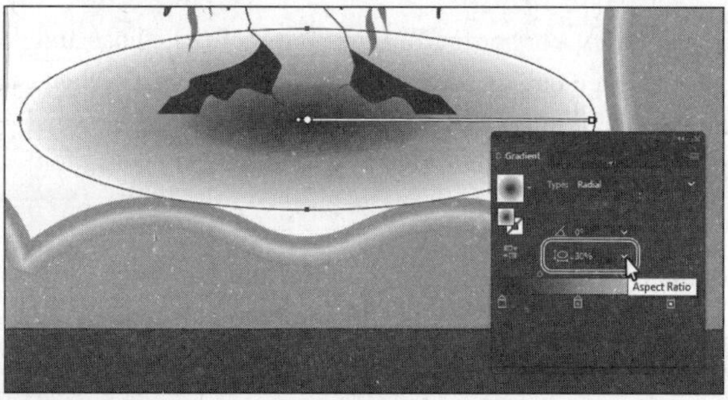

The aspect ratio changes a radial gradient into an elliptical gradient and makes the gradient better match the shape of the artwork. Another way to edit the aspect ratio is to do so visually. If you position the pointer over the gradient on the selected artwork with the Gradient tool selected and then position the pointer over the top black circle that appears on the dotted path, the pointer changes to . You can then drag to change the aspect ratio of the gradient.

Note: The aspect ratio is a value between 0.5% and 32,767%. As the aspect ratio gets smaller, the ellipse flattens and widens.

3 Select the Selection tool ( ) in the Tools panel, and double-click the Scale tool ( ) in the Tools panel. Change the Uniform Scale value to **80%**, and click OK.

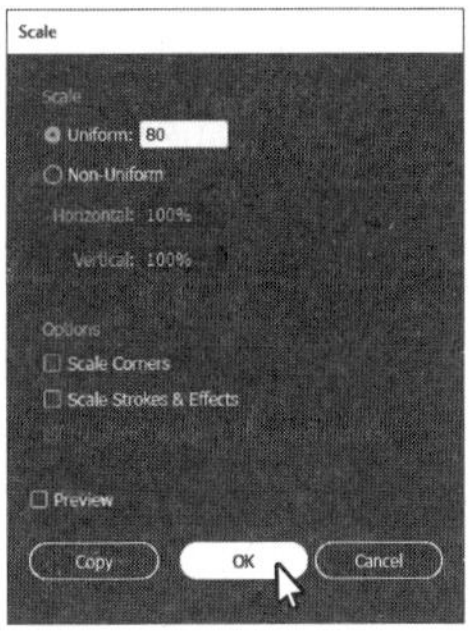

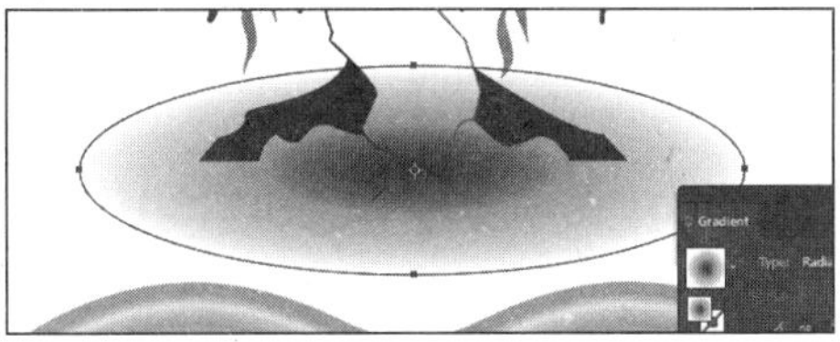

If you transform a shape with a gradient applied, such as scaling or rotating the shape (among other types of transformations), the gradient transforms as well. By the way, double-clicking the Scale tool, like other Transform tools, is the same as choosing Object > Transform > Scale (in this case).

4 Choose Select > Deselect and then choose File > Save.

Applying gradients to multiple objects

You can apply a gradient to multiple objects by selecting all the objects, applying a gradient color, and then dragging across the objects with the Gradient tool.

Now you'll apply a linear gradient fill to the two shapes that make up the cake.

1 Choose View > Fit Artboard In Window.

2 With the Selection tool ( ) selected, click the cream-colored cake shape and, pressing the Shift key, click the other cake shape to select both.

3 Click the Fill color in the Properties panel. In the panel that appears, make sure the Swatches option ( ) is selected, and select the Background gradient swatch.

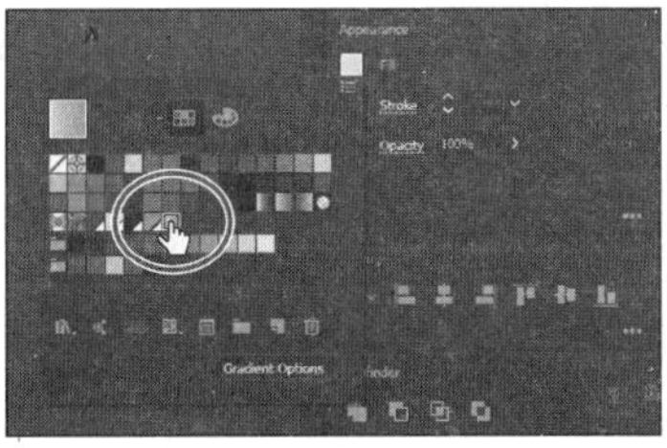

4 Select the Gradient tool ( ) in the Tools panel. Choose View > Hide Gradient Annotator so the bars that appear in the shapes are temporarily hidden.

5 Drag from the middle of the upper shape to the bottom shape. Leave the shapes selected.

Dragging across multiple shapes with the Gradient tool allows you to apply a gradient across the shapes.

Adding transparency to gradients

By specifying varying opacity values for the different color stops in your gradient, you can create gradients that fade in or out and that show or hide underlying artwork. Next, you'll apply a gradient that fades to transparent on the cake shapes. To do that, you'll copy the cake shapes and apply a gradient to the copies.

1 Select the Selection tool ( ). With the cake shapes still selected, choose Edit > Copy and then choose Edit > Paste In Front.

2 Choose Object > Arrange > Bring To Front to bring them on top of the other cake shapes.

3 In the Gradient panel, ensure that the Fill box is selected. Click the Gradient menu arrow ( ) and then select White, Black to apply the generic gradient to the fill.

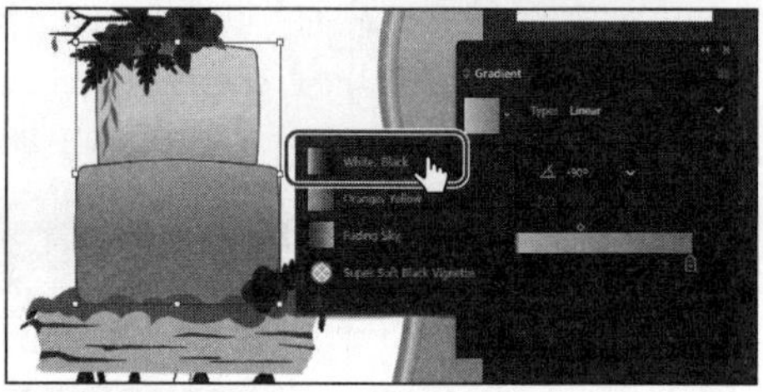

4 Click the Reverse Gradient button ( ) in the Gradient panel so the gradient starts with black (black will be the color stop on the left of the gradient slider).

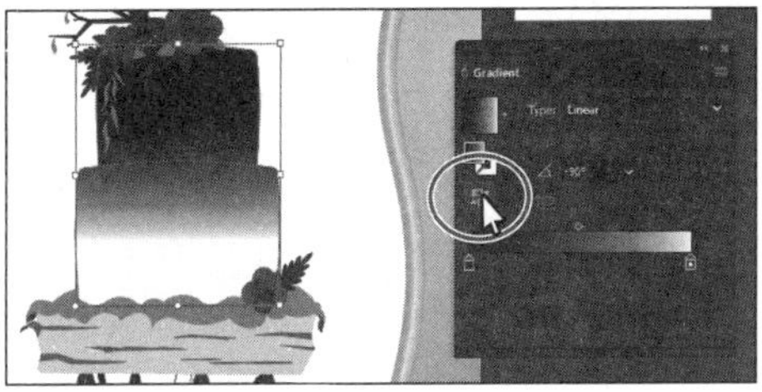

5 Select the Gradient tool ( ) in the Tools panel, and drag from the left edge of the widest cake shape to the right, going to the middle of the shapes.

6 In the Gradient panel, click the black color stop in the Gradient panel. Change Opacity to **40%** Click the white color stop and change Opacity to **0%**.

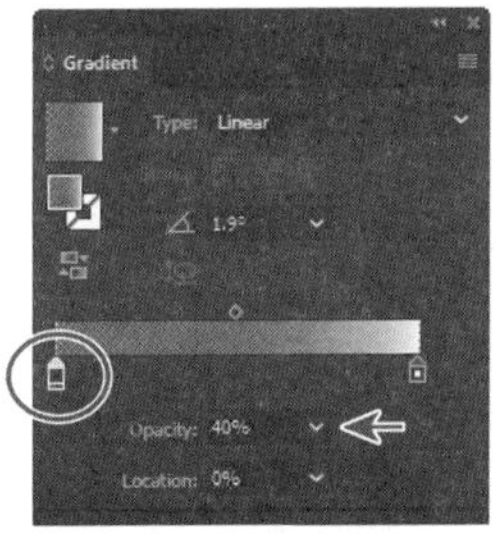

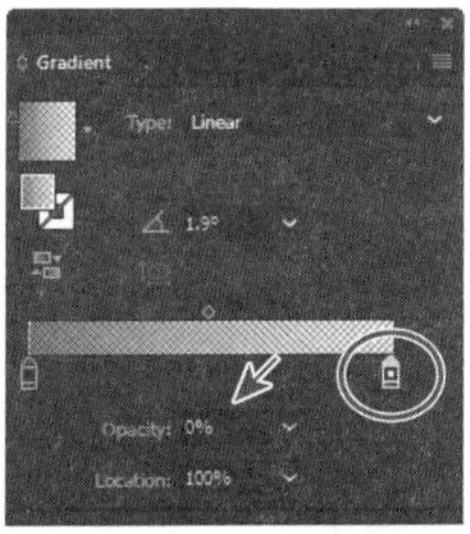

7 Drag the gradient midpoint (the diamond shape) to the right until you see a value of approximately 60% in the Location field.

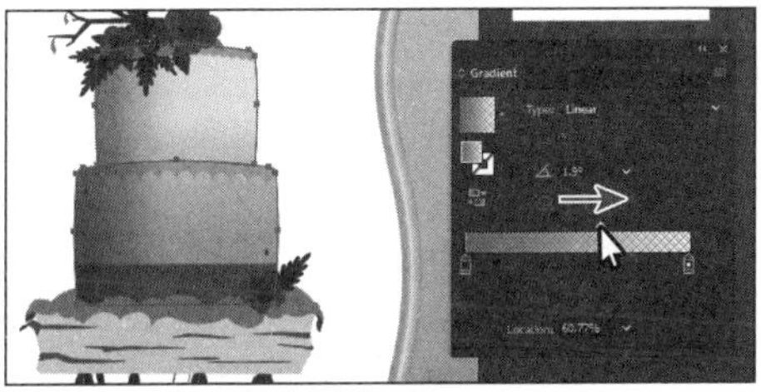

8 Choose Object > Hide > Selection.

9 Choose File > Save.

Working with blended objects

You can blend two distinct objects to create and distribute shapes evenly between two objects. The two shapes you blend can be the same or different. You can also blend between two open paths to create a smooth transition of color between objects, or you can combine blends of colors and objects to create color transitions in the shape of a particular object.

The following are examples of different types of blended objects you can create:

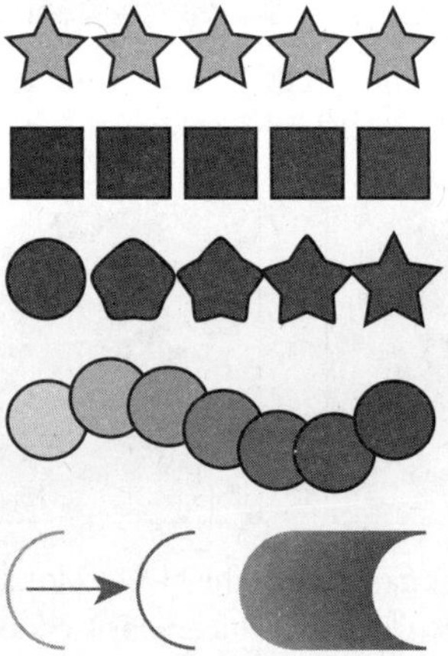

Blend between two of the same shape.

Blend between two of the same shape, each with a different color fill.

Blend between two different shapes with different fill colors.

Blend between two of the same shape along a path.

Smooth color blend between two stroked lines (original lines on left, blend on right).

When you create a blend, the blended objects are treated as one object, called a *blend object*. If you move one of the original objects or edit the anchor points of the original object, the blend changes accordingly. You can also expand the blend to divide it into distinct objects.

Creating a blend with specified steps

Next, you'll use the Blend tool ( ) to blend two shapes that you will use to create a pattern for the cake decoration.

Tip: You can add more than two objects to a blend.

Note: If you wanted to end the current path and blend other objects, you would first click the Blend tool in the Tools panel and then click the other objects, one at a time, to blend them.

1 Choose View > Zoom In a few times to zoom in closely. Make sure you can still see the two small maroon shapes on the cake (see the following figure).

2 Select the Blend tool ( ) in the Tools panel. Move the little box part of the pointer ( ) over the center of the small maroon shape on the left side of the cake and click.

3 Move the pointer away from the shape and a you'll see a plus sign next to the pointer ( ), indicating that you can add an object to the blend. Move the little box part of the pointer (not the plus) over the center of the small maroon shape on the right side of the cake and click to create a blend between these two objects.

4 With the blended object still selected, choose Object > Blend > Blend Options. In the Blend Options dialog box, choose Specified Steps from the Spacing menu, change Specified Steps to **9**, and then click OK.

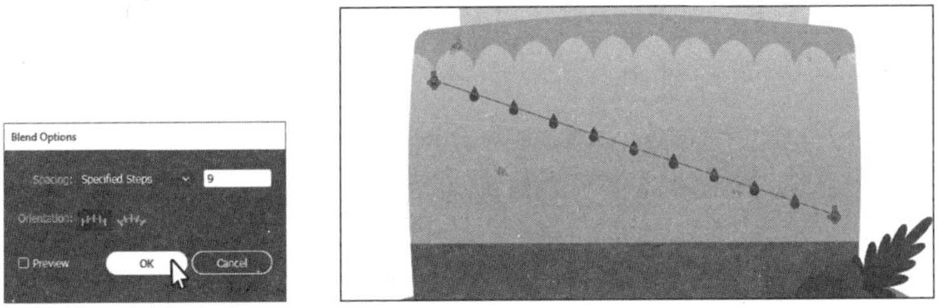

Tip: To edit the blend options for an object, you can also select the blend object and then double-click the Blend tool. You can also double-click the Blend tool ( ) in the Tools panel to set tool options *before* you create the blend object.

Modifying a blend

Now you'll edit the spine of the blend you just created so the shapes blend along a curve.

1 Select the Selection tool ( ) in the Tools panel, and click anywhere on the blend object to select it, if it's not already selected. Choose View > Zoom In, making sure you can still see the whole blend object.

2 Double-click anywhere on the blend object to enter Isolation mode.

This temporarily ungroups the blended objects and lets you edit each original shape, as well as the spine. The spine is a path along which the steps in a blended object are aligned. By default, the spine is a straight line.

3 Choose View > Outline.

In Outline mode, you can see the outlines of the two original shapes and a straight path (spine) between them. These three objects are what a blend object is composed of, by default. It can be easier to edit the path between the original objects in Outline mode.

4 Click and drag the edge of the smaller shape on the right up until it touches the cake decoration above it. See the following figure.

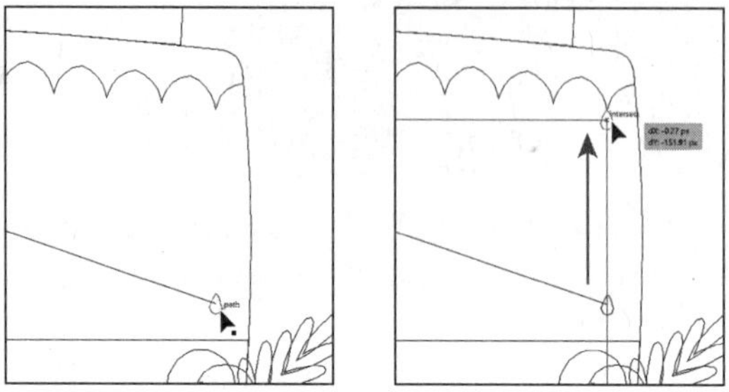

Make sure you drag the shape and not the path between the shapes.

5 Choose Select > Deselect, and remain in Isolation mode.

▶ **Tip:** Another way to reshape the spine of a blend is to blend the shapes along another path. You can draw another path, select the blend as well, and then choose Object > Blend > Replace Spine.

6 Select the Pen tool (✒) in the Tools panel. Press the Option key (macOS) or Alt key (Windows), and position the pointer over the path between the shapes. When the pointer changes (▶), drag the path up, like in the first part of the figure.

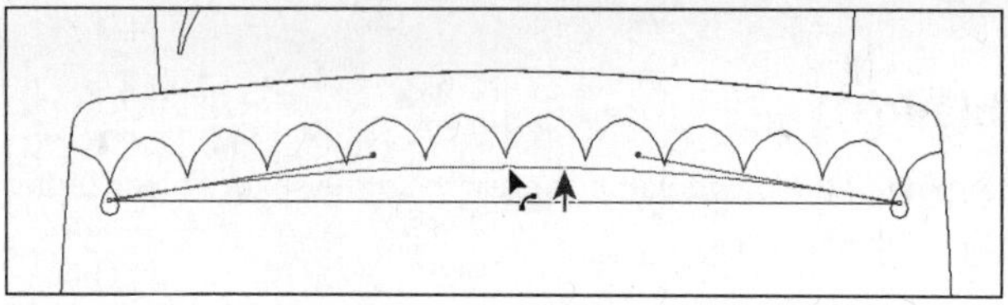

▶ **Tip:** If the maroon shapes don't align with the points on the cake shape above, you can press the arrow keys (left or right) after dragging with the Pen tool to reshape the path. You can also press the Option/Alt key with Pen tool selected, and drag the path again.

7 Choose View > GPU Preview if supported, or View > Preview On CPU (Preview) if not, to see the change.

8 Press Esc to exit Isolation mode.

9 Choose Select > Deselect, and choose File > Save.

Creating and editing a smooth color blend

You can choose several options for blending the shapes and colors of objects to create a new object. When you choose the Smooth Color blend option in the Blend Options dialog box, Illustrator combines the shapes and colors of the objects into many intermediate steps, creating a smooth, graduated blend between the original objects, like you see in the figure on the right.

If objects are filled or stroked with different colors, the steps are calculated to provide the optimum number of steps for a smooth color transition. If the objects contain identical colors or if they contain gradients or patterns, the number of steps is based on the longest distance between the bounding box edges of the two objects.

Now you'll combine two shapes into a smooth color blend to make the trunk of a tree that is the leg of the cake stand.

1 Choose View > Fit Artboard In Window.

2 Select the Zoom tool (), and drag across the paths under the cake.

   Both brown paths have a stroke color and no fill. Objects that have strokes blend differently than those that have no stroke.

3 Select the Selection tool () and click on the path on the left. Press the Shift key and click on the path on the right to select both.

4 Choose Object > Blend > Make.

   This is another way to create a blend and can be useful if creating a blend using the Blend tool proves challenging. The blend you created is using the last settings from the Blend Options dialog box (Specified Steps: 9).

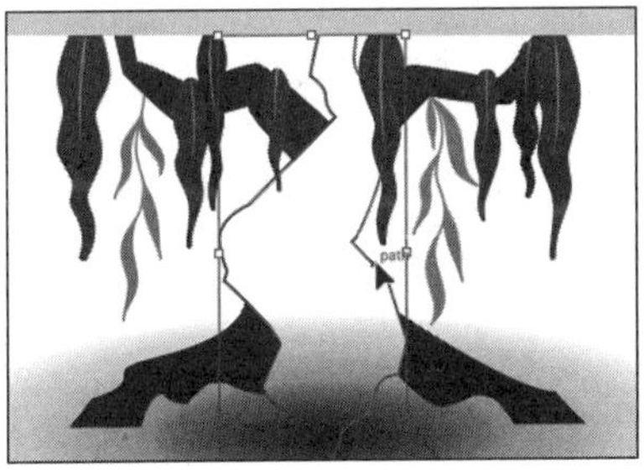

   Next, you'll change the blend settings for the tree trunk so that it blends as smooth color, rather than in specified steps.

5 With the blend object still selected, double-click the Blend tool ( ) in the Tools panel. In the Blend Options dialog box, choose Smooth Color from the Spacing menu to set up the blend options, which will remain set until you change them. Select Preview and then click OK.

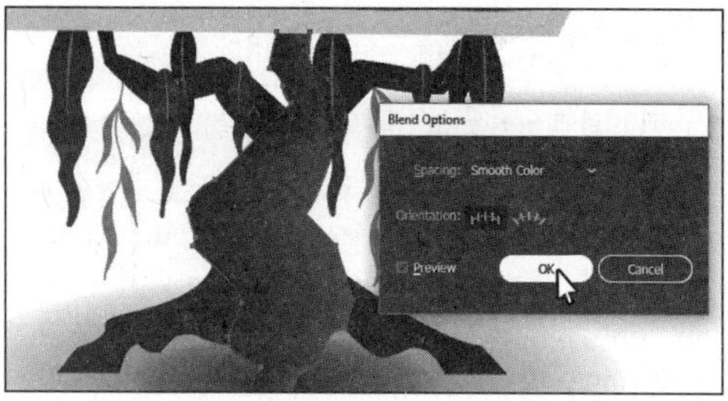

6 Choose Select > Deselect.

Once you've applied a smooth color blend to objects, you can edit it. Next, you'll edit the paths that make up the blend.

7 With the Selection tool ( ) selected, double-click within the color blend to enter Isolation mode. Click the path on the left to select it, and change the Stroke color in the Properties panel to any color you want. Press the Escape key to hide the panel. Notice how the colors are blended.

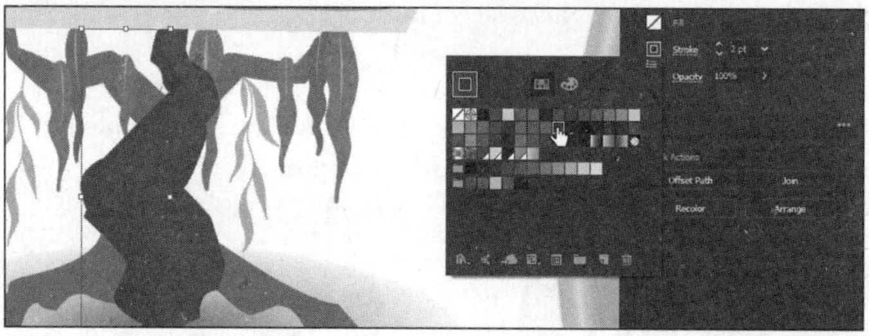

8 Choose Edit > Undo Apply Swatch until the original stroke color is showing.

9 Double-click away from the blend to exit Isolation mode, and deselect all.

10 Choose View > Fit Artboard In Window.

11 Choose File > Save.

Note: Creating smooth color blends between paths can be difficult in certain situations. For instance, if the lines intersect or the lines are too curved, unexpected results can occur.

Tip: If you're having a hard time selecting the path, choose View > Outline to enter Outline mode. Select the path, and then choose View > GPU Preview if supported or View > Preview On CPU (Preview) if not.

Painting with patterns

In addition to process colors, spot colors, and gradients, the Swatches panel can also contain pattern swatches. Illustrator provides sample swatches of each type in the default Swatches panel as separate libraries and lets you create your own patterns and gradients. In this section, you will focus on creating, applying, and editing patterns.

Applying an existing pattern

A *pattern* is artwork saved in the Swatches panel that can be applied to the stroke or fill of an object. You can customize existing patterns and design patterns from scratch with any of the Illustrator tools. All patterns start with a single tile that is *tiled* (repeated) within a shape, starting at the ruler origin and continuing to the right. Next, you will apply an existing pattern to a shape.

1 Choose Object > Unlock All.

2 Choose Select > Deselect.

3 With the Selection tool (▶) selected, click to select the background rectangle behind all of the other artwork.

4 Click More Options (•••) in the Appearance section of the Properties panel to open the Appearance panel (or choose Window > Appearance). Click the Add New Fill button at the bottom of the panel. This adds a second gradient fill to the rectangle and layers it on top of the first.

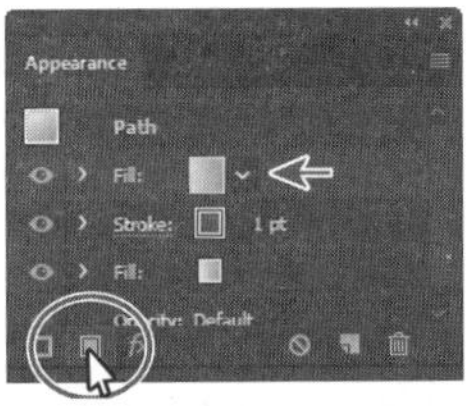

● **Note:** You'll learn all about the Appearance panel in Lesson 12, "Exploring Creative Uses of Effects and Graphic Styles."

5 In the Appearance panel, click the *top* fill box to the right of the word "Fill" to show a panel of swatches. An arrow is pointing to it in the figure. Select the Pompadour swatch.

The pattern swatch fills the shape as a second fill on top of the first. The swatch named "Pompadour" is included in the swatches for a Print document. You can find so many more pattern swatches in Illustrator by choosing Window > Swatch Libraries > Patterns and choosing a pattern library.

6 In the Appearance panel, click the arrow to the left of the *top* word "Fill." Click the word "Opacity" that appears to open the Transparency panel (or choose Window > Transparency). Change the Opacity value to **20**. Press the Escape key to hide the panel.

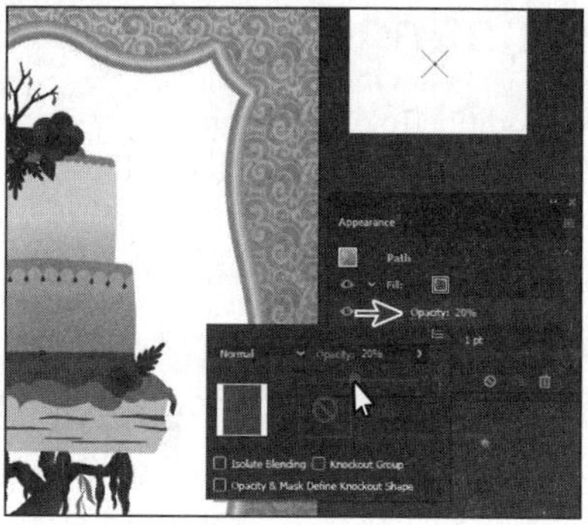

7 Close the Appearance panel.

8 Choose Object > Lock > Selection and then choose File > Save.

Creating your own pattern

In this section, you'll create your own custom pattern. Patterns you create are saved as a swatch in the Swatches panel for the document you're working in.

1 With nothing selected, click the Next Artboard button in the Properties panel to show the smaller artboard on the right.

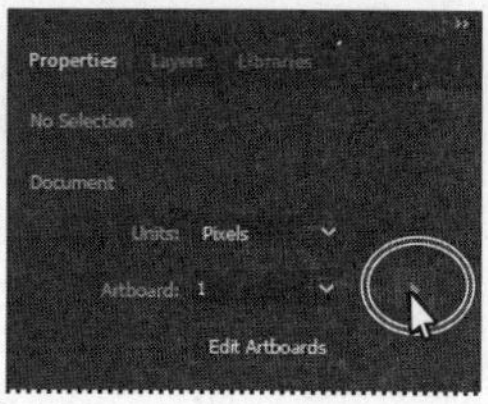

2 With the Selection tool (▶) selected, choose Select > All On Active Artboard to select the artwork you'll use to create a pattern.

3 Choose Object > Pattern > Make. Click OK in the dialog box that appears.

● **Note:** You don't need to have anything selected when you create a pattern. You can add content to the pattern when you edit it in Pattern Editing mode, as you'll see.

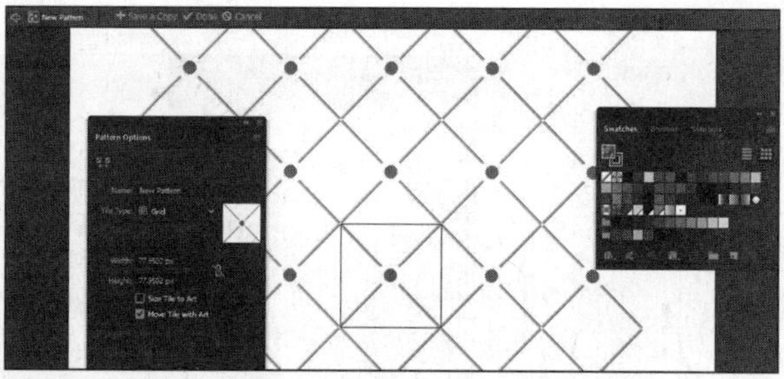

When you create a pattern, Illustrator enters Pattern Editing mode, which is similar to the Isolation mode you've worked with in previous lessons. Pattern Editing mode allows you to create and edit patterns interactively, while previewing the changes to the pattern on the artboard. All other artwork is dimmed and cannot be edited while in this mode. The Pattern Options panel (Window > Pattern Options) also opens, giving you all the necessary options to create your pattern.

4 Choose Select > All On Active Artboard to select the artwork.

5 Press Command++ (macOS) or Ctrl++ (Windows) to zoom in.

The series of lighter-colored objects around the artwork in the center are the pattern repeat. They are there for a preview and are a little dimmed to let you focus on the original. The blue box around the original group of objects is the *pattern tile* (the area that repeats).

> **Note:** A pattern can be composed of shapes, symbols, or embedded raster images, among other objects that you can add in Pattern Editing mode. For instance, to create a flannel pattern for a shirt, you can create three overlapping rectangles or lines, each with varying appearance options.

6 In the Pattern Options panel, change the Name to **Cake Top**, and try choosing different options from the Tile Type menu to see the effect on the pattern. Before continuing, make sure Grid is selected.

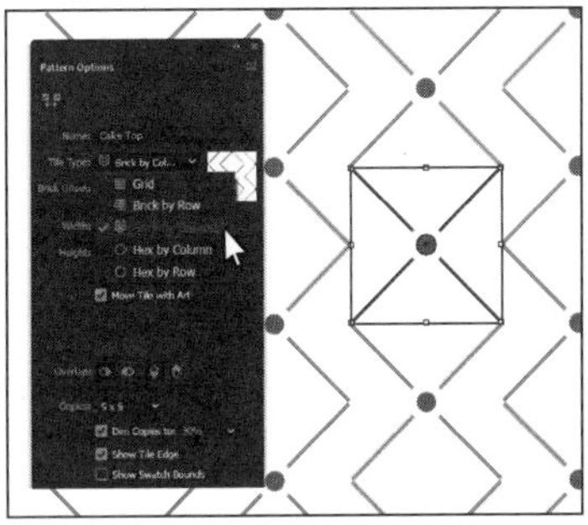

The name in the Pattern Options panel becomes the name of the swatch saved in the Swatches panel and can be useful to distinguish multiple versions of a pattern swatch, for instance. Tile Type determines how the pattern is tiled. You have three main Tile Type choices: the default grid pattern, a brick-style pattern, or the hex pattern.

7 Choose 1 x 1 from the Copies menu at the bottom of the Pattern Options panel. This will remove the repeat and let you temporarily focus on the main pattern artwork.

8 Click in a blank area to deselect the artwork.

9 Option+Shift-drag (macOS) or Alt+Shift-drag (Windows) the blue circle in the center to a little outside the upper-right corner of the blue pattern tile box.

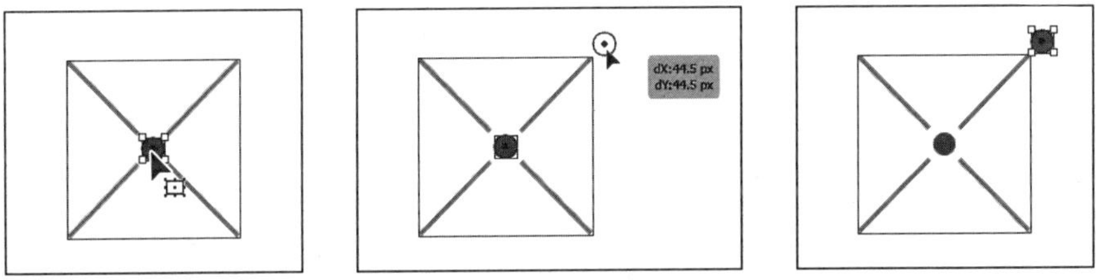

> **Tip:** The H Spacing and V Spacing values can be either positive or negative values, and they move the tiles apart or bring them closer together, either horizontally (H) or vertically (V).

10 In the Pattern Options panel, change the following options:

- Choose 5 x 5 from the Copies menu to see the repeat again.

Notice that the circle you dragged outside of the pattern tile is not repeated. That's because it's not within the pattern tile. Only artwork within the pattern tile is repeated.

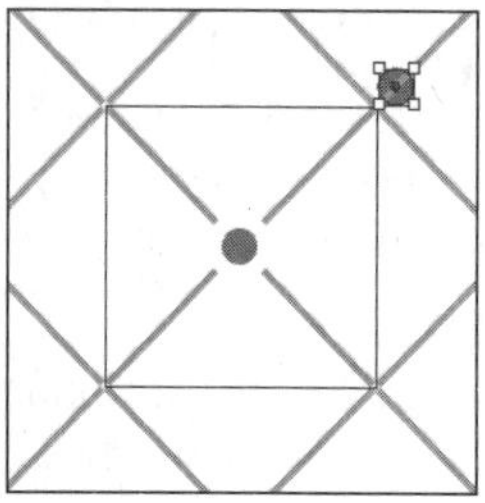

- Select the Size Tile To Art option in the Pattern Options panel.

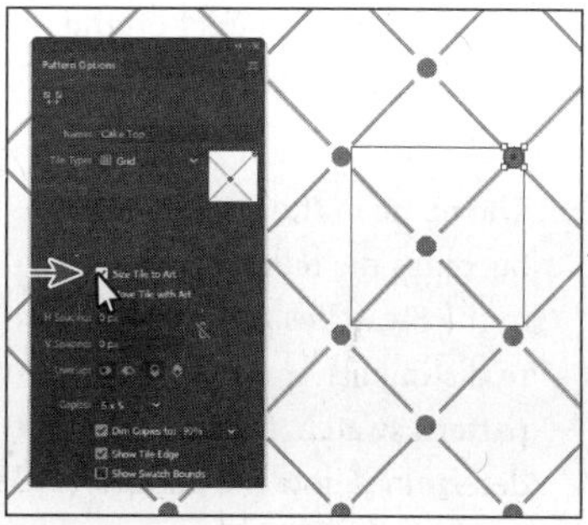

The Size Tile To Art selection fits the tile area (the blue square) to the bounds of the artwork, changing the spacing between the repeated objects. With Size Tile To Art deselected, you could manually change the width and the height of the pattern definition area in the Width and Height fields to include more content or to edit the spacing between. You can also edit the tile area manually with the Pattern Tile Tool button ( ) in the upper-left corner of the Pattern Options panel.

> **Note:** To learn more about the Pattern Options panel, search for "Create and edit patterns" in Illustrator Help (Help > Illustrator Help).

If you set the spacing values (H Spacing or V Spacing) to negative values, the artwork in the pattern tile will overlap. By default, when objects overlap horizontally, the left object is on top; when objects overlap vertically, the top object is on top. You can set the overlap values: Left In Front, Right In Front to change overlap horizontally or Top In Front, Bottom In Front to change the overlap vertically.

> **Tip:** If you want to create pattern variations, you can click Save A Copy in the bar along the top of the Document window when in Pattern Editing mode. This saves the current pattern in the Swatches panel as a copy and allows you to continue creating.

11 Click Done in the bar along the top of the Document window. If a dialog box appears, click OK.

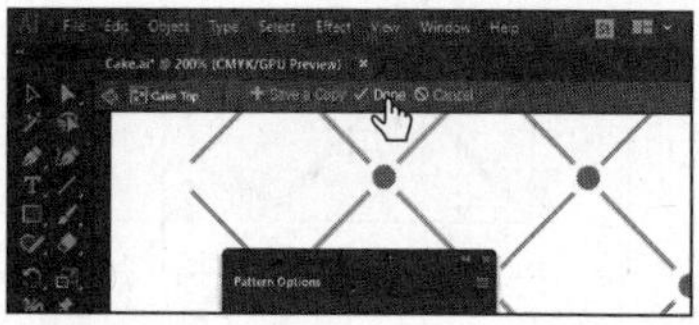

12 Choose File > Save.

Applying your pattern

You can assign a pattern using a number of different methods. In this section, you'll apply your pattern using the fill color in the Properties panel.

1 With nothing selected, click the Previous Artboard button (◀) in the Properties panel to show the larger artboard on the left.

2 With the Selection tool (▶), click the top cake shape (see the following figure). Choose Edit > Copy and then Edit > Paste In Front.

3 Select the swatch named "Cake Top" from the fill color in the Properties panel.

Note: Instead of making a copy of the shape, you could have applied a second fill to the shape like you did previously.

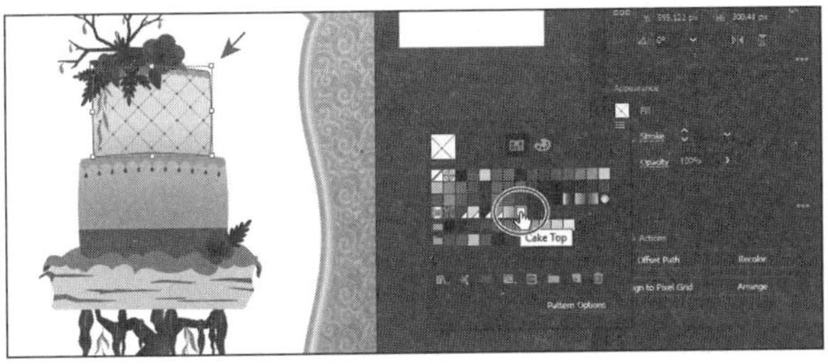

Editing your pattern

Next, you'll edit the Cake Top pattern swatch in Pattern Editing mode.

1 With the shape still selected, click the Fill color in the Properties panel. Double-click the Cake Top pattern swatch to edit it in Pattern Editing mode.

2 Press Command++ (macOS) or Ctrl++ (Windows) several times to zoom in.

3 In Pattern Editing mode, with the Selection tool (▶) selected, click one of the blue circles; then pressing the Shift key, click to select the other.

4 In the Properties panel, change the fill color to the brown swatch named "BG."

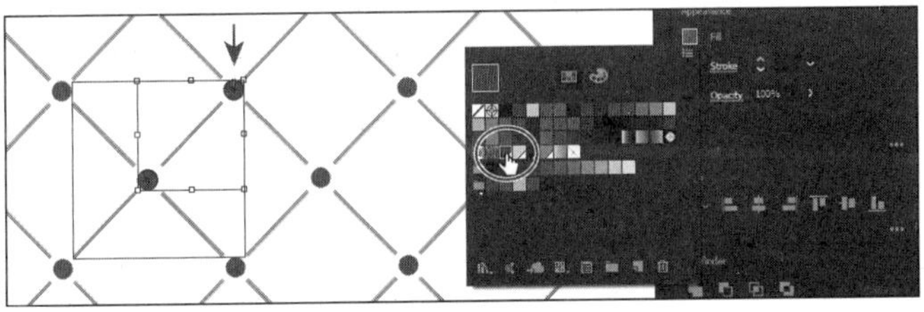

5 Click Done in the gray bar along the top of the Document window to exit Pattern Editing mode.

6 Choose View > Fit Artboard In Window.

7 Click the top cake shape with the pattern fill to select it, if necessary.

▶ **Tip:** In the Scale dialog box, if you wanted to scale the pattern *and* the shape, you can select Transform Objects and select Transform Patterns. You can also transform patterns in the Transform panel (Window > Transform) by choosing Transform Pattern Only, Transform Object Only, or Transform Both from the panel menu (☰) before applying a transformation.

8 With the shape selected, double-click the Scale tool (⤢) in the Tools panel to scale the pattern but not the shape. In the Scale dialog box, change the following options (if not already set):

- Uniform Scale: **50%**
- Scale Corners: **Deselected** (the default setting)
- Scale Strokes & Effects: **Deselected** (the default setting)
- Transform Objects: **Deselected**
- Transform Patterns: **Selected**

9 Select Preview to see the change. Click OK.

10 Choose Object > Show All.

11 Choose Select > Deselect and then choose File > Save.

12 Choose File > Close.

Review questions

1 What is a *gradient*?

2 How do you adjust the blend between colors in a gradient?

3 Name two ways you can add colors to a gradient.

4 How can you adjust the direction of a gradient?

5 What is the difference between a gradient and a blend?

6 When you save a pattern in Illustrator, where is it saved?

Review answers

1 A gradient is a graduated blend of two or more colors or of tints of the same color. Gradients can be applied to the stroke or fill of an object.

2 To adjust the blend between colors in a gradient, with the Gradient tool (■) selected and with the pointer over the gradient annotator or in the Gradient panel, you can drag the diamond icons or the color stops of the gradient slider.

3 To add colors to a gradient, in the Gradient panel, click beneath the gradient slider to add a gradient stop to the gradient. Then, double-click the color stop to edit the color, using the panel that appears to mix a new color or to apply an existing color swatch. You can select the Gradient tool in the Tools panel, position the pointer over the gradient-filled object, and then click beneath the gradient slider that appears in the artwork to add a color stop.

4 Drag with the Gradient tool to adjust the direction of a gradient. Dragging a long distance changes colors gradually; dragging a short distance makes the color change more abrupt. You can also rotate the gradient using the Gradient tool and change the radius, aspect ratio, starting point, and more.

5 The difference between a gradient and a blend is the way that colors combine together—colors blend together within a gradient and between objects in a blend.

6 When you save a pattern in Illustrator, it is saved as a swatch in the Swatches panel. By default, swatches are saved with the currently active document.

11 USING BRUSHES TO CREATE A POSTER

Lesson overview

In this lesson, you'll learn how to do the following:

- Use four brush types: Calligraphic, Art, Bristle, and Pattern.
- Apply brushes to paths.
- Paint and edit paths with the Paintbrush tool.
- Create an Art brush from a raster image.
- Change brush color and adjust brush settings.
- Create new brushes from Adobe Illustrator artwork.
- Work with the Blob Brush tool and the Eraser tool.

This lesson takes approximately 60 minutes to complete. Please log in to your account on peachpit.com to download the lesson files for this chapter, or go to the "Getting Started" section at the beginning of this book and follow the instructions under "Accessing the lesson files and Web Edition."

Your Account page is also where you'll find any updates to the chapters or to the lesson files. Look on the Lesson & Update Files tab to access the most current content.

The variety of brush types in Adobe Illustrator CC lets you create a myriad of effects simply by painting or drawing using the Paintbrush tool or the drawing tools. You can work with the Blob Brush tool; choose from the Art, Calligraphic, Pattern, Bristle, or Scatter brushes; or create new brushes based on your artwork.

Starting the lesson

In this lesson, you will learn how to work with the different brush types in the Brushes panel and how to change brush options and create your own brushes. Before you begin, you'll restore the default preferences for Adobe Illustrator CC. Then you'll open the finished art file for the lesson to see the finished artwork.

● **Note:** If you have not already downloaded the project files for this lesson to your computer from your Account page, make sure to do so now. See the "Getting Started" section at the beginning of the book.

1 To ensure that the tools function and the defaults are set exactly as described in this lesson, delete or deactivate (by renaming) the Adobe Illustrator CC preferences file. See "Restoring default preferences" in the "Getting Started" section at the beginning of the book.

2 Start Adobe Illustrator CC.

3 Choose File > Open. In the Open dialog box, navigate to the Lessons > Lesson11 folder, and select the L11_end.ai file on your hard disk. Click Open to open the file.

4 If you want, choose View > Zoom Out to make the finished artwork smaller and then adjust the window size and leave the artwork on your screen as you work. (Use the Hand tool [✋] to move the artwork to where you want it in the Document window.) If you don't want to leave the artwork open, choose File > Close.

To begin working, you'll open an existing art file.

5 Choose File > Open. In the Open dialog box, navigate to the Lessons > Lesson11 folder, and select the L11_start.ai file on your hard disk. Click Open to open the file.

6 Choose View > Fit Artboard In Window.

7 Choose File > Save As. In the Save As dialog box, name the file **CruisePoster.ai**, and select the Lesson11 folder. Leave the Format option set to Adobe Illustrator (ai) (macOS) or the Save As Type option set to Adobe Illustrator (*.AI) (Windows) and then click Save.

● **Note:** If you don't see Reset Essentials in the workspace switcher menu, choose Window > Workspace > Essentials before choosing Window > Workspace > Reset Essentials.

8 In the Illustrator Options dialog box, leave the Illustrator options at their default settings and then click OK.

9 Choose Reset Essentials from the workspace switcher in the Application bar to reset the workspace.

Working with brushes

Using brushes you can decorate paths with patterns, figures, brush strokes, textures, or angled strokes. You can modify the brushes provided with Illustrator and create your own brushes.

You can apply brush strokes to existing paths, or you can use the Paintbrush tool to draw a path and apply a brush stroke simultaneously. You can change the color, size, and other features of a brush, and you can edit paths after brushes are applied (including adding a fill).

Types of brushes

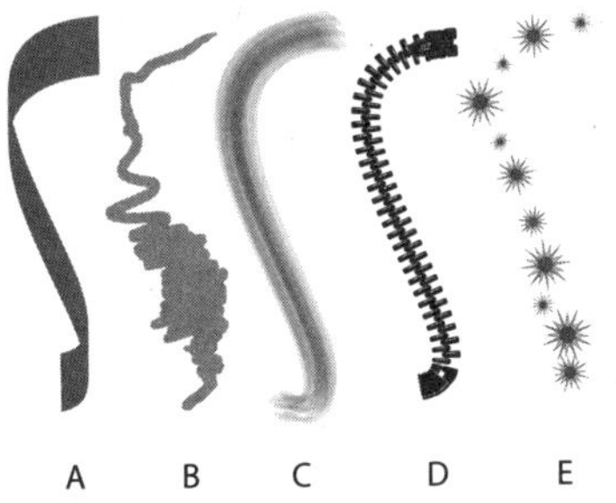

A. Calligraphic brush
B. Art brush
C. Bristle brush
D. Pattern brush
E. Scatter brush

There are five types of brushes that appear in the Brushes panel (Window > Brushes): Calligraphic, Art, Bristle, Pattern, and Scatter. In this lesson, you will discover how to work with all of these except for the Scatter brush.

▶ **Tip:** To learn more about Scatter brushes, search for "Scatter brushes" in Illustrator Help (Help > Illustrator Help).

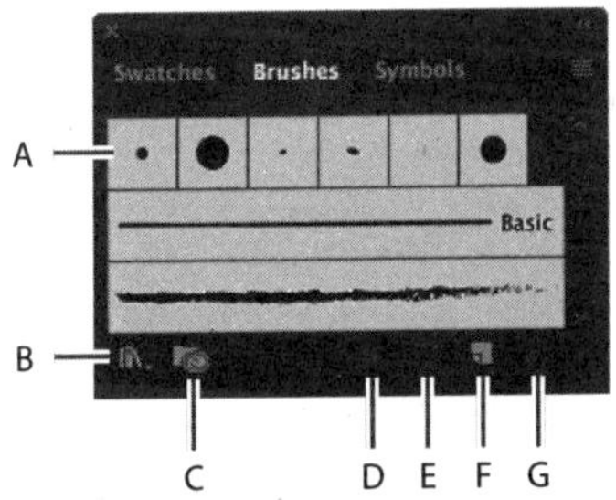

A. Brushes
B. Brush Libraries Menu
C. Libraries panel
D. Remove Brush Stroke
E. Options of selected object
F. New Brush
G. Delete Brush

Using Calligraphic brushes

The first type of brush you'll learn about is a Calligraphic brush. Calligraphic brushes resemble strokes drawn with the angled point of a calligraphic pen. Calligraphic brushes are defined by an elliptical shape whose center follows the path, and you can use these brushes to create the appearance of hand-drawn strokes made with a flat, angled pen tip.

Calligraphic brush examples

Applying a Calligraphic brush to artwork

To get started, you'll filter the type of brushes shown in the Brushes panel so that it shows only Calligraphic brushes.

1 Choose Window > Brushes to show the Brushes panel. Click the Brushes panel menu icon (▤), and choose List View.

Note: A checkmark next to the brush type in the Brushes panel menu indicates that the brush type is visible in the panel.

2 Click the Brushes panel menu icon (▤) again, and deselect Show Art Brushes, Show Bristle Brushes, and Show Pattern Brushes, leaving only the Calligraphic brushes visible in the Brushes panel. You can't deselect them all at once, so you'll have to keep clicking the menu icon (▤) to access the menu.

3 Select the Selection tool (▶) in the Tools panel, and Shift-click both of the two curved pink paths above the orange/yellow shape of a ship to select both of them.

4 Select the 5 pt. Flat brush in the Brushes panel to apply it to the pink paths.

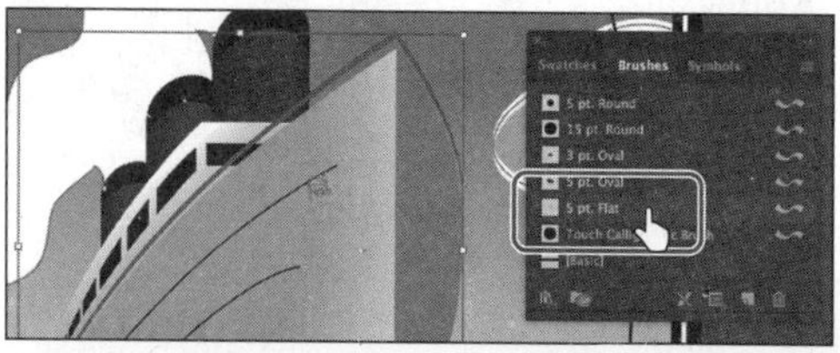

Note: Like drawing with an actual calligraphic pen, when you apply a Calligraphic brush, such as the 5 pt. Flat brush, the more vertically the path is drawn, the thinner the path's stroke appears.

5 Change the Stroke weight to **6 pt** in the Properties panel. Click the Stroke color in the Properties panel, make sure the Swatches option (▦) is selected, and select White. Press the Escape key to hide the Swatches panel, if necessary.

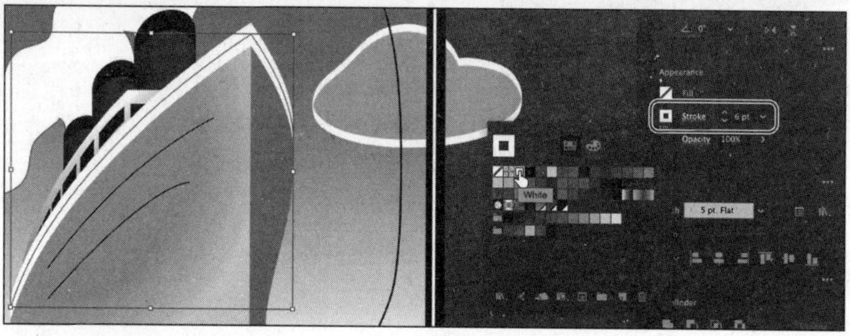

6 Choose Select > Deselect.

7 With the Selection tool, click the smaller of the white paths (an arrow is pointing to it in the figure) that you just applied the brush to. Change the stroke color to a light gray in the Properties panel (I chose the color with the tooltip value "C=0, M=0, Y=0, K=10").

8 Choose Select > Deselect and then choose File > Save.

Drawing with the Paintbrush tool

As mentioned earlier, the Paintbrush tool allows you to apply a brush as you paint. Painting with the Paintbrush tool creates vector paths that you can edit with the Paintbrush tool or other drawing tools. Next, you'll use the Paintbrush tool to paint waves in the water with a calligraphic brush from a default brush library. Your waves won't look identical to what you see in the lesson, and that's okay—*just have some fun.*

1 With the Selection tool (▶), click the darker blue water shape below the ship.

2 Choose Select > Deselect.

The water shape is on a sublayer behind the ship. Selecting the water shape selects that sublayer in the Layers panel, which means that all of the waves you create will also be on the same sublayer as the water shape.

3 Select the Paintbrush tool (🖌) in the Tools panel.

4 Click the Brush Libraries Menu button (▥) at the bottom of the Brushes panel, and choose Artistic > Artistic_Calligraphic. A brush library panel with various brushes appears.

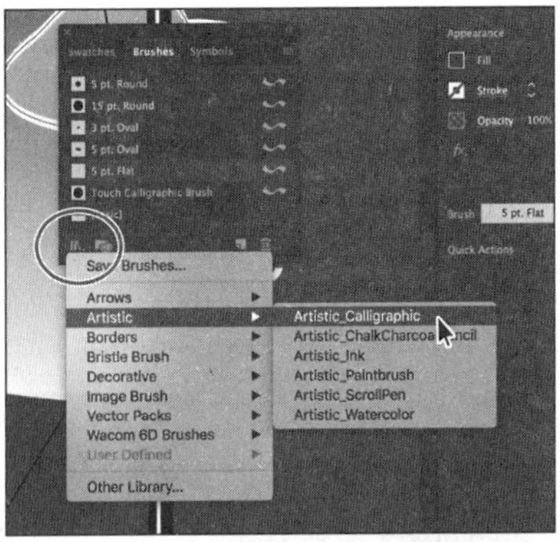

Illustrator comes with a host of brush libraries that you can use in your artwork. Each of the brush types discussed previously has a series of libraries to choose from.

5 Click the Artistic_Calligraphic panel menu icon (▤), and choose List View. Click the brush named "50 pt. Flat" to add it to the Brushes panel.

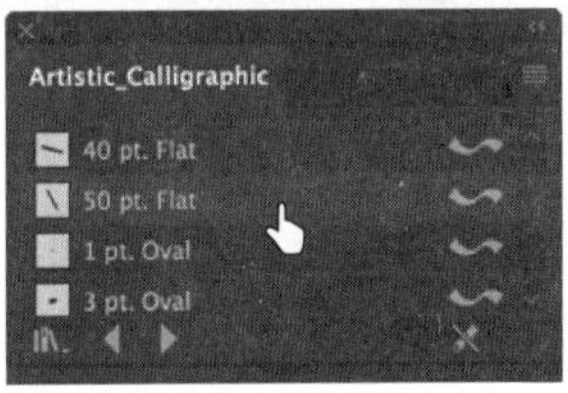

6 Close the Artistic_Calligraphic brush library.

Selecting a brush from a brush library, such as the Artistic_Calligraphic library, adds that brush to the Brushes panel for the active document only.

7 Change the fill color to None (☒), the stroke color to the swatch named "Dark Blue," and the stroke weight to **1 pt** (if necessary) in the Properties panel.

Notice that the Paintbrush pointer has an asterisk next to it (🖌*), indicating that you are about to paint a new path.

Note: This Calligraphic brush creates random angles on the paths, so yours may not look like what you see in the figures, and that's okay.

8 Position the pointer off the left side of the artboard, just below the ship. Paint a long, curving path from left to right, stopping about halfway across the water (see the figure). Try creating three more paths, painting from left to right, going all the way across the water. You can see the figure for ideas on how I painted.

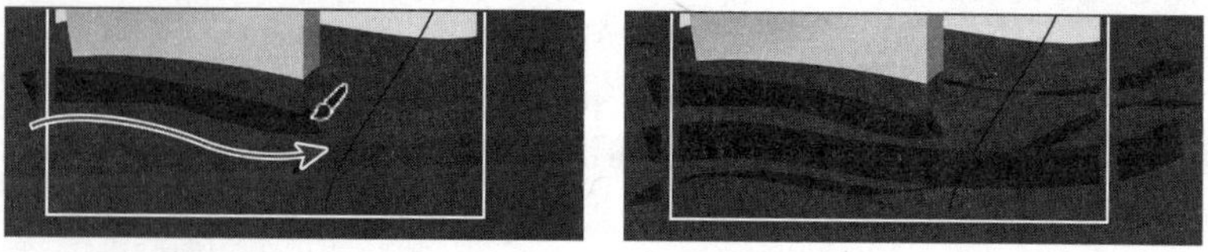

9 Choose Select > Deselect (if necessary) and then choose File > Save.

Editing paths with the Paintbrush tool

Now you'll use the Paintbrush tool to edit one of the paths you painted.

1 Select the Selection tool (▶) in the Tools panel, and click to select the first path you drew on the water (the one that is just below the bottom of the ship).

Tip: You can also edit paths drawn with the Paintbrush tool using the Smooth tool (✐) and the Path Eraser tool (✐), located under the Pencil tool (✐) in the Tools panel.

2 Select the Paintbrush tool (✐) in the Tools panel. Position the pointer near the right end of the selected path. An asterisk *will not* appear next to the pointer when it's positioned over a selected path. Drag to the right to extend the path all the way to the right edge of the artboard. The selected path is edited from the point where you began drawing.

3 Press and hold the Command (macOS) or Ctrl (Windows) key to toggle to the Selection tool, and click to select another curved path you drew with the Paintbrush tool. After clicking, release the key to return to the Paintbrush tool.

4 With the Paintbrush tool, move the pointer over some part of the selected path. When the asterisk disappears next to the pointer, drag to the right to redraw the path.

5 Choose Select > Deselect (if necessary) and then choose File > Save.

Next, you will edit the Paintbrush tool options.

6 Double-click the Paintbrush tool (🖌) in the Tools panel to display the Paintbrush Tool Options dialog box, and make the following changes:

- Fidelity: Drag the slider all the way to Smooth (to the right).
- Keep Selected: **Selected**.

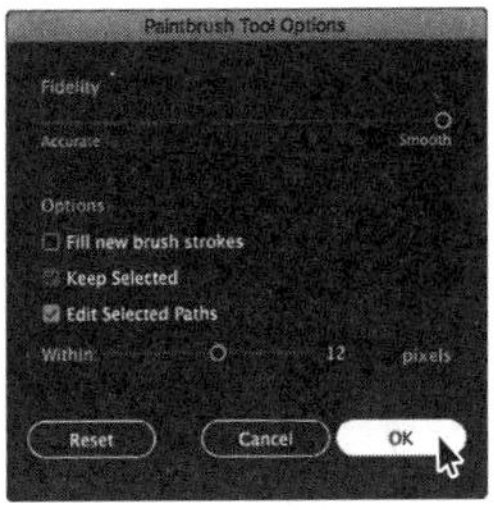

7 Click OK.

The Paintbrush Tool Options dialog box changes the way the Paintbrush tool functions. For the Fidelity option, the closer to Smooth you drag the slider, the smoother the path will be with fewer points. Also, because you selected Keep Selected, the paths remain selected after you finish drawing them.

8 Change the stroke color to the swatch named "Medium Blue," and change the stroke weight to **0.5 pt** in the Properties panel.

9 With the Paintbrush tool selected, paint three or four more paths from either left to right or right to left across the water shape below the ship.

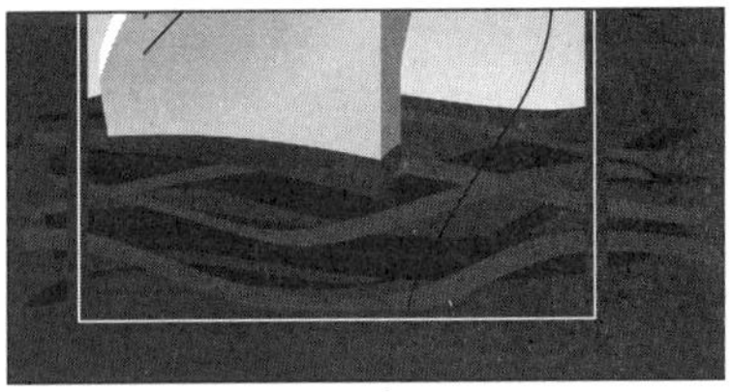

Notice that after painting each path, the path is still selected, so you could edit it if you needed. I already deselected in the figure.

10 Double-click the Paintbrush tool in the Tools panel. In the Paintbrush Tool Options dialog box, deselect the Keep Selected option, and then click OK.

Now the paths will *not* remain selected after you finish drawing them, and you can draw overlapping paths without altering previously drawn paths.

11 Choose Select > Deselect and then choose File > Save.

Note: When the Keep Selected option is deselected, you can edit a path by selecting it with the Selection tool (▶) or by selecting a segment or point on the path with the Direct Selection tool (▷) and then redrawing part of the path with the Paintbrush tool, like you saw previously.

Editing a brush

To change the options for a brush, you can double-click the brush in the Brushes panel. When you edit a brush, you can also choose whether to change artwork to which the brush has been applied. Next, you'll change the appearance of the 50 pt. Flat brush you've been painting with.

1 In the Brushes panel, double-click the brush thumbnail to the left of the text "50 pt. Flat" or to the right of the name in the Brushes panel to open the Calligraphic Brush Options dialog box.

Note: The edits you make will change the brush for this document only.

▶ **Tip:** The Preview window in the dialog box (below the Name field) shows the changes that you make to the brush.

2 In the dialog box, make the following changes:
- Name: **30 pt. Flat**
- Angle: **0°**
- Choose Fixed from the menu to the right of Angle. (When Random is chosen, a random variation of brush angles is created every time you draw.)
- Roundness: **5%** (the default setting)
- Size: **30 pt**

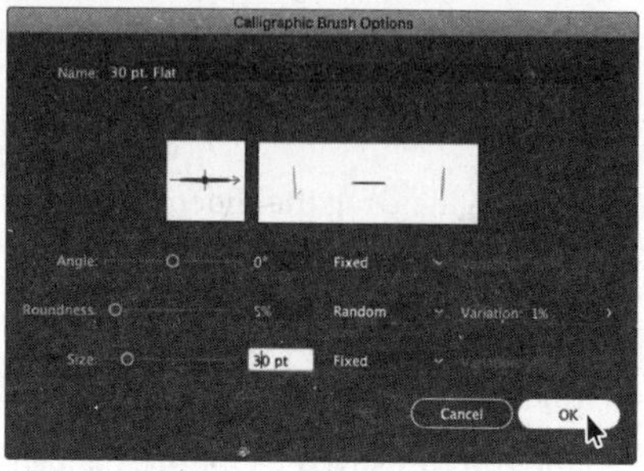

3 Click OK.

4 In the dialog box that appears, click Leave Strokes so as not to apply the brush change to the existing waves that have the brush applied.

5 Change the stroke color to the swatch named "Light Blue," and change the stroke weight to **1 pt** in the Properties panel.

6 Click the 30 pt. Flat brush in the Brushes panel to ensure that you will paint with it applied. With the Paintbrush tool (🖌) selected, paint three paths across the water to create more waves, overlapping the existing waves.

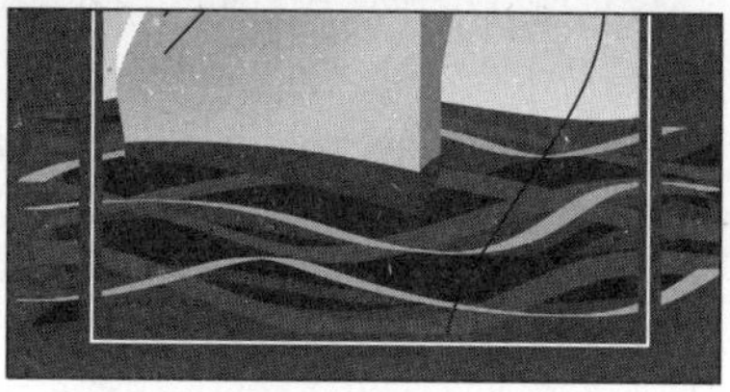

● **Note:** The artwork should be deselected already, and, if it is, the Deselect command will be dimmed (you can't select it).

7 Choose Select > Deselect, if necessary, and then choose File > Save.

Removing a brush stroke

You can easily remove a brush stroke applied to artwork where you don't want it. Now you'll remove the brush stroke on the cloud.

1 Select the Selection tool (▶), and click the blue cloud with the white stroke.

● **Note:** The figure shows the result of clicking the Remove Brush Stroke button.

2 Click the Remove Brush Stroke button (☒) at the bottom of the Brushes panel.

Removing a brush stroke doesn't remove the stroke color and weight; it just removes the brush applied.

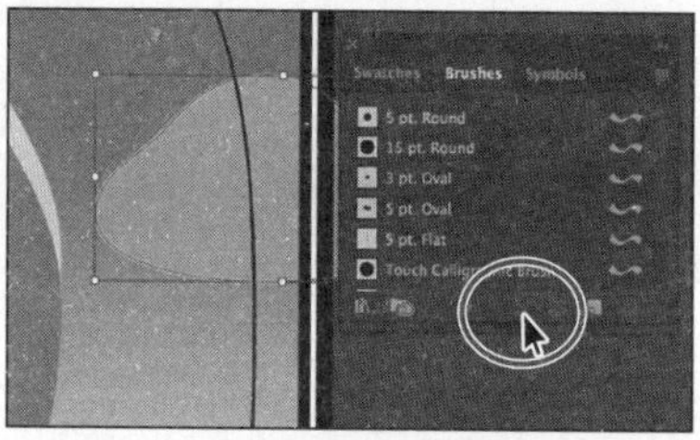

3 Change the stroke weight to **0 pt** in the Properties panel.

4 Choose Select > Deselect and then choose File > Save.

Using Art brushes

Art brushes stretch artwork or an embedded raster image evenly along the length of a path. As with other brushes, you can edit the brush options to affect how the brush is applied to artwork.

Art brush examples

Applying an existing Art brush

Next, you'll apply an existing Art brush to waves at the front of the boat.

1 In the Brushes panel, click the Brushes panel menu icon (), and deselect Show Calligraphic Brushes. Then select Show Art Brushes from the same panel menu to make the art brushes visible in the Brushes panel.

2 Click the Brush Libraries Menu button () at the bottom of the Brushes panel, and choose Artistic > Artistic_Paintbrush.

3 Click the Artistic_Paintbrush panel menu icon (), and choose List View. Click the brush named "Brush 3" in the list to add the brush to the Brushes panel for this document. Close the Artistic_Paintbrush panel group.

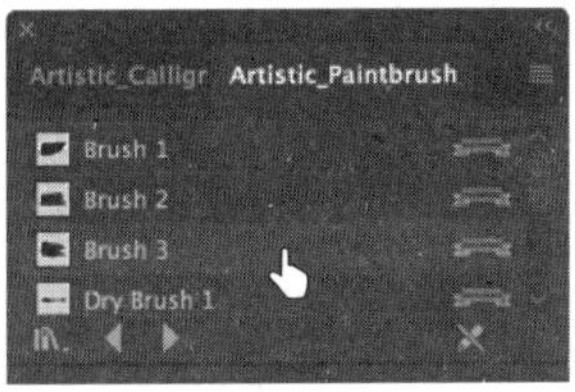

4 Select the Paintbrush tool () in the Tools panel.

5 Change the fill color to None (), the stroke color to White (if necessary), and the stroke weight to **1 pt** (if necessary) in the Properties panel.

6 Click the Layers panel tab on the right side of the workspace to open the Layers panel. Click the Spray/Tree sublayer so that the new artwork is on that layer. Click the Properties panel tab to show that panel again.

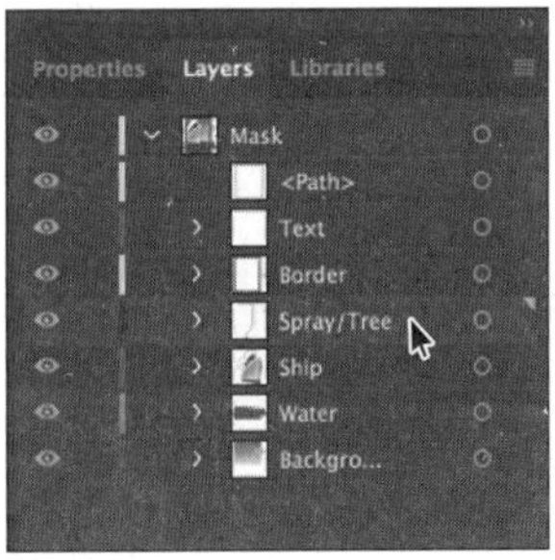

7 Position the Paintbrush pointer () at the bottom front of the ship in the red area (marked with an X in the following figure). Drag to the left along the bottom of the red strip on the ship, just along the water line. See the figure for how I painted it, and don't worry about being exact. You can always choose Edit > Undo Art Stroke and repaint the path.

Tip: With the Paintbrush pointer selected, press the Caps Lock key to see a precise cursor (X). In certain situations, this can help to paint with more precision.

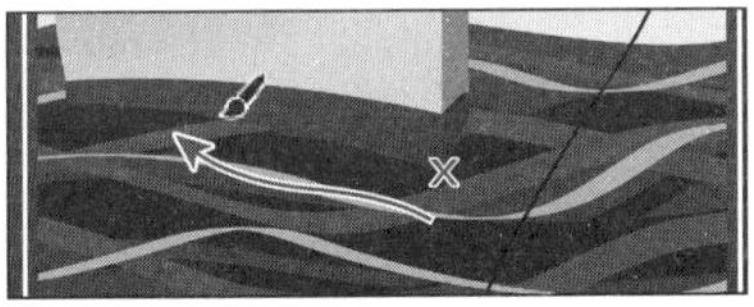

8 Paint a path from the same starting point (the red X in the *previous* figure), but drag to the right this time.

9 Paint a "U" shape from left to right to cover any red showing. See the figure—start at the X in the figure for the "U" shape.

10 Try adding a few more painted paths, always starting from the same point as the original path you painted.

11 Choose File > Save.

Creating an Art brush using a raster image

● **Note:** To learn about guidelines for creating brushes, see "Create or modify brushes" in Illustrator Help (Help > Illustrator Help).

● **Note:** You may need to click the Options button on macOS to see the Link option.

In this section, you'll place a raster image and embed it so you can create a new Art brush from it. Images you use in an art brush cannot be linked.

1 Choose File > Place. In the Place dialog box, navigate to the Lesson11 folder, and select the image named tree.psd. Make sure to deselect the Link option. Click Place.

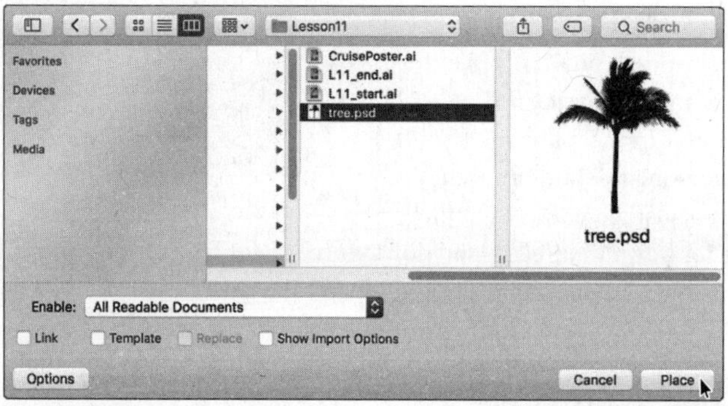

2 Move the pointer off of the right edge of the artboard. Click to place the image.

Next, you'll make an Art brush from the selected artwork. You can make an Art brush from vector artwork or from embedded raster images, but that artwork must not contain gradients, blends, other brush strokes, mesh objects, graphs, linked files, masks, or text that has not been converted to outlines.

● **Note:** When dealing with embedded images and brushes, there is a direct impact on the performance of the document in Illustrator. There is a fixed limit to the size of the embedded image that can be used for a brush. You may see a dialog box telling you that the image needs to be resampled before you can make a brush from it.

3 Select the Selection tool (▶). Choose Window > Brushes to open the Brushes panel, if it isn't open already. With the placed image still selected, click the New Brush button (◼) at the bottom of the Brushes panel. This begins the process of creating a new brush from the selected raster artwork.

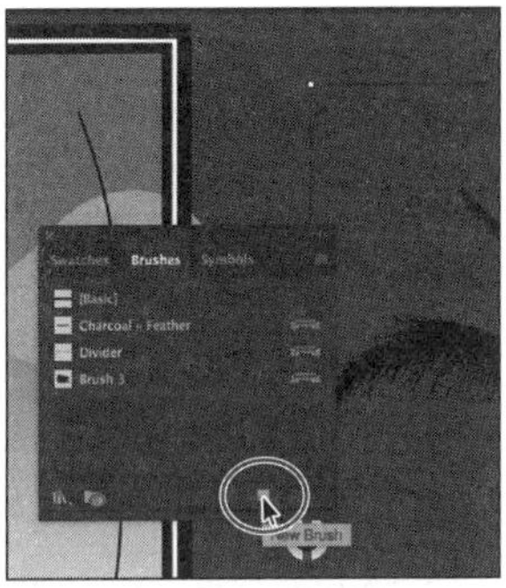

4 In the New Brush dialog box, select Art Brush and then click OK.

5 In the Art Brush Options dialog box that appears, change the name to **Palm Tree**. Click OK.

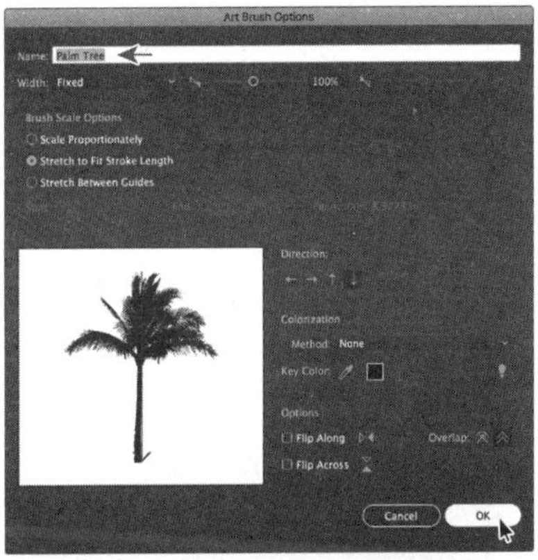

6 Delete the image you placed off the right side of the artboard since you don't need it anymore.

7 With the Selection tool selected, click to select the curved black line to the right of the ship.

8 Click the brush named "Palm Tree" in the Brushes panel to apply it.

Notice that the original tree image is stretched along the path. This is the default behavior of an Art brush.

Editing an Art brush

Next, you'll edit the Palm Tree Art brush and update the appearance of the palm tree on the artboard.

▶ **Tip:** To learn more about the Art Brush Options dialog box, see "Art brush options" in Illustrator Help (Help > Illustrator Help).

1 With the curved path still selected on the artboard, double-click the brush thumbnail to the left of the text "Palm tree" or to the right of the name in the Brushes panel to open the Art Brush Options dialog box.

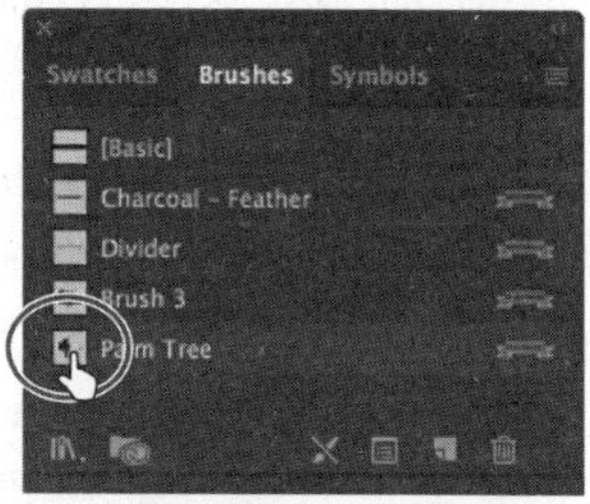

2 In the Art Brush Options dialog box, select Preview to see the changes as you make them, and move the dialog box so you can see the curvy line with the brush applied. Make the following changes:

- Stretch Between Guides: Selected
- Start: **5 in**
- End: **6 in**
- Flip Across: **Selected**

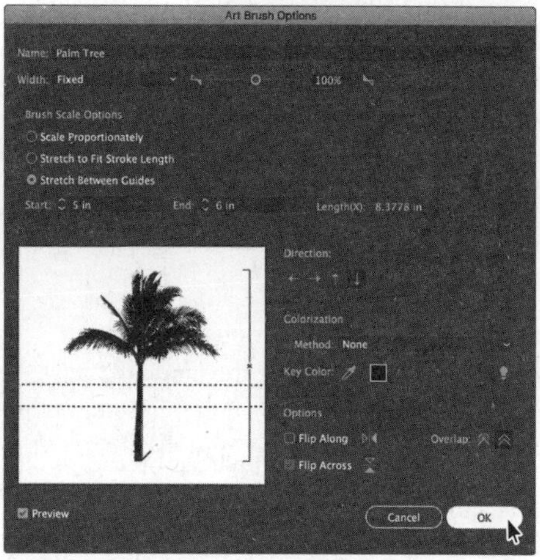

3 Click OK.

4 In the dialog box that appears, click Apply To Strokes to apply the change to the curvy line that has the Palm Tree brush applied.

5 Click the word "Opacity" in the Properties panel, and choose Multiply from the Blend Mode menu. Press Enter or Return to close the Transparency panel.

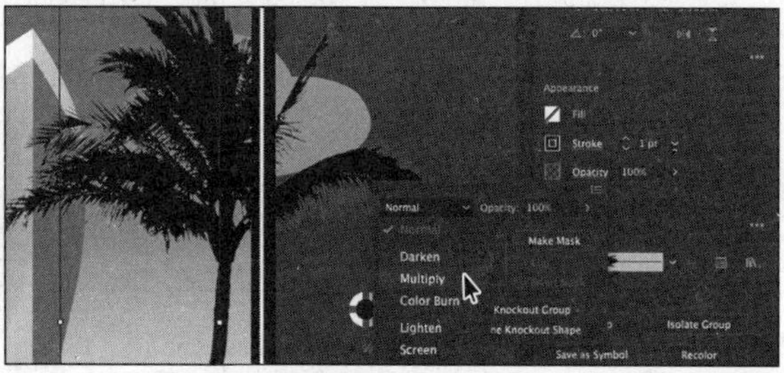

6 Choose Select > Deselect and then choose File > Save.

Using Bristle brushes

Bristle brushes allow you to create strokes with the appearance of a natural brush with bristles. Painting with a Bristle brush, using the Paintbrush tool, creates vector paths with the Bristle brush applied.

In this section, you'll start by adjusting options for a brush to change how it appears in the artwork and then paint with the Paintbrush tool and a Bristle brush to create smoke.

Bristle brush examples

Changing Bristle brush options

As you've seen, you can change the appearance of a brush by adjusting its settings in the Brush Options dialog box, either before or after brushes have been applied to artwork. In the case of Bristle brushes, it's usually best to adjust the brush settings prior to painting since it can take some time to update the brush strokes.

Note: To learn more about the Bristle Brush Options dialog box and its settings, see "Using the Bristle brush" in Illustrator Help (Help > Illustrator Help).

1 In the Brushes panel, click the panel menu icon (), choose Show Bristle Brushes, and then deselect Show Art Brushes.

2 Double-click the thumbnail for the default Mop brush or double-click directly to the right of the brush name in the Brushes panel to change the options for that brush. In the Bristle Brush Options dialog box, make the following changes:

Tip: Illustrator comes with a series of default Bristle brushes. Click the Brush Libraries Menu button () at the bottom of the Brushes panel, and choose Bristle Brush > Bristle Brush Library.

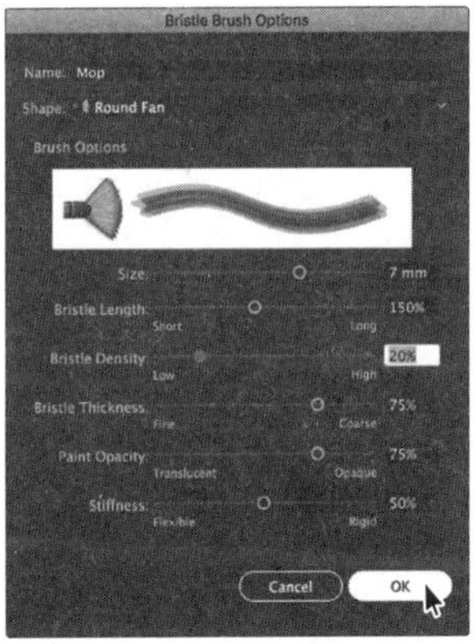

- Shape: **Round Fan** (the default setting)
- Size: **7 mm** (The brush size is the diameter of the brush.)
- Bristle Length: **150%** (the default setting) (The bristle length starts from the point where the bristles meet the handle of the bristle tip.)
- Bristle Density: **20%** (The bristle density is the number of bristles in a specified area of the brush neck.)
- Bristle Thickness: **75%** (the default setting) (The bristle thickness can vary from fine to coarse [between 1% and 100%].)
- Paint Opacity: **75%** (the default setting) (This option lets you set the opacity of the paint being used.)
- Stiffness: **50%** (the default setting) (Stiffness refers to the rigidness of the bristles.)

3 Click OK.

Painting with a Bristle brush

Now you'll use the Mop brush to draw some smoke above the ship. Painting with a Bristle brush can create an organic, fluid path. To constrain the painting, you will paint inside a shape. This will mask (hide) part of the painting to be in the shape of smoke.

1 Select the Zoom tool (🔍) in the Tools panel, and click a few times, slowly, on the smoke shape above the ship (not the cloud) to zoom in on it.

2 Select the Selection tool (▶) in the Tools panel, and click to select the smoke shape. This selects the layer that the shape is on so that any artwork you paint will be on the same layer.

● **Note:** To learn more about the drawing modes, see Lesson 3, "Using Shapes to Create Artwork for a Postcard."

3 Click the Draw Inside button (◙) at the bottom of the Tools panel.

● **Note:** If the Tools panel appears as one column, click the Drawing Modes button (◙) at the bottom of the Tools panel, and then choose Draw Inside from the menu that appears.

4 With the smoke shape still selected, change the fill color to None (☒) in the Properties panel (press the Escape key to hide the Swatches panel). Leave the stroke as is.

5 Choose Select > Deselect to deselect the smoke shape.

The dotted lines on the corners of the shape indicate that any paths you paint will be masked by the smoke shape.

▶ **Tip:** If you want to edit paths as you draw, you can select the Keep Selected option in the Paintbrush Tool Options for the Paintbrush tool or you can select paths with the Selection tool. You don't need to completely fill the shape.

6 Select the Paintbrush tool (🖌) in the Tools panel. Choose the Mop brush from the Brush menu in the Properties panel, if it's not already chosen.

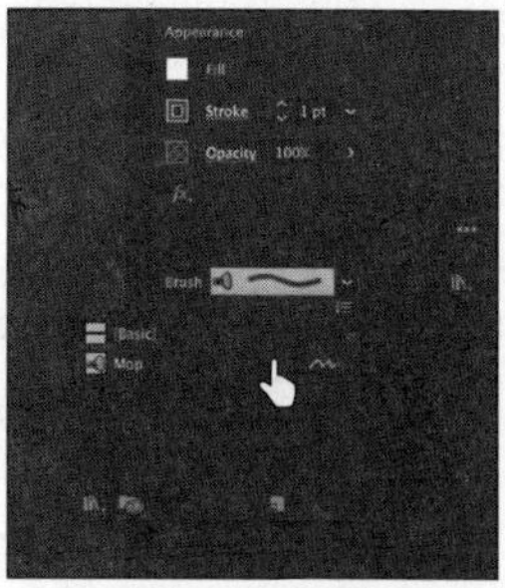

7 Make sure that the fill color is None (☒) and the stroke color is White in the Properties panel. Press the Escape key to hide the Swatches panel. Make sure that the stroke weight is **1 pt** in the Properties panel.

8 Position the pointer at the top of the largest smokestack. (See the red X in the following figure.) Drag up and then down and to the left to loosely follow the edge of the smoke shape. Release the mouse button when you reach the end of the smoke shape.

▶ **Tip:** If you don't like what you just painted, you can choose Edit > Undo Bristle Stroke.

When you release the mouse button, notice that part of the path you just painted is masked (hidden) by the smoke shape.

9 Use the Paintbrush tool to paint more paths inside the smoke shape, using the Mop brush. Try drawing from each of the smokestacks, following the smoke shape. The idea is to fill up the smoke shape with the paths you paint.

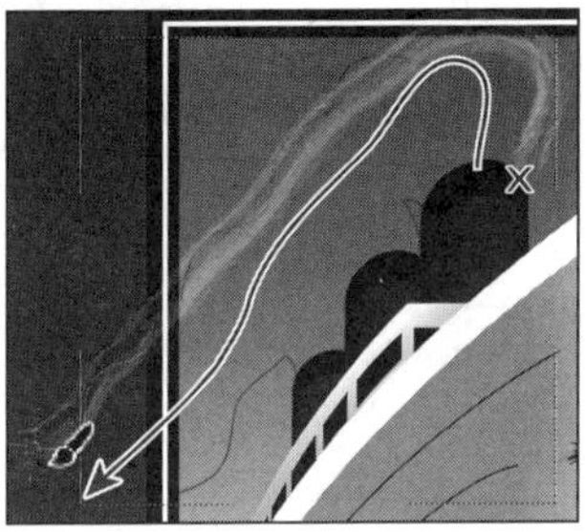

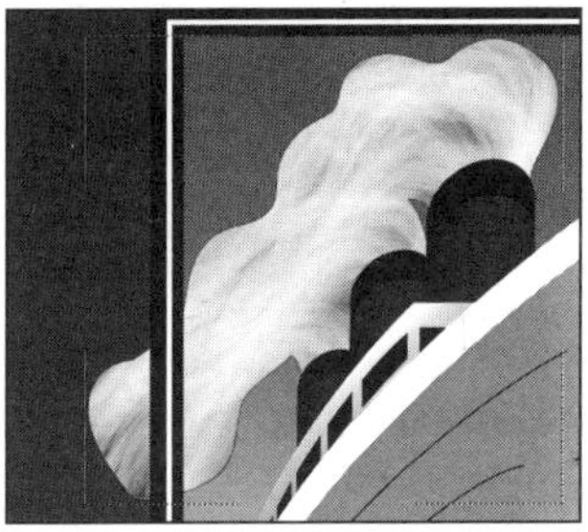

Note: In the first part of the figure, I dimmed the shape paths so you could more easily see the smoke paths.

Cleaning up the shapes

Next, you'll remove the stroke on the smoke shape.

1 Choose View > Outline to see all of the paths you just created when painting.

2 Choose Select > Object > Bristle Brush Strokes to select all of the paths created with the Paintbrush tool using the Mop brush.

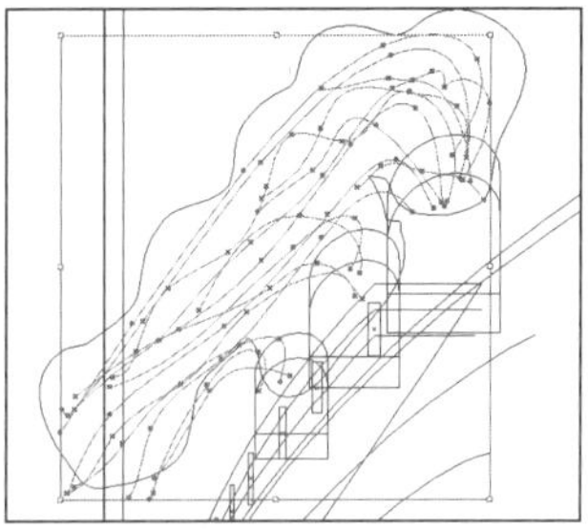

3 Choose Object > Group and then choose View > GPU Preview if supported or View > Preview On CPU if not.

4 Click the Draw Normal button ( ) at the bottom of the Tools panel.

Note: If the Tools panel appears as one column, click the Drawing Modes button at the bottom of the Tools panel and then choose Draw Normal from the menu that appears.

5 Select the Selection tool in the Tools panel. Choose Select > Deselect.

6 Double-click in the smoke shape to enter Isolation mode. Click the edge of the original smoke shape to select it. Change the stroke color to None ( ) in the Properties panel.

Note: Be careful you don't double-click on the path with the Palm Tree brush applied, since it may overlap the smoke shape.

7 Press the Escape key several times to hide the panel and to exit Isolation mode.

Tip: You can also double-click away from the artwork to exit Isolation mode.

8 Click the Layers tab on the right side of the workspace to show the Layers panel. Click the eye icon ( ) to the left of the Spray/Tree sublayer name to hide the artwork on that layer. Click the Properties panel tab to show that panel again.

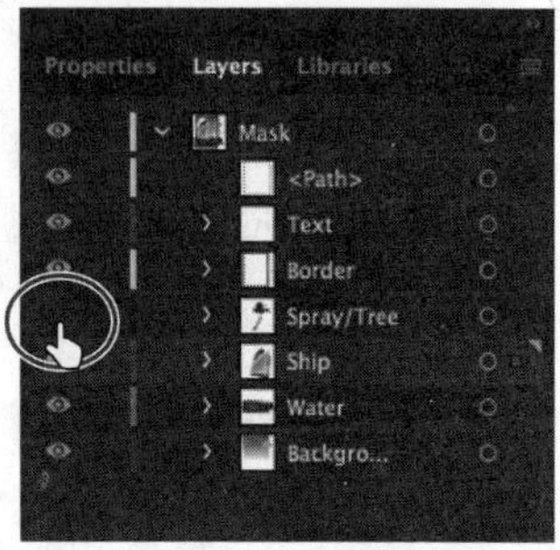

9 Choose Select > Deselect and then choose File > Save.

When saving, you may see a warning dialog box indicating that the document contains multiple Bristle brush paths with transparency. As mentioned earlier, painting with a Bristle brush creates a series of individual vector paths with the brush applied. This can lead to issues with printing or saving to EPS/PDF or legacy versions of Illustrator documents. In order to reduce the complexity and number of the Bristle Brush paths, you can rasterize paths with a Bristle brush applied. Select the path(s) with the Bristle brush applied, and choose Object > Rasterize.

The Bristle brush and graphic tablets

When you use Bristle brush with a graphic tablet, Illustrator interactively tracks the movements of the stylus over the tablet. It interprets all aspects of its orientation and pressure input at any point along a drawing path. Illustrator provides the output that is modeled on the stylus's x-axis position, y-axis position, pressure, tilt, bearing, and rotation.

—From Illustrator Help

Using Pattern brushes

Pattern brushes paint a pattern made up of separate sections, or *tiles*. When you apply a Pattern brush to artwork, different tiles of the pattern are applied to different sections of the path, depending on where the section falls on the path—the end, middle, or corner. There are hundreds of interesting Pattern brushes that you can choose from when creating your own projects, from grass to cityscapes. Next, you'll apply an existing Pattern brush to a path to create windows on the ship.

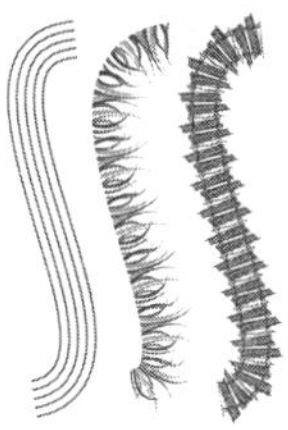
Pattern brush examples

1 Choose View > Fit Artboard In Window.

2 In the Brushes panel, click the panel menu icon (▤), choose Show Pattern Brushes, and then deselect Show Bristle Brushes.

The brush named "Windows" that appears in the Brushes panel is a brush that I created and saved with the file. Next, you'll apply a Pattern brush, and then edit its properties.

> **Tip:** Just like other brush types, there is a series of default Pattern brush libraries that come with Illustrator. To access them, click the Brush Libraries Menu button (▤), and choose a library from one of the menus (the Decorative menu, for example).

3 With the Selection tool (▶) selected, Shift-click the two black paths on the orange/yellow shape to select them both.

4 Select the Windows Pattern brush from the Brushes panel to apply the Pattern brush.

Next, you'll edit the brush properties for one of the paths.

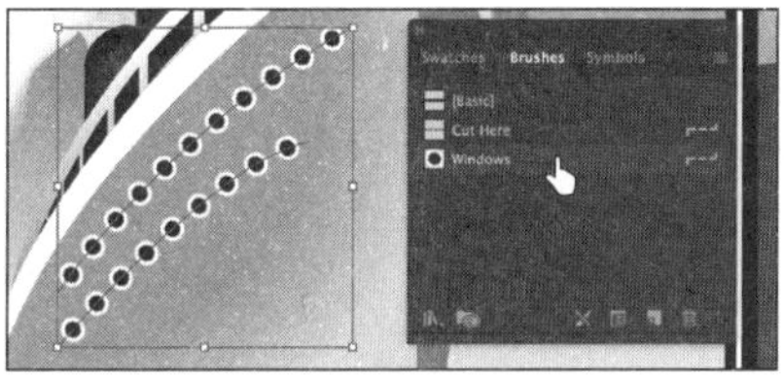

5 Choose Select > Deselect and then click the bottommost path with the Windows brush applied to select it.

6 Click the Options Of Selected Object button (▤) in the Properties panel to edit the brush options for only the selected path on the artboard.

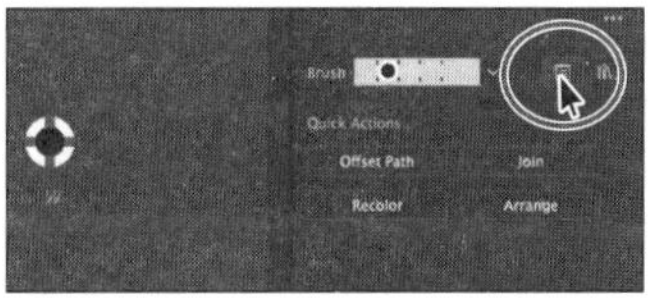

7 Select Preview in the Stroke Options (Pattern Brush) dialog box. Change the Scale to **110%** either by dragging the Scale slider or by typing in the value. Click OK.

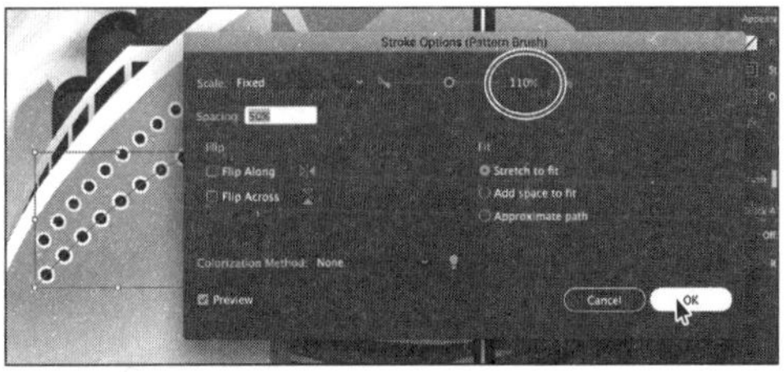

> **Tip:** You'll also see the Options Of Selected Object button (▤) at the bottom of the Brushes panel.

> **Tip:** To change the size of the windows, you can also change the stroke weight of the lines on the artboard, with the brush applied.

When you edit the brush options of the selected object, you only see some of the brush options. The Stroke Options (Pattern Brush) dialog box is used to edit the properties of the brushed path without updating the corresponding brush.

8 Choose Select > Deselect and then choose File > Save.

Creating a Pattern brush

You can create a Pattern brush in several ways. For a simple pattern applied to a straight line, for instance, you can select the content that you're using for the pattern and click the New Brush button (■) at the bottom of the Brushes panel.

To create a more complex pattern to apply to objects with curves and corners, you can select artwork in the Document window to be used in a pattern brush, create swatches in the Swatches panel from the artwork that you are using in the Pattern brush, and even have Illustrator autogenerate the Pattern brush corners. In Illustrator, only the side tile needs to be defined. Illustrator automatically generates four different types of corners based on the art used for the side tile. These four autogenerated options fit the corners perfectly. Next, you'll create a Pattern brush for the border around the poster.

● **Note:** You'll find Pattern Objects at the bottom of the View menu.

1 Choose View > Pattern objects. This should show you a zoomed-in view of the life preserver and the rope off the right edge of the artboard.

2 With the Selection tool (▶) selected, click to select the brown rope group.

3 Click the panel menu icon (■) in the Brushes panel, and choose Thumbnail View.

Notice that Pattern brushes in the Brushes panel are segmented in Thumbnail view. Each segment corresponds to a pattern tile.

4 In the Brushes panel, click the New Brush button (■) to create a pattern out of the rope.

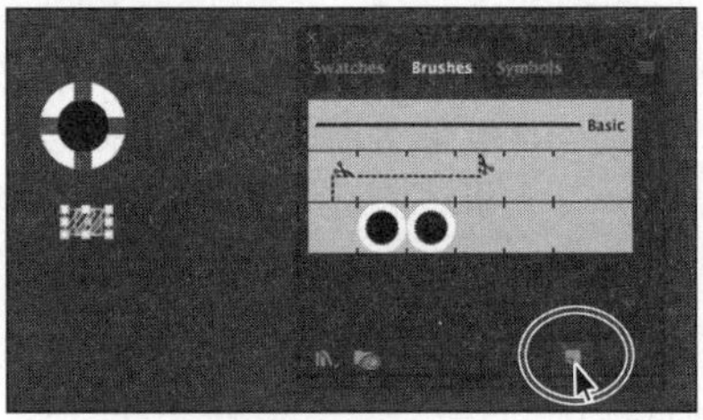

5 In the New Brush dialog box, select Pattern Brush. Click OK.

A new Pattern brush can be made regardless of whether artwork is selected. If you create a Pattern brush without artwork selected, it is assumed that you will add artwork by dragging it into the Brushes panel later or by selecting the artwork from a pattern swatch you create as you edit the brush. You will see the latter method later in this section.

● **Note:** Some brushes have no corner tiles because they are designed for curved paths.

6 In the Pattern Brush Options dialog box, name the brush **Border**.

Pattern brushes can have up to five tiles—the side, start, and end tiles, plus an outer-corner tile and an inner-corner tile to paint sharp corners on a path.

You can see all five tiles as buttons below the Spacing option in the dialog box. The tile buttons let you apply different artwork to different parts of the path. You can click a tile button for the tile you want to define, and then you select an autogenerated selection (if available) or a pattern swatch from the menu that appears.

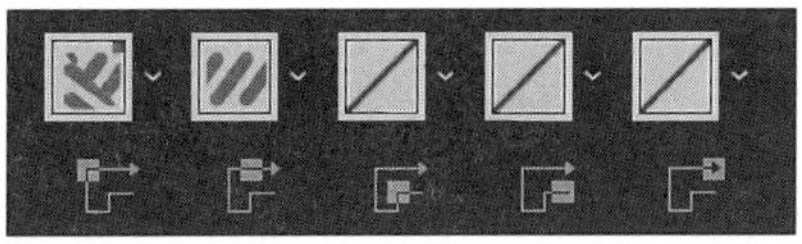

7 Under the Spacing option, click the Side Tile box (the second tile from the left). The artwork that was originally selected is in the menu that appears, along with None and any pattern swatches found in the Swatches panel. Choose Pompadour from the menu.

In the Preview area below the tiles, you will see how the new artwork affects a path.

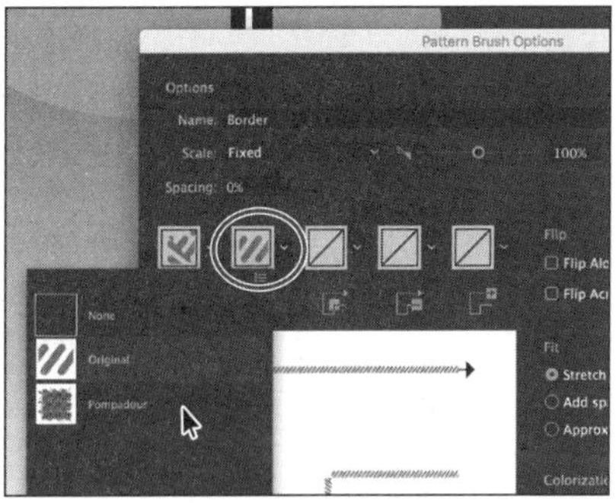

▶ **Tip:** Position the pointer over the tile squares in the Pattern Brush Options dialog box to see a tooltip indicating which tile it is.

▶ **Tip:** Selected artwork becomes the side tile, by default, when creating a Pattern brush.

8 Click the Side Tile box again, and choose the option called "Original."

9 Click the Outer Corner Tile box to reveal the menu.

The outer-corner tile has been generated automatically by Illustrator, based on the original rope artwork. In the menu, you can choose from four types of corners that are generated automatically:

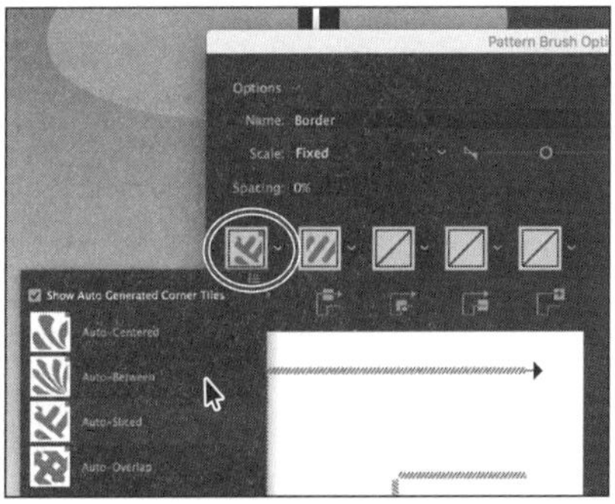

▶ **Tip:** To save a brush and reuse it in another file, you can create a brush library with the brushes you want to use. For more information, see "Work with brush libraries" in Illustrator Help.

- **Auto-Centered.** The side tile is stretched around the corner and centered on it.
- **Auto-Between.** Copies of the side tile extend all the way into the corner, with one copy on each side. Folding elimination is used to stretch them into shape.
- **Auto-Sliced.** The side tile is sliced diagonally, and the pieces come together, similar to a miter joint in a wooden picture frame.
- **Auto-Overlap.** Copies of the tiles overlap at the corner.

10 Choose Auto-Between from the menu. This generates the outer corner of any path that the Pattern brush will be applied to from the rope.

11 Click OK. The Border brush appears in the Brushes panel.

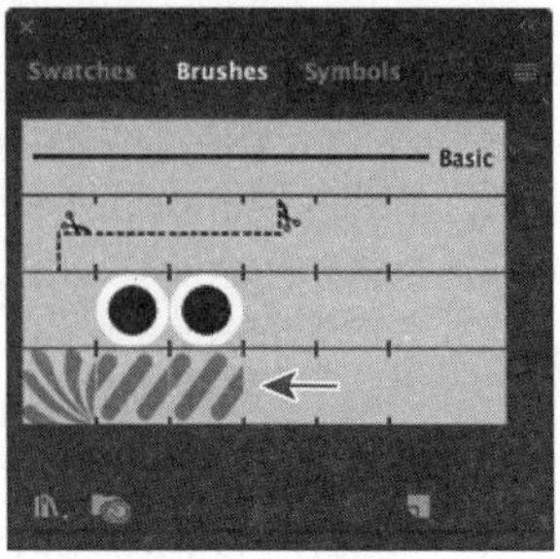

Applying a Pattern brush

In this section, you'll apply the Border Pattern brush to a rectangular border around the artwork. As you've seen, when you use drawing tools to apply brushes to artwork, you first draw the path with the drawing tool and then select the brush in the Brushes panel to apply the brush to the path.

1 Choose View > Fit Artboard In Window.

2 With the Selection tool (▶) selected, click the white stroke of the rectangle on the border.

3 In the Tools panel, click the Fill box, and make sure that None (◪) is selected. Then click the Stroke box and select None (◪).

4 With the rectangle selected, click the Border brush in the Brushes panel.

5 Choose Select > Deselect.

The rectangle is painted with the Border brush, with the side tile on the sides and the outer-corner tile on each corner.

Editing the Pattern brush

▶ **Tip:** For more information on creating pattern swatches, see "About patterns" in Illustrator Help.

Now you'll edit the Border Pattern brush using a pattern swatch that you create.

1 Choose Window > Swatches to open the Swatches panel.

2 Choose View > Pattern objects to zoom in to the life preserver off the right edge of the artboard.

3 With the Selection tool (▶), drag the life preserver into the Swatches panel.

The new pattern swatch appears in the Swatches panel. After you create a pattern brush, you can delete the pattern swatches from the Swatches panel, if you don't plan to use them for additional artwork.

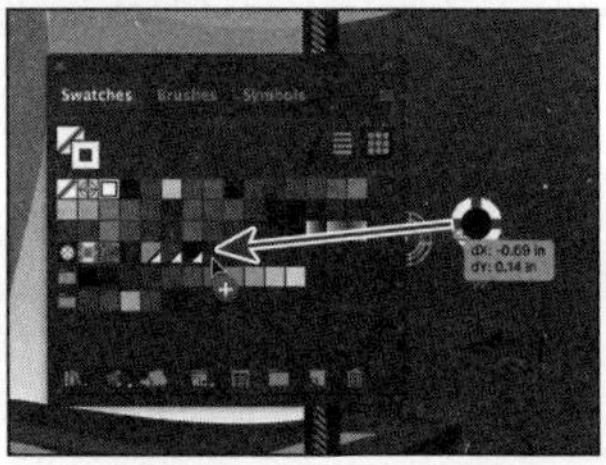

4 Choose Select > Deselect.

5 In the Swatches panel, double-click the pattern swatch that you just created to enter Pattern Editing mode.

6 In the Pattern Options dialog box, name the swatch **Corner**.

You don't have to name the pattern swatch, but it can make it easier to select when you edit the brush.

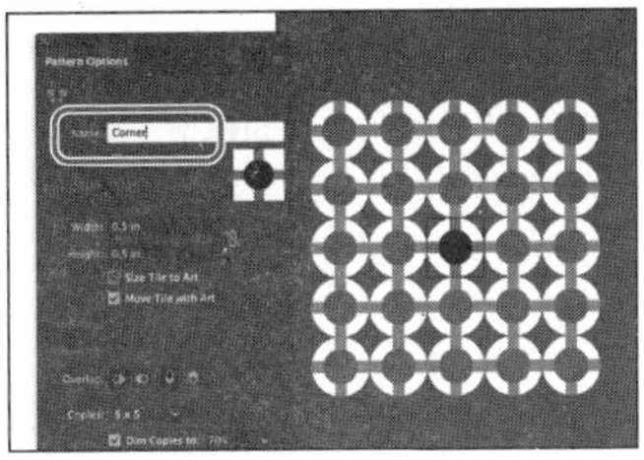

7 Click Done in the gray bar, along the top of the Document window, to finish editing the pattern.

8 Choose View > Fit Artboard In Window.

9 In the Brushes panel (Window > Brushes), double-click the Border Pattern brush to open the Pattern Brush Options dialog box.

10 Click the Outer Corner Tile box, and choose the Corner pattern swatch from the menu that appears (you'll need to scroll). Change Scale from 100% to **70%**, and click OK. The figure shows choosing the outer-corner tile.

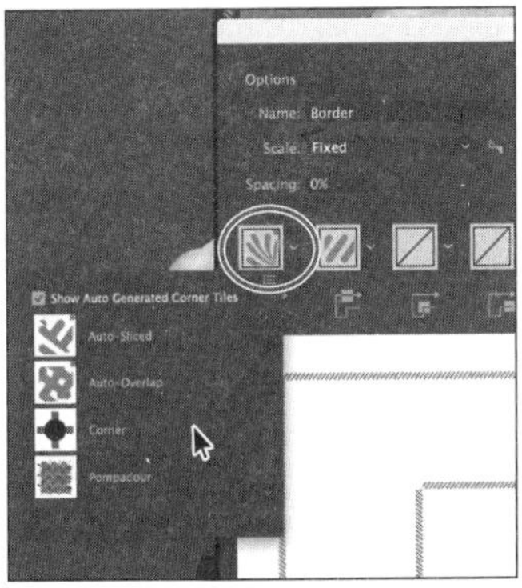

11 In the dialog box that appears, click Apply To Strokes to update the border on the artboard.

Tip: You can also change the pattern tiles in a Pattern brush by pressing the Option (macOS) or Alt (Windows) key and dragging artwork from the artboard onto the tile of the Pattern brush you want to change in the Brushes panel.

12 With the Selection tool selected, click to select one of the paths that contains a row of windows. Click the Border brush in the Brushes panel to apply it.

Notice that the life preservers are not applied to the path. The path is painted with the side tile from the Border brush. Because the path does not include sharp corners, outer-corner and inner-corner tiles are not applied to the path.

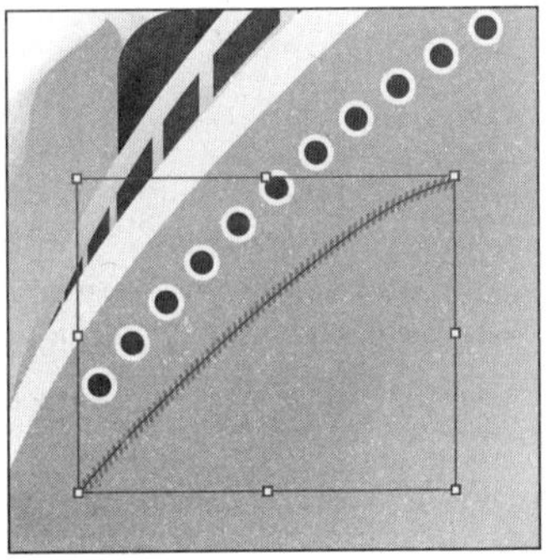

Note: Earlier in the lesson, you learned how to remove a brush from an object by clicking the Remove Brush Stroke button (■) in the Brushes panel. In this case, you chose Edit > Undo Apply Pattern Brush instead, because clicking the Remove Brush Stroke button would strip the previous formatting from the path, leaving it with a default fill and stroke.

13 Choose Edit > Undo Apply Pattern Brush to remove the brush from the path.

14 Choose Select > Deselect and then choose File > Save.

Working with the Blob Brush tool

You can use the Blob Brush tool ( ) to paint filled shapes that intersect and merge with other shapes of the same color. With the Blob Brush tool, you can draw with Paintbrush tool artistry. Unlike the Paintbrush tool, which lets you create open paths, the Blob Brush tool lets you create a closed shape with a fill only (no stroke) that you can then easily edit with the Eraser or Blob Brush tool. Shapes that have a stroke cannot be edited with the Blob Brush tool.

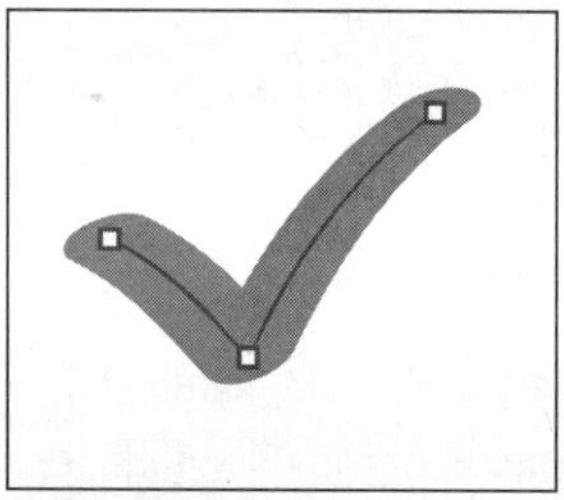

Path created with the Paintbrush tool

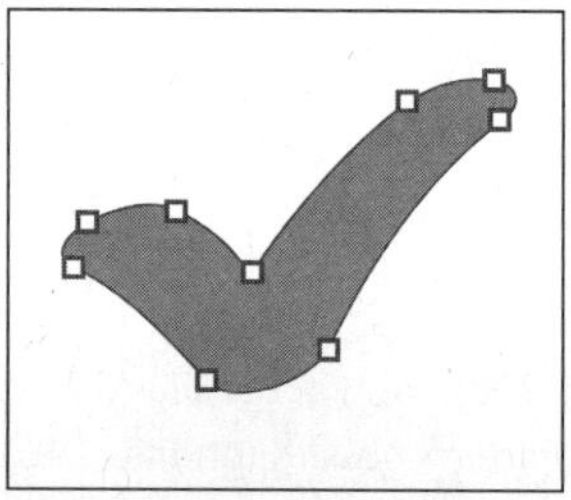

Shape created with the Blob Brush tool

Drawing with the Blob Brush tool

Next, you'll use the Blob Brush tool to create part of a cloud.

1 Click the Layers panel tab on the right side of the workspace to show the Layers panel. Click the eye icon ( ) to the left of the Ship sublayer to hide the contents of the layer. Click the Background sublayer to select it.

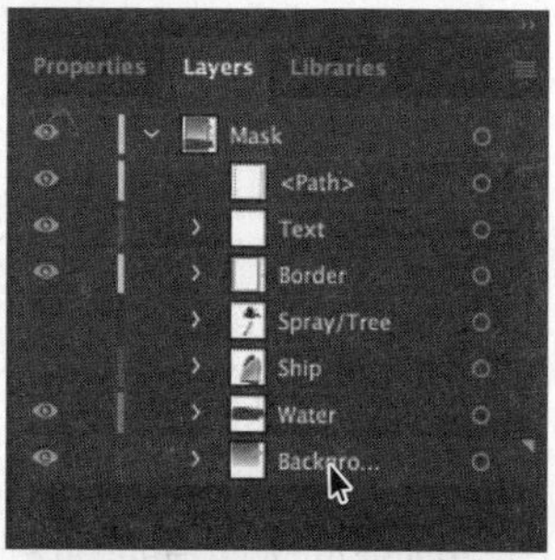

2 In the Swatches panel, select the Fill color box and then select the swatch named "Light Blue." Select the Stroke color box and select None ( ) to remove the stroke.

When drawing with the Blob Brush tool, if a fill and stroke are set before drawing, the stroke color becomes the fill color of the shape made by the Blob Brush tool. If only a fill is set before drawing, it ultimately becomes the fill of the shape created.

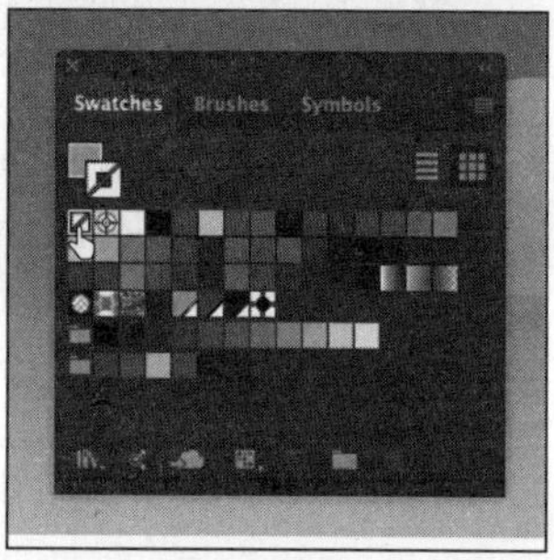

3 Click and hold down on the Paintbrush tool (🖌) in the Tools panel, and select the Blob Brush tool (🖌). Double-click the Blob Brush tool in the Tools panel. In the Blob Brush Tool Options dialog box, change the following:

- Keep Selected: **Selected**
- Size: **70** pt

4 Click OK.

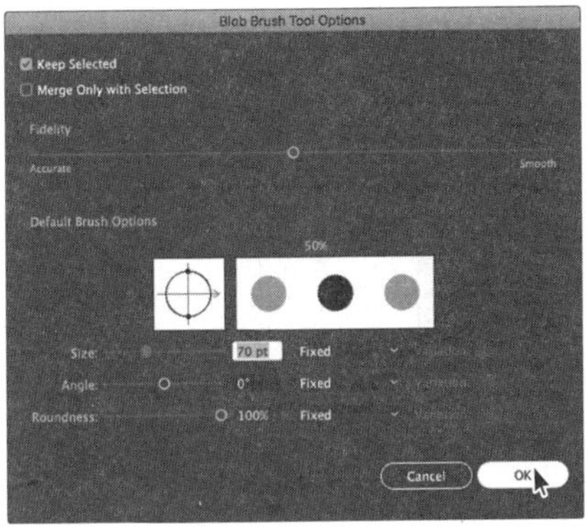

5 Position the pointer to the left of the little blue cloud in the sky. Drag to create a cloud shape that *doesn't* touch the little cloud to the right of it (see the figure).

▶ **Tip:** You can also change the Blob Brush size by pressing the right bracket key ( ]) or left bracket key ([ ) several times to increase or decrease the size of the brush.

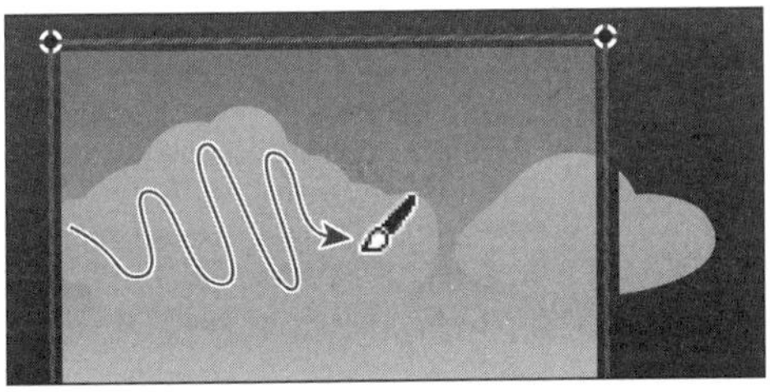

When you draw with the Blob Brush tool, you create filled, closed shapes. Those shapes can contain any type of fill, including gradients, solid colors, patterns, and more. Notice that the Blob Brush pointer has a circle around it before you begin painting. That circle indicates the size of the brush (70 pt, which you set in the previous step).

Merging paths with the Blob Brush tool

● **Note:** To learn more about Blob Brush tool guidelines, search for "Painting with fills and strokes" in Illustrator Help (Help > Illustrator Help). On that Help page, go to the section titled "Draw and merge paths with the Blob Brush tool."

● **Note:** In the figure, the cloud you drew has a blue outline. You may not see that, and that's okay.

In addition to drawing new shapes with the Blob Brush tool, you can use it to intersect and merge shapes of the same color. Objects merged with the Blob Brush tool need to have the same appearance attributes, have no stroke, be on the same layer or group, and be adjacent to each other in the stacking order.

Next, you will merge the cloud you just created with the little cloud to the right of it to create one big cloud.

1 Choose Select > Deselect.

2 With the Blob Brush tool () selected, drag from inside the cloud shape you created to the inside of the little cloud to the right, connecting the two shapes.

● **Note:** If you find that the shapes are not merging, it may be that they have different strokes and fills. You can select both the cloud you created and the small cloud with the Selection tool () and ensure that the fill color is the light blue swatch and the stroke is None in the Properties panel. Then you can select the Blob Brush tool and try dragging from one cloud to the other.

3 Continue drawing with the Blob Brush tool to make the two clouds look more like a single cloud.

If you find that new shapes are being made instead of the existing cloud shape being edited, undo what you've created. Then, with the Selection tool (), reselect and deselect the cloud shape and continue.

4 Choose Select > Deselect and then choose File > Save.

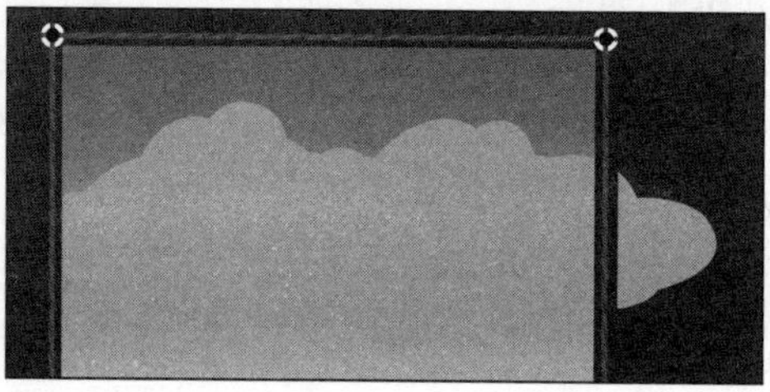

Editing with the Eraser tool

As you draw and merge shapes with the Blob Brush tool, you may draw too much and want to edit what you've done. You can use the Eraser tool (◆) in combination with the Blob Brush tool to mold the shape and to correct any changes you don't like.

▶ **Tip:** As you draw with the Blob Brush and Eraser tools, it is recommended that you use shorter strokes and release the mouse button often. You can undo the edits that you make, but if you draw in one long stroke without releasing the mouse button, an undo removes the entire stroke.

1 With the Selection tool (▶), click to select the cloud shape.

  Selecting the shape(s) before erasing limits the Eraser tool to erasing only the selected shape(s).

2 Double-click the Eraser tool (◆) in the Tools panel. In the Eraser Tool Options dialog box, change Size to **40 pt**, and click OK.

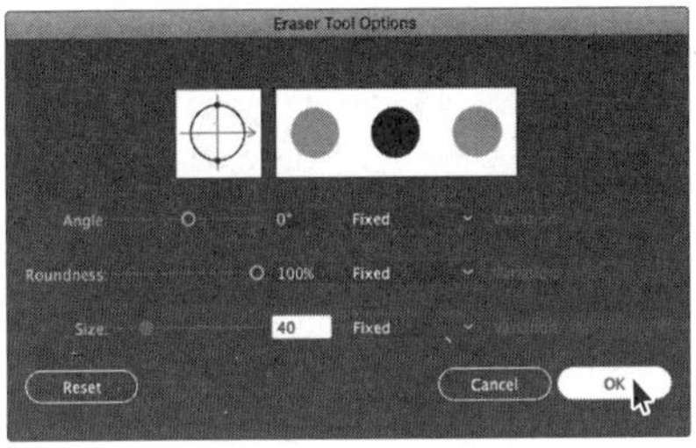

3 Position the pointer over the edge of the cloud shape and, with the Eraser tool, drag along the bottom of the cloud shape to remove some of it. Try switching between the Blob Brush tool and the Eraser tool to edit the cloud.

  The Blob Brush and Eraser tools both have pointers that include a circle, indicating the diameter of the brush.

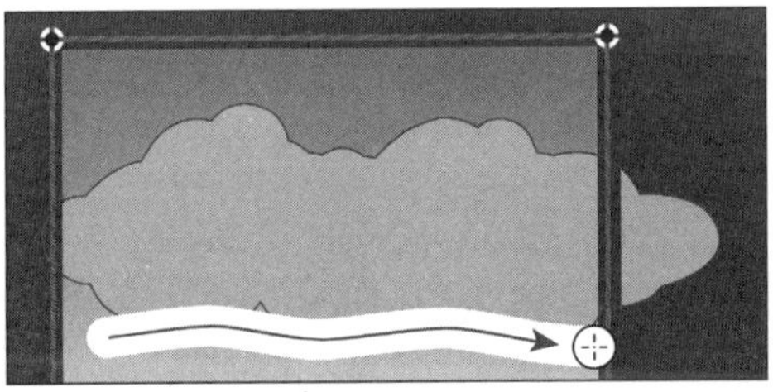

4 Choose Select > Deselect.

5 Click the Layers panel tab on the right side of the workspace to show the Layers panel, if necessary. Click the visibility columns to the left of all the sublayers to ensure that they are all showing. Click to select the main layer named "Mask" at the top of the Layers panel. Click the Make/Release Clipping Mask button (▣) at the bottom of the Layers panel.

By clicking the Make/Release Clipping Mask button, you are taking an existing rectangle shape and using it to mask content. To learn more about masking, see Lesson 14, "Using Illustrator CC with Other Adobe Applications."

6 Choose Object > Show All to show some poster text.

7 Choose Select > Deselect.

8 Choose File > Save, and close all open files.

Review questions

1 What is the difference between applying a brush to artwork using the Paintbrush tool ( ) and applying a brush to artwork using one of the drawing tools?

2 Describe how artwork in an Art brush is applied to content.

3 Describe how to edit paths with the Paintbrush tool as you draw. How does the Keep Selected option affect the Paintbrush tool?

4 What must be done to a raster image in order for it to be used in certain brushes?

5 For which brush types must you have artwork selected on the artboard before you can create a brush?

6 What does the Blob Brush tool ( ) allow you to create?

Review answers

1 When painting with the Paintbrush tool ( ), if a brush is chosen in the Brushes panel and you draw on the artboard, the brush is applied directly to the paths as you draw. To apply brushes using a drawing tool, you select the tool and draw in the artwork. Then you select the path in the artwork and choose a brush in the Brushes panel. The brush is applied to the selected path.

2 An Art brush is made from artwork (vector or embedded raster). When you apply an Art brush to the stroke of an object, the artwork in the Art brush, by default, is stretched along the selected object stroke.

3 To edit a path with the Paintbrush tool, drag over a selected path to redraw it. The Keep Selected option keeps the last path selected as you draw with the Paintbrush tool. Leave the Keep Selected option selected when you want to easily edit the previous path as you draw. Deselect the Keep Selected option when you want to draw layered paths with the paintbrush without altering previous paths. When Keep Selected is deselected, you can use the Selection tool ( ) to select a path and then edit it.

4 In order to be used in certain brushes (Art, Pattern, and Scatter), a raster image must be embedded.

5 For Art (and Scatter) brushes, you need to have artwork selected in order to create a brush using the New Brush button ( ) in the Brushes panel.

6 Use the Blob Brush tool ( ) to edit filled shapes that you can intersect and merge with other shapes of the same color or to create artwork from scratch.

12 EXPLORING CREATIVE USES OF EFFECTS AND GRAPHIC STYLES

Lesson overview

In this lesson, you'll learn how to do the following:

- Work with the Appearance panel.
- Edit and apply appearance attributes.
- Copy, enable and disable, and remove appearance attributes.
- Reorder appearance attributes.
- Apply and edit an effect.
- Apply a variety of effects.
- Save and apply an appearance as a graphic style.
- Apply a graphic style to a layer.
- Scale strokes and effects.

This lesson takes approximately 60 minutes to complete. Please log in to your account on peachpit.com to download the lesson files for this chapter, or go to the "Getting Started" section at the beginning of this book and follow the instructions under "Accessing the lesson files and Web Edition."

Your Account page is also where you'll find any updates to the chapters or to the lesson files. Look on the Lesson & Update Files tab to access the most current content.

You can change the look of an object without changing its structure simply by applying attributes, such as fills, strokes, and effects, from the Appearance panel. And because the effects themselves are live, they can be modified or removed at any time. This allows you to save the appearance attributes as graphic styles and apply them to another object.

Starting the lesson

In this lesson, you'll change the appearance of artwork using the Appearance panel, various effects, and graphic styles. Before you begin, you'll need to restore the default preferences for Adobe Illustrator. Then you'll open a file containing the finished artwork to see what you'll create.

● **Note:** If you have not already downloaded the project files for this lesson to your computer from your Account page, make sure to do so now. See the "Getting Started" section at the beginning of the book.

1 To ensure that the tools function and the defaults are set exactly as described in this lesson, delete or deactivate (by renaming) the Adobe Illustrator CC preferences file. See "Restoring default preferences" in the "Getting Started" section at the beginning of the book.

2 Start Adobe Illustrator CC.

3 Choose File > Open, and open the L12_end.ai file in the Lessons > Lesson12 folder on your hard disk.

This file displays a completed illustration of a flyer for a bike tour company.

● **Note:** You will need an Internet connection to sync fonts.

4 In the Missing Fonts dialog box that most likely will appear, click Sync Fonts to sync all of the missing fonts to your computer. After they are synced and you see the message stating that there are no more missing fonts, click Close.

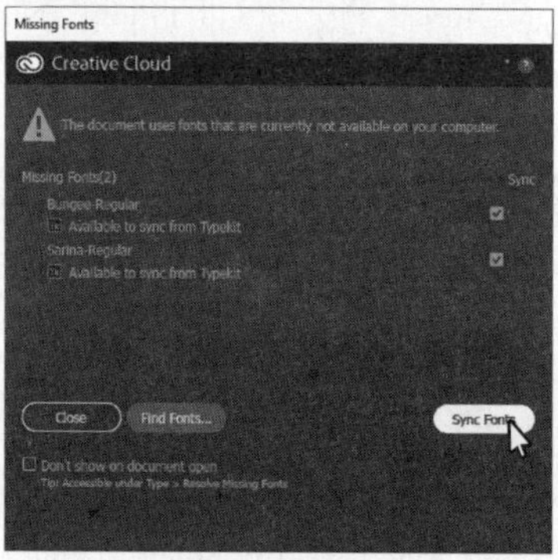

If you can't get the fonts to sync, you can go to the Creative Cloud desktop application and choose Assets > Fonts to see what the issue may be (refer to the section "Changing font family and font style" in Lesson 8, "Adding Type to a Poster," for more information on how to resolve it).

You can also just click Close in the Missing Fonts dialog box and ignore the missing fonts as you proceed. A third method is to click the Find Fonts button in the Missing Fonts dialog box and replace the fonts with a local font on your machine. You can also go to Help (Help > Illustrator Help) and search for "Find missing fonts."

5 Choose View > Zoom Out to make the finished artwork smaller. Adjust the window size, and leave it on your screen as you work. (Use the Hand tool [✋] to move the artwork where you want it in the window.) If you don't want to leave the image open, choose File > Close.

To begin working, you'll open an existing art file.

6 Choose File > Open. In the Open dialog box, navigate to the Lessons > Lesson12 folder, and select the L12_start.ai file on your hard disk. Click Open to open the file.

The L12_start.ai file uses the same fonts as the L12_end.ai file. If you've synced the fonts already, you don't need to do it again. If you didn't open the L12_end.ai file, then the Missing Fonts dialog box will most likely appear for this step. Click Sync Fonts to sync all of the missing fonts to your computer. After they are synced and you see the message stating that there are no more missing fonts, click Close.

● **Note:** For help on resolving any missing fonts, refer to step 4.

7 Choose File > Save As, name the file **BikeTours.ai**, and select the Lesson12 folder. Leave the Format option set to Adobe Illustrator (ai) (macOS) or the Save As Type option set to Adobe Illustrator (*.AI) (Windows) and then click Save.

8 In the Illustrator Options dialog box, leave the Illustrator options at their default settings and then click OK.

9 Choose Reset Essentials from the workspace switcher in the Application bar to reset the workspace.

● **Note:** If you don't see Reset Essentials in the workspace switcher menu, choose Window > Workspace > Essentials before choosing Window > Workspace > Reset Essentials.

10 Choose View > Fit Artboard In Window.

Using the Appearance panel

An *appearance attribute* is an aesthetic property—such as a fill, stroke, transparency, or effect—that affects the look of an object but does not affect its basic structure. Up to this point, you've been changing appearance attributes in the Properties panel, Swatches panel, and more. Appearance attributes like these can also be found in the Appearance panel for selected artwork. In this lesson, you'll focus on using the Appearance panel to apply and edit appearance attributes.

1 Select the Selection tool (▶), and click to select the orange shape in the background, behind the "CALL 1-800..." text.

▶ **Tip:** You can also choose Window > Appearance to see the Appearance panel.

2 Click More Options (▪▪▪) in the Appearance section of the Properties panel on the right (an arrow is pointing to it in the following figure) to open the Appearance panel.

The Appearance panel shows what the object is (a path) and the appearance attributes applied to it (Stroke, Fill, Drop Shadow, and Opacity).

▶ **Tip:** You may want to drag the bottom of the Appearance panel down to make it taller, like I did.

The different options available in the Appearance panel are described here:

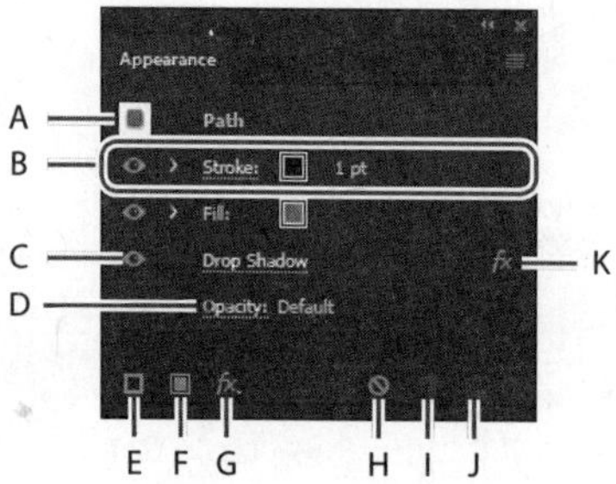

A. Selected object and thumbnail

B. Attribute row

C. Visibility column

D. Link to options

E. Add New Stroke

F. Add New Fill

G. Add New Effect

H. Clear Appearance

I. Duplicate Selected Item

J. Delete Selected Item

K. Indicates an effect applied

The Appearance panel (Window > Appearance) can be used to view and adjust the appearance attributes for a selected object, group, or layer. Fills and strokes are listed in stacking order; top to bottom in the panel correlates to front to back in the artwork. Effects applied to artwork are listed from top to bottom in the order in which they are applied to the artwork. An advantage of using appearance attributes is that they can be changed or removed at any time without affecting the underlying artwork or any other attributes applied to the object in the Appearance panel.

Editing appearance attributes

You'll start by changing the appearance of artwork using the Appearance panel.

1 With the orange shape selected, in the Appearance panel, click the orange Fill color box in the fill attribute row as many times as needed, until the Swatches panel appears. Select the swatch named "Mountain1" to apply it to the fill. Press the Escape key to hide the Swatches panel.

Note: You may need to click the Fill box more than once to open the Swatches panel. The first click on the Fill box selects the Fill row in the panel, and the next click shows the Swatches panel.

2 Click the words "1 pt" in the Stroke row to show the Stroke Weight option. Change the stroke weight to 0 to remove it (the Stroke Weight field will be blank or show "0 pt" when it's 0).

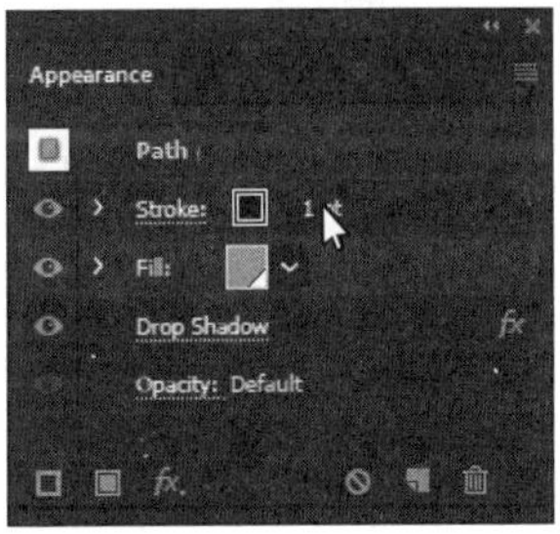

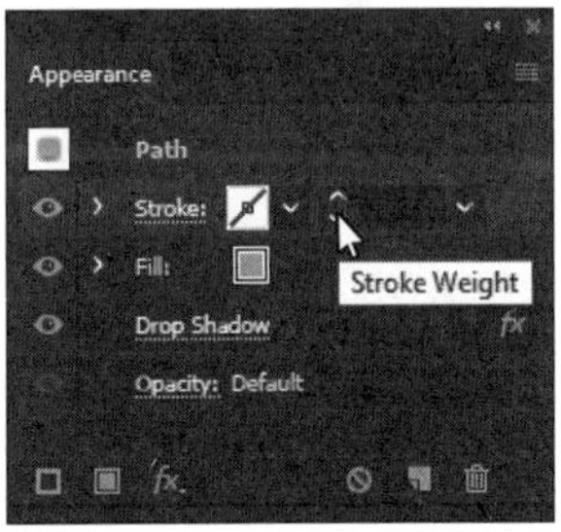

▶ **Tip:** In the Appearance panel, you can drag an attribute row, such as Drop Shadow, to the Delete Selected Item button (🗑) to delete it, or you can select the attribute row and click the Delete Selected Item button.

3 Click the visibility column (👁) to the left of the Drop Shadow attribute name in the Appearance panel.

Appearance attributes can be temporarily hidden or deleted so that they no longer are applied to the selected artwork.

▶ **Tip:** You can view all hidden attributes (attributes you have turned off) by choosing Show All Hidden Attributes from the Appearance panel menu (☰).

4 With the Drop Shadow row selected (click to the right of the link "Drop Shadow" if it isn't selected), click the Delete Selected Item button (🗑) at the bottom of the panel to completely remove the shadow, rather than just turning off the visibility.

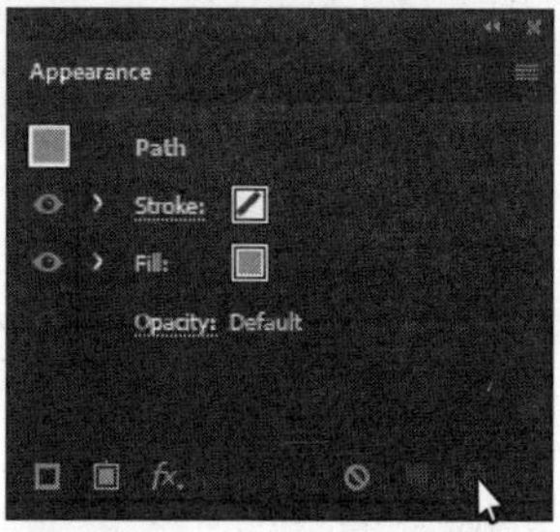

Adding another stroke and fill to artwork

Artwork in Illustrator can have more than one stroke and fill applied. This can be a great way to add interesting design elements. You'll now add another fill to an object using the Appearance panel.

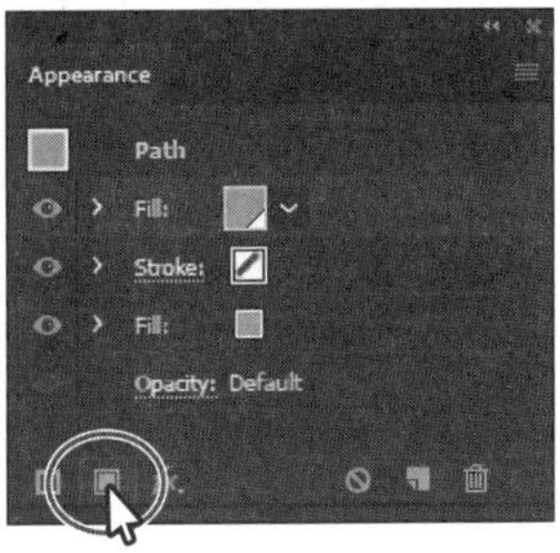

1 With the shape still selected, click the Add New Fill button (■) at the bottom of the Appearance panel.

   The figure shows what the panel looks like after clicking the Add New Fill button. A second Fill row is added to the Appearance panel. By default, new fill or stroke attribute rows are added directly above a selected attribute row or, if no attribute rows are selected, at the top of the Appearance panel list.

2 Click the *bottom* (original) Fill color box in the fill attribute row a few times, until the Swatches panel appears. Click the pattern swatch named "USGS 22 Gravel Beach" to apply it to the original fill. Press the Escape key to hide the Swatches panel.

   The pattern won't show in the selected artwork because the second fill you added in the first step is covering the "USGS 22 Gravel Beach" fill. The two fills are stacked on each other.

▶ **Tip:** Other ways to close panels that appear when clicking an underlined word, like "Stroke," include pressing the Escape key, clicking the Stroke attribute row, or pressing Enter or Return.

3 Click the eye icon to the left of the *top* fill attribute row to hide it.

You should now see the pattern fill in the shape. In the next section, you'll reorder the attribute rows in the Appearance panel so the pattern will be on top of the color fill.

4 Click where the eye icon was to the left of the *top* fill attribute row to show it.

Next, you'll add another stroke to a shape using the Appearance panel. This can be a great way to achieve interesting design effects with just one object.

5 With the Selection tool (▶) selected, click to select the black circle that will become a bicycle tire.

6 Click the Add New Stroke button (■) at the bottom of the Appearance panel.

A second stroke, which is a copy of the original, is now applied to the selected circle. This is a great way to add interest to your designs without having to make copies of shapes, changing the formatting (stroke in this case), and putting them on top of each other.

7 With the new (top) stroke attribute row selected, change the stroke weight to **10 pt**.

8 Click the word "Stroke" in the same attribute row to open the Stroke panel. Click the Align Stroke To Center button (■), select Dashed Line, and ensure that Dash is set to 12 pt. Press the Escape key to hide the Stroke panel.

Clicking underlined words in the Appearance panel, as in the Properties panel, shows more formatting options—usually a panel such as the Swatches or Stroke panel. Appearance attributes, such as Fill or Stroke, can have other options, such as Opacity or an effect applied to only that attribute. These additional options are listed as a subset under the attribute row and can be shown or hidden by clicking the disclosure triangle (▶) on the left end of the attribute row.

9 Choose Select > Deselect.

Adding another stroke and fill to text

Adding multiple strokes and fills to text can be a great way to add interest to your text. Next, you'll add another fill to text.

1 Select the Type tool (T), and select the text "MTN RIDGES."

Notice that "Type: No Appearance" appears at the top of the Appearance panel. This is referring to the type object, not the text within.

You will also see the word "Characters." Formatting for the text (not the type object) is listed below the word "Characters." You should see the stroke (none) and the fill (white). Also notice that you cannot add another stroke or fill to the text since the Add New Stroke and Add New Fill buttons are dimmed at the bottom of the panel. To add a new stroke and/or fill to text, you need to select the type object, not the text within.

▶ **Tip:** You could also click "Type: No Appearance" at the top of the Appearance panel to select the type object (not the text within).

2 Select the Selection tool (▶). The type object will now be selected (not the text).

3 Click the Add New Fill button (▣) at the bottom of the Appearance panel to add another fill above the word "Characters."

Once again, "Characters" refers to the formatting for the text within the text object. If you were to double-click the word "Characters," you would select the text and see the formatting options for it (fill, stroke, etc.).

● **Note:** If you are wondering why I would name a swatch "USGS 8B Intermit. Pond," know that I didn't. That pattern swatch can be found in Illustrator by default (Window > Swatch Libraries > Patterns > Basic Graphics > Basic Graphics_Textures).

4 Click the fill attribute row to select it, if it's not already selected. Click the Fill color box, and select the pattern swatch named "USGS 8B Intermit. Pond." Press the Escape key to hide the swatches.

▶ **Tip:** Depending on which attribute row is selected in the Attributes panel, the options in panels, such as the Properties panel, Gradient panel, and others, will affect the attribute selected.

5 Click the disclosure triangle (▸) to the left of the same fill row to show other properties, if necessary. Click the word "Opacity" to show the Transparency panel and change Opacity to **20%**. Press the Escape key to hide the Transparency panel.

Each appearance row (stroke, fill) has its own opacity that you can adjust. The bottom Opacity appearance row affects the transparency for the entire selected object.

6 Leave the type object selected.

Reordering appearance attributes

The ordering of the appearance attribute rows can greatly change how your artwork looks. In the Appearance panel, fills and strokes are listed in stacking order—top to bottom in the panel correlates to front to back in the artwork. You can reorder attribute rows in a way similar to dragging layers in the Layers panel to rearrange the stacking order. Next, you'll change the appearance of artwork by reordering attributes in the Appearance panel.

1 Select the Selection tool (▶) and click to select the bottom tan shape behind the "CALL 1-800..." text.

2 In the Appearance panel, drag the bottom fill attribute row (with the pattern swatch applied) up above the original Fill attribute row. When a line appears above the Fill attribute row, release the mouse button to see the result.

▶ **Tip:** You can also apply blending modes and opacity changes to each Fill row to achieve different results.

Moving the new Fill attribute above the original Fill attribute changes the look of the artwork. The pattern fill is now on top of the solid color fill.

3 Choose Select > Deselect and then choose File > Save.

Using live effects

● **Note:** When you apply a raster effect, the original vector data is rasterized using the document's raster effects settings, which determine the resolution of the resulting image. To learn about document raster effects settings, search for "Document raster effects settings" in Illustrator Help.

Effects alter the appearance of an object without changing the underlying artwork. Applying an effect adds the effect to the object's appearance attribute, which you can edit, move, delete, or duplicate, at any time, in the Appearance panel.

Artwork with a drop-shadow effect applied.

There are two types of effects in Illustrator: *vector effects* and *raster effects*. In Illustrator, click the Effect menu item to see the different types of effects available.

- **Illustrator Effects (vector):** The top half of the Effect menu contains vector effects. You can apply these effects only to vector objects or to the fill or stroke of a bitmap object in the Appearance panel. The following vector effects can be applied to both vector and bitmap objects: 3D effects, SVG filters, Warp effects, Transform effects, Drop Shadow, Feather, Inner Glow, and Outer Glow.
- **Photoshop Effects (raster):** The bottom half of the Effect menu contains raster effects. You can apply them to either vector or bitmap objects.

In this section, you will first explore how to apply and edit effects. You will then explore a few of the more widely used effects in Illustrator to get an idea of the range of effects available.

Applying an effect

Effects are applied using the Properties panel, the Effect menu, and the Appearance panel, and they can be applied to objects, groups, or layers. You are first going to learn how to apply an effect using the Effect menu, and then you will apply an effect using the Properties panel.

1 With the Selection tool (▶) selected, click the yellow background shape and Shift-click the grayish-brown background shape beneath it on the artboard. Arrows are pointing to them in the figure.

2 Choose Object > Group.

By grouping the objects before applying an effect, the effect is applied to the group, *not* the individual objects. You'll see later that if you ungroup, the effect will be removed.

3 Choose Effect > Stylize > Drop Shadow from the Illustrator Effects section of the menu that appears. In the Drop Shadow dialog box, change the following options:

- Mode: **Multiply** (the default setting)
- Opacity: **50%**
- X Offset: **0 in**
- Y Offset: **0 in**
- Blur: **0.25 in**
- Color: **Selected**

4 Select Preview to see the drop shadow applied to the group. Click OK.

Since the drop shadow is applied to the group, it appears around the perimeter of the group, not on each object independently. If you look in the Appearance panel right now, you'll see the word "Group" at the top and the Drop Shadow effect applied. The word "Contents" refers to the content within the group. Each object in a group can have its own appearance properties.

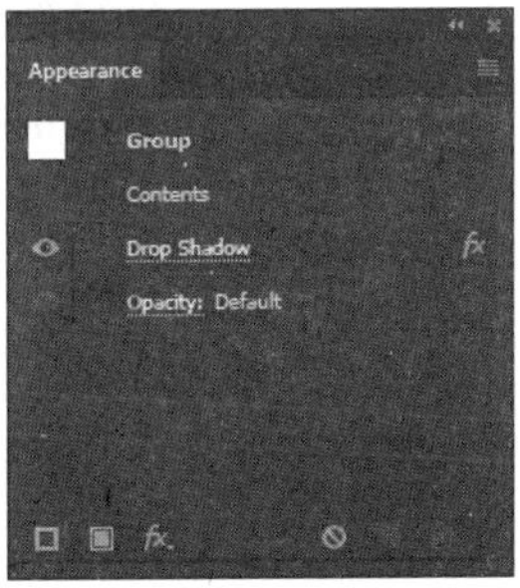

5 Choose File > Save, and leave the group selected.

Editing an effect

● **Note:** If you attempt to apply an effect to artwork that already has the same effect applied, Illustrator will warn you that you are about to apply the same effect.

Effects are live, so they can be edited after they are applied to an object. You can edit the effect in the Properties panel or Appearance panel by selecting the object with the effect applied and then clicking the name of the effect or, in the Appearance panel, double-clicking the attribute row. This displays the dialog box for that effect. Changes you make to the effect update in the artwork. In this section, you will edit the Drop Shadow effect applied to the group of background shapes.

1 With the group still selected, choose Object > Ungroup to ungroup the shapes, and leave them both selected.

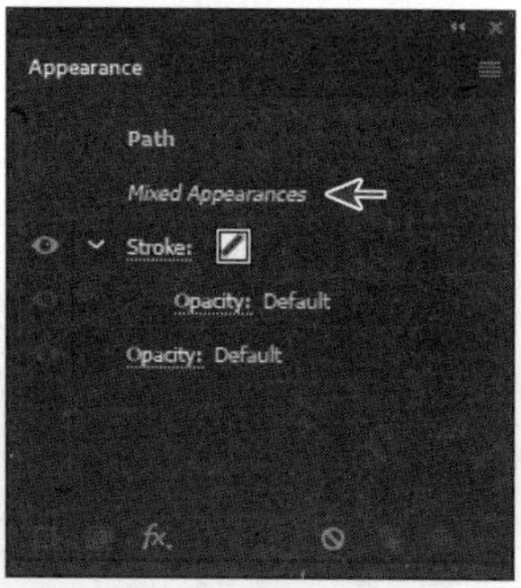

Notice that the drop shadow is no longer applied to the artwork. When an effect is applied to a group, it affects the group as a whole. If the objects are no longer grouped together, the effect is no longer applied. In the Appearance panel, you'll see "Mixed Appearances." This means that more than one path is selected currently and they have different appearances (different fills, for instance).

▶ **Tip:** If you were to choose Effect > Drop Shadow, the Drop Shadow dialog box would appear, allowing you to make changes before applying the effect.

2 With the shapes selected (and ungrouped), choose Effect > Apply Drop Shadow.

The Apply Drop Shadow menu item applied the last used effect with the same options set. The Drop Shadow effect is now applied to *each* selected object independently.

● **Note:** You could also select each shape independently to edit the Drop Shadow effect in the Appearance panel.

3 With the shapes still selected, click the text "Drop Shadow" in the Appearance panel.

4 In the Drop Shadow dialog box, change Opacity to **75%**. Select Preview to see the change and then click OK.

Styling text with a Warp effect

Text can have all sorts of effects applied, including Warp, like you saw in Lesson 8, "Adding Type to a Poster." Next, you will use a Warp effect to warp text. The difference between the warp you applied in Lesson 8 and this Warp effect is that this one is an effect and can be turned on and off, edited, or removed easily.

1 With the Selection tool (▶) selected, click the text "MTN RIDGES" and Shift-click the "BIKE TOURS" text.

2 Click the Effect option (fx) in the Appearance section of the Properties panel. Choose Warp > Arc.

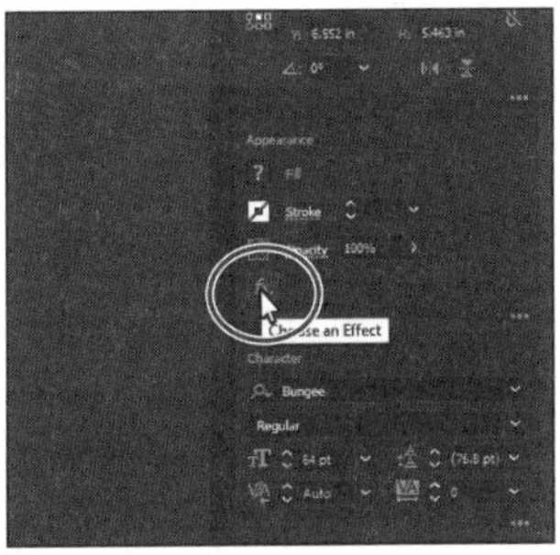

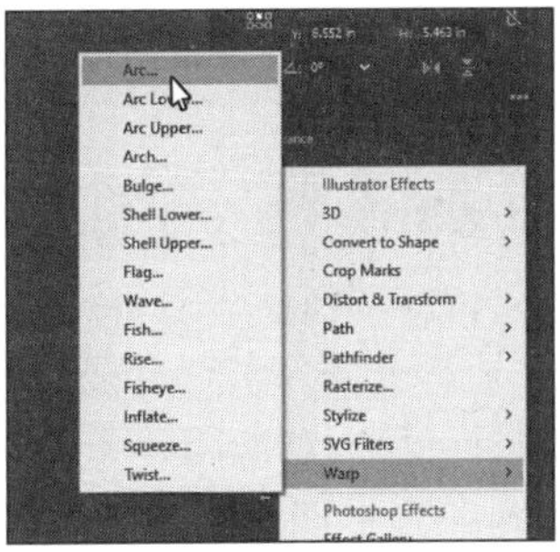

3 In the Warp Options dialog box, to create an arcing effect, set Bend to **65%**. Select Preview to preview the changes. Try choosing other styles from the Style menu and then return to Arc. Try adjusting the Horizontal and Vertical Distortion sliders to see the effect. Make sure that the Distortion values are returned to **0** and then click OK.

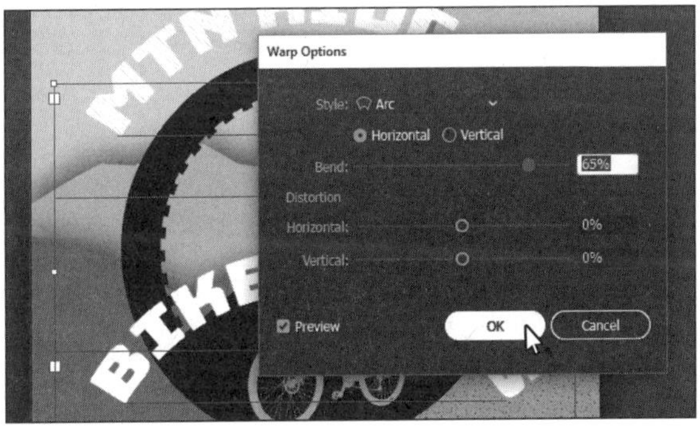

4 Choose Select > Deselect.

5 Click the "BIKE TOURS" text. In the Appearance panel, click the "Warp: Arc" text in the Properties panel (or Appearance panel) to edit the effect. In the Warp Options dialog box, change Bend to **–65%**. Click OK.

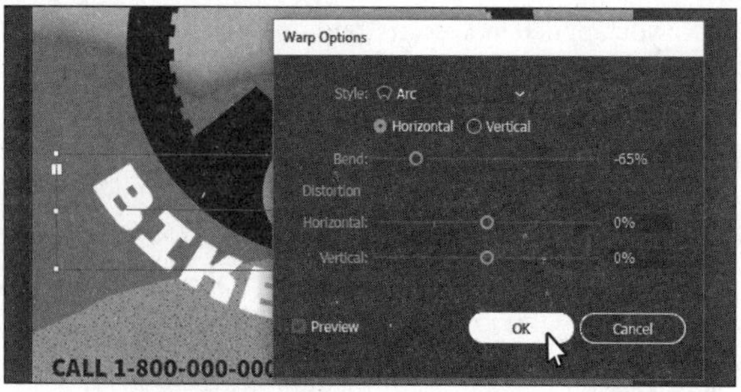

Editing text with a Warp effect

You can edit text with a Warp effect applied, but sometimes it's easier to turn off the effect, make the change to the text, and then turn the effect back on.

1 With the Selection tool (▶) selected, click the "MTN RIDGES" type object. Click the visibility icon (👁) to the left of the Warp: Arc row in the Appearance panel to temporarily turn off the effect.

Notice that the text is no longer warped on the artboard (see the following figure).

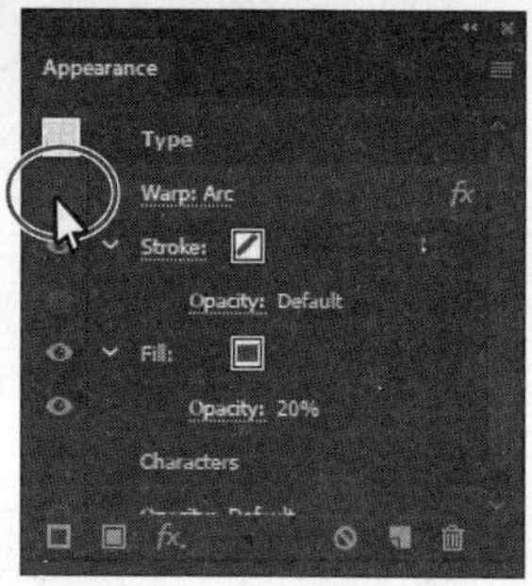

2 Select the Type tool (T) in the Tools panel, and change the text to "MTN RIDGE."

3 Select the Selection tool (▶) in the Tools panel. This selects the type object, not the text.

4 Click the visibility column to the left of the Warp: Arc row in the Appearance panel to turn on visibility for the effect so that the text is once again warped.

● **Note:** You may want to move the text closer or farther from the black wheel shape by pressing an arrow key a few times.

5 In the Appearance panel, click the "Warp: Arc" text to edit the effect. In the Warp Options dialog box, change Bend to **64%**. Click OK.

6 Choose Select > Deselect and then choose File > Save.

Applying the Offset Path effect

Next, you will offset the dashed stroke you applied to the bicycle tire (the black circle). This process allows you to create the appearance of multiple stacked shapes.

1 With the Selection tool ( ) selected, click the black circle to select it.

2 Click the Stroke row in the Appearance panel with the 10 pt Dashed stroke applied to select it.

3 With the stroke attribute row selected in the Appearance panel, click the Add New Effect button ( ) at the bottom of the panel, and choose Path > Offset Path.

4 In the Offset Path dialog box, change Offset to **0.57 in**, select Preview, and then click OK.

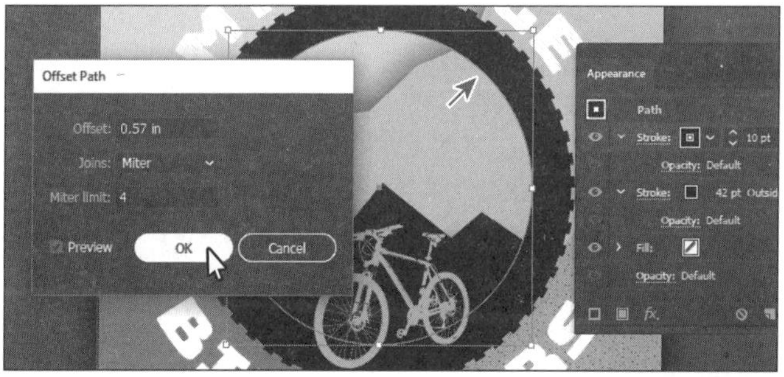

5 In the Appearance panel, click the disclosure triangle ( ) to the left of the words "Stroke: 10 pt Dashed" to toggle it open (if it's not already open).

Notice that the Offset Path effect is a subset of Stroke. This indicates that the Offset Path effect is applied to only that stroke.

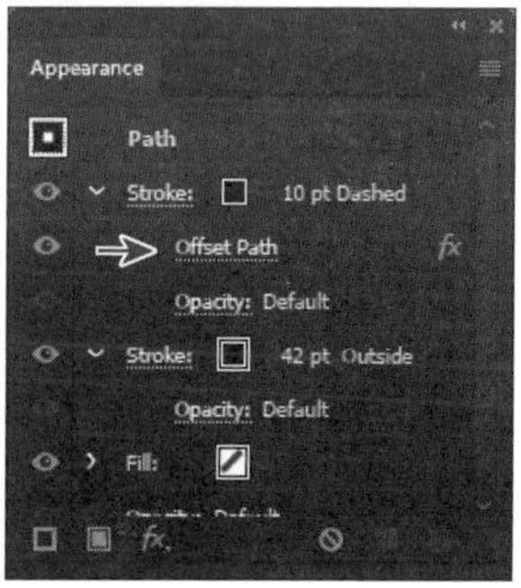

6 Choose Select > Deselect.

7 Choose File > Save.

Applying a Photoshop effect

As described earlier in the lesson, raster effects generate pixels rather than vector data. Raster effects include SVG filters, all of the effects in the bottom portion of the Effect menu, and the Drop Shadow, Inner Glow, Outer Glow, and Feather commands in the Effect > Stylize submenu. You can apply them to either vector or bitmap objects. Next, you'll apply a Photoshop effect (raster) to some of the background shapes.

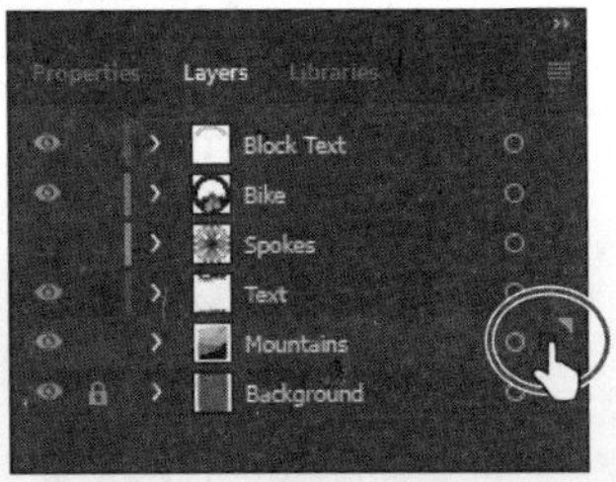

1 In the Layers panel (Window > Layers), click the selection column to the right of the Mountains layer to select the layer contents.

2 Click the Properties panel tab to show the panel again.

3 Click the Effect option (fx) in the Appearance section of the Properties panel. Choose Texture > Texturizer.

When you choose most of the raster (Photoshop) effects (not all), the Filter Gallery dialog box opens. Similar to working with filters in Adobe Photoshop, where you can also access a Filter Gallery, in the Illustrator Filter Gallery, you can try different raster effects to see how they affect your artwork.

4 With the Filter Gallery dialog box open, you can see the type of filter (Texturizer) showing at the top. Choose Fit In View from the view menu in the lower-left corner of the dialog box. That should fit the artwork in the preview area so you can see how the effect alters one of the shapes.

The Filter Gallery dialog box, which is resizable, contains a preview area (labeled A), effect thumbnails that you can click to apply (labeled B), settings for the currently selected effect (labeled C), and the list of effects applied (labeled D). If you want to apply a different effect, expand a category in the middle panel of the dialog box (labeled B), and click an effect thumbnail.

5 Change the Texturizer settings in the upper-right corner of the dialog box as follows (if necessary):

- Texture: **Sandstone**
- Scaling: **145**
- Relief: **4** (the default setting)
- Light: **Top** (the default setting)

6 Click OK to apply the raster effect to all four shapes.

7 Choose Select > Deselect.

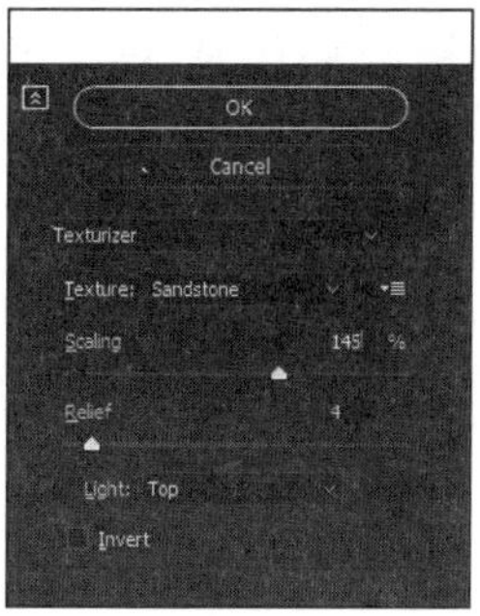

▶ **Tip:** You can click the eye icon ( ) to the left of the name "Texturizer" in the section labeled "D" to see the artwork without the effect applied.

● **Note:** The Filter Gallery lets you apply only one effect at a time. If you want to apply multiple Photoshop effects, you can click OK to apply the current effect and then choose another from the Effect menu.

Working with 3D effects

To learn about other working with 3D effects, check out the video *Working with 3D Effects* that is a part of the Web Edition. For more information, see the "Web Edition" section of "Getting Started" at the beginning of the book.

Using graphic styles

A *graphic style* is a saved set of appearance attributes that you can reuse. By applying graphic styles, you can quickly and globally change the appearance of objects and text.

The Graphic Styles panel (Window > Graphic Styles) lets you create, name, save, apply, and remove effects and attributes for objects, layers, and groups. You can also break the link between an object and an applied graphic style to edit that object's attributes without affecting other objects that use the same graphic style.

The different options available in the Graphic Styles panel are described here:

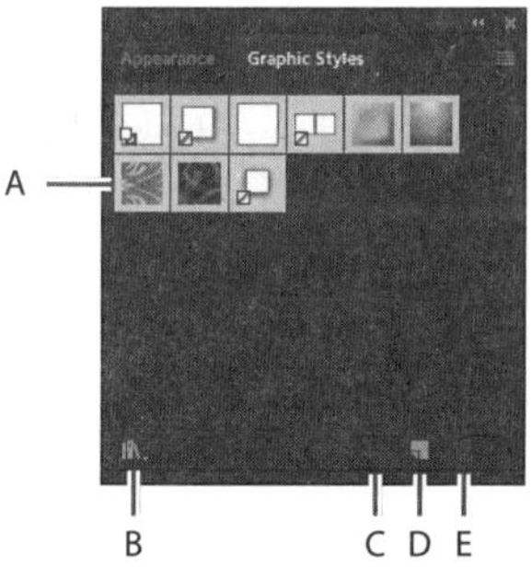

A. Graphic Style thumbnail

B. Graphic Styles Libraries menu

C. Break Link To Graphic Style

D. New Graphic Style

E. Delete Graphic Style

For example, if you have a map that uses a shape to represent a city, you can create a graphic style that paints the shape green and adds a drop shadow. You can then use that graphic style to paint all the city shapes on the map. If you decide to use a different color, you can change the fill color of the graphic style to blue. All the objects that use that graphic style are then updated to blue.

Applying an existing graphic style

You can apply graphic styles to your artwork from graphic style libraries that come with Illustrator. Next, you'll explore some of the built-in graphic styles and apply a few to artwork.

1 Choose Window > Graphic Styles. Click the Graphic Styles Libraries Menu button ( ) at the bottom of the panel, and choose Vonster Pattern Styles.

▶ **Tip:** Use the arrows at the bottom of the Vonster Pattern Styles library panel to load the previous or next Graphic Styles library in the panel.

2 With the Selection tool ( ), select the bottom background mountain shape.

3 Click the Splatterz 2 style and then click the Splatterz 3 graphic style in the Vonster Pattern Styles panel. Close the Vonster Pattern Styles panel.

Clicking the styles applies the appearance attributes to the selected artwork and adds both graphic styles to the Graphic Styles panel for the active document.

4 With the artwork still selected, look in the Appearance panel to see the fills applied to the selected artwork. Also notice "Path: Splatterz 3" at the top of the panel. This indicates that the graphic style named Splatterz 3 is applied.

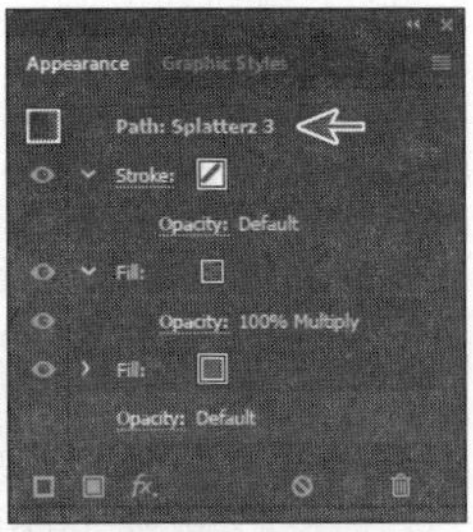

5 Click the Graphic Styles panel tab to show the panel again.

You should see the two graphic styles, Splatterz 2 and Splatterz 3, listed in the panel now.

6 Right-click and hold down the mouse button on the Splatterz 2 graphic style thumbnail in the Graphic Styles panel to preview the graphic style on the selected artwork. When you're finished previewing, release the mouse button.

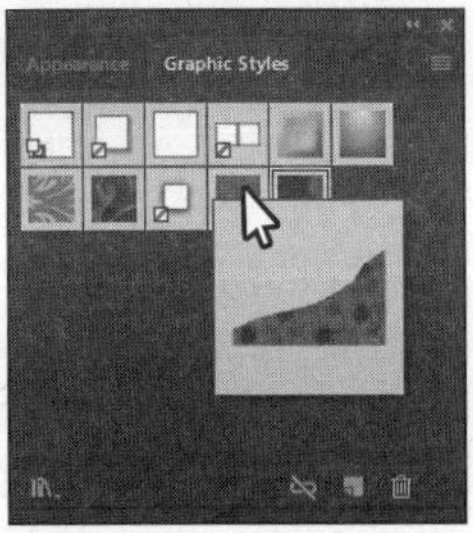

Previewing a graphic style is a great way to see how it will affect the selected object, without actually applying it.

Creating and applying a graphic style

Now you'll create a new graphic style and apply that graphic style to artwork.

▶ **Tip:** To create a graphic style, you can also click to select the object that you are using to make the graphic style. You can then either drag the object directly into the Graphic Styles panel or, in the Appearance panel, drag the appearance thumbnail at the top of the listing into the Graphic Styles panel. The panels can't be in the same panel group.

1 With the Selection tool selected, click the yellow shape that the arrow is pointing to in the following figure.

2 Click the New Graphic Style button (▣) at the bottom of the Graphic Styles panel.

The appearance attributes from the selected shape are saved as a graphic style.

3 In the Graphic Styles panel, double-click the new graphic style thumbnail. In the Graphic Style Options dialog box, name the new style **Mountain**. Click OK.

4 Click the Appearance panel tab, and at the top of the Appearance panel you'll see "Path: Mountain."

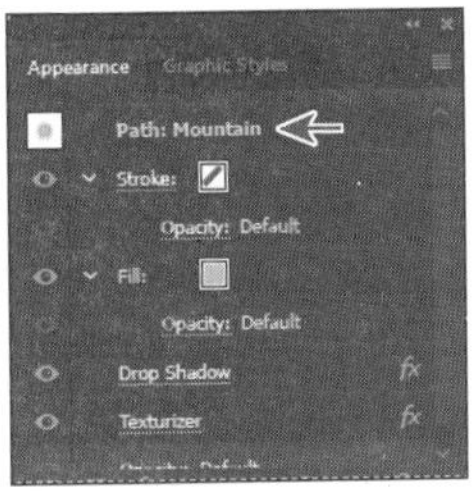

This indicates that a graphic style named "Mountain" is applied to the selected artwork.

5 With the Selection tool, click the bottom rectangle shape in the background (beneath the "Call 1-800..." text). In the Graphic Styles panel, click the graphic style named "Mountain" to apply the styling.

6 Leave the shape selected and then choose File > Save.

Applying a graphic style to text

When you apply a graphic style to a type area, the fill color of the graphic style overrides the fill color of the text by default. If you deselect Override Character Color from the Graphic Styles panel menu (▤), the fill color (if there is one) in the text will override the color of the graphic style.

If you choose Use Text For Preview from the Graphic Styles panel menu (▤), you can then right-click and hold down the mouse button on a graphic style to preview the graphic style on the text.

Updating a graphic style

Once you create a graphic style, you can update the graphic style, and all artwork with that style applied will update its appearance as well. If you edit the appearance of artwork that a graphic style is applied to, the graphic style is overridden, and the artwork will not update when the graphic style is updated.

1 With the bottom yellow shape still selected, look in the Graphic Styles panel; you will see that the Mountain graphic style thumbnail is highlighted (has a border around it), indicating that it's applied.

2 Click the Appearance panel tab. Notice the text "Path: Mountain" at the top of the panel, indicating that the Mountain graphic style is applied. Like you saw earlier, this is another way to tell whether a graphic style is applied to selected artwork.

3 Click the yellow fill color box a few times to open the Swatches panel. Select the swatch named Mountain2. Press the Escape key to hide the swatches.

Notice that the "Path: Mountain" text at the top of the Appearance panel is now just "Path," telling you that the graphic style is no longer applied to the selected artwork.

4 Click the Graphic Styles panel tab to see that the Mountain graphic style no longer has a highlight (border) around it, which means that the graphic style is no longer applied.

5 Press the Option (macOS) or Alt (Windows) key, and drag the selected shape on top of the Mountain graphic style thumbnail in the Graphic Styles panel. Release the mouse button and then release the modifier key when the thumbnail is highlighted. Both mountain shapes now look the same since the Mountain graphic style was applied to both objects.

6 Choose Select > Deselect.

7 Click the Appearance panel tab. You should see "No Selection: Mountain" at the top of the panel (you may need to scroll up).

When you apply appearance settings, graphic styles, and more to artwork, the next shape you draw will have the same appearance settings listed in the Appearance panel as the previous one.

8 Click to select the top shape in the background that has the Mountain graphic style applied. An arrow is pointing to it in the following figure.

9 Click the fill color for the Fill appearance row, and in the Swatches panel that appears, select the Mountain1 swatch.

10 Choose Select > Deselect and then choose File > Save.

Applying a graphic style to a layer

When a graphic style is applied to a layer, everything added to that layer has that same style applied to it. Now you'll apply a drop shadow graphic style to the layer named Block Text; this will apply the style to all the contents of that layer at once.

Note: If you apply a graphic style to artwork and then apply a graphic style to the layer (or sublayer) that it's on, the graphic style formatting is added to the appearance of the artwork—it's cumulative. This can change the artwork in ways you didn't expect, since applying a graphic style to the layer will be added to the formatting of the artwork.

Tip: In the Layers panel, you can drag a target icon to the Trash button ( ) at the bottom of the Layers panel to remove the appearance attributes.

1 In the Layers panel, click the target icon ( ) for the Block Text layer.

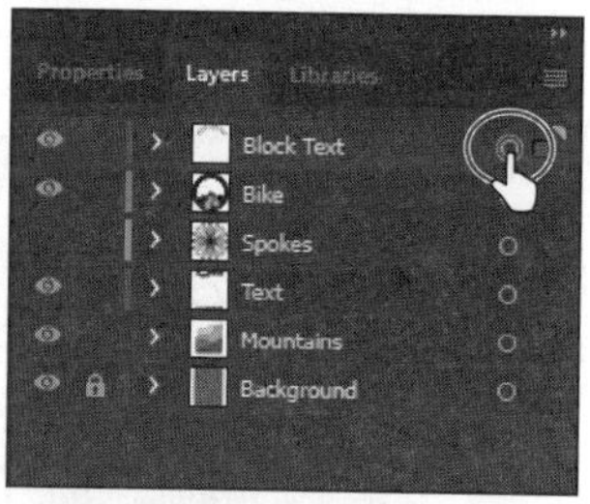

This selects the layer content and targets the layer for any appearance attributes.

2 Click the Graphic Styles panel tab, and then click the graphic style named "Shadow" to apply the style to the layer and all its contents.

The target icon in the Layers panel for the Block Text layer is now shaded.

Tip: In the Graphic Styles panel, graphic style thumbnails that show a small box with a red slash ( ) indicate that the graphic style does not contain a stroke or fill. It may just be a drop shadow or outer glow, for instance.

3 Click the Appearance panel tab, and you should see, with all of the artwork on the Block Text layer still selected, the words "Layer: Shadow."

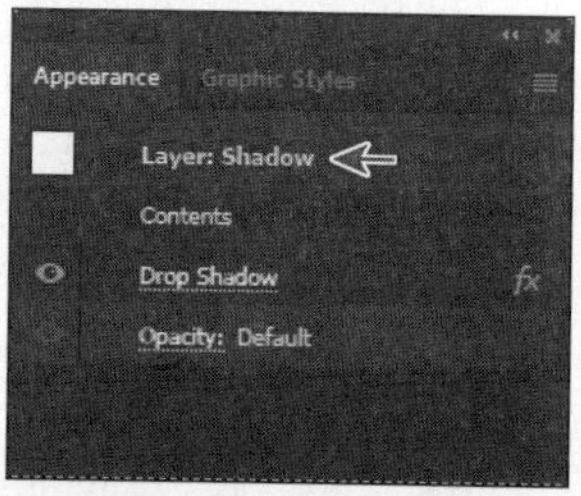

This is telling you that the layer target icon is selected in the Layers panel and that the Shadow graphic style is applied to that layer.

Note: If you want to edit the drop shadow applied to either of the text objects, you can do this a few ways. You can click the target icon in the Layers panel to see the Drop Shadow effect in the Appearance panel, or you can select the artwork (text object in this case) and click Layer: Shadow in the Appearance panel to see the appearance properties for the layer and then click Drop Shadow.

4 Choose Select > Deselect and then choose File > Save.

Applying multiple graphic styles

You can apply a graphic style to an object that already has a graphic style applied. This can be useful if you want to add properties to an object from another graphic style. After you apply a graphic style to selected artwork, you can then Option-click (macOS) or Alt-click (Windows) another graphic style thumbnail to add the graphic style formatting to the existing formatting, rather than replacing it.

Scaling strokes and effects

In Illustrator, by default, when scaling (resizing) content, any strokes and effects that are applied do not change. For instance, suppose you scale a circle with a 2-pt. stroke from small to the size of the artboard. The shape may change size, but the stroke will remain 2 pt. by default. That can change the appearance of scaled artwork in a way that you didn't intend, so you'll need to watch out for that when transforming artwork. Next, you'll make the spokes group larger.

1 Choose View > Fit Artboard In Window, if necessary.

2 In Layers panel, click in the visibility column for the layer named "Spokes" to show the artwork.

   This shows a large group of wheel spokes on the artboard.

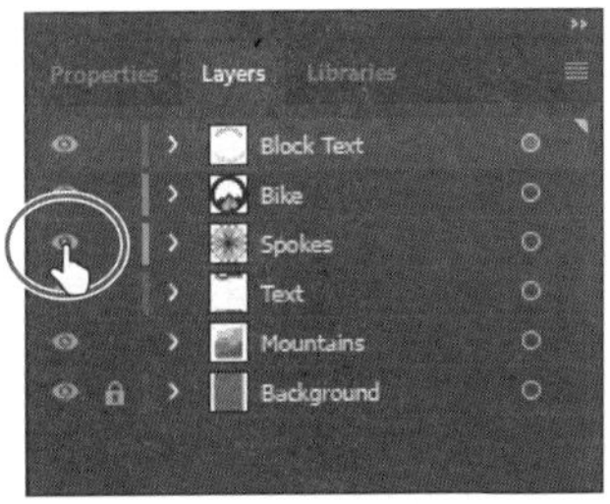

3 Click the spokes artwork, and notice the stroke weight of 6 pt in the Properties panel.

4 Click More Options in the Transform section of the Properties panel, and select Scale Strokes & Effects at the bottom of the panel that appears.

Without this option selected, scaling the spokes would not affect the stroke weights or effects when it is scaled. You are selecting this option so that the spokes will scale smaller and not remain the same stroke weight.

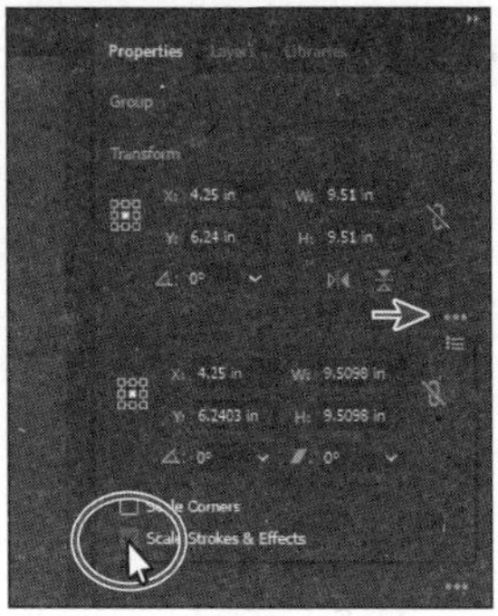

5 Click the Constrain Width And Height Proportions button ( ) to ensure it's active ( ). Change Width (W) to **5** inches. Press the Tab key to move to the next field. The height should change proportionally with the width.

After scaling the spokes, if you look at the stroke weight in the Properties panel, you will see that it has changed (scaled).

6 Choose Select > Deselect.

7 Choose File > Save and then choose File > Close.

Review questions

1 How do you add a second fill or stroke to artwork?

2 Name two ways to apply an effect to an object.

3 When you apply a Photoshop (raster) effect to vector artwork, what happens to the artwork?

4 Where can you access the options for effects applied to an object?

5 What's the difference between applying a graphic style to a *layer* versus applying it to *selected artwork*?

Review answers

1 To add a second fill or stroke to artwork, click the Add New Stroke button (■) or Add New Fill button (■) at the bottom of the Appearance panel, or choose Add New Stroke/Add New Fill from the Appearance panel menu. A stroke is added to the top of the appearance list. It has the same color and stroke weight as the original.

2 You can apply an effect to an object by selecting the object and then choosing the effect from the Effect menu. You can also apply an effect by selecting the object, clicking the Add New Effect button (fx) in the Properties panel or at the bottom of the Appearance panel, and then choosing the effect from the menu that appears.

3 Applying a Photoshop effect to artwork generates pixels rather than vector data. Photoshop effects include all of the effects in the bottom portion of the Effect menu and the Drop Shadow, Inner Glow, Outer Glow, and Feather commands in the Effect > Stylize submenu. You can apply them to either vector or bitmap objects.

4 You can edit effects applied to selected artwork by clicking the effect link in the Properties panel or Appearance panel to access the effect options.

5 When a graphic style is applied to a single object, other objects on that layer are not affected. For example, if a triangle object has a Roughen effect applied to its path and you move it to another layer, it retains the Roughen effect.

After a graphic style is applied to a layer, everything you add to the layer has that style applied to it. For example, if you create a circle on Layer 1 and then move that circle to Layer 2, which has a Drop Shadow effect applied, the circle adopts that effect.

13 CREATING ARTWORK FOR A T-SHIRT

Lesson overview

In this lesson, you'll learn how to do the following:

- Work with existing symbols.
- Create, modify, and redefine a symbol.
- Store and retrieve artwork in the Symbols panel.
- Understand Creative Cloud libraries.
- Work with Creative Cloud libraries.

This lesson takes approximately 45 minutes to complete. Please log in to your account on peachpit.com to download the lesson files for this chapter, or go to the "Getting Started" section at the beginning of this book and follow the instructions under "Accessing the lesson files and Web Edition."

Your Account page is also where you'll find any updates to the chapters or to the lesson files. Look on the Lesson & Update Files tab to access the most current content.

In this lesson, you'll explore a variety of useful concepts for working smarter and faster in Illustrator, including using symbols and working with Creative Cloud libraries to make your design assets available anywhere.

Starting the lesson

In this lesson, you'll explore several concepts such as symbols and the Libraries panel to create artwork for a T-shirt. Before you begin, you'll restore the default preferences for Adobe Illustrator. Then, you'll open the finished art file for this lesson to see what you'll create.

● **Note:** If you have not already downloaded the project files for this lesson to your computer from your Account page, make sure to do so now. See the "Getting Started" section at the beginning of the book.

● **Note:** If the Missing Fonts dialog box appears, click Close.

1 To ensure that the tools function and the defaults are set exactly as described in this lesson, delete or deactivate (by renaming) the Adobe Illustrator CC preferences file. See "Restoring default preferences" in the "Getting Started" section at the beginning of the book.

2 Start Adobe Illustrator CC.

3 Choose File > Open, and open the L13_end.ai file in the Lessons > Lesson13 folder on your hard disk.

You're going to create artwork for a T-shirt design.

4 Choose View > Fit Artboard In Window and leave the file open for reference, or choose File > Close.

5 Choose File > Open. In the Open dialog box, navigate to the Lessons > Lesson13 folder, and select the L13_start.ai file on your hard disk. Click Open to open the file.

6 Choose View > Fit All In Window.

7 Choose File > Save As. In the Save As dialog box, navigate to the Lesson13 folder, and name the file **TShirt.ai**. Leave the Format option set to Adobe Illustrator (ai) (macOS) or the Save As Type option set to Adobe Illustrator (*.AI) (Windows) and then click Save.

8 In the Illustrator Options dialog box, leave the Illustrator options at their default settings and then click OK.

9 Choose Reset Essentials from the workspace switcher in the Application bar.

● **Note:** If you don't see Reset Essentials in the menu, choose Window > Workspace > Essentials before choosing Window > Workspace > Reset Essentials.

Working with symbols

A *symbol* is a reusable art object that is stored in the Symbols panel (Window > Symbols). For example, if you create a symbol from a flower you drew, you can then quickly add multiple *instances* of that flower symbol to your artwork, which saves you from having to draw each flower. All instances in the document are linked to the original symbol in the Symbols panel. When you edit the original symbol, all instances of the flower (in this example) that are linked to it are updated. You can turn all those flowers from white to red instantly! Not only do symbols save time, but they also greatly reduce file size.

● **Note:** Illustrator comes with a series of symbol libraries, which range from tiki icons to hair to web icons. You can access those symbol libraries in the Symbols panel or by choosing Window > Symbol Libraries and easily incorporate them into your own artwork.

- Choose Window > Symbols to open the Symbols panel. The symbols you see in the Symbols panel are the symbols you can use with this document. Each document has its own set of saved symbols. The different options available in the Symbols panel are described here:

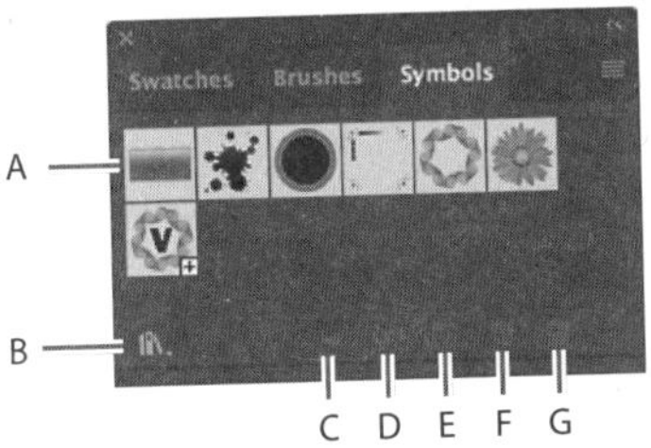

A. Symbol thumbnail

B. Symbol Libraries Menu

C. Place Symbol Instance

D. Break Link to Symbol

E. Symbol Options

F. New Symbol

G. Delete Symbol

Using existing Illustrator symbol libraries

You'll start by adding a symbol from an existing symbol library to the artwork.

1 Click the Artboards menu in the Properties panel to the right of the document and choose 1 from the menu. The larger artboard with the black T-shirt on it will show in the Document window.

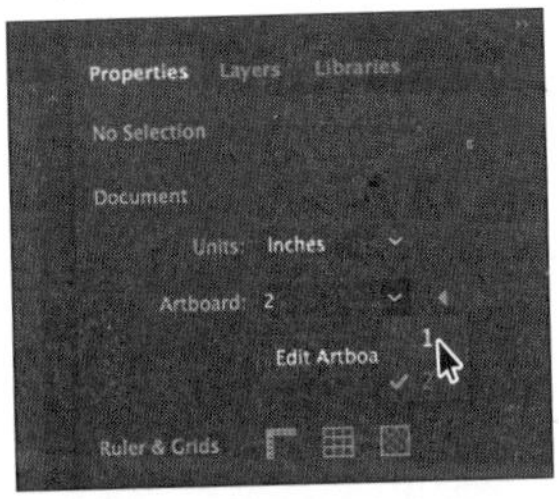

2 Click the Hide Smart Guides option in the Properties panel to turn the Smart Guides off temporarily.

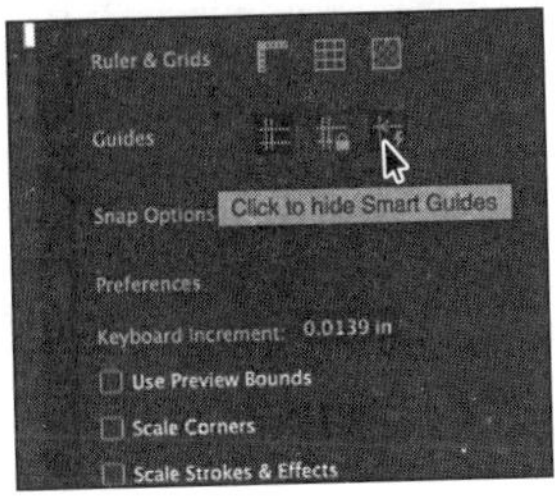

▶ **Tip:** You can also choose View > Smart Guides to turn them off.

3 Click the Layers panel tab to show the Layers panel. Click the Content layer to make sure it is selected. Make sure that both of the layers are collapsed by clicking the disclosure triangles to the left of the layer names (if necessary).

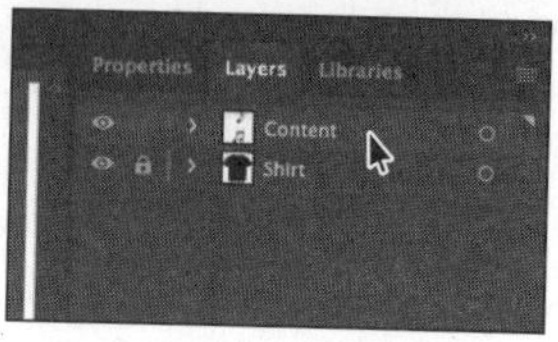

When adding symbols to a document, the layer that is selected when they are added is the same layer they become a part of.

4 In the Symbols panel (Window > Symbols), click the Symbol Libraries Menu button ( ) at the bottom of the panel, and choose Tiki from the menu.

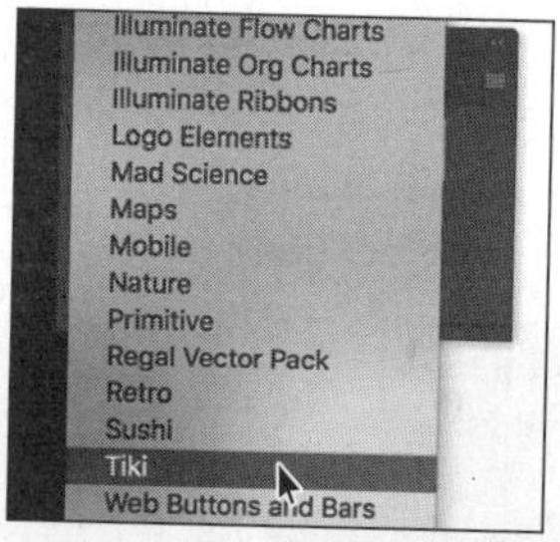

The Tiki library opens as a free-floating panel. The symbols in this library are not part of the file that you are working on, but you can import any of the symbols into the document and use them in the artwork.

▶ **Tip:** If you want to see the symbol names along with the symbol pictures, click the Symbols panel menu icon ( ), and then choose Small List View or Large List View.

▶ **Tip:** You can also copy a symbol instance on the artboard and paste as many as you need. This is the same as dragging a symbol instance out of the Symbols panel onto the artboard.

5 Position the pointer over the symbols in the Tiki panel to see their names as tooltips. Click the symbol named "Guitar" to add it to the Symbols panel. Close the Tiki panel.

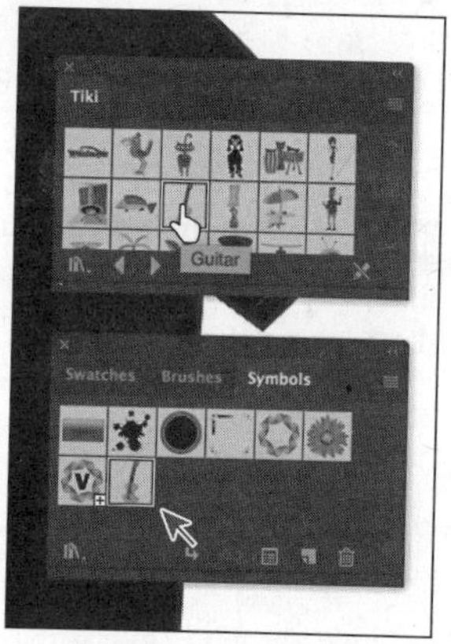

When you add symbols to the Symbols panel, they are saved with the active document only.

6 Using the Selection tool ( ), drag the Guitar symbol from the Symbols panel onto the artboard into the center of the black T-shirt. Do this *twice* to create two instances of the guitar on the T-shirt.

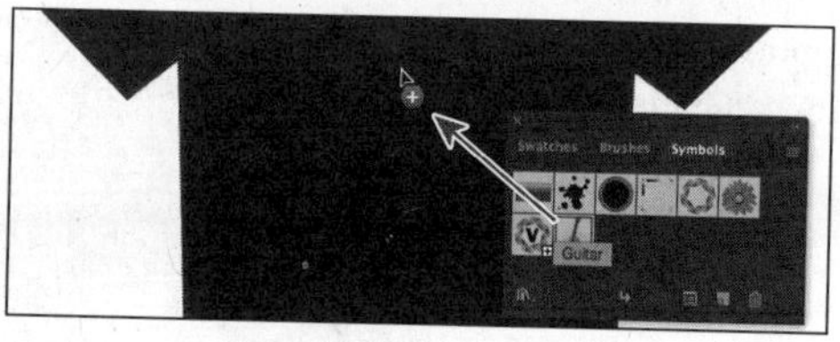

Each time you drag a symbol like the guitar onto the artboard, an *instance* of the original symbol is created. Next, you'll resize one of the symbol instances.

7 Click to select the Guitar instance on the right, if it's not already selected. Shift-drag the upper-right bounding point toward the center to make it a little smaller, while constraining its proportions. Release the mouse button and then the key.

A symbol instance is treated like a group of objects and can have only certain transformation and appearance properties changed (such as scale, rotate, move, transparency, etc.). You cannot edit the individual artwork that makes up an instance without breaking the link to the original symbol. With the symbol instance still selected on the artboard, notice that, in the Properties panel, you see "Symbol (Static)" and symbol-related options.

Note: Although you can transform symbol instances in many ways, specific properties of instances from static symbols like the guitar cannot be edited. For example, the fill color is locked because it is controlled by the original symbol in the Symbols panel.

8 With the same instance still selected, click the Flip Along Horizontal Axis option ( ) in the Properties panel to flip the guitar horizontally.

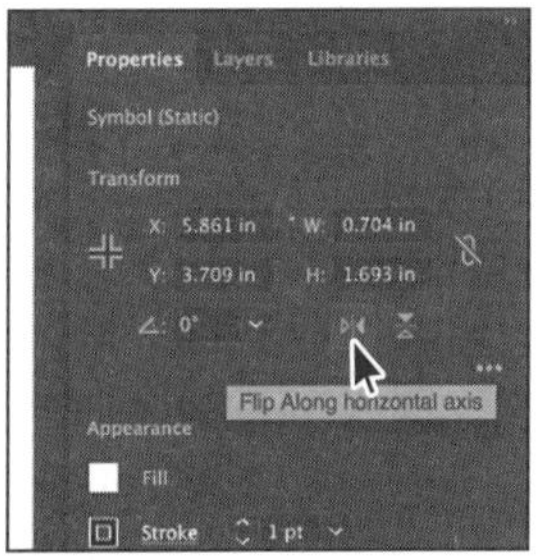

Editing a symbol

In this next section, you'll edit the Guitar symbol, and all instances in the document will be updated. There are several ways to edit a symbol, and in this section you will focus on one method.

1 With the Selection tool ( ) selected, double-click the selected Guitar symbol instance on the artboard. A warning dialog box appears, stating that you are about to edit the original symbol and that all instances will update. Click OK.

Tip: Another way to edit a symbol is to select the symbol instance on the artboard and then click the Edit Symbol button in the Properties panel.

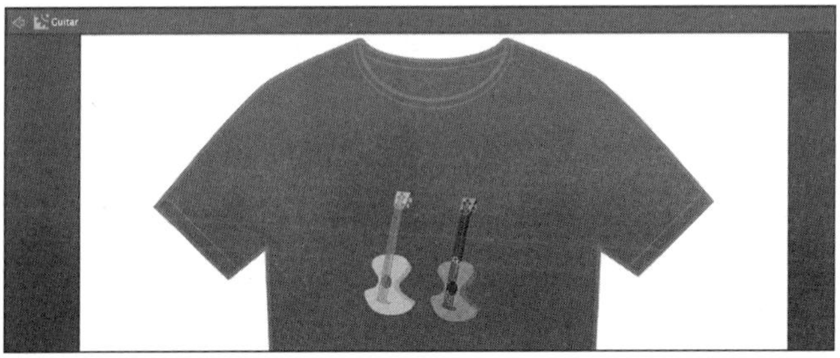

This takes you into Symbol Editing mode, so you can't edit any other objects on the page. The Guitar symbol instance you double-clicked will appear larger and will no longer be reflected. That's because in Symbol Editing mode, you are looking at the *original* symbol artwork. You can now edit the artwork that makes up the symbol.

2 Select the Zoom tool (🔍), and drag across the symbol content to zoom in closely.

3 Select the Direct Selection tool (▶), and click to select the blue body of the guitar artwork. An arrow is pointing to it in the following figure.

4 Click the Fill color box in the Properties panel, make sure the Swatches option is selected, and select the brown swatch with the tooltip "C=25 M=40 Y=65 K=0."

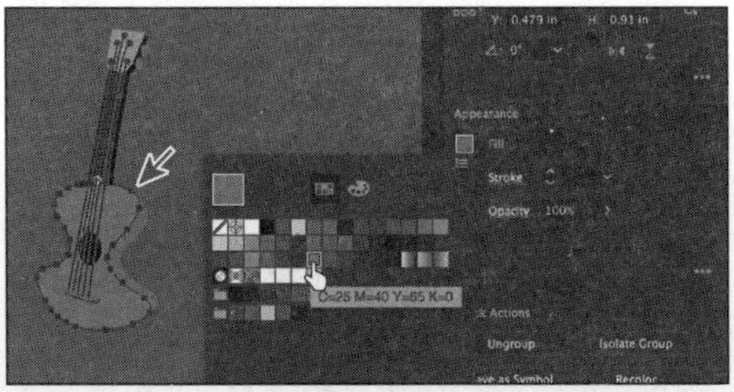

5 Double-click away from the symbol content, or click the Exit Symbol Editing Mode button (⇦) in the upper-left corner of the Document window until you exit Symbol Editing mode, so that you can edit the rest of the content.

6 Choose View > Fit Artboard In Window, and notice that both of the Guitar symbol instances on the artboard have been changed.

Working with dynamic symbols

As you just saw, editing a symbol updates all of the instances in your document. Symbols can also be *dynamic*, which means you can change certain appearance properties of instances using the Direct Selection tool (▶) without editing the original symbol. In this section, you'll edit the properties of the Guitar symbol so that it is dynamic, and then you'll edit each instance separately.

1 In the Symbols panel, click the Guitar symbol thumbnail to select it, if it's not already selected. Click the Symbol Options button (▤) at the bottom of the Symbols panel.

2 In the Symbol Options dialog box, select Dynamic Symbol, and click OK. The symbol and its instances are now dynamic.

▶ **Tip:** You can tell if a symbol is dynamic by looking at the thumbnail in the Symbols panel. If there is a small plus sign (+) in the lower-right corner of the thumbnail, it is a dynamic symbol.

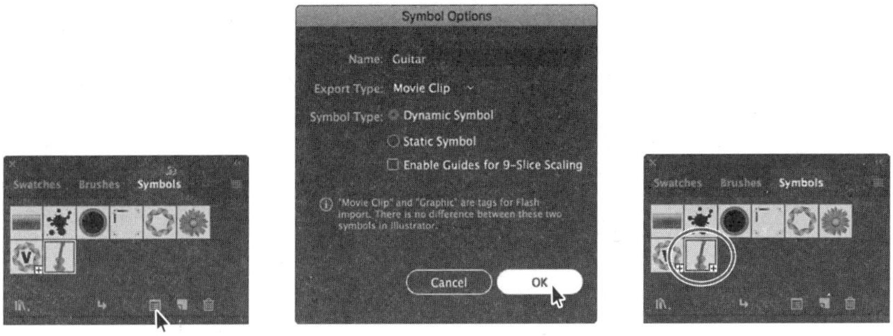

3 Select the Zoom tool (🔍), and drag across the symbol content (guitars) to zoom in.

4 Select the Direct Selection tool (▷) in the Tools panel. Click to select the blue, curved body shape of the guitar instance on the right. See the following figure.

With part of the symbol instance selected, notice the words "Symbol (Dynamic)" at the top of the Properties panel telling you it's a dynamic symbol.

5 Change the fill color to a darker brown swatch in the Properties panel.

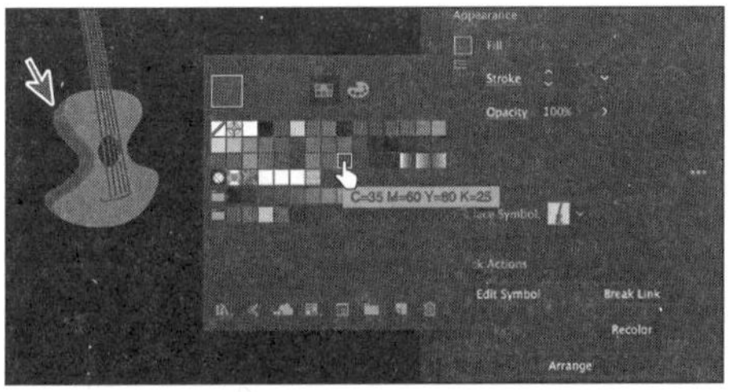

▶ **Tip:** After making edits to a dynamic symbol instance with the Direct Selection tool, you can reselect the entire instance with the Selection tool and click the Reset button in the Properties panel to reset the appearance to the same as the original symbol.

The guitar on the right now looks a little different from the one on the left. Know that if you were to edit the original symbol like you did previously, both symbol instances would still update, but that darker brown part of the right guitar instance would remain different.

Creating a symbol

Illustrator also lets you create and save your own symbols. You can make symbols from objects, including paths, compound paths, text, embedded (not linked) raster images, mesh objects, and groups of objects. Symbols can even include active objects, such as brush strokes, blends, effects, or other symbol instances. Next, you'll create your own symbol from existing artwork.

1 Choose 2 Symbol Artwork from the Artboard menu in the lower-left corner of the Document window.

2 With the Selection tool (▶) selected, click the top "musical note" shape on the artboard to select it.

▶ **Tip:** You can also drag the selected content into a blank area of the Symbols panel to create a symbol.

3 Click the New Symbol button (■) at the bottom of the Symbols panel to make a symbol from the selected artwork.

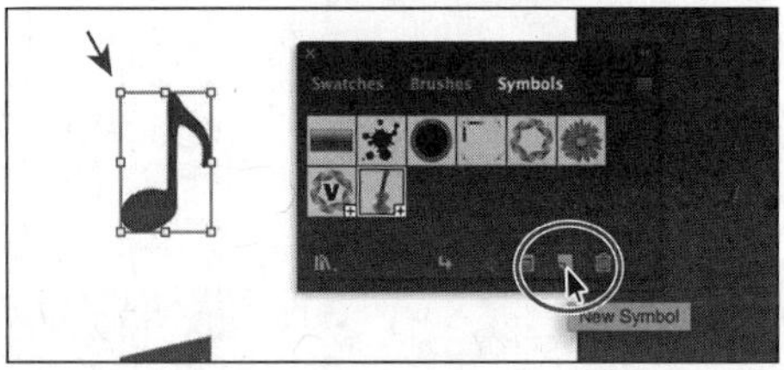

4 In the Symbol Options dialog box that opens, change the name to **Note1**. Ensure that Dynamic Symbol is selected, just in case you want to edit the appearance of one of the instances later. Click OK to create the symbol.

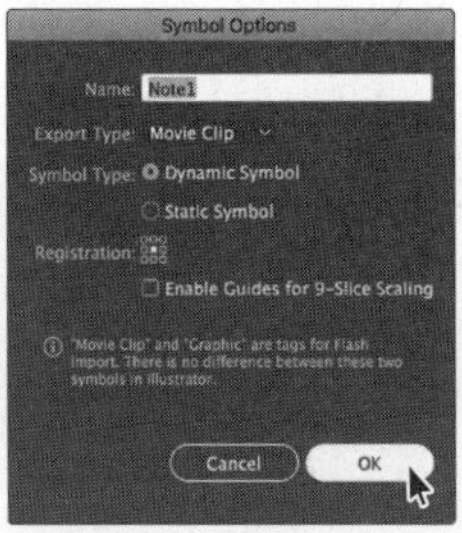

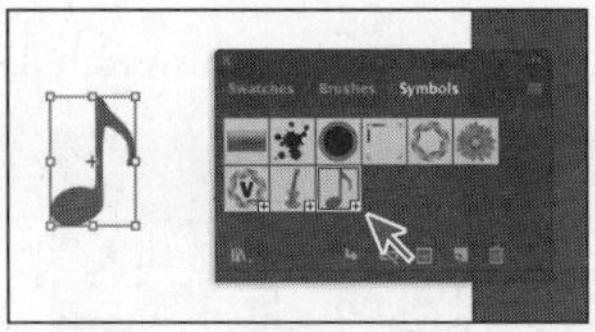

▶ **Tip:** You can drag the symbol thumbnails in the Symbols panel to change their ordering. Reordering symbols in the Symbols panel has no effect on the artwork. It can simply be a way to organize your symbols.

In the Symbol Options dialog box, you'll see a note that explains that there is no difference between a movie clip and a graphic type in Illustrator. If you don't plan on exporting this content to Adobe Animate CC, you don't need to worry about choosing an export type. After creating the symbol, the note artwork on the artboard is converted to an *instance* of the Note1 symbol. The symbol also appears in the Symbols panel.

5 Choose 1 T-Shirt from the Artboard menu in the lower-left corner of the Document window.

6 Drag the Note1 symbol from the Symbols panel onto the artboard four times, and position the instances around the guitars like you see in the following figure.

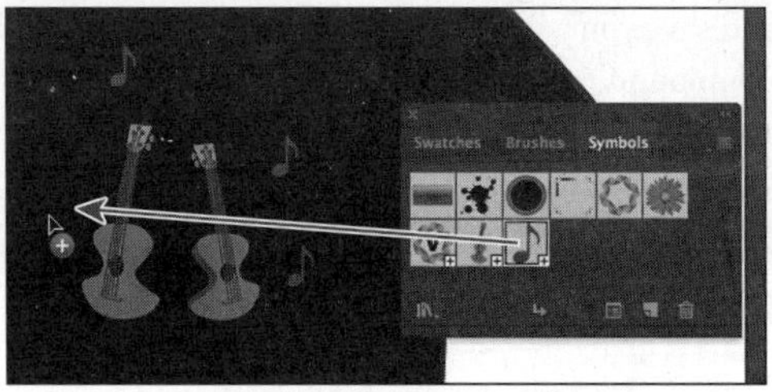

7 Resize a few of the Note1 instances on the artboard using the Selection tool.

8 Choose Select > Deselect and then choose File > Save.

Duplicating symbols

Often you will want to add a series of symbol instances to your artwork. After all, one of the reasons for using symbols is for storing and updating frequently used content like trees or clouds. In this section, you'll create, add, and duplicate a symbol that happens to be another musical note.

1 Choose 2 Symbol Artwork from the Artboard menu in the lower-left corner of the Document window.

2 Using the Selection tool (▶), click and drag the bottom "musical note" shape from the artboard into a blank area of the Symbols panel to create a new symbol.

3 In the Symbol Options dialog box, change the name to **Note2**, and make sure Dynamic Symbol is selected. Leave the remaining settings at their defaults, and click OK to create the symbol.

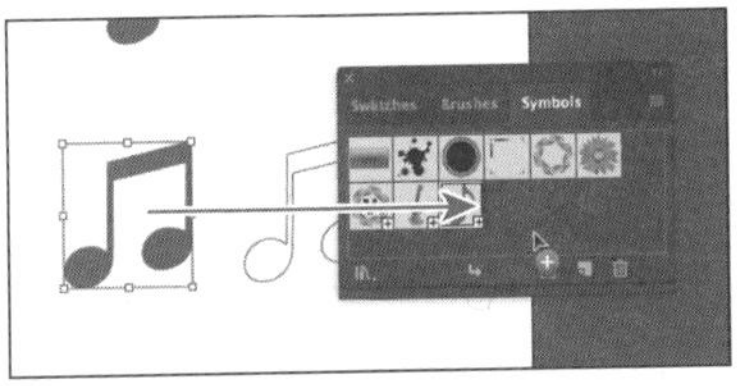

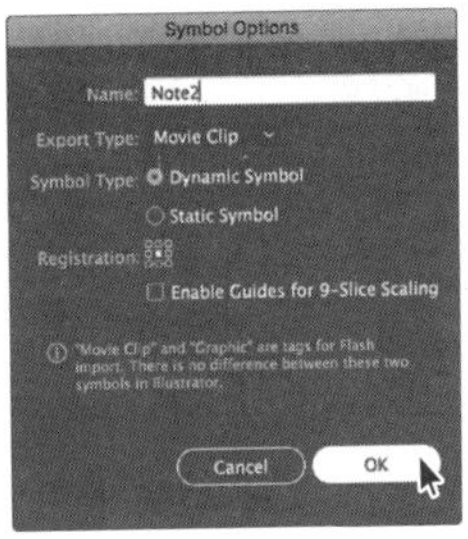

4 Choose 1 T-Shirt from the Artboard menu in the lower-left corner of the Document window to go back to the T-shirt artwork.

5 Drag one instance of the Note2 symbol from the Symbols panel onto the T-shirt, near the other notes.

6 Press Option (macOS) or Alt (Windows), and drag the Note2 symbol instance on the artboard to create a copy. When the new instance is in position (see the figure), release the mouse button and then the modifier key.

Note: Your symbol instances may not be in the same position on the artboard, and that's fine.

7 Create a few more copies by pressing Option (macOS) or Alt (Windows) and dragging any of the note symbol instances.

8 Resize and move a few of the symbol instances, making some smaller and some a bit larger, so they look different from each other.

9 Choose File > Save.

Replacing symbols

You can easily replace a symbol instance in the document with another symbol. Next, you'll replace a few of the Note2 symbol instances.

1 With the Selection tool (▶), select one of the Note2 symbol instances on the artboard.

   When you select a symbol instance, you can tell which symbol it came from because the symbol for the selected instance is highlighted in the Symbols panel.

2 In the Properties panel, click the arrow to the right of the Replace Symbol field to open a panel showing the symbols in the Symbols panel. Click the Note1 symbol in the panel.

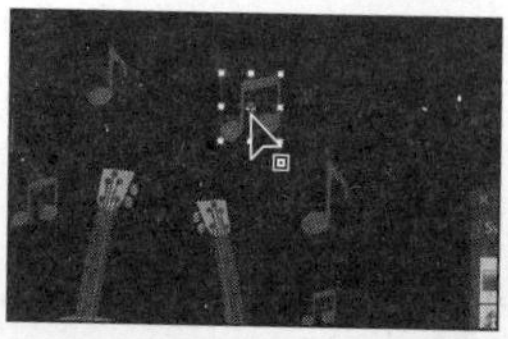

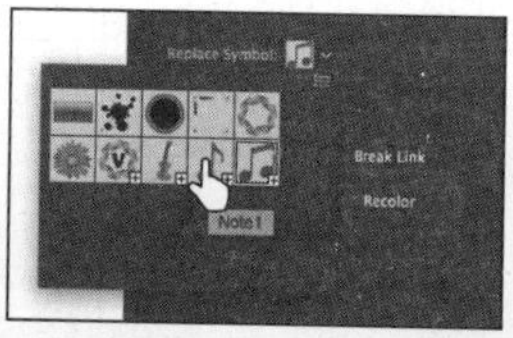

   If the original symbol instance you were replacing had a transformation applied, such as a rotation, the symbol instance replacing it would have the same transformations applied.

3 Double-click the Note2 symbol thumbnail in the Symbols panel to edit the symbol.

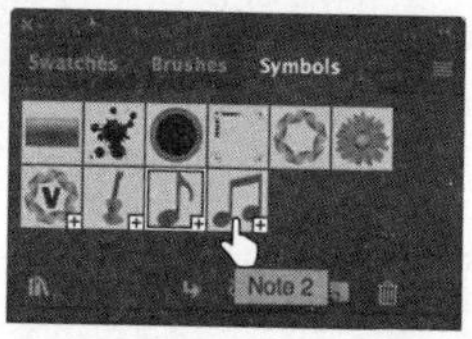

   A temporary instance of the symbol appears in the center of the Document window. Editing a symbol by double-clicking the symbol in the Symbols panel hides all artboard content except the symbol artwork. This is just another way to edit a symbol.

4 Select the Selection tool (▶) in the Tools panel, and click the note shape. Press Command++ (macOS) or Ctrl++ (Windows) a few times to zoom in.

5 Change the fill color in the Properties panel to a light gray swatch with the tooltip that shows "C=0 M=0 Y=0 K=30."

6 Double-click away from the symbol content to exit Symbol Editing mode so that you can edit the rest of the content.

7 Choose View > Fit Artboard In Window.

8 Select the Selection tool (▶), and click one of the note symbol instances. It doesn't matter which symbol (Note1 or Note2) it is. Choose Select > Same > Symbol Instance.

This is a great way to select all instances of a symbol in the document. You can see that the symbol instance on the right artboard was also selected.

9 Choose Select > Deselect.

Symbol layers

When you edit a symbol using any of the methods described, open the Layers panel, and you will see that the symbol has its own layering.

Similar to working with groups in Isolation mode, you see the layers associated with that symbol only, not the document's layers. In the Layers panel, you can rename, add, delete, show/hide, and reorder content for a symbol.

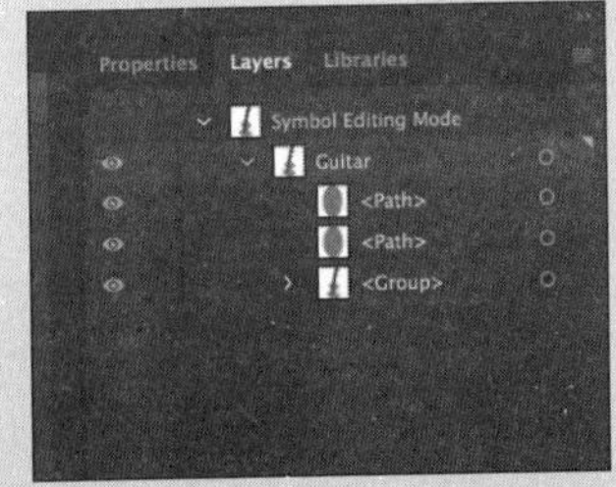

Breaking a link to a symbol

At times, you need to edit specific instances on the artboard. As you've learned, you can make changes, such as scaling, opacity, and flipping, only to a symbol instance, and saving the symbol as dynamic only lets you edit certain appearance attributes using the Direct Selection tool. In certain cases, you may need to break the link between a symbol and an instance. This breaks the instance into the original artwork on the artboard, and that instance will no longer update if the symbol is edited.

Next, you'll break the link to one of the guitar symbol instances.

▶ **Tip:** You can also break the link to a symbol instance by selecting the symbol instance on the artboard and then clicking the Break Link To Symbol button () at the bottom of the Symbols panel.

1 With the Selection tool () selected, click to select the Guitar symbol instance on the left. In the Properties panel, click the Break Link button.

This object is now a series of paths; if you click to select the artwork, you'll see "Group" at the top of the Properties panel. You should be able to edit the artwork directly now. This content will no longer update if the Guitar symbol is edited.

2 Select the Zoom tool (), and drag across the top of the selected guitar artwork on the artboard to zoom in.

3 Choose Select > Deselect.

● **Note:** I have you select the Direct Selection tool and not the Selection tool because the guitar is a group. Selecting with the Direct Selection tool usually allows you to select individual artwork in a group.

4 Select the Direct Selection tool, and click the top small blue circle toward the top of the guitar. Option-drag (macOS) or Alt-drag (Windows) the circle up to create a copy. Release the mouse button and then the modifier key.

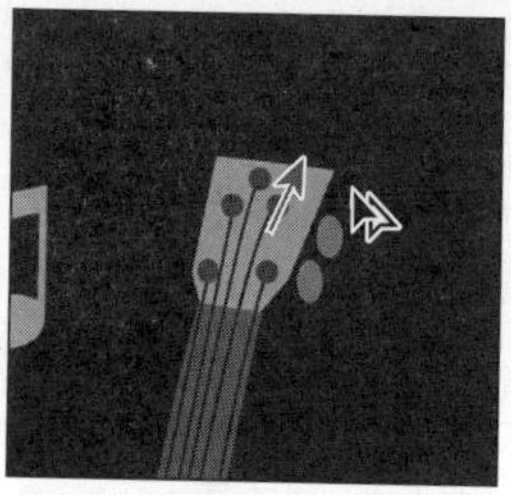

5 Choose Select > Deselect.

6 Choose File > Save.

The Symbolism Tools

The Symbol Sprayer tool () in the Tools panel allows you to spray symbols on the artboard, creating symbol sets.

A *symbol set* is a group of symbol instances that you create with the Symbol Sprayer tool. This can be really useful if, for instance, you were to create grass from individual blades of grass. Spraying the blades of grass speeds up this process greatly and makes it much easier to edit individual instances of grass or the sprayed grass as a group. You can create mixed sets of symbol instances by using the Symbol Sprayer tool with one symbol and then using it again with another symbol.

You use the symbolism tools to modify multiple symbol instances in a set. For example, you can disperse instances over a larger area using the Symbol Scruncher tool or gradually tinting the color of instances to make them look more realistic.

—From Illustrator Help

Working with Creative Cloud libraries

Creative Cloud libraries are an easy way to create and share stored content such as images, colors, text styles, Adobe Stock assets, Creative Cloud Market assets, and more between many Adobe applications like Adobe Photoshop CC, Adobe Illustrator CC, Adobe InDesign CC, and certain Adobe mobile apps.

Creative Cloud libraries connects to your Creative Profile, putting the creative assets you care about at your fingertips. When you create content in Illustrator and save it to a Creative Cloud library, that asset is available to use in all of your Illustrator files. Those assets are automatically synced and can be shared with anyone with a Creative Cloud account. As your creative team works across Adobe desktop and mobile apps, your shared library assets are always up to date and ready to use anywhere.

Note: In order to use Creative Cloud libraries, you will need to be signed in with your Adobe ID and have an Internet connection.

In this section, you'll explore CC libraries and use them in your project.

Adding assets to CC libraries

The first thing you'll learn about is how to work with the Libraries panel (Window > Libraries) in Illustrator and add assets to a Creative Cloud library. You'll open an existing document in Illustrator to capture assets from.

1 Choose File > Open. In the Open dialog box, navigate to the Lessons > Lesson13 folder, and select the Sample.ai file on your hard disk. Click Open.

Note: The Missing Fonts dialog box may appear. You need an Internet connection to sync the fonts. The syncing process may take a few minutes. Click Sync Fonts to sync all of the missing fonts to your computer. After they are synced and you see the message stating that there are no more missing fonts, click Close. If you have an issue syncing, you can go to Help (Help > Illustrator Help) and search for "Find missing fonts."

2 Choose View > Fit All In Window.

Using this document, you will capture artwork, text, colors, and type formatting to be used in the TShirt.ai document.

3 Choose Window > Libraries, or click the Libraries panel tab to open the Libraries panel.

To start, you have one library to work with called "My Library." You can add your design assets to this default library, or you can create more libraries—maybe to save assets according to clients or projects.

4 Choose Select > Deselect, if necessary.

Note: The menu that appears after clicking the Add Content icon (+) is contextual. It changes depending on what can be saved from the selected artwork.

5 Select the Selection tool (▶), and click the type area that contains the text "Rock On." In the Libraries panel, click the Add Content icon (+) and make sure all of the options are selected, except for Graphic. Click Add to capture the text and formatting, and save it in the default library. If you see a warning dialog box about text appearance, click OK.

Tip: You can change the appearance of the items (icons or list) by clicking the buttons in the upper-right corner of the Libraries panel.

The paragraph style formatting, text object, and fill color will be saved in the currently selected library. In this case, it is adding the assets to my default library called "My Library." As you save assets and formatting in the Libraries panel, notice how it is organized by asset type.

6 Double-click the name "Text 1" in the Libraries panel, and change it to **Heading**. Press Enter or Return to accept the name change.

You can change the name of the color, character style, and paragraph style saved in the Libraries panel as well. In the case of the character and paragraph styles saved, you can move the pointer over the asset and see a tooltip that shows the saved formatting.

7 Drag across the black artwork in the lower-right corner with the text "Guitar" on it to select all of the artwork.

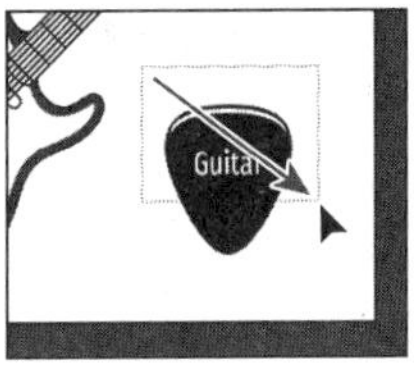

8 Drag the selected artwork into the Libraries panel. When a plus sign (+) and a name (such as "Artwork 1") appears, release the mouse button to add the artwork as a graphic.

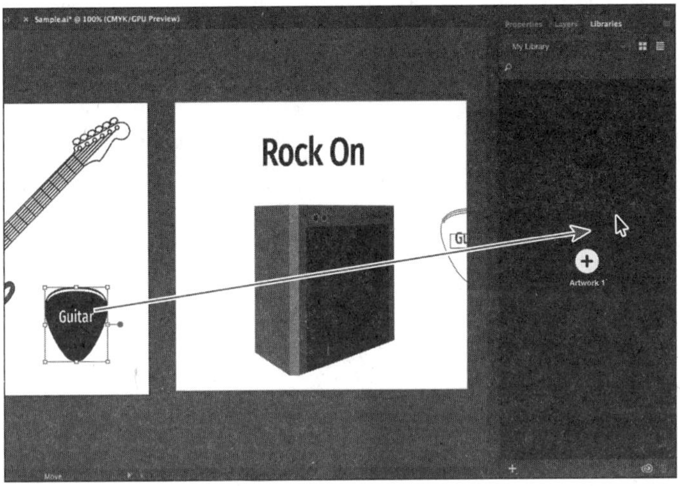

The assets you store as a graphic in a Creative Cloud library retain their vector form wherever you use the graphic.

9 Drag the amp artwork, below the "Rock On" text, into the Libraries panel to save it as a graphic asset.

10 Choose File > Close to close the Sample.ai file and return to the TShirt.ai file. Don't save the file if asked.

Notice that the Libraries panel still shows the assets in the library. The libraries and their assets are available no matter which document is open in Illustrator.

Tip: You can share a copy of your library with others by choosing the library you want to share in the Libraries panel and then choosing Share Link from the panel menu.

Using library assets

Now that you have some assets in the Libraries panel, once synced, those assets will be available to other applications and apps that support libraries, as long as you are signed in with the same Creative Cloud account. Next, you will use some of those assets in the TShirt.ai file.

1 While still on the 1 T-Shirt artboard, choose View > Fit Artboard In Window.

2 Drag the Heading text asset from the Libraries panel onto the artboard.

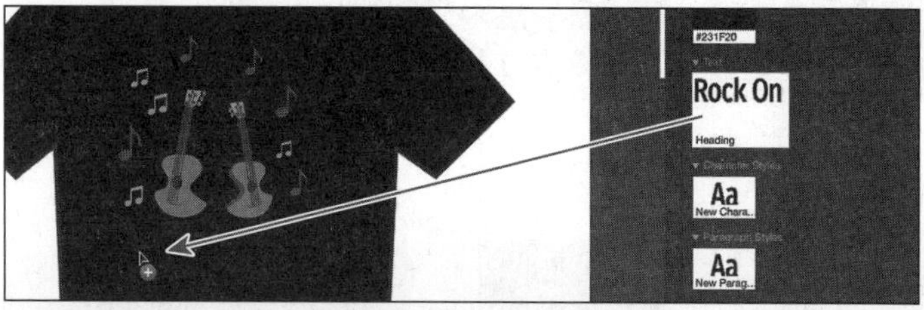

3 Click to place the text.

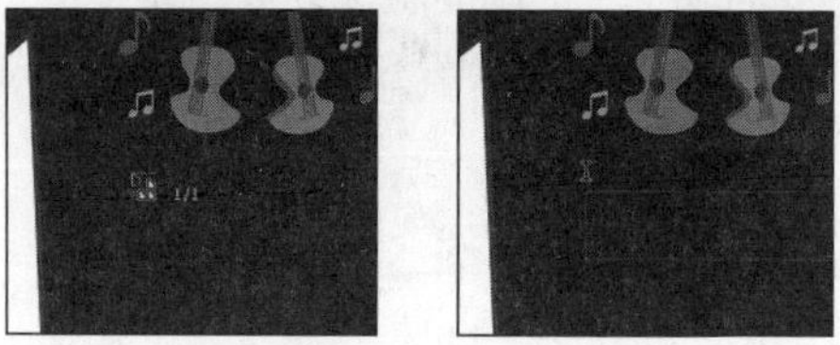

4 Press Esc to select the Selection tool and the type object. Click the Properties panel tab and change the fill color to white.

5 Double-click the "Rock On" text to switch to the Type tool. Press Command+A (macOS) or Ctrl+A (Windows) to select the text.

6 Change the text to **ROCK ON!** (with an exclamation point).

7 Click the Libraries panel tab to show the panel. Drag the pick graphic asset and then the amp graphic asset from the Libraries panel onto the artboard. Don't worry about position for now.

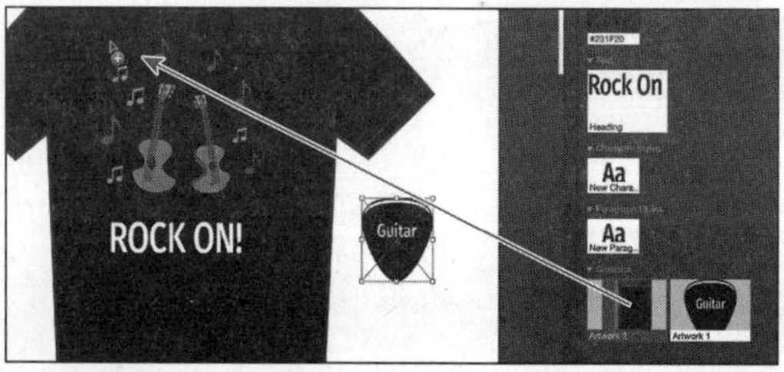

▶ **Tip:** As you'll learn in the next section, graphics you drag from the Libraries panel are linked. If you Option-drag (macOS) or Alt-drag (Windows) the artwork from the Libraries panel into a document, it will be embedded by default.

▶ **Tip:** To apply the color or styles saved in the Libraries panel, select artwork or text and click to apply. When it comes to text styles in the Libraries panel, if you apply them to text in a document, a style of the same name and formatting will appear in the Paragraph Styles panel or Character Styles panel (depending on which you selected in the Libraries panel).

● **Note:** You will most likely need to click to place the assets, like you did with the text.

Updating a library asset

When you drag a graphic from your Creative Cloud library to an Illustrator project, it is automatically placed as a linked asset. If you make a change to a library asset, the linked instances will update in your projects. Next, you'll see how to update the asset.

1 Select the Selection tool (▶), and click the pick asset on the artboard and look at the top of the Properties panel (you'll need to click the Properties panel tab to show it). Click the words "Linked File" to open the Links panel.

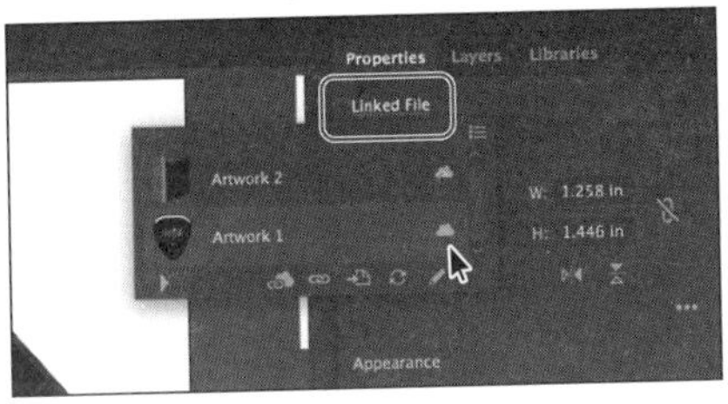

In the Links panel that appears, you will see the name of the pick asset, as well as a cloud icon to the right of the name. The cloud icon indicates that the artwork is a linked library asset.

● **Note:** You'll learn more about the Links panel in Lesson 14, "Using Illustrator CC with Other Adobe Applications."

▶ **Tip:** You can edit a linked library asset like the guitar pick by clicking Edit Original (✎) at the bottom of the Links panel.

2 Back in the Libraries panel, double-click the pick asset thumbnail. The artwork will appear in a new, temporary document.

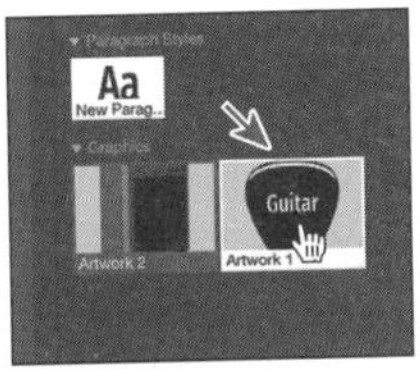

3 With the Direct Selection tool, click to select the black shape. Change the fill color to a gray with the tooltip "C=0 M=0 Y=0 K=70" in the Properties panel.

4 Choose File > Save and then choose File > Close.

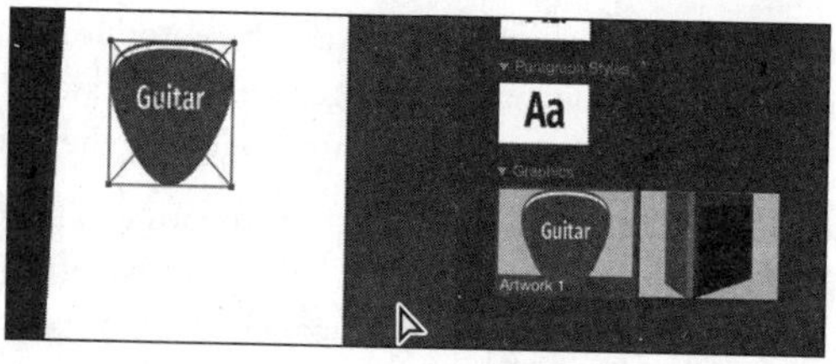

In the Libraries panel, the graphic thumbnail should update to reflect the appearance change you made. Back in the TShirt.ai document, the pick graphic on the artboard should have updated. *If it hasn't,* with the pick artwork still selected on the artboard, click the Linked File link in the Properties panel. In the Links panel that shows, with the pick asset row selected, click the Update Link button ( ) at the bottom of the panel.

5 With the artwork selected, click the Embed button back in the Properties panel.

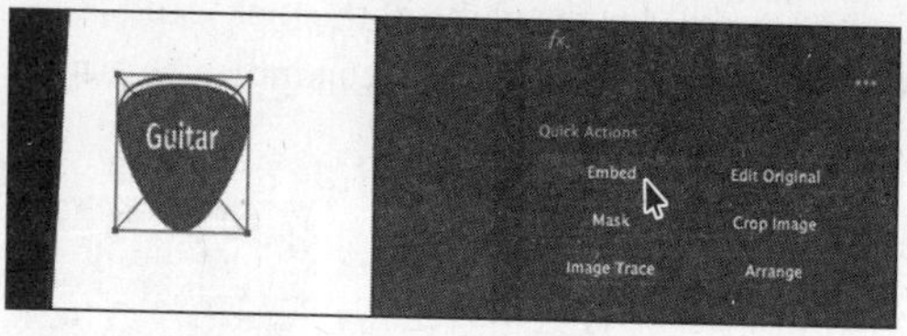

The artwork is no longer linked to the original library item and will not update if the pick library item is updated. That also means it is now editable in the TShirt.ai document. Just know that Libraries panel artwork that is embedded after it has been placed will typically have a clipping mask applied.

6 With the Selection tool, click the amp artwork and, to send it behind everything else, click the Arrange button in the Properties panel and choose Send To Back.

7 Drag all of the artwork like you see in the following figure. You may want to resize the pick and amp artwork to make them each a little smaller. If you resize any of the artwork, make sure you press the Shift key to constrain the proportions as you scale; then release the mouse button and key when finished.

8 Choose Select > Deselect and then choose File > Save.

Review questions

1 What are three benefits of using symbols?

2 How do you update an existing symbol?

3 What is a dynamic symbol?

4 In Illustrator, what type of content can you save in a library?

5 Explain how to embed a linked library graphic asset.

Review answers

1 Three benefits of using symbols are as follows:

- You can edit one symbol, and all instances are updated.
- You can map artwork to 3D objects (not discussed in the lesson).
- Using symbols reduces file size.

2 To update an existing symbol, double-click the symbol icon in the Symbols panel, double-click an instance of the symbol on the artboard, or select the instance on the artboard and then click the Edit Symbol button in the Properties panel. Then you can make edits in Isolation mode.

3 When a symbol is saved as Dynamic, you can change certain appearance properties of instances using the Direct Selection tool (▶) without editing the original symbol.

4 In Illustrator, currently you can save colors (fill and stroke), type objects, graphic assets, and type formatting.

5 By default in Illustrator, when a graphic asset is dragged from the Libraries panel into a document, a link is created to the original library asset. In order to embed a graphic asset, select the asset in the document, and click Embed in the Properties panel. Once embedded, the graphic will no longer update if the original library asset is edited.

14 USING ILLUSTRATOR CC WITH OTHER ADOBE APPLICATIONS

Lesson overview

In this lesson, you'll learn how to do the following:

- Place linked and embedded graphics in an Illustrator file.
- Transform and crop images.
- Create and edit clipping masks.
- Use text to mask an image.
- Make and edit an opacity mask.
- Work with the Links panel.
- Embed and unembed images.
- Package a document.

This lesson takes approximately 60 minutes to complete. Please log in to your account on peachpit.com to download the lesson files for this chapter, or go to the "Getting Started" section at the beginning of this book and follow the instructions under "Accessing the lesson files and Web Edition."

Your Account page is also where you'll find any updates to the chapters or to the lesson files. Look on the Lesson & Update Files tab to access the most current content.

You can easily add images created in an image-editing program to an Adobe Illustrator file. This is a great way to incorporate raster images into your vector artwork to combine the two.

Starting the lesson

Before you begin, you'll need to restore the default preferences for Adobe Illustrator CC. Then you'll open the finished art file for this lesson to see what you'll create.

● **Note:** If you have not already downloaded the project files for this lesson to your computer from your Account page, make sure to do so now. See the "Getting Started" section at the beginning of the book.

1 To ensure that the tools function and the defaults are set exactly as described in this lesson, delete or deactivate (by renaming) the Adobe Illustrator CC preferences file. See "Restoring default preferences" in the "Getting Started" section at the beginning of the book.

2 Start Adobe Illustrator CC.

3 Choose File > Open. Locate the file named L14_end.ai in the Lessons > Lesson14 folder that you copied onto your hard disk.

This is a small poster for a vacation destination.

4 Choose View > Fit Artboard In Window and leave it open for reference, or choose File > Close.

● **Note:** The fonts in the L14_end.ai file have been converted to outlines (Type > Create Outlines) to avoid having missing fonts, and the images have been embedded.

5 Choose File > Open. In the Open dialog box, navigate to the Lessons > Lesson14 folder, and select the L14_start.ai file on your hard disk. Click Open to open the file.

This is an unfinished version of the poster for a travel company. You will add and edit graphics to it in this lesson.

● **Note:** You need an Internet connection to sync the fonts. The syncing process may take a few minutes.

6 The Missing Fonts dialog box will most likely appear. Click Sync Fonts to sync all the missing fonts to your computer. After they are synced and you see the message stating that there are no more missing fonts, click Close.

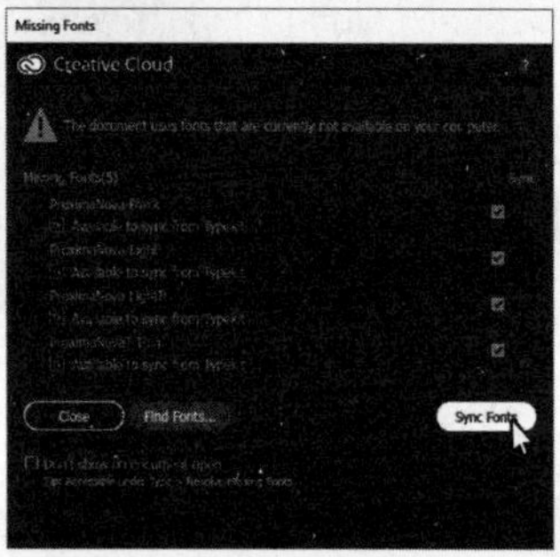

If you can't get the fonts to sync (a "Syncing Typekit fonts..." message doesn't go away), you can go to the Creative Cloud desktop application and choose Assets > Fonts to see what the issue may be (refer to the section "Changing font family and font style" in Lesson 8, "Adding Type to a Poster," for more information on how to resolve it). You can also just click Close in the Missing Fonts dialog box and ignore the missing fonts as you proceed. A third method is to click the Find Fonts button in the Missing Fonts dialog box and replace the fonts with a local font on your machine.

Note: You can also go to Help (Help > Illustrator Help) and search for "Find missing fonts.

7 Choose File > Save As. In the Save As dialog box, navigate to the Lesson14 folder, and open it. Name the file **GreenIsle.ai**. Leave the Format option set to Adobe Illustrator (ai) (macOS) or the Save As Type option set to Adobe Illustrator (*.AI) (Windows) and then click Save. In the Illustrator Options dialog box, leave the Illustrator options at their default settings. Click OK.

8 Choose View > Fit Artboard In Window.

9 Choose Window > Workspace > Reset Essentials to reset the Essentials workspace.

Working with Adobe Bridge

Adobe Bridge CC is an application available with your Adobe Creative Cloud subscription. Bridge provides you with centralized access to all the media assets you need for your creative projects.

Bridge simplifies your workflow and keeps you organized. You can batch edit with ease, add watermarks, and even set centralized color preferences. You can access Adobe Bridge from within Illustrator by choosing File > Browse In Bridge.

Combining artwork

You can combine Illustrator artwork with images from other graphics applications in a variety of ways for a wide range of creative results. Sharing artwork among applications lets you combine continuous-tone paintings and photographs with vector art. Illustrator lets you create certain types of raster images, and Adobe Photoshop excels at many additional image-editing tasks. The images edited or created in Photoshop can then be inserted into Illustrator.

Note: To learn more about working with vector and raster images, see the "Introducing Adobe Illustrator" section in Lesson 1, "Getting to Know the Work Area."

This lesson steps you through the process of creating a composite image, including combining bitmap images with vector art and working between applications. You will add photographic images created in Photoshop to a small poster created in Illustrator. Then you'll mask an image, update a placed image and then package the file.

Placing image files

You can bring raster artwork from Photoshop or other applications into Illustrator using the Open command, the Place command, the Paste command, drag-and-drop operations, and the Libraries panel. Illustrator supports most Adobe Photoshop data, including layer comps, layers, editable text, and paths. This means that you can transfer files between Photoshop and Illustrator without losing the ability to edit the artwork.

● **Note:** Illustrator includes support for DeviceN rasters. For instance, if you create a Duotone image in Photoshop and place it in Illustrator, it separates properly and prints the spot colors.

When placing files using the File > Place command, no matter what type of image file it is (JPG, GIF, PSD, AI, etc.), it can be either embedded or linked. *Embedding* files stores a copy of the image in the Illustrator file, and the Illustrator file size increases to reflect the addition of the placed file. *Linked* files remain separate external files, and a link to the external file is placed in the Illustrator file. A linked file does not add significantly to the size of the Illustrator file. Linking to files can be a great way to ensure that image updates are reflected in the Illustrator file. The linked file must always accompany the Illustrator file, or the link will break and the placed file will not appear in the Illustrator artwork.

Placing an image

First, you will place a JPEG (.jpg) image into your document.

1 Click the Layers panel tab to open the Layers panel. In the Layers panel, select the layer named "Pictures."

When you place an image, it is added to the selected layer. The layer already includes several shapes in the document.

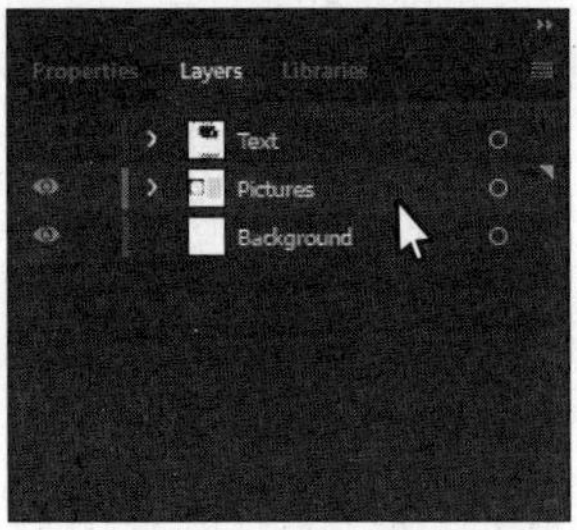

2 Choose File > Place.

● **Note:** You may need to click the Options button in the Place dialog box to reveal the Link option.

3 Navigate to the Lessons > Lesson14 > images folder, and select the Kayak.jpg file. Make sure that Link is selected in the Place dialog box. Click Place.

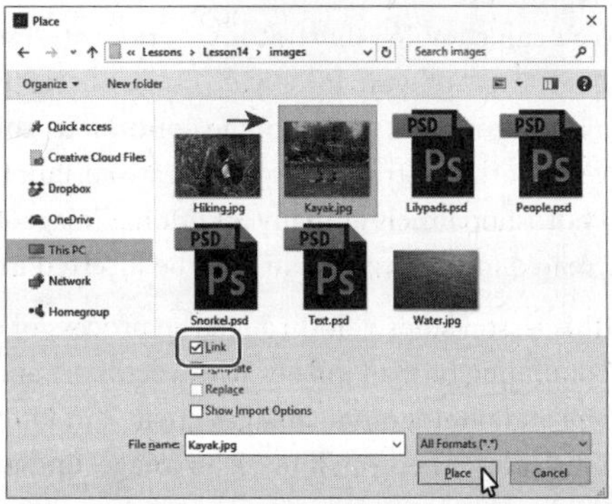

The pointer should now show the loaded graphics cursor. You can see "1/1" next to the pointer, indicating how many images are being placed (1 of 1), and a thumbnail so you can see what image you are placing.

4 Position the loaded graphics cursor near the upper-left corner of the artboard, and click to place the image. Leave the image selected.

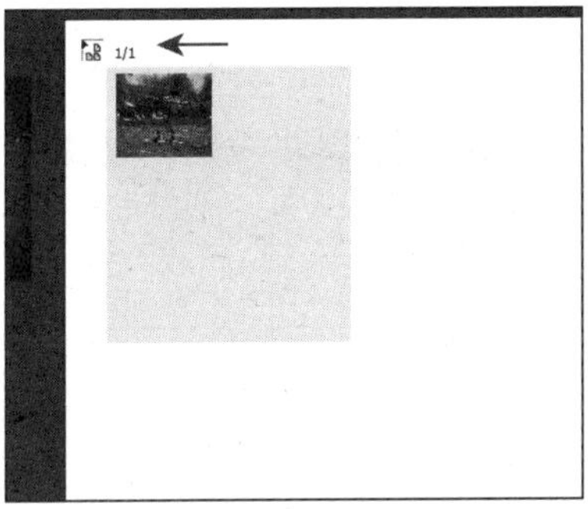

Position the loaded graphics cursor.

Click to place the image.

The image appears on the artboard, with the upper-left corner of the image placed where you clicked. The image is 100% of its original size. You could also have dragged with the loaded graphics cursor to size the image as you placed it.

Notice in the Properties panel that, with the image selected, you see the words "Linked File," indicating that the image is linked to its source file, together with other information about the image. By default, placed image files are linked to their source file. So, if the source file is edited (outside of Illustrator), the placed image in Illustrator is updated. Deselecting the Link option while placing embeds the image file in the Illustrator file.

Tip: The X on a selected image indicates that the image is linked (with edges showing, View > Show Edges).

Transforming a placed image

You can duplicate and transform placed images just as you do other objects in an Illustrator file. Unlike vector artwork, you need to consider the resolution of the raster image content in your document since raster images without enough resolution may look pixelated when printed. Working in Illustrator, if you make an image smaller, the resolution of the image increases. If you make an image larger, the resolution decreases. Next, you will transform the Kayak.jpg image.

Note: Transformations performed on a linked image in Illustrator, and any resulting resolution changes, do not change the original image. The changes apply only to the image within Illustrator.

1 Holding down the Shift key, use the Selection tool (▶) to drag the lower-right bounding point toward the center of the image until the measurement label shows a width of approximately 5 in. Release the mouse button and then release the key.

Tip: To transform a placed image, you can also open the Properties panel or Transform panel (Window > Transform) and change settings in either.

▶ **Tip:** Much like other artwork, you can also Option+Shift-drag (macOS) or Alt+Shift-drag (Windows) a bounding point around an image to resize from the center, while maintaining the image proportions.

2 Click the Properties panel tab to show that panel.

3 Click the text "Linked File" at the top of the Properties panel to see the Links panel. With the Kayak.jpg file selected in the Links panel, click the Show Link Info arrow in the lower-left corner of the panel to see information about the image.

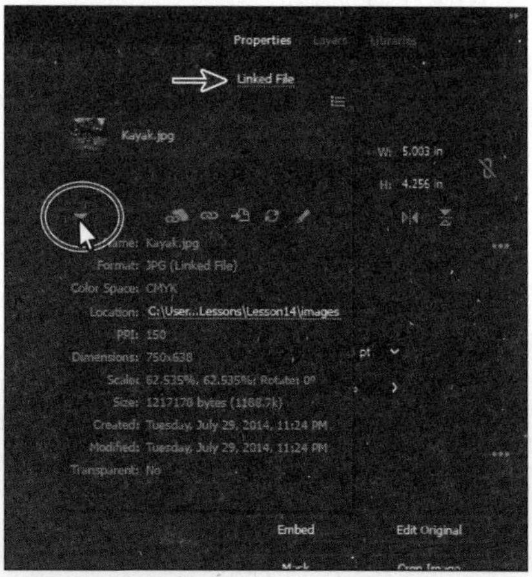

You can see the scale percentage as well as rotation information, size, and much more. Specifically, notice the PPI (Pixels Per Inch) value is approximately 150. PPI refers to the resolution of the image. Other transformations like rotation can also be applied to images using the various methods you learned in Lesson 5, "Transforming Artwork."

4 Press the Escape key to hide the panel.

5 Click the Flip Along Horizontal Axis option (▶◀) in the Properties panel to flip the image horizontally, across the center.

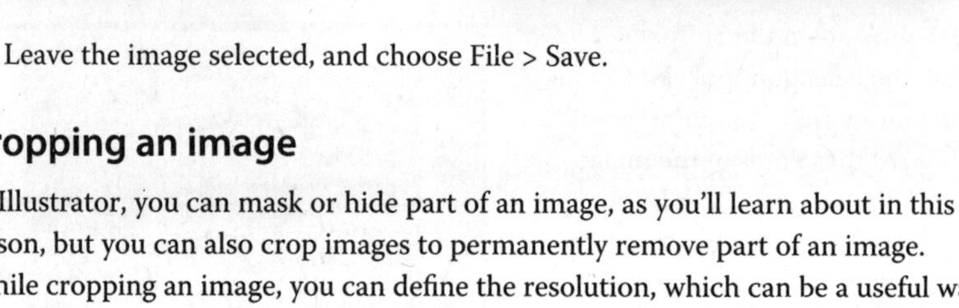

6 Leave the image selected, and choose File > Save.

Cropping an image

In Illustrator, you can mask or hide part of an image, as you'll learn about in this lesson, but you can also crop images to permanently remove part of an image. While cropping an image, you can define the resolution, which can be a useful way to reduce file size and improve performance. Next, you'll crop part of the image of the kayakers.

1 With the image still selected, click the Crop Image button in the Properties panel. Click OK in the warning dialog box that appears.

Linked images, like the kayak image, become embedded after you crop them. That means that if you update the original image, Kayak.jpg, outside of Illustrator, say in Photoshop, the image in Illustrator will not be affected. You should now see a dotted box with eight handles around the selected image. The rest of the artwork is dimmed, and you cannot select it until you are finished cropping.

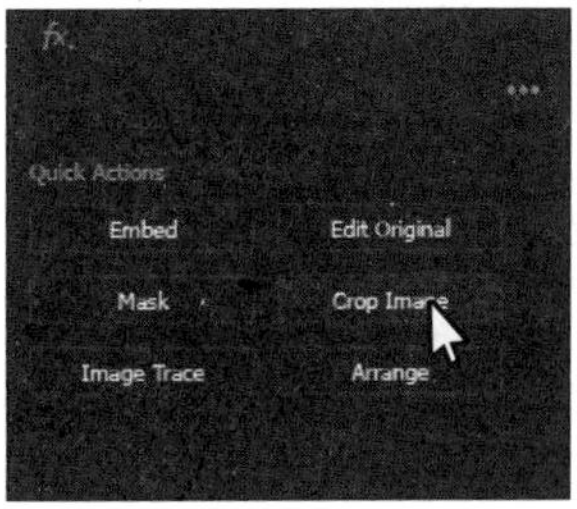

▶ **Tip:** To crop a selected image, you can also choose Object > Crop Image or choose Crop Image from the context menu (right-click or Ctrl-click on the image).

2 Drag the top crop handle down to cut off a bit of the trees at the top of the image.

You can drag the handles that appear around the image to crop different parts of the image. You can also define a size in the Properties panel (width and height) to crop to.

3 Click the PPI (resolution) menu in the Properties panel.

The PPI is the resolution of the image. Any options in the PPI menu that are higher than the original resolution of the image you are cropping are disabled. The maximum value that you can enter equals the resolution of the original image or 300 PPI for linked artwork. Choosing a lower resolution than the original can be useful if you want to save file size.

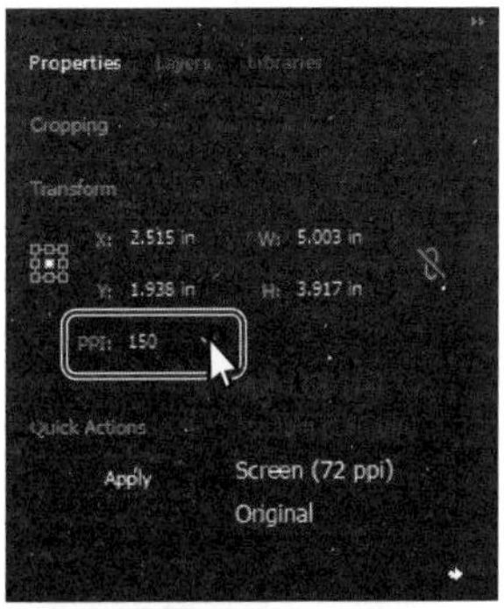

● **Note:** A lower PPI may result in an image that is not suitable for printing.

● **Note:** Depending on the size of your kayak image, the "Medium (150 ppi)" option may not be dimmed and that's okay.

4 Move the pointer over the image, and drag the crop area to make it more centered, vertically on the image.

5 Click Apply in the Properties panel to permanently crop the image.

6 Choose Select > Deselect and then choose File > Save.

Placing a Photoshop image with Show Import Options

When you place image files in Illustrator, you have the ability to change image options when the file is imported (when available). For instance, if you place a Photoshop file (.psd), you can choose to flatten the image or even to preserve the original Photoshop layers in the file. Next, you'll place a Photoshop file, set import options, and embed it in the Illustrator file.

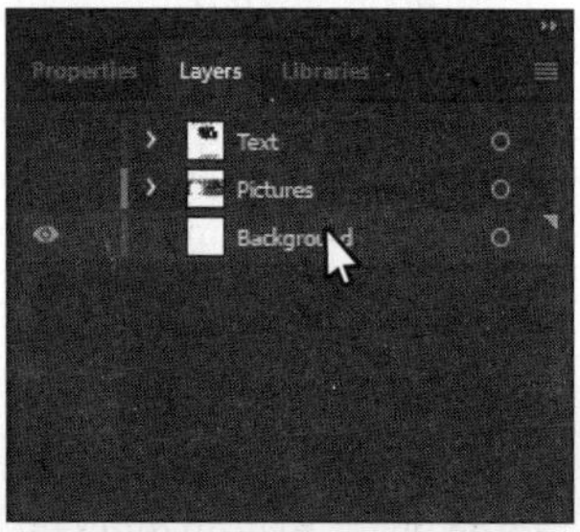

1 In the Layers panel, click the eye icon ( ) for the Pictures layer to hide the content, and then select the Background layer.

2 Choose File > Place.

3 In the Place dialog box, navigate to the Lessons > Lesson14 > images folder, and select the Lilypads.psd file. In the Place dialog box, set the following options (if you don't see the options, click the Options button):

- Link: **Deselected** (Deselecting the Link option embeds an image file in the Illustrator file. Embedding the Photoshop file allows for more options when it is placed, as you'll see.)
- Show Import Options: **Selected** (Selecting this option will open an import options dialog box where you can set import options before placing.)

4 Click Place.

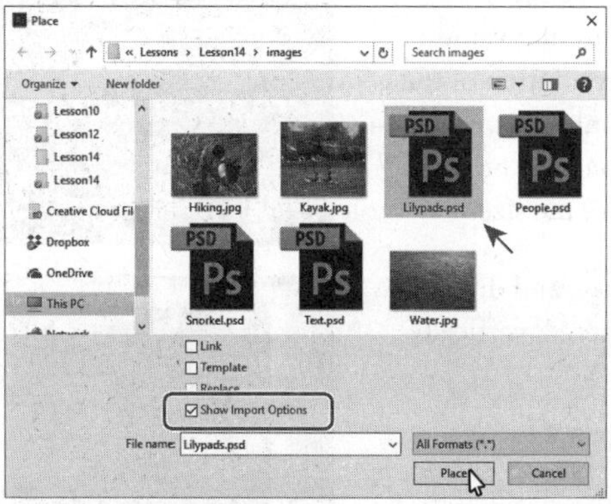

The Photoshop Import Options dialog box appears because you selected Show Import Options in the Place dialog box.

Note: Even though you select Show Import Options in the Place dialog box, the Import Options dialog box will not appear if the image doesn't have multiple layers.

5 In the Photoshop Import Options dialog box, set the following options:

- Layer Comp: **All** (A layer comp is a snapshot of a state of the Layers panel that you create in Photoshop. In Photoshop, you can create, manage, and view multiple versions of a layout in a single Photoshop file. Any comments associated with the layer comp in Photoshop will appear in the Comments area.)
- Show Preview: **Selected** (Preview displays a preview of the selected layer comp.)
- Convert Layers To Objects: **Selected** (This option and the next one are available only because you deselected the Link option and chose to embed the Photoshop image.)
- Import Hidden Layers: **Selected** (to import layers hidden in Photoshop)

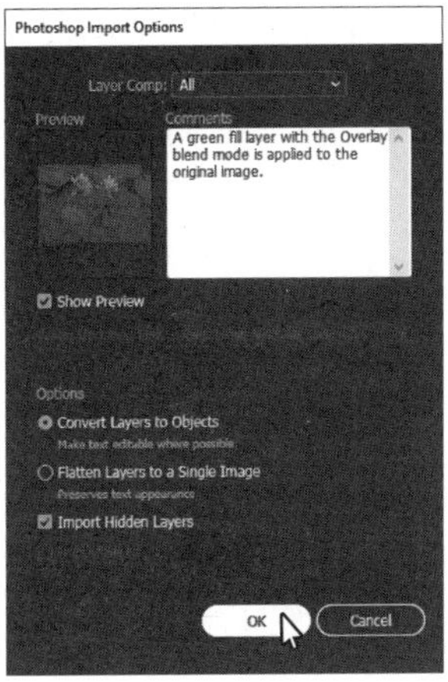

▶ **Tip:** To learn more about layer comps, see "Importing artwork from Photoshop" in Illustrator Help (Help > Illustrator Help).

● **Note:** A color mode warning may appear in the Photoshop Import Options dialog box. This indicates that the image you are placing may not be the same color mode as the Illustrator document. For this image (and going forward), if a color warning dialog box appears, click OK to dismiss it.

6 Click OK.

7 Position the loaded graphics cursor in the upper-left corner of the artboard, and click to place the image.

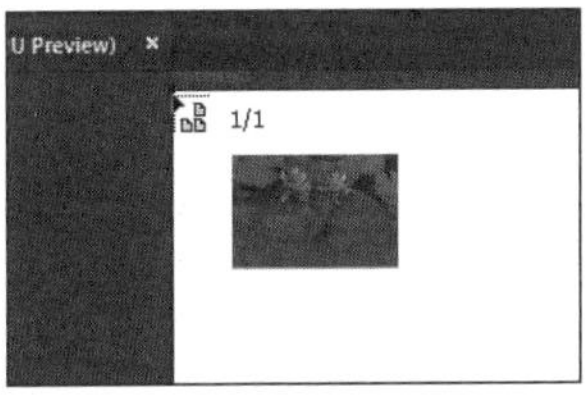

Rather than flatten the file, you have converted the Lilypads.psd Photoshop layers to layers that you can show and hide in Illustrator. When placing a Photoshop file in particular, if you had left the Link option selected (to link to the original PSD file), the only option in the Options section of the Photoshop Import Options dialog box would have been to flatten the content.

● **Note:** When the pointer snaps to the upper-left corner of the artboard, the word "intersect" may appear. It may also be hidden by the top edge of the Document window.

8 In the Layers panel, click the Locate Object button ( ) to reveal the image content in the Layers panel.

Notice the sublayers of Lilypads.psd. These sublayers were layers in Photoshop and appear in the Layers panel in Illustrator because you chose not to flatten the image when you placed it. Also notice that, with the image still selected on the page, the Properties panel shows the word "Group" at the top.

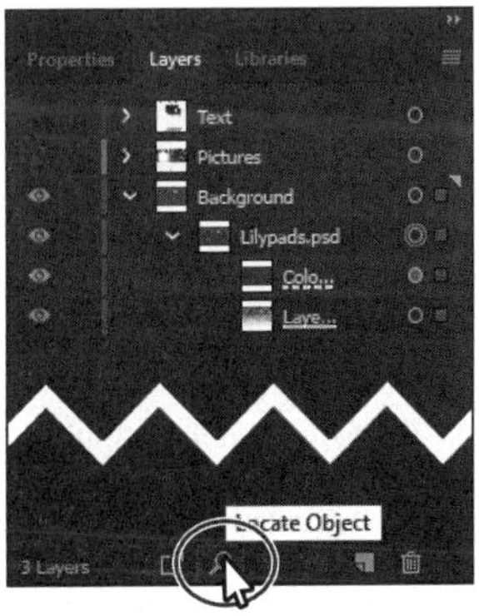

When you place a Photoshop file with layers and you choose to convert the layers to objects in the Photoshop Import Options dialog box, Illustrator treats the layers as separate sublayers in a group. This particular image had a layer mask in Photoshop applied to Layer 0, which is why the image appears to fade.

Note: The Color Fill 1 sublayer was a layer in Photoshop that was filled with a green color and blended via Blend Mode into the lily pad image beneath it.

9 In the Layers panel, click the eye icon ( ) to the left of the Color Fill 1 sublayer to hide it. You may want to drag the left edge of the Layers panel to see more of the layer names.

10 Choose Select > Deselect and then choose File > Save.

Placing multiple images

In Illustrator you can also place multiple files in a single action. Next, you'll place two images at once and then position them.

1 In the Layers panel, click the disclosure triangle ( ) to the left of the Background layer to collapse the layer contents. Click the visibility column of the layers named "Pictures" and "Text" to show the contents for each and then ensure that the Background layer is selected.

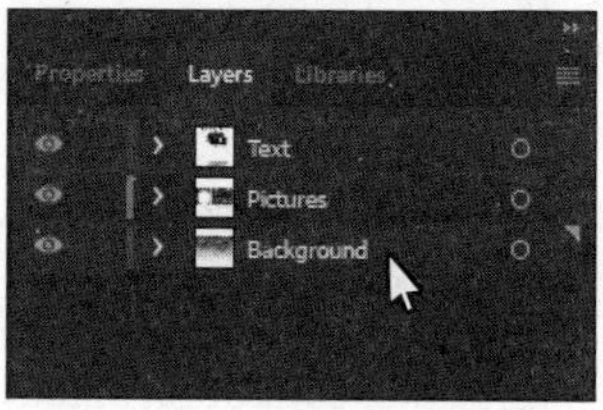

2 Choose File > Place.

Tip: You could also select a range of files in the Place dialog box by pressing the Shift key.

Note: The Place dialog box you see in Illustrator may show the images in a different view, like a List view, and that's okay.

3 In the Place dialog box, select the Water.jpg file in the Lessons > Lesson14 > images folder. Command-click (macOS) or Ctrl-click (Windows) the image named Text.psd to select both image files. On macOS, click the Options button, if necessary, to reveal other options. Deselect Show Import Options, and make sure that the Link option is *not* selected. Click Place.

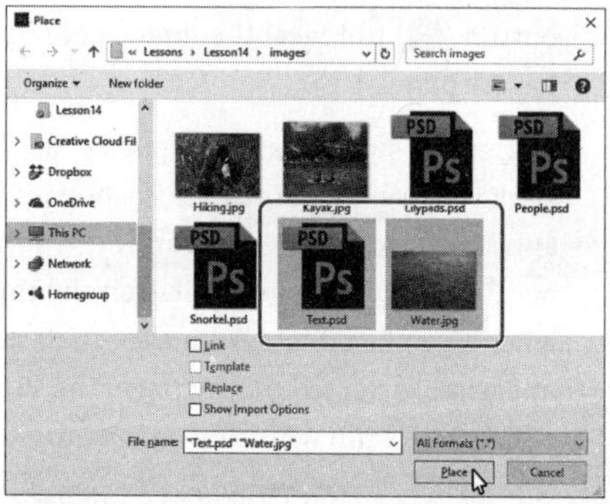

Tip: To discard an asset that is loaded and ready to be placed, use the arrow keys to navigate to the asset, and then press the Escape key.

4 Position the loaded graphics cursor on the left side of the artboard. Press the Right or Left Arrow key (or Up and Down Arrow keys) a few times to see that you can cycle between the image thumbnails. Make sure that you see the water image thumbnail, and click the left edge of the artboard, about halfway down, to place the image.

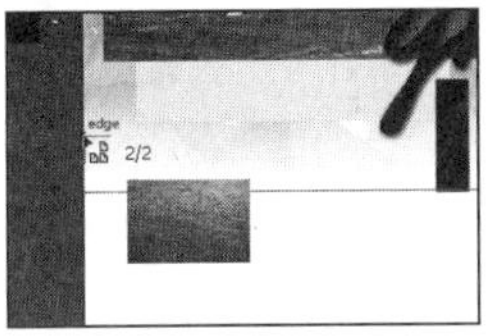

Whichever thumbnail is showing in the loaded graphics cursor when you click in the Document window is placed.

5 Press and hold the spacebar and drag to the left so that you see the area off the right side of the artboard. Release the spacebar.

6 Move the loaded graphics cursor off the right side of the artboard. Click and drag down and to the right, stopping when the image is roughly as big as you see in the figure. Leave the image selected.

You can either click to place an image at 100% or click and drag to place an image and size it as you place it in the Document window. By dragging when you place an image, you are resizing the image. Resizing an image in Illustrator will most likely result in a different resolution than the original.

7 With the Text.psd image (the image of the green leaf) still selected, drag the selected art indicator (the colored box) in the Layers panel up from the Background layer to the Text layer to move the image to the Text layer.

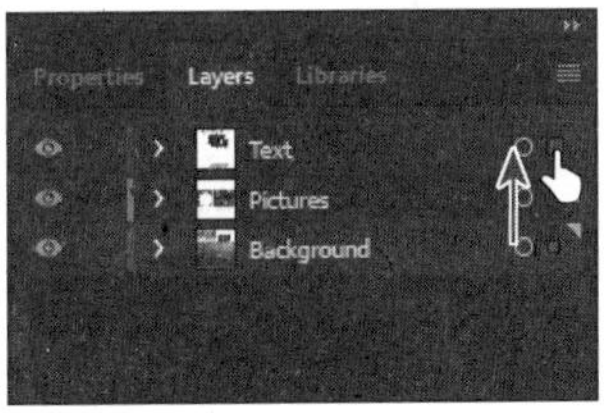

Later, you will mask the image with text on the Text layer.

8 Choose View > Fit Artboard In Window.

Masking images

● **Note:** You will hear people use the phrases "clipping mask," "clipping path," and "mask." The way most of us refer to them, they mean the same thing.

To achieve certain design effects, you can apply a clipping mask (clipping path) to content. A *clipping mask* is an object whose shape masks other artwork so that only areas that lie within the shape are visible. In the first part of the figure to the right is an image with a white circle on top. In the second part of the figure, the white circle was used to mask or hide part of the image.

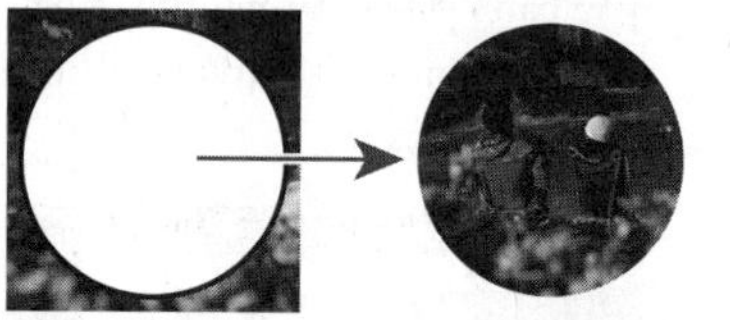

Image with a white circle on top.

The circle masking part of the image.

Only vector objects can be clipping paths; however, any artwork can be masked. You can also import masks created in Photoshop files. The clipping path and the masked object are referred to as the *clipping set.*

Applying a simple mask to an image

In this section, you'll see how to let Illustrator create a simple mask for you on the Kayak.jpg image so that you can hide part of the image.

1 With the Selection tool (▶) selected, click the Kayak.jpg image to select it (the first image you placed).

▶ **Tip:** You can also apply a clipping mask by choosing Object > Clipping Mask > Make.

2 Click the Properties panel tab to show that panel. Click the Mask button in the Properties panel.

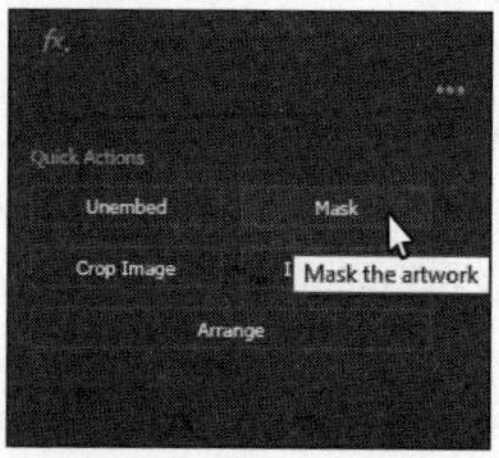

Clicking the Mask button applies a clipping mask to the image in the shape and size of the image. In this case, the image itself does not look any different.

3 In the Layers panel, click the Locate Object button () at the bottom of the panel.

Notice the <Clipping Path> and <Image> sublayers that are contained within the <Clip Group> sublayer. The <Clipping Path> object is the clipping path (mask) that was created, and the <Clip Group> is a set that contains the mask and the object that is masked (the cropped, embedded image).

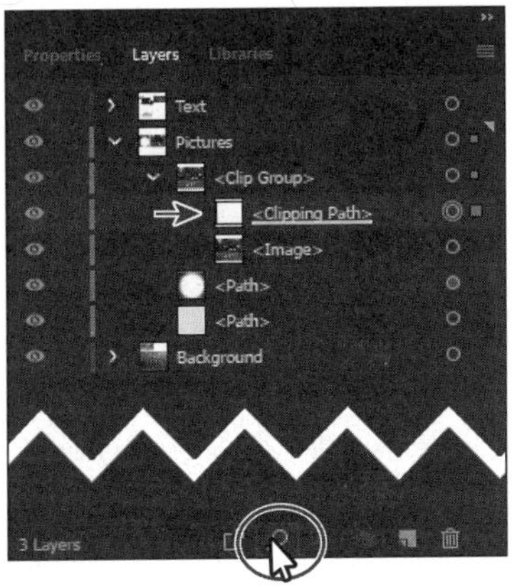

● **Note:** You may need to drag the left edge of the Layers panel to the left to see more of the names, like I did for the figure.

Editing a clipping path (mask)

In order to edit a clipping path, you need to be able to select it. Illustrator offers several ways to do this. Next, you'll edit the mask you just created.

1 Click the Properties panel tab to show the panel. With the kayak image still selected on the artboard, click the Edit Contents button () at the top of the Properties panel.

2 Click the Layers panel tab, and notice that the <Image> sublayer (in the <Clip Group>) is showing the selected-art indicator (small color box) to the far right of the sublayer name.

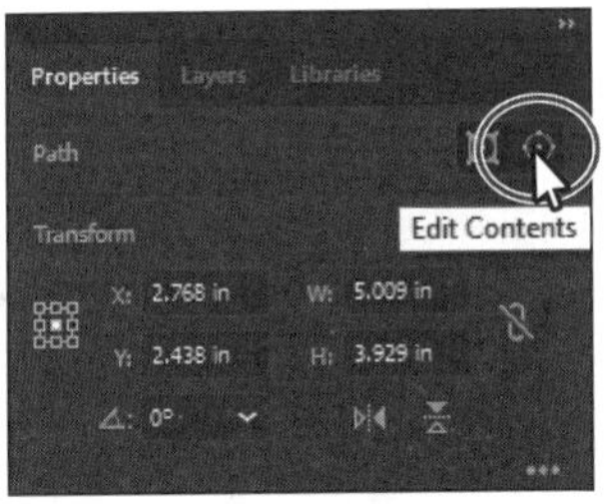

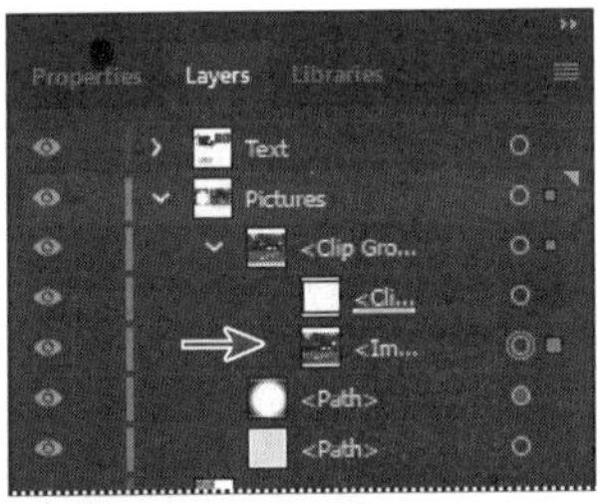

▶ **Tip:** You can also double-click a clip group (object masked with a clipping path) to enter Isolation mode. You can then either click the masked object (the image in this case) to select it or click the edge of the clipping path to select the clipping path. After you are finished editing, you can then exit Isolation mode using a variety of methods as discussed in previous lessons (like pressing the Escape key).

3 Back in the Properties panel, click the Edit Clipping Path button () at the top of the Properties panel, and <Clipping Path> will now be selected in the Layers panel.

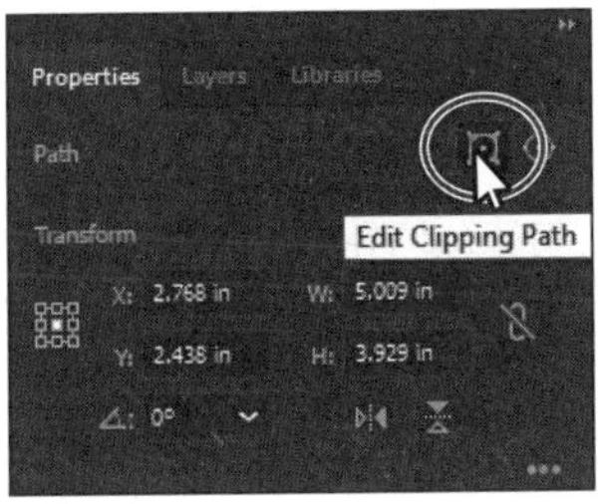

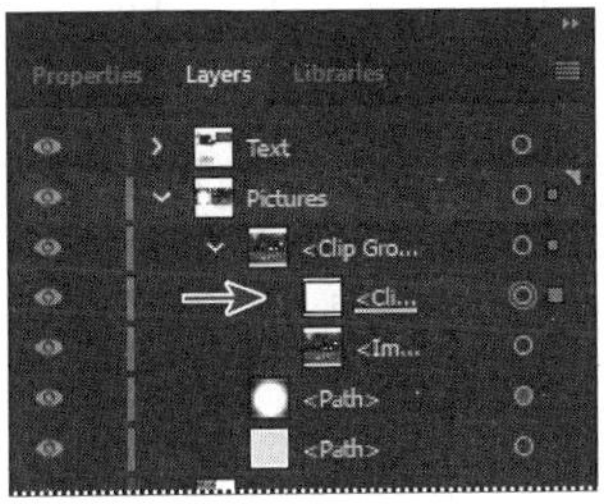

When an object is masked, you can edit the mask, the object that is masked, or both. Use these two buttons to select which to edit. When you first click to select an object that is masked, you will edit both the mask and the masked object.

4 Choose View > Outline.

▶ **Tip:** You can also edit a clipping path with transformation options, like rotate, skew, etc., or by using the Direct Selection tool (▷).

5 With the Selection tool (▶) selected, drag the top-middle bounding point of the selected mask down until the measurement label shows a height of approximately 3.25 in.

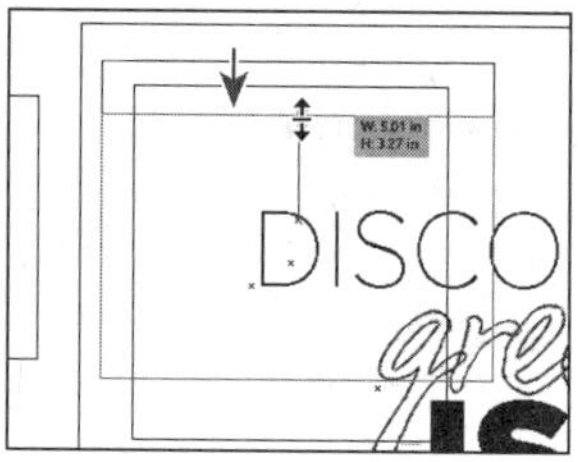

6 Choose View > GPU Preview (or Preview On CPU if that is all that is available).

7 Make sure that the center of the reference point is selected (▦) in the Properties panel. Make sure that Constrain Width And Height Proportions is off (▯), and change Width to **3.5 in**. If you see that Height is not **3.25 in**, go ahead and make it so.

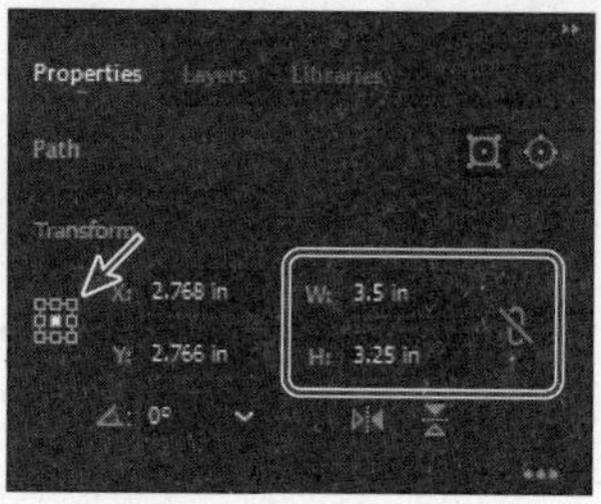

8 Click the Edit Contents button (◉) at the top of the Properties panel to edit the Kayak.jpg image, *not* the mask.

▶ **Tip:** You can also press the arrow keys on the keyboard to reposition the image.

9 With the Selection tool (▶), be careful to drag from within the bounds of the mask down a little bit and release the mouse button. Notice that you are moving the image and not the mask.

With the Edit Contents button (◉) selected, you can apply many transformations to the image, including scaling, moving, rotating, and more.

10 Choose Select > Deselect and then click the image again to select the entire clip group. Drag the image onto the light gray rectangle, and position it like you see in the figure.

11 Choose Select > Deselect and then choose File > Save.

Masking an object with text

In this section, you'll use text as a mask for an image you placed. To create a mask from text, the text needs to be on top of the image, as you'll see.

Note: If the image Text.psd is not as wide as the "ISLE" text, make sure you resize the image, holding down the Shift key to constrain the proportions. Don't worry if it's larger than you see in the figure.

1 With the Selection tool (▶) selected, drag the green leaf image (Text.psd) from off the right side of the artboard on top of the "ISLE" text.

2 Choose Object > Arrange > Send To Back. You should see the "ISLE" text now. Make sure that the image is positioned roughly like you see in the figure.

3 With the image still selected, Shift-click the "ISLE" text to select them both.

4 Click the Make Clipping Mask button in the Properties panel.

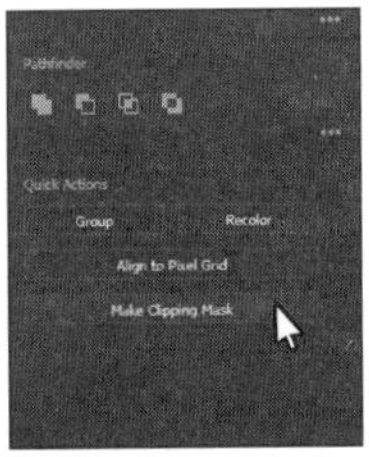

You can edit the Text.psd image and the clipping mask separately, just as you did previously with the masked Kayak.jpg image.

Tip: You can also right-click over the selected content and choose Make Clipping Mask from the context menu or choose Object > Clipping Mask > Make.

5 With the text still selected, choose Window > Graphic Styles to open the Graphic Styles panel. Select the Text Shadow graphic style to apply a drop shadow. Close the Graphic Styles panel.

6 Choose Select > Deselect and then choose File > Save.

Masking an object with multiple shapes

You can easily create a mask from either a single shape or multiple shapes. In order to create a clipping mask with multiple shapes, the shapes first need to be converted to a compound path. This can be done by selecting the shapes that will be used as the mask and choosing Object > Compound Path > Make. Ensure that the compound path is on top of the content to be masked and both are selected. Choose Object > Clipping Mask > Make.

Creating an opacity mask

An *opacity mask* is different from a *clipping mask* because it allows you to mask an object and also alter the transparency of artwork. You can make and edit an opacity mask using the Transparency panel. In this section, you'll create an opacity mask for the Water.jpg image so that it fades into the water lilies image.

1 In the Layers panel, click the disclosure triangles for all layers (▾) to hide the content for each layer, if necessary. Click the eye icon (◉) to the left of the Text and Pictures layers to hide their contents.

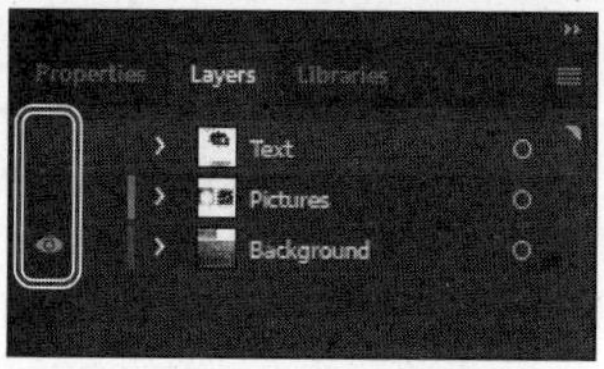

2 Choose View > Zoom Out.

3 With the Selection tool selected, drag the water image into the center of the artboard. Make sure the bottom of the image is aligned with the bottom of the artboard.

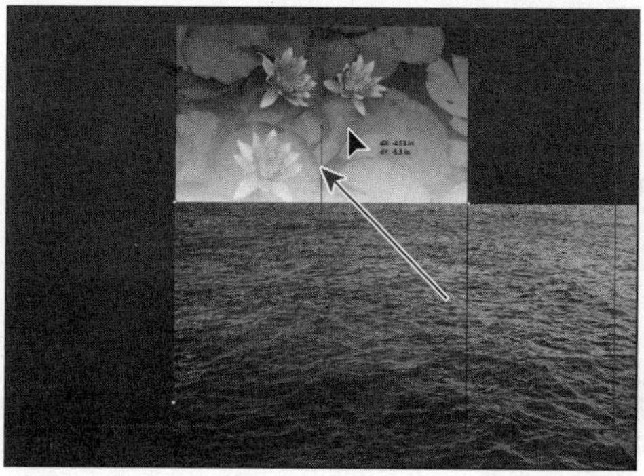

4 Select the Rectangle tool ( ) in the Tools panel, and click in the approximate center of the artboard. In the Rectangle dialog box, make sure the Constrain Width And Height Proportions is off ( ), change Width to **9 in** and Height to **8 in**. Click OK. This will become the mask.

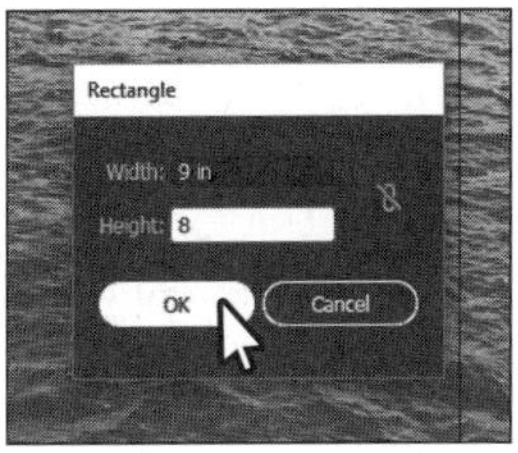

5 Press the D key to set the default stroke (black, 1 pt) and fill (white) for the new rectangle to more easily select and move it.

6 Select the Selection tool ( ), and drag the rectangle to align it into the bottom center of the artboard.

Note: The object that is to become the opacity mask (the masking object) needs to be the top selected object on the artboard. If it is a single object, like a rectangle, it does not need to be a compound path. If the opacity mask is to be made from multiple objects, they need to be grouped.

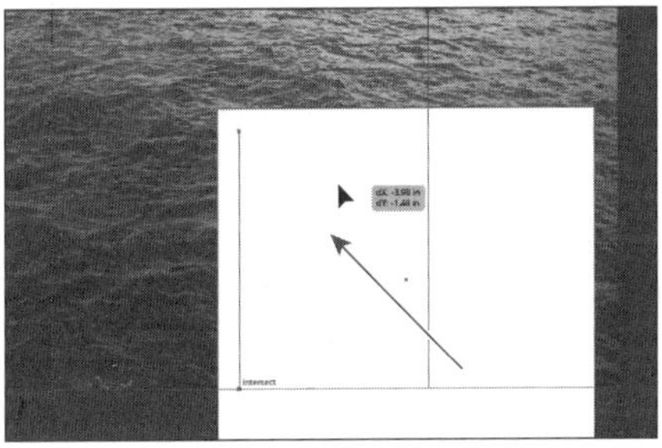

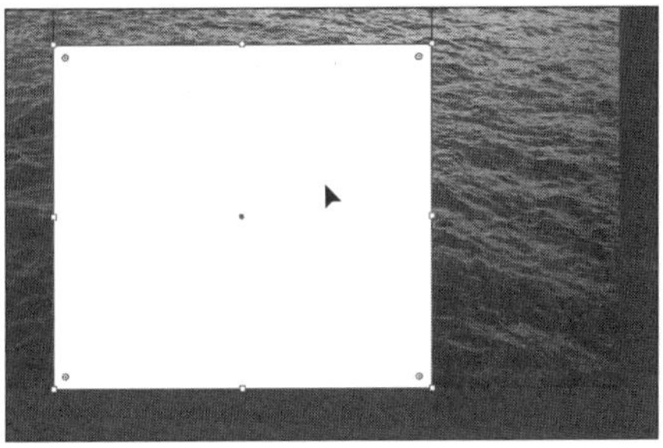

7 Press the Shift key, and click the Water.jpg image to select it as well.

8 Choose Window > Transparency to open the Transparency panel. Click the Make Mask button, and leave the artwork selected.

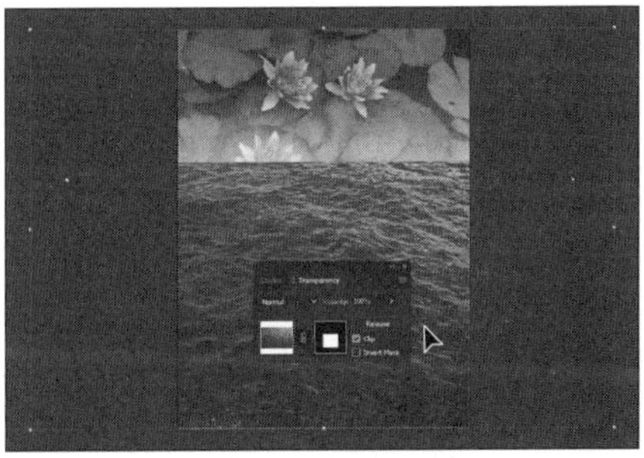

After clicking the Make Mask button, the button now shows as "Release." If you were to click the button again, the image would no longer be masked.

Tip: You can also click the word "Opacity" in the Properties panel to reveal the Transparency panel.

Note: If you wanted to create a mask that was the same dimensions as the image, instead of drawing a shape, you could have simply clicked the Make Mask button in the Transparency panel.

Editing an opacity mask

Next, you'll adjust the opacity mask that you just created.

Tip: To disable and enable an opacity mask, you can also choose Disable Opacity Mask or Enable Opacity Mask from the Transparency panel menu.

1 In the Transparency panel, Shift-click the mask thumbnail (as indicated by the white rectangle on the black background) to disable the mask.

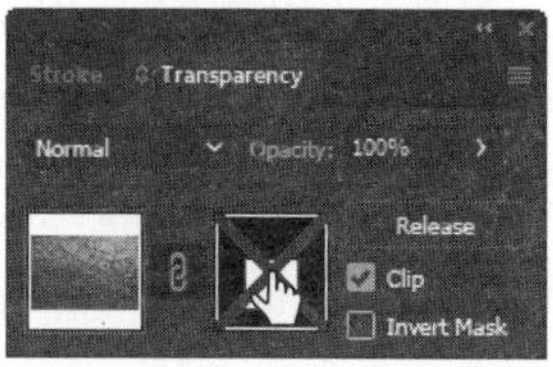

Notice that a red X appears on the mask in the Transparency panel and that the entire Water.jpg image reappears in the Document window.

2 In the Transparency panel, Shift-click the mask thumbnail to enable the mask again.

Tip: To show the mask by itself (in grayscale if the original mask had color in it) on the artboard, you can also Option-click (macOS) or Alt-click (Windows) the mask thumbnail in the Transparency panel.

3 Click to select the mask thumbnail on the right side of the Transparency panel. If the mask isn't selected on the artboard, click to select it with the Selection tool ( ).

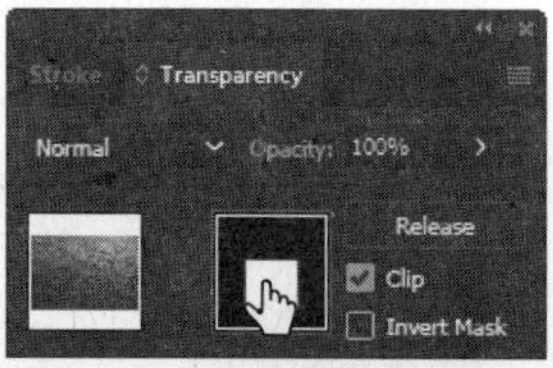

Clicking the opacity mask in the Transparency panel selects the mask (the rectangle path) on the artboard. With the mask selected, you can't edit other artwork on the artboard. Also, notice that the document tab shows (<Opacity Mask>/Opacity Mask), indicating that you are now editing the mask.

4 Click the Layers panel tab and click the disclosure triangle ( ) for the <Opacity Mask> layer to reveal the contents, if necessary.

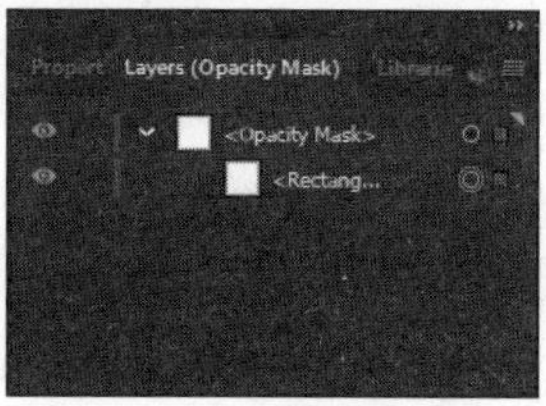

In the Layers panel, notice that the layer <Opacity Mask> appears, indicating that the mask—rather than the artwork that is being masked—is selected.

5 With the mask selected in the Transparency panel and on the artboard, change the fill color to a white-to-black linear gradient, called White, Black, in the Properties panel.

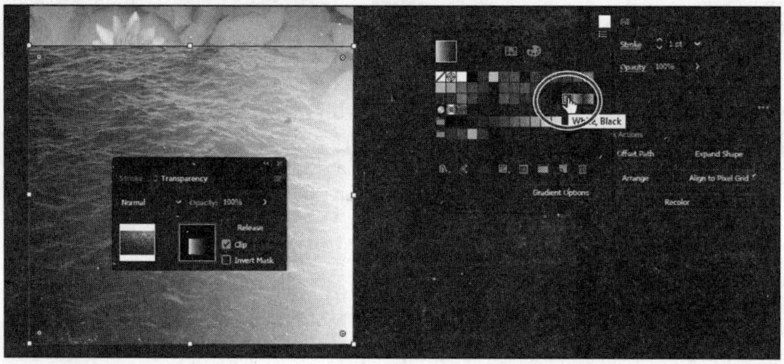

You'll now see that where there is white in the mask, the Water.jpg image is showing, and where there is black, it is hidden. The gradient mask gradually reveals the image.

6 Make sure that the Fill box toward the bottom of the Tools panel is selected.

7 Select the Gradient tool ( ) in the Tools panel. Holding down the Shift key, position the pointer close to the bottom of the Water.jpg image. Click and drag up to just below the top of the mask shape, as shown in the figure. Release the mouse button and then release the Shift key.

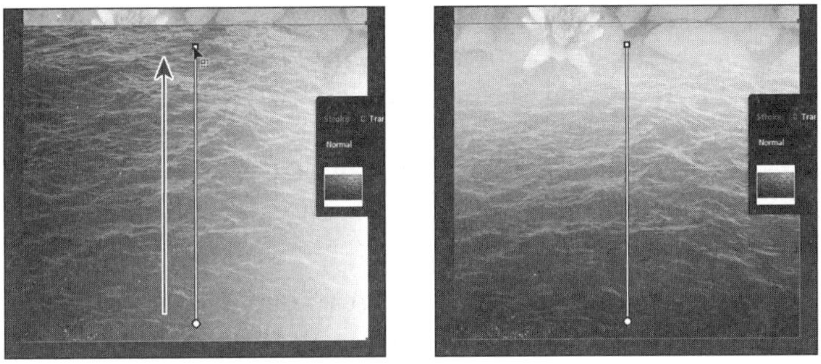

Notice how the mask has changed appearance in the Transparency panel. Next, you'll move the image but not the opacity mask. With the image thumbnail selected in the Transparency panel, both the image and the mask are linked together by default so that if you move the image, the mask moves as well.

8 In the Transparency panel, click the image thumbnail so that you are no longer editing the mask. Click the link icon ( ) between the image thumbnail and the mask thumbnail. This allows you to move just the image or the mask but not both.

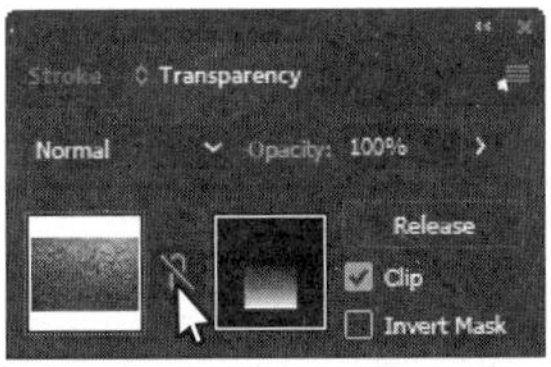

Note: You have access to the link icon only when the image thumbnail, not the mask thumbnail, is selected in the Transparency panel.

9 With the Selection tool, drag the Water.jpg image down. After dragging a little, release the mouse button to see where it's positioned.

10 In the Transparency panel, click the broken link icon ( ) between the image thumbnail and the mask thumbnail to link the two together again.

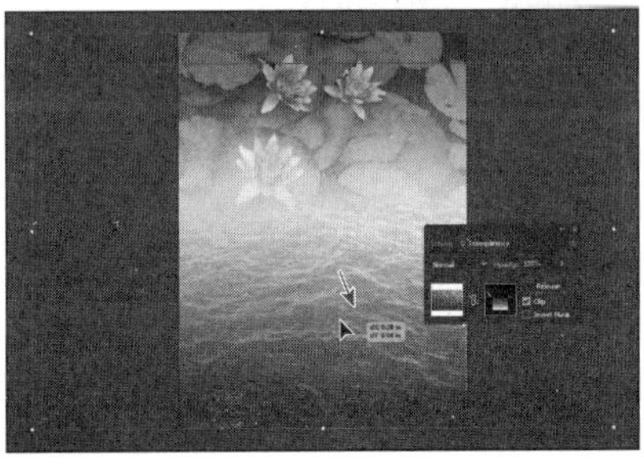

Note: The position of Water.jpg does not have to match the figure exactly.

11 Choose Object > Arrange > Send To Back to send the Water.jpg image behind the Lilypads.psd image.

It probably won't look like anything has changed on the artboard, but later you will attempt to select the Lilypads.psd image, and it will need to be on top of the Water.jpg image.

12 Choose Select > Deselect and then choose File > Save.

Working with image links

- **Note:** Learn about working with links and Creative Cloud library items, in Lesson 13, "Creating Artwork for a T-Shirt."

When you place images in Illustrator and either link to them or embed them, you can see a listing of these images in the Links panel. You use the Links panel to see and manage all linked or embedded artwork. The Links panel displays a small thumbnail of the artwork and uses icons to indicate the artwork's status. From the Links panel, you can view the images that have been linked to and embedded, replace a placed image, update a linked image that has been edited outside of Illustrator, or edit a linked image in the original application, such as Photoshop.

Finding link information

When you place an image, it can be helpful to see where the original image is located, what transformations have been applied to the image (such as rotation and scale), and more information. Next, you'll explore the Links panel to discover image information.

1 In the Layers panel, make sure that all of the layers are collapsed and then click the visibility column to the left of the Text and Pictures layers to show the layer contents on the artboard.

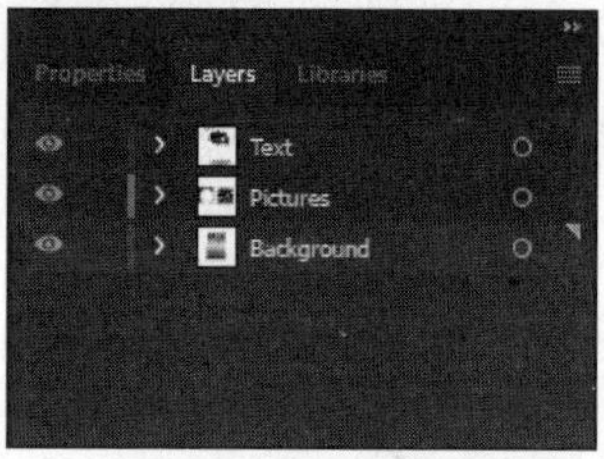

2 Choose Window > Workspace > Reset Essentials.

3 Choose Window > Links to open the Links panel.

- **Tip:** You can also double-click the image in the Layers panel list to see the image information.

- **Note:** The link information you see may be different than what you see in the figure, and that's okay.

4 Select the Kayak.jpg image in the Links panel. Click the toggle arrow in the lower-left corner of the Links panel to reveal the link information at the bottom of the panel.

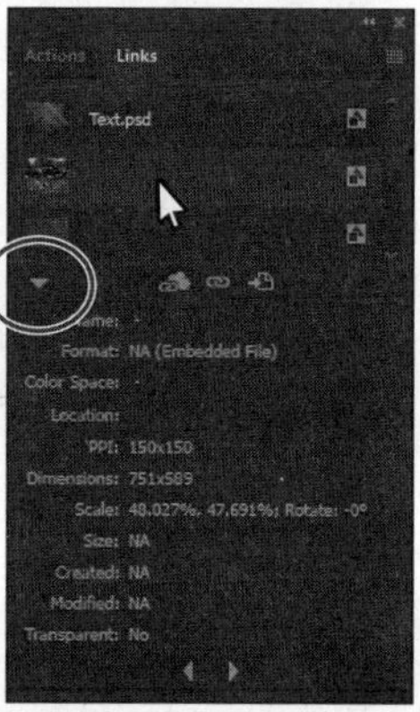

Looking in the Links panel, you'll see a listing of all the images you've placed. You can tell whether an image has been embedded by the embedded icon (). You'll also see information about the image, such as the fact that it's embedded (Embedded File), the resolution, transformation information, and more.

5 Click the Go To Link option ( ) below the list of images.

The Kayak.jpg image will be selected and centered in the Document window.

6 Choose Select > Deselect and then choose File > Save.

Embedding and unembedding images

As was mentioned previously, if you choose not to link to an image when placing it, the image is embedded in the Illustrator file. That means that the image data is stored within the Illustrator document. You can choose to embed an image later, after placing and linking to it, if you choose. Also, you might want to use embedded images outside of Illustrator or to edit them in an image-editing application like Photoshop. Illustrator allows you to unembed images, which saves the embedded artwork to your file system as a PSD or TIFF file (you can choose) and automatically links it to the Illustrator file. Next, you will unembed an image in the document.

1 Choose View > Fit Artboard In Window.

2 Click to select the water image at the bottom of the artboard.

The water image was embedded when you originally placed it. With an image embedded, you may realize that you need to make an edit to that image in a program like Adobe Photoshop. You can just as easily unembed an image, which is what you'll do next to the water image.

3 Click the Unembed button in the Properties panel.

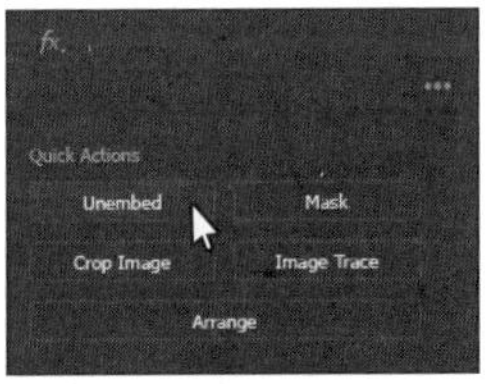

4 In the Unembed dialog box, navigate to the Lessons > Lesson14 > images folder (if you are not already there). Make sure Photoshop (*.PSD) is chosen in the File Format menu (macOS) or the Save As Type (Windows) menu, and click Save.

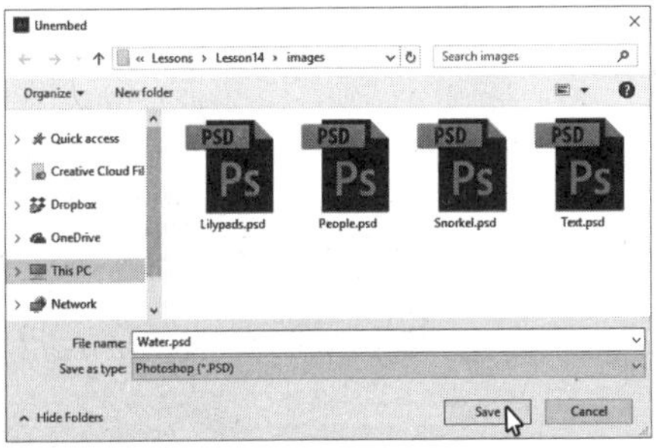

5 Choose Select > Deselect.

Tip: You can also choose Unembed from the Links panel menu ( ).

Note: The embedded Water.jpg image data is unembedded from the file and saved as a PSD file in the images folder. The water image on the artboard is now linked to the PSD file.

Replacing a linked image

You can easily replace a linked or embedded image with another image to update the artwork. The replacement image is positioned exactly where the original image was, so no adjustment should be necessary if the new image is of the same dimensions. If you scaled the image that you are replacing, you may need to resize the replacement image to match the original. Next, you'll replace an image.

1 Select the Selection tool (▶) and drag the gradient-filled rectangle off the left edge of the artboard on top of the Kayak.tif image, centering it on the image using the Smart Guides.

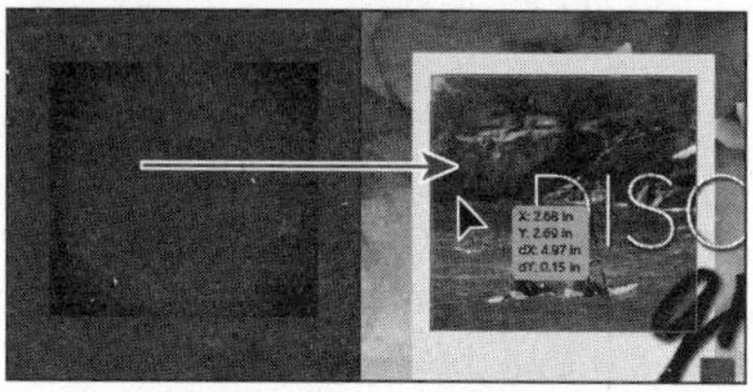

2 Choose Object > Arrange > Bring To Front to bring the gradient-filled rectangle on top of the image.

3 In the Layers panel, click the edit column to the left of the Background layer to lock the layer content on the artboard.

4 Drag across the kayak image, the gradient-filled rectangle, and the light gray rectangle beneath it to select the artwork. Make sure not to select the text.

5 Choose Object > Group.

6 Choose Edit > Copy and then choose Edit > Paste to paste a copy.

7 In the Links panel, with one of the kayak images selected, click the Relink button (🔗) below the list of images. In the Place dialog box, navigate to the Lessons > Lesson14 > images folder, and select another image like People.psd. Make sure that the Link option is selected. Click Place to replace the kayak image with the People.psd image.

● **Note:** The figure shows the image already replaced. The pointer is simply pointing to the Relink button for reference.

8 Drag the kayak image group and the image group with the people into position like you see in the figure.

9 Position the pointer just off the upper-right corner, and when you see the rotate arrows (↶), click and drag to rotate. Alternate the rotation like you see in the figure.

10 Choose File > Save.

Packaging a file

When you *package* a file, you create a folder that contains a copy of the Illustrator document, any necessary fonts, copies of the linked graphics, and a report that contains information about the packaged files. This is an easy way to hand off all necessary files for an Illustrator project. Next, you'll package the poster file.

1 Choose File > Package. In the Package dialog box, set the following options:

- Click the folder icon (▬), and navigate to the Lesson14 folder, if you are not already there. Click Choose (macOS) or Select Folder (Windows) to return to the Package dialog box.
- Folder name: **GreenIsle** (remove "_Folder" from the name)
- Options: Leave at default settings.

Note: If the file needs to be saved, a dialog box will appear to notify you.

2 Click Package.

The Copy Links option *copies* all the linked files to the new folder it creates. The Collect Links In Separate Folder option creates a folder called Links and copies the links into there. The Relink Linked Files To Document option updates the links within the Illustrator document to link to the new copies.

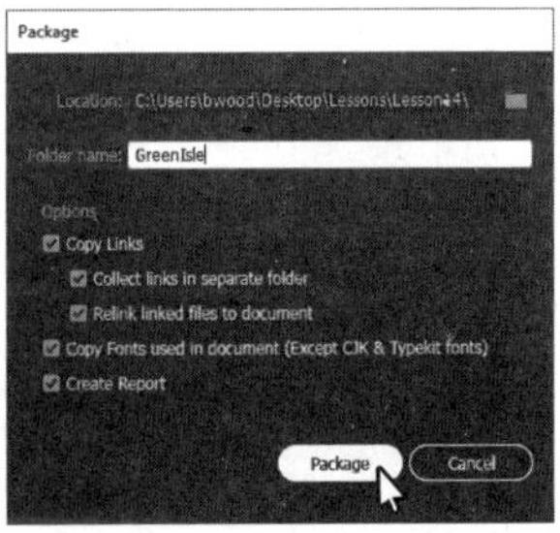

Note: The Create Report option, when selected, will create a package report (summary) in the form of a .txt (text) file, which is placed in the package folder by default.

3 In the next dialog box that discusses font-licensing restrictions, click OK.

Clicking Back would allow you to deselect Copy Fonts Used In Document (Except CJK & Typekit fonts).

4 In the final dialog box to appear, click Show Package to see the package folder.

In the package folder should be a copy of the Illustrator document and a folder named Links that contains all the linked images. The GreenIsle Report (.txt file) contains information about the document contents.

5 Return to Illustrator.

Creating a PDF

Portable Document Format (PDF) is a universal file format that preserves the fonts, images, and layout of source documents created on a wide range of applications and platforms. Adobe PDF is the standard for the secure, reliable distribution and exchange of electronic documents and forms around the world. Adobe PDF files are compact and complete and can be shared, viewed, and printed by anyone with software such as the free Adobe Reader.

You can create different types of PDF files from within Illustrator. You can create multipage PDFs, layered PDFs, and PDF/x-compliant files. Layered PDFs allow you to save one PDF with layers that can be used in different contexts. PDF/X-compliant files ease the burden of color, font, and trapping issues in printing. Next, you'll save this project as a PDF so that you can send it to someone else to view.

1 Choose File > Save As. In the Save As dialog box, choose Adobe PDF (pdf) from the Format menu (macOS) or Adobe PDF (*.PDF) from the Save As Type menu (Windows). Navigate to the Lessons > Lesson14 folder, if necessary. Notice that you have the option, at the bottom of the dialog box, to save all of the artboards in the PDF or a range of artboards. Click Save.

● **Note:** If you want to learn about the options and other presets in the Save Adobe PDF dialog box, choose Help > Illustrator Help and search for "Creating Adobe PDF files."

2 In the Save Adobe PDF dialog box, click the Adobe PDF Preset menu to see all of the different PDF presets available. Ensure that [Illustrator Default] is chosen, and click Save PDF.

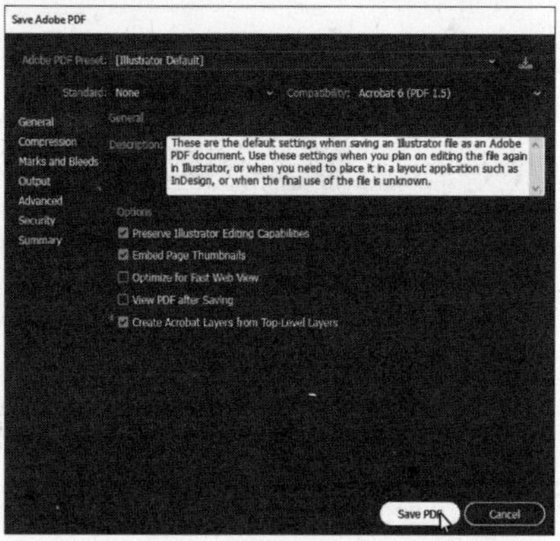

There are many ways to customize the creation of a PDF. Creating a PDF using the [Illustrator Default] preset creates a PDF in which all Illustrator data is preserved. PDFs created with this preset can be reopened in Illustrator without any loss of data. If you are planning on saving a PDF for a particular purpose, such as viewing on the Web or printing, you may want to choose another preset or adjust the options.

● **Note:** You may notice that the file currently open is the PDF (GreenIsle.pdf).

3 Choose File > Save, if necessary, and then choose File > Close.

Review questions

1 Describe the difference between *linking* and *embedding* in Illustrator.

2 What kinds of objects can be used as masks?

3 How do you create an opacity mask for a placed image?

4 Describe how to replace a placed image with another image in a document.

5 Describe what *packaging* does.

Review answers

1 A *linked file* is a separate, external file connected to the Illustrator file by a link. A linked file does not add significantly to the size of the Illustrator file. The linked file must accompany the Illustrator file to preserve the link and to ensure that the placed file appears when you open the Illustrator file. An *embedded file* is included in the Illustrator file. The Illustrator file size reflects the addition of the embedded file. Because the embedded file is part of the Illustrator file, no link can be broken. You can update linked and embedded files using the Relink button ( ) in the Links panel.

2 A mask can be a simple or compound path, and masks (such as an opacity mask) may be imported with placed Photoshop files. You can also create layer clipping masks with any shape that is the topmost object of a group or layer.

3 You create an opacity mask by placing the object to be used as a mask on top of the object to be masked. Then you select the mask and the object(s) to be masked, and either click the Make Mask button in the Transparency panel or choose Make Opacity Mask from the Transparency panel menu.

4 To replace a placed image with a different image, select the image in the Links panel. Then click the Relink button ( ), and locate and select the replacement image. Click Place.

5 *Packaging* is used to gather all of the necessary pieces for an Illustrator document. Packaging creates a copy of the Illustrator file, the linked images, and the necessary fonts (if desired), and it gathers the copies into a folder.

15 EXPORTING ASSETS

Lesson overview

In this lesson, you'll learn how to do the following:

- Create pixel-perfect drawings.
- Use the Export For Screens command.
- Work with the Asset Export panel.
- Generate, export, and copy/paste CSS (Cascading Style Sheets) code.

This lesson takes approximately 30 minutes to complete. Please log in to your account on peachpit.com to download the lesson files for this chapter, or go to the "Getting Started" section at the beginning of this book and follow the instructions under "Accessing the lesson files and Web Edition."

Your Account page is also where you'll find any updates to the chapters or to the lesson files. Look on the Lesson & Update Files tab to access the most current content.

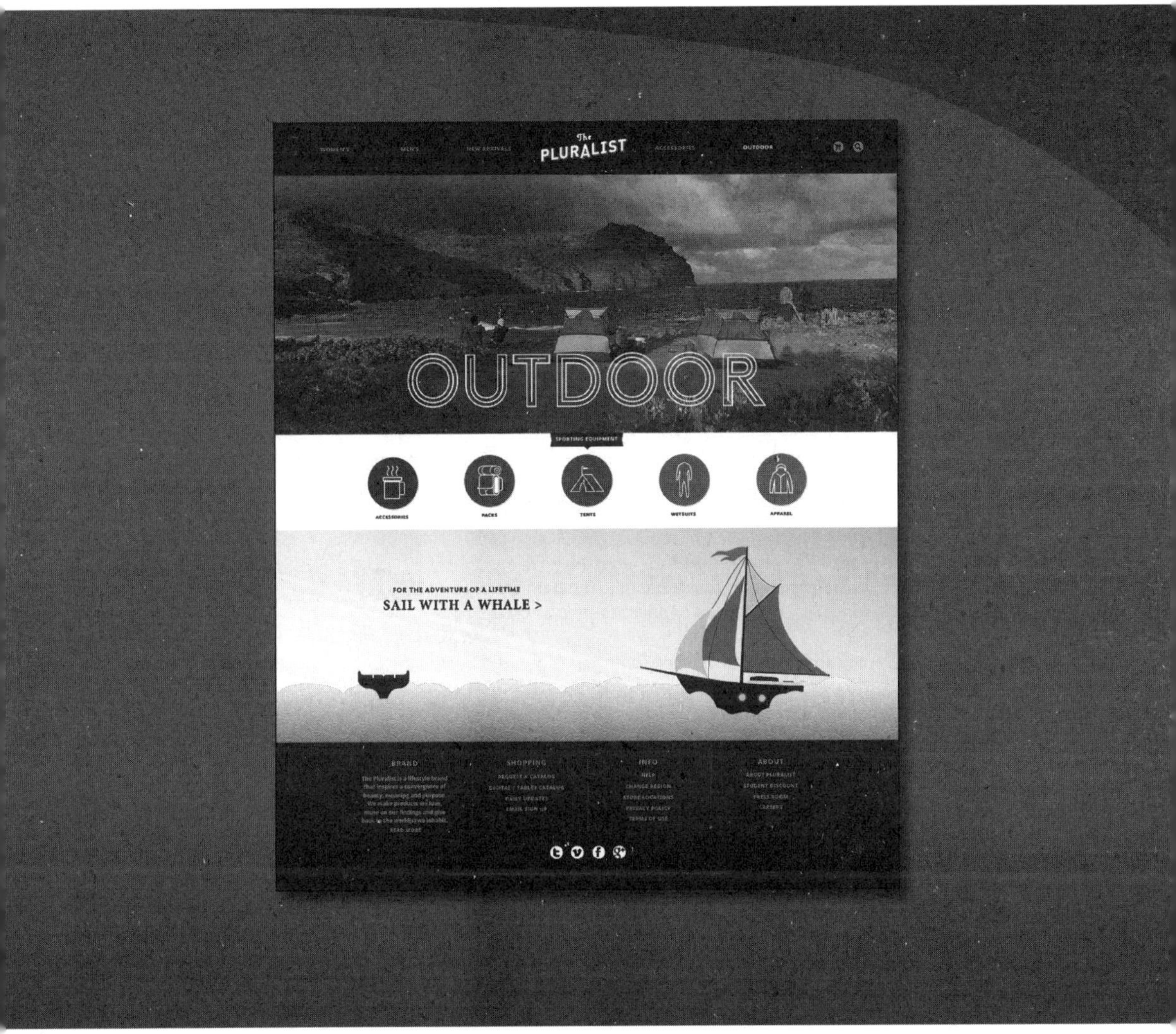

You can optimize your Illustrator CC content for use on the Web, in apps, and in screen presentations using various methods. For example, you can easily export assets and save them for the web or apps, export CSS and image files, and generate SVG (Scalable Vector Graphics).

Starting the lesson

Before you begin this lesson, you'll restore the default preferences for Adobe Illustrator CC and open the lesson file.

● **Note:** If you have not already downloaded the project files for this lesson to your computer from your Account page, make sure to do so now. See the "Getting Started" section at the beginning of the book.

1 To ensure that the tools function and the defaults are set exactly as described in this lesson, delete or deactivate (by renaming) the Adobe Illustrator CC preferences file. See "Restoring default preferences" in the "Getting Started" section at the beginning of the book.

2 Start Adobe Illustrator CC.

3 Choose File > Open. In the Open dialog box, navigate to the Lessons > Lesson15 folder. Select the L15_start.ai file, and click Open. This lesson contains a fictitious business name, address, and website address for the purposes of the project.

4 The Missing Fonts dialog box will most likely appear. Click Sync Fonts to sync all the missing fonts to your computer (your list may not match the figure). After they are synced and you see the message stating that there are no more missing fonts, click Close.

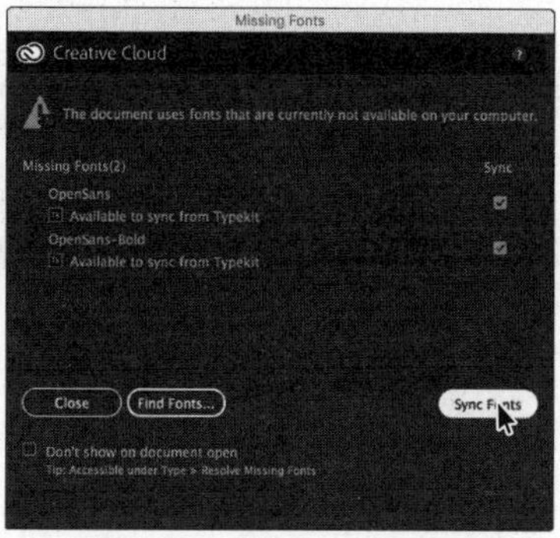

● **Note:** If you can't get the fonts to sync, you can go to the Creative Cloud desktop application and choose Assets > Fonts to see what the issue may be (refer to the section "Changing font family and font style" in Lesson 8, "Adding Type to a Poster," for more information on how to resolve it). You can also just click Close in the Missing Fonts dialog box and ignore the missing fonts as you proceed. A third method is to click the Find Fonts button in the Missing Fonts dialog box and replace the fonts with a local font on your machine.

● **Note:** If you don't see Reset Essentials in the Workspace menu, choose Window > Workspace > Essentials before choosing Window > Workspace > Reset Essentials.

5 Choose Window > Workspace > Reset Essentials to ensure that the workspace is set to the default settings.

6 Choose View > Fit Artboard In Window.

7 Choose File > Save As. In the Save As dialog box, navigate to the Lessons > Lesson15 folder, and name the file **AssetExport.ai**. Leave the Format option set to Adobe Illustrator (ai) (macOS) or the Save As Type option set to Adobe Illustrator (*.AI) (Windows) and then click Save. In the Illustrator Options dialog box, leave the Illustrator options at their default settings and then click OK.

8 Choose Select > Deselect, if necessary.

Creating Pixel-Perfect Drawings

When creating content for use on the Web, in mobile apps, in onscreen presentations, and more, it's important that images saved from vector art look sharp. To enable designers to create pixel-accurate designs, you can align artwork to the pixel grid using the Snap To Pixel option. The *pixel grid* is a grid of 72 squares per inch, vertically and horizontally, that is viewable when you zoom to 600% or higher with Pixel Preview mode enabled (View > Pixel Preview).

Pixel-aligned is an object-level property that enables an object to have its vertical and horizontal paths aligned to the pixel grid. This property remains with the object when the object is modified. Any vertical or horizontal path in the object gets aligned to the pixel grid as long as the property is set for it.

Aligning new artwork to the pixel grid

When Snap To Pixel (View > Snap To Pixel) is enabled, shapes that are drawn, modified, or transformed appear crisp. This makes most artwork, including most Live Shapes, align to the pixel grid automatically. In this first section, you'll explore the pixel grid and how to align new content to it.

1 In the AssetExport.ai file, choose File > Document Color Mode, and you will see that RGB Color is selected.

When designing for onscreen viewing (web, apps, etc.), RGB (Red, Green, Blue) is the preferred color mode for documents in Illustrator. When you create a new document (File > New), you can choose which color mode to use with the Color Mode option. In the New Document dialog box, choosing any document profile, *except* for Print, sets Color Mode to RGB by default.

Tip: After you create a document, you can change the document color mode using File > Document Color Mode. This sets the default color mode for all new colors you create and the existing swatches. RGB is the correct color mode to use when creating content for the Web, for apps, or for onscreen presentations.

2 Select the Selection tool (▶), and click to select the brown circle with the word "ACCESSORIES" beneath it. Press Command++ (macOS) or Ctrl++ (Windows) several times to zoom in closely to the selected artwork.

3 Choose View > Pixel Preview to preview a rasterized version of the design.

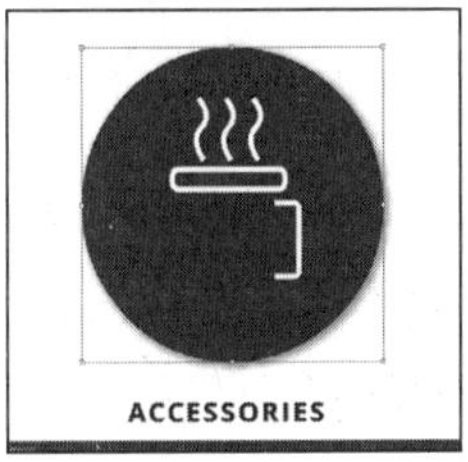

Preview mode

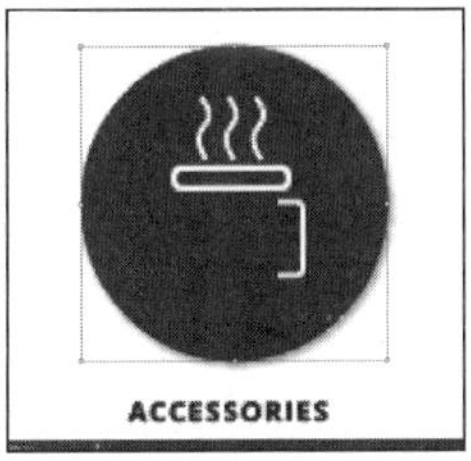

Pixel Preview mode

When you export assets in a format such as GIF, JPG, or PNG, any artwork that was vector is rasterized in the resulting file. Turning on Pixel Preview is a great way to be able to see what the artwork will look like when it's rasterized.

▶ **Tip:** You can turn off the pixel grid by choosing Illustrator CC > Preferences > Guides & Grid (macOS) or Edit > Preferences > Guides & Grid (Windows) and deselecting Show Pixel Grid (Above 600% Zoom).

4 Choose 600% from the View menu in the lower-left corner of the Document window (in the Status bar), and make sure you can still see the brown circle above the "ACCESSORIES" text.

By zooming in to at least 600% and with Pixel Preview turned on, you can see a pixel grid appear. The pixel grid divides the artboard into 1 pt. (1/72-inch) increments. For the next steps, you need to see the pixel grid (zoom level of 600% or greater).

5 Click to select one of the white paths on the brown circle.

This is an easy way to set the stroke and fill formatting for the next object drawn to match the selected artwork.

● **Note:** As of the writing of this book, the creation tools affected by Snap To Pixel are the Pen tool, the Curvature tool, shape tools like the Ellipse tool and the Rectangle tool, the Line Segment tool, the Arc tool, Grid tools, and the Artboard tool.

6 Select the Rectangle tool (■) in the Tools panel. Draw a simple rectangle on the brown circle.

You might notice that the edges of the rectangle look a little "fuzzy." That's because in this document, Snap To Pixel is turned off.

7 Press Delete or Backspace to remove the rectangle.

▶ **Tip:** You can also click the Snap To Pixel option in the Properties panel with nothing selected and the Selection tool selected, or you can select the Align Art To Pixel Grid option (▣) on the right end of the Control panel (Window > Control).

8 Choose View > Snap To Pixel to turn on Snap To Pixel.

Now, any shapes that are drawn, modified, or transformed will snap to the pixel grid if possible. By default, Snap To Pixel is turned on when you create a new document that uses the Web or Mobile document profile.

9 With the Rectangle tool selected, draw a simple rectangle to complete the coffee cup on the brown circle, and notice that the edges are "cleaner."

The vertical and horizontal segments of the drawn artwork snap to the pixel grid. In the next section, you'll see that you can snap existing artwork to the pixel grid. In this case, I had you redraw the shape just to see the difference.

10 Select the Selection tool (▶), and drag the rectangle into position like you see in the figure. You may need to resize the rectangle to look better.

Aligning existing artwork to the pixel grid

You can also align existing artwork to the pixel grid in several ways, as you will do in this section.

1 Select the Selection tool (▶), and click to select the rounded rectangle above the rectangle you drew.

2 Click the Align To Pixel Grid button in the Properties panel to the right (or choose Object > Make Pixel Perfect).

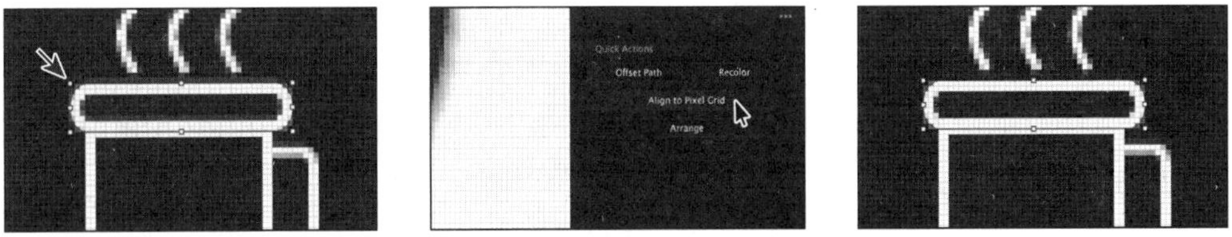

The rounded rectangle was created when Align To Pixel Grid wasn't selected. After the rectangle was aligned to the pixel grid, the horizontal and vertical straight edges were snapped to the closest pixel grid lines. Live Shapes and Live Corners are preserved when doing this.

Objects that you pixel-align that do not have any straight vertical or horizontal segments are not modified to align to the pixel grid. For example, because a rotated rectangle does not have straight vertical or horizontal segments, it is not nudged to produce crisp paths when the pixel-aligned property is set for it.

Note: The Align To Pixel Grid button does not appear in the Properties panel when an open path is selected.

3 Click to select one of the wavy white lines above the rounded rectangle, which selects a group of lines. Choose Object > Make Pixel Perfect.

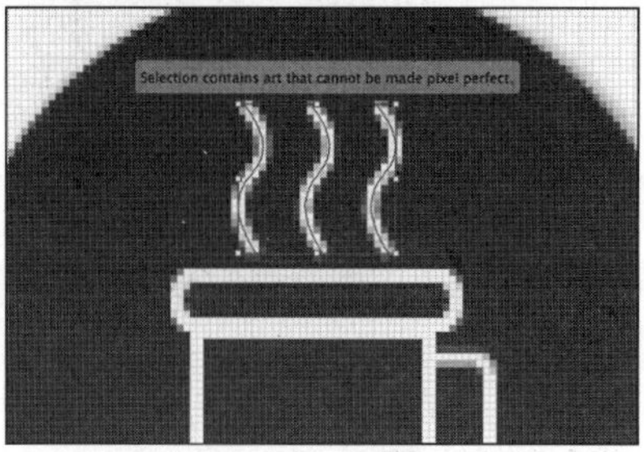

You will see a message in the Document window, "Selection Contains Art That Cannot Be Made Pixel Perfect." In this case, this means there are no vertical or horizontal straight edges to align.

4 Click the white "handle" shape on the right side of the coffee mug. Press Command++ (macOS) or Ctrl++ (Windows) several times to zoom in closely to the selected artwork.

5 Drag the upper-right corner bounding point to make the handle a bit larger.

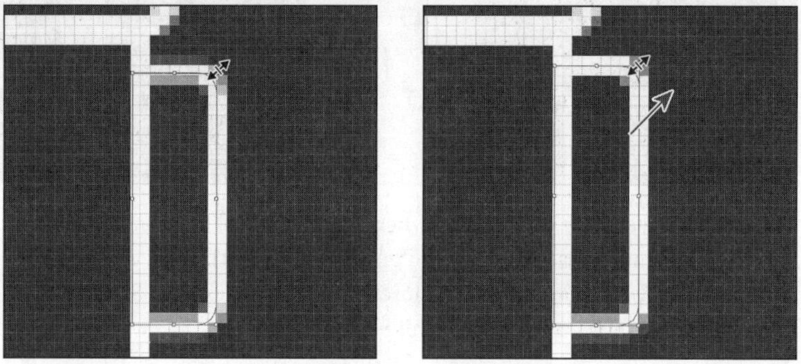

After dragging, notice that resizing the shape using the corner or side handles fixes the *corresponding* edges (snaps them to the pixel grid) but not all of them.

Note: Moving artwork is constrained to be in whole pixels when transforming via the Selection tool, Direct Selection tool, Live Shape center widget, arrow keys, and Artboard tool. The Direct Selection tool snaps anchor points and handles to pixel or subpixel locations depending on the stroke settings of the path. This snap is similar to the Pen tool snap during creation.

6 Choose Object > Make Pixel Perfect to ensure that all of the vertical or horizontal straight edges are aligned to the pixel grid.

7 Choose Select > Deselect (if available) and then choose File > Save.

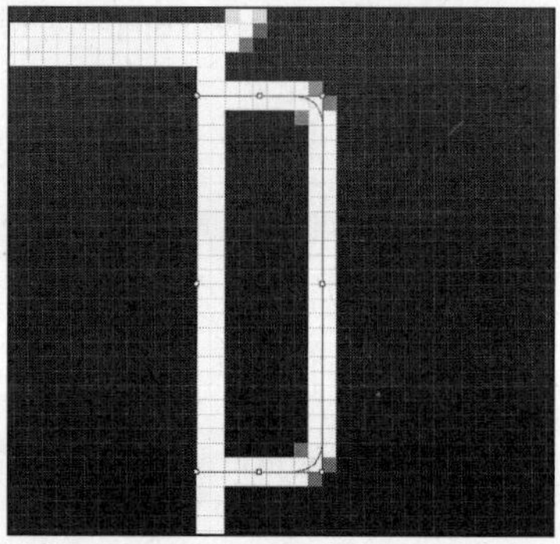

Exporting artboards and assets

In Illustrator, using the File > Export > Export For Screens command and the Asset Export panel, you can export entire artboards, perhaps to show a design in progress, or selected assets. The exported content can be saved in several file formats, such as JPEG, SVG, PDF, and PNG. These formats are optimized for use on the Web, devices, and onscreen presentations and are compatible with most browsers, yet each has different capabilities. The selected artwork is automatically isolated from the rest of the design and saved as an individual file.

Tip: To learn more about working with web graphics, search for "File formats for exporting artwork" in Illustrator Help (Help > Illustrator Help).

Slicing content

In the past, before the Export For Screens command or the Asset Export panel, you needed to isolate artwork you wanted to export. This was done by placing the artwork on its own artboard or by slicing the content. In Illustrator, you can create slices to define the boundaries of different web elements in your artwork. When you save the artwork using the File > Export > Save For Web (Legacy) command, you can choose to save each slice as an independent file with its own format and settings.

It is not necessary to isolate artwork by slicing when using the File > Export > Export For Screens command or Asset Export panel since artwork is isolated automatically.

Note: To learn more about creating slices, search for "Create slices" in Adobe Illustrator Help (Help > Illustrator Help).

Exporting artboards

In this section, you'll see how to export artboards in your document. This could be useful if you want to show someone a design you are working on or to capture a design for use in a presentation, website, app, or other.

1 Choose View > Fit Artboard In Window.

2 Choose File > Export > Export For Screens.

In the Export For Screens dialog box that appears, you can choose between exporting artboards and exporting assets. Once you decide what to export, you can set export settings on the right side of the dialog box.

3 With the Artboards tab selected, on the right side of the dialog box, ensure that All is selected.

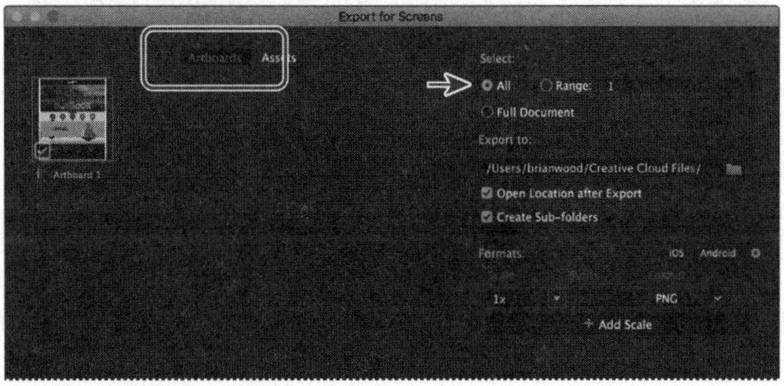

You can choose to export all or a specific range of artboards. This document has only one artboard, so selecting All is the same as selecting a range of 1. Selecting Full Document will export all artwork in a single file.

4 Click the folder icon (■) to the right of the Export To field. Navigate to the Lessons > Lesson15 folder, and click Choose (macOS) or Select Folder (Windows).

5 Click the Format menu, and choose JPG 80.

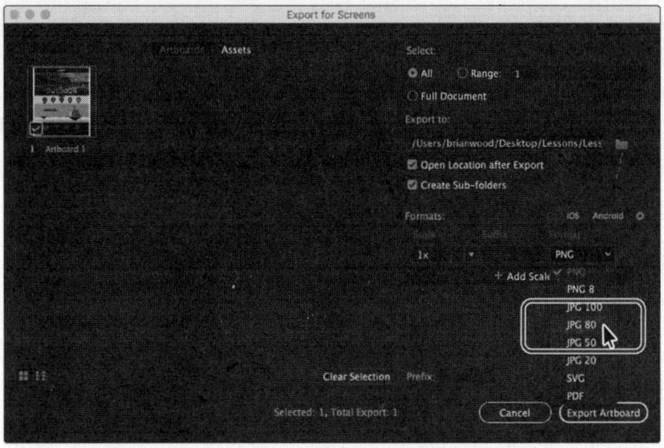

In the Formats section of the Export For Screens dialog box, you can set a Scale factor for the exported asset, create (or in this case edit) a suffix for the filename, and change the format. You can also export multiple versions with different scale factors and formats by clicking the + Add Scale button.

6 Click Export Artboard.

The Lesson15 folder should open, and you should see a folder named "1x" and, in that folder, an image named "Artboard 1-80.jpg." The "-80" suffix refers to the quality you set when exporting.

7 Close the folder, and return to Illustrator.

▶ **Tip:** To avoid creating subfolders, like the folder "1x," you can deselect Create Sub-folders in the Export For Screens dialog box when exporting.

Exporting assets

You can also quickly and easily export individual assets in file formats such as JPG, PNG, and SVG using the Asset Export panel. The Asset Export panel lets you collect assets that you might export frequently and can be a great tool for web and mobile workflows because it allows for the export of multiple assets with a single click. In this section, you'll open the Asset Export panel and see how to both collect artwork in the panel and use it to export that collected artwork.

Note: There are several methods for exporting artwork in a variety of formats. You can select artwork in your Illustrator document and choose File > Export Selection. This adds the selected artwork to the Asset Export panel and opens the Export For Screens dialog box. You can choose from the same formats you saw in the previous section.

1 With the Selection tool (▶) selected, click to select the white "Pluralist" logo at the top of the artboard.

2 Press Command++ (macOS) or Ctrl++ (Windows) several times to zoom in closely to the logo.

3 With the logo selected, choose Window > Asset Export to open the Asset Export panel.

The Asset Export panel is where you can save content for export now or later. It can work in conjunction with the Export For Screens dialog box to set export options for the selected assets, as you'll see.

4 Drag the selected Pluralist logo into the top part of the Asset Export panel. When you see a plus sign (+) appear, release the mouse button to add the artwork to the Asset Export panel.

Tip: To add artwork to the Asset Export panel, you can also right-click the artwork in the Document window and choose Collect For Export > either As Single Asset or As Multiple Assets.

Tip: To delete an asset from the Asset Export panel, you can either delete the original artwork in the document or select the asset thumbnail in the Asset Export panel and click the Remove Selected Assets From This Panel button.

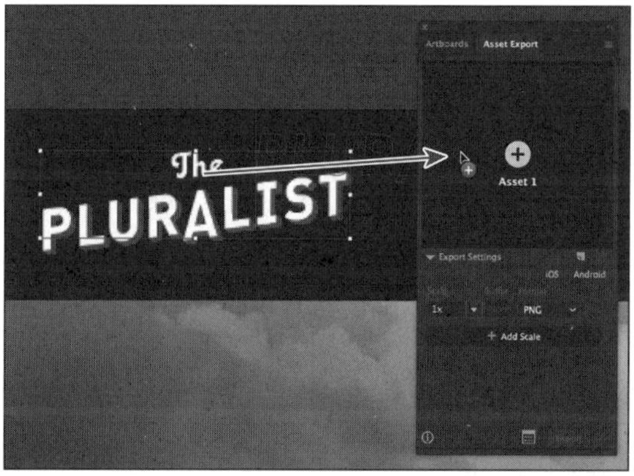

The artwork you added to the panel is now called "pluralist" or something similar. The asset is tied to the original artwork in the document. In other words, if you update the artwork in the document, the asset is updated in the Asset Export panel. Every asset you add to the Asset Export panel is saved with the panel and will be in there until you delete it from either the document or the Asset panel. You can also drag multiple objects into the Asset Export panel, and each will be saved as a separate asset.

Tip: If you Option-drag (macOS) or Alt-drag (Windows) multiple objects into the Asset Export panel, the selected content will become a single asset in the Asset Export panel.

● **Note:** You may need to double-click to edit the name.

5 Click the name of the asset in the Asset Export panel, and rename it **PluralistLogo**.

The asset name that appears is based on what the artwork is named in the Layers panel. Also, how you name assets in the Asset Export panel is up to you. I name them so later I can more easily keep track of what each asset is used for.

6 Click the Pluralist logo asset thumbnail to select it in the Asset Export panel.

As you add more and more assets to the panel using various methods, you will need to first select the assets you'd like to export.

● **Note:** If you are creating assets for use on iOS or Android, you could also click the iOS or Android options to create a series of scaled export options, by default.

7 In the Export Settings area of the Asset Export panel, choose SVG from the Format menu, if necessary.

The SVG is perfect for the website, but in this case, a co-worker has asked for a PNG version of the same logo as well.

8 Click the + Add Scale button below the SVG option in the panel to export the artwork in another format (in this case). Change Scale to 1x and ensure that Format is PNG.

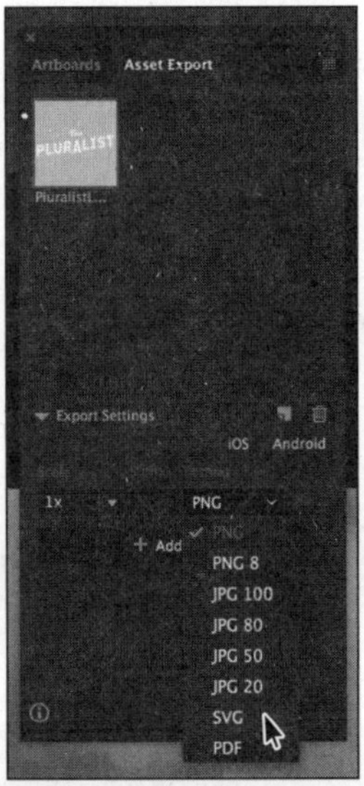

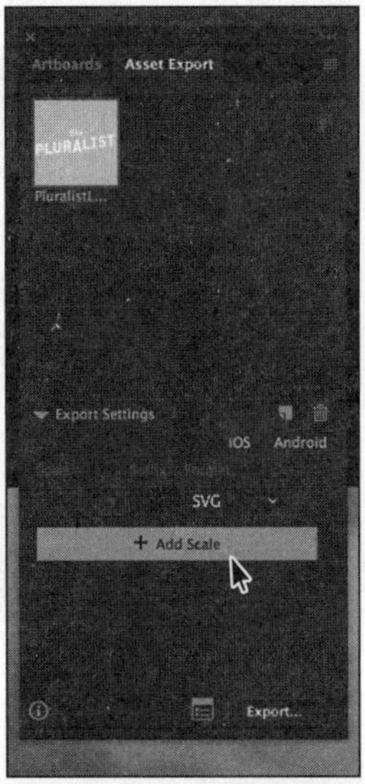

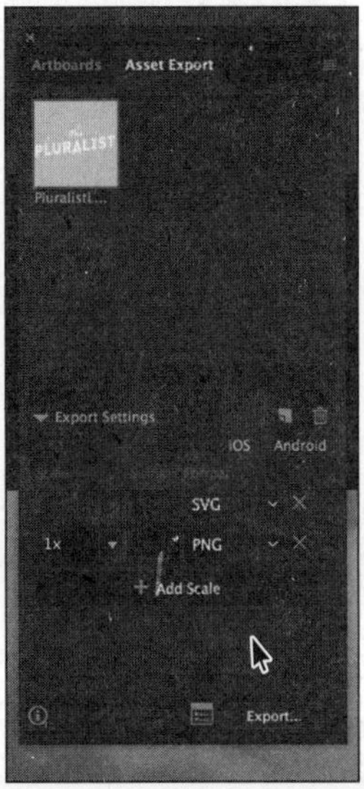

This sets the format for all of the selected assets in the Asset Export panel. You can also set a scale (1x, 2x, etc.) if you need multiple scaled versions of the selected assets—perhaps for Retina and non-Retina displays when it comes to formats like JPEG or PNG. You can also add a suffix to the exported file name. A suffix could be something like "@1x" to indicate the 100% scaled version of an exported asset.

9 With the PluralistLogo thumbnail selected at the top of the Asset Export panel, click the Export button at the bottom of the Asset Export panel to export the selected asset. In the dialog box that appears, navigate to the Lessons > Lesson15 > Asset_Export folder, and click Choose (macOS) or Select Folder (Windows) to export the assets.

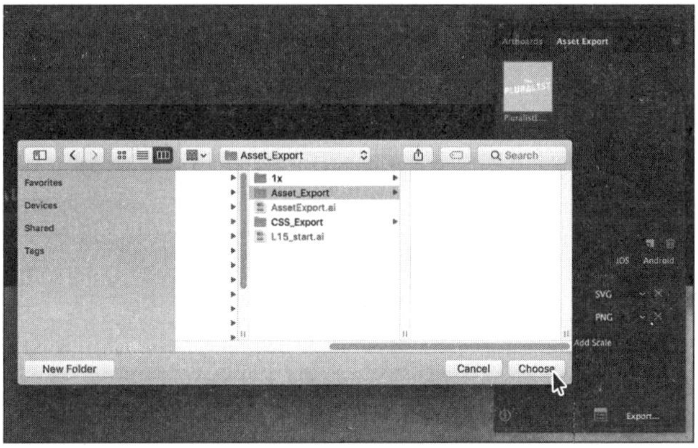

Both the SVG file (PluralistLogo.svg) and the PNG file (PluralistLogo.png) will be exported to the Asset_Export folder in separate folders.

You can also click the Launch The Export For Screens Dialog button (▤) at the bottom of the Asset Export panel. This will open the Export For Screens dialog box where you can set all of the same settings, including a few more.

Creating CSS from your design

Note: Exporting or copying CSS from Illustrator CC *does not* create HTML for a web page. It is intended to create CSS that is applied to HTML you create elsewhere, such as in Adobe Dreamweaver.

If you are building a website or want to hand off content to a developer, you can transform the visual designs you create in Illustrator to Cascading Style Sheets styles using the CSS Properties panel (Window > CSS Properties) or File > Export > Export As command. *Cascading Style Sheets* is a specification for formatting rules, much like paragraph and character styles in Illustrator, that control the appearance of content in a web page. Unlike paragraph and character styles in Illustrator, CSS can control not only the look and feel of text but also the formatting and positioning of page elements found in HTML.

```
html {
    font-family: sans-serif;
    -webkit-text-size-adjust: 100%;
    -ms-text-size-adjust: 100%;
}
body {
    margin: 0;
}
a:focus {
    outline: thin dotted;
}
a:active, a:hover {
    outline: 0;
}
h1 {
    font-size: 2em;
    margin: 0 0 0.2em 0;
}
```

An example of CSS code.

The great thing about generating CSS from your Illustrator artwork is that it allows for flexible web workflows. You can export all of the styling from a document, or you can just copy the styling code for a single object or a series of objects and paste it into an external web editor, like Adobe Dreamweaver. This can be a great way to move the styling from your web design in Illustrator straight to your HTML editor or to hand it off to a web developer. But creating CSS styling and using it effectively requires a bit of setup in your Illustrator CC document, and that's what you'll learn about next.

Note: To learn more about CSS, visit the "Understand Cascading Style Sheets" section of Adobe Dreamweaver Help (https://helpx.adobe.com/dreamweaver/using/cascading-style-sheets.html).

Setting up your design for generating CSS

If you intend to export or copy and paste CSS from Illustrator CC, setting up the Illustrator CC file properly before creating CSS allows you to name the CSS styles that are generated. In this section, you'll look at the CSS Properties panel and see how you can set up the content for style export using *named* or *unnamed* content.

1 Choose Window > Workspace > Reset Essentials.

2 Choose Select > Deselect, if available.

3 Choose View > Fit Artboard In Window and then press Command+– (macOS) or Ctrl+– (Windows) to zoom out.

4 Choose Window > CSS Properties to open the CSS Properties panel. Using the CSS Properties panel, you can do the following:

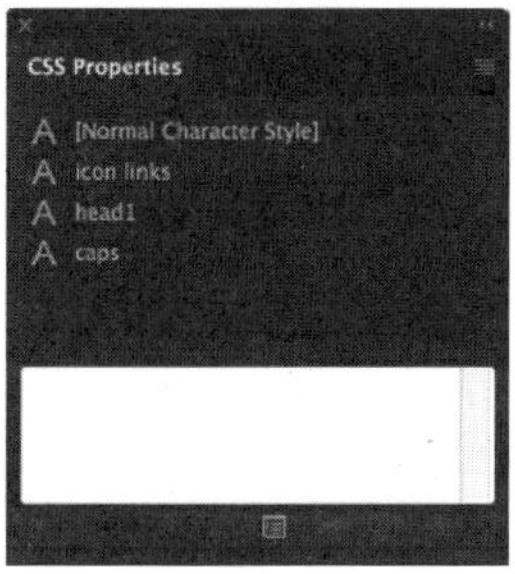

- Preview CSS code for selected objects.
- Copy CSS code for selected objects.
- Export generated styling for selected objects to a CSS file (along with any images used).
- Change options for the CSS code exported.
- Export the CSS for all objects to a CSS file.

5 With the Selection tool (▶) selected, click to select the blue rectangle behind the navigation and logo at the top of the artboard (see the following figure).

In the CSS Properties panel you'll see a message in the preview area. Instead of CSS code (which is what the preview area typically shows), the message states that the object needs to be named in the Layers panel or you need to allow Illustrator to create styling from "unnamed objects."

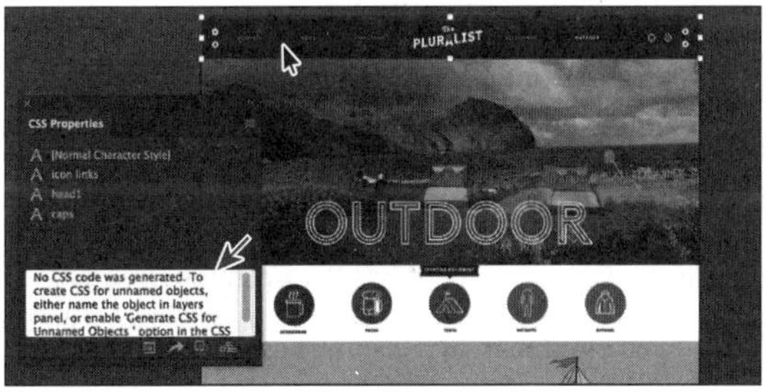

6 Open the Layers panel (Window > Layers), and click the Locate Object button (🔍) at the bottom of the panel to easily find the selected object in the panel.

● **Note:** You may need to drag the left edge of the Layers panel to the left to see the entire name of the object.

● **Note:** The content for the sublayer named "pluralist" may be showing in your Layers panel and that's okay.

7 Double-click directly on the name of the selected <Rectangle> object in the Layers panel, and change the name to **navbar** (lowercase). Press Return or Enter to make the change.

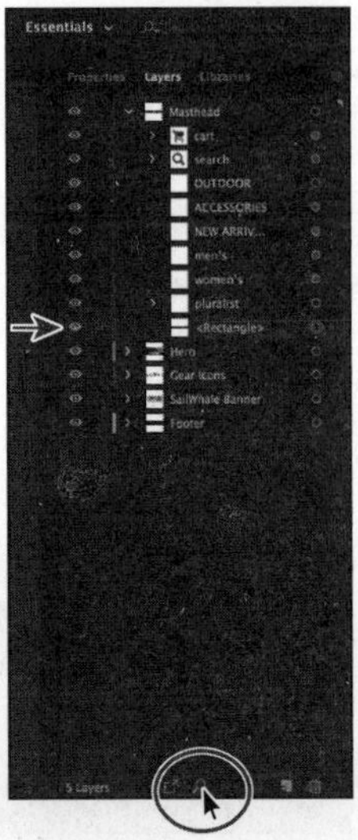

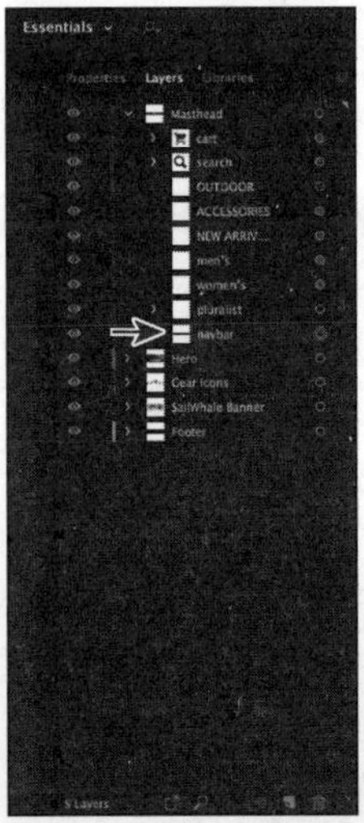

8 Look in the CSS Properties panel again, and you should see a style named .navbar in the preview area. Drag the bottom of the panel down to show more.

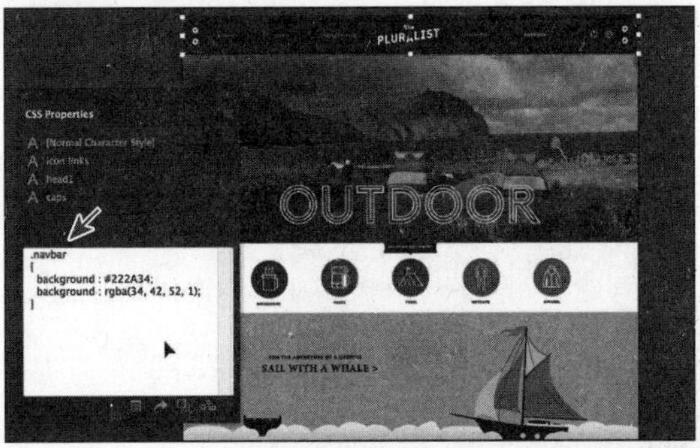

● **Note:** If you see a style named ".navbar_1_," it's usually because there is an extra space after the name "navbar" in the Layers panel.

▶ **Tip:** You can tell a style is a *class* in CSS because the name has a period (.) before it.

When content is unnamed in the Layers panel (it has the default naming), a CSS style is not created for it, by default. If you name the object in the Layers panel, the CSS is generated, and the name of the style created matches the object name in the Layers panel. Illustrator creates styles called *classes* for most content.

For objects in the design (not including text objects, as you will see), the name you give them in the Layers panel should match the class name in the HTML that is created in a separate HTML editor, like Dreamweaver. But, you can also forgo naming the objects in the Layers panel and simply create generic styles that you can then export or paste into an HTML editor and name there. You will see how to do that next.

9 With the Selection tool, click to select the brown circle behind the cup you worked with earlier. In the CSS Properties panel, a style will not appear since the object is unnamed in the Layers panel (it just has the generic <Path> name).

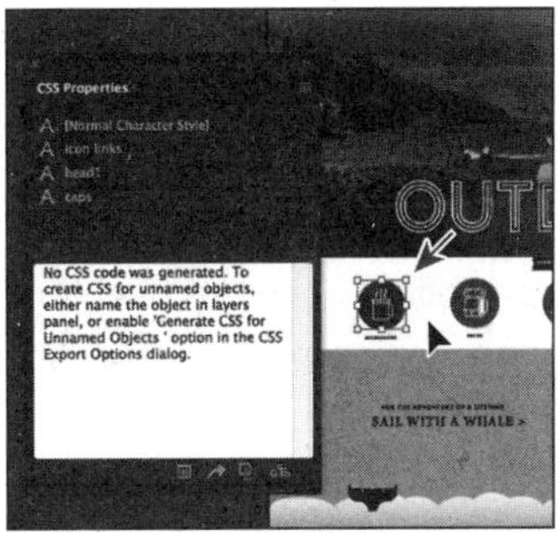

10 Click the Export Options button (▤) at the bottom of the CSS Properties panel.

The CSS Export Options dialog box that appears contains export options that you can set, such as which units to use, which properties to include in the styles, and other options, such as which Vendor prefixes to include.

11 Select Generate CSS For Unnamed Objects, and click OK.

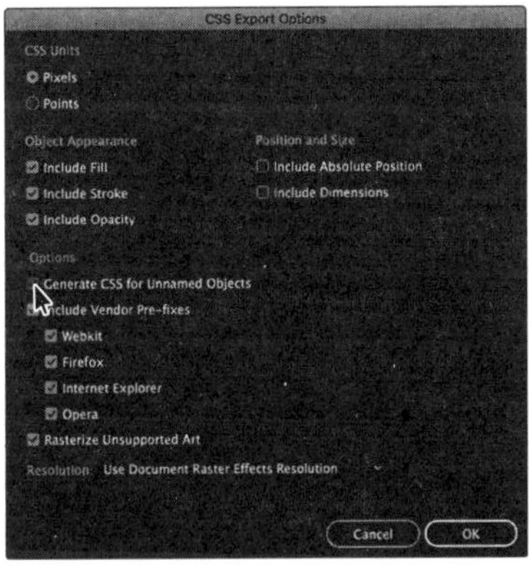

12 With the brown circle still selected, a style named ".st0" appears in the preview area of the CSS Properties panel.

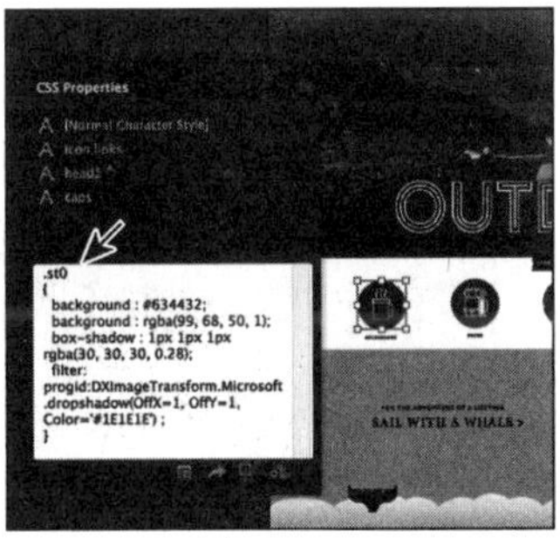

.st0 is short for "style 0" and is a generic name for the formatting that is generated. Every object that you don't name in the Layers panel will now be named .st1, .st2, and so on, after turning on Generate CSS For Unnamed Objects. This type of style naming can be useful if, for instance, you are creating the web page yourself and you are going to paste or export the CSS from Illustrator and name it in your HTML editor or if you simply needed some of the CSS formatting for a style you already have in your HTML editor.

13 Choose Select > Deselect and then choose File > Save.

Working with character styles and CSS code

● **Note:** Currently, paragraph styles are not taken into account when naming styles in the CSS code that is generated.

Illustrator will create CSS styles based on text formatting, as well. Formatting, such as font family, font size, leading (called *line-height* in CSS), color, kerning and tracking (collectively called *letter-spacing* in CSS), and more, can be captured in the CSS code. Any character styles that are applied to text in your design are listed in the CSS Properties panel as a CSS style and have the same name as the character style. Text that has formatting applied, without a character style applied, will have a generic CSS style name when Illustrator generates the style.

Next, you'll create and then apply a character style to text.

1 In the CSS Properties panel, notice the style named [Normal Character Style], toward the top of the panel.

   In the CSS Properties panel, only character styles that are applied to text appear. The Normal Character Style is applied to text by default, so it appears in the CSS Properties panel. If you create character styles but don't apply them to text, they will not appear in the CSS Properties panel.

2 Choose Window > Type > Character Styles to open the Character Styles panel.

3 With the Selection tool (▶) selected, click to select the paragraph of text *below* the heading "BRAND," on the left end of the footer.

4 Press Command++ (macOS) or Ctrl++ (Windows) several times to zoom in to the text.

5 Select the Type tool (T) in the Tools panel. Select the entire paragraph that begins with "The Pluralist is a lifestyle brand...."

6 Click the style named "p" in the Character Styles panel to apply it to the selected text.

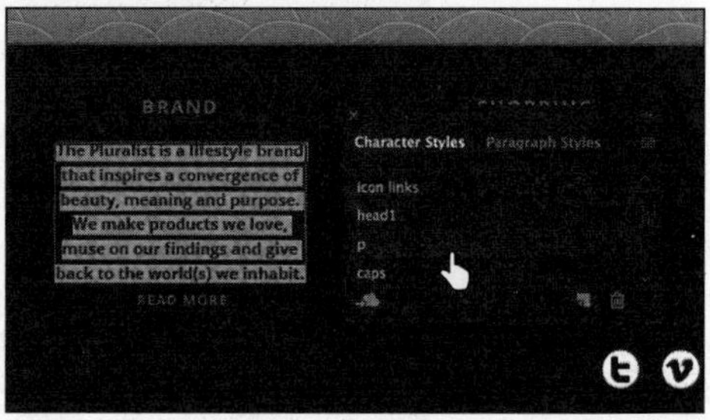

7 Select the Selection tool (▶), and with the text object still selected, you will see the character style named "p" in the CSS Properties panel list. This indicates that it is applied to text in the design. You will also see CSS code in the preview area of the panel.

▶ **Tip:** You can also use the character styles listed in the CSS Properties panel as a way to apply the styles to text.

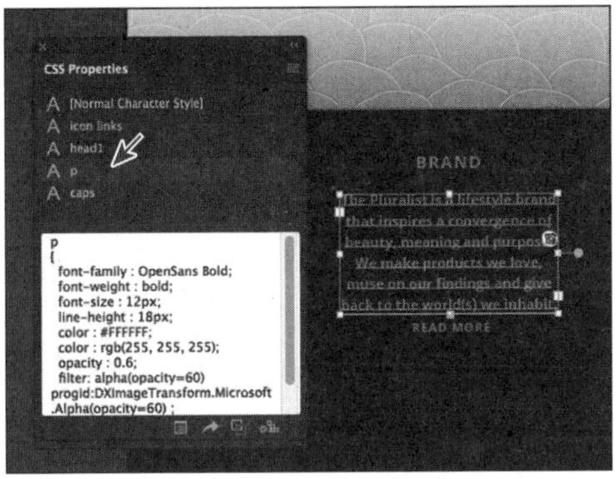

Selecting a text object (not the text) will show all the generated CSS code for the styling used in the entire text area. With the text selected, the CSS is not shown in the CSS Properties panel.

8 With the Selection tool, click the type object in the footer that contains the "Shopping" heading. Look in the CSS Properties panel, and you will see a series of CSS styles listed. These are the styles applied to *all* the text in the type area. You may want to drag the bottom of the CSS Properties panel down to see more of the styling.

● **Note:** The ordering of the styles you see in the CSS Properties panel may not match the figure and that's okay.

Selecting a type area gives you the ability to see all the CSS code generated from the styling. It is also a great way to be able to copy or export all the text formatting from a selected type area.

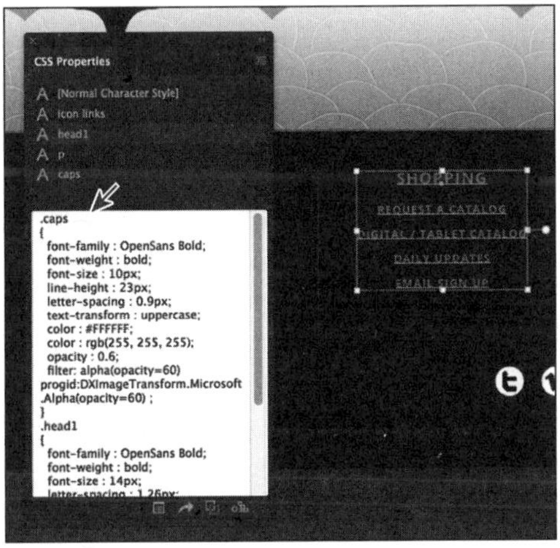

Working with graphic styles and CSS code

CSS code can also be copied or exported for any graphic styles that are applied to content. Next, you'll apply a graphic style and see the generated CSS code.

1 Choose View > Fit Artboard In Window. With the Selection tool (▶), click to select the blue rectangle behind the ship. You may want to zoom out a bit.

▶ **Tip:** Like selecting a character style in the CSS Properties panel to apply the formatting, you can also select content and select a graphic style listed in the CSS Properties panel to apply it.

2 Choose Window > Graphic Styles. In the Graphic Styles panel, click the graphic style named "GradientBox." You can close the Graphic Styles panel group.

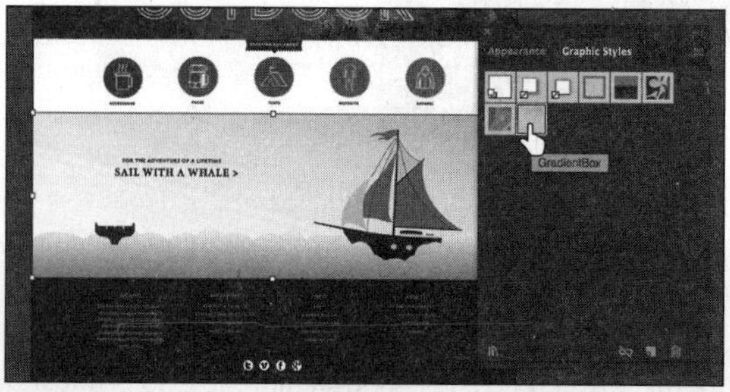

Looking in the CSS Properties panel, you will see the graphic style named "GradientBox" now listed, because it is applied to content in your document.

You will also see CSS code for a style. Mine is named ".content_1_," but yours may be different. The CSS code is generated from the GradientBox graphic style you just saw since that graphic style is applied. But it's not naming the style with the "GradientBox" name since the graphic style is just a way to apply formatting. Remember, this is an unnamed CSS style because you didn't rename the selected object (the rectangle) in the Layers panel.

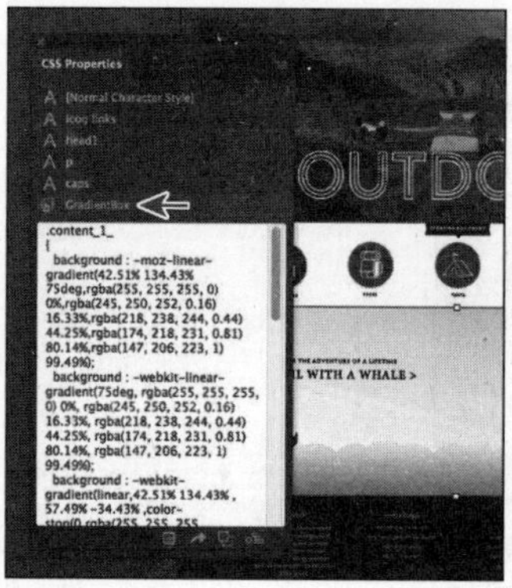

3 Leave the rectangle selected and then choose File > Save.

Copying CSS

At times, you may need to capture only a bit of CSS code from part of your design to paste into your HTML editor or to send to a web developer. Illustrator lets you copy and paste CSS code easily. Next, you'll copy the CSS for a few objects and learn about how grouping can change the way CSS code is generated.

1 With the rectangle still selected, click the Copy Selected Style button ( ) at the bottom of the CSS Properties panel. This copies the CSS code currently showing in the panel.

  Next, you will select multiple objects and copy the generated CSS code at the same time.

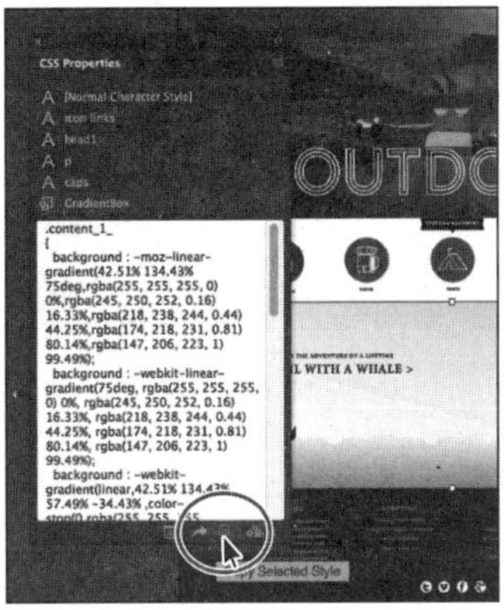

2 With the Selection tool ( ) selected and the rectangle still selected, Shift-click the brown circle to select both objects.

  In the CSS Properties panel, you will not see any CSS code since you need to tell Illustrator to generate CSS code for more than one selected object.

3 Click the Generate CSS button ( ) at the bottom of the panel.

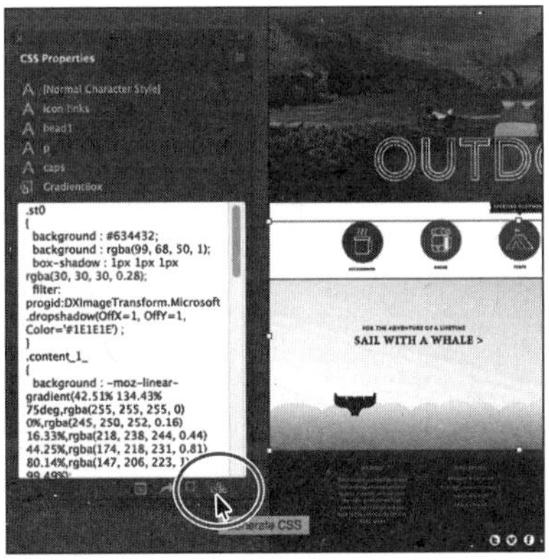

  The code for two CSS styles, .st0 and .content_1_, now appears in the preview area of the CSS Properties panel. Your style names may be different, and that's okay. To see both styles, you may need to scroll down in the panel. Yours may also be in a different order, and that's okay.

  With both styles showing in the CSS Properties panel, you could copy the styles and paste them into your HTML editor code or paste them into an email to send to a web developer, for instance.

Note: You may see a yield sign icon ( ) at the bottom of the panel when certain content is selected. It indicates that not all of the Illustrator appearance attributes (such as the multiple strokes applied to the shape) can be written in the CSS code for the selected content.

Tip: When CSS code appears in the CSS Properties panel for selected content, you can also select part of the code, right-click the selected code, and then choose Copy to copy just that selection.

Note: The styling or naming you see may be different, and that's okay.

4 With the Selection tool, click to select the ship.

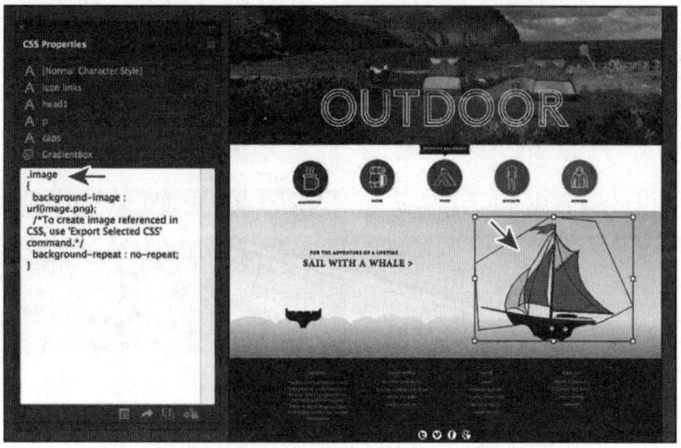

In the CSS Properties panel, you will see CSS code for an .image style. That code contains a background-image property. When Illustrator encounters artwork (or raster images) that it can't make CSS code from or a group of objects, it rasterizes the exported content (*not* the artwork on the artboard) when you export the CSS code. The CSS code that is generated can be applied to an HTML object, like a div, and the PNG image will be applied as a background image in the HTML object.

5 Drag a marquee selection across the brown circle and cup shapes to select them.

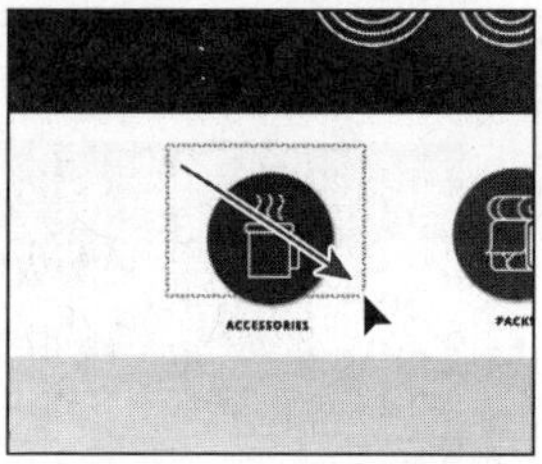

Note: The styling you see may be different, and that's okay.

6 Click the Generate CSS button ( ) at the bottom of the CSS Properties panel to generate the CSS code for the selected artwork.

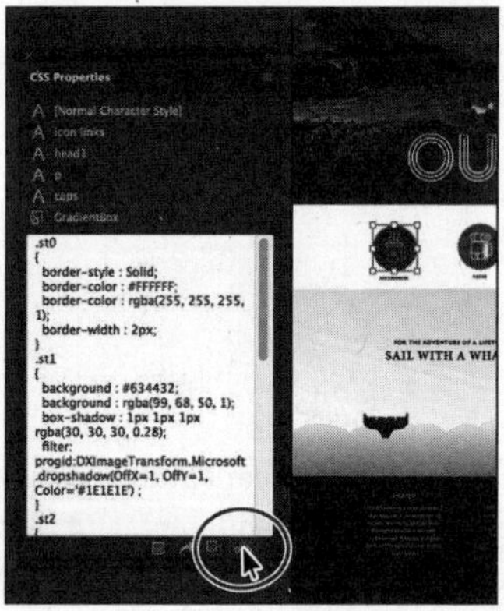

You will see the CSS code for all the selected objects in the panel. If you were to copy the CSS code now, the images would not be created, only the code referring to them. To generate the images, you need to export the code, which you will do in the next section.

7 Choose Object > Group to group the objects together. Leave the group selected for the next section.

Notice that, in the CSS Properties panel, a single CSS style is now showing (.image). Grouping content tells Illustrator to create a single image (in this case) from the grouped content. Having a single web image would most likely be better if you intend on placing it on a web page.

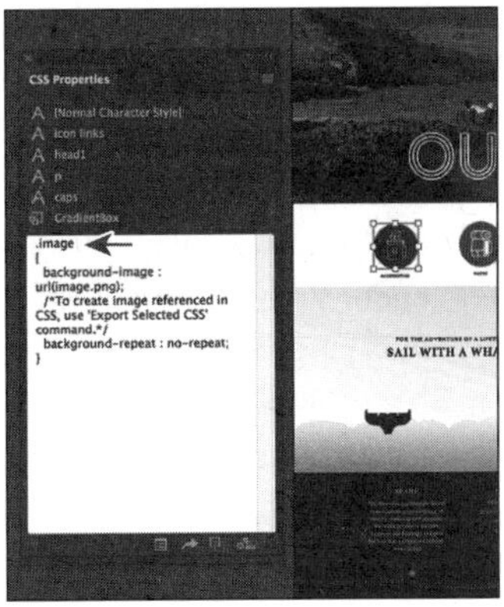

Exporting CSS

You can also export part or all of the CSS code for your page design. Exporting CSS code has the distinct advantages of creating a CSS file (.css) and exporting PNG files for content that is considered unsupported. In this section, you will see both methods.

1 With the group still selected, click the Export Selected CSS button (icon) at the bottom of the CSS Properties panel.

2 In the Export CSS dialog box, make sure that the filename is AssetExport. Navigate to the Lessons > Lesson15 > CSS_Export folder, and click Save to save a CSS file named AssetExport.css and a PNG image file.

3 In the CSS Export Options dialog box, leave all settings at default, and click OK.

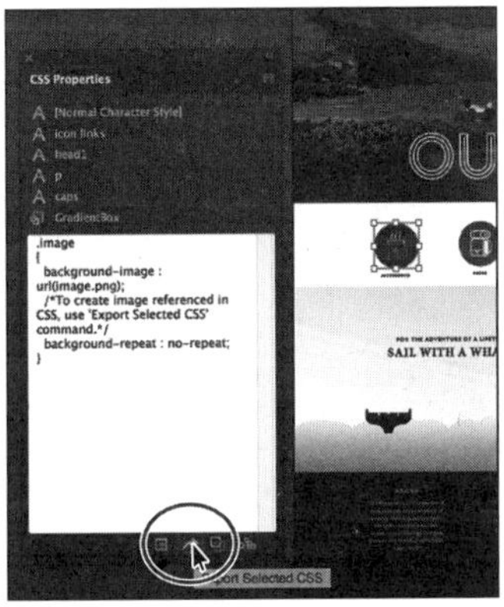

4 Go to the Lessons > Lesson15 > CSS_Export folder on your hard drive. In that folder, you should now see the AssetExport.css file and an image named image.png.

As stated earlier, the CSS code that was generated assumes that you are going to apply the CSS styling to an object in your HTML editor and that the image will become a background image for the object. With the image generated, you can use it for other parts of your web page as well. Next, you'll export all the CSS from the design.

5 Back in Illustrator, choose File > Export > Export As. In the Export dialog box, set the Format option to CSS (css) (macOS) or the Save As Type option to CSS (*.CSS) (Windows). Change the filename to **AssetExport_all**, and make sure that you navigate to the Lessons > Lesson15 > CSS_Export folder. Click Export.

Tip: You can choose a resolution for rasterized artwork in the CSS Export Options dialog box. By default, it uses the Document Raster Effects resolution (Effect > Document Raster Effects Settings).

Note: You can also export all of the CSS from your design by choosing Export All from the CSS Properties panel menu. If you want to change the export options first, you can set them by clicking the Export Options button (icon) at the bottom of the CSS Properties dialog box.

6 In the CSS Export Options dialog box, leave all the options at their default settings, and click OK. You most likely will see a dialog box telling you that images will be overwritten. Click OK.

Position and size properties are not added to the CSS code by default. In certain situations, you will need to export CSS with those options selected. The Include Vendor Pre-fixes option is selected by default. *Vendor prefixes* are a way for certain browser makers (each is listed in the dialog box) to add support for new CSS features. You can choose to exclude these prefixes by deselecting them.

● **Note:** Your file sorting and icons may look different in the CSS_Export folder, and that's okay.

7 Go to the Lessons > Lesson15 > CSS_Export folder, and you will see the new CSS file named AssetExport_all.css and a series of images created because the Rasterize Unsupported Art option was selected in the CSS Export Options dialog box.

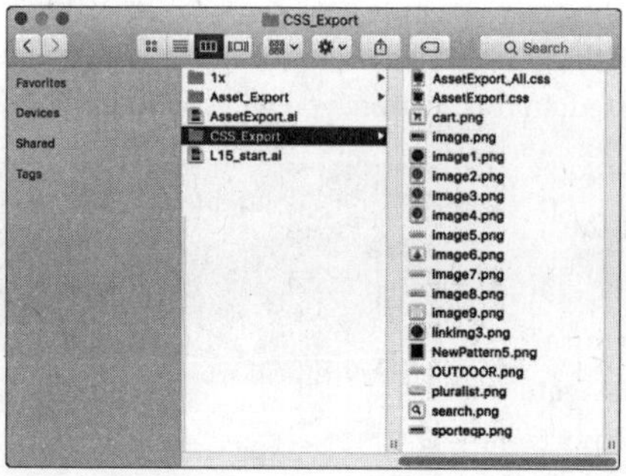

8 Return to Illustrator, and choose Select > Deselect.

9 Choose File > Close to close the file. Save the file if asked.

Review questions

1 Why do you align content to the pixel grid?

2 Name three image file types that can be chosen in the Export For Screens dialog box and Asset Export panel.

3 Describe the generic process for exporting assets with the Asset Export panel.

4 What is CSS?

5 Describe the difference between *named* and *unnamed* content when it comes to generating CSS.

Review answers

1 Aligning content to the pixel grid is useful for providing a crisp appearance to the edges of artwork. When Snap To Pixel is enabled for supported artwork, all the horizontal and vertical segments in the object are aligned to the pixel grid.

2 The image file types that can be chosen in the Export For Screens dialog box and the Asset Export panel are PNG, JPEG, SVG, and PDF.

3 In order to export assets using the Asset Export panel, the artwork to be exported needs to be collected in the Asset Export panel. Once in the panel, you can select the asset(s) to be exported, set the export settings, and then export.

4 If you are building a website or want to hand off content to a developer, you can transform the visual designs you create in Illustrator to CSS styles using the CSS Properties panel (Window > CSS Properties) or File > Export > Export As command. Cascading Style Sheets is a specification of formatting rules, much like paragraph and character styles in Illustrator, that control the appearance of content in a web page. Unlike paragraph and character styles in Illustrator, CSS can control not only the look and feel of text but also the formatting and positioning of page elements found in HTML.

5 Named content is content whose layer name in the Layers panel has been changed. When content is unnamed in the Layers panel (the default layer name is used), a CSS style is not created for the content by default. If you name the object in the Layers panel, the CSS is generated, and the name of the style created matches the object name in the Layers panel. To generate CSS styles for unnamed content, you need to enable this in the CSS Export Options dialog box by clicking the Export Options button (▤) in the CSS Properties panel.

INDEX

B

D

G

M

N

O

P

R

S

T

U

V

W

Y

Z

Contributors

Brian Wood is a web developer and the author of fourteen training books (Adobe Illustrator, Adobe InDesign, Adobe Muse, Adobe XD, and Adobe DPS), as well as numerous training videos on Dreamweaver & CSS, InDesign, Illustrator, Acrobat, Adobe Muse and others.

In addition to training many clients large and small, Brian speaks regularly at national conferences, such as Adobe MAX and the HOW conference, as well as events hosted by AIGA and other industry organizations. To learn more, check out www.youtube.com/askbrianwood or visit www.brianwoodtraining.com.

Production Notes

The *Adobe Illustrator CC Classroom in a Book (2018 release)* was created electronically using Adobe InDesign CC 2017. Art was produced using Adobe InDesign CC, Adobe Illustrator CC, and Adobe Photoshop CC.

References to company names, websites, or addresses in the lessons are for demonstration purposes only and are not intended to refer to any actual organization or person.

Images

Photographic images and illustrations are intended for use with the tutorials.

Typefaces used

Adobe Myriad Pro and Adobe Warnock Pro are used throughout this book. For more information about OpenType and Adobe fonts, visit www.adobe.com/type/opentype/.

Team credits

The following individuals contributed to the development of this edition of the *Adobe Illustrator CC Classroom in a Book (2018 release)*:

Writer/Design: Brian Wood
Executive Editor: Nancy Davis
Senior Production Editor: Tracey Croom
Copyeditor: Kim Wimpsett
Keystroking: David Van Ness
Keystroking/Technical Editor: Victor Gavenda
Technical Editor: Jean-Claude Tremblay
Design: Danielle Fritz
Compositor: Brian Wood
Proofreader: Patricia Pane
Indexer: James Minkin
Cover design: Eddie Yuen
Interior design: Mimi Heft

Lesson project credits

The following individuals contributed artwork for the lesson files for this edition of the *Adobe Illustrator CC Classroom in a Book (2018 release)*:

Danielle Fritz (www.behance.net/danielle_fritz): The hand lettering for "A Quick Tour of Adobe Illustrator CC (2018 release)."